ABHINAVAGUPTA
THE KULA RITUAL

ABHINAVAGUPTA

THE KULA RITUAL

As Elaborated in Chapter 29 of the Tantrāloka

JOHN R. DUPUCHE

MOTILAL BANARSIDASS PUBLISHERS
PRIVATE LIMITED • DELHI

Reprint: Delhi, 2006
First Edition: Delhi, 2003

ISBN: 81-208-1979-9

MOTILAL BANARSIDASS
41 U.A. Bungalow Road, Jawahar Nagar, Delhi 110 007
8 Mahalaxmi Chamber, 22 Bhulabhai Desai Road, Mumbai 400 026
236, 9th Main III Block, Jayanagar, Bangalore 560 011
203 Royapettah High Road, Mylapore, Chennai 600 004
Sanas Plaza, 1302 Baji Rao Road, Pune 411 002
8 Camac Street, Kolkata 700 017
Ashok Rajpath, Patna 800 004
Chowk, Varanasi 221 001

Printed in India
BY JAINENDRA PRAKASH JAIN AT SHRI JAINENDRA PRESS,
A-45 NARAINA, PHASE-I, NEW DELHI 110 028
AND PUBLISHED BY NARENDRA PRAKASH JAIN FOR
MOTILAL BANARSIDASS PUBLISHERS PRIVATE LIMITED,
BUNGALOW ROAD, DELHI 110 007

In respect
and affection
this work is dedicated
to
my parents
who gave me an upbringing
full of variety and gentleness.

ACKNOWLEDGEMENTS

Thanks first and foremost to my supervisor, Dr. Greg Bailey, of the Asian Studies Department at La Trobe University, Melbourne. He encouraged me from the start to pursue this area of interest and gave every support both by his advice and particularly by the many hours spent in reading the text with me.

Thanks also to Professor Alexis Sanderson of Oxford who pointed out the value of Chapter 29.

Thanks to my mentor and friend, Fr. Chris Barnett, Pastor Emeritus, who supported me in pursuing this unusual endeavour and who, during the preparation of this work, provided a roof over my head and the pleasure of his conversation.

Thanks to Archbishop Emeritus of Melbourne, T. Frank Little, who allowed me to open this door and provided the necessary financial support. Thanks also to his successor, Archbishop George Pell, who continued to provide financial assistance.

Thanks to Pandit Hemendranath Chakravarti of Varanasi, India, whose knowledge of the Sanskrit language and of the literature of Kashmir Shaivism was invaluable in disclosing this arcane text. Over the three months we spent together his frankness and delicacy were always appreciated.

Thanks to Dr. Anita Ray of the Asian Studies Department, La Trobe University, for providing finish to the text, but above all for her constant friendliness during the time of study.

CONTENTS

PART I

PROLEGOMENA TO THE *TANTRĀLOKA* 29 AND TO JAYARATHA'S INVESTIGATION

PART II

The Translation of the *Tantrāloka* 29 and Jayaratha's Investigation

PREFACE

This monograph is a first reading of one chapter of the *Tantrāloka* written a thousand years ago in remote Kashmir. Yet this chapter occupies an important position in a book which itself is the greatest work of the greatest thinker of his day for it was into the Kula ritual that Abhinavagupta was initiated by Śambhunātha and which he prized above almost all the rest. Abhinava states in *TĀ* 13.300cd-301ab:

> *'Sequentially and according to the descent of power, one is initiated in the Siddhānta, then in the Left, in the Right, in the Mata, in the Kula, in the Kaula, then in the Trika which is in the Heart.'*

A first glance is bewildering. The mixture of images and themes and codes makes the text unreadable. A second glance scandalises. The use of wine and sexual fluids, the use of women and the disregard for conventions—what have they to do with the great Abhinavagupta? Are they perhaps an aberration, the shadow side of genius?

Inescapably, however, we are forced to admit that Abhinava placed the Kula ritual almost at the summit of divine revelation. Only the Trika, i.e. the single mantra *SAUḤ*, stood higher. We are forced to attend more closely to the ritual. How does it, in fact, express the grandiose vision set out in the first half of the *Tantrāloka*? Or again, how does the theory of the first five chapters work out in practice?

This monograph will show that the Kula ritual, properly understood, is an exalted and simple way of life. It does involve wine etc. but not so as to create a dichotomy between body and spirit, enjoyment and liberation. The aim of the Kula ritual is to overcome the dualism of pure and impure, sacred and profane, divine and human, even good and evil. It wishes to show how ordinary life is the expression of consciousness, of Śiva himself in union with his śakti.

HOW TO READ THIS MONOGRAPH

The focus of this monograph is not a theme such as the concept of the word fully studied in the work of André Padoux nor the theme of the heart studied in its various aspects by Paul Eduardo Muller-Ortega.[1] They draw on a number of authors and texts to study a theme, whereas this work is directed above all to the text of *TĀ* 29 and its investigation alone. The chapters in Part I of this work aim only to lead the reader to appreciate the text more fully. They will help situate the text in its various settings—the life and work of Abhinavagupta, the currents of his day and his basic world view. The introductory chapters which are meant to accompany the text will explain certain words in more detail and provide some assistance regarding those texts where the density of language or wealth of imagery at first confuses the reader. The structure is of major importance in showing the direction of the chapter and the interrelationship of its sections. The notes and the appendices will further help to explain the mass of terms and codes in *TĀ* 29 and its investigation. In particular the glossary with its references to the text will help to explore the various meanings and usages of a word and so draw up a fuller presentation of a particular theme. By combining these various tools the reader will be able to analyse the text at greater depth.

The text of the Tantrāloka is written in couplets so that each *śloka* consists of two whole lines or four half-lines. Gnoli, in his translation of the *Tantrāloka* indicates the first whole by the letter 'a' and the second whole line by the letter 'b' but this monograph sees a value, especially for the glossary, in referring to half-lines. Thus *TĀ* 29.1b refers to the second half-line of

1. André Padoux, *Vāc, The concept of word in selected Hindu tantras,* Translated by Jacques Gontier, Albany, State University of New York Press, 1990. Paul Eduardo Muller-Ortega. *The Triadic Heart of Śiva.* Albany, State University of New York Press, 1989.

CHAPTER 1

ABHINAVAGUPTA

We are unusually well-informed about the life and background of Abhinavagupta. He himself provides the autobiographical details in places scattered throughout his work and especially at the conclusion of the *Tantrāloka* and the *Parātriṃśikāvivaraṇa*.[1] Pandey and others have set out these details clearly and there is no need to repeat them.[2] Only those points of particular relevance to *TĀ* 29 are given here.

Abhinava stems from an illustrious background for his distant ancestor, Atrigupta, a Brahman[3] famous for his erudition and culture, was invited by Lalitāditya, king of Kashmir, the 'World Conqueror',[4] to leave the prestigious capital Kanauj which Lalitāditya had conquered. Atrigupta was provided with a great house in the capital, Pravarapura (modern Srinagar) near the temple of Śītāṃśumaulī[5] on the banks of the Jhelum.[6]

The opening hymn of the *Tantrāloka*, repeated in the *Tantrasāra* and found again at the start of the *Parātriṃśikāvivaraṇa*, sings of the union of Śiva and śakti from whose bliss the whole universe

1. See *TĀ* 37.33-85 and the 21 *ślokas of Parātriṃśikāvivaraṇa* pp.283 line 20 - p.286 line 7.
2. K.C.Pandey, *Abhinavagupta: an historical and philosophical study*, 2nd edn. Varanasi, Chowkhamba Sanskrit Series Office, 1963, pp.5-26. Lilian Silburn, Le *Paramārthasāra*, 2nd revised edn. Paris, E. de Boccard, 1979, pp.8-9. Daniel H.H. Ingalls, ed. *The Dhvanyāloka of Ānandavardhana with the Locana of Abhinavagupta*, Cambridge, Massachusetts, Harvard University Press, 1990, pp.2-4 and p.30. Navjivan Rastogi, *Introduction to the Tantrāloka*, Delhi, Motilal Banarsidass, 1987, pp.19-55.
3. *TĀ* 37.38.
4. Ingalls, ed. *The Dhvanyāloka*, p.3.
5. *TĀ* 37.52.
6. Ingalls, ed. *The Dhvanyāloka*, p.30.

derives. The same hymn can equally be understood to refer to his parents, Narasiṃhagupta and Vimalā. In their union he regarded them as Śiva and śakti. From them, in their state of transcendent union he, Abhinava, has sprung. He is their *yoginī*-child, the 'depository of knowledge', who 'even as a child in the womb ... has the form of Śiva.'[7] He was born about 960 C.E. and died about 1020 C.E.[8] He is named Abhinavagupta. In giving the etymology of his name he perhaps reveals his own self-image.

> '*That wise man alone is suited to this sacrifice who is protected* (gupto) *on all sides* ('bhi) *by praise* (nav).' [9]

Jayaratha glosses that seemingly banal etymology of the name and Silburn summarises his gloss as follows:

> '*That person is 'Abhinavagupta' who remains vigilant in the course of every day activities; who is present everywhere* (abhi), *in the objective domain as much as in the subjective domain, and dwells there without limitation. He sings the praise* (nu) *without ceasing to concentrate on the energies of knowledge and activity. He is protected* (gupta) *by this praise even though he lives under the pressure of temporal affairs.*'[10]

Jayaratha's interpretation is reflected in Qt.100b.4 which is a description of the practitioner of Sacrifice 3.

Vimalā, Abhinava's mother, dies when he is two years old and his father rears him. He also has a brother Manoratha and a sister Ambā.[11] Abhinava describes his father, Narasiṃhagupta, as 'outstandingly adorned with devotion to Maheśvara'.[12] He goes on to note that he himself, following his father, was 'spontaneously seized

7. *TĀ* 29.163a. This last point is underscored by Jayaratha in his investigation of *TĀ* 1.1. See Raniero Gnoli, *Luce delle sacre scritture*, (*Tantrāloka*), Torino, Unione Tipografico-Editrice Torinense, 1972, p.67 footnote 1.
8. P.V. Kane, *The history of Sanskrit poetics*, 4th edn. Delhi, Motilal Banarsidass, 1971, pp.242-243, gives his life span as 950 C.E. - 1020 C.E.
9. *TĀ* 4.278cd.
10. Silburn, *Le Paramārthasāra*, p.54.
11. For these and other details on his family, see Rastogi, p.32.
12. *TĀ* 37.54d.

by devotion to Maheśvara'.[13] The devotional attitude, found in *TĀ* 29.176, is evident in all his works and especially in his hymns.

Abhinava acclaims his father as his first teacher. Narasiṃhagupta introduced the young boy to Sanskrit grammar.[14] Afterwards he was introduced to all the intellectual currents of his day. He himself notes that

> *'out of curiosity', he '... frequented the logicians, the followers of the Veda* (śrauta), *the Buddhists, the Jains, the Vaiṣṇavas, etc.'* [15]

and he explains the purpose of his curiosity was '... to fill out [his] consciousness'.[16] In *TĀ* 37.62, he lists a host of other teachers.[17] This does not mean that he travelled widely outside of Kashmir[18] since the vale was itself experiencing a Golden Age of intellectual ferment.

In *TĀ* 36, Abhinava portrays the vast sweep of traditions which descend from Bhairava. Śrīkaṇṭha, i.e. Śiva, is the guru of the three Perfected Beings, Āmardaka, Śrīnātha and Tryambaka. At Śrīkaṇṭha's command, these promulgate the dualist, dualist-non-dualist and the non-dualist Śaiva traditions respectively. Furthermore, Tryambaka himself has two children, a son and a daughter who is called Half-Tryambaka or Ardhatryambakā so that there are, in fact, 'three and a half streams of tradition' (*adhyuṣṭa-saṃtatisrotaḥ*).[19] The lineage of the daughter is called the 'three-and-a-half' tradition (*adhyuṣṭa-pīṭha*)[20] and is identified with the

13. *TĀ* 37.58d.
14. Ingalls, ed. *The Dhvanyāloka*, p.30.
15. *TĀ* 13.345cd-346ab. Jayaratha glosses 'logicians' as 'the followers of the Nyāya and the Vaiśeṣika etc.'
16. *TĀ* 13.342cd.
17. Pandey, p.12. Rastogi, p.54-55.
18. Alexis Sanderson, 'The triadic heart of Śiva: kaula tantricism of Abhinavagupta in the non-dual shaivism of Kashmir, by Paul Eduardo Muller-Ortega' [review] *Bulletin of the School of Oriental and African Studies* 53: 354-357, 1990, p.356.
19. *TĀ* 36.15a.
20. See *TĀ* 29.68c. The word adhyuṣṭa is invented as the Sanskrit equivalent of the Prakrit *addhuṭṭha* which is derived from *ardha-caturtha*, 'three-and-a-half'. Monier Monier-Williams, *Sanskrit English Dictionary*, Delhi, Motilal Banasidass, 1993, p.23.3.

Kula tradition. Her tradition forms the subject matter of Tantrāloka 29. Those schools attracted his particular interest. In *TĀ* 37.60-61, he speaks of his education in them. Vāmanātha, 'son' of Erakavara, taught him the dualist tradition; the 'son' of Bhūtirāja taught him the dualist-non-dualist tradition; Lakṣmaṇagupta, 'son' of Utpala who himself was the 'son' of Somānanda, taught him the non-dualist tradition which goes back to Tryambaka. Finally, Śambhunātha, 'son' of Somadeva, taught him the fourth or the 'three-and-a-half' tradition.[21]

The vast *Tantrāloka* begins with the customary acknowledgment of the divine origins, the Perfect origins and the human origins from which the work derives. In the encomium of the human origins, *TĀ* 1.7-21, Śambhunātha receives the most frequent and complete mention. Again, at the end of the vast work, he is mentioned as the high point in the series of his gurus:

> *'The omniscient Śambhunātha, 'son' of Somadeva, like the full moon over the sea, expounded [for him] the so-called 'Fourth Tradition'.*[22]

Śambhunātha and Abhinava must have met though it is not clear where they did so.[23] Did the master travel all the way to Kashmir[24] or, rather, did the disciple make the journey?[25] In Jr.29b.1, Jayaratha identifies the sacred site mentioned in *TĀ* 29.28b with Jālandhara and says that this is the place

> *'... from which the doctrine [of the Kula tradition] was propagated by the lineage of the [eternal] Perfected Beings and the [eternal] yoginīs'.*

And so he gives the slight weight of evidence in favour of Abhinava making the journey to Jālandhara.

---

21. It is worth noting that Śambhunātha's own guru, Sumati, originated from South India. Bettina Bäumer, *Wege ins Licht*, Zü rich, Benziger, 1992, p.33.
22. *TĀ* 37.61cd. See also *Tantrasāra* p.204.
23. In *TĀ* 29.243b, he states that: 'such a procedure, presented in the *Dīkṣottara*, was explained to me by Śambhu'.
24. See B umer, *Wege*, p.33.
25. See Silburn, *Le Paramārthasāra*, p.6.

It was Śambhunātha who initiated Abhinava into the Kula tradition.[26] Thus it is altogether appropriate that, in *TĀ* 29.95cd, at the very heart of the Kula ritual, at the juncture of Sacrifices 2 and 3, Abhinava should acclaim his master as 'the moon shining over the ocean of Trika knowledge.' It was at Śambhunātha's command,[27] as well as at the request of his students and colleagues, *TĀ* 1.15, that Abhinava composed the *Tantrāloka.*

Abhinava did not marry. He states concerning himself that:

> '..*he was a celibate throughout his life and as such the question of having wife or son etc. never did arise.*'[28]

We cannot, however, conclude that he did not have direct experience of all the Kula rituals. In fact, in the concluding line, *TĀ* 29.292ab, he refers to the authority of his own experience and seems to scotch the accusation that he knows the rituals only at second hand.

Abhinava lived out his life as a writer and teacher. Although he was a Brahman like his ancestor Atrigupta, there is no evidence in *TĀ* 29 that he exercised a function at any temple. Rather, the context of *TĀ* 29 is the house, the 'hall of sacrifice',[29] or the gathering of Kula practitioners, i.e. the circle-sacrifice,[30] the gathering of heroes surrounding the guru who is the 'Chief of Heroes'.[31]

26. Lilian Silburn, L. *Hymnes de Abhinavagupta*, Paris, Editions E. de Boccard, 1970, p.2. Padoux, Vāc, p.60.
27. *TĀ* 1.19.
28. *dārātmajaprabhṛtibandhukathāmanāptaḥ. Īśvarapratyabhijñāvivṛtivimarśinī* III, concluding verse 2, quoted in Rastogi, p.32 footnote 1 and translated in *op.cit.* p.32
29. *TĀ* 29.18a.
30. *TĀ* 29.99d.
31. *TĀ* 29.286bc.

CHAPTER 2

THE HISTORY OF THE TANTRIC TRADITION

Abhinavagupta entitles his great work *'Tantrāloka'*, 'Light on the Tantras'. By so doing he places it in a precise historical context. No attempt is made here to give a full picture of that historical context.[1] The following pages only trace the trajectory of the tantric traditions to point out how they surface both in *TĀ* 29 and in Jayaratha's investigation.

(a) Other Traditions

The *Tantrāloka* falls within the tradition of tantric Śaivism. It should be seen firstly in contrast to the 'orthodox', Vedic, tradition which Abhinava the Brahman does not totally reject. Rather, he eliminates it from his concern by relegating it to the lowest position in the hierarchy of revelations Śiva has granted to mankind. The purpose of incorporating the Vedic element is firstly to maintain social conventions of life in the world, out of compassion for those who know no better and secondly to protect the reputation of the Śaiva gurus.[2] The Veda is embodied in the ideal Brahman whom Sanderson describes as follows:

> *'Brahmanhood in its orthodox form as the basis of the path of purity was of two levels, the physical and*

1. The most complete presentation is given in Alexis Sanderson, 'Śaivism and the tantric traditions', in Stewart Sutherland, Leslie Houlden, Peter Clarke and Friedhelm Hardy, eds., *The world's religions*, London, Routledge, 1988, pp.660-704.
2. Alexis Sanderson, *Annuaire, Résumés des conférences et travaux. Ecole pratique des Hautes Etudes, V-iéme Section-Sciences Religieuses, XCIX (1990-1991)*, 141-144: *Conférences de M. Alexis Sanderson, Directeur d'études associé*, p.143.

> *the social. The first, conferred by birth from Brahman parents and seen as an inalienable property of the body, is necessary but not sufficient for the second, participation in the society of Brahmans through the study of Vedic revelation, marriage and commensality. This could be achieved, maintained and perfected only by conformity to the corpus of rules derived directly or indirectly from the infallible Veda and embodied in the conduct of the orthodox.'*[3]

The ritual of *TĀ* 29 inveighs against this ideal as the Kula ritual has no regard for purity or impurity. It uses forbidden foods and forbidden women. It completely overturns the meaning of *brahmacarya*. It downgrades the Vedas and does not see marriage, in the Vedic sense, as the most honourable estate. In addition, it opposes the Vedas in those movements such as the later Siddhānta which try to revive the Vedic viewpoint and it attends to the Vedic ritual only to reinterpret it along Kula lines.[4]

Smārta ceremonies were the domestic rituals every twice-born or initiated person, whether *Brahman*, *kṣatriya* or *vaiśya*, was expected to perform after his marriage. The tantric ritual claimed an essential superiority over such rituals but in fact vied with them by providing equivalents in the external conduct of its own ceremony.[5] The *smārta* tradition is explicitly rejected as dualist in Qt.75b.3 whilst in Qt.79d.1 it is dismissed as irrelevant since the Kula version of the Krama process in its third Cycle is not bound by time and place. Indeed, in the Kula rituals of *TĀ* 29 the external act is reduced to a minimum. The desire for equivalence remains

3. Alexis Sanderson, 'The category of purity and power among the Brahmins of Kashmir', in M. Carrithers, S. Collins and S. Lukes, eds., *The category of the person; anthropology, philosophy, history*, Cambridge, Cambridge University Press, 1985, p.192.
4. Thus, in the first part of the quotation, Qt.110b.1, the goddess lists the elements of the Vedic ritual. In the second part, Qt.110b.2, Śiva gives his revelation: those elements are replaced by the various aspects of love-making. Lilian Silburn, *La kuṇḍalinī, l'énergie des profondeurs,* Paris, Les Deux Océans, 1983, p.216.
5. Alexis Sanderson, 'Meaning in tantric ritual', in A.-M. Blondeau and K. Schipper, eds., *Essais sur le rituel III: colloque du centenaire de la section des sciences religieuses de l'Ecole Pratique des Hautes Etudes*, Louvain-Paris, Peeters, 1995, Vol.3. p.27.

but the equivalence is not in observable form. The words *tarpaṇa*, satiation; *yāga*, sacrifice; *homa*, oblation into the fire; and all the language of ritual are reinterpreted to refer to internal experience. Indeed, the internal sacrifice replaces and surpasses the outward observance.

The tantric traditions contrast significantly with those based on the Vedas and include a whole range of types. Their history runs through three stages: oral, scriptural and exegetical. Between the years 400 C.E. and 800 C.E.[6] many of the *tantras* were written but it is uncertain by whom they were composed and where. They are called scriptural in the sense that they are revelations from a divine source, either spoken by the deity to his consort or, less frequently, granted by the goddess to her god.

In *TĀ* 4.248 ff., in the general context of a discussion on pure and impure, Abhinava compares the scriptures and concludes that there is a hierarchy of all the sacred texts. These, in ascending order of importance, consist of the Vedas, the Vaiṣṇava scriptures and the Śaiva scriptures.[7] Nevertheless, in *TĀ* 29.74c, the Vaiṣṇavas will feel the edge of Abhinava's tongue because of their dualism. In the *Tantrasāra*, quoting the *Parameśvaratantra* in terms reminiscent of *TĀ* 29.74c, he elaborates on the reasons for his rejection of the Vaiṣṇava tantras:

> *'The Vaiṣṇavas etc. who all are tainted by attachment to impure knowledge do not come to know the supreme category: they are deprived of the knowledge of the One who knows all.'*[8]

He criticises the Vaiṣṇava school throughout the *Tantrāloka*, a fact which indicates its importance in the life of Kashmir. Indeed, it will eventually cohabit with his thought and survive through to modern times.

(b) The Śaiva Tantric Scriptural Traditions

The many strands of the Śaiva tantric tradition are like the

6. Sanderson, 'Śaivism', p.663.
7. The Vaiṣṇava tantras follow the Pāñcarātra system. ibid. p.661.
8. Sanderson', 'Śaivism' p.666.

channels of the Gangetic delta which shift and change with every monsoonal flood. Nevertheless Sanderson has managed to map their course. In what follows there is no attempt to repeat this history in its complexity but only to touch on those things which are strictly relevant to *TĀ* 29.

Sanderson begins his survey of the tantric traditions by describing the Atimārga, the 'outer' or 'transcendent' path which concerns only the ascetic and provides only for salvation. The Lākula division of the Atimārga is expressed in the *Niśvāsatattvasaṃhitā* which states that the ascetic

> '*... may eat and drink anything. No action is forbidden to him. For he is immersed in contemplation of Rudra, knowing that no other deity will save him.*'[9]

Sanderson goes on to note that the Lākula ascetic '... was to abandon the more basic notion of the pure and the impure.'[10]

However, the *Tantrāloka* is not concerned with the ascetic so much as with the householder and for that reason it is situated within the tradition of the Mantramārga. This strand comprises a whole ramification of traditions which constitute a trajectory towards the feminine and move towards ever more powerful and more esoteric systems of ritual.[11] The ramification can be set out as follows:

The Mantramārga divides into:

- Śaivasiddhānta
- Bhairava-tantras, these latter bifurcate into:

- Mantrapīṭha
- Vidyāpīṭha, this latter sub-divides into:

- Yāmala-tantras
- Śakti-tantras, these latter divide into:

- Trika-tantras and Kālī-tantras.

9. *Tantrasāra* p.22 lines 6-7.
10. *ibid.* In Jr.100b.4, Jayaratha quotes a passage which refers to the Kula practitioner 'who is perfectly acquainted with the rules of unlawful behaviour mentioned in the Atimārga'.
11. Sanderson 'Śaivism', p.669.

Thus, the first division of the Mantramārga is occupied by the Śaivasiddhānta who have Sadāśiva as their highest deity. They do admit the existence of his female consort but she is largely an abstraction and the daily ritual does not incorporate her worship. The 'mantra', i.e. the deity, is without śakti.[12] Furthermore, the ritual conforms to the Veda and is the least esoteric of the tantric rituals.

However, one must clearly distinguish between the early Śaivasiddhānta texts and their later reinterpretation according to a Vedic orientation by the Śaivasiddhāntins of Abhinava's day. In *TĀ* 29.74cd-75ab, the later Śaivasiddhāntins receive his strongest criticism:

> *'The mantras given by the Siddhāntas and the Vaiṣṇavas etc. are therefore impure. Because they cannot bear so much splendour, they are lifeless, according to the non-dual tradition'.*

The Kāpālika tradition had a profound influence on the progress of these tantric traditions. It is closely linked with the Lākula branch of the Atimārga[13] and is also found in the earlier tradition of Svacchandabhairava but in the Vidyāpīṭha it comes to the fore.[14] The Kāpālika tradition has been thoroughly studied by Lorenzen who proposes that the movement originated in South India or on the Deccan plateau perhaps in the fifth or sixth centuries. He describes the devotee:

> *'... a typical Kāpālika. He smears his body with the ashes of the dead; he carries a trident and a skull bowl; he worships Bhairava and Mahākapālin; his text is the Bhairavāgama; he honours this god with liquor and offerings of human heads; and he imagines salvation as the indescribable bliss of an endless embrace in the arms of Umā.'*[15]

12. This point is made in Qt.3d.1.
13. Sanderson, Annuaire, pp.141-142.
14. Sanderson, 'Śaivism', p.670.
15. David N. Lorenzen, *The Kāpālikas and Kālāmukhas. Two lost Śaivite sects*, New Delhi, Thomson Press (India) Ltd., 1972, p.43.

'The paradoxical identity of the Kāpālika saint and Brahman sinner finds its divine archetype in the curious myth of the beheading of the god Brahmā by Śiva.'[16]

In the Vidyāpīṭha the devotee worships as the principal deity a male figure who presides over 'predominantly female pantheons'.[17] He adopts the customs of the Kāpālika:

'With his hair matted and bound up with a pin of human bone, wearing earrings, armlets, anklets and a girdle, all of the same substance, with a sacred thread ... made of twisted corpse-hair smeared with ash from the cremation-pyres, carrying the skull-bowl, the skull-staff and the rattle drum ..., intoxicated with alcohol, he alternated periods of night-wandering ... with worship ... in which he invoked and gratified the deities of the maṇḍala into which he had been initiated. This gratification required the participation of a dūtī, *a consecrated consort, with whom he was to copulate in order to produce the mingled sexual fluids which, with blood and other impurities of the body, provided the offering irresistible to this class of deities.'*[18]

The Yoginī Cult also forms part of the background of the Vidyāpīṭha which is of particular significance for *TĀ* 29. The *yoginīs* of legend are fearsome apparitions who are both wildly dangerous and the source of great boons.[19] They radiate from the heart of the deity[20] as sources of power which govern time and space and send out further emanations of female powers which are visible in the sacred sites (*pīṭha*) and cremation grounds (*śmaśāna*). These thus became the most favourable place for

16. *ibid.* p.77.
17. Sanderson, 'Śaivism', p.670.
18. *ibid.* pp.670-671.
19. Marie Thérése de Mallmann, *Les enseignements iconographiques de l'Agni-Purāṇa*, Paris, Presses Universitaires de France, 1963, pp.169-182. André Padoux, *Le coeur de la yoginī*, Paris, Diffusion de Boccard, 1994, pp.55-58. For the legendary aspects, see Alain Daniélou, *Hindu polytheism*, London, Routledge and K. Paul, 1964, p.288 and p.301.
20. Sanderson, 'Śaivism', p.671.

ritual while the most auspicious time was the darkest moment of the lunar cycle. By placating these hordes with horrific substances, even with the vital fluids of one's own body, and perhaps even by copulating with them, the devotee gained the ascendancy and so secured their powers over the cosmos etc. The male deity worshipped in this ritual is Rudra or Bhairava, '... the wild ascetic who leads the Yoginī hordes (*yoginīgaṇanāyaka*).'[21]

The cult of the *yoginīs* seems to have been the earliest form of what becomes the Kula tradition. They are usually sixty-four in number, a traditional number usually interpreted as eight times the eight 'mothers' (*mātṛkā*).[22] All the yoginīs belong to a family (*kula*) or to a clan (*gotra*) grouped into 63 [64?] sisterhoods.[23] However there are 8 major families who have Brāhmī etc. as their 'Mothers' (*mātṛ*) and who are of particular importance at the moment of initiation, for the guru ascertains, by the manner in which the flower falls, to which of the families and to which of the 'Mothers', the initiate belongs and which of the *yoginīs* he is to seek and which powers he will receive.

The cult of Tumburu-Bhairava, called the 'Vāma', is in fact a third ramification of the Vidyāpīṭha along with the Yāmala-tantras and the Śakti-tantras although it is not listed in Sanderson's ramification given above. It occupies a significant place in the thought of Abhinava who often includes it in his listing of the hierarchy of traditions.[24]

The Trika belongs to the group of the Śakti-tantras and has three stages of development. At a first stage, it is based simply on the

21. *ibid.*
22. Padoux, *Le coeur*, p.58.
23. Sanderson, 'Śaivism', p.672.
24. The Bhairava school has two streams: Right Hand (*dakṣiṇa*) or Southern, and Left Hand (*vāma*) or Northern. The four goddesses of the Dakṣiṇa school, whose deity is called Bhairava, are Śuṣkā, Siddhā, Utpalā, Raktā/Caṇḍikā. Alexis Sanderson, 'Maṇḍala and Āgamic identity in the Trika of Kashmir', in A. Padoux, ed. *Mantras et diagrammes rituels dans l'Hindouisme*, Paris, Editions du Centre National de la Recherche Scientifique, 1986, p.186 footnote 84. The four goddesses of the Vāma school are Jayā, Vijayā, Jayantī and Aparājitā. They are 'sisters' or female attendants of the deity Tumburu and are associated with the directions—east, south, west and north respectively—of the sky which surrounds him. Teun Goudriaan, *The Vīṇāśikhatantra*, Delhi, Motilal Banarsidass, 1985, p.138 note 6.

three goddesses Parā, Parāparā and Aparā. At a second stage, those three goddesses are subsumed into Kālī who transcends them as the fourth goddess. At the third stage, the Trika is influenced to a profound degree by the *Īśvarapratyabhijñākārikā*.

The first stage is expressed in the *Siddha-yogeśvarīmata* as well as in the *Mālinīvijayottaratantra* and the *Tantrasadbhāva* in which the *trika*, 'the set of three' goddesses and their emanations of lesser *yoginīs* comprise the whole array of cosmic levels and are imagined as present within the body of the worshipper. His own central axis is the staff of their *maṇḍala* while above his head are three lotuses which represent the three goddesses.[25] Parā is worshipped both as 'one of the three and as their sum and source'.[26] In this last capacity she is also called Mātṛsadbhāva, 'Essence of the Mothers'. By supplying them with alcohol and meat on a surface such as a cloth, the worshipper ascends the levels of beings and so arrives at the absolute.

The other main division of the Śakti-tantras concerns the cult of the single goddess Kālī as found in the *Jayadrathayāmala* alias the *Tantrarājabhaṭṭāraka*. The first quarter of this immense work of 24,000 verses describes Kālī or Kālasaṅkarṣiṇī, Destroyer of Time, in terms of the Yoginī Cult. The remaining three quarters go far beyond this understanding. Here Bhairava is superseded, even dismembered. The goddess is 'the hidden emaciated [*kṛśā*] destroyer who embodies ... consciousness.' Thus she is also called Kṛśā.[27] Shc both emits and reabsorbs.[28] The emaciated goddess, Kṛśā, is worshipped in *TĀ* 29.76 and Qt.77d.1.

(c) The Kula Reform

Abhinava gives two sources for the origins of the Kula tradition. Firstly, in *TĀ* 1.7, he praises Macchanda as the source of his own doctrine, a point Jayaratha takes up in his commentary and extends

25. Sanderson, 'Śaivism', 673.
26. *ibid.* p.674.
27. *ibid.* p.675.
28. *Parātriṃśikāvivaraṇa* p.243 lines 10-12. In his article 'Śaivism', pp.675-676, Sanderson sums up her presentation in the second part of the *Jayadrathayāmala* and provides a sketch.

by quoting a text which gives Kāmarūpa in Assam as the place of origin.[29] Secondly, in *TĀ* 1.8, Abhinava goes on immediately to praise Tryambaka without explaining this latter's connection with Macchanda. It has already been noted above that the daughter of Tryambaka is the source of the Kula tradition.

The word *kula* refers to the family or grouping of the *yoginīs* and of the 'Mothers'. It is also taken to mean the corporeal body, the body of power, the cosmic body, the totality of things so that by entering into a 'family', a *kula*, the worshipper enters into the totality of cosmic powers, the kula. He himself, in his own body, is the embodiment of the 'Mothers' and of the whole of reality. By being initiated into a 'Mother' he also enters into one or other level of his own body and becomes master of the powers identified with it. By piercing all the circles of his body he is master of the totality[30] and attains the central deity which is identified with the true self of the worshipper, his 'blissful inner consciousness'[31] of whom the eight 'Mothers' are the projections.

Abhinava distinguishes between the Kula and the Kaula in his listings of the hierarchy of tradition. The Kula tradition, Sanderson holds, belongs to ascetics who are close to the Kāpālika and preserve a connection with the cremation ground and wear various insignia. Contrary to this, the Kaula tradition is a reformed version which makes allowance for the householder.[32] This being said, the distinction is not so clear. The ritual described in *TĀ* 29 is called Kula and yet is applicable to the householder. The original Yoginī Cult suited those who were removed from everyday life. By contrast, the Kaula reform allows the Yoginī Cult to become available to the householder by placing the emphasis on inner experience.

29. *Tantrāloka* with the Commentary of Jayaratha, reprinted in 8 volumes, enlarged with an Introduction by Navjivan Rastogi and re-edited by R.C. Dwivedi and Navjivan Rastogi, Delhi, Motilal Banarsidass, 1987, vol.2, p.24. See also André Padoux, *La Parātrīśikālaghuvṛtti*,Paris, E. de Boccard,1975, p.4 footnote 4, and P.C. Bagchi ed., *Kaulajñānanirṇaya*, Prachya Prakashan, Varanasi, 1986, pp.1-69. *Tantrāloka* vol.2, p.25 line 5. Padoux, *Le coeur*, p.37 footnote 48.

30. *ibid.* p.680.

31. *ibid.*

32. Sanderson, 'The category', p.214 footnote 110. See also Padoux, *Vāc*, p.73.

If the householder could experience what the Kāpālika experienced but more simply and indeed more powerfully, his domestic ritual was deemed to be at least equivalent. The terminology of the Kāpālika or Yoginī cult could then be transferred to his domestic ritual and the externals of those cults could be justifiably abandoned as superfluous. The Kaula version of the Trika thus understood itself to be the essence of tantric practice.[33]

At some unknown date,[34] the Kaula developed four transmissions, each with its own set of deities, mantra, *maṇḍala*, mythic figures etc.[35] These four are the eastern or 'earliest' *(pūrva)* whose chief divinity is Kuleśvarī; the northern *(uttara)* whose chief divinity is Kālikā, i.e. the twelve Kālīs; the western (*paścima*) whose chief divinity is Kubjikā; and the southern *(dakṣiṇa)* whose chief divinity is the goddess Kāmeśvarī /Tripurasundarī.[36] Of these four transmissions, the Eastern and Northern are found in *TĀ* 29.

The Eastern Transmission *(pūrvāmnāya)* is contrasted with the earlier or first stage of the Trika which is called *tantra-prakriyā*.[37] This Kaula reform of the Trika is well-established in Kashmir by about 800 C.E.[38] and is entitled *kula-prakriyā*. Jayaratha reports that Abhinava considered the Kula to be superior to the Tantra:

> *'And in this way, he esteems more highly the guru who follows the Kula ritual procedure* (kulaprakriyā)*—because of [its] restfulness—in comparison with the guru who is devoted to tantra ritual procedure* (tantraprakriyā).*'*[39]

This statement is born out by even a cursory comparison of *TĀ* 15-16, two chapters full of ritual activity, with *TĀ* 29 where the ritual is largely reduced.

The Kaula Kālī Cult, i.e. the Northern Transmission

33. Sanderson, 'Śaivism', p.681.
34. Padoux, *Le coeur*, p.36.
35. Sanderson, 'Śaivism', p.680.
36. Padoux, *Le coeur*, p.38.
37. Sanderson, 'Śaivism', p.681.
38. *ibid.*
39. *Tantrāloka* vol.2, p.31 lines 12-13.

(*uttarāmnāya*), comprised three Kaula variants of the Kālī cult: the Mata, the Krama and the Cult of Guhyakālī,[40] of which the most significant for *TĀ* 29 is the Krama. The Mata is described in the *Ciñciṇīmatasārasamuccaya* which consists of two short passages[41] associated with the bodiless gurus Vidyānandanātha and Niṣkriyānandanātha mentioned in Qt.42d.1. The Krama is traced to Oḍḍiyāna in the valley of Swat, three hundred kilometres northwest of Kashmir,[42] and its main scriptural authority is the *Devyāyāmalatantra*.[43] It is based on the four phases of emission, maintenance, dissolution and the Nameless and reinterprets the Trika to produce its second stage in which one worships Kālasaṃkarṣiṇī as a fourth, resorptive goddess above Parā, Parāparā and Aparā.[44]

(d) Abhinava's Hierarchy of Traditions

Many of these strands and streams have been arranged by Abhinava in a hierarchy observable in *TĀ* 29.51. He is consistent in his several listings of the arrangement[45] except for the so-called Mata which varies its position, being placed usually before or sometimes after the Kula. But what does 'Mata' mean? Does it refer to that variant of the Northern Transmission called 'the Mata' or to the other variant of the Northern Transmission called 'the Krama' which features so frequently in the Tantrāloka. Moving upwards, the order is: Veda, Siddhānta, Left (*vāma*), Right (*dakṣina*, Bhairava), Mata, Kula, Kaula, Trika. Sanderson continues the list, moving downwards:

> *'below the Siddhānta are the various Pāśupata systems (Lākula, Vaimala, Mausala and Kāruka); below Śaivism is the Vaiṣṇava Tantric system of the Pañcarātra; and finally there is the universal prescription (sāmānyo*

40. Sanderson, 'Śaivism', p.682.
41. *ibid.* p.683.
42. *ibid.* p.684.
43. *ibid.* p.683.
44. Alexis Sanderson, 'The visualisation of the deities of the Trika', in *L'Image divine*, Paris, Editions du Centre National de la Recherche Scientifique, 1990, p.71.
45. TĀ 13.300cd-301ab. TĀ 13.319cd. TĀ 15.319-320. TĀ 37.25cd-27ab. *Parātriṃśikāvivaraṇa* p.217 lines 24-25 and *ibid.* p.217 lines 27-28 which is a quotation from the *Niśācāra*. *Parātriṃśikāvivaraṇa* p.269 lines 5-6. *Parātrīśikālaghuvṛtti* p.56.

> *dharmaḥ) of the smārta and śrauta traditions. Thus the Trika locates itself at the furthest remove from neutral 'vedic 'orthodoxy.'*[46]

At the apex of that hierarchy stands the Trika, surpassing both the Kula and the Kaula. This point is made explicitly in *Parātriṃśikāvivaraṇa* p.217 line 22 where, before listing the hierarchy of schools Abhinava quotes the phrase: 'The Trika is higher than the Kula,' (*kulāt parataraṃ trika*), where the word 'Trika' refers to *SAUḤ*[47] and not to the rituals and *maṇḍala* etc. associated with the Trika. The inner knowledge of the single mantra *SAUḤ* surpasses in simplicity and effectiveness all other mantras, rituals and traditions, even those of the Kula.

(e) The Exegesis of the Śaiva Tantric Traditions

The third stage of the tantric traditions is the post-scriptural or exegetical stage which occurs in the middle of the ninth century C.E.[48] and produces two major streams, on the one hand the Śaivasiddhānta and on the other the Trika and Krama.[49] Both streams are directed at the householder who seeks not the supernatural powers of the ascetic but liberation.

According to the later Śaivasiddhānta, liberation consists in being like Śiva, equal to Śiva, yet essentially other than Śiva.[50] Similarly, the Śaivasiddhānta exegetes establish a division between the individual and the world such that the Siddhānta is fundamentally dualist. The endless cycle of birth and rebirth is due to the stain (*mala*) which is a substance (*dravya*). As such it can only be removed by what is equally material, namely the Śaivasiddhānta ritual. The initiatory ritual removes this stain whilst the daily and the occasional ceremonies continue to remove any persisting impurity. Complete liberation occurs only at death when the practitioner is at last free of the world.

46. Sanderson, 'The visualisation', p.50.
47. Pandey, p.601.
48. Sanderson, 'Śaivism', p.690.
49. *ibid.*
50. ibid. p.691.

The Krama reinterprets the three goddesses of the Trika such that Parā is understood to be the knower (*pramātṛ*); Parāparā as the means of knowledge (*pramāṇa*); and Aparā as the known (*prameya*). The supreme goddess of the Trika, Parā, is then assimilated to the supreme goddess of the Krama who absorbs and transcends the other goddesses and is called Śrī Parā. By a play on the word *mātṛ* which can mean either 'mother' or 'knowing subject', Śrī Parā is now understood, in fact, to be the 'Essence of Knọwing Subjects', Mātṛsadbhāva. When these four, Śri Parā, Parā, Parāparā and Aparā, are multiplied by the three stages of emanation, preservation and reabsorption (*sṛṣṭi, sthiti* and *saṃhāra*) they constitute a group of twelve but in fact the twelve can be calculated in two ways, as a multiple either of 3 x 4 or of 4 x 3. These are equivalent[51] since the fourth goddess, Mātṛsadbhāva and the fourth phase, 'ineffable' (*anākhyā*) or 'nameless' (*anāma*) are the same. The multiple of 4x3 can be put schematically as follows:

	emanation	*preservation*	*reabsorption*	*'ineffable'*
known	1.	2.	3.	4.
knowing	5.	6.	7.	8.
knower	9.	10.	11.	12.

Sacrifice 2 of *TĀ* 29 in particular will be arranged around this schema so that the worshipper rediscovers in himself the sequence (*krama*) of twelve stages and in so doing rises above it to attain the divine state.[52]

The Trika adopts a third form under the impact of Vasugupta, 875-925 C.E., who commences a new tradition with the *Śivasūtra* and with the *Spandakārikā,* although there is dispute over whether this last text was composed by Vasugupta himself or by his pupil Kallaṭa whom Abhinava mentions in *TĀ* 29.124a.[53] The

51. Sanderson, 'Maṇḍala', p.200
52. Silburn, L., *Hymnes aux Kālī, La Roue des Energies Divines*, Paris, E. de Boccard, 1975, pp.125-148 and Sanderson, 'Maṇḍala', p.200.
53. In *TĀ* 28.338cd, Abhinava mentions 'the guru Kallaṭa who belongs to our lineage'. As to whether the *Spandakārikā* is due to Vasugupta or Kallaṭa, see Pandey, pp.155-156, 204, 622.

Spandakārikā propounds that the ultimate reality is a vibration (*spanda*) which manifests itself both in the transcendent state of consciousness and in the panoply of the external world. Liberation consists in attaining that source and in realising it. The next stage of the development occurs with Somānanda who composed the *Śivadṛṣṭi*, the seminal work of what will eventually be called the Pratyabhijñā school. Somānanda gives a more philosophical cast to the movement which began with Vasugupta.[54] Somānanda's pupil, Utpaladeva, develops a classical formulation of the movement in his *Īśvarapratyabhijñāsūtra* written towards the beginning of the tenth century.[55] The Pratyabhijñā school takes its name from that work.

In opposition to the later Śaivasiddhānta, the Trika allows that a person can achieve liberation through ritual as well as through insight alone. These two, ritual and insight, are not opposed for ritual is the mirror of hidden realities and can reveal to the practitioner his own innate nature. This knowledge is the act of salvation, it is an awareness that the practitioner is truly Śiva. He does not become like Śiva or even become Śiva, but rather he comes to realise he is Śiva. Liberation is the moment of recognition (*pratyabhijñā*).[56] Similarly, liberation from bondage is not a release from the world but the realisation that the world is simply the expression of oneself. Just as the practitioner and Śiva are one, so the practitioner and the world are one reality which is free, conscious, omnivalent. Although by coming to knowledge the practitioner regains the original state of consciousness, he does not remain at this level. Although he is essentially Śiva and all reality is simply the expression of his self, he freely 'contracts', he lessens his glory and manifests himself in limited subjects such that 'this' and 'that' appear in dualist fashion.

The majority of Śaiva devotees in Kashmir followed the cult of Svacchandabhairava and his consort Aghoreśvarī as expressed at length in the *Svacchandatantra* and adopted in a domesticated form.[57] The later Śaivasiddhāntins set about reinterpreting the cult

54. Dyczkowski, *The doctrine of vibration*, p.18.
55. *ibid.* p.17.
56. The word *pratyabhijñā* does not occur in *TĀ* 29 or its investigation.
57. Sanderson, 'Śaivism', p.700.

according to their own outlook and succeeded in establishing it, during the tenth century C.E.,as the principal interpretation of the Svacchandabhairava tradition so that it took on a form compatible with the Veda.[58]

The protagonists of the non-dualist Trika and Krama rejected this interpretation and held that the true interpretation of the ancient Śaivasiddhānta, was to be found in the Trika and the Krama. Yet in fact the Śaiva tantras are in the main dualist[59] so that this 'true interpretation' in non-dualist terms is itself an imposition foisted by the Kaula minority and considered justified by the teaching of the Trika and the Krama and by the writings of Somānanda and Utpaladeva.[60]

58. Sanderson, 'The category', p.204.
59. 'If then any doctrine may be said to represent the mainstream of the Śaiva Tantras it is dualism. Non-dualism takes over only at the Kaula fringe, to be superimposed by scholastic artifice on the rest of the non-Siddhāntika literature.' Alexis Sanderson, 'The Doctrine of the Mālinīvijayottaratantra,' in Teun Goudriaan, ed. *Ritual and speculation in early tantrism. Studies in honour of André Padoux*, Albany, State University of New York Press, 1992, p.308. See also Sanderson, *Annuaire*. p.144. Abhinava superimposes the non-dualism of his school also on the *Mālinīvijayottaratantra*. Sanderson, 'The Doctrine', p.306.
60. The history of modern research on the non-dual Shaivism of Kashmir has been described in Muller-Ortega, *The Triadic Heart*, pp.18-24.

CHAPTER 3

THE *TANTRĀLOKA*

(a) The Purpose of the *Tantrāloka*

In the context of the long tantric tradition and its many competing schools, Abhinavagupta composes the 'Light on the Tantras', the *Tantrāloka*. He does so at the request of his disciples and, according to *TĀ* 1.19, at the command of his guru.

After describing the circumstances of the composition, Abhinava himself explains the title:

> *'[Abhinavagupta] therefore composed this great work which expounds the truth on the Tantras according to logic and tradition* (āgama). *Guided by the light which emanates from it, people can easily be engaged in the rituals.'*[1]

In this way he gives a double emphasis: truth and ritual. Accordingly, the first half of the work, Chapters 1-13, deals with the exposition of a world view whilst the second half, Chapters 14-37, describes the rituals.

The *Tantrāloka* is destined for his own disciples and is therefore directed to those who are already acquainted with the subject-matter. It is not a work of popularisation, not even of *haute vulgarisation* and, trying to cover the whole range of tantric lore, summarises and does not elaborate. What was perhaps clear to his entourage is allusive and cryptic to readers who do not have their background.

1. *TĀ* 37.83cd.

(b) Models of Composition

Rastogi suggests that Abhinava uses four models in composing his *Tantrāloka*.[2] It is a *saṅgrahagrantha*, a 'digest of tantric literature and lore'; a *prakriyā-grantha* or *paddhati-grantha*, a manual of practice; a *śāstra-grantha*, a religious treatise or fully structured text; a *stuti-grantha*, a hymn of praise.

The *Tantrāloka* combines elements of all these genres. In first place, it can be truly described as 'A Digest of Tantric Literature and Lore'. The list of works mentioned by Abhinava in the *Tantrāloka* is long and he draws on them to form a compendium and to show that his own work gives their true meaning and is correctly entitled 'The Light on the Tantras'. Abhinava himself defines the *Tantrāloka* as a *vārttika*[3] which is defined as the exposition of what is said, what is left unsaid or what is inadequately said.[4] Quite specifically the *Tantrāloka* is a gloss on the *Mālinīvijayottaratantra* for he says: 'There is nothing here [in the *Tantrāloka*] which is not in the illustrious *Mālinīvijayottara*'[5] which text provides the essence, he says in *TĀ* 1.19, of the three Śaiva currents: the dual current represented by ten scriptures; the dual-non-dual current expressed in eighteen scriptures; and the non-dual current represented in the sixty-four scriptures. This being said, *TĀ* 29 can hardly be classed as a simple commentary on the *Mālinīvijayottaratantra* since from *śl.*21 till *śl.*187cd he does not quote from the *Mālinīvijayottaratantra* and when he does quote it is sometimes with a notable slant.[6] The word *vārttika* applies, therefore, in the sense of ' that which is left unsaid'. In fact, as far as *TĀ* 29 is concerned, Abhinava prefers texts such as the *Mādhavakula*, the *Vīrāvali* or the *Yogasañcāra* but until these texts become available we cannot say if he adheres to them more closely than he does to the *Mālinīvijayottaratantra*.

---

2. Rastogi, pp.4-12.
3. *Īśvarapratyabhijñāvivṛtivimarśinī* I, p.33 quoted in *ibid.* p.3 footnote
4. Monier-Williams, *Sanskrit English dictionary*, p.945.2.
5. *TĀ* 1.17.
6. See for example *TĀ* 29.197cd which refashions the phrase *kara-stobha*, 'release of the hand', to read *kara-kampa*, 'trembling of the hand'.

Abhinava's attitude to the texts is ambiguous. On the one hand he reveres them and is at pains to support his argument by appealing to their authority. On the other hand he submits the texts to his own structures so that various parts of *TĀ* 29 do not fit well together, as for instance sections A and B of Sacrifice 2 which depend on the *Mādhavakula* and the *Yogasañcāra* respectively. The same occurs within a single passage as in the case of the second rite of ordinary initiation where he refers to the *Ratnamālā* alone but does not seem to present a coherent ritual so that one wonders whether he may have inserted material from an unnamed source.

The second half of the *Tantrāloka* presents the various initiations and consecrations in great detail and so constitutes a sort of manual of tantric practice. *TĀ* 29 itself is clearly a manual of practice and is divided into two major sections: the rituals for the initiate and the rituals of initiation. This being said, *TĀ* 29 is not a set of rubrics. Sacrifice 1 and the rituals of initiation do make use of a clearly defined pattern but the sequence of the rituals moves increasingly towards the internal forum which functions according to its own spontaneity.

Jayaratha describes Abhinava as the 'composer of a religious treatise' (*śāstrakāraḥ*)[7] and shows how the initial statement (*ādivākya*) given in *TĀ* 1.1-21, presents the four purposes of a religious treatise.[8] Likewise, the second sentence of *TĀ* 29, *śl.* 1cd-2ab, is the *ādivākya* which defines the Chapter as a religious treatise on Kula ritual procedure. Just these two lines contain the four indispensable elements (*anubandhacatuṣṭaya*)[9] required in any religious treatise.

1. *prayojana*, the purpose: defined here as 'is described', a purpose Jayaratha expresses more fully in Jr.02 with the word *abhidātuṃ*, 'to expound';
2. *adhikārī*, one who is qualified to receive the subject matter: defined here as 'the most advanced gurus and disciples';

7. Tantrāloka vol.2, p.3 lines 8-9.
8. Rastogi, p.9-11, examines this in detail.
9. These are given in Jaideva Singh, trans. *Parātriṃśikāvivaraṇa*, Bettina Bäumer ed., Delhi, Motilal Banarsidass, 1988, p.19 note 6.

3. *abhidheya*, the subject-matter: defined here as 'Kula ritual procedure';
4. *sambandha*, the connection between the title (*abhidhāna*) of the *Tantrāloka*, and the subject-matter (*abhidheya*): defined here as the reinterpretation of 'the whole of the preceding service' in the light [*āloka*] of Kula ritual procedure.

The structure of *TĀ* 29 is set out as a whole in Appendix 15 and together with the overview of *TĀ* 29 given in Chapter 6 shows how fitting the title 'religious treatise' is for *TĀ* 29.

The final model to be considered is that of the *Tantrāloka* as a 'hymn of praise'. It is the weakest of the models since the number of hymns is very small. Abhinava places a prayer at the beginning (*upakrama*) and end (*upasaṃhāra*) of the *Tantrāloka*.[10] Just as every one of his works includes a blessing,[11] so too *TĀ* 29 has a hymn of praise strategically placed at the conclusion of the sections which deal with intercourse. In imitation of his master, Jayaratha introduces all thirty-seven chapters of the *Tantrāloka*-except Chapter1—with a verse of two lines.

(c) Generalities on Style

Although the *Tantrāloka* and *TĀ* 29 are finely structured, the work is conceived as an integrated whole such that it cannot be broken into detached sections.[12] Since Abhinava wishes to avoid isolating one Chapter from the next he makes use of the technique of what Jayaratha calls *saṃcayanyāya*, 'aggregate' or 'accumulation',[13] where the one *śloka* is divided into two halves, the first serving as the end of one chapter or section and the second beginning the next Chapter or Section. This occurs between every Chapter of the *Tantrāloka* and frequently within *TĀ* 29.[14]

---

10. Rastogi, pp.11-12.
11. Pandey, p.105.
12. Rastogi, p.76.
13. *Tantrāloka* vol.2, p.309 line 9.
14. Rastogi, pp.76-77. The technique produces a complication in the numbering of *ślokas*, for which see *ibid.* p.164 ff. For example, *TĀ* 28 ends with a half *śloka* and *TĀ* 29 begins with a half *śloka* so that in a sense *TĀ* 28.435cd is *TĀ* 29.1ab.

Abhinava's first device in presenting an esoteric matter is to disperse its discussion over many Chapters.[15] 'An important secret should not be divulged all at once. Nor should it be kept completely secret'.[16] The reader is thus obliged to read the whole text before one topic can be fully appreciated or sometimes even understood and so the fine structuring of the text goes hand in hand with a certain obscuration.

The verses are compact so that the sentences and phrases need to be read both backwards and forwards, with reference to what precedes and what follows. The words also have various levels of meaning: being interpreted both in an obvious and in a symbolic sense, applying on the gross, subtle and supreme levels, understood as object, means and subject of knowledge, such that a text is not so much to be read as mulled over. Once these initial difficulties are overcome the passages can be read and reread with increasing profit. This monograph attempts only to overcome the initial difficulties and to provide at least one intelligible reading.

(d) The Manuscript

Many of the manuscript texts discovered in Kashmir were written in the *śāradā* script.[17] Indeed, Jayaratha makes the point that Abhinava actually refers to the morphology of that script.[18] This fact is significant in understanding the symbolism of the phoneme *Ḥ* in *TĀ* 29. The *Tantrāloka* of Abhinavagupta in its entirety together with Jayaratha's investigation or commentary (*viveka*) was presumably transliterated from the *śāradā* script and was certainly first published in 12 volumes between 1918-1938. Its editor, Mukund Ram Shastri, does not provide any editorial note or preface so that little is known about the manuscript sources. He seems to have used a base text plus three other manuscripts designated by the *nāgarī* letters Ka, Kha and Ga. These three are referred to in footnotes and give the variant readings. On the other hand he

15. Rastogi, pp.83-84.
16. *Tantrasāra* p.31 lines 1-3.
17. Pandey, p.653.
18. *ibid.* p.652

may have used just these three manuscripts.[19] From the fourteenth chapter onwards, and therefore including *TĀ* 29, no variant readings are indicated. Are we to conclude that the manuscripts all agree? In any case, '... a largely readable and complete text of an important treatise is in our hands.'[20]

The text of *Tantrāloka* used in this monograph is a reprint of the original edition to which Navajivan Rastogi has added an introduction. There is no critical edition of the whole text[21] or, to my knowledge, of any part of the text.

19. Rastogi, p.160.
20. *ibid.* p.161.
21. *ibid.* pp.xii-xiii.

CHAPTER 4

JAYARATHA

Jayaratha's ancestor is Pūrṇamanoratha, minister to King Yaśaskara in Kashmir, c.930 C.E. His father, Śṛṅgāraratha, was minister to King Rājarāja who is probably the same as Jaya Siṃha and who lived around 1200 C.E. while Jayaratha himself flourished around 1225-1275 C.E.[1] He was initiated by Subhaṭa Datta and his teacher in Śaivism was Kalyāṇa. At the instigation of the king he studied the *Tantrāloka*[2] and without royal patronage could not have concluded the task.[3] Besides the *viveka* on the *Tantrāloka* he wrote the *Alaṅkāra Vimarśinī*, a commentary on the *Alaṅkāra Sarvasva* of Ruyyaka, and the *Alaṅkārodāharaṇa*.[4] He also wrote the *Vāmakeśvarīmata-vivaraṇa*, a commentary on the *Nityāṣoḍaśikārṇava*, the basic scripture of the South Transmission of Tripurasundarī.[5]

Rastogi tries to reconstruct the circumstances that surrounded Jayaratha's massive undertaking in commenting on the *Tantrāloka*. He proposes in the first place that the text of the *Tantrāloka* had become corrupt[6] and that Jayaratha restored both the text and the correct order of the *ślokas*.[7] He proposes furthermore that Jayaratha's *viveka* was not the first commentary and that other commentaries existed[8] which either assisted him or against which he

1. Sanderson, 'Śaivism', p.689.
2. Pandey, p.262.
3. Rastogi, p.102.
4. Pandey, p.263. For further biodata on Jayaratha, see Rastogi, pp.895. For his teachers etc. see *ibid.* pp.95-100. For a tabular chart of his family and preceptorial lineage, see the chart following *ibid.* p.92.
5. Sanderson, 'Śaivism', p.689.
6. Rastogi, p.143.
7. *ibid.* p.109.
8. *ibid.* pp.103-104.

inveighed. Rastogi proposes, therefore, that quite different points of view were entertained concerning the *Tantrāloka*.[9] If so, there is little evidence of contention in Jayaratha's commentary for he gives the impression of being focussed and unassailable. These other commentaries have not survived so that the *Tantrāloka* is in the unusual position of having only one commentary or investigation which is yet thorough and complete. In a sense the *viveka* is not just a commentary but is an extension of the *Tantrāloka*.[10] For example, the long intervention on the meaning and use of alcohol, Jr.13d.1-13 and Qt.13d.1-25, explains the multiple meanings and uses of alcohol and defends it against what must have been severe criticism. There is no such defense concerning the use of the sexual partner. Indeed, although Jayaratha accepts that he is writing a *viveka*, investigation, he prefers to call his work *prakāśana*, elucidation,[11] and rightly so for his work is illuminating and without it *TĀ* 29 would be most difficult to understand.[12]

As already noted earlier, Abhinava gives to the *Tantrāloka* the style and character of a *śāstra*. Jayaratha follows suit and proposes, in Jr.166b.2, that *TĀ* 29 or rather Sacrifices 3 and 4 constitute a *śāstra* since the two sacrifices provide the *vidyā*, mantra, *mudrā* and *maṇḍala* which establish the four-fold base that every *śāstra* must have.[13]

Abhinava has himself divided the *Tantrāloka* into its topics and sub-topics. Jayaratha also provides connotative titles for all the chapters of the *Tantrāloka*[14] and so highlights the meaning of the chapter. For example in Jr.0.2 he adds the title 'the ritual of the secret study'. He also clearly signposts the Sub-topics. In Jr.2b.1 and Jr.2b.2, he scarcely refers to the Sub-topic 'the category 'qualified' '.

---

9. *ibid.* pp.107-108.
10. *ibid.* p.102.
11. 'Jayaratha's titles are invariably followed by the word '*Prakāśana*'. It lends credence to the view that Jayaratha perhaps preferred '*Prakāśa*' to '*Viveka*' as a title for his investigation. *ibid.* p.170.
12. *ibid.* p.118. See also Padoux, *La Parātrīśikālaghuvṛtti*, p.7 footnote 4.
13. Kṣemarāja, commenting on the word *catuṣpīṭhaṃ* found in *Svacchandatantra* 1.5c, characterises the *Svacchandatantra* as the compendium of a religious treatise which has these four bases. The same classificatory system is expounded in *TĀ* 37.18 ff.
14. Rastogi, p.138.

However, in Jr.17d.3, he indicates the actual commencement of the 'Kula procedure concerning the Perfected Beings and their wives' and in Jr.55d.3 he clearly explains that it has just been completed. In Jr.55d.3, he introduces the Sub-topic: 'the ritual of adoration', and in Jr.95d.2 he introduces 'the ritual with the sexual partner'. Jr.186b.2 notes the conclusion of 'the ritual of the secret teaching' and introduces the Sub-topic 'initiation'. Jr.224d.2 introduces 'consecration' while Jr.235d.2 introduces 'penetration'.

Furthermore he clearly marks the sub-divisions within a sub-topic. For example, the divisions within the ritual of adoration are clearly noted by Jayaratha in Jr.57d.4, Jr.70b.7, Jr.77d.3 so that these three constitute three varieties of the 'ritual of the sacred sites'. Furthermore, Jr.81d.3 notes the conclusion of the ritual of adoration and the beginning of a distinct but relevant discussion on recitation. Jr.95d.2 repeats the clear distinction. Again, Jayaratha, by the way in which he positions his interventions, divides the text into short units, into what might loosely be called *kārikās* which are somewhat self-contained and so allow a coherent commentary. All these smaller divisions are important for understanding the text since the larger divisions into topic and sub-topics do not adequately present the argument for a reader who is unacquainted with the subject matter. By and large this monograph follows the divisions into *kārikās* suggested by Jayaratha.

After having made these divisions into *kārikās*, Jayaratha proceeds to surround them with both an introduction and an elucidation. He first introduces the lines by providing the bridge, which is not always self-evident, between the preceding statement of Abhinava and the following. In doing so he may take on the role of a disciple and ask for clarification or take on the role of an opponent and raise an objection which is sometimes couched in the form of a quotation. The objection is often introduced by the word *nanu* which need not be translated. To these questions Abhinava is imagined to give his reply. The interventions are well chosen and show that Jayaratha has understood the precise issue at hand. After giving the verses of the text Jayaratha proceeds to comment upon them. He first of all explains the meanings of words.

For example, he will explain that the 'ejaculated form' (*abhyuditaṃ rūpaṃ*) in Jr.128b.1 refers to the sexual fluid. He also provides alternative terms for well-known words that have occurred in the text or in order to prepare the reader for words in a quotation. For example, Jayaratha gives six quotations, Qt.39d.1-6, from the *Kulakriḍāvatāra* which list somewhat differing details on the hermitages etc. In order to prepare the reader for these quotations he gives, in Jr.39d.1, a list of equivalents. He is speaking about textual and functional equivalents, not necessarily about geographical equivalents. Again, the list of equivalents in Jr.66d.1 is given not only to explain the meaning of *śl*.66 but also to square the text of *śl*.66 with Qt.66d.1-3. This being said, the harmonisation of Abhinava's text and a quotation can be tortuous, as in Jr.72b.1.

After explaining the meanings of individual words and phrases of a verse Jayaratha may also give a paraphrase wherein he displays all his skill. The text of Abhinava is often in code or symbolic language and is extremely compressed so that it can only be understood in the light of the paraphrase. For example, *śl*.83-88 can hardly be understood without Jr.88d.1. Again, *śl*.278cd-281 needs Jr.281d.1-2. In his paraphrase he interpolates definitions of terms as well as references to other passages from *TĀ* 29. He suggests the various levels on which Abhinava's text may be read. For example, Jr.104b.1 shows that *śl*.104ab can be understood both as a description of sexual intercourse and as a summary of the five levels of consciousness. He equally suggests that the five levels are in fact experienced in intercourse. The paraphrase is not only a commentary on the verses preceding but also a preparation for the verses which follow. The elucidation needs to be read both backwards and forwards. Thus, the same paraphrase just mentioned, Jr.104b.1, prepares the reader for the description of intercourse which starts at *śl*.104cd-105ab.

Does Jayaratha read more into Abhinava's text than is present? In general the answer is no. The most notable example of over-interpreting is his commentary on the word 'if', in *śl*.96, which he interprets as 'must'. Does he read all that is available in them? It is most unlikely since a finely wrought text such as *TĀ* 29 admits of many readings.

The commentary from Jayaratha's own pen amounts to more than 1150 lines of about 18 syllables each. It is a significant contribution. A most notable aspect of the investigation is Jayaratha's use of quotations. The longest quotation, Qt.100b.5, occupies 29 lines while the shortest is one half-line. He makes a total of 172 quotations from various sources and these amount to a total of 422 lines. By comparison, the text of Abhinavagupta amounts to 583 lines. Thus the original text of Abhinavagupta has been considerably amplified. Some of the quotations are taken from other parts of *TĀ* 29 or from other chapters of the *Tantrāloka* just as parts of *TĀ* 29 such as *śl.*66 and *śl.*162cd-163ab are quoted in earlier chapters of the *Tantrāloka*. This shows Jayaratha's complete familiarity with the whole of the immense work while it implies that the reader should draw together the meaning of the various contexts in which the same quotation is found. That comment applies also to repeated quotations from sources other than Abhinava, such as Qt.81d.1: 'His śaktis are the whole universe', or Qt.98b.1: 'Bliss is the form of *brahman*'. The various contexts of the one quotation are significant to each other.

At times the quotations are given in a straightforward manner. At other times the quotations are woven into Jayaratha's paraphrase so as to produce very complex sentences which are always grammatically correct, just as the Sanskrit is always accurate, but which lack smoothness of flow. This technique also shows his skill and comprehension. A good case in point is Jayaratha's investigations following on *śl.*109ab, *śl.*126 and *śl.*153ab.

CHAPTER 5

PARAMETERS OF THE *TANTRĀLOKA*

The following contextualisation of *TĀ* 29 is not a summary of the *Tantrāloka*.[1] Rather, it presents the several concepts and structures within which *TĀ* 29 functions. These are drawn from the *Tantrāloka* as a whole and use the main terms found in *TĀ* 29.

1. The Absolute

(a) As a Unitary Reality

'I' (*aham*) is the primary consideration of *TĀ* 29. Reality is not to be reduced to mere objects. It is not just the projection of the faculties of knowledge, of sub-conscious impulses or of a mind conditioned by social forces. The essence of reality is personal: 'I am'. However, the personal 'I am' is not to be confused with the individual, the atomic, limited self. The universally personal knows no such limitation. It says 'I am' and cannot say 'I am not'.

The 'I' stands as the basis of the three forms, 'subject of knowledge' or 'knower' (*pramātṛ*); 'means of knowledge' or 'knowing' (*pramāṇa*); and 'object of knowledge' or 'the known' (*prameya*) or the world of objectivity designated by pronouns such as 'he' 'she', 'it'. The three forms may be understood in some sort of opposition to each other but there is yet a fourth term (*pramiti*) which refers to the unity of all three such that the knower knows by means of his own self and at the same time is the known. Thus Kashmir Śaivism is not so much a doctrine of being as a doctrine of revelation.

1. A recent summary of the contents of each chapter of the *Tantrāloka* is available in Lilian Silburn and André Padoux, *La Lumiére sur les tantras, chapitres 1 á 5 du Tantrāloka,* Paris, É. de Boccard, 1998, pp.31-37.

Before ever the world is emanated, the Light knows its Light by means of its own Light. Since Śiva is identical with his emanation, when he contemplates the world he contemplates his own self. All lesser means of knowledge, such as the faculties, logic etc., are particular forms of his own universal Light. The perceiving subject of whom all is a manifestation is, by definition, unsurpassable (*anuttara*). There is no other perceiver who could reduce him to an object of knowledge or define him.[2] The unsurpassability is not the same as transcendence for which, strictly speaking, there is no place since all reality is a revelation of the supreme knower. He is his revelation.[3]

Knowledge (*jñāna*), is the basis of the whole construction of Abhinava's world view. It refers first and foremost to the knowledge which is all-inclusive such that nothing is excluded from its range of vision. It can also refer to category 33 in the thirty-six divisions of reality[4] which already involves a limitation of boundless knowledge. It can refer to differentiated thought (*vikalpa*) and to the knowledge of phenomena such as 'blue' and 'pleasant'. These vastly different meanings of the word *jñāna* can easily lead to confusion. They must not be confused, neither must they be opposed since all forms of knowledge are expressions of the supreme knowledge and all relate to each other. The terms linked to *jñāna* are many. *TĀ* 29 prefers the word *saṃvit*, consciousness, which captures something of the totality (*saṃ*) of knowledge and refers to what unites all forms of knowledge in one act of perception.

The term 'idealism' is sometimes used to describe the Śaivism of Abhinava. The term may conjure up several nineteenth century Western schools of thought and may also seem to be the opposite of 'realism'. However, in the thought of Abhinava, objects are not unreal or illusory. They are real, not because they are dualistically separate from the subject but because they are truly projected from the subject's own being. The cosmos derives from the antecedent supreme 'I'. Objects take their reality and their meaning from him. He is not reduced to their inertia.

2. *Parātrīśikālaghuvṛtti* p.49.
3. Padoux, *Vāc*, p.235 footnote 25.
4. See Appendix 1.

(b) As a Mutuality

The pair of terms 'splendour' (*prakāśa*) and 'reflection' (*vimarśa*) are used to express the ineffable consciousness. That is, the knowing subject knows that he knows. Consciousness is not ignorant of its consciousness. If consciousness is splendour then *vimarśa* is the awareness of the splendour. It is the self-evidence of light, a sort of reflection but not an introspection or introversion. There is no obscurity, no room for doubt, and because of this assurance there is an infinite capacity to act which is called śakti and is of paramount importance throughout *TĀ* 29.

A certain ambiguity attaches to consciousness. It can be understood as the splendour whose counterpart is reflection. It is possible, however, to go a step further back, so to speak, and to acknowledge the void, the altogether apophatic, about which nothing is said and yet which is known to be the fount of all. The consciousness which arises in this context is śakti, who is the goddess (*TĀ* 29.118ab).

Just as consciousness knows no limit so it knows no restriction. It does not resist and is irresistible, it remains the subject and cannot be subject to another. It enjoys an essential freedom (*svā-tantrya*). As the self-evidence of consciousness it occurs naturally, spontaneously. It 'happens'. Consciousness and freedom are a fundamental pair. The divine śakti is the freedom of Śiva and all her emanations are made in utter freedom. The mastery of Śiva expresses itself in doing what is impossible and extremely difficult[5] taking on the form of limited subjects or even in using the impurity of things in order to realise the pure light of consciousness.

Reflection (*vimarśa*) is simply the self-revelation of consciousness and so is the primary act of revelation. As such it is a dynamic reality and is appropriately called śakti since the word '*śakti*' derives from the verbal root *ŚAK* 'to be able' and can be translated as 'energy', 'power' etc. However, by definition śakti cannot adequately be defined since she herself is the defining agent. From śakti as self-revelation, derive all the other revelations, the

5. Paramārthasāra śl.15.

whole manifestation of the universe which is like a shower of light. Everything is śakti.[6]

The will (*icchā*) is not involved in the foremost manifestation of śakti. Voluntarism has no part to play in this system. Rather, the śakti spontaneously arises, of her own volition, so to speak. Yet consciousness is not a detachment, an uninvolved observation. The śakti is consciousness recognising itself and assenting to itself.

The term *śaktimān* means, literally, 'the person (masculine gender) who possesses energy'.[7] It stands in relation to śakti as does Śiva or as consciousness does to self-revelation. It occurs frequently in *TĀ* 29 where it refers to the male practitioner in union with his sexual partner, for these have become assimilated to the divine pair.

Among the more useful and fully expounded[8] similes is that of the mirror. Strictly speaking, the mirror cannot be seen and becomes apparent, in a sense, only when an image appears on its surface. Precisely because it has no particular form it is capable of an infinity of forms. On this analogy Śiva is the mirror which has no form while śakti, prior to any particularisation, is the capacity of the mirror to take on any form. In terms of language, Śiva is the ineffable which is the starting point of any statement, and in terms of art he is the king of dancers (*naṭarāja*). The postures he adopts are not something apart from him yet he is not limited to any one posture and he transcends them all. He is essentially void.

In ordinary language, the reflection (*pratibimba*) seen in a mirror is the reflection of something external to the mirror-a face, a vase of flowers-which is the original object being reflected (*bimba*). By extension, the word *pratibimba* refers also to the 'reflection' found in the mirror of consciousness which is the *bimba*. In this extended sense, however, there is strictly speaking no *bimba* since

6. Nevertheless, in *Tantrasāra* p.27 line 9 - p.28 line 2, in the chapter on *śakti* method (*śāktopāya*) Abhinava gives a long list of words to describe *śakti*. Many of these words will reappear in *TĀ* 29 and its investgation.
7. *TĀ* 1.69-74.
8. *TĀ* 3.1-64.

there is no object apart from consciousness. Furthermore, consciousness is 'void' and cannot be reflected. In fact nothing is reflected and there is no reflection, neither *bimba* nor *pratibimba*. Rather, the image arises spontaneously in the 'mirror' of consciousness.[9] Nevertheless the term *pratibimba* is used to refer to any expression of a higher reality. Therefore, Śiva and śakti are related as *bimba* and *pratibimba*, the original and its reflection.

This imaging forth occurs at every stage of the emanation. Each category of reality (*tattva*) is the source of the one which follows, and each later category is a reflection of its source.[10] Thus action, category 32, is an expression of the previous category, knowledge, which is category 33. That is, knowledge is the source of action since a person acts according to what he has in mind. Or again, the practitioner who has reached the state of Bhairava may wish to express himself in an external ritual which thus becomes a reflection of his divine self, as noted in Jr.24d.2.

(c) As a Unity

The pairs of terms we have been considering must not lead to a sense of dichotomy. The words *eka*, one; *advaita*, non-dual; *anavacchinna*, undivided; *tadātmya*, identity, are often used precisely in order to prevent any sense of dualism at the highest level. The polarities noted above are not dualities for the highest reality is not a sameness but a relationship of such sort that one term essentially involves the other. Other terms which come now for consideration bring our attention back to the essential unity of consciousness.

The first such term is *kaula*. In ordinary usage it is interchangeable with *kula* but since the term *kaula* can also mean 'combination', it can refer to the union of Kula and Akula. In *TĀ* 29.117b, *kaula* refers to Kula and Akula, to śakti and the one who possesses śakti, to Śiva and śakti in their union. All emanates from them in such a way that the emanation is not divided from them. Rather, the panoply of the world is simply the revelation of themselves.

9. Silburn, *Hymnes de Abhinavagupta*, p.35.
10. Padoux, *Vāc*, p.231.

Thus the *kaula*, the union of Śiva and śakti, is at the same time the totality of knowledge and the objects of knowledge.

The relationship of Śiva and śakti is one of complete harmony and repose, (*viśrānti*). The term 'repose' does not signify idleness but effortless act. Each category rests in the one in which it was originally contained, from which it has proceeded and to which it returns.[11] All reality rests in śakti which in turn rests upon the void of Śiva. This relationship, though a perfect repose, is also expressed by the term *spanda*, vibration, since the elements of an oscillation are essentially related to each other. The play of cognition and recognition is a constant vibration of which the vibrating cosmos is a reflection. The term *spanda* can be taken at various levels. It is Śiva and śakti, awareness, creative awareness,[12] and the outflow of the whole world.[13]

At the very highest level, before any expression, cognition and recognition are perfectly related to each other so that nothing more is needed. The adequacy of one to the other is bliss (*ānanda*). The adequacy or bliss is experienced (*anubhava*) and cannot be described nor proven. In *TĀ* 3.68, bliss is noted as the first effect of the union of Śiva and śakti and as their most characteristic aspect.

> *'The paired* (yāmalaṃ) *form of [Śiva and śakti] is called union* (saṃghaṭṭa). *It is the energy of bliss from which all is emitted.'*[14]

Indeed, *TĀ* 3.71 ff. show how the emanation occurs and how it is symbolised by the series of phonemes of the Sanskrit alphabet. In the process of emanation the divine bliss produces particular forms of bliss. Yet earthly bliss, though limited, is particularly able to open a person to eternal bliss.

In *TĀ* 29, the term *ānanda*, bliss, has several meanings. It can refer to the ultimate relationship of Śiva and śakti and their perfect

11. *ibid.* p.192. See also Padoux, *La Parātrīśikālaghuvṛtti*, p.92 note 114.
12. *Parātrīśikālaghuvṛtti* p.52.
13. *TĀ* 4.182cd-183.
14. See also *TĀ* 29.49c, *TĀ* 29.53c, Jr.79.d.1. In *Īśvarapratyabhijñāvivṛtivimarśinī* 1.5, Abhinava defines bliss. '... that is known as bliss which is but the fullness of the self-revelation of one's own nature, accompanied with a reflective awareness, a self-representation of one's own nature.' Padoux, *Vāc*, p.245 footnote 52.

fusion (*sāmarasya*)[15] the experience of wonder (*camatkāra*) at one's own self.[16] It is freedom.[17] It can also refer to the experience of the relationship of Śiva and śakti which is experienced in the bliss of sexual intercourse and to the 3 M's which are linked to bliss and in particular to the sexual fluids arising in intercourse. These various levels of meaning interpenetrate each other and the single use of the word ānand can refer to one or to all of them.

The unity of Śiva and śakti is powerfully expressed by the phoneme *A* which now introduces the symbolism of the Sanskrit alphabet. It is a feature of Kashmir Śaivism, as indeed universally in India, that language and revelation are intimately associated so that the phonemes of the Sanskrit alphabet in particular are taken to symbolise all revelation. Furthermore, since in the idealism of Kashmir revelation and reality are co-terminous, the study of the phonemes is the study of being. The phonemes *A* and *Ā*, the first two letters of the Sanskrit alphabet, are given a rich variety of meanings which summarise the teaching on Śiva and śakti and their bliss. The phoneme *A* can refer to Akula alone or to Kula alone or to their inseparable union. The phoneme *Ā* can refer to the goddess herself or to the union of Śiva and śakti or to their bliss. From them, in the bliss of their union, all reality, i.e. all other phonemes proceed, as shall be described shortly.

A further notable phonetic symbolism can be mentioned at this point. The word 'I' (*aham*) is the fountainhead of all and the summation of all and in its very components symbolises that totality. It can be divided in two ways: *A* + *HA* and *A* + *Ḥ*. Since *A* and *HA* are the first and last letters of the Sanskrit alphabet[18] the word *AHAM* symbolises the beginning and end of all things. The phonemes *A* and *HA* also signify all the intervening letters of the

15. Jr.79d.1, Jr.117b.1.
16. Jr.50d.1.
17. *Tantrasāra* p.6 line 11.
18. Strictly speaking, the Sanskrit alphabet has only 49 phonemes, the last of these being *HA*. To round off this number, a further phoneme is 'invented': *KṢA*. Thus either *HA* or *KṢA* can be considered to be the last phoneme. The speculations differ according to the stance taken in this matter. See Padoux, *Vāc*, p.112 footnote 79 and ibid. p.241 footnote 43.

alphabet.[19] Therefore *AHAM*, 'I', contains within itself the whole emanation. Secondly, as *A* + *Ḥ*, the word *AHAM* can also be read dynamically in two directions, for the 'I' is an oscillation. Therefore *A*+*Ḥ* can be read in its emitting aspect when the union of Śiva and śakti is expressed in external revelation. That is, *A* the first phoneme of the alphabet leads to the sixteenth phoneme, *Ḥ*, which emits the following thirty-four phonemes of the alphabet and so manifests the cosmos. 'Ḥ is the projection of reality.'[20] On the other hand, *A* + *Ḥ* can also be read in the direction of reabsorption for the 'I' draws all into itself. In this way *Ḥ* is a portal out of which reality emerges and back through which all returns.[21] Similarly, the *bindu* *Ṃ* can symbolise either the result of the emanation, i.e. the individual, *aṇu*,[21b] or the supreme undivided union of Śiva and śakti.[21c]

2. The Emanation of the Absolute

Śiva and śakti in their very essence and at the highest level are a vibration, a mutuality and a unity but they also express their vibration in limited form. The question may be asked as to why they should do so, but no answer is given except that it pleases Śiva through his śakti to perform feats impossible and improbable. These feats or emanations (*sṛṣṭi*) can be considered from a number of different angles.

(a) As a Contraction of Splendour

Cognition recognises itself by the act of self-awareness (*vimarśa*), an act both total and abiding. This awareness is to be distinguished from creative awareness (*parāmarśa*) which is awareness expressed in emanation. The creative awareness itself is further to be distinguished from the will (*icchā*) which is a limitation of creative awareness, a focussing on one possibility among many.

19. In *TĀ* 3.204cd-205ab, Abhinava applies to *AHAM* the grammatical rule called *pratyāhāra* whereby the whole is indicated by its start and finish.
20. *Parātriṃśikāvivaraṇa* p.253 lines 2-3.
21. Pandey gives an extensive analysis of *AHAM* in his book *Abhinavagupta*, pp.286-293. He notes significantly that the contex of the Kula ritual is *śāmbhavupāya*, the 'means of Śambhu', whose main goal is the realisation of *AHAM*. *ibid.* p.91.
21b. Lilian Silburn, *Le Vijñāna Bhairava*, Paris, E. de Boccard, 1983, p.69.
21c. Silburn, *Le Vijñāna Bhairava*, p.164

The creative awareness is exercised through what are commonly called 'the five acts of Śiva', namely emission, stability, destruction, darkening and grace.[22] The two acts, emanation (*sṛṣṭi*) and destruction or reabsorption (*saṃhāra*) are particularly associated with śakti and Śiva respectively since śakti in her infinite capacity is the fountainhead of all manifestation while Śiva, the perfect stillness of the void, is the end point of all reabsorption. The same basic concepts of 'emission' and 'reabsorption' are expressed by the terms *saṃkoca*, 'contraction', and *vikāsa*, 'expansion'. Permanence or stability (*sthiti*) refers to the maintenance of the fabric of the universe. The third of the five acts of Śiva is reabsorption (*saṃhāra*), a dissolution (*laya*) of the emanation. The reabsorption is a reconciliation of all into their essential unity. All is merged (*līna*) into the being of Śiva who holds all in the oneness of his undivided self. All things cease their restlessness and find repose (*viśranti*) in the tranquillity (*śānta*) of Śiva and śakti who are perfectly fused (*sāmarasya*) in a harmony which is yet an eternal vibration without beginning or end. The fourth act is a darkening (*tirodhāna*) since no expression is able to reveal the greatness of the divine splendour. Any manifestation is, in fact, an obscuration until such time as the person, by a later grace, attains the original light and comes to the condition of Śiva (*śivatā*). The fifth act of Śiva is grace (*anugraha*). It is the free benevolence of Śiva who wishes to bring the confused human being to the realisation (*pratyabhijñā*) of his divinity. He is freed by grace from darkness and from its consequences, from *mala*, stain, and *karma*.

The terms *udita*, 'rising', and *śānta*, 'resting', which are often used in *TĀ* 29, bear much the same meaning as emanation and reabsorption. The 'rising' is the coming into existence, the manifestation and the appearing and so is particularly associated with śakti and her emanations while *śānta* is the disappearing from view and so is particularly associated with the ineffability of Śiva.

(b) As Word and Alphabet

The self-evidence (*vimarśa*) of consciousness constitutes the

22. *TĀ* 14.24.

supreme word (*parāvāc*) which is not a stage of the word but of which all other stages of the word are an expression. To the unenlightened individual, all this external reality appears to be obscure, unmanifesting, a world of objects and facts without meaning but to the enlightened person reality is symbolic, suggestive and transparent. Indeed, when he has come to recognise his true nature as Śiva, reality is seen as the revelation of his own nature. All becomes his supreme word and all words speak of him. The first stage or particularisation of the supreme word is *paśyanti*, literally 'the [word] which sees [something limited]', in other words 'insight'. Here subjectivity predominates but objectivity has begun to appear. From this comes a further 'coagulation' or 'hardening' of the word which is called *madhyamā*, literally 'the middle' [word], i.e. the word in its stage between subjectivity and total objectivity, where subjectivity still lingers but objectivity predominates, as when a person is about to say something. The final stage is the 'gross word' (*vaikharī*) where objectivity alone is found, as for example in the spoken or written word.

The series of phonemes in the Sanskrit alphabet imitates the process of emanation. Indeed the sequence is understood to bring about the emanation and in fact to be the emanation so that the phonemes can be called 'seed' (*bīja*) on the analogy of the small seed which contains within itself the essence (*sāra*) of the mighty banyan and which makes the tree appear in the course of time. The emanation is divided into two stages, that of the vowels and that of the consonants while the juncture of these two stages is the *visarga*, *Ḥ*, a phoneme of great importance.

The short vowel *U* is the beginning of the knowledge (*jñāna*) of what is to be emanated while the long vowel *Ū* represents the stage when the manifestation becomes more evident as a specification and therefore as a limitation or deficiency (*ūnatā*), a wave (*ūrmi*) on the limpid surface of consciousness. It is like the udder (*ūdha*) of the Celestial Cow which grants every boon[23] and symbolises the first six vowels.[24] It is not yet the emanation itself, which only takes place with the appearance of the consonants.

23. Padoux, *Vāc*, p.252.

24. *Ibid*. p.253.

The vowels are deemed to be seeds while the consonants are wombs.[25] However, the phonemes *Ṛ*, *Ṝ*, *Ḷ*, *Ḹ* are classed as neither seed nor womb and therefore are 'neuter' (*ṣaṇtha* or *napuṃsaka*).[26] They are not part of the emitting process, as are all the other vowels, but rather they are a pause within the will (*icchā*) which is symbolised by the phoneme *I*.[27] That is, the neuter vowels represent a stage in the process of emission, where the will—the more remote source of emission—considers the various possibilities displayed by knowledge and does not proceed with some of them.[28]

It is appropriate to break the order at this point and to consider two semivowels which are intimately linked with the neuter vowels *Ṛ* and *Ḷ*, namely the phonemes *YA* and *RA* employed in the initiatory rituals of *TĀ* 29. *YA* is the conjunction of the power of will, *I* or *Ī*, with the Absolute, *A*. It has the character of a swift movement which is an attribute of the wind so that it is a dessicating force. The phoneme *RA* (*repha*)[29] derives from the vowel *Ṛ* and has the nature of heat.[30]

The phoneme *E*, in *devanāgarī* and even more in the *śāradā* script, has the form of a downward pointing triangle and is called a triangular 'seed' (*trikoṇabīja*).[31] Abhinava explains its meaning:

> *'The thoughts of the unsurpassable* [A] *and of bliss* [Ā] *joined to the energy of the will* [I] *enunciate the 'triangle'* [E] *which, they say, is beautiful with the perfume of emission.'*[32]

In his investigation of that text Jayaratha identifies *trikoṇa* with 'the mouth of the yoginī' (*yoginīvaktra*), 'generative organ' (*janma*), 'womb' (*yoni*), 'vulva' (*bhaga*), 'secret maṇḍala' (*guptamaṇḍala*).[33]

25. *ibid.* p.257.
26. *ibid.* The term *ṣaṇḍha* [*sic*], eunuch, is also a grammatical term meaning the same as *napuṃsaka*, neuter. *ibid.* p.258 footnote 97.
27. *ibid.* p.259.
28. *TĀ* 3.78-81. *Parātrīśikālaghuvṛtti* p.51. Padoux, *Vāc*, pp.254-262.
29. *ibid.* p.148. footnote 170.
30. *ibid.* p.299.
31. *ibid.* p.116 footnote 92.
32. *TĀ* 3.94cd-95ab.
33. *ibid.* p.266 and *ibid.* footnote 126.

The phoneme *AI* is deemed to come from the addition of *A* or *Ā* to *E* and so contains even more powerfully the movement of emanation.[34] The phoneme *A* or *Ā* which represents Śiva or seed is already triangular. It is joined to *E* which represents śakti or womb (*yoni*) so that the resulting double triangle represents Śiva and śakti in their inseparable union. The phoneme *AI* is said to have six rays[35] and is called *ṣaṭkoṇa*[36] even though the orthography of the phoneme *AI* does not have a six-angled shape.[37]

The energies of Śiva are will (*icchā*), knowledge (*jñāna*) and activity (*kriyā*). All these three energies are particularly intense in the phoneme *AU* at the moment when the emanation is about to take place.[38]

The fifteenth *kalā*, the fifteenth vowel, the phoneme *Ṃ* occupies a special position in the symbology. It contains the value of all the preceding phonemes and is the moment of transition when the whole energy of sound gathers to a point (*bindu*) and is ready to explode in the emission of the universe.[39] The act of emitting– but not that which is emitted–is symbolised by the two points of the *visarga*, : , which we shall discuss later. The term *bindu* can be interpreted in the two directions of emission and reabsorption. In the latter case it represents the summation of the whole emission, when all is concentrated once more into a point and is about to be finally reabsorbed into the void of Śiva,[40] so that *bindu* takes on the sense of pure consciousness from which all originally comes.[41]

---

34. *ibid.* p.269.
35. *TĀ* 3.96ab.
36. Padoux, *Le coeur*, p.351 footnote 286.
37. Padoux, *Vāc*, p.28.
38. Padoux, *La Parātrīśikālaghuvṛtti*, p.84 note 72.
39. *ibid.* p.85 note 79.
40. In *Tantrasāra* p.14 line 6 - p.15 line 1, Abhinava puts it very clearly: 'And so, when the whole of creatable reality—right up to the power of action, *kriyā*—is about to return to the Unsurpassable, at that very point, before it does return, it halts, since it is the fullness of consciousness, pure light, a point. It is called '*AM*'.
41. In *TĀ* 3.133cd-134ab, light (*prakāśa*) is called the '*bindu* of Śiva' (*śivavindu* [sic]).

The phoneme *Ḥ* (*visarga*), 'emission', is one of the keys to *TĀ* 29 and in particular to Sacrifice 3. The phonemes *Ḥ, HA, HĀ* are similar in sound while *HA* and *S* belong to the class of fricatives. Thus, although they are distinct sounds, they tend to become interchangeable.

The phoneme *Ḥ*, pronounced as a faint emission (*visarga*) of breath, is called 'half-of-*HA*' (*ha-kalā*) and is written as ' : ' in both the *śāradā* script and the *devanāgarī* script.[42] The form ' : ' is halved, so to speak, to produce the shape '.', which is called half-of-half-of-*HA*,[42a] and which is the *bindu*. These phonetic and morphological details provide the symbolism.

Siva and śakti together constitute *AHAM*. If śiva is *A*, Śakti is *HA*. Consequently *HA* comes to represent the whole range of the word,[43] all the mantras, the whole emanation and every manifestation of bliss. Furthermore, as the last letter of the alphabet, *HA* represents the moment of transition from emanation to reabsorption.

The manuscripts of the *Tantrāloka* were written in *śāradā*, the script of Kashmir. In this script, *HA* is written in the shape of the Roman letter S[44] and is therefore curved in shape (*kuṭila*), like an ear-ring (*kuṇḍala*). Since *Ḥ* is half-of-*HA* it is possible to speculate on the *visarga* as *kuṇḍalinī*.

In *TĀ* 3.165cd, Abhinava notes that '... the entire universe shines within the letter *sa*.' However, the *S* is also the eternal, supreme word which is known spontaneously in sexual union.[45] When *S* is understood as referring to the experience of the Absolute in sexo-cosmic rituals, it is called *sīt-kāra*, 'making the sound *sīt*'.

In the list of phonemes, *Ḥ* precedes the list of consonants which are deemed to proceed from it and, by a reverse movement, all the consonants lead to it. It is the point of balance, the spot where the

42. Padoux, *Vāc*, p.277.

42a. Gnoli, *Il Commento*, p.254 line 18.

43. Padoux, *Le coeur*, p.244 footnote 246.

44. Singh, *Parātriṃśikāvivaraṇa*, p.60 note 6. For the shape of the phoneme, see Walter Slaje, *Indische Schriften, Band 1, Śāradā*, Reinbek, Dr. Inge Wezler Verlag für Orientalische Fachpublikationen, 1993, p.27.

45. Padoux, *Vāc*, p.302.

vibration is most intense and yet harmonious, and therefore symbolises the junction of the emanation and reabsorption, the divine pulsation.[46] The two dots in the morphology of *visarga* are deemed to represent Śiva and śakti. The upper dot represents the moon or Śiva which is resorptive whereas the lower dot is śakti, the sun, emitting.[47] They are called 'moon and sun',(*somasūryau*).[48] The two points are joined in the *visarga*, ' : ', which is thus a *saṃghaṭṭa*, union.[49]

The idea of the term 'sixteenth vowel', *Ḥ*, symbolising the union of Śiva and śakti is further emphasised by speculation on the lunar cycle. The sixteenth 'day' of the lunar month corresponds to the night of the new moon and therefore to the darkness during which the sun and moon are supposed to live together. Their union and the *amṛta*, nectar, which results are the hidden reservoir of the fifteen *kalā*, i.e. of the objective world.[50]

In short, the term *visarga*, the phoneme *Ḥ* or the two dots, ' : ', can refer to a triple emission, a threefold *visarga*. The term 'emission' refers either to the process of emanation, to the process of reabsorption or to the eternal union (*melaka*) and pulsation of Śiva and śakti, which already contains in principle the subsequent emanation and reabsorption.

Finally, the emission can also refer to the emission of sexual fluids so that these acquire all thc symbolic value attached to the various meanings of *visarga*, *Ḥ*.[51]

(c) As Cosmology

The emanation proceeds from the void of Śiva to the earth. This emanation or flow (*sāra*) in all its diversity can be classified

46. *ibid.* p.281.
47. Singh, *Parātriṃśikāvivaraṇa*, p.88 note 4. *Parātriṃśikāvivaraṇa* p.257 line10.
48. Padoux, *La Parātrīśikālaghuvṛtti*, p.81 note 60.
49. TĀ 3.136cd-143. TĀ 5.68ab.
50. Raniero Gnoli, 'Alcune tecniche yoga nelle scuole Śaiva', in *Rivista degli studi orientali* 29: 279-290, 1956, pp.286-287. Padoux, *Vāc*, p.91.
51. 'Thus *visarga*, which is the emission of the cosmos by the divinity is also the emission of sperm. This allows certain texts to function in two ways, to having meaning on two levels, a fact which is essential in the descriptions of tantric practices.' André Padoux, 'Le monde hindou et le sexe - symbolisme, attitudes, pratiques', in *Cahiers Internationaux de Sociologie* 76: 29-49, 1984, p.39.

according to categories, worlds, *kalā*, and causal deities which present a more 'physical' outline of the emanation.

The whole of reality consists of 36 categories (*tattva*)[52] as set out in Appendix 1. In fact, Abhinava speculates about a 37th and 38th category but these are logical considerations rather than realities.[53] The term *tattva* constantly recurs in *TĀ* 29 and its investigation but also acquires another quite different meaning. The knowledge of Śiva, the supreme category, the category *par excellence*, produces bliss and a sexual flow which thus signifies all the categories from the highest to the lowest and also grants access to them and to all their powers. The sexual fluid is therefore called *tattva*, 'substance'.

A category is a grouping of worlds (*bhuvana*), portrayed in *TĀ* 8[54] as a complex *maṇḍala* or throne for Śiva. These constitute an intricate system of enjoyments into which the disciple is initiated in *TĀ* 29 but they cannot be listed here. They extend, in varying numbers according to various texts, from Sadāśiva down to the lowest level, Kālāgni, from which the reabsorption starts. Each world is distinct with its own deities, its own qualities and pleasures into which a person is reborn according to his attitude of

---

52. The whole of *TĀ* 9 is an exposition of the categories.

53. There are two numbering systems.
The first is as follows. Śiva is essentially united with śakti and inseparable. As such he is classed as the thirty-sixth category. However, if for the sake of discussion he is regarded as separate from śakti, he may be classed as a thirty-seventh 'category'. Yet the very act of consideration involves a thirty-eight 'category' which is the subject who is considering Śiva as separate from śakti. This is stated simply in *Tantrasāra* p.110 line 13-p.111 line 5. It is also dealt with in *TĀ* 11.20ab-27 and in *TĀ* 6.179 cd-181ab. See also Padoux, *Vāc*, pp.78-81.
Secondly, if Śiva is considered to be a distinct thirty-sixth category, the totality of categories is classed as 'thirty-seventh'. When he is all that he emits, he is a thirty-eighth category. See *TĀ* 15.314b. See also *Tantravaṭadhānikā* 3.17cd.

54. *TĀ* 8 explores the various worlds (*bhuvana*) and is dependent on a number of sources, in particular the *Svacchandatantra*. See Gnoli, *Luce*, p.247 footnote1. After describing the cosmic *maṇḍala* in its immense variety, Abhinava summarises his description from *śl*.407cd onwards. Then, in *śl*.436cd-452, he gives a further summary taken from *Mālinīvijayottaratantra* chapter 5 which lists 118 worlds. In that summary he states that above the hells which are ruled by Kālāgni and Kūṣmāṇḍa is the level of earth, *bhūtala*, whose Lords are Hāṭaka and 'Śiva', *śl*.437cd. The highest world is that of Sadāśiva, *śl*.451, while the category of Śiva does not contain any worlds, *śl*.452b.

mind, his initiation, his mantra etc. Each person must pass through these worlds to achieve liberation but by the appropriate means a person can proceed speedily through them all at once.

Just as a category is a grouping of worlds so the *kalā* is a grouping of categories.[55] There are five *kalā*: 1. *nivṛtti* has the one category: earth; 2. *pratiṣṭhā* extends from water through to *prakṛti*; 3. *vidyā* involves the categories from *puruṣa* to *māyā*; 4. *śānta* extends from *śuddhavidyā* to *śakti*. The fifth *kalā*, corresponding to the category 'Śiva', is called *śāntātītā* since it transcends *śānta* and contains all the *kalā*.[56]

The causal deities (*kāraṇa*) govern the various levels of being. As such they are tied to limitation so that they do not enjoy the liberty the practitioner of the Kula ritual will eventually enjoy. Abhinava lists six lords which Jayaratha explains in his accompanying investigation.[57] They are associated with the various modalities of the subtle-breath, the diverse positions in the body and the steps of the life-cycle.[58] They are also linked with the five well-known states of consciousness to which a sixth state is added.[59] Again, in the *Tantrasāra,* Abhinava links them with the various eons of time, with the levels of the body, with the categories, with the subtle-breath and the stages of sound.[60]

The categories, worlds, *kalā* and causal deities cover the range of emanated realities. Attention must now be given to certain elements within that range, the first to be considered being *māyā* because of its pivotal importance in the process of Śiva's self-concealment. The word is often translated as 'illusion' but in the mind

55. *TĀ* 11.2-3.
56. See *TĀ* 11.8-9. See also Padoux, *La Parātrīśikālaghuvṛtti*, p.109-110 note 241. These *kalā* are set out in Appendix 1.
57. *TĀ* 8.9-10. There are variations in the listings. In *TĀ* 9.57cd-58a, Abhinava lists the six causal forces under alternative names: *brahma-viṣṇu-hara-īśāna-suśiva-anāśrita-ātmani\ṣaṭke kāraṇasaṃjñe* ... In *Tantrasāra* p.57 line 10, they are listed in the same way as in Jr.235d.1, namely Brahmā, Viṣṇu, Rudra, Īśvara, Sadāśiva and *Anāśriśiva*, and are called *kāraṇa-ṣaṭkam* as in TĀ 29.233a.
58. *Tantrasāra* p.57 lines 8-12.
59. *ibid.* p.141 lines 4-6.
60. Raniero Gnoli, *L'essenza dei Tantra (Tantrasāra)*, Torino, Boringhieri, 1960, pp.143-146.

of Abhinava the world is a reality about which only the ignorant individual has false views. *Māyā* refers to the error of the latter's understanding and not to the object about which the error is held. *Māyā* can be considered internally from the point of view of knowledge as a stain with its *karma* or externally from the point of view of the coverings.

There are three impurities or stains (*mala*) which are also called knots (*granthi*). If the highest reality is knowledge (*jñāna*), the fundamental 'stain is ignorance' (*malam ajñāna*).[61] Abhinava quotes an unknown text which puts it well:

> *'The wise describe the stain of ignorance, i.e. [the stain of] individuality, as the root cause of the stains of* māyā *and* karma. *That same seed of the worn out tree of [transmigratory] existence is consumed instantly in the blazing fire of supreme consciousness.'*[62]

For the non-dualist the basic impurity is individualism, whereby either the Self, in its increasing self-obscuration, thinks it is only an individual or the individual self presumes that itself, *qua* individual, is the Self. The ignorance consists in either underestimating or over-estimating. It opposes self and Self in a dualism. It is the *āṇava-mala*, the stain concerned with the erroneous sense of individuality. The subject who has succumbed to the primary error of particularity now takes on the stain of illusion (*māya-mala*) and its limitations which are described as follows: 'The 'I' (*so 'ham*) knows this now, does this and is attached to this.'[63] It is the admission of the limitations involved in the five 'coverings'. From this, in turn, comes the third stain, *kārma-mala*, the stain of false action, defined as 'taking on attitudes of mind which are concerned with pure and impure ...'[64] The actions that flow from ignorance are vitiated and one is condemned to the cycle of rebirth.[65]

---

61. *Mālinīvijayottaratantra* 1.23c. Abhinava quotes the phrase in *Parātriṃśikāvivaraṇa* p.223 line 10. In TĀ 1.23a, he states: *malam ajñānam icchanti.*
62. *Parātriṃśikāvivaraṇa* p.223 lines 5-8.
63. *Īśvarapratyabhijñāvimarśinī*, vol.2, p.237.
64. *Parātriṃśikāvivaraṇa* p.199 line 30 - p.200 line 1.
65. *Īśvarapratyabhijñāvimarśinī*, vol.3, p.205

There are three stages of *karman*[66] : the past, present and future. The past and future *karman* are not yet operative (*anārabdha-kārya*). The process of initiation for both the Son and the Adept destroys the past *karman*. The initiation as a Son destroys the future *karman* as well whereas the Adept wishes to enjoy his future *karman*, at least in its advantageous aspects.[67] As regards the present *karman*, the *prārabdha-karman*, the *karman* in the process of maturation (*ārabdha-kārya*), the initiation under discussion does not destroy it[68] for if the guru were to destroy the present *karman* as well—in a type of initiation called *sadyonirvāṇa-dīkṣā*[69] —the disciple would immediately die (*dehapātaḥ*).

The 'coverings' (*kañcuka*) which obscure consciousness and give shape to external reality are six in number: *māyā* itself, restricted activity, desire, limited knowledge, time and necessity.[70] If *māyā* is excluded in the sense of being a blanket term, the coverings are five in number. They may also be referred to as *kalā* so that the word *kalā*, as used in the terms *sakala* and *niṣkala*, refer to the five coverings. Thus, Śiva 'without parts' or simple, *niṣkala*, is Śiva prior to his subjection to *māyā*. He is active in the world of limited beings, but as a sort of invisible, effective presence. When Śiva takes on the limitations of objective reality, Śiva 'with parts' or composite, *sakala*, he acts through the faculties and sense organs.[71] Notice that Śiva in this case is not burdened by the ignorance of *māyā* but is liberated while alive.

However, the person who does not recognise his true nature and who continues to be dominated by the three stains, ends as a 'bonded animal' (*paśu*). He lives in a dualist world and is trapped by every limitation. Like the ox at the mill, he moves round in an endless cycle of activity which leads to nothing. He is under the control of other forces and greedily satisfies himself with food and drink, as noted in Qt.100b.2.[72]

66. Abhinava studies *karman* at length in *TĀ* 9.88cd-144ab.
67. *TĀ* 15.28 ff. *Tantrasāra* p.158 lines 10-11.
68. *TĀ* 9.131ab.
69. Héléne Brunner, 'Le *sādhaka*, personnage oublié du Śivaïsme du sud', in *Journal Asiatique* 263: 411-443, 1975, p.417.
70. *TĀ* 9.204. *Paramārthasāra*, *śl.*16cd, *śl.*17c.
71. *TĀ* 28.225d-226.
72. See also *Īśvarapratyabhijñāvimarśinī*, vol.3, p.204.

The categories of reality continue to move into darkness and inertia. Śiva, who is *AHAM*, 'I am', unlimited, unsurpassable consciousness, has concealed himself by a sort of forgetfulness and takes on the stain of the limited self (*āṇava-mala*) becoming *puruṣa*, the individual person, which is numbered as category twenty-five. He then enters further into darkness by subjecting himself to the processes of intellect (*buddhi*). From this he derives an image of the self, the ego (*ahaṃkāra*) which is category twenty-two.[73] The ahaṃkāra is a natural reduction, so to speak, of Śiva's infinite *AHAM* but is not incompatible with *AHAM*. Indeed, when the whole cycle we are examining is complete, the ego will be reconciled with the 'I' just as all the categories will be brought into the harmony of the person who is liberated while living and who is Śiva.

The term *ahaṃkāra* is not to be confused with the term *ahaṃyu*, egoism or conceit. Such a person is attached to his self-image and will allow nothing to disturb it so that neither emanation nor reabsorption can occur. The vibration ceases and reality remains fragmented.

The emanation of the categories reaches its final point where Śiva becomes inert (*jaḍi*). In that state there is neither the spontaneity of consciousness nor any expansiveness of heart, no subjectivity nor sense of the harmony of things but only fragmentation, lethargy and impotence. Inertia is the dominance of matter (*pṛthvī*) and the petering out of emanation.[73b]

(d) As the Human Being

The process of emanation is set out in the body itself. Starting from the tuft of hair and ending with the soles of the feet, the human person is a microcosm, a symbol of the whole. The harmonious complexity of reality or of the body with all its combinations and phases is symbolised by the wheel (*cakra*). This word has a variety of meanings: 'wheel', 'cycle', 'circle', 'vortex', 'radiation', 'group',

---

73. Abhinava links the two concepts, *AHAM* and *ahaṃkāra*, in his derivation of *ahaṃkāra*. The ego, *ahaṃkāra*, is a product, *kāra*, of the 'I am', *AHAM*. Gnoli, *L'essenza*, p.170 footnote .

73b.Padoux, *La Parātrīśikālaghuvṛtti*, p.72 note 18.

'network', 'hierarchy' or even 'pair'.[74] At the centre of the wheel is the hub or the space (*kha*). The wheel involves other 'wheels', all arranged in a hierarchy. The principal circle (*mukhya-cakra*) is consciousness from which all comes or is identified with the sex organ since it too, like consciousness, is the source of bliss. On the principal circle the many sub-circles (*anucakra*) depend so that one circle leads to another in an harmonious system.

The codes given in *TĀ* 29.37cd are of particular importance for understanding the circles in the body. *Svacchandatantra* 15 gives a large number of codes and their meaning[75] none of which correspond to anything in *TĀ* 29. That being said, *Svacchandatantra* 15.24-31 gives the illuminating example of an Adept pointing to a particular part of the body, tuft of hair or skull or forehead or palate, and so indicating a category: *śakti, bindu, īśvara, rudra* etc.[76] In Jr.195d.3, Jayaratha describes the ritual of the 'hand of Śiva' which touches one or other of the circles of the initiate's body causing conviction in that place and making it the focus of his practice,[77] and therefore of his level of power. By referring to one or other of these locations in his body, the *yogī* reveals both the initiatory experience he has received and the corresponding supernatural powers and rights that have been granted to him.

The parts of the body are emanated in the followng way. Twelve finger-widths above the head is the 'end-of-twelve', the place beyond the visible body where consciousness rests.[78] The term *śikhā* which means tuft of hair, flame, subtle-breath, śakti, Śiva himself[79] etc. also symbolises the source of the emanation[80] and the end point of the reabsorption, consciousness in its plenitude.

---

74. See *śl.*88d, *śl.*158b and Jr.88d.1, Jr.158b.1.
75. See also *Hevajra Tantra* I.7.
76. *Svacchandatantram, with commentary 'Uddyota'*, by Kṣemarājācārya, V.V. Dwivedi, ed. Delhi, Parimal Publications, 1985, vol.2, p.429.
77. Pandey interprets the *chummā* as different parts of the '... physical organism, where they primarily practised concentration...' Pandey, p.545.
78. *TĀ* 16.112 bcd-113ab.
79. TĀ 6.22cd-23ab.
80. In *Parātriṃśikāvivaraṇa* p.277 lines 3-5, Abhinava states that *śikhā* is '...the freedom to imagine all the categories down to the earth and is applied to various things such as supreme consciousness, intelligence, 'touch', subtle-breath, the 'aperture of Brahmā' and the currents ...'.

The aperture of Brahmā (*brahma-randhra*) or the 'pit-of-Brahmā' (*brahma-bila*) and the aperture of Ka (*ka-randhra*) is situated above the *suṣumṇa*, the central axis of the body[81] at the top of the head, at the place leading beyond the limitations of *māyā*.

The three principal channels (*nāḍī*)[82] are *iḍā* on the left; *piñgalā* on the right; and the dominant *suṣumṇā* in the centre.[83] From these come innumerable other channels by which the subtle-breath leaves and enters the practitioner and the guru enters the disciple. *TĀ* 29 and its investigation refer to other openings in the body.

The upper *kuṇḍalī* is to be distinguished from the lower *kuṇḍalī*. The former is at the top of the head[84] and is the 'pit-of-Brahmā' as distinct from the lower Brahmā at the generative organ. Viewed experientially, it is the *kuṇḍalinī* in its raised state[85] as distinct from *kuṇḍalinī* in its dormant state in the 'bulb' (*kanda*) where it lies in repose.

The eye-brow centre (*bhrū-madhya*) is particularly associated with *bindu* and with the mind. It is the place where all the manifestations of consciousness as well as all the operations of intelligence etc. have their starting and concluding point. To affect this point is to affect all the thought processes.

The words *raśmi*, *ara* and *marīcī* in their ordinary sense mean a 'spark', a 'beam' or a 'ray'. They can also refer to the secondary divinities which emanate as rays of light from the principal divinity such as, for example, the twelve goddesses of the Krama or the eight goddesses Brāhmī etc.,[86] and can refer to levels of consciousness, *gocara*, *bhūcara* etc. They often designate the faculties which proceed from consciousness like rays of light in order to make contact with their objects.[87] Principal among these faculties are the three internal faculties (*antaḥ-karaṇa*), *buddhi, ahaṃkāra* and

81. *TĀ* 8.394a.
82. *Tantrasāra* p.58 line 2.
83. Gnoli, *L'essenza*, p.147 footnote 3.
84. In *TĀ* 7.68cd-69a and investigation.
85. Silburn translates the expression *ūrdhvagakuṇḍali* as 'the kuṇḍalinī in its raised state'. Silburn, *La kuṇḍalinī*, p.209.
86. Padoux, *La Parātrīśikālaghuvṛtti*, p.92 note 116 which gives various listings.
87. See Padoux, *Le coeur*, p.193 footnote 54.

manas and the five faculties of knowledge (*jñānendriya or buddhendriya*), and the five faculties of action (*karmendriya*). The *puryaṣṭaka*, the 'eight', are traditionally listed as the three internal senses, *buddhi*, *ahaṃkāra*, *manaḥ*, and the five subtle elements (*tanmātra*).[88]

The sexual organ and sexual area is of special importance and is designated by a number of terms. It is called the 'bulb' which is not so much a part of the anatomy as a place of experience. For this reason there are different localisations of the 'bulb', (*kanda*).[89] The male, but particularly the female organ, is called a lotus, since the flower has the property of expanding and contracting.[90] It is also called 'root' (*mūla*) in the sense of being the place of origin. The female sexual organ, called 'mouth of the *yoginī*' (*yoginī-vaktra*), the Picu-mouth (*picu-vaktra*), the generative organ (*janma-ādhāra*) etc., symbolises the womb of the universe and is particularly associated with the *visarga*, *Ḥ*. The downward pointing triangle (*tri-koṇa*) which is reminiscent of the region in which the womb is located, also symbolises the emanation of the universe. Indeed, just as the sound seed (*bīja*) in fact contains and emits the universe, so too the *tri-koṇa* of the woman conceives and gives birth to the universe. The symbol enacts what it represents.

The feet and in particular the toe are intimately connected with the earth and with the last stage of emanation and for that very reason they also symbolise the starting point of reabsorption so that the Fire of Time, Kālāgni, Kālānala, begins from that point.[91]

3. Reabsorption of the Absolute

The process of emanation is reversed by the process of reabsorption and the one mirrors the other. There are a number of frameworks which are more often weighted in the direction of reabsorption.

---

88. Gnoli, *Luce*, p.606 footnote 7. Padoux, *Le coeur*, p.151 footnote 228. For these, see Appendix 1. In *Īśvarapratyabhijñāvimarśinī*, vol.3, p.212, Abhinava gives another listing which comprises eighteen elements.
89. Padoux, *Vāc*, p.413 footnote 89.
90. *Parātriṃśikāvivaraṇa* p.281 lines 18-19.
91. See *TĀ* 29.63cd, *śl.*259 and *Vijñānabhairava* 52.

(a) Six Pathways

Perhaps the grandest of the frameworks is the set of six pathways (*adhvan*) which set out the whole structure of reality and therefore the manner in which the great vibration of emanation and reabsorption takes place. The pathway is usually understood as the means of arriving at consciousness but it must first be understood as an emanation from consciousness.[92] The pathway is described[93] as the way by which, in reverse direction so to speak, a person who is still caught in duality reaches the highest level. Rather than being a painful journey, for those who are enlightened the pathway is something to be enjoyed or 'devoured' (*adyate*) whence, Abhinava explains, comes the word *adhvan*. Throughout the *Tantrāloka* 6-11,[94] he develops a schema of the manifestation of the pathways which, following *TĀ* 6.34-36, can be set out in this fashion:

A. Pathway of time (*kāla-adhva*) based on subtle-breath (*prāṇa*)	B. Pathway of space (*deśa-adhva*) based on bodily forms (*mūrti*)
1. phonemes (*varṇa*)	4. *kalā*
2. *mantra*	5. categories (*tattva*)
3. *pada*[95]	6. worlds (*pura, bhuvana*)

The guru initiates his disciple into one or other of the pathways which are not exclusive of each other. In point of fact Abhinava

92. *TĀ* 6.29.

93. *TĀ* 6.30.

94. In *TĀ* 6, Abhinava deals at length with subtle-breath and time, lunar day, month, year, eons etc. He deals with phonemes, mantras and *pada* in *TĀ* 6 and 7. He deals with worlds in *TĀ* 8, with categories in *TĀ* 9 and 10 and with *kalā* in *TĀ* 11. The arrangement of the sixfold pathway with the numbers of worlds, categories etc. according to the *Tantrāloka*, the *Mālinīvijayottaratantra* and the *Svacchandatantra* is set out in Padoux, *Vāc*, pp.358-359.

95. '... for neither the term *word*, it most-frequent sense, or any other term, is able to convey the meanings of *pada* in the *ṣaḍadhvan*, where it may be a word, or a syllable or a group of syllables sometimes even a sentence.' *ibid.* p.348.

notes that the guru must perform the purification of one pathway in such a way that all the pathways are included in it.[96] The aim is to have the disciple eventually pass through them all so as to arrive at consciousness which is their source.

(b) Five Forms of Subtle-breath

The subtle-breath (*prāṇa*) is of first importance in the *Tantrāloka* and is examined in great detail in both *TĀ* 5 and *TĀ* 6. The words *prāṇa* or *prāṇana* refer to the subtle-breath, 'life' (*jīvana*), before it has differentiated into the varieties of subtle-breath such as *prāṇa*, *apāna* etc.[97] It is a vital energy, a spiritual energy particularly associated with the heart and indeed is assimilated to the energy of the cosmos.[98] The term can refer to the first of the subtle-breaths, *prāṇa*, or to all five: *prāṇa, apāna, samāna, udāna, vyāna*. The *prāṇa*, exhalation, is a movement towards externalisation. The *apāna* starts from externality and is the beginning point towards internalisation and feeds the *prāṇa* just as the waning moon feeds the sun.[99] When these two movements are brought into harmony or balance with each other, there is an experience of *samāna*. In this state, they are both restrained (*nirodha*) from their normal trajectory: *prāṇa* from its tendency to externality and its *īḍā* channel; *apāna* from its tendency to internality and its *piñgalā* channel. Then there is an experience of 'breath', which is the *udāna* rising within its central channel, the *suṣumṇā*, towards the highest level of consciousness. This involves a devouring of limited subjectivity etc. and the attainment of supreme subjectivity, *AHAM*, where there is no limitation of any sort, no dualism in any sense. The *AHAM* is all inclusive, reigning over all.

Abhinava connects the five stages of subtle-breath with the five levels of consciousness[100] in the following schema:

96. *TĀ* 11.82cd-85ab. Gnoli, *Luce*, p.375 footnote 15. Padoux, *Vāc*, p.370.
97. Gnoli, *Luce*, p.653 footnote 82.
98. Padoux, *La Parātrīśikālaghuvṛtti*, p.105 note 203.
99. *TĀ* 6.92cd-94ab.
100. *Īśvarapratyabhijñāvimarśinī*, vol.3, pp.215-218 commenting on *Īśvarapratyabhijñā* III.2.19 ff.

	Breath	Level of consciousness
1.	*prāṇa* and *apāna*	wakefulness, *jāgrat*
2.	*prāṇa* and *apāna*	dreaming sleep, *svapna*
3.	*samāna*, equal breath	deep sleep, *suṣupti*
4.	*udāna*, rising breath	Fourth, *turya*
5.	*vyāna*, permeating breath	Beyond-Fourth, *turyātīta*

This schema is tied to the one described directly below and to several others emerging in the course of this book.

(c) Seven Levels of Bliss

The bliss of Śiva and śakti, the relationship of cognition and recognition, may proceed through seven levels described in *TĀ* 5.43-52ab and is linked to the five forms of subtle-breath. They are set out schematically as follows:

Bliss	Place of repose	Breath	Image
1. *nijānanda*	subject (*pramātā*),		heart (*hṛt*)
2. *nirānanda*	void (*śūnyatā*)		
3. *parānanda*	objects of knowledge (*prameya*)	*prāṇa*	[sun]
	all objects of knowledge	*apāna*	moon
4. *brahmānanda*	union (*saṃghaṭṭa*) of all objects	*samāna*	
5. *mahānanda*	devouring of the means (*māna*) and objects of knowledge (*meya*)	*udāna*	fire
6. *cidānanda*	nothing is inert (*jaḍa*)	*vyāna*	
7. *jagadānanda*			

The first level of bliss is that of the supreme subject, *AHAM*, the personal bliss (*nijānanda*) which belongs to Śiva and śakti. Out of freedom the divine reality wishes to express itself in the great *maṇḍala* of the world. It abandons, so to speak, the bliss it possesses eternally and begins the process of self-expression. This intermediate stage is called *śūnyatā*, emptiness, since bliss is found neither in the subject nor yet in the object. It is rightly called 'non-bliss' (*nirānanda* or *a-nanda*).[101] Progressing further, the divine emanation manifests the world of objects and therein finds *parānanda*, pleasure in the object. The objective world is limited by nature and so pleasure in a limited object comes to an end. This is the starting point of a return movement called 'the bliss of Brahmā' (*brahmānanda*) since Brahmā is the starting point of the movement toward consciousness. This process of returṇing to subjectivity, of seeing the object of knowledge and the means of knowledge as simply the result of one's own subjectivity, is the fifth form of bliss called *mahānanda*. The sixth stage is called *cidānanda*, the bliss of consciousness when the realisation of 'I' is predominant. The seventh form of bliss, *jagadānanda*, is a total bliss, the unity of all the forms of bliss. Bliss is found in the world as in the self, since the self has been experienced in the world. To delight in the one is to delight in the other.

(d) Four Aspects of the Krama Cycle

Somewhat comparable to those seven stages of bliss are the four moments of the Krama cycle of emission and reabsorption. These are not different from the twelve stages of the Krama but are a different way of looking at them. The first is *udyoga* where consciousness emits the object. The second stage is *avabhāsa*, the manifestation of reality. The third is the reabsorption, the relishing or savouring (*carvaṇa*) of reality. The final stage is the dissolution when reality is reabsorbed in its every aspect into the rest (*viśrānti*) of subjectivity.[102] For example,

---

101. *TĀ* 5.44cd states: 'since he rests on the void alone, he experiences an absence of bliss', *śūnyatāmātraviśrānter nirānandam vibhāvayet* || In his investigation of that text, Jayaratha glosses as follows: 'absence-of-bliss (*nirānandaṃ*), moving out from own-bliss (*nijāt*) which is experienced in the knowing subject, is particularised as [end-of-]ten.' It is slightly removed from the 'end-of-twelve' and is a state intermediate between that based on the subject, *nijānanda*, and that based on the object, *parānanda*, and is the state connected with the means of knowledge. See Pandey, p.646.
102. Padoux, *Vāc*, p.238 footnote 37. In *Dehasthadevatācakrastotra* 5, Abhinava proclaims 'I make homage to Ānandabhairavī who, as awareness (*vimarśa*), forever plays at arousing (*udaya*), manifesting (*avabhāsa*) and devouring (*carvaṇa*) the universe.' *Parātriṃśikāvivaraṇa* p.255 lines 23-24 has the terms *udyoga-avabhāsa-saṃkrāma-vilāpana*.

'... at first there is will to perceive a jar (udyoga), then there is actual perception of the jar (avabhāsa), relishing of the perceptive experience (carvaṇa), and finally assimilating the perceptive experience of the jar to the essential nature of the Self.'[103]

(e) Five States of Consciousness

The theory of the four states of consciousness—wakefulness, sleep, deep-sleep and the Fourth—has a history going back to the oldest *Upaniṣads*.[104] To these four states the Trika adds a fifth, the Beyond-Fourth, which permeates and transcends them. The first three are grouped together since all three are transient.[105] The other two stages, Fourth and Beyond-Fourth, are linked together because subjectivity, the 'I' (*ahaṃbhāva*), shines forth in them. In short, the wakened state is the world of multiplicity and division whereas the movement towards the deeper states of consciousness is a progression towards unity.[106] The first three states are simply described. Wakefulness (*jāgrat*) is the state

'wherein an object is perceived by the external senses and where there is an object of perception common to perceiving subjects.'[107]

Dreaming sleep (*svapna*):

'... because it derives from a mental state alone, this emanation is not an object seen by other perceiving subjects.'[108]

---

103. Singh, *Parātriṃśikāvivaraṇa*, pp.197-198 note 7.
104. For a survey of the history of this theory, see the work of Anne-Marie Esnoul, 'Les songes et leur interprétation dans l'Inde', in Anne-Marie Esnoul, Paul Garelli, Yves Hervouet, Marcel Leibovici, Serge Sauneron, Jean Yoyotte eds., *Les songes et leur interprétation, Sources orientales*, Paris, Editions du Seuil, 1959, Vol.2, pp.208-247.
105. *Īśvarapratyabhijñāvimarśinī*, vol.2, p.257.
106. Bäumer, *Wege*, p.179.
107. *Īśvarapratyabhijñāvimarśinī*, vol.2, p.268. See also *TĀ* 10.231246.
108. *Īśvarapratyabhijñāvimarśinī*, vol.2, p.266. See also *TĀ* 10.247-257ab.

Dreamless sleep (*suṣupti*):

> *'the state of deep sleep, however, does not have a clear object of knowledge.'*[109]

The Fourth is so named because of its place in the list. It does not come after the other three states but rather suffuses them.[110] Thus, whereas the first three exclude each other, the Fourth can be found in each of them and, indeed, the aim of the Kula ritual is to attain the condition wherein the Fourth and especially the Beyond-Fourth are universally present. The Fourth (*turya*) is particularly associated with the dynamism of śakti and is a process of transforming all perception into consciousness.[111] The fifth state of consciousness, Beyond-Fourth, is *AHAM*, Śiva-śakti, eternal cognition and recognition. It is defined as

> *'... that state ... in which the same principle of free-consciousness* [svātantryātmanā] *or self consciousness* [ahaṃbhāvena], ... *shines, in its full freedom ... and there is full consciousness of the presence of qualities of omnipresence and eternality etc. ...'*[112]

Abhinava adds a sixth level: 'namely the 'unsurpassable' (*anuttara*) which is the state of self-existence.'[113]

(f) Five Fields of Knowledge

Vyomeśvarī, also called Vyomavāmeśvarī or Vāmeśvarī, presides over four fields or lesser states of consciousness. Sanderson, basing himself on Kṣemarāja,[114] defines thus:

---

109. *Īśvarapratyabhijñāvimarśinī*, vol.2, p.265. See also *TĀ* 10. 257cd-264ab.
110. 'The Fourth must be poured, like sesamum oil, on the [other] three.' Śivasūtra 3.20.
111. *Īśvarapratyabhijñāvimarśinī*, vol.3, p.209. See also *TĀ* 10. 264cd-269.
112. *Īśvarapratyabhijñāvimarśinī*, vol.3, p.209. See also *TĀ* 10.278-284ab.
113. *Tantrasāra* p.141 lines 2-3.
114. In fact it is not Abhinava but his disciple, Kṣemarāja, who analyses the terms in detail. He does so in the *Pratyabhijñāhṛdayam*, for which see Jaideva Singh, *Pratyabhijñāhṛdayam*, 4th edn. Delhi, Motilal Banarsidass, 1982, p.81-82, and especially in the *Spandasaṃdoha*, for which see Mark Dyczkowski, *The stanzas on vibration*, Varanasi, Dilip Kumar Publishers, 1994, pp.69-70. In *Il commento di Abhinavagupta alla Parātriṃśikā*, Traduzione e testo, Roma, Instituto Italiano per il Medio ed Estremo Oriente, 1985, pp.287-289, Gnoli deals with the matter in some detail and gives the relevant translation from the *Spandasaṃdoha*.

'In Kṣemarāja's Krama Vāmeśvarī is identified with the power of consciousness in its absolute, uncontracted state and is said to give rise to four circuits of subordinate deities: the Khecarīs, the Gocarīs, the Dikcarīs and the Bhūcarīs. These are the same power of consciousness but projected towards and into plurality on the levels of the (i) the subject, (ii) the mental apparatus (antaḥkaraṇam), (iii) the faculties of sense perception (buddhīndriyam) *and action* (karmendriyam), *and (iv) the sense elements* (tanmātram).*'*[115]

(g) Twelve Stages of Sound

The twelve stages of sound (*nāda*) are divided into a set of eight and a set of four. The set of eight when expressed in the direction of emanation are: 'the transmental' (*unmanā*); 'association with mind' (*samanā*); 'the pervasive' (*vyāpinī*); 'energy' (*śakti*); 'end-of-sound' (*nādānta*); 'sound' (*nāda*); 'the obstructing' (*nirodhinī*); 'half-moon' (*ardhacandra*). To these eight are added a set of four stages, making a total of twelve. These four, still in the direction of emanation are *bindu*, and, in the case of *OṂ*, the three phonemes *M, U, A*. The set of twelve are experienced in the direction of emanation or of reabsorption. While it will be described here in terms of emanation, the terminology sometimes makes more sense when described in terms of reabsorption.

12. The stage of *unmanā* corresponds to the supreme word, the acknowledgement of the self (*svātmavimarśa*).[116] It is the pure word without any movement towards emanation and where any exteriority has ceased. It transcends all comprehension, as the word *unmanā*, transcendental, suggests.

11. Stages 11, 10 and 9, i.e. *samanā, vyāpinī* and *śakti,* are the bridge between the supreme word and sound and are sometimes implied together as a trio[117] so as to form the '*śakti*-spike' on which *unmanā* is enthroned. In stage 11, *samanā*, the word

115. Sanderson, 'Meaning', pp.69-70.
116. Silburn, *Le Vijñāna Bhairava*, p.51.
117. *Parātriṃśikāvivaraṇa* pp.228-229. Jr.271d.1.

begins to manifest itself. It is the first stage in a movement towards sound but it is a complete indetermination with regard to any particular sound or form of manifestation and due to its association with mind is called *samanā*. In the direction of reabsorption it signifies the moment of indifference to any manifestation.

10. The word continues its process of manifestation. There is a first sense of particularity or variety but the word still pervades all equally and is called *vyāpinī*, permeation. In the direction of reabsorption it is the cessation of any will to emanate.

9. The word limits itself still further into energy (*śakti*) which is also called *sparśa-vyaptī*[118] or simply *sparśa* (Jr.160b.2). It is a concentration of the inherent dynamism of the word and is a determination to express. In the direction of reabsorption it is the cessation of any determination.

8. The next two stages, *nādānta* and *nāda*, are paired. *Nādānta* is the 'end of sound', the end of any sense of expressing. Conversely, in the direction of emanation it could be called 'beginning of sound'.

7. Sound (*nāda*) is the first condensation of the supreme word (*parāvāc*).[119] It is the act of saying, the expressing without any indication of what is expressed. If *nāda* is the statement, *nādānta* is the withdrawal of the statement.

6. Sound moves towards its self-expression. The command is being given. It still has a universality and has not yet been particularised. This sixth stage is called *nirodha*, obstruction, because the causal deities, whose nature is particularised and who hold sway over various particular groupings of categories are prevented from entering this indeterminate stage.[120] In the direction of reabsorption it is the end of any subject matter.

5. The 'half-moon' (*ardhacandra*) is understood in association with *bindu*. It is the beginning of the impulse to manifestation

118. Silburn, *Le Vijñāna Bhairava*, p.50.

119. Padoux, *Vāc*, pp.96-97.

120. *ibid.* p.103.

which is *bindu*. It is a transition stage between the universality of *nirodha* and the particularity of *bindu*. In terms of reabsorption it is the cessation of impulse towards audible sound.

4. The *bindu* is the concentration of the audible sound. Since *bindu* is the concentrated mass of the expression it is more powerful than the audible sound. In the direction of reabsorption it is the moment of silence wherein the audible sound has ceased but which contains all that was said.

3-2-1. At this point sound becomes audible. The last three stages should properly be considered in terms of reabsorption. In the case of the sacred sound *OM* they are constituted by the phonemes *A, U, M.*

(h) Four Means to Reach the Highest State

The last of the frameworks which structure reality and emphasise the process of reaching the highest state is arguably the most important since it is treated at the outset of the *Tantrāloka*, in chapters 2-5. It consists of the 'four means' (*upāya*). The first 'means' is totally transcendent. Each of the other *upāya* in turn reflects one of the three external activities of Śiva: will (*icchā*), knowledge (*jñāna*) and action (*kriyā*). Each also reflects one of the three levels of being: '*śiva*', '*śakti*', and '*nara*'. The latter in this list of three is an expression of the former but the practitioner need not proceed from one method to the next since each is a valid means to attaining Śiva himself.[121]

The first method is, strictly speaking, a 'non-method' (*anupāya, nirupāya*) whose description in *TĀ* 2 is given mainly in apophatic terms. This method is both means and end at once since it is an immediate and total effectiveness. Abhinava gives the example of a person who hears one word of the guru (*guruvacanam*) and is there upon brought to realisation by an intense descent of energy and enjoys an absorption into Śiva (*samāveśa*) without other means of realisation.[122] He is not bound by any other activities such as mantra, worship, meditation or discipline.[123] The agency in the 'non-means' belongs entirely to Śiva himself without any activity

121. Bäumer, *Wege*, pp.62-63.
122. Gnoli, *L'essenza*, p.8.
123. *ibid.* p.9.

on the part of the disciple. The 'non-method' does, however, have indirect methods (*parikaratvam*) as for example the 'oblation' (*caru*) which is mentioned in Jr.200d.2.

The second means, 'the method of Śambhu' (*śāmbhavopāya*), is particularly associated with the will, with an attitude of mind and heart, a fundamental orientation. This method too is described largely in the negative, as the method of non-discursive thought (*nirvikalpa*).[124] To put it in positive terms, undifferentiated or non-discursive thought is 'pure thought, direct perception (*pratyakṣa*) of the ultimate reality'.[125] Abhinava also excludes all ritual action from the *śāmbhavopāya*.[126] The Kula ritual derives from the attitude involved in *śāmbhavopāya* and leads to it, but being ritual, is itself the 'fourth method'. It is concerned with the contemplation of *AHAM*.[127]

The third method, the 'method of śakti' (*śāktopāya*), uses *vikalpa*[128] which means differentiated thought, that sort of mental activity which opposes the various aspects of things and emphasises one thing to the exclusion of another. It questions, hesitates, it divides and is dualist in tendency.[129] It is nevertheless a means since a valid reflection, even though differentiated as in the statements 'I am omniscient' or 'I am omnipotent', unifies all aspects of reality so that the non-duality of consciousness arises[130] in a manner described according to the steps of the Krama tradition which is closely associated with the third means.[131]

Fourthly, 'the individual method' (*āṇavopāya*) uses *kalpa* which is action in a broad sense.

124. *TĀ* 3.274ab. See also *Mālinīvijayottaratantra* 2.23.
125. Padoux, *Vāc*, p.180.
126. *TĀ* 3.289cd-291ab.
127. Pandey, p.461.
128. *Mālinīvijayottaratantra* 2.22.
129. Padoux, *Le coeur*, p.148 footnote 219.
130. Alexis Sanderson, 'Śivasūtra et Vimarśinī de Kṣemarāja: traduction et introduction, by L. Silburn' [review] *Bulletin of the School of Oriental and African Studies* 46: 160-161, 1983, p.161. Sanderson, 'Meaning', p.46.
131. Pandey, p.534.

> *'The absorption which makes use of acts* (prakalpana) *such as rising breath* (uccāra), *the sense-organs, concentration, phonemes, locations is properly called 'individual'.'*[132]

Are not all these acts involved in the Kula rituals? Yes, but it is a question of the starting point. The absorption is not the result of rising, breath, concentrations etc. but is given directly by the guru during initiation. The ritual expresses and fortifies the absorption by means of various actions but is not the means of attaining it in the first place.

(i) Three Attitudes

Although the four means all lead to consciousness, Śiva is not divorced from the world. The attainment of Śiva is not simply a return to the previous condition but rather is a discovery of states such as universal bliss (*jagadānanda*) and especially the 'attitude of Bhairava' (*bhairavī-mudrā*) which is best understood in connection with two other attitudes, *khecarī-mudrā* and *krama-mudrā*.

Just as cognition is the basis of recognition, so too the person who attains (*carī*) the illimitation of space (*kha*) brings about the presence of many *śaktis*. In *khecarī-mudrā* the practitioner attains the space of pure consciousness so that the goddesses arise before him. He enjoys them and secures all their powers[133] and has no need of other ritual obligations (*nirācāra*). This state is *khecarī-mudrā*.

As the term *krama* suggests, the attitude called *krama-mudrā* involves a progression from the emanation of the objective world through twelve stages to pure subjectivity. If *khecarī-mudrā* is absorption into the absolute, *krama-mudrā* is a fluctuation[134] in that it involves both emanation and reabsorption.

---

132. *Mālinīvijayottaratantra* 2.21.

133. *TĀ* 32.7cd-8ab. In *TĀ* 32.30-31, Abhinava quotes the *Yogasañcāra's* description of *khecarīmudrā*: 'The *yogī*, due to the sound *HA*, sees his self moving in other bodies and another's self in his own body, sees his self coming and going through the nine apertures, single, resonating, permeating, abiding. As a result of this [*mudrā*] he is a *khecarī*. So it is said in the illustrious *Yogasañcāra*.'

134. Bäumer, *Wege*, p.188. See also Sanderson, 'Meaning', p.58.

Kṣemarāja in his *Pratyabhijñāhṛdayam* defines *bhairavī-mudrā* by quoting the verse: '... focused within, gazing out, neither opening nor closing [his eyes].'[135] Kṣemarāja goes on to quote a further text, from the *Kakṣyāstotra*, which is less lapidary:

> *'Throwing by will all the powers like seeing etc. simultaneously and on all sides into their respective objects and remaining (unmoved) within like a gold pillar, you (O Śiva) alone appear as the foundation of the universe.'*[136]

In other words, *khecarīmudrā* is the state of absorption. *Kramamudrā* is the process of externalisation and internalisation. *Bhairavīmudrā* is neither: the outer and the inner are one. It is the preferred state in *TĀ* 29.

---

135. *antarlakṣyo bahirdṛṣṭirnimeṣonmeṣavarjitaḥ* | Singh, *Pratyabhijñāhṛdayam*, p.98. English translation of *antarlakṣyo* ... etc. from Sanderson, 'Meaning', p.67.
136. Singh, *Pratyabhijñāhṛdayam*, p.98. This is the state of *jīvanmukti* and is also called *śāmbhavīmudrā*. Bäumer, *Wege*, p.172. For a description of *śāmbhavīmudrā*, see *Anubhavanivedana*,, *śl.*1.

CHAPTER 6

TANTRĀLOKA 29

The first impression on reading *TĀ* 29 is confusion. However, once the structure is perceived, the chapter is seen to be admirably arranged. Accordingly this overview will firstly present the structure in broad outline and then take each section of the chapter, present its structure and describe the main terms and procedures operating in that section. The structure is also incorporated into the translation and is provided as a whole in Appendix 15.

(a) Structure of *Tantrāloka* 29

Abhinava himself provides the basic structure[1] for the *Tantrāloka* in *TĀ* 1.278-327ab where he gives the 'table of contents' (*anukramaṇikā*) divided into two sections. In the first section, *TĀ* 1.278-284ab, he gives the list of the general topics (*purvajoddeśa*) of the *Tantrāloka*. *Śloka* 283cd reads: *rahasyacaryā mantraugho maṇḍalaṃ mudrikavidhiḥ* I 'the secret ceremony, the host of mantras, the *maṇḍala*, the ritual concerning the *mudrā*.' These four topics form an ensemble occupying chapters 29-32. The general topic of *TĀ* 29 is 'the secret ceremony' (*rahasyacaryā*). The general topic of *TĀ* 30 is the host of mantras (*mantraugho*) which, according to *TĀ* 30.123cd, includes both mantra and *vidyā* etc. *TĀ* 31 studies the *maṇḍala* and *TĀ* 32 studies the *mudrā*. *TĀ* 29 touches on all these topics but in less detail. The second section, *TĀ* 1.284

1. The four categories, *jñāna, yoga, kriyā, caryā*, i.e. knowledge, yoga, ritual and conduct, are sometimes considered to form the tantric quadrilateral of themes, 'on which topic see Héléne Brunner-Lachaux, 'Analyse du *suprabhedāgama*', in *Journal Asiatique* 155: 31-60, 1967 and Héléne Brunner 'The four pada of saivagama', in *Journal of Oriental Research* (*Madras*) 56-62: 260-278, 1986-1992. The four categories do not determine the structure of *TĀ* 29 nor, indeed, of the *Tantrāloka* as a whole, as Rastogi notes in his *Introduction*, p.195.

bc-324ab, gives the list of Sub-topics (*anujoddeśa*). *TĀ* 1.323cd-324cd gives the list of the Sub-topics of *TĀ* 29:

> *'the category 'qualified'; the Kula lineage of the Perfected Beings and their wives; the ritual of adoration; the ritual with the sexual partner; the procedure of the secret teaching; initiation and anointing; and penetration: such are [the Sub-topics] in the twenty-ninth chapter.'*[2]

A further elaboration of the structure is given in *TĀ* 29.7 where Abhinava lists six supports for the Kula sacrifice: 'on external reality, on the śakti and on the pair; on the body, on the course of the subtle-breath, on the mind', *bahiḥ śaktau yāmale ca dehe prāṇa-pathe matau* I These will be called Sacrifice 1, Sacrifice 2 etc.[3]

---

2. *ādhikāryātmano bhedaḥ siddhapatnīkulakramaḥ* II
arcāvidhirdautavidhī rahasyopaniṣatkramaḥ II
dīkṣābhiṣekau bodhaścetyekonatriṃśa āhnike II
For *bodha* Rastogi reads *vedha*. Rastogi, p.184 footnote 3.

3. The various summaries of the *Tantrāloka* give slightly different listings of these Sacrifices. *Tantrasāra* ch.22 summarises *Tantrāloka* 29. It states: '[*Kula* sacrifice] is of six kinds: in external [surface], in the *śakti*, in one's own body, in the pair, in the subtle-breath and in consciousness'. *saca* [*kulayāgaḥ*] *ṣoḍhā-bāhye śaktau svadehe yāmale prāṇe saṃvidi ca iti*I *Tantrasāra* p.198 lines9-10. The *Tantrasāra* mentions a seventh sacrifice: 'The seventh Kula sacrifice, the best of all, is celebrated with respect to the guru's body.' *guruśarīre saptamaḥ kulayāgaḥ sarvottamaḥ*. *Tantrasāra* p.207 line 5. This seventh sacrifice is absent from *TĀ* 29 unless the second ritual of conclusion is classed as the seventh sacrifice. The *Tantroccaya* summarises the *Tantrāloka* even further. In *Tantroccaya* ch.8 p.177, the list of supports reads as follows: *sthaṇḍile maṇḍale svaśaktigurudehacakraprāṇāntarātmasu ... ārcayet* However, it is not clear how that list should be divided since the *Tantroccaya* describes only the first three sacrifices: 'on the sacrificial surface, in the *maṇḍala*, and in his *śakti*'. A translation which reconciles the three texts, the *Tantrāloka*, the *Tantrasāra* and the *Tantroccaya*, would read that list of supports as follows: 'He should make adoration with regard to the sacrificial surface, in respect of the *maṇḍala*, of his own *śakti*, of the guru, of the circle of the body, of the subtle-breath and of the self (*ātma*).' In Raniero Gnoli and Raffaele Torella, eds. 'The *Tantroccaya* of Abhinavagupta' in *Indo-Sino-Tibetica*, Roma, Bardi, 1990, on p.177 footnote 166, the editors note that the text has *maṇḍale* where one might expect *yāmale*. However, the discrepancy is not so great if we consider that the word *maṇḍala* can mean 'circle' and that the word 'circle' can also mean pair, *yāmala*. The *Tantravaṭadhānikā* is an even briefer summary of the *Tantrāloka* but has no details on the rituals of *TĀ* 29.

Most of the overall structure of *TĀ* 29 falls thus neatly into place. However, Sub-topic 2, *TĀ* 29.18-55, has a structure requiring closer examination. It is a development of the ritual of *Mālinīvijayottaratantra* 11.3-16. A comparison of these two texts suggests the following sequential structure:

	Mālinīvijaya 11		*TĀ* 29
i.	Introductory comments:	1-2	2cd-17
ii.	Preliminary ritual	3-7	18-24
iii.	External ritual	8-16	25-55

This sequence is elucidated by the following comments on each of those elements :

(i) In *TĀ* 29.2cd, Sub-topic 2 is called 'the essence [of the Kula ritual procedure]' and is also the daily ritual. It is appropriate, therefore, that the introductory comments should be attached to it in the first instance, but they apply also to all the Kula rituals which follow.

(ii) In Jr.17d.3, Jayaratha notes that the preceding verses, *śl.*2cd-17, constitute the setting for the sacrifice. He also notes that *śl.*18 is the beginning of the description of the Kula ritual. He notes later, in Jr.23d.3, that 'the sacrifice is complete' (*siddhaḥ kulayāgaḥ*). *Śl.*18-23 would seem, therefore, to constitute a ritual which is, in a way, complete and separate.

By contrast, in Jr.19d.2, he refers to *śl.*18 ff. as 'the daily worship' (*nityād*). He confirms this in Jr.132d.1 where he notes that *śl.*24-55, for the most part at least, constitute the daily ritual of the Kula ritual. Furthermore, the comparable section of *Mālinịvijayottaratantra* 11.3-16 is reflected in *TĀ* 29.18-55. In *Tantrasāra* p.198 line 15, Abhinava begins the summary of *TĀ* 29.24-55. Immediately afterwards, on p.199 line 1, he changes the focus and describes *TĀ* 29.18-23. He only returns to his discussion of *TĀ* 29.24-55 on p.200 line 6. Alḷ this would bind 18-24 and 25-55 closely together.

How then do 18-24 and 25-55 fit? The answer is to be found in the meaning of the term *siddhaḥ* which is used in Jr.23d.3. In *TĀ* 29.5-6, Abhinava discussed the meaning of sacrifice (*yāga*).

In *śl.*5 he defined sacrifice as what is done 'as a result of seeing all things from that point of view', i.e. from the point of view of *śl.*4 or, as Jr.5d.1 says, '... in terms of the outflow from the pulsation of Śiva and *śakti*'. He went on, in *śl.*6, to state that: 'Whatever a hero performs with mind, word and body in order to evoke such a frame [of mind] is said to be the Kula sacrifice.' In Jr.23d.3, therefore, Jayaratha is pointing out that this outlook has been achieved by following the prescriptions of *śl.*18-24 and that the Kula sacrifice has been performed. If the ritual does continue, it is not because something needs to be done in order for the practitioner to achieve the state mentioned in śl.6 but rather because he wishes to express that state. He does so in what may be called Sacrifice 1. *Śloka* 24 describes the transition and could be counted either with *śl.*18-24 or *śl.*25-55. Thus *TĀ* 29.18-55 constitute the daily ritual which consists of two parts, the first of which, *śl.*18-23, achieves the state of *bhairavī-mudrā* intended by the Kula ritual, while the second, *śl.*24-55, is the external expression of that state.

(iii) The verses 25-55 correspond more clearly to what is called the 'Kula procedure concerning the Perfected Beings and their wives'. However, those verses differ distinctly from *Mālinīvijayottaratantra* 11.8-16 because of the long insertion of the Kula hierarchy found in *śl.*29c-45ab.

Therefore, there would seem to be three parts to Sub-topic 2: namely Introduction, Opening Ritual and Sacrifice 1. That being said, the three parts are not sealed off from each other. In particular, Abhinava notes in the *Tantrasāra* that the Opening Ritual and Sacrifice 1 stand in a special relation to each other. Firstly there is a movement from the external, i.e. the hall of sacrifice (*śl.*18a), to the state of Bhairava (*śl.*22d) and thence back to the external such as the cloth (*śl.*25a). The cloth provides the starting point for a return to the centre, for a throne upon which *śakti* and Bhairava (*śl.*49ab) will be seated. Next there is an externalisation as far as the placing of the 'lamps' (*śl.*55). Thus there is a double enclosure, a chiasm, A-B-A'-B'-A'', where the external, A, and consciousness,

B, enclose each other. It is an expression of the vibration (*spanda*).[4]

TĀ 29 is divided into two sections of unequal length. The first two thirds are devoted to the rituals for the initiated, the last third to the rituals of initiation. The two sections are closely linked since the rituals of the initiate cannot be performed without prior initiation while the ritual of initiation is performed by the guru after he has performed the rituals of the initiate.

Accordingly, the overall structure of *TĀ* 29 is as follows:

śl. 1ab	*General Topic*	'The Secret Ceremony' (*rahasyacaryā*)
śl. 1cd-2ab	*Sub-topic 1*	'The Category 'qualified' (*ādhikāryātmano bhedaḥ*)

Part I: The Rituals for the Initiated

	Sub-topic 2	The Kula lineage of the Perfected Beings and their wives, (*siddhapatnīkulakramaḥ*)
śl. 2cd-17		Introduction
śl. 18-23		The Opening Ritual
śl. 24-55		Sacrifice 1external (*bahiḥ*)
śl. 56-95	*Sub-topic 3*	The ritual of adoration (*arcāvidhir*) Sacrifice 2 based on the śakti (*śaktau*)
śl. 96-166ab	*Sub-topic 4*	The ritual with the sexual partner (*dautavidhī*) Sacrifice 3 based on the pair (*yāmale*)
	Sub-topic 5	The rite of the secret teaching (*rahasyopaniṣatkramaḥ*):

4. *Tantrasāra* p.200 line 13 ff.

śl. 166cd-177		Sacrifice 4 based on the body (*dehe*)
śl. 178-180		Sacrifice 5 based on the subtle-breath (*prāṇe*)
śl. 181-186ab		Sacrifice 6 based on the mind (*matau*)

Part II : The Rituals of Initiation

śl. 186cd-224	*Sub-topic 6*	Initiation (*dīkṣā*)
śl. 225-235	*Sub-topic 7*	Consecration (*abhiṣeka*)
śl. 236-281	*Sub-topic 8*	Penetration (*bodha = vedha*)
śl. 282-292ab		Rites to conclude the initiation

Finally, in *TĀ* 1.246-277, just before listing the general topics of the *Tantrāloka*, Abhinava discusses one of the structural principles of his encylopaedic work: the threefold[5] division into enunciation, definition and examination. These three steps are relevant to the detailed structuring of the Sub-topics. For example, at the beginning of Sub-topic 3 he enunciates the Sub-topic (*śl*.56) and proceeds to define it (*śl*.57). He goes on to examine the three Cycles but first defines Cycle 1 (*śl*.58) and then examines it (*śl*.59-63). Another example: in *śl*.201ab he enunciates the initiation as Son and in *śl*.201cd-*śl*.202ab defines the ritual while in *śl*.202cd-206 he examines it. The systematic nature of this elaboration gives great clarity to his work and earns it the title of *śāstra*.

(b) General Topic 'The Secret Ceremony'

From the outset Abhinava reserves the ritual to those who are qualified (*adhikārī*) and the first Sub-topic of *TĀ* 29 concerns 'the category 'qualified'' about which Abhinava says practically nothing.

---

5. 'Abhinavagupta bases himself on the three steps of knowledge in Nyāya, namely *uddeśa*, 'enunciation', *lakṣaṇa* 'definition', and *parīkṣā*, 'examination'. Bettina Bäumer, 'Vāc as saṃvāda. Dialogue in the context of advaita śaivāgamas', in D'Sa, F.X. and Mesquita, R. eds., *Hermeneutics of encounter*, Vienna, Publications of the De Nobili Research Library, vol.XX, 1994, p. 13. Bäumer refers to *Nyāyasūtra* I 1.2.

It is Jayaratha who defines the suitability, stating that a person is qualified if he 'dwell[s] in a state of undifferentiated (*nirvikalpaka*) thought',[6] and so indicating that the Kula sacrifices pertain to the second of the means, the method of Śambhu (*śāmbhavopāya*).

Abhinava gives a second quite different meaning to the term 'qualified' in connection with his description of the Kula hierarchy in *TĀ* 29.29cd-33 where he lists the six 'qualified' gurus and six 'non-qualified' gurus. The non-qualified have neither consorts nor lineages whilst the qualified do transmit their potency, their 'seed' (*vīrya*) which is to be understood in two senses. Jayaratha explains, in Jr.42d.1, that the transmission of 'seed' means the transfer of semen (*carama-dhātoś*) and the transmission of the vibrating power (*sphārasya*) of Śiva and śakti from which the entire universe proceeds. For that reason, *śl.*34 lists the six śaktis or consorts of the qualified and *śl.*35 refers to their lineage of disciples and grand-disciples. By contrast, those who are 'not functioning'[7] or inactive do not hand on the Kula tradition in any sense: they are celibate and do not have disciples, they are not opposed to the tradition nor outside of it but remain 'at rest within the self', (*sva-ātma-mātra-viśrānti*) Jr.42d.1.[8] In short, the person is qualified to practise the ritual if he has the 'seed' or 'potency' (*vīrya*) of the Kula tradition. He is 'functioning' within the tradition if he communicates 'seed'. The term *vīra*, 'hero' is thus appropriately used to describe the Kula practitioner.

Because they are qualified they may practise the secret (*rahasya*) ritual. It is secret in a first sense because it is the hidden knowledge granted by a god at the request of his consort and then revealed to mankind in a tantra. However, the secrecy referred to in *TĀ* 29 is also societal. The Kula ritual had to be kept secret since its 'impure' practices involved grave social consequences for the practitioner and his whole extended family.[9] Something of the social horror is expressed in Qt.10d.1:

---

6. Jr.2b.1. He elaborates in Jr.102d.6.
7. Gnoli translates the term *adhikāro* as 'functioning'. Gnoli, *Luce, passim.* Hélène Brunner also translates it in that way in her article 'Un tantra du nord: le Netra Tantra', in *Bulletin de l'Ecole Française d'Extreme-Orient* 61: 125-197, 1974, p.154.
8. This phrase is used to refer to those who have reached the highest state. See Jr.24d.1, Jr.79d.1 and Jr.185d.2.
9. Jean Varenne, *L'enseignement de la divine shakti*, Paris, Grasset & Fasquelle, 1995, p.151.

> *"This lineage [of the Perfected Beings] is to be worshipped with ingredients that are both hated by people and forbidden according to the scriptures, that are both disgusting and despised."*

Nevertheless, the secret Kaula societies were 'no fringe phenomenon in the Kashmir of our period' and had clearly penetrated into learned society and even into court circles.[10] This penetration was possible precisely because of the secrecy which allowed public decorum to prevail in a manner described by a well-known saying:

> *'Secretly* (antaḥ) *a kaula, outwardly a Śaiva-*[siddhānta], *but publicly a follower of the Vedas'.*[11]

(c) Sub-topic 1 'The Category 'qualified''

In *TĀ* 29.1cd, Abhinava undertakes to recast the previous ceremonial ritual (*upāsa*) which means what is described either in *TĀ* 28 or *TĀ* 15 ff. or indeed in the whole of the *Tantrāloka*, in terms of the Kula ritual procedure. But what is the Kula ritual procedure? Was there a Kula ritual properly speaking or was it a trend which defies any categorisation? Until such time as the various Kula texts, the *Ratnamālā*, the *Yogasañcāra*, the *Vīrāvali* etc., on which Abhinava draws are available, it will be difficult to know how far he has departed from his sources and what he means by 'The Kula Ritual'. As it is, he departs considerably from the *Mālinīvijayottaratantra*, the basic source text of the *Tantrāloka*, in composing *TĀ* 29. Accordingly this present study analyses *TĀ* 29 without detailed reference to other works that contain the word *kula* or show similarities.

Within the category 'qualified', Abhinava lists gurus and disciples. The term 'guru' is preferred to the terms 'Master' or 'Adept' who are minor figures in *TĀ* 29. Indeed, the authentic guru performs

---

10. Sanderson, 'The category', p.203.
11. Quoted by Jayaratha in *Tantrāloka* vol.3, p.643 line 11 and quoted again in *ibid.* vol.3, p.894 line 5. A similar phrase is given in *Yonitantra* 4.20 and in the *Śyāmārahasya*. J.A. Schoterman, *Yonitantra*, New Delhi, Manohar, 1980, p.16.

all functions. He bestows liberation, and enjoyments, he initiates and teaches, he performs rituals and receives the worship of Adepts, Sons and ordinary initiates. The word 'guru' is also used to refer to the Master and the Adept and to others who exercise a function. The Master and the Adept will be described later in looking at the rituals of consecration where Abhinava specifically names them. The *yogī*, *jñānī* and *karmī* are named only by Jayaratha and may suitably be treated here in order to clarify the parameters of the word 'guru'. The terms *yoga*, *nirācāra* and *sācāra* are also reviewed since they are used in our text and further describe the variety of persons who are qualified to perform the Kula ritual. The diverse personages are all outstripped by the guru who remains the person of choice.

In *TĀ* 13.326cd-340, Abhinava discusses the different capabilities of the *yogī* and the knowledgeable person (*jñānī*). In brief, the *yogī* is essentially concerned with enjoyment (*bhoga*) while the knowledgeable person is essentially concerned with liberation (*mokṣa*) and discriminating knowledge (*vijñāna*). The guru *par excellence* has all these roles. Abhinava puts the matter very clearly:

> *'He who wishes both enjoyment and liberation and discriminating knowledge, should seek a guru who is well-practised* (svabhyasta) *in knowledge* (jñāninaṃ) *and accomplished in yoga* (yogasiddhaṃ). *However, if such a person does not exist, he should seek [a guru] who is a knowledgeable person as regards discriminating knowledge and liberation; as regards a particular enjoyment, [he should seek out] a* yogī *who is able to grant that result.'*[12]

As the name implies, the *yogī* is concerned with *yoga* which Abhinava defines as the particular expression of ultimate reality. Consciousness shines forth in differentiated thoughts which in turn imply particular realities.[13] Involvement with these limited realities

12. *TĀ* 13.338-339.
13. *Tantrasāra* p.27 lines 5-9.

brings equally limited enjoyments which cannot simply by themselves lead to consciousness.[14] That sort of *yoga* is to be distinguished from the yoga of Pātañjali, discussed in *TĀ* 4.86-109ab under the heading 'the irrelevance of the limbs of yoga'. Abhinava notes that the eight limbs are of no direct use in attaining consciousness but rather the reverse: they are the manifestations of an already existing consciousness.[15]

The distinction between *jñānī* and *yogī* is echoed in the distinction between *nirācāra*, the person who is not attached to any ritual, and *sācāra*, the person who is so attached. When the *sācāra* performs an initiation, an external manifestation or sign occurs which convinces the recipient that he, the recipient, has attained Śiva. By contrast the *nirācāra*, who is also called 'independent' (*avadhūta*), does not have any particular ritual to perform and his initiation does not provide any proof other than the inner experience of self-evident consciousness.[16] Abhinava describes the *nirācāra*:

> '*Free, not attached to any ritual* (nirācāro), *without doubt* (niḥśaṅko), *free of worldly concerns, pure* (avadhūto), *not attached to any ritual, reflecting that 'I am not'* (na-aham-asmi), *relying solely on the mantra, viewing all the goddesses who reside in his body... always seeing* (paśyan) *these things as the perceiving subject, he is clearly made perfect by means of* khecari-mudrā.'[17]

That description of the practitioner who is not attached to any ritual is further illustrated by those women who are called *nirācārāḥ*, who are not restricted by food laws or moral codes and so are to be worshipped as goddesses.[18]

14. *TĀ* 13.330.
15. *TĀ* 4.97.
16. *TĀ* 20.8-10ab.
17. *TĀ* 32.20cd-24ab.The importance of *TĀ* 32.20cd-24ab in the thinking of Abhinava is shown by the fact that it is quoted, with variations, both in *Tantrasāṛra* ch.22 on the Kula ritual, p.206 lines 7-10, and in *Tantroccaya* pp.180 lines 4-7 at the end of the description of Sacrifice 3.
18. *TĀ* 15.554, quoting the *Gama-tantra*.

The term 'officiant' (*karmī*) is very similar to the *yogī*. Where the *yogī* is concerned with particular powers, the officiant is concerned with particular rituals. In *TĀ* 23.12cd-14ab, Abhinava notes that the officiant must perform certain actions and avoid others, he must follow a particular ritual code if he wishes to achieve his purpose.[19] He is to be distinguished from the knowledgeable person and the *nirācāra*. In *TĀ* 23.25a, Abhinava makes the blunt statement: 'The guru who is an officiant is without knowledge' (*jñānahīno guruḥ karmī ...*). This is softened, however, by his statement in *TĀ* 28:

> *'The characteristic quality of a guru is fullness of knowledge* (jñānatā). *The distinction* (avāntarā) *which does in fact exist between the [guru who is] an officiant* (karmī) *and the [guru who is] a knowledgeable person is secondary and always presupposes that knowledge.'* [20]

In his commentary on the word *sācāra*, 'he who follows a ritual', in *TĀ* 20.9c, Jayaratha similarly softens this classification and notes that the officiant, 'places emphasis on ritual' (*kriyāpradhāna*) so that it is a question not of exclusion but of emphasis. The officiant would seem to be particularly concerned with the proper performance of the ritual rather than with understanding and expounding his insight. Jayaratha emphasises this point of view in Jr.130b.1 which is an investigation of the phrase in *śl.*129c, 'those who have not received enlightenment'. Abhinava goes on, in *TĀ* 23.25b-26ab, to note that once the officiant has passed on his qualification, he can no longer perform initiations without asking the permission of his successor whereas the knowledgeable person, even though he has passed on his qualification, can continue to function as before.[21]

---

19. Gnoli considers that this text may be corrupt but that he has given its general meaning. Gnoli, *Luce*, p.592 footnote 6. I have adopted his interpretation.
20. *gurorlakṣaṇametāvatsampūrṇajñānataiva yā| tatrāpi yāsya cidvṛttikarmibhit sāpyavāntarā* || *TĀ* 28.389. This translation is dependent on Gnoli, *Luce*, p.674.
21. *TĀ* 23.26cd-27ab.

The distinction between ritual and knowledge thus leads to a set of equations. On the one hand are the *yogī*, *yoga*, the *sācāra* and the officiant. On the other hand are the knowledgeable person and the *nirācāra*.[22] However, all these gurus have insight and the ideal remains the person who is liberated while alive.

(d) Sub-topic 2 'The Kula Lineage of the Perfected Beings and their Wives'

Introduction

	A. 1.	Definition of the Kula sacrifice
śl. 2cd-3		a. The essence of the Kula ritual
śl. 4		b. The *kula*
śl. 5		c. The sacrifice i. As knowledge
śl. 6		ii. As action
	2.	Examination of the Kula sacrifice
śl. 7		a. The six supports
śl. 8		b. Rejection of supports of *tantra*
śl. 9	Transition:The *kaula* as the basis of all	
śl. 10	B. 1.	Definition of the ingredients
	2.	Examination:
śl. 11-13		a. Alcohol
śl. 14-16		b. The triple secret: 'vessel', 'sacred place', 'lamp'
śl. 17		c. Conclusion: The absence of doubt

The introduction is divided into two sections, the first of which introduces the key ideas of the Kula ritual while the second presents the essential ingredients. The manner of presentation is an unfolding because the latter term is involved in the earlier. Abhinava's world is a vibrating reality revealing its hidden essence and later resuming the objective reality into its subjective heart.

---

22. Sanderson, 'Meaning', p.78 footnote 203.

Abhinava first defines the essence (*sāratva*) of the whole Kula ritual[23] as the worship of the Perfected Beings. Initiation is of first importance because, by giving the mantra, it communicates the lineage and its power[24] and this is more important than the theoretical doctrine or the mechanics of the ritual. Sub-topic 2 in large part follows: *Mālinīvijayottaratantra* 11.1-16 whereas Sub-topics 3-5 do not, but since Sub-topic 2 is the essence of the Kula ritual, the later topics are seen as an expression of the essence, a sort of gloss.

Who are these Perfected Beings? The mantra is passed on to the disciple by his guru who in turn obtained it from his guru and so on back through the human stream, the symbolic figure of 64 generations of Masters[25] who themselves obtained it from the stream of the Perfected Beings (*siddha*) who in their turn ultimately obtained the mantra from the divine stream. The Perfected Beings thus occupy a place midway between the gods and mankind. They enjoy supernatural powers (*siddhi*) and lead others to the same condition they enjoy.[26]

The term 'Perfected Being' has a wider scope. In Jr.29b.1, Jayaratha mentions the 'eternal (*anādi*) Perfected Beings and the 'eternal *yoginīs*' on the left hand side of the worshipper who are historical beings since they lived at Jālandhara yet are different from Khagendra etc. who are worshipped at the cardinal points. Jayaratha does not say what he means by 'eternal'. Finally there is

---

23. Brunner studies the phrase "essence of the Veda" found in the *Kāmikāgama*. She concludes that, according to that text, the term 'essence' does not mean a summary but a source. Accordingly, the Śaivasiddhānta texts are, in the view of the *Kāmikāgama*, the foundation of the Vedas. Hélène Brunner, 'Le Śaiva-Siddhānta, "essence" du Veda (Etude d'un fragment du *Kāmikāgama*)', in *Indologica Taurinensia* 8: 51-66, 1980, p.63.

24. '... there are hardly any schools, but rather initiatory traditions - *guruparamparā* - ... it is the principal divinity and its cult which count ... and not the doctrine which may well be largely personal and is often composed ... of materials drawn from different traditions.' André Padoux, '*Le Yoginīhṛdaya* et la *Dīpikā* d'Amṛtānanda: quelques problémes', in *Bulletin d'Etudes Indiennes* 1: 89-95, 1983, p.94. See also Padoux, *Vāc*, p.40 footnote 24.

25. *TĀ* 29.54a; Jr.54d.4, Jr.54d.5.

26. Padoux, *La Parātrīśikālaghuvṛtti*, p.107 notes 226-227.

the so-called Perfected Being who is simply anyone committed to religious practices.[27]

The Perfected Beings communicate the mantra which must now be considered. The supreme word (*parāvāc*) is the revelation of consciousness to itself, the acknowledgement of knowledge so that the supreme word is itself the mantra of consciousness.[28] All the manifestations of the supreme word are words and all revelations of the divine śakti are deities. Abhinava defines the mantra to mean both the world and its supreme Lord, pure consciousness as well as discursive thought. It is the energy of the phonemes.[29] As a result the mantras are able to bring a person to identity with himself and so to freedom and in turn to grant him authority and power.[30] The ritual 'setting out' of the phonemes is an imitation of the emanative process—the *varṇaparāmarśa*—whereby the earlier phoneme contains and emits the later phoneme. Just as there is a progression in emanation or a hierarchy of *tattvas*, so too there is a hierarchy of deities and their *mantras*. The goddess presides over her *vidyā* or *mūla-mantra* which is her very substance and is surrounded by subsidiary goddesses who in turn preside over their own *vidyā*.

A mantra is received, individually and privately from the mouth of the guru during initiation. Indeed, initiation consists primarily in the communication of this word[31] which is at the same time one's deity and one's personal mantra. It is received orally and cannot be written (*alekhya*)[32] for to write it down is to dissociate it from the living tradition and from the guru who imparts it and consequently to weaken it.[33] Nor can it be coined[34] for it is the

---

27. Gnoli, *Luce*, p.671 footnote 132.
28. '... the great *mantra*, *mahāmantra*, is essentially the autonomy of awareness ...' *Parātriṃśikāvivaraṇa* p.250 line 1.
29. Padoux, *Vāc*, p.376.
30. *TĀ* 30.2-3.
31. Agehananda Bharati, *The tantric tradition*, London, Rider & Co., 1965, p.101.
32. This was already asserted concerning the Veda. Padoux, *Vāc*, p.xiv. 'It must not be written down', (*alekhyaṃ*) says Abhinava in *TĀ* 29.125c and in Gnoli. *Il commento* p.269 line 7 and p.273 line 13.
33. *TĀ* 26.20-21. However an exemption is given in *TĀ* 26.23cd-24ab: 'Those who come to know the potency contained in a mantra even when it is read in a book are purified by Bhairava himself. As said above, they are naturally endowed.'
34. André Padoux, 'Mantras - What are they?', in Harvey P. Alper, ed. *Understanding mantras*, Delhi, Motilal Banarsidass, 1991, pp.295-318, p.309.

communication of a tradition stretching back in time to the void itself. Ordinarily the mantra is received during the ceremony of initiation, such as the one described in *śl.*187cd ff., but there it is not so much the guru who whispers it into the ear of the disciple. Rather, the guru by his silent concentration causes the goddess to make the disciple drop the flower upon the *maṇḍala* and so to reveal which mantra, which goddess, which *kula* and its attendant ritual, have been chosen for the disciple. The guru discerns the *kula* and then, one may suppose, utters to the disciple the phonic form of the mantra so that the mantra is both visual and aural. [35]

Just as the mouth of the guru utters the mantra which leads to consciousness so too the 'mouth' of the *yoginī*, the *yoginī-vaktra*, *yoginī-mukha*, *yoginī-vadana*, communicates the unique experience of consciousness, immediately.[36] Just as the guru considers the initiate to be his son, so too the *yoginī* by her 'mouth' brings him into the family (*kula*) of the 'Mothers' or into the clan (*gotra*) or into the Kula tradition whose eponymous ancestor is Khagendra or Macchanda.

The initiate proceeds to perform the various Kula rituals which, like so many others,[37] are primarily concerned with the communication or awakening of the mantra. They are so organised that the latter ritual surpasses the former in subtlety and power. Sub-topic 2 leads to the personal mantra while Sacrifice 2 leads to recitation. Sacrifice 3 leads to the supreme Bhairava of sound which is universally pervasive. Sacrifices 4, 5 and 6 which are linked together as Sub-topic 5 lead finally to the supreme mantra, the goddess who is consciousness (*citi*). After the guru has reached the highest form of the mantra, consciousness itself, in the company

---

35. Padoux, *Vāc*, p.xiv. In *TĀ* 21.19cd-20ab, Abhinava notes that the sight of the *maṇḍala*, even without the mantra, can make a person an ordinary initiate, while *Parātrīśikā* 18ab will say the converse: the knowledge of *SAUḤ* even without the sight of the *maṇḍala* initiates a person as a *yogī*.

36. See *śl.*124c ff., Jr.126b.3.

37. In *Tantrasāra* p.166 lines 6-11, Abhinava lists the causes which bring about the presence (*saṃnidhaye*) of the mantra, such as flowers, the image, the company of the *yogī* .

of the *yoginīs* and of the Perfected Beings, he is able to impart the mantra to the disciple.

The protagonists of the various systems, the Trika, the Śaivasiddhānta and the Vaiṣṇava vie with each other, trying to demonstrate the superiority of their tradition and of their mantras.[38] The simpler[39] and the more effective the mantra, the more it commands assent. Power rather than doctrinal consistency is the trump card and the mantras of the Kula tradition are supremely effective because, when understood as Kula and Akula united in an eternal embrace,[40] they 'cause an immediate conviction'.

The mantra leads to supernatural powers (*siddhi*) which are of central interest in Indian thought.[41] They are found already in the Vedas,[42] but the tantras are particularly interested in them. They include power over various dangerous forces, over women and over enemies[43] or the control of *mantras* and *mudrās*, the knowledge of events hidden in the past or in the future.[44] In his commentary *Parātriṃśikāvivaraṇa*[45] Abhinava presents a lengthy interpretation of the various forms of supernatural powers pertaining to the Kula tradition but the supernatural power he mentions first and which comes first in his estimation is bliss.[46] He does not deny the value of the *siddhis* such as smallness, lightness etc., or of lesser manifestations of the descent of energy

38. In *TĀ* 11.88, Abhinava contrasts the mantras of the Siddhānta and of the Left and Right schools etc. with the mantras of the Trika. Those mantras involve various stages of purification. 'However, the *mantras* based upon the unsurpassable Trika are all, at every moment and in any place, the source of every good.'
39. Wade T. Wheelock, 'The mantra in vedic and tantric ritual', in Harvey P. Alper, ed. *Understanding mantras*, Delhi, Motilal Banarsidass, 1991 p.119. Even more, the greater the concentration of the *yogī* the fewer times need he repeat the mantra (Jr.89d.2). Thus the one mantra, the supreme word, is uttered once and eternally from consciousness.
40. Padoux, *Le coeur*, p.60.
41. *ibid.* p.84 footnote 162.
42. Padoux, *La Parātrīśikālaghuvṛtti*, p.14 footnote 2.
43. Sanderson, 'Meaning', p.24.
44. *Parātrīśikā* 12-18.
45. *Parātriṃśikāvivaraṇa* p.197 line 15 - p.199 line 5.
46. *op.cit.* p.197 lines 20-21.

such as trembling or reeling.[47] However, the supreme supernatural power is the bliss of consciousness in every circumstance. The greatest value is to become liberated while alive and to be able to communicate this state to all creatures and so to attain the state of Śiva (*śivatā*),[48] the final purpose of the whole sweep of rituals of *TĀ* 29.

The various worlds have their respective powers and the various parts of the body, heart, navel, eye-brow centre etc., have their respective powers just as one's *kula* determines the powers one may enjoy,[49] but the aim is to progress rapidly through all levels so as to arrive at the highest level of consciousness which confers all powers. Thus, although the mantra can achieve all things, its greatest effectiveness is seen in bringing the practitioner to consciousness without the delay of ritual and so to enter the inner circle of initiates and gain access to all the lesser supernatural powers.

The mantra is the basis for the term 'sacrifice' (*yāga*) which Abhinava defines essentially as knowledge and whatever is done in relation to that knowledge. In two sentences (*śl.*5-6) he both relativises all ritual action and ritualises all human activity[50] so that the Kula sacrifice is universally applicable. The various rituals of *TĀ* 29 are the more limited and externalised forms of that essential sacrifice. This teaching is the equivalent of the instruction given in the *Parātriṃśikā* 18 and 20 which says that merely knowing *SAUḤ* is to be initiated and to know and perform all rituals.

Since all proceeds from the union of Śiva and śakti, towards what could Śiva be hesitant? Knowledge which is clear and complete leaves no room for doubt (*śaṅkā*). Kula knowledge is a conviction, a universal awareness which inspires confidence so

47. *TĀ* 29.208cd.
48. *TĀ* 29.281.
49. In *TĀ* 4.268cd-269ab, he teaches that the member of one branch should keep to his branch and must refrain from seeking the enjoyments and ritual that pertain to another branch (*parasaṃtāninā*). This restriction underscores the import of the initiation ceremony which determines one's *kula* and therefore one's range of enjoyments and privileges.
50. This point will be echoed in *TĀ* 29.65cd, 89 and 161cd-162ab.

that nothing is impure. The regulations of the Vedas and their proscriptions, the injunctions of the *Manusmṛti* have no value in his eyes, for he is lead by a higher revelation. While the Vedas are not entirely rejected as revelation they are far superceded by the revelaton due to Śiva who is essentially pure such that nothing makes him impure. So the practitioner ignores the multitude of doubts[51] and rises above any fear. If, however, a person cannot free himself of doubt he is adjudged not yet to be initiated or able to perform the Kula ritual. At best he can become an ordinary initiate and eventually bringing himself to the state of readiness where he can accept the requirements of the Kula ritual without hesitation.

The mantra and its outlook are the perfect sacrifice and whatever is done in order to attain that outlook is a Kula sacrifice. That being said, Abhinava goes on, in *śl.*7, to list six particular forms of activity or ritual which will assist the Kula practitioner to strengthen the universal sacrificial outlook. It is the radiation of the one splendour of the mantra. As already noted, these six forms provide one of the structural divisions of *TĀ* 29.

Traditionally there are three categories of ritual: the daily or regular (*nitya*), the occasional (*naimittika*) and the optional (*kāmya*).[52] The regular or daily ritual must be performed at fixed times. According to Jayaratha, Sub-topic 2 is a daily ritual.[53] The occasional ritual must be performed in certain eventualities,[54] e.g.

51. In *TĀ* 13.198ab, Abhinava lists a number of doubts: 'concerning mantra, self, elements, ingredients, food, rites, categories etc. ...' *mantra-ātmā-bhūta-dravya-āśa-divya-tattva-ādi* ... This list is extended in Jayaratha's investigation, *Tantrāloka* vol.5, p.2326 line15 - p.2327 line 3. On the basis of those lists, Sanderson writes: 'As that which holds the Brahman back from the path of power it is fear of loss of identity (*ātma-śaṅkā*), or participation in non-Vedic rites (*divya-karmaśaṅkā*), of impure Tantric incantations (*mantraśaṅkā*), fear of contact with the forbidden substances that are offered and consumed in Tantric worship (*dravyaśaṅkā*), fear of contamination by untouchables in caste-promiscuous sexual rites (*jātiśaṅkā*), fear of entering the cremation grounds and the other impure sites in which the cult of power is celebrated (*sthāna-śaṅkā*), fear of assault or possession by the forces that inhabit these sites and are handled in the Tantric liturgies (*bhūta-śaṅkā, śarīraśaṅkā*) and finally, fear of an alien taxonomy of reality (*tattvaśaṅkā*) ...' Sanderson, 'The category', p.212 footnote 69.
52. Gnoli, *Luce*, p.614 footnote 6.
53. See Jr.19d.2 and Jr.132d.1.
54. Sanderson, 'Meaning', pp.30-31.

the visit of the guru. The 23 occasional rituals of *TĀ* 28[55] are referred to in a general way in *TĀ* 29.291c so that they must form part of the Kula ritual but Abhinava does not clearly state how they do so. Jayaratha refers to some of the occasional rites: no.10, the posthumous rites, in Qt.13d.15, Jr.13d.11; no.11, a misfortune, in Qt.13d.14; and no.23, the reparation for an infringement of a rule, in Qt.13d.11, Qt.13d.12, Qt.13d.13. Finally, the optional rituals are performed for a purpose of one's choosing, e.g. to capture elephants or to secure a beautiful woman.[56] *TĀ* 29.75cd-77 has aspects of an optional ritual as when Abhinava states: '... he should recite the 'The Hymn of the Sacred Site' in order to invoke good fortune'.

Abhinava terminates this first part of the introduction by defining the term *kaula*. If *kula* refers to śakti and her manifestations, *kaula* refers to *Kula* and Akula and their manifestations all of which form the one reality. The *kaula* is knowledge in all its aspects, the knower, the knowing and the known. *Śl.*9 sums up the idealist position and provides the basis for the use of 'unclean' ingredients, for, if the *kaula* in fact constitutes the whole of reality, nothing is impure.

The Veda distinguishes between the 'pure and 'impure' (*śuddhy-aśuddhī*) and is constantly concerned with purity. The Siddhānta

55. In *TĀ* 28.6-8, Abhinava lists twenty-three 'occasional' rituals. The translation which follows depends on Gnoli's rendition and on Gnoli, *Luce*, p.632 footnotes 1-11. The *śloka* numbers give the places in *TĀ* 28 etc. where these matters are dealt with to some extent. [1] The receiving of knowledge; [2] the receiving of the scriptures; [3] the visit of the guru, [4] of his brother and hisfamily, *śl.*192-212; [5] the day of the guru's birth, *śl.*213-216, [6] of his consecration, [7] of his union (*abheda*) [with Śiva, i.e. of his death, for which see also *TĀ* 25.11-12]; [8] the day of one's own birth, *śl.*213-216; [9] the day of festival, *śl.*368; [10] the posthumous rites, [see also *TĀ* 25]; [11] a misfortune; [12] a sickness; [13] the joy of recuperation; [14] the sight of a portent, *śl.*369-370; [15] a meeting with the *yoginīs*; [16] a meeting with those who belong to one's own lineage, *śl.*370-385ab; [17] the beginning, [18] middle and [19] end of an explanation of the scriptures, *śl.*385cd-407; [20] the gradual appearing of a circle (*kramodaya*); [21] the sight of a deity in a dream; [22] the authorisation [on the day of one's consecration]; [23] [as reparation for] an infringement of a rule.' Of these rituals *Tantrasāra* p.179 mentions only nos. 1, 2, 3, 4, 5, 6, 7, 9, 15-16,17-19, 21, 22, 23.
56. Gudrun Bühneman, 'Tantric worship of Gaṇeśa according to the *Prapañcasāra*', in *Zeitschrift der Deutschen Morgenländischen Gesellschaft* 137: 357-382, 1987, describes such optional rituals.

ritual follows suit and considers that purity and impurity are somehow 'material', but the Trika considers knowledge to be purity and ignorance to be impurity[57] and that the Siddhāntins' idea of purity is in fact an impurity because it is an ignorance.[58] Nothing can overwhelm the pure light of consciousness so that the Kula practitioner is without fear before what is deemed profane. Indeed, he makes use of what is reprehensible so that by being involved in sin—yet not in the manner of the 'bonded animal'—he realises the transcendence of consciousness. Far from involving a person in sin, the unlawful ingredient 'destroys great sins' (*pātaka*) as noted in *TĀ* 29.282d. Yet the Kula ritual, although it decries the concepts 'permitted' and 'forbidden' (*niṣiddha*) needs them and defines itself partly in terms of them so that it is counter-ritual rather than revolutionary. How can power derive from the act of transgression if there is no such thing as transgression.[59]

The concept of purification does, however, have its place but in a quite different sense. The process involves dissolving the lower categories into the higher ones, seeing the lower levels as contained in the higher levels, till one reaches the state of Śiva,[60] and then regenerating the body by expressing the higher categories in the lower ones. Purification consists in regenerating all as light.

The rejection of the terms 'pure' and 'impure' is first expressed in the use of the forbidden ingredients and particularly in the use of wine which is described as ambrosia or nectar-of-the-left (*vāma-amṛta*). It is called 'left' (*vāma*) not only because the left hand is to be used in the ritual but also because 'left' has the added sense of 'foreign to ordinary day life', 'secret',[61] antinomian or heterodox.[62] The word *vāma* also has the meaning of 'vomiting' or 'emitting' so

57. *TĀ* 4.118cd-119ab reads: 'The idea that those things which in fact consist of Śiva are separated from him: that is called impurity. Purity is the suppression of that idea.' See also *TĀ* 4.227.
58. Sanderson, 'The category', p.198.
59. Padoux, *Vāc*, p.35 footnote 14.
60. *ibid.* p.126 footnote 111.
61. *TĀ* 15.278cd-283ab. He then goes on to stress the importance of doing all the rituals -installations, sprinklings etc. - with the left hand, in particular with the left thumb and left ring-finger. See also *Tantrasāra* p.200 lines 3-5 which requires the use of the fourth finger and thumb of the left hand.
62. Sanderson, 'Meaning', p.18.

that the wine is associated with emanation and the creation of a set of pure categories for enjoyment.[63]

Wine has a series of other associations which start with *soma*, the mysterious and illustrious liquor without which none of the principal rites of the Aryans could be performed.[64] The gods enjoyed its intoxicating effect and the brahmans, just like the gods, became drunk on such occasions.[65] However, generally speaking alcohol is proscribed so that the significance of alcohol in the Kula ritual lies not so much in its intoxicating effect as in its sinfulness, for even a small amount, even a whiff, is gravely wrong.[66]

The most important of the alcohols is wine which takes on all the ambiguity associated with alcohol. However, the term *vāma-āmṛta* takes on further meanings, as in Qt.13d.21 where it symbolises the sexual union of Śiva and śakti and their fluids. Occasionally, as in Jr.166b.1 the term *amṛta* by itself refers to the sexual fluid. See also Qt.110b.2. The lesser alcohols, grain spirit, rum and mead, [67] are designated 'masculine' 'feminine', 'neuter' in a grammatical sense only and refer to the world of objectivity.[68]

---

63. *Tantrasāra* p.147 lines 2-3.
64. Pentti Aalto, 'Madyam Apeyam', in *Jñānamuktāvali* (Commemoration Volume in Honour of Johannes Nobel), New Delhi, 1963, p.18.
65. *ibid.* p.24.
66. *Manusmṛti* 11.91-98 and 147-151 list the penances for drinking *surā* intentionally or unintentionally. For example, just to smell wine causes a Brahman to lose caste. *Manusmṛti* 11.68. Indeed, if he should swallow anything that has only touched *surā*, he must be initiated again. *Manusmṛti* 11.151.
67. Aalto, pp.20 - 21. O. Prakash, *Food and drinks in ancient India*, Delhi, Munshi Ram Manohar Lal, 1961, p.41 and p.216. These three are specifically forbidden in the *Manusmṛti* 95.84.
68. Gnoli, *Il commento*, p.292 footnote 141 quotes the comments of Patañjali and of Helārāja in his investigation of Bhatṛhari. These see the masculine *guṇa* as associated with increase (*upacaya*) and the feminine *guṇa* with decrease (*apacaya*). In that footnote also, Gnoli states that Abhinava, in *Parātriṃśikāvivaraṇa* p.212 lines 12-16, applies these same notions to the words 'more' (*adhikam*) and 'less' (*ūnam*). The neuter is seen as a state mid-way between the two (*mādhyasthyam*). In the *Parātriṃśikāvivaraṇa* p.212 lines 16-17, Abhinava goes on to make an observation on Sanskrit grammar noting that the world of objectivity, *jaḍa, nara*, is expressed in the masculine, feminine and neuter genders while in Sanskrit grammar the addressee 'you' and the subject 'I' do not have gender. 'The senses of 'I' - which are identical forms of consciousness - do not correspond to that state described as 'this-ness' which is growth, diminution and [all] between. The sense of 'you', though distinct, is [viewed] similarly. For that reason, 'you' and 'I' are used without gender.' These points help to explain *TĀ* 29.11cd-12, Jr.13d.3, Qt.13d.4, Qt.13d.5 and also *TĀ*

Abhinava explains the import of alcohol by associating it with both liberation and enjoyment. He further explains the overriding importance of wine by linking it with consciousness and with Bhairava. Liberation and enjoyment are appropriately discussed here before going on to look at the triple secret which consists of the 'vessel', the sacred place and the 'lamp'.

Śiva seeks neither enjoyment (*bhukti*) nor liberation (*mukti*) since they preexist in him and proceed from him. He does not seek what he already has. Although the word *mukti* is commonly translated as 'liberation', Abhinava gives the word a quite different thrust:

> *'The term* mokṣa, *liberation, is nothing else than the revelation of one's nature and one's nature is quite simply consciousness of the self.'*[69]

It comes from intuition and not, strictly speaking, from initiation since initiation does not give anything that is not already known but rather cuts the bonds which might hinder a person from self-recognition. Liberation can be obtained either without differentiated thought or within all the variety of the world[70] so that liberation is not opposed to enjoyment. Indeed, the purpose of *TĀ* 29 is to show how the seeming dualism is overcome by becoming 'liberated-while-living' (*jīvan-muktaḥ*) a term which appears in *śl.* 161cd-162ab and reappears in Jr.277b.1. This state is thus shown to be the climax of both major sections of *TĀ* 29, namely the rituals of the initiate and the rituals of initiation.

29.282-283. The three lesser forms of alcohol express the passing world of objectivity, of increase and decrease, of mere passing enjoyment suited to a certain sort of Adept. Since the objective world is divided into three genders, each desires the other two in order to regain the primal unity. By contrast, the highest level of light, consciousness and bliss, expressed by wine, is that of the supreme subject, *para-pramātṛ*, Bhairava himself, who is beyond any limitation of gender. There is no basis for associating spirit, mead and rum with female, neuter and male in a sexual sense.

69. *TĀ* 1.156. In *TĀ* 13.164cd-195, Abhinava quotes the *Nandi-śikhātantra* at length. This text makes the point that 'liberation comes from intuition', *prātibhato muktau* (*śl.*193c). In the Doctrine of Recognition, (*Pratyabhijñā*) initiation, strictly speaking, does not, give liberation but only frees a person from the bonds which hinder it. 'As a result of the cutting of the bonds, they are liberated', *pāśacchedādvimucyante* (*śl.*194c).

70. *Īśvarapratyabhijñāvimarśinī*, vol.3, p.227.

'Bhairava' and 'Śiva' are the names most commonly used in *TĀ* 29 to refer to the ultimate reality and indeed are identified in the mind of Abhinava.[71] The name Bhairava is to be distinguished from the noun bhairava for there are many bhairavas who surround the one Bhairava as his circle of attendants. The name Śiva means 'the Auspicious One', while the term Bhairava has the opposite meaning: 'awesome', 'fearsome'.[72] The opposition is merely apparent since the grace of Śiva is a destruction of every limitation, while to be torn away from the concepts 'pure' and 'impure' is a moment of blessing. In this sense the term *bhairava* is fittingly associated with wine, the forbidden drink, the deicide and brahmanicide.[73] Indeed the word becomes synonymous with wine, as in Qt.13d.8, or becomes synonymous with bliss, as in Qt.13d.6.

In *TĀ* 29 and its investigation, the term *argha-pātra*, vessel, refers either to the container or more significantly to the contents. These are the 'fearless essences'[74] which consist especially of the sexual fluid immersed in wine. In *TĀ* 15.164cd-167ab, Abhinava broaches the theme of *kuṇḍa-golaka*. He states that the gurus recommend

> *'... the nectar* (amṛtam) *which comes from the union of the heroes and their counterpart [viz. their sexual partner]'.*[75]

In his investigation of this text, Jayaratha clearly states that

> *'... the nectar is the so-called sexual fluid* (kuṇḍa-golaka) *which arises during the perfect fusion of the [hero and the* yoginī*],*[76]

71. *TĀ* 1.90ab.
72. In *TĀ* 1.95-105, Abhinava gives the traditional etymology (*nirukta*) of the divine names. The first in the list and the one given the longest *nirukta* (*śl.*96-100ab) is 'Bhairava'. In *Tantrāloka*, vol.3, p.1064, in his investigation of *TĀ* 5.135, Jayaratha also gives a series of meanings to 'Bhairava'.
73. The mythology of Bhairava is given in H. von Stietencron, 'Bhairava', in *Vorträge / Deutscher Orientalistentag, Supplementa* I, vol.3, 1968, pp.863-71, and Lorenzen, *The Kāpālikas, passim.*
74. *TĀ* 27.42c. Jayaratha glosses them as the five nectars, *pañcāmṛtādibhir.*
75. *TĀ* 15.166cd.
76. *Tantrāloka* vol.6, p.2524 lines 14-15.

and he specifies that '... it occurs 'as a result of the six-rayed shape', i.e. as result of intercourse.[77]

Closely associated with the *kuṇḍa-golaka* is the menstrual blood, *rakta*. It is used both in the vessel and as the context of copulation[78] as indicated in Qt.109b.2. The word *aruṇa*, which also means blood, can also refer to the female procreative sexual power, as in *TĀ* 29.195ab.

The fluids derive from a 'sacred place'. The term *dhāman*, sacred place, means 'light', 'glory', 'power as related to function', '... a self-luminous place (for instance, a star), a point where energy is manifested',[79] a place of divine splendour. It is a word of first importance and will be used with great frequency in *TĀ* 29 and its

---

77. *ibid.* vol.6 p.2524 lines 13-15. 'At the moment of orgasm, women ejaculate a liquid through the urethra that is chemically similar to male ejaculate but contains no sperm.' Alice Kahn Ladas, Beverly Whipple, John D. Perry, *The G Spot and otherrecent discoveries about human sexuality*, New York, Holt, Rinehart and Winston, 1982 p.20. 'One woman ... reported that "...the flavour changes four times during the month. Tangy, sour, tart, and very, very sweet. The sweet taste lasts about three days and is right before my period. It is absolutely delicious. This sweet taste is better than any honey and not nearly as thick.' ibid. pp.70-71. 'In ancient times, the word "semen" was used to describe the "seed" or "ejaculate" of either sex. You may recall that de Graaf refers to his predecessors' supposition that this ejaculate contained "female semen", but when the microscope revealed that only the male ejaculate contained sperm, the word previously used to describe the fluids of both sexes was allocated in the scientific literature to males alone.' *ibid.* p.78.
   It may be of interest to note the following extract from the description of a modern day 'tantric' ritual at Puri, in Orissa. 'The officiant, reciting mantras and sprinkling water in the same manner as previously, purifies the woman's *yoni*. With a blade of grass the officiant touches the *yoni* while reciting a Vedic *mantra* to make the womb fertile ... Then looking at the *yoni* he recites a *mantra* stating that the nectar flows. As a rule then the female sexual fluid (*raja*) should fall down itself (*swatah raja pāta*). But if it does not the officiant then engages in sexual intercourse (without ejaculating, information given orally). This brings out the sexual fluid which he collects on a betel leaf to which he adds several perfumes. To that leaf he does the same purificatory actions as for the other substances.' Frédérique Apffel Marglin *Wives of the god-king: the rituals of the deva-dasis of Puri*, Delhi, Oxford University Press, 1985, p.222. The central ritual of *Yonitantra* is the production of the *yonitattva*, the vaginal substance.
78. '... ritual coition with a woman during her monthly periods is recommended in *Yonitantra*. Although much abhorred in Hindu society, the fact itself is certainly not unknown in mythology and in reality.' Schoterman, *Yonitantra*, p.31.
79. Padoux, *Vāc*, p.274 footnote 145. Padoux, *Le coeur*, p.104 footnote 48. Jan Gonda *Meaning of the Sanskrit term dhāman*, Amsterdam, Maatschappij, 1967, pp.94-95.

investigation. Its uses are many, they cross refer and can be taken at various levels. In the first instance it refers to the trio consisting of earth, cloth and skull which themselves can be taken as referring to object of knowledge, means of knowledge and subject of knowledge. It can refer to the sexual organ, especially to the female sexual organ, or to the central axis, the *suṣumṇā* and also to consciousness, the knowing subject, to the source of emission, to the world, etc. It can bear this variety of meanings because any location where the divine glory becomes apparent is indeed a sacred place.

The word *dīpa*, 'lamp', can bear its ordinary sense but another meaning is suggested in *TĀ* 29.282a where Abhinava speaks of 'having cooked *dīpaka*'. Sanderson states [80] that the *dīpa-caru* was a lamp

> '... *shaped out of dough with red wicks fuelled with clarified cow's butter ... intended as a substitute for the flesh of a human sacrifice ... to be eaten by the worshipper at the end of the cult.*' [81]

As regards the wick, he goes on to refer to the Krama where

> '... *the wicks were to contain camphor, musk, aloe and olibanum mixed with the blood of a man or of an animal substitute and the lamps themselves were to be made from the flour of red rice kneaded with fermented liquor and mixed with ginger and pepper. Both red rice and ginger were substitutes for flesh.*' [82]

All this suggests that the 'lamp' is more than just an ordinary ritual lamp. The matter will become clearer after considering the term *caru*.

---

80. He does so perhaps with reference to Jr.54d.5 and other texts of *TĀ* 29 and its investigation.
81. Sanderson, 'Meaning', p.83. 'Some cults may even require an offering of human flesh (thus *Svacchanda-tantra*. 8.14-15).' Padoux, *Vāc*, p.48 footnote 40. See *Hevajra Tantra* I.11,8.
82. Sanderson, 'Meaning', pp.82-83. See also Jr.54d.5 and notes.

Ordinarily, *caru*, oblation, is 'rice, barley or pulse boiled with butter and milk'[83] but not so in the Kula ritual. In Jr. 200d.1, Jayaratha explains that the 'oblation' consists of the 'five jewels'[84] which are listed as 'male urine, semen, menstrual blood, phlegm, faeces'.[85] It is taken as the human equivalent of the *pañçagavya*, the five products of the cow, milk, curd, ghee, urine and dung, all referred to in Qt.16d.3 in connection with the 'lamp'. The 'lamp' and the 'oblation' would, therefore, seem to be identical.[86]

The Opening Ritual

A. Preparation

śl. 18ab	1.	He enters
śl. 18cd-19	2.	He purifies himself with the mantras
śl. 20ab		- on occasion he may initiate
śl. 20cd	3.	He purifies the instruments
śl. 21		- comment on the three *mantras*
śl. 22ab	4.	He prepares the vessel

B. Sacrifice

śl. 22cd	5.	He becomes Bhairava
śl. 23	6.	He satiates the self and the goddesses
śl. 24	7.	He externalises

The Opening Ritual is a self-contained ritual which also serves as an introduction also to the procedures of the whole chapter. It

83. S.C. Banerji, *Tantra in Bengal*, 2nd edn, New Delhi, Manohar Publications, 1992, 175 note 37. See also Gnoli, *Luce*, p.489 footnote 196.
84. Traditionally, the 'five jewels' are gold, silver, coral, diamond, pearl. Monier-Williams, *Sanskrit English Dictionary*, p.864.3
85. Compare the phrase from the *Kaulajñānanirṇaya* 11.11: 'Traditionally in the Kaula tradition the five means of purification are faeces, the nectar of the generative organ (*dhāra*), semen, menstrual blood and marrow (*majja*) mixed together.'
86. Compare *Kaulajñānanirṇaya* 18.2: 'I will speak of the methods relating to the Kula Dīpa (*kulaṃ dīpasya*), as well as the cake made of rice flour or wheat ...' The god goes on to refer to various cakes including combinations of *rakta* and *śukra*, *kuṇḍa*, *gola*. Bagchi, *Kaulajñānanirṇaya*, pp.102 ff.

has a preparatory section as well as a moment of worship properly speaking. The preparatory section involves a cleansing or regeneration of the practitioner followed by a preparation of the instruments, whatever these may be, and in particular a filling of the vessel. After these preparations the practitioner performs the most important part of the ritual which takes place in two stages. Firstly, he brings himself into the state of Bhairava and, secondly, sprinkles himself and the circles with droplets taken from the vessel. Some elements require a more extensive comment.

The location of ritual is not public but private. Abhinava speaks of 'entering the hall of sacrifice' (*yāga-okas*) but this need not be elsewhere than in a house. It is filled with incense etc. but what counts is that 'the heart is filled with peace and is disposed to full absorption into Śiva'. That is the true place of sacrifice.[87] Even if performed with a partner or with disciples or in the context of a circle of worshippers, the ritual is private worship (*ātmārthapūjā*) and it contrasts with '*āgamic*', dualistic, ritual which usually involves the temple and public worship (*parārthapūjā*).[88]

Although there is no calendar in the Kula ritual, there is considerable specification concerning direction. At least in this Opening Ritual, the practitioner faces north-east since north is the direction of liberation while east is the direction of enjoyment[89] so that the Kula practitioner is liberated-while-living. In Jr.29b.3, Jayaratha adds a further detail. The personages who are worshipped are ranged on his left whatever his direction so that rather than the practitioner facing a particular direction, the direction is determined by his own body. Like Śiva, the divinised practitioner is the point from which all directions are measured.

Just as there is no public place of sacrifice, there is no calendar of sacrifice. *TĀ* 28 attaches great importance to the 'junctures' (*parvan*) or feast days,[90] whereas in the Kula ritual the calendar is

87. *TĀ* 15.80 ff., which correspond to *TĀ* 29.18, refer to various sites such as mountain-tops, river-banks, places sanctified by a liṅga etc., but goes on to speak of the body as the principal sacred site for sacrifice. In *Tantrasāra* p.133 lines 2-3, Abhinava defines the *yāgasthānaṃ* as '... wherever the heart is filled with peace and is disposed to full absorption into Śiva.'

88. Padoux, *Vāc*, p.33.

89. *TĀ* 15.194 ff. See also *TĀ* 15.193 and 231b-232a.

90. *TĀ* 28.10-60ab.

excluded as Abhinava states in *TĀ* 29.65. This being said, the feast of *TĀ* 28 called the 'Ceremony of the Cord' is the occasion for obtaining the ingredients, especially the sexual fluid, to be used in the Kula daily ritual and other Kula rituals.[91]

These matters are best understood as the context for using the mantras which, at this first stage in the Opening Ritual, are explicitly named and of which the first is Mālinī the principal *vidyā* of the *Mālinīvijayottaratantra*. It is a set of 50 Sanskrit phonemes in which vowels and consonants are mixed as a garland (*mālā*). The first phoneme of the set is *NA* and the last is *PHA* whence the frequently used alternative name *Nādiphānta*. In *TĀ* 15.140c, Abhinava states that, instead of the long form of fifty phonemes, Mālinī may be used in the abbreviated form: *NA-PHA HRĪṂ*.

Although the origin of *Mālinī* is unknown,[92] Abhinava states that there are many other arrangements of alphabets where vowels and consonants are mixed and he even names one of them, Kulaputtalikā, without further elaboration. He goes on to affirm that Mālinī is the principal one of these arrangements.[93]

He also explains that this mixing, where vowels are the seed and consonants are the womb, produces the emission (*visarga*)[94] so that the object predominates and Mālinī is primarily emanating, cooling, nourishing. This explains the predominance of Mālinī in *TĀ* 29 which is more concerned with union and emission in all its meanings than with the reabsorption which predominates in *Mātṛsadbhāva*.

---

91. The Ceremony of the Cord is specifically mentioned in Qt.22b.1 in connection with obtaining the sexual fluid and is described at length in *TĀ* 28.112-186ab. In *TĀ* 28.139cd-142ab he mentions great celebrations, feasting, dancing etc., at the conclusion of which there must be a Circle Sacrifice. In *Parātriṃśikāvivaraṇa* p.280 lines 28-29, Abhinava stresses the importance of taking part in the *pavitraka* ceremony. It would seem that the ingredients were obtained at least on such an occasion and were kept for later use, perhaps in the form of pills as suggested by the word *vidrāvya* in Qt.129b.3.
92. Teun Goudriaan, '*Vāc*. The concept of Word in selected Hindu tantras, by A. Padoux' [review] *Wiener Zeitschrift für die Künde Südund Ostasiens* 37:238-240, 1993, p.238.
93. *TĀ* 15.129cd-130ab.
94. *TĀ* 15.126cd and *TĀ* 3.199ab.

The second mantra to be examined is Parā whose phonic form is *SAUḤ*. It is called 'seed of the heart' (*hṛdaya-bīja*) 'seed of nectar' (*amṛta-bīja*). *Parātrīśikā* 10b calls it 'the heart of Bhairava himself' while *Parātrīśikā* 35b calls it Rudrayāmala.[95] It is also called *trika* which can cause confusion with the system called '*Trika*' of which it is the crown.

The phonemes of the mantra take their meaning from what has been said above concerning the forms of emanation. When Parā is recited in the direction of reabsorption, *S* represents the objective world; *AU* the three energies of will, knowledge and action; *Ḥ* is the supreme *brahman* who emits the universe.[96] From another point of view, *S* represents the first three cosmic spheres (*aṇḍa*): *pṛthvī*, *prakṛti* and *māyā*. The phoneme *AU* represents the fourth sphere of śakti, namely the three powers of action, will and knowledge or the deities *Śuddhavidyā*, *Īśvara* and *Sadāśiva* while *Ḥ*, consisting of two dots, : , represents Śiva and śakti. Thus *SAUḤ* contains the whole of reality in every aspect.[97]

When Parā is recited in the direction of emission, *S* symbolises Śiva as the highest *brahman*,[98] *AU* retains its meaning as the three energies of will, knowledge and action, while *Ḥ* represents the emission. However, all this takes place within consciousness.[99] While Parā can be recited in the directions both of reabsorption and emission, the emitting aspect predominates, as reflected in Jr.21d.1.[100]

A different interpretation is available for Parā. In *Parātriṃśikāvivaraṇa* p.266 lines 4-9, Abhinava interprets *Parātrīśikā* 9cd-10ab, and therefore *SAUḤ*, as referring to the

95. Sanderson, 'The Triadic Heart', p.356.
96. Padoux, *La Parātrīśikālaghuvṛtti*, pp.112-113 notes 261, 263, 264.
97. Singh, *Parātriṃśikāvivaraṇa*, p.168 footnote 2. *Mālinīvijayottaratantra* 4.25 speaks to this effect.
98. *Parātriṃśikāvivaraṇa* pp.260-265.
99. Padoux, *La Parātrīśikālaghuvṛtti*, p.114 note 275.
100. 'Thus Abhinavagupta's interpretation of *sauḥ* is in keeping with the aesthetics of creation, creativity and invigoration encoded in Parā's āgamic icons and *sādhanas*; and it is so in spite of a general tendency in his exegesis to assimilate the understanding of the Trika into the doctrines of the Krama with their emphatically reabsorptionist orientation.' Sanderson, 'The visualisation', p.58.

liquids of the Kula ritual. The point is especially significant since *Parātrīśikā* 18 will point out that the knowledge of *SAUḤ* alone is sufficient to secure every supernatural power (*siddhi*), so just to consume the liquids is to attain the fullness of power.

Although Parāparā and Aparā feature in *TĀ* 29 they are minor mantra-deities since the ritual is concerned above all with the subject.[101]

The third principal mantra to be examined in Mātṛsadbhāva. Now, the first expression of the union (*saṃghaṭṭa*) of Śiva and śakti is the energy of bliss (*śakti-ānanda*) from which all is emitted.[102] Abhinava gives[103] a variety of names for bliss: 'goddess' (*devī*), 'essence' (*sāra*), 'heart' (*hṛdaya*), 'emission' (*visarga*). He also notes that, according to the *Devyāyāmalatantra*, she is called *Kālakarṣiṇī*, 'she who pulls time to herself'. He also calls her *Śrī Parā* and notes that in the *Mālinīvijayottaratantra* she is called 'Mātṛsadbhāva' which originally meant 'The Essence of the Mother Goddesses' but which Abhinava interprets to mean 'The Essence of (All) Agents of Cognition'.[104] She is also called Kālī.[105] Her phonic form (*vidyā*) is the one syllable *KHPHREṂ*[106] which is also called Piṇḍanātha or Pañcapiṇḍanātha[107] since it consists of one syllable comprising five phonemes. She also has a *vidyā* of seventeen syllables, *hrīṃ mahācaṇḍayogeśvari thṝ dhṝ thṝ phaṭ phaṭ phaṭ phaṭ phaṭ*, which is given in Qt.70b.2.[108]

These three great mantras of the Kula tradition are not only self-standing but are also inter-connected. To begin with, Parā and Mātṛsadbhāva are closely associated. In TĀ 31.97ab, Abhinava

101. The mantric form, *vidyā*, of Parāparā is given in *TĀ* 30.20-26ab and is fully spelt out in Gnoli, *Luce*, p.719 footnote 16. From the body of Parāparā come the eight gods, *ibid.* p.719 footnote 16, who will be mentioned in *TĀ* 29.53a. The *vidyā* of Aparā is given in *TĀ* 30.26cd and is fully spelt out in Gnoli, *Luce*, p.719 footnote18.
102. *TĀ* 3.68.
103. *TĀ* 3.69-71.
104. Sanderson, '*Maṇḍala*', p.194. *TĀ* 4.176b-177ab.
105. *TĀ* 4.176c.
106. *TĀ* 4.189cd-191ab and 30.45b-46.
107. Gnoli, *Luce*, p.176 footnote 84. See also Padoux, *Vāc*, p.416.
108. Sanderson, 'The visualisation', p.59.

adopts the Krama position and places Kālāntakā, i.e. Mātṛsadbhāva, above Parā.[109] However, Abhinava's exegesis of his base text, the *Mālinīvijayottaratantra*, shows, according to Sanderson, that '... the pantheons of the Trika and the Krama are ultimately identical.'[110] When Abhinava treats of these two mantras together, he first speaks of *SAUḤ* and then goes on to speak of *KHPHREṂ*.[111] Their intimate relationship is perhaps best explained by his comment, at *TĀ* 4.191cd, that *SAUḤ* is 'the heart of emission' (*sṛṣṭau ca hṛt* ...') and that *KHPHREṂ* is 'the heart of dissolution' (*saṃhārahṛdayaṃ*). It is this power of dissolution that places Mātṛsadbhāva at the apex.

In second place, a mantra may be used by itself or combined with other mantras, as for example in the practice of enclosing (*sampuṭa*) one mantra in another. On the analogy of a substance which is enclosed by two bowls, a mantra or the personage who embodies the mantra is further empowered when enclosed by the principal mantra which is its origin and end.[112] The enclosing can be done in two ways. The principal mantra can be placed before and after the lesser mantra. Thus the mantra *rudra-śakti* is Mālinī enclosed either by Parā or by Mātṛsadbhāva and is explained in Jr.21d.1 as a means of acquiring both liberation and enjoyment. Alternatively the principal mantra can be interspersed throughout the lesser mantra.[113] This second method can be given a circular

109. See also Padoux, *Vāc*, p.422 footnote 110. Table VI on p.75 of Sanderson, 'Meaning', shows how Mātṛsadbhāva, the highest goddess of the Krama, transcends Parā, the highest goddess of the Trika.

110. *ibid.* p.73.

111. See, for example, *TĀ* 4.186cd-189ab and 189cd-191ab; *TĀ* 5.142-144 and 5.146; *TĀ* 30.27-28ab and 30.45cd ff.

112. Brunner, 'Un tantra du nord: le Netra Tantra', p.159. For example, in *Parātriṃśikāvivaraṇa* p.272 lines 8-10, Abhinava notes that '... those who are perfect in the use of a mantra from another school ...' can also become liberated-while-alive by the use of *SAUḤ* which surrounds their mantra and empowers it. In *Tantrasāra* p.135, he notes that even the dualist and impure mantras of the followers of Garuḍa and Viṣṇu are made pure and capable of giving liberation when they are associated with Mālinī.

113. See *Parātriṃśikāvivaraṇa* p.278 lines 2-3.

form if at the end of the lesser mantra the practitioner repeats the procedure.[114]

By extension, the word *sampuṭa* may be given a cosmic meaning. Since the bliss of Śiva and śakti stands at the beginning and end of the whole process of emanation and reabsorption, the cosmos is enfolded in bliss.[115] So too, the universe and consciousness mutually enclose each other. [116]

This notion is further extended to refer to Śiva and śakti who are joined, as two bowls, to form a whole.[117]

The idea of enclosure, where the outlying element is dominant and the centre (*madhya*) is weak, must be distinguished from another idea of the centre where the central element transcends and governs the attendant realities. For example, when Abhinava refers to the central position of Śiva in contrast to the surrounding four faces of Tatpuruṣa, Aghora, Sadyojāta and Vāmadeva, he states that '... to occupy the central position means to preside over all things...' [118] Again, when the *prāṇa* and *apāna* come to harmony, the *udāna* rises in the central channel (*madhya-nāḍī*) and leads to consciousness.

While, in Abhinava's recension, the principal mantras of the Kula ritual are Mālinī, Parā and Mātṛsadbhāva, another more basic mantra is found in the groan of love, *HĀ-HĀ*, which expresses in a more spontaneous fashion the experience of the bliss of consciousness.

The word *kūṭa* means 'peak', or 'combination'[119] and can also refer to a grouping of two consonants without their accompanying vowel.[120] The most prominent of these is the combination of *K* and *S* to form *KṢ*, such that *kūṭa* becomes almost synonymous with *KṢ*, as in Jr.213d.1. Its significance lies firstly in the fact that

114. An example of the circular arrangement of mantras is given in *TĀ* 29.215 which describes the twelves vowels as a sort of china rose.
115. *Parātriṃśikāvivaraṇa* p.278 line 4.
116. *Tantrasāra* p.200 lines 13-14.
117. *TĀ* 3.205cd-206ab. See Padoux, *La Parātrīśikālaghuvṛtti*, p.120 note 315.
118. *Tantrasāra* p.139 lines 4-5.
119. See Padoux, *Le coeur*, p.294 footnote 107.
120. Singh, *Parātriṃśikāvivaraṇa*, p.187 note 15 and *ibid.* p.152.

it combines the two phonemes *K*, which is in essence the Unsurpassable or Akula, and *S*, the emission or Kula. Thus *KṢ* symbolises the union of Śiva and śakti and all the emanation arising from their union.[121] Secondly, according to a certain reading of the alphabet, *KṢA* is the last phoneme and so symbolises the starting point of reabsorption.[122]

In the Opening Ritual, the three great mantras are used as a form of bath (*snāna*) the external sort of which is discounted in the Kula ritual.[123] The internal bath is used in *TĀ* 29.18cd-19 and is performed with the mantra whereby the practitioner identifies himself with all the categories by placing the mantra upwards and downwards in the directions of reabsorption and emission.[124] The third sort, the principal bath, which features in *TĀ* 29.22-23, is described as follows :

> *'... after transforming, by means of contemplation, the ingredient of bliss within the hero's receptacle into Śiva, he worships therein the circle of the mantra; then, by means of the same ingredient, he satiates the circle of goddesses in his body and his subtle-breath. That is the principal bath.'*[125]

In *TĀ* 29, the act of bathing is performed by installation (*nyāsa*) which occurs in a variety of ways in *TĀ* 29. For example, the

121. Padoux, *Vāc*, p.304 and *loc.cit.* footnote 227. *ibid.* p.312.
122. *ibid.* p.304.
123. *Mālinīvijayottaratantra* 8.4-15a lists six types of external bath. In *TĀ* 15.38 ff., Abhinava expands the list and gives eight sorts of bath. For the hero, however, these eight are replaced by '... the dust of the battlefield, hero's water [alcohol], the breeze of a crematory, the ashes of a hero, the air of a cremation ground, the moon and sun of a cremation ground, the self which is without differentiated thought.' *Tantrasāra* p.130 line 11- p.131 line 1.
124. See also *Tantrasāra* p.131 line 8.
125. *Tantrasāra* p.131 lines 4-7. *Tantrasāra* p.200 lines 3-5, which is the comparable text to *TĀ* 29.22-23, describes this bath in detail: '... with the drops [contained in the vessel] he should worship the sacrificial surfaces and with the liquid (*rasena*) [in the vessel] he should, by joining the fourth finger and the thumb of the left hand, worship and satiate the circle of the mantras contained in the circles of the body, then within the subtle breath, ...'. Note that the phrase 'the circle of the mantras contained in the circles of the body' refers to the the five gods located in five positions in the body.

mantra, sacred sites, the circle of the śakti or even the faculties of the guru are installed on the whole body or on parts of the body or on the faculties of the person.[126] The effect is to communicate the sacred power of what is placed, indeed to transform the location into what is placed. The act of installation unites the location and the located so that the place becomes the sacred site and acquires its character and its enjoyments. When, for example, the sacred site Aṭṭahāsa, also a name for Śiva, is installed on the tuft of hair, the tuft becomes consciousness. When the mantra Parā is installed on the body in both an upwards and downwards direction, the body is reabsorbed and emitted as a pure body.

The last preparatory action of the Opening Ritual is the filling of the vessel. All is contained in the mantra so that the filling of the vessel is an expression of the inner reality of the mantra which is the bliss of Śiva and śakti. The practitioner fills the vessel with wine, meat and sexual fluid for they lead to bliss (*ānanda*) and result from bliss and come simply to mean bliss. To come in contact with the contents of the vessel is to arrive at bliss and to sprinkle droplets from the chalice is to communicate that blessedness.

Bliss refers in the first instance to the very highest reality, the union of Śiva and śakti so that in *TĀ* 29.97c Abhinava states that 'Bliss is the supreme *brahman*'[127] for it is the source of all other realities.[128] The experience of their bliss produces various reactions such as the sexual fluid or the cry *HĀ-HĀ* which is the savouring of bliss, as in Qt.160b.2. These experiences and expressions of bliss lead to each other in a constant cycle of vibration.

Although the 3 M's are involved with bliss, the Kula practitioner is not dependent on them because he first discovers bliss within himself. Indeed, the use of the 3 M's is not so much a means to acquire the bliss of consciousness as an expression of the bliss which is already possessed. It is not the false bliss of 'bonded animals' which is based on delusion and the absence of consciousness and which the 'bonded animals' think they attain by

126. 'External placement, is always done with a gesture of the hand - or hands - touching the place where the *mantra* is deposited. In the case of touching the subtle body, however, an *antarnyāsa*, the act is done mentally, it is imagined.' Padoux, *Le coeur*, p.188 footnote 44.

127. This sentence is explored in Jr.98b.1, Qt.98b.1, Qt.100b.3 and Qt.110b.4.

128. *TĀ* 3.68.

indulgence. The two forms of bliss, the bliss of consciousness and the 3 M's, presume each other. In that sense, to abstain from the 3 M's is to abstain from consciousness.

After this preparation, the practitioner embarks on the sacrifice properly so called. He brings himself to the state of Bhairava by an internal act. Three inter-related internal acts may be considered here since they are the essential method of all the Kula sacrifices. The first of these to be considered is *bhāvanā* which basically means 'that which causes to be',[129] but it is a complex word for it can mean 'realisation', 'creative visualisation', 'contemplation', 'identification' etc.[130] Abhinava defines it as follows:

> *'The wise call this realisation 'the cow which fulfils all desires'. It brings into reality the object which existed only as a desire.'*[131]

All preexists in consciousness and is externalised by a mental act. It is not make-believe or external manufacture but yogic projection, a gradual bringing into reality by means of repetition and is comparable to the act of impregnation or saturating.[132] A reality which is glimpsed momentarily is brought into prominence by being dwelt upon and seen in every circumstance so that the fleeting reality is in fact seen to constitute the whole.

The term recollection (*smaraṇa*) is closely connected with *bhāvanā*. In the act of recollection the worshipper brings to mind the higher principle and reabsorbs the lower into it. It is a return to the heart, an act of integration whereby the object is brought into harmony with the supreme subject and so frees a person from ritual, or rather turns all into ritual. The aim of the worshipper is to attain the state whereby all his acts and words are done with recollection and so are turned into worship.

Meditation (*dhyāna*) is another major technique advanced in TĀ 29 and is defined as 'a continuum of uniform knowledge ...'[133]

---

129. Bernard Parlier, *Le Ghaṭakarparavivṛti d'Abhinavagupta*, Paris, E. de Boccard, 1975, p.47.
130. Gnoli, *Luce*, p.155 footnote 2. Padoux, *Vāc*, p.205 footnote 93.
131. *TĀ* 4.14.
132. Parlier, *Le Ghaṭakarparavivṛti*, p.47.
133. *TĀ* 4.93cd.

Even though Abhinava asks the question: 'How can one meditate on the One who has no form?',[134] he does make good use of the method because it can be understood at different levels. One of these is attentiveness (*anusaṃdhir*) 'to the whole nature [of consciousness]',[135] a form of meditation emphasised in *TĀ* 29 since the Kula ritual is based on undifferentiated thought. Attentiveness takes place on the 'undivided level' (*anavacchinna-pada*) and there is no attempt to provide a visual meditation on some form of the goddess holding weapons, for example, because these things are created objects.[136] He does allow meditation on a form of the formless, a sort of coagulation, *mūrti*, or projection from one's own self[137] such as the square, circle, triangle and point etc. of the *maṇḍala* or in slightly more imaginative forms of visualisation.[138]

Abhinava also makes use of satiation (*tarpaṇa*) which refers in its primary meaning to the offering of food and drink to the ancestors and to the gods, a sort of libation.[139] In the Trika it is given the wider sense of the reabsorption of the lower categories into the higher categories or of object of knowledge into the means of knowledge which itself is reabsorbed into the subject of knowledge. The satiation takes the form of either an external act or an internal act. When he performs the external act the practitioner projects his inner reality or identifies the outer object with the bliss symbolised by the droplets. He does this by sprinkling (*prokṣa*) droplets of wine etc. from the consecrated vessel. It is also performed by consuming food and drink, satisfying of the lower 'circles' so that the highest circle, consciousness, may become manifest. He may also, in a more internal fashion, perform the sprinkling with a mantra such as *rudra-śakti*. Again, it may be done simply by acknowledging the object with full consciousness

134. *Mahopadeśaviṃśatikā* 12c.
135. *TĀ* 12.9.
136. *Parātriṃśikāvivaraṇa* p.278 lines 9-10.
137. Abhinava defines meditation as '... whatever [the *yogī*] fashions, as he pleases, from his own being, interiorly or exteriorly ...' *TĀ* 4.195. Padoux, *Le coeur*, p.175 footnote 310.
138. See for example *TĀ* 29.241cd-241ab, *śl.*245b, *śl.*259-260, *śl.*261-262.
139. See Padoux, *Le coeur*, p.391 footnote 415.

so that the object is incorporated into consciousness and acquires all its power.[140] Whatever the method the outer and the inner reality are made identical so that there is a harmony and an appropriateness at every level of reality.

Externalisation follows from the idea of sprinkling and is one of the principal themes of *TĀ* 29. By means of the Opening Ritual the practitioner has brought himself to the awareness of his state as Bhairava and so is now able to engage in Sacrifice since divinisation is a precondition for true worship, as in the phrases: 'Having become Śiva he should worship Śiva',[141] 'He who is not god may not worship god'.[142] If he is Śiva it is natural for him to express himself in Sacrifice 1, since Śiva freely expresses himself in his five acts, not just emanation, preservation and reabsorption but also in the two acts which emphasise the role of grace: his varied and multiple acts of concealment and revelation.[143] The ritual is not performed in order to attain a state of liberation or enjoyment as though these were absent but is a manifestation of the real condition the practitioner has received through initiation and the mantra. He now wishes to show (*didṛkṣur, śl.*24d) that the external world and the inner world coincide, to demonstrate the 'attitude of Bhairava' (*bhairava-mudrā*). Yet in a sense the external sacrifice is also needed. In the *Tantrasāra*, while discussing the relationship of external and internal, Abhinava notes that if the sacrifice were performed only interiorly there would be a lack of externality and therefore limitation[144] and dualism.[145]

---

140. *Tantrasāra* p.199 line 18 - p.200 line 2.
141. Bäumer, *Wege*, p.156.
142. Padoux, *Vāc*, p.47. 'The general Tantric principle [is] that only one who has become the deity may worship the deity.' Sanderson, '*Maṇḍala*', p.176.
143. In *TĀ* 15.262cd ff., Abhinava rejects the idea of a transcendent Śiva who remains so. In *Tantrasāra* p.141, he tackles the objection as to why, after attaining the state of Śiva which is the *bimba*, the practitioner would proceed to express this state through emanation or reflection, *pratibimba*. To that objection he replies that the motionless body of Bhairava already manifests within itself, *svātmani*, millions upon millions of creations and dissolutions. Of his very nature Bhairava manifests within, and with equal freedom chooses to manifest without.
144. *Tantrasāra* p.143 lines 4-5.
145. Although Abhinava does not use the words *bimba* and *pratibimba* in *TĀ* 29 - Jayaratha does in Jr.24d.2 - he uses the word *bimba* in *Tantrasāra* p.179 line 15 - p.180 line 2 when describing a daily ritual.

Sacrifice 1 external, *bahiḥ*

śl. 25-27ab — 1. The external setting
2. The ritual:

A. Reabsorption into the centre:

śl. 27cd-29ab — 1. The personages on the square
śl. 45cd-46ab — 2. The mantras in the circle: Mālinī and Mātṛkā
3. The goddesses in the triangle: Parā, Parāparā and Aparā
śl. 46cd-48 — 4. Kuleśvarī in the centre

B. Emanation from the centre:

śl. 49-50 — 1. Śakti and Bhairava at the centre
śl. 51 — 2. Deities in triangle: 12, 64, 4 etc.
śl. 52-54c — 3. The 8 goddesses and their consorts on the lotus
śl. 54d-55 — 4. The 'lamps' :
a. According to 64 Masters
b. According to one's *vidyā*

Sacrifice 1 is the external celebration of the splendour of consciousness and consists of a vibration, moving from the emission represented by the setting out of the instruments of sacrifice and proceeding by reabsorption through various stages to the centre where Kuleśvara and Kuleśvarī rule. According to another image, it is the construction of a throne for the divine pair.[146]

146. *Tantrasāra* p.200 lines 6-10, which refers to *TĀ* 29.25 ff, reads as follows: 'Then on the sacrificial surface he should construct a throne finishing with the three śaktis, who are the trident. In other words, he should construct, on the flood of [the phoneme] *S* and on the phoneme *AU*, a throne finishing with the three śaktis who conclude *māyā*. And on the three śaktis who conclude *māyā*, who [themselves] are on the flood of [the phoneme] *S* and on the phoneme *AU*, the sakti is to receive sacrifice, she who is the form of awareness (*vimarśa*) [*Ḥ*].' In *Tantrasāra* p.200 line 13 ff., he goes on to note that the process of emanation and reabsorption, which is a vibration between the inmost and outmost poles, means that there is a double enclosure, *saṃpuṭa*: external reality is enclosed within consciousness, consciousness is enclosed within external reality.

Then by a new emission the practitioner goes through the various stages till he sets out the 'lamps' on the sacrificial surface. Into this overall pattern taken from the *Mālinīvijayottaratantra*, Abhiṇava inserts what may be called the Kula hierarchy. Some of these elements require closer analysis.

From the large range of supports available,[147] Abhinava has selected those which suit the nature of the Kula ritual,namely the ground with its design (*maṇḍala*), the cloth (*paṭa*) and the skull which is the vessel containing the fearsome ingredients. These constitute the sacred space appropriate to the external Sacrifice. The *liṅga* is not mentioned here in *TĀ* 29 as an instrument of sacrifice.[148] The *maṇḍala* and the skull require further comment.

According to Jayaratha in Jr.27b.1 and Jr.27b.2, the *maṇḍala* of *śl.*26d refers to a dot or circle (*śl.*25c) or dot and circles (Qt.27b.1) drawn on the ground. On the cloth which is placed over the diagram on the ground, the practitioner sets out the Kula *maṇḍala* consisting of a square, circle, triangle and point. Thus there are two *maṇḍala*. The first *maṇḍala* consisting of a dot or circle represents Śiva and śakti and their act of emitting. The square of cloth is the conclusion of the emission and the starting point of the reabsorption enacted by the practitioner.

The term *maṇḍala* has many other meanings in *TĀ* 29. They draw on the basic meanings of 'circle or 'diagram': a group of goddesses, the union of a Perfected Being and a *yoginī*, the structure of the body and its channels, the design of the triple trident, the faculties, a triangle, the coverings such as *māyā* etc.

The skull is a significant item for it is a reminder of the Kāpālika background of the Kula tradition but its relatively minor role in the ritual shows how distant that background is. The skull is in fact called the 'sacred site of the body' (*kāya-pīṭha*) because it is deemed to be the seat on which the deity is enthroned.[149] This

147. See *TĀ* 6.3, TĀ 2.42-43ab, *TĀ* 21.16-22ab and *TĀ* 27.44-46.

148. Nevertheless, the *liṅga* still remains a possibility. *Tantrasāra* p.198 line 15 - p.199 line 1, which provides the setting for the Kula ritual and which is the equivalent passage to *TĀ* 29.14-16, reads as follows:'... the external reality consists of a sacrificial surface, a hero's cup full of wine (*ānanda*), a blood-red cloth or a *liṅga* etc. as mentioned above.'

149. See Jr.27b.2 and Qt.16d.1

'sacred site of the body' may be a skull taken from a cremation ground or a substitute such as a coconut or conch-shell and it contains-precisely in what condition it is not quite clear-the ingredients of the ritual, the heroic and horrific substances which include wine etc.[150] The skull can also be one's own head (Jr.16d.1).

Insertion of the Kula Hierarchy

The outer section of the *maṇḍala* or the square of the cloth is the world of objectivity, in particular the history of the Kula tradition in its divine, Perfect and human streams. At first Abhinava follows the pattern given by *Mālinīvijayottaratantra* 11.8-16, but before leaving the outer square and following that text further into the centre he inserts the Kula hierarchy. After all, the essence of the Kula ritual consists in the worship of the Perfect Beings and their wives and it is appropriate to give more details on the lineages than are provided by the *Mālinīvijayottaratantra*. He does not indicate what other text, if any,[151] he is following. The hierarchy may be first considered in order not to break the flow from the outer limit of the *maṇḍala* to its central point. The hierarchy proceeds as follows:

śl. 29cd-32ab	a. The 4 Perfected Beings and wives
śl. 32cd-33	b. The 6 qualified gurus
śl. 34	i. Thcir śaktis
	ii. The marks of the lineages
śl. 35	a. Definition
śl. 36-39	b. Examination
śl. 40	iii. Advantage of these marks
śl. 41	c. The 6 non-qualified gurus;
śl. 42	difference between qualified and non-qualified
śl. 43-45ab	d. The bodiless gurus

150. Abhinava gives an interpretation of drinking from the skull: 'He drinks from a skull, from the fragment of an object of knowledge which he holds in his hand, full of the wine of the essence of the universe ...' *Paramārthasāra*, śl. 80.

151. *TĀ* 4.212-278 is Abhinava's commentary on his own paraphrase of *Mālinīvijayottaratantra* 18.74-81. Very often in that commentary, he contrasts the *Śaivasiddhānta* and the Kula tradition and, in so doing, refers to details which reappear in *TĀ* 29.29cd-39 and will be pointed out as appropriate.

The six active princes, who are uncertainly connected with the four Perfected Beings, Khagendra etc., govern six sets of dynasties, gestures, codes, hermitages, begging places and sacred sites. The arrangement is so neat that it seems fabricated rather than factual. Yet Abhinava goes on to give some historical plausibility noting, in *TĀ* 29.40, that those who make use of the gestures etc. when they travel to various sacred sites obtain whatever they want from the *yoginīs*.

The term 'Perfected Being' is particularly associated with the figure of the *yoginī* who differs vastly in *TĀ* 29 from the type described in the section above dealing with the *yoginī* cult. Yet these fantastic creatures provide the basis for the role of the *yoginī* in *TĀ* 29 and its investigation.[152] In particular, from her 'mouth' the *yoginī* provides the sexual fluid, the awesome substance which destroys the ego. She is the sexual partner and grants supernatural powers of which the bliss of consciousness is the greatest and she gives birth to the *yoginī*-child who is the receptacle of all knowledge, a Rudra. The domestication of the Kula ritual and its reinterpretation by Abhinava means that the female sexual partner is invested with all the imagery of another era. She has the essential role of the mythical *yoginī* but not her outward appearance. Thus to be associated in sexual rites with the female partner is effectively to enter the cremation ground and to join the company of the Perfected Beings and their preferred partners, the *yoginīs*.

152. Some of the characteristics listed by de Mallmann, *Les enseignements*, pp.169-182, are found in the *yoginīs* of *TĀ* 29: 'they have superhuman powers': the *yoginīs* grant powers to the hero of their own kula (*śl.*40d.); 'moving through the sky': they dwell in the sky where they receive those who deserve them (Qt.64d.1); 'preferring to dwell in cemeteries': they frequent cremation grounds (*śl.*183b, *śl.*72b, Qt.72b.2, Jr.185d.1); 'they can take on the shape of all sorts of animals': they devour flesh when unsatiated (Qt.13d.24); 'they compete for the attentions of the same man': they are lovers of men (Qt.129.1) and love certain rituals in particular, (śl.150d); 'they protect children': they are celestial beings who engender children in women of their own kula (Jr.46b.1) while the human female sexual partner who is identified with the *yoginī* gives birth to a child who is *yoginī-bhūḥ* (*śl.*163a).

The bodiless gurus are intimately involved in handing on the tradition. Indeed they are the sky-travellers (*khecarī*) who bring about the birth of the receptacles of Kula knowledge, among whom Jayaratha places Abhinava, and so ensure in their own way the transmission of the tradition. The bodiless gurus and their wives, for example Svabhāva and Bhagavatī, exist in an eternal union. However, they freely choose that there should be knowledge and then bring about the birth of the child such that the knowledge is now received in bodily form by human beings. The attendant *yoginīs* witness and take part in the events at each stage, at conception, birth etc. until the *yoginī*-child[153] reaches full maturity at the age of twenty-seven.[154] In this way there is a progression down every level of being from will to knowledge, then to action and so to the historical birth. In this way the hierarchy does full circle.

Resumption of Sacrifice 1 :

After inserting the Kula hierarchy, Abhinava resumes in very general terms the pattern provided by *Mālinīvijayottaratantra* 11.10 ff. He moves out of the history of the Kula lineages and into the circle formed by the more subtle sets of alphabet deities, Mālinī and Mātṛkā from whom all emanate and into whom all are reabsorbed as is indicated by the way in which they move between north-east and south-west.[155] The goddesses are also mediators between the centre and the periphery, subject and object.

The term *mātṛkā* is originally associated with the mythological figures, the Seven Mothers or *mātṛkā* who govern the universe

153. Gnoli, *Luce*, p.685 footnote 31.

154. The number twenty-seven has symbolic value in the Trika, being the result of the calculation 3x3x3. In *Parātriṃśikāvivaraṇa* p.277 lines 1-3, Abhinava explains the derivation of the number. The three goddesses Parā, Parāparā, Aparā are 'multiplied' by the three activities of will, knowledge and activity and are 'multiplied' again by the three acts of emanation, maintenance and reabsorption. Gnoli, *Il commento*, p.169. Padoux, *La Parātrīśikālaghuvṛtti*, p.117 note 296.

155. Kṣemarāja in his commentary on the *Netratantra* interprets the contrary movements as indicating both emanation and destruction. Brunner, 'Un Tantra du Nord', p.155.

and who recur in various roles and with various names.[156] However, the phonematic speculation of Kashmir Śaivism will profoundly alter the meaning of the term to denote the set of 50 phonemes in their normal order, from *A* to *KṢA*.[157] It is the principal *vidyā* of the *Svacchandatantra*,[158] not to be confused with Mātṛsadbhāva the *vidyā* of the Krama, and is also called Pūrvamālinī, not to be confused with Mālinī proper also called Uttaramālinī.

Mātṛkā and Mālinī are associated. In Mātṛkā the subject predominates and therefore Mātṛkā is absorptive, fiery, whereas in Mālinī emission predominates and therefore Mālinī is cooling. Abhinava identifies Mālinī with śakti and identifies Śabdarāśi or Mātṛkā with Śiva[159] but these alphabets do not exclude each other any more than Śiva excludes śakti. Indeed, after having described the two alphabets Mātṛkā and Mālinī, Abhinava goes on to say that even if Mātṛkā does consist of Śiva and Mālinī of śakti, both have the nature of Śiva and śakti since both alphabets are complete.[160]

The pair, Mātṛkā and Mālinī, form the circle which surrounds the triangle formed by the Trika deities Parā, Parāparā and Aparā in their transcendent state. They in turn are the last entourage

156. Daniélou, Hindu polytheism, p.287. 'Perhaps the best-known mythological account of these *Mātṛkās* in the mediaeval period is found in the third episode of the *Devīmahāhātmya*.' David Kinsey, *Hindu goddesses*, Delhi, Motilal Banarsidass, 1987, p.156. The gods create seven śaktis who resemble themselves but they are to be understood '... not primarily as the divine consorts of śaktis of the male deities but rather as extensions or forms of the Devī herself.' *ibid.* pp.157-158. The seven mothers, (*mātaraḥ*) are listed in the *Agni-Purāṇa* as Brāhmī, Śāṅkarī, Kaumārī, Lakṣmī, Vārāhī, Aindrī and Cāmuṇḍā. Mahālakṣmī is added as an eighth. Their depiction is given in the *Agni-Purāṇa*, ch.50. See de Mallmann, *Les enseignements de l'Agni-Purāṇa*, p.150 The 'Mothers' (*mātṛkā*) are listed frequently in tantric texts but the names vary. Compare *Mālinīvijayottaratantra* 3.14, *TĀ* 8.241cd-244 and *TĀ* 30.20-26ab.

157. Kṣemarāja, in his commentary on *Śivasūtra* 1.4, explains: 'The mother unknown [to those who are fettered by the triple impurity] ....is *mātṛkā*, the begetter of the universe, who assumes the form of the phonemes from *A* to *KṢA*.' Padoux, *Vāc*, p.151-2. It is expounded in *TĀ* 15.117ab-120.

158. M.S. Kaul, ed., *Mālinīvijayottara Tantram*, Delhi, Butala & Co. 1984, p.xiv.

159. *Tantrasāra* p.134 lines 2-3.

160. *TĀ* 15.133c-134b.

protecting and expressing the highest, all-transcending deity, Kuleśvarī, who pervades these three goddesses and all the circles which eddy out from them.

The worshipper has now come to the point, the source and origin of all things whether in her single form or in its equivalent, her coupling with Kuleśvara. At this point the nomenclature changes and Abhinava speaks of Bhairava and śakti but the same realities are intended. The practitioner contemplates the bliss of the divine pair which derives from their union (*saṅghaṭṭa*) but, as Jayaratha points out in Jr.50d.2, the contemplation of the couple is equivalently the contemplation of the self full of consciousness and bliss.

Reality is also a vibration such that the concluding moment of arrival at the centre is also the beginning of an emanation to the periphery. The worshipper acknowledges the light streaming from the centre in the form of a hierarchy of traditions all of which, in their lessening degrees, express consciousness and bliss. Firstly, the twelve goddesses of the Krama or an alternative set of twelve, as Jr.51d.1 allows; the sixty-four Masters or *tantras* or deities of the Bhairava tradition; the four deities of the Right or Left traditions and then one's own tradition, all located within the triangle.[161]

The lotus petals which emanate in a circle from around the triangle are thrones for the eight goddesses who occupy an

---

161. In Jr.51d.2, Jayaratha introduces the set of eight goddesses by raising an objection which runs as follows. The traditional teaching states that the triangle contains an infinite number of rays which radiate from the single mass of consciousness and bliss. Why then specify the limited numbers twelve, sixty-four or four within the triangle, for any departure from traditional teaching will invalidate the ritual. Jayaratha admits the force of the objection and must, therefore, mitigate the significance of the numbers which he does by highlighting Abhinava's rhetorical question: 'What number do they [viz. other gurus] assign to the rays [of light]?' (*śl*.51d) and so concluding that the statement about the limited number of rays is just a concession to other gurus such as those of the Krama, the Left, the Right etc., while Abhinava's own teaching concerns the limited number outside the triangle, namely the two sets of eight.In another context, Jayaratha will give a different argument. *TĀ* 33, the synoptic chapter, lists many sets of rays, six, twenty-four, sixteen, thirty-four etc., and gives their names which are those of male and female divinities. He then notes that Abhinava understands these circles of divinities to be in fact unreal. Gnoli, *Luce*, p.758 footnote 16. Consciousness, says *TĀ*33.20a,is one, *eka eva cidātmaiṣaḥ*.

important place in *TĀ* 29. As Mātṛkās they are emanations of the supreme goddess but since the phonemes are also the cause of the universe they may also be interpreted as the eight classes of phonemes.[162] They can also be understood as the three internal senses and the five subtle elements [163] in the sense that the faculties of knowledge move out from the heart and bring the various objects of perception back to it. They are the intermediaries between consciousness and the world of objectivity.[164] Again, the goddesses are temporal deities, each governing a specific day of the lunar fortnight[165] and also have a directional significance as *lokapāla*, protectors of the points of the compass. Thus, from these eight come the whole external world.

Each goddess and her bhairava has an entourage (*āvaraṇa*) of eight Masters with their consorts, the propagators of the Bhairava scriptures,[166] to a total of sixty-four, whose names are omitted but who were referred to within the triangle (*śl*.51b).[167]

---

162. *Īśvarapratyabhijñāvimarśinī*, vol.3, p.226. In *Tantrasāra* p.17 line 7, Abhinava also associates the number eight with the eight classes of phonemes and adds a ninth class, the single phoneme *KṢ*, as Gnoli notes in *L'essenza*, p.112 footnote 2. Padoux also explains that such goddesses are the energies which preside over the eight classes of phonemes which in turn are the mother-energies of creation. He notes also that the lists vary between different texts. Padoux, *Vāc*, p.51 and p.155 note 194. See *Svacchandatantra*, 1.34-36.
163. See *Dehasthadevatācakrastotra* 6-13 which uses somewhat different names.
164. Silburn, *Hymnes de Abhinavagupta*, p.92.
165. *TĀ* 28.10cd-14ab.
166. In his investigation, *Tantrāloka* vol.2, pp.39-44, Jayaratha lists the sixty-four *bhairavatantras*. These are set out in eight groups of eight and the discrepancies are noted in Rastogi, p.324. Mark Dyczkowski, *The canon of saivagama and the Kubjika Tantra of the Western kaulạ tradition*, Delhi, Motilal Banarsidass, 1989, p.121 gives a slightly different list of the sixty-four *tantras* and names the teachers of each *tantra*.
167. At this point Jayaratha raises another objection. The essence of the Kula worship was stated in *śl*.2d to consist in the worship of the succession of the Perfected Beings. Why then is the listing of the Masters absent from the description of the *maṇḍala*? To answer this point, Jayaratha first admits, in Jr.54d.3, that the'sixty-four' refer to Masters and then refers to the endless number of Kula texts and their inconsistency in their lists of names and reinforces his argument by noting in Jr.54d.4 that a certain scripture even changes the number, admitting only fifty-six names. The actual numbers and names therefore, he argues in Jr.54d.5, are not important so that Abhinava is justified in not giving them.

It is from these Masters and scriptures that the worshipper has received his *vidyā* which now he worships, presumably on the square, by setting out 'lamps' considered as the outermost expression of the original bliss. Qt.54d.5 suggests that these 'lamps' primarily involve wine, meat and menstrual blood.

The Opening Ritual and especially Sacrifice 1 form the heart of the Kula ritual procedure so that the other Sacrifices flow from it. In displaying this essence, Abhinava has followed the pattern of *Mālinīvijayottaratantra* 11.3-16. But now, at the conclusion of Sacrifice 1, a complete break is made so that neither Abhinava nor Jayaratha will quote or paraphrase from that text again until *śl.*187cd resumes with *Mālinīvijayottaratantra* 11.17.

(e) Sub-topic 3 'The Ritual of Adoration'

śl. 56	Enunciation of the sub-topic
śl. 57	Definition of the sub-topic : The four stages of the Krama cycle

Sub-topic 3 or Sacrifice 2 is divided into two major sections. The first deals with the Krama cycle and is based on the *Mādhavakula* which is the fourth section of the *Tantrarājabhaṭṭāraka*. The second draws from the *Yogasañcāra* and deals more particularly with recitation. It also shows the influence of the Krama. Although the two sections are related they do not fit with complete ease. Abhinava follows his usual pattern and introduces the key elements of the ritual. Some of these require special comment.

Sacrifice 2 is based 'on the śakti' (*śaktau*) which has a wide reference but it does not refer to an actual woman. It is based on the 'internal śakti' which is, in the first instance, a recollection of outcaste women but is also any act of any faculty. In the *Tantrasāra* Abhinava makes the point,[168] firstly, that the preeminent and purest object of adoration in Sacrifice 2 is the union of heroes and śaktis, but adds that the same adoration can be applied to the eye's act of looking, for example. In *śl.*96a by contrast, he

168. *Tantrasāra* ch.22, p.201 lines 5-7.

states that Sacrifice 3 which is based 'on the couple' (*yāmale*) is performed 'with an external śakti' (*bāhya-sthayā śaktyā*) who is an actual sexual partner.[169]

Sacrifice 2 is also associated with sacred sites (*pīṭha*)[170] whose symbolism relies on an extensive body of legends. One aspect particularly relevant to *TĀ* 29 is the legend that the sacred sites contain the relics of the dismembered Satī, consort of Śiva. The sacred site is deemed to be the place where the goddess dwells in union with Bhairava.[171] It should be possible to travel to these various sacred sites and there to acquire the powers of the goddess or *yoginī* who dwells there.[172] It is more convenient and equally

169. In *TĀ* 28.78cd-82ab, Abhinava lists the five types of Circle Sacrifice: 'solitary', 'paired', 'mixed', 'circle', 'intermixture of heroes'. Regarding the fourth type, he says: '[The sacrifice celebrated with] a potter's wife etc. (*cakriṇyādyāś*), i.e. performed with the respective śaktis, will be described later. The Circle Sacrifice which takes place through their presence gives every result.' In his investigation of that text, Jayaratha explains the phrase 'potter's wife etc.' by quoting *TĀ* 29.66 and explains the phrase 'later on' by naming *TĀ* 29. Later on in his gloss on the phrase 'but without regard to castes etc.' (*TĀ* 29.101b) he also refers to *TĀ* 29.66. It transpires that both Sacrifice 2 and Sacrifice 3 are adaptations of the fourth Circle Sacrifice. The first adaptation, Sacrifice 2, is performed with an internal śakti and occurs by recollection only. Just as the worshipper recalls the twenty-four sacred sites, so too he recalls the śaktis listed in *śl*.66. They are therefore internal or intentional rather than materially present. The second adaptation, Sacrifice 3, is a domestic and private equivalent performed with an external śakti, with an actual woman. By quoting *TĀ* 29.66 in his commentary on *TĀ* 28.79b, Jayaratha is only indicating what sort of śaktis are involved in the fourth Circle Sacrifice. They are not the wife nor the prized courtesanof the second and third forms of the Circle Sacrifice but are from the lowest ranks of society. Gnoli confirms the point, stating that in the second sacrifice the śakti is contemplated whereas in the third there is sexual intercourse. Gnoli, *L'essenza*, p.280 footnote 2.
170. The tantric texts always use *pīṭha* and never *tīrtha*. P. Pal, *Hindu religion* and *iconology*. According to the *Tantrasāra*, Los Angeles, Vichitra Press, 1981, p.27.
171. D.C. Sircar, *The śākta pīṭhas*, 2nd edn. Delhi, Motilal Banarsidass, 1973, pp.6-7.
172. The *Kaulajñānanirṇaya* 16.7-10 states: 'It is said that female *sādhakas*, adept in yoga, dwell at Kāmākhyā Pīṭha. If one joins with one, one achieves Yoginī Siddhi, obtaining consciousness, mind, the ability to assume various shapes and Aṇimā with the other of the eight siddhis. Whatsoever is desired may be obtained here. ... Similarly the fivefold essence of siddhi, which is secret, may be obtained in these places.' Bagchi, *Kaulajñānanirṇaya*, p.86.
It may be of interest to refer to the sanctuaries of the Mātṛcakra or the Cauñṣaṭ Yoginī at Hirāpur near Bhubaneswar, or to Rānīpur Jhariāl in the Balangir District of Orissa. K.S. Behera, 'Evolution of Śakti Cult at Jajpur, Bhuvaneswar and Puri,' in D.C. Sircar, ed., *The śākti cult and Tārā*, Calcutta, Calcutta University

effective to identify these sites with one's own body by the ritual of installation (*nyāsa*) and so transform the body into the sacred sites.

The word *pīṭha* has another sense. It signifies the tradition expressed in the four elements: *vidyā*, mantra, *mudrā* and *maṇḍala*.[173] The goddess, specifically Kuṇḍalinī, presides over this tradition and makes it produce its fruit, the oil or essence which is pleasing to consciousness.

In Sacrifice 2, the term *pīṭha* more specifically focusses on the sexual dimension of the body so that the union of the sacred sites of the male practitioner, on the one hand, and of the group of nine impure women, on the other, symbolises the sexual union of the hero and the *yoginī* or of the faculty and its object. It is performed by recollection and constitutes the sacred region (*kṣetra*) or cremation ground.[174] Or again, the heart is both the sacred region and the cremation ground because all is absorbed into the fire of consciousness and all proceeds from consciousness which is the heart. Like the term 'sacred region', the term 'cremation ground' (*śmaśāna*) can refer to the union of the male and female practitioner or the faculty and its object.

Section A of Sacrifice 2 follows the three major steps of the Krama process, i.e. the objects of knowledge, means of knowledge and subject of knowledge, each of which in turn follows the cycle of emanation, permanence, reabsorption and the 'nameless'. Cycle I is concerned with action (*kalpa*) and starts with the emanation of the objects of knowledge and leads to Saṅkarṣiṇī, the goddess of the Krama. Cycle II is concerned with knowledge (*vikalpa*) and

---

Press, 1967, p.81. Almost all of these sanctuaries, dating from 9th - 11 cent. CE, were circular, consisting of a cloister containing statues of 64 or more *yoginīs*, surrounding a pavilion containing an image of Śiva. For a detailed account see de Mallmann, *Les enseignements*, pp.172-182. See also H.C. Das, *Tāntricism, a study of the yoginī cult*, New Delhi, Sterling Publishers, 1981. Some of these sorts of sanctuaries existed in Kashmir, although no remains survive. de Mallmann, *Les enseignements*, loc.cit.

173. *TĀ* 37.18c.

174. In his investigation of *TĀ* 4.259c, Jayaratha glosses *kṣetra* as *melāpasthānaṃ*, the place where the Perfected Beings and the *yoginī* meet. Gnoli, *Luce*, p.185 footnote 105.

starts from the emanation of the means of knowledge and finishes with the same goddess under the title of Kṛśā. Cycle III, which is without differentiated thought (*nirvikalpa*), starts from the emanation of the subject of knowledge and leads to 'the sacred place of his śakti' (*śl.*81cd).

A. Cycle I: Object of Knowledge

śl. 58	Definition of the ritual
	Examination
śl. 59-63	1. Emanation
	a. 24 sites on one's body
śl. 64	i. 'I' am not
śl. 65	ii. By recollection
śl. 66	b. Śakti-circle of 9 wives
śl. 67	their 9 sacred sites
śl. 68-69a	2. Maintenance: Cakriṇī /Kuṇḍalinī
śl. 69b	3. Reabsorption: Kuleśvarī
śl. 69cd	4. 'Nameless': Saṅkarṣiṇī
śl. 70ab	alone or paired

The first step of the Krama cycle consists in the emanation of the world. This is ritually symbolised by the installation of the sacred sites. The body of the male practitioner is transmuted in an orderly and harmonious way into the twenty-four sacred sites according to the order of emanation, starting from the tuft of hair and finishing with the foot. Likewise reabsorption starts from the toe so that reference to the Fire of Time (*kālāgni*) gives a hint of the reverse process of reabsorption which forms the inclusion at the end of Sacrifice 2 (*śl.*92-95). This is done by recollection.

The nine wives are carefully selected. Each of them is involved with the instruments of the Kula ritual, the twelve ingredients listed in Qt.17d.1 or the five 'jewels' listed in Qt.200b.1 and the skull, so that the significance of the women lies not only in their adulterous character but also in the fact that they are ritually impure. Like the ingredients they allow the practitioner to transcend the concepts of pure and impure and so to reach supreme consciousness. Whereas the sacred sites are installed upon the practitioner and confer their power on him, these reprobate women, these goddesses, are enthroned on the sacred sites and sanctify them.

Once the two sets of 'sacred sites' have been joined to form the 'sacred region', or once the male and female or the faculty and its object or any complementary sets have been joined, the return to the 'nameless' begins. As a result of their joining the 'wheel' begins to function.

In *śl.*66-70ab, the word *cakra* is used in three separate images. The first image (*śl.*66-67, 70ab) views the nine wives as forming a circle around the worshipper who has become the god. Eight of them are placed on the practitioner just as the eight petals of the lotus are placed on the square of the *maṇḍala* while the ninth, *cakriṇī*, occupies the centre as the most significant of them. Among its various meanings, the term *cakriṇī* can mean either the wife of the potter [175] or the wife of the oil-presser. Of these two possibilities, wife of the oil-maker or oil-presser applies best to śl.68 ff. The *cakriṇī* or *cākrikī* sits on a seat which presses down on the sesamum seeds while the ox, moving round and round the trampled floor, turns the mill. The oil is thus extracted and is used for worship etc. but the husk is used as fodder.

The second image (*śl.*68) is that of a wheel turning in the cycle of emission-dissolution wherein Cakriṇī/Kuṇḍalinī plays the principal role. In 70b.1, Jayaratha sketches three forms of the activity of Kuṇḍalinī / Cakriṇī. Firstly, with the emphasis on the cycle of emanation and reabsorption, Kuṇḍalinī manifests the universe as far as objects such as blue etc. and then reabsorbs all back into consciousness. Secondly, by transforming the seed into *prāṇa* she circulates through the body. She also produces the

175. The potter belongs to the lowest class of Indian society, but within this group he occupies an important position for the pot was not only an important utensil but it was often looked on as a representation of Devī herself. J.A. Schoterman, The *Ṣaṭsāhasra Saṃhitā*, chapters 1-5, Leiden, E.J.Brill, 1982, pp.7-8.

'flower', the menstrual or sexual fluid, which is consumed. The emphasis here is on internal experience. Then, in a third paragraph, Jayaratha explains the image of the oil-presser (*cākrikī*).

The third image (*śl.*69) is that of radiation from a central point and of contraction back to that point. In the radiation there are three stages: 1. the appearance of the 'circle' or the emanation and maintenance where Kuṇḍalinī is dominant; 2. the middle of the 'circle' or the reabsorption, where Kuleśvarī or Kālakṛntanī is dominant; 3. the very end of the 'circle', the 'nameless', where Saṅkarṣiṇī is dominant [176] and transcends Kuleśvarī, the principal goddess of Sacrifice 1.

In the *Tantrasāra*, Abhinava changes the image and expresses the same in terms of the triangle. Where Kuleśvarī, in Sacrifice 1, occupied the centre of the triangle formed by Parā etc., in Sacrifice 2, Saṅkarṣiṇī is at the apex of the triangle.[177]

Cycle II: Means of Knowledge

śl. 70cd-71ab	1. Emanation:
	the 24 sacred sites in 8 directions
śl. 71cd-72ab	the triads - their code
śl. 72cd-73ab	2. Maintenance:
	'lamps' are placed there
śl. 73cd-75ab	Insertion of one's private ritual
śl. 75cd-76ab	3. Reabsorption:
	setting aside the instruments
	4. 'Nameless': Goddess Kṛśā
śl. 76cd-77	aside: Hymn of the Sacred Site

176. According to *TĀ* 29.68-69, the goddesses Kuṇḍalinī, Kuleśvarī and Saṅkarśiṇī are associated with the stages of emission / maintenance, reabsorption and 'nameless' respectively but in Qt.70b.5 the goddesses are associated with the object of knowledge, the means of knowledge and the subject of knowledge. Thus the goddess who presides over the means of knowledge is Kālakṛntanī: 'she who knows', *jñā*. The object of knowledge had emanated from her so that she is described as 'after knowing', *jñātvā*. The goddess who presides at the very end, from the point of view of pure subject, is Saṅkarśiṇī.

177. *Tantrasāra* p.201 lines 9-11.

The opening act of the second Cycle is the emanation of the means of knowledge symbolised by the construction of a *maṇḍala* in eight directions so that the means of knowledge governs all the objects of knowledge and forms a bridge to the one subject of knowledge. The emanation starts from the heart or 'cremation ground' and leads in two contrary directions, to two sacred sites, to the lower *kuṇḍalī* and to the group of *yoginīs*, the upper *kuṇḍalī*. This is repeated in each of the eight directions so that the twenty-four sacred sites are used again, but in order to signify that the whole range of the means of knowledge and in particular the whole range of *prāṇa* is being set out in every sense.[178]

The next step symbolises the second stage, maintenance, which is done by joining twenty-four 'lamps' to the *maṇḍala*. Note that, according to Qt.73b.1, these are edible. At the same time Abhinava allows the practitioner to perform the ritual he may have obtained from a previous initiation and to make it effective by enclosing it in the ritual of Cycle II. From the comments in *TĀ* 29.75cd, Abhinava seems to have the tantric initiations of *TĀ* 15 ff. particularly in mind. The joining of the *maṇḍala* and the lamps evokes the third stage, the elimination, of which there are two moments.

The first act of elimination is to set aside the tantric instruments of sacrifice and is a moment of reabsorption when the practitioner acquires an unspecified supernatural power. He then focusses on Kṛśā, the fourth stage of Cycle II and consumes the hero's meal, the contents of the cup consisting of wine and sexual fluids etc. It is the moment of complete dissolution into subjectivity when all power is given to him and his mantras succeed without effort.

---

178. Many of these twenty-four are repeated in *TĀ* 15.83cd ff. which refers to *Niṣisaṃcarātantra*. Their arrangement helps understand *TĀ* 29.70cd ff. In *TĀ* 15.84, Abhinava notes that 'the will of [Parameśvara] is the basis of the sacred sites' and that this will corresponds externally to Kāmarūpa. He goes on to note that two other sacred sites, Pūrṇagiri and Uḍḍīyāna, develop out of Kāmarūpa, *dvayaṃ tataḥ*, so that the central sacred site gives rise to two others. He goes on to review their arrangement. These sets of three are arranged in two ways. First of all there is a set of 3x3, then, more significantly to our purpose, there is a set of 3x8=24 located on the petals of the lotus of the heart, on the tips of the petals of the lotus and on the connecting points of the petals.

Cycle III Subject of Knowledge

śl. 78	1. Emanation	:	Śaktis by themselves
śl. 79	2. Maintenance	:	Pairing with śaktis:
śl. 80	3. Reabsorption	:	a. No time
śl. 81ab			b. No throne
śl. 81cd	4. The 'nameless'	:	His śakti *(sva-śakti)*

Cycle III involves the subject alone, without the use of the faculties and without the objects of knowledge. The śaktis, the latter of the twelve goddesses of the Krama, are worshipped or emanated just 'by themselves', without the *maṇḍala* of the sacred sites, the cup of wine or the 'lamps'. They and the practitioner are without ritual (*nirārcārāḥ*) and differentiated thought. This stage may be compared to the moment of *parāmarśa*, creative awareness without any further emanation.

Abhinava moves swiftly at this point and notes that there is neither time, nor place because everything is reabsorbed into what may be compared with *vimarśa* simple awareness, the state of pure consciousness where, at last, 'Parameśvara works vigorously, above all within the sacred place of his śakti' (*śl.*81cd). The cleverness of this phrase is evident when it is seen not only as the climax of the Krama process but also as the bridge to recitation.

B. Recitation

śl. 82	Enunciation and Definition
śl. 83-88	1. The objects of focus
	2. The *haṃsa*.
śl. 89	a. Enunciation of *haṃsa*
śl. 90ab	b. Definition of *haṃsa*
śl. 90cd-91	note: no distinctions
śl. 92-95ab	3. Oblation in fire of consciousness

The practitioner recognises in himself the continual resting of Parameśvara in his śakti, the a-temporal throbbing of consciousness which is the proper state for recitation (*japa*). The treatment of recitation takes place in three steps. According to Jayaratha in Jr.81d.3, they are related in a general way to the three cycles of

Sacrifice 2. *śl.* 82-88, which give details on the focal points of the recitation and the numbers of recitations, are oriented to objects such as face and heart. *Śloka* 89-91 describes the *haṃsa* or the subtle-breath as the means of arriving at consciousness. The third step (*śl.*92-95ab) takes up again the twelve stages of the Krama which are performed in the context of oblation into the fire. These various steps require some elaboration.

The recitation is grouped into sets. The items listed in the sets of 5, 6, 7, 8 and 9 are set out below in a table which relies heavily on Jayaratha's interpretation of the words and symbols.

5	6	7	8	9
face	mouth	mouth	mouth	mouth
	eyes	eyes	eyes	eyes
		ears		ears
				breasts
				hands
				feet
			navel	
heart	heart	heart	heart	
'thread'	'thread'			
breath	breath	breath	breath;	breath;
			pit-of-	pit-of-
			Brahmā;	Brahmā;
Śaiva couple;	Śiva+śakti;	union of	private	private
		Śiva+śakti;	place +	place+
			aperture	end-of-
			of Ka;	twelve;

It becomes immediately apparent that the more numerous the sets of repetitions the more externalised is the focus of the recitation. Conversely, the less the number the more internalised is the focus. This accords with the comment made in Jr.89d.2 to the effect that the more competent the *yogī* the fewer repetitions does he need to make. Subtle-breath is the source of time which is a veil over consciousness[179] so that the reduction of the number of recitations and the stilling of the subtle-breath allow consciousness to appear.

Although the term *haṃsa* in fact refers to the goose which floats on the waves but dives its head under the water and in this sense has symbolic value, the term has many other meanings as well. *Haṃ* symbolises exhalation (*prāṇa*), while *sa* symbolises inhalation (*apāna*)[180] so that *haṃsa* is uttered twenty-four hours every day.[181] The connection of exhalation and inhalation with *prāṇa* and *apāna* ties *haṃsa* to the various meanings of those two forms of subtle-breath. Thus *haṃsa* is the cycle of emanation and reabsorption[182] as well as the whole range of phonemes and since emanation and reabsorption involve all reality, *haṃsa* contains all reality.[183] However, both emanation and reabsorption are themselves the work of Śiva-śakti with the result that *haṃsa* is also the heart (Jr.88d.1), the supreme self in perfect union with reality.[184] Finally, the word *haṃsa* can be divided into *HA*

---

179. In *Tantrasāra* p.60 lines 4-6, Abhinava says: 'When the acts of breathing disappear, when time is devoured, complete, truly single consciousness shines in all its splendour.' In the *Tantrasāra*, time, the number of arisings of subtle-breath and the number of phonemes in the mantra are linked. Similarly, in *TĀ* 7.39cd ff., Abhinava gives explicit details about the number of breaths and the number of recitations.
180. Gnoli, *L'essenza*, p.134 footnote 1. Singh, *Parātriṃśikāvivaraṇa*, pp.28-29.
181. Bagchi, *Kaulajñānanirṇaya*, p.ix.
182. *TĀ* 3.142 and *TĀ* 29.89d.
183. 'Kṣemarāja, in his commentary [on the *Svacchandatantram*], explaining *haṃsa* as *hāna*, 'forsaking', and *samādāna*, 'taking back', says that Śiva, indeed, gives out and takes back the universe in his cosmic activity of emanation and reabsorption, that the sun gives out and takes back its life-giving warmth, that the Self is in the nature of Śiva, and finally that the breath gives and takes back air through respiration, and that it is an aspect of Śiva in the form of his unlimited energy identical with the "unstruck" sound (*anāhata*). This shows that *haṃsa* is not the breath itself but the energy of breath.' Padoux, *Vāc*, p.141.
184. Gnoli, *Luce*, p.170 footnote 59. "He [the subject] drinks this[emitted reality] joyfully, declaring '*haṃsa haṃsa*' [I am this, I am this!].' *TĀ* 4.136cd.

and *SA*, both associated with ritual sexual union.[185]

By adopting the whole meaning of *haṃsa* the practitioner's subtle-breath is involved with every reality and every power. It can start from the lowest and lead to the highest and in this sense is closely allied to the term *uccāra*, 'arousing'. This word has several meanings including the 'subtle-breath' which rises as *udāna* [186] and moves from the base to the highest place, from the location of the dormant śakti, to the place where śakti and Śiva unite, at the end-of-twelve. This *uccāra* is also identified with sound which proceeds upwards in the direction of reabsorption, moving through the twelve or eight stages of sound to reach the supreme personal word. Since all aspects of the practitioner are associated with the subtle-breath, he too, in his body as in all his faculties, is reabsorbed and all becomes purely personal, subjective. The arousing is therefore the reabsorption into the personal so that the practitioner becomes the supreme person, 'I', *AHAM*. The various aspects are in fact the one event, the *uccāra*, which occurs spontaneously under the inspiration of śakti who is the freedom of Śiva.[187]

The practitioner once again goes through the twelve stages of the Krama process, gradually withdrawing from the external world of sound. At first he recites out loud, then he murmurs and so on, withdrawing progressively from sound till he reaches the last two moments which are in fact one autonomous consciousness. This is the real oblation into the fire, of which all other forms are mere echoes.[188] Is there also an exterior fire? The answer is uncertain. The bald statement that 'he both makes oblation and performs the recitation' (śl.92d) seems to imply a real oblation into a real fire.[189] Jayaratha's separation of the two in Jr.95d.2 further suggests an objective distinction.

---

185. Padoux, *Vāc*, p.302-303.
186. Silburn, *Hymnes de Abhinavagupta*, p.43 footnote 1.
187. Padoux, *La Parātrīśikālaghuvṛtti*, p.10 note 177.
188. The oblation into the fire, *homa*, is described at length in *TĀ* 15.388b-436a. The fire ritual is an externalisation of the transcendent fire of consciousness as Abhinava notes in *TĀ* 15.429. Recitation is treated in *TĀ* 4.194-211 in the context of the śakti method and in *TĀ* 4.202, Abhinava states: The various realities (*bhāvā*), entering into that fire of consciousness (*bodha*) and increasing its brightness, are used as its oblation.'
189. Pandey, p.619, understands it to be a visible act.

(f) Sub-topic 4[190] 'The Ritual with the Sexual Partner'

śl. 96	Enunciation of the Sub-topic
	Introduction
	1. The participants:
śl. 97ab	a. Enunciation of *brahmacarya*
śl. 97cd-98ab	i. Definition of *brahman*
śl. 98cd	ii. Definition of *brahmacarya*
śl. 99-100ab	iii. Contrast of'bonded animal'
śl. 100cd-101ab	b. Definition of the term śakti
śl. 101cd-102	examination of the term śakti
śl. 103	concluding bibliography and effect
	2. The ritual[191]
śl. 104ab	a. i. Definition of the ritual as
	1. Emanation,
	2. Reabsorption and
	3. Blending
śl. 104cd-105ab	ii. Brief examination of ritual
śl. 105cd-106ab	b. i. Definition of 'principal circle' and 'sub-circle'
śl. 106cd-107ab	ii. Etymology of *cakra* (circle)

190. In the description of the Sacrifices in the *Tantrasāra*, Abhinava quickly passes over the Introduction and barely mentions Sacrifices 4,5 and 6. He summarises the Opening Ritual and Sacrifices 1 and 2 but quotes large sections of Sacrifice 3 *verbatim* so that it seems he attaches great importance to Sacrifice 3. Note that Gnoli adds sections from *TĀ* 29 to his translation of the *Tantrasāra*. The importance of Sacrifice 3 is further emphasised by its handling in *Tantroccaya* ch.8 where, after naming the six or seven sacrifices of the Kula ritual, Abhinava passes very quickly over Sacrifices 1 and 2, and does not treat of Sacrifices 4,5 and 6, but devotes about one third of the chapter to Sacrifice 3, again quoting from and alluding extensively to *TĀ* 29. The *Tantravaṭadhānikā*, a further summary of the *Tantrāloka*, has no literary connections with *TĀ* 100cd-166ab.

191. Although there is no known connection between *Yonitantra* and the *Tantrāloka*, the description of the *yonipūjā* may help to understand Sacrifices 3 and 4. In *Yonitantra* pp.26-27, Schoterman summarises the *yonipūjā*.

According to his usual custom, Abhinava begins by defining the key elements. Various terms, especially the Circle Sacrifice and the śakti require clarification.

He defines the word *brahmacarya* by describing *brahman* as the bliss that belongs to Śiva and śakti in their union. He goes on to interpret bliss as wine, meat and especially the sexual fluid emitted during intercourse, since these lead to bliss and result from bliss.[192] The words 'bliss' and '*brahman*' have, therefore, a double connotation and can refer to the inner experience as well as to the fluid which results from it.[193] The word *brahman* is interchangeable with the word *parabrahman*. Therefore, the true *brahmacarya* is not celibate,which is the usual meaning of the word,[194] nor is he

---

Preliminary rites:

1. The Adept procures a woman who is wanton.
2. He places her in the *maṇḍala* and
3. offers her a narcotic drink.
4. He places her on his left thigh and
5. honours her *yoni* which is to be unshaven.
6. He anoints the *yoni* with sandal paste to look like flower or menses, *puṣpam*.
7. He gives her wine to drink.
8. He paints a 'half-moon', *ardhacandra*, on her forehead with vermilion.
9. He places his hands on her breasts and mutters the *bhagabīja* [which Schoterman identifies with the *māyābīja HRĪM*].
10. He kisses her on the cheeks and moulds her breasts.
11. He recites the mantra or a *stotra*.
12. The śakti anoints the *liṅga* with sandal paste and saffron

Central ritual:

1. The Adept conducts the ritual coition.
2. 'The object of ... this ritual coition is the production of the fluid called *Tattva Uttama* ... or *Yonitattva*.'

Concluding Rite:

1. The Adept pays his respects to the *yonimaṇḍala* and to the guru.
2. He utters some final lines expressing that he has accomplished his purpose and has been saved from *saṃsāra*.Schoterman notes, op.cit. pp.28-29, that the point of the ritual is to secure the *yonitattva* which has two applications:
   a. The Adept uses it to form his *tilaka* in his daily ritual.
   b. He uses it to worship the śakti in three stages. Firstly he worships the *yoni* with water used for cleansing the *yoni* and the *liṅga*. Secondly, he offers the vessel containing the *yonitattva* to the śakti. This is then divided into three parts of which the Adept presents one part to the śakti while he himself drinks the other two parts mixed with wine.

192. In *Anuttarāṣṭikā* 4 line 1, Abhinava weakens the identification: '[This] bliss [which comes from the Unsurpassable (*anuttara*)] is not like the intoxication which comes from wealth or wine nor even like the bliss that comes from joining with the Beloved (*aṅga*).'
193. This double meaning dominates the two quotes Qt.100b.3, Qt.100b.4 which in turn very adequately describe the meaning of 'the 'bliss of *brahman*'.
194. Mircea Eliade, *Rites and symbols of initiation: the mysteries of birth and rebirth*, NewYork, Harper and Row, 1965, p.53.

involved with the 5 M's[195] but rather makes use of the 3 M's: wine, meat and intercourse.

Abhinava goes on to contrast the *brahmacarya* with the 'bonded animal' (*paśu*) whom he defines (*TĀ* 29.99) as someone who either does not use any of the 3 M's or who may indeed use the 3 M's outside of the ritual but refuses them during the ritual. Jayaratha explicates these points. Two types of person are envisaged. Some do not consume the three M's at any stage, either during the ritual or in ordinary life. They totally abstain in accordance with the recommendation given in the *Manusmṛti* which is quoted in Qt.98d.1.[196] Far from being truly free they are no more than 'bonded animals', like oxen who do not feed on wine or meat. Others do consume the three M's in ordinary life but do not share it in the sacred setting.[197] They are 'bonded animals' in a moral sense or, as Qt.100b.2 says, are 'like dullards'.

Abhinava is flexible. It may be that someone who does not make use of the 3 M's finds his way into the ritual. Is he a complete outsider, uninitiated, someone who has strayed into the meeting?[198] Should that be the case, Abhinava holds that he is usually not to be ejected from the meeting. In *TĀ* 28.20cd ff., he makes a comparison. Just as the late-comer to a spectacle can become quickly involved because of the infectious enthusiasm of the other spectators who have been only gradually involved, so too someone who joins a meeting of the *yoginīs* and the *siddhas* may suddenly arrive at consciousness.

Jayaratha gives an important complement to those basic points. The true Kula practitioner is already possessed of bliss for he has experienced absorption during the course of his initiation. He performs the ritual, as Jayaratha notes in Jr.100b.3, 'for the reason

195. The *pañcamakāra*, the five M's, are wine; *madya*; meat, *māṃsa*; fish, *matsya*; parched grain, *mudrā*; and intercourse, *maithuna*. In *TĀ* 29, there is no reference to the five M's but in *TĀ* 28, in the description of the Circle Sacrifice, fish is mentioned.

196. This group is described in *śl.*99ab, Jr.100b.1 and Qt. 100b.1.

197. This other group is described in *śl.*99cd, Jr.100b.2, Qt.100b.2.

198. On the matter of the stray entrant, see *TĀ* 28.373cd-385ab and especially 381cd-383ab, which will be noted shortly in the description of the Circle Sacrifice.

that he is in every way committed simply to manifesting his own bliss'. He makes ritual use of the 3 M's in order to manifest an interior bliss just as in *śl.* 24 the practitioner who is Bhairava wishes to manifest his true nature by performing the external ritual of Sacrifice 1. This contrasts with the person who has not experienced bliss by the grace of Śiva but wishes to attain it by the inappropriate and ineffective use of the 3 M's: 'Without a guru, without a deity, like dullards ... forever consuming wine and meat ...' Qt.100b.2.

It is appropriate at this point to give details concerning the Circle Sacrifice (*cakra-yāga*) described in *TĀ* 28.60cd-111 as it forms an important background to Sacrifice 3. It is the same as the Subsequent Sacrifice (*anuyāga*) and the Image Sacrifice (*mūrti-yāga*),[199] and of all the daily, occasional and optional ceremonies[200] it is by far the principal rite. Its preferred participants are the knowledgeable person (*jñānī*) or the *yogī* since they will perform the ritual in the fullest fashion but the ordinary initiates and outsiders should be avoided. The guru should be knowledgeable.[201] The Circle Sacrifice or Image Sacrifice should be celebrated on the following occasions:

> *'On the occasion of the Ceremony of the Cord, of the rite performed after death, on the days of juncture* (parvan), *at the eclipses of the sun and moon etc., even at the ordinary junctures, on the occasion of a feast [e.g. celebrating the guru's birth etc., notes Jayaratha], of a marriage, of the ritual sacrifice and initiation of Brahmans, at the installation [of a temple, a liṅga], on the day that the rules are abrogated, and finally in order to bring about one's special desires: [on these occasions] the Image Sacrifice should be performed. It consists of five types.'*[202]

199. *TĀ* 28.60cd-61ab. *Tantrasāra* p.184 lines 8-9.
200. *TĀ* 28.61cd-62ab.
201. *TĀ* 28.62cd-75cd.
202. *TĀ* 28.76cd-78.

The five types of Circle Sacrifice are 'solitary', 'paired', 'mixed', 'circle' and 'intermixture of heroes'.[203] These he defines in the following manner:

1. 'Solitary': a sacrifice in which gurus alone take part.
2. 'Mixed': a sacrifice performed with the Adepts etc. and their wives.
3. 'Paired' is of two kinds, according as wives or prized courtesans take part.
4. "Circle' is celebrated with a potter's wife etc. It gives every result, i.e. both liberation and enjoyment.
5. 'Intermixture of heroes': the sacrifice is performed with all of the above.[204]

The fourth of these lies behind Sacrifices 2 and 3.

It is not clear how the participants of these sacrifices are arranged. Comparing *TĀ* 28.82cd-84 and *Tantrasāra* pp.184-185, it would seem that there are three concentric circles. The first is constituted by the gurus, i.e. the Masters and Adepts and the second comprises the *tattvavit*, i.e. the Sons, while the third involves the ordinary initiates, even though Abhinava prefers only the knowledgeable person and the *yogī*. The matter is not clear but that arrangement would seem to concur with the description of the group given in *TĀ* 29.282 ff. and its investigation. The various circles of participants are satiated with the contents of the vessel, one after the other, starting from the guru and extending as far as the outermost circle and then returning back to the guru, in imitation of the cycle of emission and reabsorption.[205] First the heroes are worshipped and then their śaktis (*śl.*92a). This constitutes one 'complete cycle'.[206] Next, the celebrant distributes food such as meat, fish etc. (*māṃsamatsyādi*, *śl.* 92d).

203. *TĀ* 28.79ab.
204. *TĀ* 28.79cd-82ab.
205. Gnoli, *L'essenza*, p.263 footnote 1.
206. *TĀ* 28.91b.

Abhinava goes on, in *śl.*93cd-98, to consider various situations. What if there is no vessel? What if drops fall to the ground? What if someone enters who has no right to be there? The answer to this last is that if, through lack of due precaution, someone does enter the circle, one should not question him.[207] In *śl.*99-101ab, he concludes the description of the ceremony by mentioning the remuneration (*dakṣiṇā*) consisting of money, betel nut, cloth etc. In *śl.*104cd-106ab, Abhinava gives further details. The heroes and the *yoginīs* are to meet at night in a secret house (*gupte gṛhe*, *śl.*104a) addressing each other with a secret, unconventional language (*asaṃketa*, *śl.*105a).

Later, in *śl.* 373cd-385ab, Abhinava resumes the subject of the Circle Sacrifice, and discusses the theatrical aspect of the gathering. That is, just as during a performance of dance or song, the various spectators are caught up in the spectacle as a group and not as separate individuals, so too during the sacrifice consciousness arises in each person as part of a community. For this reason, if someone whose 'consciousness is in a state of contraction'[208] does enter the group, the ceremony should continue since he may be caught up in the experience of the group (*śl.*381cd-383ab). If the person will certainly not become involved, the ceremony should be interr-upted.[209]

Abhinava goes on to define the external śakti or sexual partner (*dūtī*).[210] The phrase 'she is 'caused', 'cause' and 'co caused' ' (śl.102a) and indeed the whole of *śl.*101cd-102 and the investigation which follows it, have caused great difficulty.

(a) One kind of interpretation is literal. Pandey states that the *dūtī* '...could be mother, sister, daughter, grand-mother, sister's daughter or daughter's daughter'[211] with which Masson and

207. *TĀ* 28.98d.
208. *TĀ* 29.380ab.
209. *TĀ* 28.384cd-385ab.
210. In *TĀ* 1.13, Abhinava gives tribute to his guru Śambhunātha and to his guru's consort who is referred to by the epithet *bhagavatī*. In his investigation of this text, Jayaratha glosses *bhāgavatī* as *dūtī*.
211. Pandey, p.618.

Patwardhan agree.[212] Gnoli accepts this and explains that the three when considered *sakṣāt*, 'directly', refer to daughter, mother and sister. The three when considered *paramparā*, 'indirectly', refer to grand-daughter, grand-mother and sister's daughter.[213] Sanderson agrees with Gnoli[214] and *Kulacūḍāmaṇi* 3.49-50 seems to support this interpretation,[215] while *Manusmṛti* 11.59 acknowledges the fact of incest.[216] Its strong prohibition is an argument in favour of interpreting śl.101cd-102 etc. as incest since the Kula ritual uses what is forbidden. A second interpretation is echoed in *Hevajra Tantra* II.5.58-59 which interprets the words as codes[217] concerning which the *Yogaratnamālā* gives the clues, stating for instance that 'Mother' refers to the Master's consort or that 'Daughter' refers to the Master's female disciple.[218] Thirdly, Silburn holds that the phrase must be understood in a spiritual sense only so that the 'mother' is the *dūtī* who inspires the partner; the 'daughter' is the *dūtī* who is inspired by the partner; the 'sister' is the *dūtī* who is equal to the partner: they inspire each other.[219]

(b) Another possible interpretation leads to the conclusion that the phrase in question refers to one woman in her various capacities.[220]

---

212. J.L. Masson and M.V. Patwardhan, *Śāntarasa and Abhinavagupta's philosophy of aesthetics*, Poona, Bhandarkar Oriental Research Institute, 1969, p.43.
213. Gnoli, *Luce*, p.692 footnote 61.
214. Sanderson, 'Meaning', p.83.
215. *Kulacūḍāmaṇi Nigama*, ed. Arthur Avalon, Madras, Ganesh and Co. 1956, p.14.
216. G. Bühler, *The Laws of Manu*, Delhi, Motilal Banarsidass, 1964, pp.441-442.
217. D.L. Snellgrove, *The Hevajra Tantra*, London, Oxford University Press, 1959, vol.1, p.113.
218. G.W. Farrow and I. Menon, *The Concealed Essence of the Hevajra Tantra, with the commentary Yogaratnamālā*, Delhi, Motilal Banarsidass, 1992, p.257.
219. Silburn, *La kuṇḍalinī*, p.212.
220. The texts which are particularly important in this present matter, *TĀ* 28.194-195, *TĀ* 29.101-102, 123 and Jr.102d.1, contain a number of words which revolve around basically similar concepts and can be put into two tables.

28.194	womb	*yoni*	knowledge	*vidyā*
28.195	ego	*ahantā*	consciousness	*bodha,*
29.101	worldly	*laukika*	non-worldly	*alaukika*
29.102	perceptibly	*sākṣāt*	indirectly	*paramparā*
29.123	being	*bhāva*	meditated upon	*bhāvitām*
Jr.102d.1	from womb	*yaunād*	from knowledge	*jñānīyāc*

(i) In *TĀ* 28.194 ff., Abhinava describes the guru and his family—wife, brother, sons etc. These are assembled as a group but the basis of their grouping is not so much the womb (*yoni*) or the family bond as knowledge (*vidyā*), not so much their blood connection as their common tradition. They form a sort of dualistic association of 'worldly' and 'unworldly', terms which refer to family and knowledge. In *TĀ* 28.195, he goes on to justify the statement given in *śl.*194 by contrasting the *ahantā*, the ego-identity, which is connected to the body, with the *ahambhāva*, the 'I' which is consciousness (*bodha*). Since consciousness is greater than the body, *vidyā* is a stronger bond than the family tie. For that reason, the disciple who shares the consciousness of the guru is truly of his line (*santāna*, *śl.*197c).

He then explains that the guru passes on his knowledge to his disciples by the fact that his consciousness enters into the very self [of the disciple][221] and communicates its particular characteristic.[222] The guru does this in the same way that a *yogī* can enter into another person's body without leaving his own.[223] In this process of making the disciple a member of the family, there is the 'cause', the 'assistant cause' and the 'co-caused' (*kāraṇaṃ sahakāri ca\ eka-kāraṇa-kāryaṃ ca*).[224] The 'cause' and the 'assistant cause', are the guru and his wife.[225] The fellow disciples are called 'brothers'[226] while a person who is associated with the disciple 'is also considered to form part, indirectly (*paramparāyogād*), of the guru's family.'[227]

Thus the terms, 'cause', 'assistant cause' and 'brothers', are concerned with initiation into the guru's wider 'family' which consists not of blood relations but of people with the same *vidyā*,

221. *TĀ* 28.204b.
222. *TĀ* 28.204cd.
223. *TĀ* 28.206cd-207ab.
224. *TĀ* 28.208d-209b.
225. *TĀ* 28.209cd. In *TĀ* 28.210a, Abhinava emphasises the point by stating that normally the guru is without qualification for this sacrifice if he is without a śakti (*niḥśaktikasya*).
226. *TĀ* 28.211c.
227. *TĀ* 28.211d-212ab.

knowledge. Furthermore, a person can form part of the guru's family by a mere association with one of its members.

(ii) In *TĀ* 29. 123cd, Abhinava quotes the saying of Kallaṭa:

> *'[The guru] should ritually prepare* (bhāvitām)
> *[the śakti] because by her very being* (sva-bhāva)
> *she is superior to his own body.'*

In Jr.124b.1, Jayaratha notes that this sentence sums up the definition of the śakti which started in *śl.*100. The śakti is female by her very nature (*sva-bhāva*) and for that reason she is ritually prepared (*bhāvitām*). As female she is the source of the *kuṇḍagolaka* and is therefore ritually prepared in a ceremony noted in *TĀ* 29.123ab and in Jr.124b.1 which tells us that 'the guru should ritually prepare the śakti, i.e. should purify her' (*saṃskṛtāṃ*). Already in *TĀ* 15.577, Abhinava has given the rule that 'one must 'avoid the woman who is not purified' (*nāsaṃskṛtāṃ vrajet*). '[Her lack of purification] would render useless the fluid which comes from her.' The śakti affects the practitioner by providing the sexual fluid and bringing him to consciousness and so she is the 'cause'. Her act is in keeping with the Kula tradition in which the daughter of Tryambaka communicates the knowledge. On the other hand she is 'ritualy prepared' (*bhāvitām*) so that she is both 'cause' and 'caused'. She affects the practitioner and is affected by him so that they are both 'co-caused'.

Someone may come to the ritual who has not been initiated just as someone might be brought to a spectacle by a friend. He comes as an associate of one of the disciples and so he is considered indirectly (*paramparāyogād*) to form part of the group. He is not directly involved with the śakti but nevertheless she has an effect on him. His presence is a tacit approval or ritual preparation of her so that he too is both 'caused' by her and 'causes her' and they are both 'co-caused'.

In short, according to this interpretation the one śakti, the one woman, has the six qualities listed in *TĀ* 29.101cd-102. The guru of *TĀ* 28 has a 'worldly', a sexual or physical, relationship with his family whereas the relationship with his disciple is 'unworldly' only, based on consciousness. The śakti of *TĀ* 29, however, has a relationship with her male partner based both on sexuality and on consciousness and so she is superior to the male guru.

(c) How then should one understand Qt.102d.2 which reads: "One's wife, sister, mother or daughter can be the beautiful mistress". This quotation can be understood to mean either: '[The same man can have] either his wife, sister, mother or daughter as his beautiful mistress' or: 'The wife, sister, mother or daughter can function as a beautiful mistress [in the Kula ritual but not necessarily to the same man].' In other words, the meaning of the quotation is not clear. Next, the question must be asked: does the quote actually refer to the three categories, 'caused', 'cause' and 'co-caused'? In fact Jayaratha's discussion on *śl.* 101cd-102 finished in Jr.102d.2 with a comment on the word *tulyā*, 'like that' so that the quotation should rather be understood to introduce a new issue which is elaborated over the following interventions and quotations,[228] namely: why is one's own wife excluded from this ritual? That question concerning the wife is best viewed in the context of the five Circle Sacrifices. The second of these is performed with 'the Adepts etc. and their wives'. The third is performed with 'wives or prized courtesans'. The fourth is performed with outcasts such as the potter's wife. What is the particular advantage of the fourth sacrifice? Qt.102d.2, then, is not at all concerned with mother or daughter but with the advantage of the fourth Circle Sacrifice.

The Vedic teaching is that the upright man who observes the *dharma* will have as one of his highest duties to join with his wife who is of the same caste as himself and by the emission of seed with its accompanying pleasure (*riraṃsā*) to continue the family line. It is against this particular norm of conduct that the fourth Circle Sacrifice and Sacrifice 3 inveigh. It proposes just the opposite situation: to join with a woman of whatever caste or condition who is not the wife, and to have sexual intercourse with her but without seeking the pleasure of orgasm, Qt.102d.7, and without

228. Jr.102d.5-6, Qt.102d.3-7.

the intent of procreation.[229] The aim is to engage in sexual activity simply in order to arrive at consciousness and to attain the state of being liberated while living. Even if there is procreation, as in the example quoted in Qt.102d.6 and allowed for in *TĀ* 29.162cd - 163, it is without the intent of pleasure. The sexual partner provides the satisfaction which allows the practitioner to become still even as he is roused. He must not alter the balance and experience orgasm which causes intense pleasure, on the one hand, but breaks the stillness of absorption, on the other. Rather than seek the fluctuating mental stages of excitement and abatement, the practitioner seeks intimacy with the sexual partner while focussing on their eternal identity as Śiva and śakti, joined together in bliss.

(d) In short, the evidence would seem to hold that the śakti of *śl.*101cd-102 is not the mother, sister, daughter or wife etc. but is a woman who takes on the position of a consecrated female vis-á-vis the practitioner. The one woman has six aspects just as the divine śakti manifests herself in many ways and has innumerable further aspects depending on how she is viewed. As was forecast in the fourth Circle Sacrifice where Abhinava states that 'the Circle Sacrifice which takes place through their presence gives every result', the one woman 'bestows both enjoyment and liberation' (*TĀ* 29.103).

After presenting the ingredients and the participants of the ritual, the text goes on to define the ritual itself: it consists of three types of emission: emanation, reabsorption and union (*melakam*). This briefest of definitions can be understood, according to Jr.104b.1, as the stages of sexual intercourse or as the five forms of subtle-breath or the five stages of consciousness which finish with the ultimate state, the union of Śiva and śakti. Similarly, in *śl.*104cd-105ab, Abhinava summarises the ritual in terms which are both erotic and sacred. The various meanings are possible because of the inter-relationship of the lower and higher circles which lead to each other.

229. Indeed one of the descriptions of the perfect sexual partner is that she is 'without children' (*aprasūtā*, Qt.100b.6).

The texts which now follow will occasionally require an analysis of some of the terms or require the accompaniment of a commentary which will help unravel a compact statement.

Examination of the Ritual

The First Emission: Emanation (*sṛṣṭi*);
the 'arisen' (*udita*);

There are three Emissions just as there are three ways of understanding the phoneme *Ḥ*. The First Emission is concerned with emanation, with *Ḥ* as the source of the other phonemes, the Second Emission with reabsorption, with *Ḥ* as the moment of transition which leads to the state of Śiva. Finally, the Third Emission is concerned with Ḥ as the two points, ' : ', as the union of things, as the union of Śiva and śakti who are the upper and lower dots respectively.[230]

The First Emission actually consists of three Trajectories, each more subtle than the other, each able to lead to the fullness of consciousness. Again, the three Trajectories tackle the Emission from the point of view of action, differentiated thought and the immediacy of the sexual fluid. A few points need to be made with regard to each Trajectory.

Trajectory 1. Emphasis on Action

śl. 107cd	Definition: Satiation (*tarpaṇa*) expansion (*vikāsa*)
	Examination Level of bliss 3: *parānanda*
śl. 108-109ab	i. Satiating subcircle with 3 M's etc.
śl. 109cd-110ab	ii. Satiating subcircle in other ways
śl. 110cd-111ab	summary quotation for levels 4-7
śl. 111cd-112ab	Level of bliss 4: *brahmānanda*
śl. 112cd-113ab	Contrasting example: the egoist:
śl. 113cd-114ab	Level of bliss 5: *mahānanda* i. Sub-circles lead to principal circle
śl. 114cd-115ab	ii. Principal circle affects sub-circle
śl. 115cd-117ab	Levels of bliss 6: *cidānanda* and 7: *jagadānanda*

230. *TĀ* 3.215-9.

The first Trajectory is particularly concerned with the circles, i.e. the higher and lower faculties. In introducing this subject in Jr.107b.3, Jayaratha raises a significant objection. In *śl.*105cd-106ab, Abhinava had said that the supreme bliss comes from within, from the principal circle..On the other hand, Qt.107b.1 states that it comes from outside. Does bliss come from outside or from inside? Abhinava will answer this dilemma by his definition of sacrifice in *śl.*108-109ab:

> *'And the sacrifice, viewed externally, is called 'satiation'; and as a result there is an expansion.'*

He notes that while satiation or pleasure is significant it is ordered according to its capacity to prepare for the experience of consciousness so that a pleasure which does not lead to consciousness is useless and is to be discarded. Yet the pleasure is not the cause of consciousness but the circumstance in which consciousness freely arises, for consciousness is not controlled by pleasure but is essentially autonomous. The focus lies, therefore, not on the pleasure but on its possible result. Pleasure is a sacrifice in response to which the divinity draws close and blesses the practitioner. In this way, Abhinava avoids the charge of hedonism and reconciles both enjoyment and liberation. Purity and pleasure are not necessarily opposed. On the contrary, when the pleasures are experienced on the unsullied basis of true consciousness, the practitioner attains the state of Rudra, the divinity who in his essence combines or rather transcends enjoyment and liberation.

On the basis of such a definition, Abhinava describes the ritual from the experiential point of view according to levels 3, 4,5,6 and 7 of the seven levels of bliss which have been described in Chapter 5 above. The third stage, *parānanda*, is a satiation of the various sub-circles or lower faculties with the 3 M's and also with sandal-wood, incense etc. It is quite different from the seventh stage, *jagadānanda*. In *parānanda* pleasure is found in external objects (*para*) but so far without the sense of 'I am', *AHAM*. Since consciousness is the source of all, there is a movement of attention, *brahmānanda*, towards consciousness. The practitioner becomes amazed as his own true self begins now to be revealed and the goddesses begin to absorb reality and lead in the direction of the bliss of consciousness.

Abhinava now introduces the significant contrasting figure of the person who is fixated at the level of *parānanda*. In point of fact it is not possible to remain at that point for the stages of bliss are essentially mobile and the experience of pleasure in external objects becomes jaded if it does not move on. The egoist who is fixated upon his ego (*ahaṃkāra*) becomes in fact *ahamyuḥ*, haughty, and is not fit for the Kula ritual which is focussed on *AHAM*. A practitioner of this sort does not experience the movement to higher levels, nor does he experience the expansiveness which belongs to the seventh stage, *jagadānanda*, universal bliss. 'His sense of self is not complete nor does it well up' (*śl.*113ab).

The practitioner and his partner who do proceed along the stages of bliss now allow their mutual pleasuring to enter a new phase and become intensely aware of each other, indeed become absorbed in each other. This is the *mahānanda*. Their intentness upon each other does not mean, Abhinava is quick to note, that they are abstracted from the sub-circles, from the body etc. but on the contrary, the sub-circles are agitated by the heightened consciousness the pair now enjoy so that the erotic experience is expressed in all the faculties, in movement, touch etc. and involves a more passionate form of exchange, as Jayaratha notes in Jr.115b.2. The experience of *cidānanda* now occurs whereby the couple lose all sense of differentiation and their union is complete. They are taken to the highest form of consciousness, the uniting form of emission, the condition of Śiva and śakti, a subject dealt with more particularly in the Third Emission. This condition is not a transcendence which denies the reality of the world but an entry into universal bliss (*jagadānanda*). The whole world is seen as coming from them and destined for them. They are the supreme *kaula*, the union of Akula and Kula and all that is emitted. They transcend emanation and reabsorption and are the source of these so that all is reconciled in their perfect fusion. The bliss of Śiva and of the world is the same.

Trajectory 2. Emphasis on Knowledge,

śl. 117cd-118ab	Enunciation:
	Self and the goddess 'consciousness'
śl. 118cd-119ab	Brief examination of the procedure
	Examination in detail
śl. 119cd	i. The differentiation
śl. 120ab	ii. The merging
śl. 120cd	iii. The identity
śl. 121	iv. The emission

A number of points will help unpack the dense language of this Trajectory. Whereas the first Trajectory (*śl.*107cd-117ab) emphasised action (*kalpa*) and led to universal bliss, the second Trajectory starts from differentiated thought (*vikalpa*) and leads to absorption and the emission of the fluid. The terms 'risen' and 'rested' dominate this Trajectory and variously mean 'apparent' and hidden', 'emanated' and 'reabsorbed', 'awareness of the self' and 'awareness of the other'. The Trajectory is described in four stages.

(i) The couple becomes particularly aware of sexual difference and of their symbolism as Śiva and śakti and so engage in the movements of intercourse which symbolise the ceasing and arising of emanation and dissolution, the whole rhythm of the pulsating universe.

(ii) The couple become aware of the emotions of the heart as they go out to each other or return to their own self-awareness in a mutual giving and receiving. Each is aware of the 'rising', i.e. of the outgoing to the other, and of the 'resting', i.e. the return to self-awareness.

(iii) This fluctuation, the intercourse, does not stay at a dualism but results in a unity where they become each other, truly a pair and not two monads. They are at the highest level where Śiva and śakti are not two but one, just as the fire and its capacity to burn are one. They rest in each other and this resting is wholly manifest, or—as Abhinava who is a virtuoso with words expresses it—the 'resting' is 'risen', is apparent.

(iv) This experience produces a particular effect in the śakti so that there is an 'emanation'. While this term can be understood at many levels including the manifestation of the universe, it also refers to the sexual fluid which may flow at this intense moment of unity and symbolises bliss as well as the whole universe, so that it acquires an evocative power, as shall be seen next.

Trajectory 3. Emphasis on the śakti

	1. Descriptions of the śakti
śl. 122ab	i. Her nature
śl. 122cd-123ab	ii. Her ritual preparation
śl. 123cd-124ab	quote: śakti as *bhāvā* and *bhāvitā*
	2. Brief description of the ritual
śl. 124cd-125ab	i. At the mouth of the *yoginī*
śl. 125cd-126ab	ii. Result: consciousness etc.

The third Trajectory is concerned with the śakti and the immediacy of her impact. Because of the immediacy, the Trajectory goes beyond *kalpa* and *vikalpa* to undifferentiated or immediate knowledge (*nirvikalpa*). The Trajectory is extensive and varied and begins with two descriptions of the śakti. The first focuses on her very nature (*bhāva*), the fact that she has the 'fully opening and closing central path' which links her so intimately with the *visarga*, : *Ḥ*. The body of the guru may well be the object of worship in the seventh Kula sacrifice proposed in the *Tantrasāra*, but the body of the śakti is superior even to the guru's body. The second description focusses on the fact that she is ritually prepared (*bhāvitā*) as the means by which the Kula tradition is transmitted so that every śakti is an image of Ardhatryambakā who received the Kula tradition from her father and passed it on to her disciples.

The very nature of the śakti and of her capacities gives rise to a number of intended ambiguities. Consciousness, the 'mouth of the *yoginī*' and the sexual fluid which is emitted, all correlate with each other. This needs to be spelled out. Consciousness is the *kaula*, the union of Śiva and śakti and is the place where the 'rested' and the 'risen' preexist. Just as from them and their pulsation the world is emitted, so too from the śakti the fluid is emitted. The emitting of the sexual fluid is its 'saying' by the 'mouth of the *yoginī*'. Just as consciousness cannot be put into writing, so too the fluid deriving from the experience of consciousness is an immediate reality which must be experienced and so cannot be 'put into writing'. And just as consciousness is the preeminent circle because it produces the highest bliss, so too the 'mouth of the *yoginī*' which emits the fluid is the principal circle. To taste the fluid is to engage in 'mouth to mouth' and therefore to arrive at the preexisting 'rested' and 'risen'. In another sense, when the practitioner joins his 'mouth' to the 'mouth of the *yoginī*', when the sexual organs are joined, he comes to consciousness. The sexual fluid since it results from consciousness and leads to consciousness can also be called the 'rested' and the 'risen' and derives its power from all these meanings.

Examination of the Ritual:

	1. For one who seeks liberation
śl. 126cd-127ab	- focus on the ejaculating
	2. For one who seeks enjoyment
śl. 127cd-128ab	- focus on the ejaculate
śl. 128cd-129ab	(i) For the knowledgeable
	- consuming the ejaculate
	(ii) For the officiant
	- anointing the organ
śl. 129cd-130ab	definition of the ritual;
śl. 130cd-132	examination:
	a. On her sex organ
śl. 133ab	b. On his own body.

On the strength of union with the śakti or the use of her fluid a number of rituals are elaborated which show her universal effectiveness. These rituals are for the person who desires liberation and for the two types who seek enjoyment.

Desiring liberation, the *mumukṣu* seeks to attain that state which precedes any movement of consciousness to objectivity. Therefore, while being involved with the 'mouth of the *yoginī*' and the resultant 'rested' and 'risen' sexual fluid, he focusses his attention on the experience which made the śakti emit the fluid. By focussing on her experience of that prior emitting reality, as later the practitioner will focus on the sound *HĀ-HĀ* (*śl.*158cd), he comes to experience what she has known, the bliss of 'the undivided level', so that she is truly the door and the means to liberation.

The *bubhukṣu*, by contrast, is concerned with enjoyment and therefore with the world that has been emanated. Appropriately, the ritual for the two types of *bubhukṣu*, the knowledgeable person and the officiant, involves handling the actual sexual fluid, the 'ejaculated form', which results from the experience of consciousness. It is endowed with all the powers of consciousness among which one of the most prized is 'bodily stability' (*piṇḍa-sthairya*) or immortality and youthful vigour, especially sexual vigour and attractiveness.

The knowledgeable person knows the Kula tradition and especially its categories and is particularly involved in teaching that knowledge. Accordingly, the ritual involves the mouth and the consumption of the fluid which, coming as it does from the body called *kula*, is itself called *kula*. It is obtained either directly from the body or in the form of a pill or paste and is consumed in very specific rituals. Jr.129b.3 and Qt.129b.3 are very illuminating and fill out Abhinava's arcane statement 'mouth to mouth'.[230a]

The officiant does not, in fact, have the knowledge or discriminating knowledge which distinguishes the knowledgeable person but he does have insight and therefore he is able to participate in the Kula ritual which is based on undifferentiated thought. Since he is involved with action rather than with knowledge, his ritual is concerned with action and the external. Thus he uses the fluid to delineate, on the sex organ of the śakti as well as on his own, the process of reabsorption and emanation

230a. In her commentary on *śl.*128-129, Silburn notes the following marriage custom from Kashmir. The young couple are together. The bridegroom's mother places a morsel of food in her son's mouth. The young man then cuts it in half and places a piece in his bride's mouth. She, in her turn, places a piece in her bridegroom's mouth. Silburn, *La kuṇḍalinī*, p.224.

which the knowledgeable person understands so much better. Although he does not fully appreciate what he is doing, the deities do come to discriminating knowledge and grant him all he desires. In other words, the officiant understands at a level more profound than thought.

The Second Emission: Reabsorption (*saṃhāra*) 'rested' (*śānta*)

śl. 133cd-134ab	Level 1 : The 'rested' state
śl. 134cd-135ab	Level 2 : Non-bliss (*nirānanda*)
	a. The principal circle stops,
śl. 135cd-136ab	b. The sub-circles stop,
śl. 136cd-137ab	c. The desire for bliss.
śl. 137cd-138ab	Levels 3, 4, 5, 6 or the Krama
śl. 138cd-139	Level 7 : The surging

The Second Emission, emphasising reabsorption or the 'rested', is described in some six verses, a rather brief presentation compared with the twenty-five verses of the First Emission. Abhinava makes use of two patterns—the seven levels of bliss and the four stages of the Krama.

He begins by positing the state of 'rested', the first state of bliss (*nijānanda*) which is the repose in the self or in the 'sea of subsiding billows' (*taraṅga*). However, it is a human being of flesh and blood who has reached that state of repose. The faculties, the central circle in the first place but also all the other sub-circles which depend on it, cease to function and are therefore dissatisfied since their natural condition is to act and take pleasure in the objective world. They are plunged in non-bliss (*nirānanda*), the second of the seven stages of bliss, but this situation cannot continue. The faculties, or rather the deities of the faculties, like the artist, create their own objects. The next four steps, which might be expressed as levels 3, 4, 5 and 6 of bliss, are described in terms of the four steps of the Krama, namely: *udyoga*, creative outburst; *avabhāsa*, manifestation; *carvaṇa*, devouring; *viśrānti*, repose. Not only does the faculty absorb its object—the eye sees, the mouth tastes—but the process continues and the whole experience is brought into union with consciousness, the true self: 'I see', 'I taste'.[231] As a consequence there occurs the next stage which might be called the seventh level of bliss, *jagadānanda*. Here it is described by the expression 'the lord of the circles surges vigorously', or as Jayaratha puts it: 'he quite suddenly turns his attention outwards'. Rest does not mean inactivity or non-involvement. Repose and activity are not mutually exclusive. In fact, Śiva is perfectly active because he is perfectly at rest, just as the consummate musician plays effortlessly.

The Third Emission: Union (*saṅghaṭṭa*), blending (*melaka*)

Transition and Introduction

śl. 140	1. Enunciation
	(a) Three emissions (*visarga*)
	(b) Etymology of *visarga*
śl. 141-142ab	2. Definition of the three emissions

The Ritual

	1. The 'mantra', i.e. the practitioner:
śl. 142cd-146ab	a. (i) Coupling all diversity
śl. 146cd-147ab	(ii) Constant perception
śl. 147cd-149ab	(iii) Creative awareness appears (*parāmarśa*)
śl. 149cd-150ab	b. Recitation
	2. Six rayed *mudrā*, i.e. intercourse:
śl. 150cd-153ab	a. (i) Intercourse
śl. 153cd-154ab	(ii) Stability at Fourth
śl. 154cd-156ab	(iii) Awareness appears (*vimarśa*)
śl. 156cd-157ab	b. The natural recitation: Enunciation
śl. 157cd-158ab	Examination: (i) 8 circles (*cakra*)
śl. 158cd-160ab	(ii) 8 phases (*uccāra*)
śl. 160cd-161ab	(iii) 8 bhairavas (*unmanā*)

231. See Padoux, *Le coeur*, p.397 footnote 440.

Abhinava wishes now to look at the greatest of the three Emissions, namely union. He appropriately examines the term *visarga* and gives its etymology. The emissions are listed as 'rested', risen' and union; or to use other words, emanation, reabsorption and what is called 'that', namely the ineffable.

The Third Emission takes place in two steps. The first concerns the 'mantra', the practitioner who is identified with the mantra. By reconciling all the diversity of nature, the contrasting forces of *prāṇa* and *apāna*, 'sun' and moon', the joints and veins, and all else, he attains the highest level where he recognises his state of Śiva and experiences immediately the most evident reality, Being itself, the knowing subject, 'I'.

In this context something further happens. Of itself, the creative awareness (*parāmarśa*), which is the 'resonance' (*dhvani*),[232] the first movement of consciousness to objectivity, becomes evident. Since it is a first movement to objectivity it contains in itself the triple emission, the three aspects of the phoneme *Ḥ*, namely awareness (*vimarśa*) and the two emissions that proceed from it - absorption and becoming or, to use other words, reabsorption and emanation. Since this creative awareness is the fountainhead of all other mantras, it is their potency (*mantra-vīryam*). When it shares its splendour even one's own individual mantra is empowered to acquire every fruit.

The practitioner proceeds to recite his mantra in such a way that the whole outflow of creative awareness becomes united with consciousness. The recitation is in three stages. It starts with the goddesses of the sub-circles, the whole objective reality. It proceeds according to the modalities of sound, the twelve or eight stages of the *uccāra* which have been noted already in Chapter 5 and, by

---

232. In *TĀ* 4.181cd-193, Abhinava discusses the potency of the mantra (*mantravīryam*). He begins his discussion with a definition of *dhvani* which is the foundation of the potency: '[Consciousness], because by nature it is creative awareness, spontaneously possesses a resonance (*dhvaniḥ*) which is ever arising and which is called 'the great supreme Heart.' Potency is given to a mantra, any mantra, if it is associated with the great mantra of the Heart. In *TĀ* 4.193ab, he concludes his discussion on the potency of the mantra with the succinct phrase: 'The potency of all mantras consists of the Heart.' See also Padoux, *La Parātrīśikālaghuvṛtti*, p.99 note 171.

means of the creative awareness which is the principle of unity, all enters into consciousness. In this way, the practitioner has indeed become Śiva in a way imitating *śl.*22 of the Opening Ritual.

The second step largely develops *śl.*23 of the Opening Ritual. The practitioner who has become the mantra now couples with the śakti so that together they form the six rayed *mudrā* which phonically is expressed as the sixth vowel, *AI*, and together they attain the state of *khecarīmudrā*. Abhinava begins by describing the sexual organ and the pleasure zones of the female and the male in terms reminiscent of the *maṇḍala* of the Kula tradition. The couple then begin their intercourse consisting of three moments. The first is the movement, the friction of the organs, after which the male and female fluids, the 'moon' and 'sun' fluids,[233] are emitted and then in the third moment are united. In the 'fire', which results from all of this, comes the 'sprout', the emanation. These matters can be understood at many levels hence Abhinava's use of symbolic language. At one level, *śl.*151-153ab is a description of intercourse leading to the procreation of a child or to the sense of producing the whole universe which is called the Fourth.[234] At another level, it is the joining of the object and means of knowledge. These coincide in such a way that the 'fire', the conscious subject arises.

Another step now occurs. Just as the creative awareness (*parāmarśa*) arises during the attentiveness to Being, so awareness (*vimarśa*) appears during the stable attention to the Fourth. This awareness is higher than creative awareness since the couple in their union more clearly symbolise Śiva and śakti, or, as Jayaratha puts it in Jr.154b.2, the interplay (*lolībhāva*)[235] of mantra and *mudrā* in copulation leads to the first and highest form of consciousness, the supreme sound.

Abhinava then goes on to describe the recitation which is most appropriate to this context. It is a natural recitation in the sense

233. The moon has 16 'portions'. The sun has 12 phases, one for each month of the solar year. de Mallmann, *Les enseignements*, p.7.

234. The sexual fluid is suggested perhaps in Qt.153b.5, the idea of the *yoginī*-born is found in *śl.*162cd-163ad and the sense of the Fourth is mentioned in *śl.*154ab.

235. '*Lolībhāva* in this system is a technical word. This means that both word (*vācaka*) and its referent (*vācya*) are so closely tied that the one signifies the other.' Singh, *Parātriṃśikāvivaraṇa*, pp.121-122. The same applies to mantra and *mudrā*.

that it is not something learned such as the mantra received in initiation but rather it is spontaneous and innate (*sahaja*). It is *sahaja*, natural, in another sense, namely that it derives (*ja*) from *SA* and *HA* or, to invert the phonemes, from *HA* and *SA*, *haṃsa*, the subtle-breath. The analysis of the recitation takes place in three stages, namely the eight circles, the eight levels and the eight bhairavas, which express in greater detail the recitation mentioned briefly in *śl.*149cd-150ab. Abhinava uses the number eight because the number eight has a sense of totality in that eight elements are deemed to completely surround the centre of which they are the complete expression. The first stage is objectivity. The term 'circle' means 'pair' or 'two' or in this case 'male and female'. The eight circles of *śl.*157cd-158ab refer to eight stages in the act of intercourse and to eight levels in the body where the intercourse is experienced, ending with consciousness itself, the end-of-twelve. The list is given not in order to limit the number of circles but to show the completeness of this level. The second stage is the subtle level of the arousing of sound (*uccāra*). Here too the number eight is symbolic since the whole range of sound from the audible to the supreme is intended. Where normally the *yogī* attends to his own recitation, here he concentrates on the reaction of his sexual partner. He is led by her natural recitation, her cry of love which is the inarticulate sound (*avyakta*) and the primordial syllable (*akṣara*), to the highest level of bliss which is the third stage, the perfect fusion of Śiva and śakti, an ineffable state referred to as 'that' (*tat*), a neuter pronoun. Accordingly the highest level, the supreme Bhairava, is envisaged as surrounded by eight bhairavas whose names are listed in the neuter form, and who are the eight stages or phases of sound, the expression of that perfect fusion.

	Results:
śl. 161cd-162ab	1. Liberated-while-living, Bhairavī
śl. 162cd-163	2. The *yoginī*-child
	Conclusion:
śl. 164-166ab	1. Etymology of *ādi-yāga*, (Primordial Sacrifice)
	2. Concluding bibliography

The lengthy description of Sacrifice 3 has now reached its climax with two principal effects. The first is the pervasion of consciousness. Since the practitioner is not tied (*alepo*) to any audible mantra or to any particular ritual, he is able to transform every state and circumstance. Being free of any particular ritual, all becomes ritual and every word is his mantra. All is sacred and so the practitioner is always pure (*alepo*). He is Bhairava, and his state is that of *bhairavī-mudrā* where the interior and the exterior are the same, the one subject, 'I'. He is liberated-while-living. A second result is the conception of the child, the *yoginī*-born. Because the practitioner and his partner have attained the perfect fusion of Śiva and śakti, the child so conceived is an expression of this transcendent unity, a Rudra, and so has all knowledge. The couple and the child are the counterparts of the *khecarī* and their offspring mentioned in Jr.46b.1.

(g) Sub-topic 5 'The Ritual of the Secret Teaching'

Sub-topic 5 is divided into three parts, Sacrifices 4, 5 and 6, dealing with the trio of body, subtle-breath and consciousness respectively which are commonly found joined together.[236] Sacrifice 4 can also be performed separately[237] as is suggested by the bibliography given in *śl*.177. Many of the terms have already been treated above and only a few points need explanation.

Sacrifice 3 brings the practitioner to a state where in all the actions of every-day life he is '... ever unattached, liberated-while-living, the supreme Bhairava', *TĀ* 29.162ab. He is free because he has joined male and female in the six rayed *mudrā* of intercourse and his only method therein is recollection which had been so prized in *śl*.64-65. This is reflected in both the *Tantrasāra* and the *Tantroccaya* where, at the conclusion of Sacrifice 3 which is described largely by quoting verbatim from the *Tantrāloka*, Abhinava quotes from *TĀ* 32.20cd-24ab as follows:

---

236. See for example *TĀ* 5.17cd-19ab, *Tantrasāra* p.35 lines 8-9 and *Parātrīśikālaghuvṛtti* p.59.

237. Sanderson views Sacrifices 4, 5, 6 as separable. Indeed, he states that Sacrifice 6 is a daily ritual and that Sacrifice 4 occurs only on special occasions. Sanderson, 'Meaning', p.90. He does not elaborate.

> *'Free* (tyaktāṃśako), *not attached to any ritual* (nirācāro), *without doubt, free of worldly concerns, pure, not attached to any ritual, reflecting that 'I am not', relying solely on the mantra, viewing all the goddesses who reside in his body .... always seeing these things as the perceiving subject, he is clearly made perfect by means of the* khecarī-mudrā.'

Sacrifice 4 Based on the Body (*dehe*)

śl. 166cd-168	1. Installation of *vidyā* and mantra
śl. 169	note: secrecy on this matter
śl. 170-173	2. The *maṇḍala*
śl. 174-175	3. Satiation of the self and deities
śl. 176	aside: a hymn
śl. 177	Concluding bibliography

The two terms *cakra* and *maṇḍala* both mean a circle and both refer to the *yoni* and to the group of goddesses which gathers there. Hence they are called 'supreme' and 'principal'. The circle is identified in particular with the very heart, the centre, the starting point and end point of the Krama cycle. From it rises the *liṅga*[238] which is composed of all the categories. From it also radiate the lotus, circle and space, three increasingly abstract patterns which represent the three dimensions of object, means and subject of knowledge. The triple trident of this kind indicates that the practitioner of Sacrifice 4 is at least a Son and that he is engaged in the totality of the Krama cycle. The male and female sex organs correspond to the *liṅga* and *yoni*, symbols of reality in all its dimensions, and around which devotees assemble in the countless shrines of India.

---

238. *TĀ* 31.28. For a graphic design of this particular *maṇḍala* and for further details, see Sanderson, *'Maṇḍala'*, 194 ff. Sanderson notes that while the single trident with three lotuses is designed for the ordinary initiate, the triple trident etc. is designed for initiation as Son. *ibid.* p.196. *TĀ* 31.52 associates the triple trident with emanation, stability and dissolution, while at the centre is the fourth state (*turyaṃ*) which brings all to completion (*paripūrakam*) and so associates the triple trident with the Krama cycle.

Although the matter is not clear, it seems that the sexual fluid is produced only in Sacrifice 3, the Primordial Sacrifice, but not in Sacrifice 4, the Subsequent Sacrifice (*anuyāga*) even though the practitioner does engage in intercourse[239] The sexual fluid used in Sacrifice 4 may have been obtained on an earlier occasion.[240]

Sacrifice 5 Based on the Subtle-breath (*prāṇa*)

śl. 178	1. Definition
śl. 179	2. Examination
śl. 180	3. Effect: powers of knowledge

Sacrifice 5 is described with utmost brevity, in only three *ślokas*. It is said, in Jr.177d.3 and *śl.*178c, to imitate the ritual performed in the body. One may presume, therefore, that the satiation of the self and the deities with sexual fluid is the model for satisfying the goddesses of the *prāṇa* with *apāna*. Just as the moon is supposed to feed the sun, so too the *apāna*, the 'moon breath' penetrates into the body through all the apertures, satisfies the *prāṇa*[241] and allows the practitioner to rise to a new level of consciousness, but not yet to the highest level so that only the supernatural powers of knowledge are given (*śl.*180d).

Sacrifice 6 Based on the Mind (*matau*)

śl. 181	1. Definition	
śl. 182	2. Examination:	i. In brief
śl. 183-185c		ii. In detail
śl. 185d	3. Effect: perfection	
śl. 186ab	Concluding bibliography	

239. In *TĀ* 15.498-508, Abhinava lists forty-eight ritual acts (*saṃskāras*). The first (*ādi-yāga*) is the union of the couple in order to emit the fluid and to bring about the conception of a child while the last sacrifice (*antyeṣṭi*) is the funeral rite. Abhinava applies the term *ādi-yāga* to Sacrifice 3. By contrast, *anuyāga*, the Subsequent Sacrifice, is the ceremonial occasion on which the sexual fluid is used. *Tantrāloka* vol.7, p.3125 lines 15-17. However, the matter is not so simple. In *TĀ* 28.42ab ff. and 45cd-46a, Abhinava also distinguishes between Subsequent Sacrifice and Primordial Sacrifice on the basis of time, but it is not clear how he does so.

240. See *Yonitantra* especially the Concluding Rite.

241. In *Parātriṃśikāvivaraṇa* p.281 lines 20-23, Abhinava repeats the meditation.

It is in Sacrifice 6 that the highest level, consciousness (*citi*), is attained. If the *apāna* was offered as satiation to the many goddesses of the *prāṇa*, now the whole of reality, every enjoyment, is offered to the one goddess of consciousness. Abhinava describes the process of worship firstly in a brief presentation and then in a detailed description which seems, from Jr.186b.1, to follow the Krama stages of reabsorption. Jayaratha himself (Jr.185d.1-2) seems to recapitulate the whole procedure in terms of the Krama.[242] The description depends significantly on the pun formed by the word *citi* which can mean either funeral pyre or consciousness. By consuming all in the fire of pure subjectivity, the practitioner achieves the highest state. The dissolution of everything in the fire of consciousness is the true initiation.[243]

(h) Sub-topic 6 'Initiation'

śl. 186cd-187ab Enunciation of the sub-topic

Having performed the rituals for the initiate, the guru has arrived at the highest state of consciousness and so is in a state of perfection

242. In Jr.186b.1, Jayaratha refers to the stages of the Krama and in Jr.185d.1-2 he takes all the key words of *śl.*183-185 and reorganises them according to those stages. His investigation is divided into two parts, the multiple of which gives the twelve stages.
1.The first part goes from 'In this [body]' and finishes with 'will not be brought to perfection?' It is an investigation particularly of the phrase 'located within the body' (*śl.*182c). The four major stages of the Krama, namely emanation, maintenance, reabsorption and 'the ineffable', are reflected, within the limitations of his text, by the words 'filled', 'transience', 'abandonment' and 'this', which last relates to 'the ineffable', the fourth stage of the Krama. 'The ineffable' is reflected again in the word 'in that' which occurs in the second part of the investigation.
2. The second part is introduced by the question 'what sort of reality' and goes from the phrase 'in the sense of simply of turning inwards' and finishes with the phrase 'to the place of repose in one's self alone' and is an investigation of the phrase 'radiant as the Fire of Time', *śl.*182d. It dwells on the three spheres of 'object of knowledge', 'means of knowledge' and 'subject of knowledge'. The first of these is reflected in the phrase 'the passing bodily form of all things'; the second in the phrase 'free of all differentiated thoughts ... the faculties'; the third in the phrase 'the single form of the knowing subject'.

243. In *Parātriṃśikāvivaraṇa* p.279 lines 9-10, for which see Gnoli, *Il commento*, p.174 notes 530a and 530b, Abhinava, after describing the dissolution of all into consciousness, quotes the following text: 'Acknowledgment of one's essential nature: this is mantra in the highest sense, this is initiation and this is the sacrifice, this is the ritual action, it is unsurpassable.'

(*śl.*185c) and is therefore in a position to perform initiation, for if it is true that only Śiva can worship Śiva it is also true that only Śiva can initiate into the worship of Śiva.

The whole *Tantrāloka* is basically divided into two parts. Chapters 1-12 deal primarily with knowledge (*jñāna*) while chapter 13 is an important bridge to chapters 14-34 which deal with the ritual, more specifically with the various forms of initiation (*dīkṣā*).[244] Chapter 15 deals with ordinary initiation. Chapters 16 and 17 describe the initiation of the Son. Chapter 18 deals with initiation in its shortened form. Chapter 19 describes initiation at the hour of death. Chapter 20 is an excursus on the symptoms of effective initiation which will be mentioned briefly in *TĀ* 29.207-208. Chapter 21 describes the initiation of those who are absent, either through distance or because of death. Ch.22 discusses the initiation of converts from inferior rituals. In Ch.23, Abhinava momentarily moves out of the field of initiation strictly speaking and into the topic of consecration. Ch.24 deals with the initiation of those who have been sent to a hell. Ch.25, the rite performed after death (*śrāddha*), is the last of the initiations. Thus the rites of initiation occupy a large part of the *Tantrāloka*.

In *TĀ* 1.43 ff., Abhinava considers the relationship of initiation and knowledge and emphasises that the only initiation which gives liberation in life is the one preceded by knowledge. Indeed he notes[245] that for some disciples the mere knowledge of chapters 1-10 of the *Tantrasāra* on the four methods of attaining Śiva and the pathways etc. will be sufficient to procure liberation. Similarly, he considers that the highest form of initiation occurs by intuition (*pratibhā*) which comes either from a 'very intense' or from an 'intense' descent of energy. It is a direct initiation by the goddesses themselves so that there is no need for such a person to undergo the ritual of initiation. Again, in rare cases there can also be a

244. In *Parātriṃśikāvivaraṇa* p.273 line 17, Abhinava provides the traditional etymology: '*Dīkṣā* is defined as the granting (*dāna*) of knowledge and the destruction (*kṣapaṇa*) of *māyā*. For the linguistic etymology of *dīkṣā*, see Jan Gonda, *Change and continuity in Indian religion*, The Hague, Mouton and Co., 1965, pp.341-342 footnote 122.

245. *Tantrasāra* p.115.

self-initiation.[246] Normally, however, there is a need to undergo the ritual of initiation of which there are two basic types: initiation into enjoyment or initiation into liberation. In *TĀ* 13.296cd-299ab, Abhinava lists the two forms of initiation, ordinary initiation and initiation as Son, and the two forms of consecration, as Adept and as Master, all of which he relates to the descent of energy in its various degrees. Ordinary initiation and initiation as a Son are treated in Sub-topic 6 while the consecration of the Adept and the Master is given in Sub-topic 7.

I. Ordinary Initiation

śl. 187cd-192ab	1. In the *Mālinīvijayottaratantra* - by means of mantra and flower
śl. 192cd-195	2. In the *Ratnamālā* - by means of mantra, 'oblation' etc.
	Transition
śl. 196-197ab	a. Assessing the absorption
śl. 197cd-198ab	b. Ordinary initiate and Son
śl. 198cd-199ab	3. In the *Ānandeśvara* - by means of the 'oblation' alone
śl. 199cd-200	Result: the way of life for an ordinary initiate

In point of fact, Abhinava does not use the word initiation (*dīkṣā*) to describe the ritual of *TĀ* 29.187cd ff. but reserves it to initiation as Son. So-called ordinary initiation [247] is essentially transitional.

---

246. *TĀ* 16.195a. It is a 'self-initiation by a process of consciousness' (*TĀ* 4.61cd). He goes on, in *TĀ* 4.62cd ff., to note that this is exceptional and is to be sought only if a suitable guru is not available.

247. In her article 'Analyse du *suprabhedāgama*', p.44, Héléne Brunner-Lachaux uses the phrase 'ordinary initiate' to translate the word *samayī*. Gnoli, *Luce*, *passim* translates it as 'regular'.

If it does not produce an experience of absorption the disciple is restricted to the level of the rule (*samaya*)[248] and will proceed to the next level only later.

Ordinary initiation is described according to three different texts which progress from the more external and gentle to the more interior and shocking. The first is according to *Mālinīvijayottara-tantra* 11.17cd ff. with which Abhinava now resumes after the long break of Sacrifices 2-6. Given the information provided in the rituals for the initiate, the rituals of initiation are fairly self-explanatory. A few items need special consideration, however.

In *TĀ* 15.456cd-474ab, Abhinava describes the so-called ritual of the 'hand-of-Śiva'. Firstly, the guru sacrifices to the circle of the mantra (*mantra-cakraṃ*) located on his right hand and then places his hand on the head of the disciple, on his heart and navel and afterwards on every limb of the disciple's body so that the disciple becomes an ordinary initiate. By contrast, in the more interior and more powerful rituals of *TĀ* 29, the rite of the 'hand of Śiva' is performed by the disciple himself. The guru does not touch him but is there silent and immobile for he acts from within, he reflects (*vicintayet*) and manipulates the *rudraśakti* which is *Mālinī* enclosed by *Parā* or *Mātṛsadhbāva* and is also called the 'circle of the goddess' or is described as a curved flame and is deemed to have the form of an elephant goad (*aṅkuśa*)[249] designed to both prod and pull. The guru directs the *rudraśakti*, the circle of the goddess (*devī-cakram*) so that the disciple places his own hands on his own head. The disciple is moved to touch not some lower centre but the highest so that the illumination will be of the highest order and both hands are used because the disciple is being

248. *TĀ* 15.520cd-521ab, Abhinava states that 'An ordinary initiate is qualified for study, for hearing the scriptures, for daily worship and for service of the guru.' Further rules of conduct are given in *TĀ* 15.521cd-611cd which apply, *mutatis mutandis*, to the ordinary Kula initiate.

249. 'The Elephant Goad is a manifestation of the god's powers of attraction and subjugation.' Goudriaan, The *Vīṇāśikhatantra*, p.139 note 19.

regenerated as one who is liberated while living.[250] It is the moment of absorption (*āveśa*). The 'hand of Śiva' has therefore several meanings in *TĀ* 29. It refers to the internal act of the guru with its resultant external effects, to the *rudraśakti*, the 'elephant goad' which the guru manipulates and to the hands of the disciple which have been so empowered.

The significance of ordinary initiation lies not so much in the external events as in the experience so that the principal task of the guru is to observe the descent of energy (*śaktipāta*) and therefore the degree of absorption.

Śiva expresses himself in the emanation of the universe which eventually peters out in inertia and conversely he draws all back to himself by the revelation of his splendour. All this is performed out of grace (*anugraha*) for he is essentially free. The revelation is performed in nine ways according as he pleases. These are the descent of energy. Even though Śiva is free, the attitude of the recipient is not irrelevant. For example, if the recipient desires only liberation, the circumstances of his life—birth, family, bodily health, wealth, even his karma—are of no account whereas if he wishes enjoyments, these matters influence the type of *śaktipāta*.[251]

Abhinava notes in general terms, that the descent of energy is classed into three groups: *tīvra* which means 'strong', 'violent', 'severe'; *madhya*, 'medium'; and *manda* 'weak', 'slow', 'sluggish'.[252] Each of the three is divided again according to the same classification to form nine categories.[253] In general Abhinava rings

---

250. In *Tantrasāra* p.163, in discussing the ritual to be performed in the case of a dying person, Abhinava describes how the 'hand of Śiva' is to be used: the right hand alone is transformed into a triangular *maṇḍala* which is made to blaze with fire and wind and is then placed on the head of the dying person in order to burn away every impurity and lead him to the highest level.

251. *TĀ* 29.116cd-117cd ff.

252. *TĀ* 13.129cd-130ab.

253. Since it is hardly possible to translate *tīvra-tīvra* by 'strong-strong', a different set of terms has been used in this translation such as 'very intense', 'intense', 'slightly intense' instead of 'strong-strong', 'medium-strong' and 'weak-strong'. His discussion on these nine forms is given in the following *ślokas*:

	strong	medium	weak	
strong	i. 130cd-131ab	iv. 131b-217	vii. 218-222ab	medium
	ii. 240-242ab	v. 242cd-243ab	viii. 243cd-244ab	
weak	iii. 245cd-246ab	vi. *ibid.*	ix. *ibid.*	

through the various changes allowed by the concepts 'Śiva', 'liberation', 'intuition', 'conviction', 'enjoyment', 'body', 'death', 'category' and notes that there can be immediate results or delays, but only the details especially relevant to *TĀ* 29 are given, as follows:

(i) Very intense: This grants liberation and involves the physical death, a death either immediate or delayed according to the intensity of this form of descent of energy. Identity with Śiva is the result.

(ii) Intense: This eliminates all ignorance and is a sudden intuition (*pratibhā*) and such a person is called 'an intuitive guru'.[254] Abhinava continues with a long discussion—many elements of which he had already presented in *TĀ* 4.33-85—on the quality of such a person. Given the importance he attaches to this ideal figure throughout *TĀ* 29, some of the major features must be mentioned.

(a) Such a person receives illumination independently of all levels of initiation, of exterior purifications, of teachers, scriptures etc.: - 'he has been initiated by the goddesses'.[255] He is like the moon, dispelling both darkness and heat (*tapas*) in his disciples; his look is full of bliss; he is acquainted with all the sciences, with tradition, grammar, astronomy, *kula* etc.[256] In his presence other gurus 'lose their qualification'.[257]

(b) Significantly, Abhinava distinguishes between a hesitant and firm intuition. The hesitant intuition received from an intense descent of energy may be made brilliant and clear by means of teachers, the scriptures, by '*yoga*, sacrifice and recitation'.[258]

(c) The person who receives an intense descent of energy acquires extraordinary supernatural powers, such as hearing from afar, penetration (*vedha*), playful acts such as immense size,[259] but 'turns from those powers with disgust, intent only on having the nature of Śiva'.[260] That being said, the supernatural powers do,

254. *Tantrasāra* p.120 line 5.
255. *TĀ* 13.142a.
256. *TĀ* 13.134dcd.
257. *Tantrasāra* p.122 line 1.
258. *TĀ* 13.175cd-176.
259. *TĀ* 13.179cd-180ab.
260. *TĀ* 13.181ab.

nevertheless, have a value: 'All these accomplishments are said to bring about conviction in others.'[261]

(d) Abhinava notes that among those with an intense descent of energy some are more suited to knowledge (*jñānayogyās*) and others are more suited to discipline (*caryāyogyās*).[262] The same descent of energy may be expressed in knowledge or action. The private worshipper at the shrine who presents his offering of flowers can have received intuition of Śiva no less than the teacher who expounds the scriptures to the assembled throng.

(iii) Slightly intense: In this case the disciple cannot proceed on the basis of his own intuition but is inspired to find an authentic guru (*sadgurum̩*) who will initiate him and grant him liberation. Abhinava lists some ways in which this initiation may occur:

> *'This [initiation] - which can be obtained from any one of the following or all together - is divided as follows: resulting from an exposition, from a meeting, from a look, from a scripture, from a transmission, from the sight of a ritual act [which excludes no one by reason of birth etc. (?)]* (sāmya), *from the oblation, from the efficacy of a mantra and of a* mudrā *etc., from a ritual act, from penetrating into the interior subtle-breath.'*[263]

Abhinava describes the six lesser varieties of descent of energy in the space of about seven *ślokas*. These show an increasing concern with enjoyments and a decreasing lack of conviction about Śivahood, the lynch pin of the Kula ritual. In consequence the six lesser forms need not be described further except to make the final point that even the very weak descent of energy is still an act of grace on the part of Śiva such that the person who is so little favoured will also attain liberation in the end.

261. *TĀ* 13.183ab.
262. *TĀ* 13.163ab.
263. *TĀ* 13.227cd-229ab.

Lastly, there is another group, so to speak: those who have received no descent of energy at all. They are like stone and are to be abandoned.[264]

Finally, the disciple's attitude towards the 'oblation' is of particular importance in the second form of ordinary initiation. If he is hesitant (*kampa*) he will remain an ordinary initiate but if he is fearless the guru will give him initiation as a Son. This is brought out more fully in the third form of ordinary initiation where the guru quite simply proffers the 'oblation'. As Jayaratha notes in Jr.200d.2, the awesome 'oblation' is a most powerful means for attaining consciousness. Indeed it is an indirect means of the 'non-means' which is the highest and first of the *upāyas*.[265] By taking the oblation the disciple shows he has been absorbed into consciousness and so rises above the concepts of pure and impure, above social convention and even natural repugnance. He has gone beyond *māyā*, has been absorbed into śakti and has become a member of one of the clans (*gotra*) of śaktis.

II. Initiation as a Son

śl. 201ab Enunciation

The initiation as Son (*putraka*)[266] is the dividing point of all the initiations and consecrations of *TĀ* 29. Thus ordinary 'initiation' is a prelude to initiation as Son. These two stages form a whole and there is no need to go further. The disciple may wish simply to remain in the state of liberation obtained by his initiation but he may also choose to adopt a public role and seek to become either

264. *TĀ* 29.211b.

265. In *TĀ* 2, which deals with the 'non-means', Abhinava states that '... the teaching occurs once only' (*sakṛtsyāddeśanā*, śl.2c) so that nothing more is needed to come to full consciousness. In *Tantrāloka* vol.2, p.312 line 13, in his investigation of this phrase, Jayaratha quotes a source, which states: 'for the *siddhas* and *yoginīs* the eating of the 'oblation' (*carubhojanam*) is revelation', and goes on to say that nothing else is needed. The 'oblation' has the same impact as the teaching.

266. The word *putraka* is simply a diminutive of *putra*, son. However, it is also held to derive from a compound, put-tra, 'preserving from the hell called Put'. Monier-Williams, *Sanskrit English dictionary*, p.632. It also has the ordinary meaning of 'son', 'offspring' etc., from *putra*. For that reason Gnoli translates *putraka* as 'figlio spirituale' [spiritual son].

an Adept or a Master. He need not first become an Adept but may directly go on to become a Master. It is also possible for the one who has first chosen to be an Adept to seek further consecration as a Master[267] but by contrast there is no point in a Master seeking consecration as an Adept, as Jr.232d.1 makes clear. Initiation as Son must precede initiation-by-penetration. He must first be brought to liberation and only then can he properly receive the enjoyments which penetration procures.

There are four subdivisions of the term 'Son'. In *TĀ* 15.23-26, on the basis of ritual, Abhinava contrasts the Son who is *nirbīja* and the Son who is *sabīja*. The *nirbīja* has no ritual obligation etc. so that children, women and the sick, for example, fit into this class. The *tattva-jña*, 'the person who knows reality', can also be placed in this class because he transcends the limitations of ritual obligation. The *sabīja*, who receives initiation into a 'seed' (*bīja*) has various ritual duties and a rule of life. Thirdly and fourthly, in *TĀ* 29.205d, Abhinava distinguishes between the *niṣkala-putraka* and the *sakala-putraka*, according as the Son seeks either liberation only or seeks enjoyments as well as liberation.

The Son is called a *mumukṣu*, one who seeks liberation, a term often opposed to the term *bubhukṣu*, the person who desires enjoyments. Can a *mumukṣu* desire enjoyments? Are not enjoyment and liberation so opposed as to exclude each other? Abhinava deals with this question in *śl*.219 ff. and explains that the liberated person knows both liberation and enjoyment by proceeding through the five stages of consciousness. In other words, because he has experienced consciousness in his initiation as a Son he will want to express it by knowing every level of being and the enjoyments of every level. It is called 'the Kula tradition of sacrifice' (*śl*.220c). The successful combination of both 'enjoyment and liberation' (*bhoga-mokṣau, śl*.276d) is the climax of *TĀ* 29.

The word *tattva-jña*[268] with its synonym, *tattva-vid*, recurs

267. This somewhat complex topic is dealt with in *TĀ* 29.231-232 and Jr.232d.1.

268. In *L'essenza*, p.269, Gnoli translates the word *atattvajñānī* as someone who does not have the 'consciousness of reality'. In Gnoli, *Luce*, p.584, he translates *tattvavin*, *tattvajña* and *jñāni* as 'gnostic'. Women also belong to this category and are called *tattvavedinī*.

constantly in the *Tantrāloka* and the *Tantrasāra* and is appropriately treated here since it is equivalent to the term Son. It revolves around the meaning of *tattva* which normally means category but is also a code word. In Jr.166b.1, Jayaratha defines the essence involved in the Primordial Sacrifice: 'it consists of the 'substance' (*tattva*) of consciousness and it appears as 'nectar' ', meaning sexual fluid. Accordingly, the *tattva-jña*, the one who knows the *tattva*, refers to the person who has taken the 'oblation' and who has been absorbed into the highest category, consciousness itself and so has become a Son.

	1. According to the *Ratnamālā*
śl. 201cd-202ab	a. Definition of the ritual
śl. 202cd-206	b. Examination of the ritual
śl. 207-208	c. Result: i. 5 possible effects
śl. 209	ii. Enjoyment
śl. 210-211ab	2. Another method: a surrounding fire
śl. 211cd-212ab	3. In the *Sadbhāva*
śl. 212cd-213	a. Enunciation: 3 phoneme masses
śl. 214-216	b. Examination of the ritual
śl. 217-218ab	Results: a. He is Bhairava
śl. 218cd	b. He is a guru

Abhinava gives three rituals of initiation as Son. Some points need elaboration and the ritual according to the *Sadbhāva* needs some explanation.

The first point for elaboration is the word *kalā* which has two different meanings in the description of initiation according to the *Ratnamālā* and its investigation.[269] The first meaning refers to the whole range of categories grouped into five *kalā* starting from the lowest, earth, to the highest, *śānty-atīta*. It is according to this pathway that the disciple is regenerated and 'nourished'.[270] The second meaning refers to the five coverings (*kalā*) and to the scope of the regeneration, as follows. Śiva is said to be of two sorts composed (*sakala*) or simple (*niṣkala*) which means with or without

269. For the two groups of *kalā*, see Appendix 1.

270. *TĀ* 16 deals with initiation as a Son. The cleansing of the pathway of the *kalā* is treated in *TĀ* 16.147ab-150ab.

those five coverings. Jayaratha explains that the person who is merged into Śiva in his simple form is initiated as a Son without more ado. The person who is merged in Śiva in his composite form is initiated with reference to a later consecration as an Adept who will be involved in obtaining and conferring enjoyments in the world of multiplicity.

In his survey of initiation as a Son (*śl*.201cd-202ab) Abhinava had mentioned the absorption (*āveśa*) which causes the initiate to fall to the ground. In fact, he lists five signs,[271] of which the reeling is the least significant but perhaps the most spectacular. The five are bliss, lightness, trembling, sleep and reeling.[272] If the disciple is particularly attached to the body, the descent of energy will have its effect there, releasing him from his attachment to the body and making him fall. The bliss which is experienced in the

271. In *TĀ* 13.214-215, Abhinava gives a different list. 'Under the term 'penetrated by *rudraśakti*', the following list of signs, according to [the *Mālinīvijayottaratantra*], is implied in due order: perfectly unwavering devotion to Rudra, the supernatural power of the mantra, dominion of all the categories, the successful accomplishment of any undertaking, the gift of poetry, understanding the meaning of all the scriptures.'

272. In *TĀ* 28.218cd-219ab, in the context of a discussion about the life-cycle, Abhinava states that: ' Incarnation is [the appearance of the subtle-breath] within the body which is located in the womb. The subtle-breath first arises from consciousness which is within the void.' The sequence is, therefore, consciousness, void, subtle-breath, [internal and external] body which is reflected in *śl*.207cd. In *Tantrasāra* p.63 lines 6-7, Abhinava gives the reverse procedure. In *Tantrasāra* p.40, he links these five effects with the five levels of consciousness and with the five locations in the body. These, along with the place where the energy enters, are schematised as follows:

Place of Energy	Effect	Level of Consciousness	Place in Body
external body *bahis-tanu*	reeling *ghūrṇi*	wakefulness *jāgrat*	triangle *trikoṇa*
internal body *antar-tanu*	sleep *nidrā*	dreaming sleep *svapna*	'bulb' *kanda*
subtle-breath *prāṇana*	trembling *kampa*	deep sleep *suṣupta*	heart *hṛt*
space *vyoma*	lightness *udbhava*	Fourth *turya*	palate *talu*
mind	bliss	Beyond-Fourth	upper *kuṇḍalinī*
citi	*ānanda*	*turyātīta*	*ūrdhva-kuṇḍalinī*

mind may not be spectacular in the same way but is more significant. Indeed, in Jr.208d.1, Jayaratha links the effects with the degrees of the descent of energy so that a very intense descent of energy will enter the mind and produce bliss while a very weak descent of energy can only touch the body.

The burning of the bonds (Jr.208d.1) is the elimination of *karma* and of rebirth. But which aspect of *karma*? There is a past, present and future *karma* encompassing the acts and their consequences in all the dimensions of time. If all of these are eliminated the disciple must die, as Jayaratha notes in Jr.208d.2. However, the guru who has joined the disciple to Śiva and has liberated him from the consequences of ignorant action in the past and from the prospect of error in the future does not eliminate the present condition of the disciple which is the 'remainder' but regenerates the disciple with pure categories. Just as Śiva who is immanent to the world is pure so too the disciple who is joined to Śiva is equally immanent to the world and enjoys it. For that reason Abhinava, after completing the discussion of initiation as a Son, goes on to speak of enjoyments (*śl*.219-224). The ideal throughout *TĀ* 29 is not to be absent from the world but to be fully present.

After giving the three masses of phonemes (*piṇḍa*) each of which leads to complete liberation, Abhinava describes the third ritual in detail with specific reference to installation, meditation and recitation. Firstly, the guru installs the *śaktibīja*, *ĪṂ*,[273] on the whole body of the disciple. Then the twelve vowels are enclosed by *HA* in circular fashion and installed on the circle of the heart so that consciousness arises from the centre. These three steps resemble the formation of the Kula *maṇḍala*. At a second stage the guru meditates on the dessicating and burning force of *YA* and *RA* in

273. There seems to be a disagreement as to the meaning of *śakti-bīja*. In Jr.216d.1, Jayaratha explains that *śakti-bīja* consists of a double *bīja*: the phoneme *Ī* and *māyā*. Bühneman, p.372, states that *śakti-bīja* is *HRĪṂ* but Padoux, *Le coeur,* p.382 footnote 389 and Agehananda Bharati, p.119, note that *HRĪṂ* is called *māyā*.

order to release the paralysing grip of *karma*[274] which holds the disciple back from regeneration and condemns him to rebirth. At a third stage, the guru recites one or other of the masses of phonemes, enclosing the disciple's name within the mass such that the disciple is absorbed into śakti and thus attains liberation.

The first result of initiation as a Son concerns the disciple alone. Before initiation he was attached to a particular category and was thus held in bondage but by his release from every limitation 'he does not see'. The phrase 'he does not see' signifies *bhairavīmudrā*, the attitude of Bhairava. The disciple no longer 'sees' if 'to see' means seeing something separate from himself, but he is now the totality of all, he is what he sees, he sees what he is, he sees by means of himself. The inner and the outer are the same, all is *AHAM*.[275] The second result is that he also comprehends all the scriptures. As Bhairava he speaks the scriptures and the scriptures speak of him so that he is a guru in the fullest sense.[276]

III. On the Son who Desires Enjoyments

śl. 219-220	1. a. Enjoyment in a category
	b. Enjoyment in all categories
	c. Enunciation of Kula sacrifice
śl. 221	2. Definition of the Kula sacrifice
śl. 222-223	3. Examination of the sacrifice
śl. 224	4. Further instruction on five states

274. The phoneme *YA* dessicates and the phoneme *RA* burns. The seed of *karma*, when affected by these influences, is made unable to produce its fruit and so the disciple is liberated from the cycle of rebirth. *TĀ* 20.5-6a reads: 'The [seed] which is burnt in this way is not able to germinate. For the same reason, the *karmas* which derive from the stain [of individuality] and *māyā*, and which have been burnt by virtue of mantra, meditation and ritual action are not able to produce their effect.'

275. *Anubhavanivedana* 1 describes *bhairavīmudrā* as follows: "When the *yogī*, his subtle-breath and mind dissolved in the internal [object], sees (*paśyann*) the external [world] with unwavering perception (*dṛṣtyā*) while not seeing it (*apaśyann*): that is truly the *mudrā* of Śambhu which is brought about through your favour, O Guru. This category (*tattvaṃ*), without void or non-void, is the level of Śambhu.' See also *Tantrasāra* p.68 lines 5-8: 'He who sees this pathway in all its parts (*sakalaṃ*), in the body and in the subtle-breath, in the mind, in the great emptiness and in consciousness, becomes Bhairava in the fullest sense.'

276. In consequence of becoming Bhairava, the initiate is truly a guru and so he is

The purpose of the Kula ritual is for the practitioner to overcome the dualism of liberation and enjoyment and to attain the state of *jīvan-mukta*, being liberated while alive. The person who has achieved liberation through initiation as a Son may therefore proceed in three ways. He may seek his own eventual personal enjoyment whether at a particular level, as in *śl.*219 or at all levels, as in *śl.* 220, or seek his personal enjoyment within the public context of obtaining enjoyment for others as an Adept, or, finally, he may seek immediate enjoyments through initiation-by-penetration, as in *śl.* 236 ff.

Abhinava passes quickly over the initiation into enjoyment within a particular category, whether this be at the lowest level such as mastery over a world or at the highest level such as that of *Sadāśiva*, as Jayaratha notes in Jr.220d.1. Such enjoyment is achieved by the appropriate ritual, which Abhinava does not describe, and by the appropriate exercise of concentration (*dhāraṇa*) which will procure the enjoyment. But Abhinava is interested in the larger picture, that of obtaining every enjoyment. This goal is achieved by means of the Kula tradition of sacrifice which is directed, as Abhinava notes in *śl.*223cd, to those who are completely involved with their own sexual partner or śakti. The practitioner has been liberated through his initiation as a Son and is directed to practise the Kula tradition of sacrifice in its five states, not in order to attain liberation but to show that he is liberated while living. He is given this single life-long practice which both classes him as a *sabīja putraka* and explores every level of enjoyment. In union with his śakti the practitioner proceeds through the five levels of consciousness. These extend from the lowest level of wakefulness with all its mantras or divinities or realities to the

---

authorised to initiate others. See *TĀ* 13.134 and TĀ 28.386cd-387ab and *Tantrasāra* p.122 lines 6-8. In *TĀ* 4.41b, in the description of the guru, Abhinava uses the phrases *svapratyayātmakaḥ*, 'conviction comes from himself', which Jayaratha explains as 'not due to [another] guru etc.'. Another person, however, who has a slightly intense descent of energy will come to him for initiation and conviction. This is the 'other person' referred to in Jr.218b.2.

highest level, Beyond-Fourth, which is pure consciousness, the basis of all the mantras and deities.[277] Since he has traversed the whole range of being, every enjoyment is his. It is a practice suited to both the yogī and the knowledgeable person since both are involved in 'what all always enjoy, in the same way as the god and the goddess do' (*śl.*170ab).

(i) Sub-topic 7 'Consecration'

	1. In the *Mālinīvijayottara*—external ritual
śl. 225-227	a. The ritual
	i. Anointing the Adept
śl. 228-229	ii. Anointing the Master
śl. 230	b. Acclaim by the group of *yogīs*
śl. 231	c. After the ritual
	i. Their respective roles
śl. 232	ii. Further instruction
śl. 233-235	2. In the *Vīrāvalibhairava*—internal ritual

The rituals of consecration of both Adept and Master are similar.[278] Abhinava gives two rituals of consecration. The first is an 'external' version taken from the Mālinīvijayottaratantra while

277. The 'mantra' is not only the verbal form but also the deity. In his article 'Meaning', p.90, Sanderson interprets śl.222-223 as follows:

waking state:	the initiate worships 'the entire pantheon, i.e. Kuleśvara and his consort Kuleśvarī together with the three goddesses Parā, Pārāparā and Aparā, their bhairavas and all their retinues of yoginīs etc.';
dream:	he worships one of the goddesses with her bhairava and retinue;
deep sleep:	he worships the core of the pantheon without the retinues, i.e. Kuleśvara, Kuleśvarī, the three goddesses and their bhairavas;
Fourth:	he worships only Kuleśvarī;
Beyond-Fourth:	he worships only Kuleśvara.

278. In *TĀ* 23.17cd-20ab, Abhinava describes the consecration of the Master and notes, in *śl.*101cd, that the consecration of the Adept imitates it. Indeed, Brunner holds that the ritual for the consecration of the Master is the model for that of the Adept. Brunner, 'Le sādhaka', p.422.

the second, 'internal',[279] seems to apply only to the consecration of the Master because it mentions the number sixty-four which is particularly associated with the Master. Both the Adept and the Master are mentioned at this point in *TĀ* 29 but Abhinava has very little role for them in the rest of the chapter.

The Adept devotes himself to the assiduous practice of the mantra (*mantra-sādhana*)[280] and so obtains the super-natural powers inherent in his mantra. He is able to grant attainments to others and so acquires a public role.[281] In *TĀ* 29.231ab, Abhinava clearly defines that role and notes also that the Adept is authorised to give the teaching of the guru and to perform the rituals which, according to Jr.232d.1, include initiation. His role is limited, nevertheless. 'There is no transmission of competence' and there is no 'vow of wisdom'.[282] According to *TĀ* 15.23cd there are two types of Adept: the *śivadharmin* stands outside the ordinary customs of life and the *lokadharmin* leads a life 'in the world'.

The Adept in *TĀ* 29 is a minor figure. If his role is to grant attainments, the Master's role is to grant liberation (*śl*.231cd) but since Abhinava is interested in those who function on the basis of liberation, it is the Master who is the more important figure of the two. Although the Adept is termed a guru in *śl*.231c, the guru *par excellence* is the one who grants liberation. Jayaratha, in Jr.232d.1, takes this a step further and explains that the Master can bestow both attainments and liberation and can adopt any role as he is an

279. In *TĀ* 13.144cd, in the course of his discussion of the intense descent of energy, Abhinava makes the point, while referring to *Vājasineya*, that a person who has received such a descent of energy 'is consecrated in that way not with the waters contained in an external jar.' Jayaratha then quotes the relevant text of *Vājasineya* which refers to the consecrator performing the consecration by meditating, *dhyātvā*.

280. According to *TĀ* 23.102cd-103ab he is given the mantra which he must practice. He is taught the rites he must perform and receives the necessary instruments. The *mantra-sādhana* is described in detail in Brunner, 'Le sādhaka', pp.423-435.

281. Brunner makes this point in ibid. p.434 footnote 74. She goes on to note the role of the Adept at moments of public crisis where he must intervene with the power of his word, his mantra.

282. *TĀ* 23.102ab.

officiant and a knowledgeable person. What value, then, is the Adept?[283]

(j) Sub-topic 8 'Penetration'

śl. 236	Enunciation of the sub-topic
śl. 237-239ab	Definition of initiation by penetration

The ritual of penetration (*vedha*) occupies an important place in *TĀ* 29 yet features very little in the rest of the *Tantrāloka*.[284] In the few passages where it does feature, penetration takes place in the context of the dying and the dead and is performed in order to secure their liberation. At a certain point it produces spectacular effects such as when the corpse trembles or raises the left hand, bringing the doubting bystander to an experience of liberation.[285] The context of *TĀ* 29 is not the dying or the dead or the unliberated but the living person who is already liberated and who desires immediate enjoyments.[286] The purpose and content of penetration in *TĀ* 29 is therefore quite different and has only this in common: that the method produces immediate enjoyments such as minuteness. These in turn, if need there should be, perfect the conviction of the already convinced Son, making his conviction firm and bringing him to the self-evidence of consciousness, pure knowledge.

Abhinava distinguishes between three types of guru: the guru who most properly deserves the name, the knowledgeable person

283. Indeed, Brunner suggests that this growing irrelevance of the Adept is one of the reasons why he becomes a forgotten person in the traditions of South India. ibid. pp.441-442.

284. *Vedha-dīkṣā* is not mentioned in the *Tantrasāra* or in the *Tantroccaya*.

285. *TĀ* 24.13cd-15. This ritual is mentioned in a few other places such as *TĀ* 13.234cd-235 and *Tantrasāra* p.175 line 9 - p.176 line 2.

286. These are the customary eight supernatural powers which Gnoli, *Luce*, p.275 footnote 144, describes as follows: *aṇimā*, smallness; *laghimā*, lightness; prāpti, the ability to obtain everything; *prākāmyam*, irresistible will; *mahimā*, immensity; *īśitvam*, supremacy over body and mind; *vaśitvam*, domination over the elements; and *kāmāvasāyitā*, realisation of all one's desires. See also Vyāsa, ad *Yoga Sūtra* 3.45. Minoru Hara 'La bhakti et le Stavacintāmaṇi de Bhaṭṭanārāyaṇa: texte traduit et commentṛ, by L. Silburn' [review] *Indo-Iranian Journal* 9: 211-218, 1966, p.215. Monier-Williams, *Sanskrit English Dictionary*, p.1216.3, notes that the list can be considerably lengthened.

and the *yogī*. The *yogī* is essentially concerned with enjoyment whereas the guru has the qualities of both the *yogī* and the knowledgeable person. The initiation-by-penetration is entrusted either to the guru as such or to the *yogī* who is most practised with regard to enjoyments and the conviction they bring.[287]

Examination

I Penetration According to the *Gahvara*

śl. 239cd-240ab	Enunciation of the 6 forms	
	Examination:	
śl. 240cd-241ab	1. Mantra	a. From the *Gahvara*
śl. 241cd-247		b. From the *Dīkṣottara*
	2. Sound	
	3. *Bindu*	
	4. Śakti	
śl. 248	5. Cobra	a. In brief
śl. 249-252		b. In detail
śl. 253-254ab	6. Supreme	

The six methods and the nine methods of initiation-by-penetration relate to the various structures of reality Abhinava presented in the first half of the *Tantrāloka*. In particular, the set of six forms of penetration is associated by Jayaratha with the six pathways.[288] Most of the six and nine forms are self-explanatory

287. See *TĀ* 20.1-15.

288. The pathways are six in number. Three are based on the subtle breath: 1. phonemes (*varṇa*); 2. mantra; 3. pada; while three are based on space: 4. *kalā*; 5. categories (*tattva*); 6. worlds (*bhuvana*, *pura*). Each of these has a gross, subtle and supreme form. They can be set out as follows:

	penetration:	**pathway:**
240cd-241ab	1. By mantra	2. Mantra
241cd-242	1. By mantra	2. Mantra
243cd-244ab and Qt.247d.1	2. By sound (*nāda*)	1. Phonemes
244cd-245	3. By *bindu*	3. *Pada*
246-247l.	4. By śakti	6. Worlds
248+249-251	5. By cobra	4, 5. Categories and *kalā*;
252+254ab	6. By *para*	

Jayaratha does not make the same sort of comment regarding the nine forms of penetration given in śl.254cd-271.

on the basis of information given earlier in this monograph but several of them need further commentary.

The first of the six methods, 'by mantra', is related to the eight or twelve levels of sound as given in Appendix 3. The guru reflects how he himself is composed of all these levels and by yogic penetration communicates these to the disciple who is thus taken through all these levels and moves from the state of mere objectivity, caused by his attachment to some object, to the state of pure subjectivity.

The second of the six forms is penetration by sound for which Jayaratha's explanation is essential. The guru pronounces Mālinī or at least its abbreviation, *NA-PHA*, in a prolonged manner so as to arouse the 'sound' *Ḥ* in the disciple such that the sound which arises in him cleanses the pathway of the phonemes and penetrates through the disciple's mind.

The fourth method depends on *Ḥ* which is located in the triangle, at the very basis of the person, the generative organ. The guru somehow inhabits the disciple such that the coiled energy of this place, the dormant subtle-breath, moves upwards of its own volition, rising in a circular movement which encompasses every level and therefore every reality till it reaches the end-of-twelve, the full expansion of the disciple's awareness. Since the body of the disciple symbolises the whole universe, by circulating in every place of the body the energy, *Ḥ*, penetrates the whole universe.

The fifth form follows on smoothly from the fourth. The energy, the 'cobra' is described as moving from the generative organ to the space above the head. Abhinava goes on to describe this in more detail. He refers to sets of realities which he says come to a total of five but it is not clear how these five are composed and it is even less clear how, according to Qt.252d.1, there are five sets of five making a total of twenty-five. Whatever about the manner of counting, the groupings variously involve the whole of reality: the five *kalās*; the categories or rather spheres; [289] the auspicious lunar

289. As Jr.252d.1 points out, these 'categories' do not refer to the usual thirty-six categories separately considered, but rather to the grouping of the categories in four sets or spheres or 'eggs' (*aṇḍa*) for which see Appendix 1. The fifth 'category' is not a sphere but is Śiva himself who contains them all.

days[290]; the spaces within the body;[291] the *kula*-s;[292] the causal deities;[293] the faculties. The śakti penetrates though all of these, moving from the lowest abode of Brahmā to the highest abode of Brahmā[294] so that every circle is pierced and the disciple arrives at full consciousness.

Although the first five forms involve very little external activity- only the second form involves audible sound - the sixth form mentions no internal activity on the part of the guru but only presence, for in his presence all the activities of the mind and indeed the mind itself disappears. It is the supreme penetration since there is no dualism of any sort,not even the dualism of initiate and initiator.

---

290. Gnoli notes that nanda is the name of one of the five auspicious lunar days. Gnoli, *Luce*, p.709 footnote 161. He does not elaborate.
291. In 252d.1, Jayaratha mentions only four locations. On the presumption that there must be five locations, perhaps we are further to presume that space itself is a location. There are different combinations of five places for which see *TĀ* 19.15b, *TĀ* 30.58d-59a and *Tantrasāra* p.199 line 5.
292. A number of interpretations of the term *kula*-s can be given. In Jr.252d.1, Jayaratha glosses the term *kula*-s with the phrase *mahākaulakaulākulakulākula* which cannot, it seems, be divided except as *mahākaula, kaula, akula, kula, kula-akula*. This division involves double counting in that *kula* is first counted separately and then is counted as part of the pair *kula-akula*. The resulting set of five imitate Jr.223d.1 where Kuleśvara and Kuleśvarī are worshipped separately and then together. The *kaula*, on the basis of Jr.223d.1, would consist of the group of attendant deities and the *mahākaula* would refer to the whole range of deities or mantras etc. so that the phrase in question refers to the five levels of consciousness. A second line of interpretation is suggested by the phrase *kula-kaula-mahākaula-siddhakaula-ādi śāsanam* which is found in an alchemical text, *Rasārṇava* 1.4b, quoted in David G. White, *The Alchemical Body, Siddha Traditions in Medieval India*, Chicago, University of Chicago Press, 1996, p.421 footnote 77, and is understood to refer to various schools within the Kula tradition. Thirdly, in the Buddhist Tantras generally five *kulas* or families are referred to, namely Naṭī, Rajakī, Ḍombī, Caṇḍalī and Brāhmaṇī. Bagchi, *Kaulajñānanirṇaya*, p.66.
293. The six causal deities may be listed as Brahmā, Viṣṇu, Rudra, Īśvara, Sadāśiva and Anāśriśiva although the nomenclature varies. In Jr.252d.1, Jayaratha excludes Anāśriśiva from the list but without indicating a replacement.
294. The two types of Brahmā are earth (*pṛthivī*) and Śiva.

II Penetration According to Some Gurus

śl. 254cd-255ab Enunciation of the 9 forms
śl. 255cd-271 Examination:

1. Mantra
2. Śakti
3. World
4. Form
5. Discriminating knowledge
6. Mass
7. Place
8. Channel
9. Supreme

In the first of the nine forms the guru places the disciple in a mantra which surrounds him as a foetus is surrounded by the womb. The flames release him from the stains or knots and from the karma that hinders him and out of this triangle the disciple is reborn. Although most of the methods of penetration are interior, it seems that menstrual blood is fittingly used here.

In the second form, the guru imaginatively concentrates himself as a small ball and by yogic penetration enters the disciple at the very basis of the disciple's being. With all his faculties raised to the highest level of consciousness compatible with some diversity, namely at the level of *śakti*, *vyāpinī* and *samanā* which constitute the śakti spike, the guru moves around the disciple and brings him to conviction.

In the fourth penetration, the guru imagines some form, for example the image of a deity, emerging from his forehead where all exists in a concealed state[295] and refashions the disciple according to that image. The disciple in turn sees himself as refashioned in that image and becomes the deity itself with all the enjoyments the deity possesses.

According to the sixth form, the disciple has three sorts of body or mass (*piṇḍa*): the gross body of flesh and bones; the subtle body

---

295. *TĀ* 4.196.

which consists of the faculties, and the supreme body which consists of the *kalā* such as time, necessity etc.[296] The invisible is made manifest in the visible so that by a reverse process the gross is reabsorbed into the subtle and the subtle into the supreme.[297]

The eighth form relies on the many channels of the body which fan out from the *īḍā*, *piñgalā* and *suṣumṇā*. The guru, by yogic projection, moves along one or other of these channels, for example the eye, and then masters the channel, releasing it from illusion and bringing it to consciousness. For example, the master's glance is initiatory.

III Supreme Penetration in the *Vīrāvalibhairava*

śl. 272ab	Enunciation
	Examination
śl. 272cd-273ab	i. The guru
śl. 273cd-274ab	ii. How penetrate the disciple
śl. 274cd-275	iii. The result: disciple is one with centre

In *TĀ* 16.23cd-26ab, the guru, in preparing himself for the initiation

296. This list of three differs from the trio given in *Paramārthasāra śl.*24 which consists of stain, *māyā* etc. and body. In Jr.271d.1, Jayaratha notes that the *kalā* of *śl.*265a are categories 26-31, the coverings (*kañcuka*).

297. *Śl.*265cd reads : 'The self [which is seen] in the reflection is [in fact] invisible. But it is thought to be visible when it is [seen] in the mirror etc.' A number of texts will help to elucidate this difficult line such as the long section *TĀ* 3.1-64 and also *TĀ* 13.182ab, *Parātriṃśikāvivaraṇa* p.234 lines 19-21, *Īśvarapratyabhijñāvimarśinī*, vol.3, p.174, *Paramārthasāra śl.*9. See also *Īśvarapratyabhijñākārikā* II.IV.19 quoted in Silburn, *Hymnes de Abhinavagupta*, p.35. On the basis of these texts it would seem that the quotation under discussion uses the analogy of a persons' reflection in the mirror in order to describe the subject, means and object of knowledge. The transcendent subject (*parā*) is supreme. The reflection is *aparā* and gross whereas the mirror, the means of knowledge (*parāparā*) is subtle. That is clear enough, but in *śl.*265cd Abhinava applies that same line to a different context, namely the three levels of the body explained as the coverings, the faculties and the flesh, so that Jayaratha has a point in stating, in Jr.271d.1, that the quote is out of context. Yet Abhinava is hardly making a mistake for every emanated category is a reflection of its emanator and can be reabsorbed into it. The line in question may be taken as the particular application of a general rule: just as *aparā* and *parāparā* are absorbed into *parā*, so too the gross is absorbed into the subtle and this into the supreme, the supreme being understood here as the five *kalā*. The final absorption into truly supreme Śiva is described in *śl.*271.

of a Son, contemplates the triple trident and goes out of himself from his right into the left of the divinity residing in that trident and leaves the divinity from its right and returns to himself through his left, etc., with the result that a single consciousness shines forth, a single throbbing (*aikyasphurattātma*). That text and the third and much fuller presentation of supreme penetration according to the *Vīrāvalibhairava* help explain the circumstances that surround the set of six and the set of nine forms of penetration.

Abhinava first describes the guru's preparation for the initiation in which he moves beyond the fluctuation of *prāṇa* and *apāna* and comes to a knowledge of the centre which governs all. In the process he comes to know all the lesser levels of reality through which he has passed, their deities and mantras.[298] The disciple then comes before him as a person might come before the deity or before the triple trident. The guru communicates to him his own being, as a father upon his death bed does to his son.[299] The guru communicates all his faculties, including the very highest, nothing less than his 'mouth' which is his śakti[300] so that the disciple becomes one with the centre the guru embodies. Since all has been totally communicated, the minds of the guru and disciple experience perfect fusion (*samarasī*)[301] at the highest level, at

298. This sort of experience is described in the Kula tradition of sacrifice connected with the five states, *śl.*221-223.

299. In her introduction to initiation-by-penetration, Silburn quotes from *Kauṣītaki-Upaniṣad* II.15 which describes the sacrificial ceremony during which the dying father identifies himself with his son by every part of his body: 'Or else [the father] can perform the transmission (with the son) sitting before him. He transmits to him, therefore: "I want to put my voice in you, says the father. - I receive your voice into myself, says the son, - I want to place my breath in you, says the father. - I receive your breath into myself, says the son" (Similarly for sight, hearing, taste, action, pleasure and suffering, procreation, conduct, intellect, and the son receives them ...).' Silburn, *La kuṇḍalinī*, pp.107-108. See also *TĀ* 28.296-298.

300. In a quotation from a lost version of the *Mālinīvijayottara-tantra*, see Gnoli, *Il commento*, p.115 footnote 347, Abhinava identifies the mouth of the guru with the 'circle of the śakti', viz. yoni, by which Śiva emits the world. '... [emission (*visargo*)] ... is said to be the mouth of the guru; it is called the 'circle of the śakti'.' *Parātriṃśikāvivaraṇa* p.248 lines 20-21.

301. Silburn commonly translates the term by 'of the same flavour throughout', as for example when salt flavours the whole dish or when the two beams of a balance have ceased their oscillation and have become still. Padoux translates this term by 'total fusion, common and / or shared enjoyment'. *Le coeur*, p.138 footnote 179. In *Vāc*, p.285, he uses the term 'perfect fusion'.

unmanā, supreme consciousness. This attainment of supreme consciousness is the true and ultimate initiation so that the disciple, like his guru, is liberated while living.

IV The Initiation to Śivahood of All Living Beings

śl. 276ab	Enunciation
śl. 276cd-277ab	Definition
śl. 277cd-278ab	Examination
	i In brief
śl. 278cd-281	ii In detail
	iii Result: all acquire Śivahood

The initiation just described emphasises the attainment of the highest level, consciousness. It is a feature, however, of *TĀ* 29 that the level of *cidānanda*, the bliss of consciousness, leads on to *jagadānanda*, universal bliss. Accordingly, Abhinava completes his description of initiation-by-penetration by presenting the procedure leading to the initiation of all living beings. It is the highest form of initiation and it grants the highest state of liberation which exceeds all that is available to the causal deities. These govern and enjoy the worlds within their purview but by definition are limited to the lower spheres, their authority is limited, their worlds divided. They rule their subjects but fail to grant them the fullness of Śivahood and so their governance is partial.[302]

After giving a brief summary of the method, Abhinava gives a more extended description and takes up the fives stages of the subtle breath. The externalisation occurs with the emission of *prāṇa* which is a darkening (*timira*), a fragmenting[303] of the natural splendour of infinite consciousness, a reduction of infinite subjectivity to the status of a limited self. After an involvement with all the levels of creation and with all the causal deities, the practitioner

302. Padoux, *Vāc*, p.103.

303. In *Paramārthasāra* śl.25, the term *timira* is given a technical meaning. 'As a result of the blindness (*timira*) of ignorance (*ajñāna*) he imagines himself to be a multiplicity of subjects and objects whereas he is unique and identical with himself'. See also Silburn, *Le Paramārthasāra*, p.71 footnote 2.

harmonises both *prāṇa* and *apāna* and so becomes attentive to the more interior forms of subtle-breath. All differentiation disappears and he comes to know the supreme, self-evident consciousness, pure subjectivity. Since however he has been involved with every living creature and is identified with them, these too acquire the state of Śiva. He is present among all creatures but motionless (*niḥspandaḥ*), untroubled by the movements of *prāṇa* and *apāna*. He enjoys all things but is unwavering in his self-awareness which is an infinite vibration (*spanda*). It is the highest state, that of being liberated while alive, a fitting conclusion, indeed the climax of the rituals of *TĀ* 29.

(ḳ) Rites to Conclude the Initiation

śl. 282-283	The First Ritual : with Masters and Adepts - oblation
	The Second Ritual : with all the heroes - wine
śl. 284-285ab	Enunciation
	Examination
śl. 285cd-287ab	1. The ritual
	a. Guru and initiate partake
śl. 287cd-289ab	b. All the heroes partake
śl. 289cd-290	2. Notes:
	a. Exclusion text
śl. 291	b. Timing of the Second Ritual

In *TĀ* 29, the rituals for the initiate take place in the privacy of the home, the rites of initiation occur in the presence of the guru while the consecration seems to occur in the gathering of the *yogīs*. It is not clear to what extent the Masters, the Adepts and the ordinary initiates have been present at the initiation-by-penetration but they are much involved in the concluding ceremonies. Only a couple of points require further comment.

Initiation-by-penetration is undertaken for the sake of immediate enjoyments. It may happen that the initiate and even the others present during the ritual have become caught up in the passing world of objectivity, of increase and decrease, of mere passing enjoyment expressed by the terms 'defective or excessive' (*ūna-adhika*). They may not have fully acquired the ability to retain the sense of liberation while enjoying what is limited. By receiving the 'oblation' the participants regain awareness consciousness. Sin (*pātaka*) consists not in what others call sin[304] but in being ignorant of consciousness so that to eat the forbidden 'oblation' does not cause sin but instead frees one from sin.

The sacrifices listed in the *Tantrasāra* include a seventh sacrifice. *Tantrasāra* p.207 line 5 states: 'The seventh Kula sacrifice, the best of all, is celebrated with respect to the guru's body.' Likewise, the list of supports given in the *Tantroccaya* mentions 'the body of the guru'. Neither the *Tantrasāra* nor the *Tantroccaya*, in the sections involved with the Kula ritual, say more on this matter. What is the status of the second ritual which is a 'sacrifice to be celebrated in honour of the guru'? In answer to this question two texts need to be considered. Firstly, in *TĀ* 23.24, Abhinava states that a remuneration (*dakṣiṇā*) must be given to the guru after the ceremony of consecration. The act of remuneration is called an 'ancillary aspect of the sacrifice' (*yāga-aṅgatvam*) and should not be confused with the occasional rite called *gurupūjanam*, a point implied in *Tantrasāra* p.191 lines 5-6. The second text is *TĀ* 28.423cd ff. It describes the *gurupūjanam* or *gurupūjāvidhiḥ*, the ritual of worship of the guru, which should take place the day after the initiation or consecration or an occasional rite. Here the disciple offers the remuneration (*dakṣiṇā*) that forms an integral part of the worship of the guru and which should please him personally (*tattuṣṭaye tvidam*, *śl*.431d). On the basis of those two texts it appears that there are two forms of remuneration: on the one hand the ancillary aspect of sacrifice which forms part of a ritual such as initiation andon the other the gift for personal pleasure which forms part of guru worship. This is borne out by Jr.285b.1 where Jayaratha states that *śl*.284-285ab is the ancillary aspect (*aṅgatvam*) and is not the gift given for personal pleasure (*na-tu tat-tuṣṭi-kāritvam*).

---

304. According to the *Smṛti* there are five great sins: murder of a Brāhmaṇa, drinking of alcohol, theft, committing adultery with the wife of one's guru and association with those who have committed such offences. Banerji, *Tantra in Bengal*, p.171.

Therefore the second concluding ritual, even though it may be a sort of seventh Kula sacrifice, is an ancillary aspect of sacrifice in keeping with *TĀ* 23.24.

śl. 292ab Summation of the Whole Chapter.

Finally, Abhinavagupta concludes the chapter of the secret ritual by noting that it is not described on the basis of eliminate hearsay but is given on the basis of his own experience.[305] He knows what he says.

305. Similar sorts of phrases are found in TĀ 7.71, Īśvarapraty-abhijñāvimarśinī, vol.2, p.310 and p.317. Since Abhinava-gupta was initiated by Śambhunātha into the Kula ritual it may be assumed he knew the ritual from experience.

PART II

The Translation of the *Tantrāloka* 29 and Jayaratha's Investigation

Heading

Here begins the Twenty-Ninth Chapter of the *Tantrāloka* composed by the illustrious worshipper of Mahāmaheśvara, the Master Abhinavagupta, [and] presented through a sub-commentary called 'investigation' written by the illustrious Jayaratha.

Blessing

Jr.0.1 Let the time of blessing, whose course is ever immeasurable, bring forth blessings. Even though [the time of blessing] is present in the non-Kula [ritual], it rushes suddenly [and] vigorously towards the Kula [ritual].

GENERAL TOPIC: The Secret Ceremony

Jr.0.2 At this point he states, with the second half [of the *śloka*], his agreement to expound the ritual of the secret 'study'.

> *Next, the secret ritual, which is intended for those who are suitably qualified, will be described in the [following verses].* ||1ab||

Jr.1b.1 [The word] 'secret' refers to the Kula ritual procedure. 'Ritual': sacrifice.

SUB-TOPIC 1 The Category 'qualified'

Jr.1b.2 He explicates that [half *śloka*] :

> *Next, the whole of the preceding service is described according to the Kula ritual procedur* ||1|| *which, as such, is suited to the most advanced gurus and disciples.*

Jr.2b.1 'Service ... according to the Kula ritual procedure': the Kula sacrifice. '[Which] as such [is suited] to the most advanced.......': according to this phrase [the Kula ritual procedure] is set forth with respect to those who are advanced in the sense that they dwell in a state of undifferentiated thought held at the supreme level; the category 'qualified' is also being defined. And in order to draw attention to the gloss he had promised on the *sūtra*, the word 'next is used in that [line].

PART I: THE RITUALS FOR THE INITIATED

SUB-TOPIC 2 The Kula Lineage of the Perfected Beings and their Wives

Introduction

A. 1. Definition of the Kula Sacrifice

śl. 2cd-3 **a. Essence of the Kula Ritual**

Jr.2b.2 What exactly differentiates Kula ritual procedure from other ritual procedures? It follows [from the answer to this question] that the category 'qualified' for such [a ritual] will further be described. To this question he says :

> *And the essence [of the Kula ritual procedure] is said by Parameśa to be [found] in the worship of the lineage [of the Perfected Beings].*[1] ||2||

Jr.2d.1 Therefore he says:

> *Thus, what results in a month with a single [mantra] given in the lineage of the Perfected Beings is not [achieved] over thousands of years with different torrents of mantras* ||3||

Jr.3d.1 'In the lineage of the Perfected Beings': in the lineage, i.e. in the Kula ritual procedure which derives from the tradition of the Perfected Beings, i.e. of the illustrious Khagendranātha and the others who have descended successively from the Golden Age

1. Gnoli, *Luce*, p.680, translates the phrase *krama-pūjane* as the name of a text as does Rastogi in his *Introduction*, p.256. However, no such text is listed in Teun Goudriaan and Sanjukta Gupta, *Hindu tantric and śakta literature*, Otto Harrassowitz, Wiesbaden, 1981, (A history of Indian literature vol.II - fasc.2) ix+245 p., or Dyczkowski, *The canon*. Jr.3d.1 would suggest that it is to be taken in the sense of 'the worship of the series' of the Perfected Beings and their wives, which is the subject matter of Sub-topic 2.

etc. 'Different': which have arisen in various other ritual procedures. Therefore it is said:

> Qt.3d.1 "The mantras mentioned in the tantras of the Siddhānta etc. are all impotent since they all lack the splendour of Śakti. The great mantras of the Kaula tradition, by contrast, are splendid with innate fire; they shine with a divine splendour, immediately causing conviction."

śl. 4b. **Definition of the *Kula***

Jr.3d.2 He now explains the word '*kula*' used in the [phrase] 'according to Kula ritual procedure' [which was mentioned] above.

> *And the kula is the śakti of Parameśa, his capacity, eminence, freedom, vitality and potency, mass, consciousness*[2] *and body.* ||4||

Jr.4d.1 'Capacity': the function of dissolving and arising. 'Eminence': superiority, through being the cause of all things. 'Freedom': consisting of universal agency etc. 'Mass': since all things are perfectly fused within the [*kula*]. 'Consciousness': the self. Therefore it is said :

> Qt.4d.1 "*Kula* is the supreme śakti ..."

> Qt.4d.2 "Dissolving and arising constitute the nature of consciousness. Therefore *kula* is said to be the [dissolving and arising]."

> Qt.4d.3 "*Kula*, the unsullied consciousness within the self-existent, is the universal cause."

> Qt.4d.4 "The sovereign maker of all in a subtle way: such is *kula*, O Varavarṇinī."

---

2. In *TĀ* 29.128b, Abhinava states '... [the fluid] is a most pure substance because of its proximity to consciousness' while Jayaratha, in Jr.129b.2, explains that the substance is the kuṇḍagolaka. In other words, the term 'body' in *TĀ* 29.4d can also mean the sexual fluid.

Qt.4d.5 "But *kula* is the ruler of all, O Goddess, is all, abiding in all. Its splendour is utterly terrible ..."

Qt.4d.6 "Potency is present in the internal faculties of the śakti. Acknowledge it as the *kula* which is everywhere present."

Qt.4d.7 "*Kula* is the supreme bliss ...."

Qt.4d.8 "*Kula* is the nature of the self ...."

Qt.4d.9 "*Kula* is called 'body' ...."

śl. 5 **c. Definition of the Sacrifice**

i. As Knowledge

Jr.4d.2 Having explained the word '*kula*' in this way, and wishing to explain the word 'sacrifice' which is implied in the words 'ritual', 'service' etc., he says:

> *As a result of seeing all things from that point of view the sacrifice of the person whose multitude of doubts has been destroyed is truly of that kind [viz.is a Kula sacrifice].* ||5||

Jr.5d.1 'From that point of view': in terms of the outflow from the pulsation of Śiva and śakti.

śl. 6 **ii. As Action**

Jr.5d.2 What significance is given to the phrase 'As a result of seeing things in that way his sacrifice is truly of that kind'? To this question he says:

> *Whatever a hero performs with mind, word and body in order to evoke such a frame [of mind] is said to be the Kula sacrifice.* ||6||

2. Examination of the Kula Sacrifice

śl. 7 **a. The Six Supports**

Jr.6d.1 And what is the support of the sacrifice which has been accurately described in that way? To this question he says:

> *[The sacrifice is based] on external reality, on the śakti and on the pair; on the body, on the artery of the subtle-breath, on the mind. The Kula sacrifice is of those six kinds. The divisions [of the sacrifice] have further sub-divisions.* ||7||

Jr.7d.1 'On the pair': 'on the intercourse' which is raised to the level of the Primordial Sacrifice. 'On the artery of the subtle-breath': 'on the central channel'. 'On the mind: 'on the intellect', i.e. what occurs [in the intellect] by means of various apprehensions. 'These divisions have further subdivisions': for example, earth, cloth etc. are sub-divisions just of 'external reality'.

śl. 8 b. Rejection of the Supports of Tantra

Jr.7d.2 The different supports [listed] in this way constitute the actual procedure to be followed. Is anything in this [procedure] distinguishable from Tantric ritual procedure or not? To this question he says:

> *The bath, the* maṇḍala, *the fire-pit etc., the six installations etc.*[3] *are of no use in this [Kula ritual procedure]. On the other hand, if [the tantric ritual is] performed, it does not invalidate [the Kula ritual].* ||8||

Jr.8d.1 Therefore it means he may perform that [tantric ritual] if he wishes. As has been said:

> Qt.8d.1 "The maṇḍala, the fire-pit, etc. are of no use at all in this [initiation]; neither are the installation etc. and the bath etc. which precedes [the installation]. [He may perform the ritual] as he wishes."[4]

---

3. The six installations etc. are described in detail at *TĀ* 15.239cd-258, following the base text, *Mālinīvijayottaratantra* 3.35.
4. This exact quote of *Mālinīvijayottaratantra* 11.2 has already been quoted by Jayaratha in his investigation of *TĀ* 2.41. The phrase 'in this' (*asyām*) refers to the initiation mentioned in *Mālinīvijayottaratantra* 11.1b.

śl. 9 Transition: The *Kaula* as the Basis of All

Jr.8d.2 What is the reason for the unsuitability of the external bath etc. [as mentioned] in [*śloka* 8]? To this question he says:

> *The* kaula *which is without the six* maṇḍalas,[5] *which is beyond every delimitation, consists of knowledge and the object of knowledge, as has been mentioned above in the teaching found in the* Traiśirasa. ||9||

Jr.9d.1 Knowledge, according to the Kula tradition, consists of the perfect fusion of Śiva and śakti. Being without the six *maṇḍala*-

> Qt.9d. 1 "Supremacy over the six circles is attributed to the Lord in the teaching of the *Traiśirasa*."

Jr.9d. 2 Which are listed in the text starting with that [quote], i.e. being without the circles [mentioned] in that [quotation, viz. Qt.9d.1], [that knowledge] is unmanifest, is therefore beyond every delimitation. It follows that knowledge, when it is outwardly directed, is perception in the sense of 'means of understanding'. The object of knowledge is the object of perception such as 'blue', 'pleasant' etc. [The *kaula*] consist of these. The whole world, i.e. the subject and the object of perception etc., is simply the essence of the pulsation of [Śiva and śakti]. But there is nothing apart from [the subject and the object of perception]. Therefore it is said:

> Qt.9d.2 "O Beloved, if there are no subjects of perception how can there be objects of perception? However, the subject and the object of perception are one. Reality, therefore, is not unclean."[6]

---

5. The Krama teaches that there are three goddesses, Parā, Parāparā, and Aparā who function in four phases. This allows a variety of arithmetical combinations. In *TĀ* 1.110-112ab, Abhinava notes some of them. *TĀ* 1.114bcd. reads: ... *traiśirase mate* | *ṣaḍ-cakra-īśvaratā nāthasya-uktā...* : In point of fact, *TĀ* 1.114, following on the *Traiśirasa* which Jayaratha quotes more fully, refers to six circles of 4, 6, 8, 12, 16 and 24 śaktis which are various categories of manifestations based on the one Lord. See Gnoli, *Luce*, p.82 footnote 58. In other words, Jayaratha interprets the phrase 'without the six *maṇḍalas*' as referring to the state of pure sujectivity beyond any manifestation.
6. In his investigation of *TĀ* 10.165-166, Jayaratha quotes Qt.9d.2. In Qt.153b.4, the word *śucis* is used as the name of fire, or rather of the knowing subject so that the

.śl. 10 B. 1. Definition of the Ingredients

Jr.9d.3 And so, given that all derives from the essence of consciousness alone, purity and impurity do not in fact exist. Such being implied, even the distinction [between the terms pure and impure] is not entertained in this [next *śloka*]. He says:

> *And in this sacrifice, the wise man should use the very ingredient which is forbidden in the series of scriptures. It is immersed in the nectar-of-the-left.* ||10||

Jr.10d.1 Therefore it is said:

> Qt.10d.1 "This lineage [of the Perfected Beings] is to be worshipped with ingredients that are both hated by people and forbidden according to the scriptures, that are both disgusting and despised."[7]

2. Examination:

śl. 11-13 a. Alcohol

Jr.10d.2 According to that [last *śloka*], the ingredient excluded by the scripture etc. is to be [used]. But what is the value of its being in contact with liquor? To this question he says:

> *And it is said in the illustrious* Brahmayāmala: *"Alcohol is the external essence of Śiva". Without alcohol] there is neither enjoyment nor liberation. It is made with flour, honey or treacle.* ||11||
> *It has a 'feminine', 'neuter' and 'masculine' form which gives a passing enjoyment. What comes from the grape, however, is splendour to a supreme degree, it is 'Bhairavic',*[8] *without the restriction [viz. of being 'feminine', 'neuter' or*

---

last phrase of the quotation could also be translated as: 'Reality is none other than the knowing subject'.

7. In his investigation glossing *TĀ* 4.246 - within the general context of a discussion on pure and impure - Jayaratha gives a similar quote. He then goes on to give another quote which is repeated as Qt.102d.7.

8. This could also be tranlsated 'pertains to Bhairava', 'is Bhairava', 'is fearsome'. In

> *'masculine'].* ||12|| *[Wine] is by nature the essence, it is pure, it is composed of splendour, bliss and consciousness. It is forever cherished by the gods*[9] *for which reason [the practitioner] should always drink it.* ||13||

Jr.13d.1 'The essence of Śiva': it is said in this regard:

> Qt.13d.1 "Alcohol is the supreme śakti; wine is said to be Bhairava. The self is turned into liquid form since Bhairava is great-hearted."

Jr.13d.2 'Without [alcohol] there is no external enjoy-ment and liberation'. Therefore it is said:

> Qt.13d.2 "Without it there is no liberation; without it [consciousness] does not have objective form;[10] without it there is no supernatural power, especially in the Bhairava tradition."

> Qt.13d.3 "Since, O Maheśvarī, [alcohol's] gift of enjoyment and liberation is smelt, heard, seen, drunk and touched ..."

Jr.13d.3 And [alcohol] is of two kinds: processed and natural. Of these, the processed is of three kinds: grain alcohol, mead and rum. However, the natural, the single produce of the grape, which is designated by the words 'Bhairavic' etc., surpasses [the other alcohols] to a supreme degree, which is the reason why he mentions [the alcohols which are made from] flour etc. In the case of the 'masculine', [for example], enjoyment is found in the 'feminine' and 'neuter', for which reason it is said: 'it gives a passing enjoyment'. 'Without restriction': the one form of the supreme

---

TĀ 37.42-44, Abhinava praises the wine of his native Kashmir as *mahābhairava*.

9. The phrase 'cherished by the gods' also means 'legitimate, or blood-related to god'. Minoru Hara, 'A note on the Sanskrit phrase devānāṃ priya', in *Indian Linguistics*, 30: 13-26, 1969, p.17.
10. The word *gatiḥ* has many meanings, one of which is defined as '... the cognition or the taking by the consciousness of the form of particular objects ...' V. Raghavan, *Abhinavagupta and his works*, Varanasi, Chaukhambha Orientalia, 1981, (Chaukhambha Oriental Research Studies no.20), p.57.

knowing subject is without the restriction of the respective forms: 'feminine', 'neuter' etc. Therefore it is said:

> Qt.13d.4 "Grain spirit, rum and mead are called processed alcohol which gives enjoyment to the Adept in terms of what is 'feminine', 'masculine' and 'neuter'."
>
> Qt.13d.5 "Wine from the grape, however, is natural, single. Its splendour is Bhairavic. Supreme Vibhu is neither 'feminine', 'neuter' nor 'masculine'."
>
> Qt.13d.6 "Rum, mead and grain alcohol: Ānandabhairava[11] [viz. wine] is above [them all]."
>
> Qt.13d.7 "The substance has four types which form a system proper to the four ages. Of the four liquors, bliss [viz. wine] is totally concerned with tranquillity."[12]

Jr.13d.4 Due to its supreme splendour alone, [wine] is by nature the 'mercurial' [13] essence, i.e. it has a greatness which is similar to ['mercury']. 'Pure': the [essence] is unmixed with any other accidental ingredient. If it were [mixed with any other ingredient], its effectiveness would be quite limited. For that reason it was said: 'It is composed of splendour, bliss and consciousness'. Therefore it is said:

> Qt.13d.8 "Just as Śiva-Bhairava is the leader among the circles of bhairavas; just as, in the gathering of the circle of goddesses, Kālāntakī [14] is supreme, so these two [viz.

11. In the *Dehasthadevatācakrastotra* 3d, Abhinava identifies Ānandabhairava with consciousness just as in *TĀ* 29.13b, Bhairava, wine and consciousness are equated.
12. The four ages (*yuga*) are the Kṛta, Tretā, Dvāpara and Kali. The three lesser alcohols are suited to lesser ages whereas bliss, wine, pertains to the world beyond time, to tranquillity.
13. Mercury is identified with the essence or sap or semen of Śiva and is united with mica which is identified with the sexual fluid of his consort. It gives the practitioner an immortal body and makes him liberated while living. Arion Rosu, '*Mantra* et *yantra* dans la médecine et l'alchimie indiennes', in *Journal Asiatique* 274: 206-268, 1986, pp.250-251.
14. Kālāntaka [*sic*] is synonymous with Kālasaṃkarṣiṇī. Gnoli, *Luce*, p.741.

wine-alcohol] are called leaders of all the finest essences. However, wine as Bhairavanātha is the finest essence, being 'mercurial'."

Jr.13d.5 'It is cherished by the gods': as has been said:

Qt.13d.9 "It is ever cherished by Bhairava and by the multitudinous group of mothers."

Jr.13d.6 'For which reason [the practitioner should always drink it]': because of that sort of greatness. But [he should] not [drink it] like a bonded animal, because of greed.
As it is said:

Qt.13d.10 "After neglecting to worship the god Bhairava, after failing to satiate the mantras, after drinking in the manner of watering a bonded animal, even the hero will go to hell."

Jr.13d.7 [The phrase] 'should drink' is a command. Therefore, not to drink would truly be a sin. As it is said:

Qt.13d.11 "A brahman who takes part in the Kula ceremony, or even a warrior, if he is not touched by liquor, should perform a rite of reparation."[15]

Qt.13d.12 "If [his] mouth is without the smell of wine and meat, he acquires the condition of a bonded animal. He should perform a rite of reparation."

Jr.13d.8 'Always': at the time of the [Kula] sacrifice. Otherwise, if he abstains from drinking wine even for a moment [viz. at the appropriate moment during the Kula sacrifice], sin would result. Accordingly:

15. The rite of reparation, one of the occasional rituals, is treated at length in *TĀ* 28.408-423ab.

> Qt.13d.13 "If he stops drinking liquor for one day or half a day or for a quarter [of a day] or just an [eighth of a day], the man should become a penitent."

Jr.13d.9 [That quote] is understood only with reference to the duration of the [Kula] sacrifice. By contrast [the statement]:

> Qt.13d.14 "The finest drink is on every occasion. The drink of average value is at the 'junctures'. The worst is only once a month. Beyond a month he becomes a 'bonded animal'."

Jr.13d.10 etc., is made with respect to misfortune.[16] However, as it is said:

> Qt.13d.15 "[The ceremony is performed] with sandalwood for brahmans and with saffron for warriors, liquid camphor for peasants, with spoiled liquor for slaves, O Beloved."

> Qt.13d.16 "[Alcohol is used] on the occasion of the initiation of a brahman, during battle in the case of a warrior, at the peasant's ritual of blessing the earth, at the funeral rite of a slave."

Jr.13d.11 etc.: - [this last quotation, Qt.13d.16, especially the phrase 'on the occasion of the initiation of a brahman'] refers to the uninitiated [brahman],[17] while in the earlier [quotation, viz. Qt.13d.15,] we made special reference [to the legitimacy of substitution] in the case of a person who is particularly faithful to the posthumous rite[18] of ceremonial libation. In any other respect the

16. Occasional rite no.11 concerns the time of misfortune (*vipat*).
17. '... the ritual sacrifice and initiation of Brahmans (*viprāṇāṃ*)' is mentioned as an occasion on which a Circle Sacrifice should be held. *TĀ* 28.77d-78.
18. The posthumous rite is occasional rite no.10 where according to *TĀ* 28.76cd-78 a Circle Sacrifice should be held. *TĀ* 25.3 notes that in the case of just one deceased person the posthumous rite should be celebrated on the third, fourth and tenth days of every month for the first year and every year after that. Libations and offerings of food are involved. Clearly, if this ceremony is to be performed in the case of several deceased persons, there must be some substitute for wine.

division into castes would be unjustified. 'On the occasion of the initiation': during the *sautrāmaṇi*[19] etc. Therefore it is said:

> Qt.13d.17 "Ever since and from the moment when [drink] was spoiled by the Master of the demons,[20] from that time on the separative designation of the castes was taught. The use of drink is admitted during the *sautrāmaṇi* sacrifice of the brahmans, during a great battle in the case of warriors, during farming in the case of the peasants, at great family celebrations and in the gathering of friends and at the conclusion of the cremation ground [ritual] in the case of slaves, on the occasion of a marriage, at the birth of a son. That limitation [on the use] of drink, O Lovely One, belongs to deluded people [such as those just mentioned]. Those, however, who have been initiated in the tradition of Śaṅkara[21] and in the tradition of the goddess, who obey the guru's command, who are hidden [from public scrutiny], engrossed in recitation and worship, skilled in knowledge and discriminating knowledge, whose attitude is true, not deriving from greed [for wine]: these twice-born bear no hostility to always [using drink], O Beloved."

Jr.13d.12 etc.-That is enough on that topic [viz. 'always']! Accordingly, more is indicated by this [text viz. śl.11-13]. Such [*evaṁ*] a range of ingredients which is excluded by the scriptures etc. does not bring about the sacrifice if it is prepared without wine. On the other hand, wine just by itself, even without such a range of ingredients, does [bring about the sacrifice]. For that reason it was said: 'He should use [the ingredient] immersed in nectar-of-the-left'. As the *āgama* [states]:

---

19. In *TĀ* 4.246ab, Abhinava notes that, according to the Veda, alcohol (surā), '... in the context of the *sautrāmaṇi*, is considered to be 'pure' for the celebrant but wrong for anyone else.'
20. The demon Master is identified as Śukra according to the familiar story in which the demons drink wine and kill Kaca the guru of the gods. Śukra thinks that wine is the cause of death and so curses it. Marglin, p.328 footnote 8. The wine, therefore, is the cause of deicide and its consumption assents to the greatest of sins.
21. In *TĀ* 4.366d, Abhinava locates the Kula tradition, the college or *māṭhikā* which derives from the daughter of Tryambaka, 'within the line of Śaṅkara'.

Qt.13d.18 "On one side [put] all the 'oblations', on the other just wine by itself. The [sacrifice] may be performed even without the 'oblation'. Without wine it is impossible."

Qt.13d.19 "Worship is celebrated every day without these ingredients. [If it is celebrated] without the one [item], i.e. without wine who is Lord, [the sacrifice] is thereby fruitless."

Qt.13d.20 "If there be no offering of incense, flowers etc., O Lovely Eyes, let him satiate the mantra with liquor ......"

Qt.13d.21 "O Goddess, what is the use of other combinations of ingredients suitable for sacrifice. They are not worth a sixteenth part of one [drop of] nectar-of-the-left."[22]

Qt.13d.22 "The vessel and the flower, the incense, the lamp and the ritual offering of food itself, any 'heroic' ingredients etc.: all is based on wine."

Qt.13d.23 "O Beloved, the person who desires the [divine] presence should always, in every way, worship the Lord of śaktis with his śaktis by means of just wine alone."

Qt.13d.24 "The *yoginīs* of him who worships the series of 'footprints'[23] without liquor sink down and devour blood and flesh."

Qt.13d.25 "Those who are without wine, O Goddess, are not finally[24] made perfect. According to the teaching of the *Thohakāsa* they are forever excluded from the *kula* of Svayaṁbhū."

---

22. The phrase 'They are not worth a sixteenth part' is a stereotyped expression. Teun Goudriaan and Sanjukta Gupta, *Hindu tantric and śakta literature*, p.30.

23. Presumably they are the traces of the Perfected Beings who have visited this world. Padoux, *Le coeur*, p.256 footnote 296. In a transferred sense the phrase *pūjayet-pādukā-kramam* could mean: 'whoever would worship the lineage of the Perfected Beings' or take part in the Kula ritual.

24. The word 'finally' could also be translated as: 'according to the [Kaula] Western Tradition'.

Jr.13d.13 In this [tradition] everyone's religious practice depends just on wine. In this matter we rely on the tradition of the *āgamas*. For that reason one should not look askance at us.

śl. 14-16 b. Triple Secret: 'Vessel', 'Sacred Place', 'Lamp'

Jr.13d.14 Even whilst [wine] is given preeminence in this way, with regard to lesser items something else too is mentioned in the scripture as having importance. He says:

> *And the matter has been defined by Parameśī in the illustrious* Kramarahasya. *The 'vessel', the sacred place of sacrifice, the 'lamp' are said to constitute the triple* ||14|| *secret in the Kula sacrifice. Of those, the 'vessel' derives from association with a śakti; and the sacred place is said to be the earth, the cloth and the skull*[25] *the one is placed over the other, in due order;* ||15|| *the 'lamps' are prepared from ghee: the cows that move upon the earth are said to be goddesses. The practitioner of the Kula, once he has understood such matters, should be diligent in [obtaining] this set of three.* ||16||

Jr.16d.1 'Of those': with reference to the three. 'Vessel': the particular[26] ingredient called 'sexual fluid'. 'From association with a śakti': as a result of what will be designated[27] by the term 'Primordial Sacrifice'. 'Skull': the head, one's own or someone else's. Therefore it is said.

> Qt.16d.1 "The head is acknowledged as the support of all the goddesses. Devīkoṭṭa is their abode. One should always worship there."

25. In Jr.27b.2, Jayaratha quotes the phrase 'the sacred place is said to be the earth, the cloth and the skull' in order to show that Sacrifice 1 exemplifies *śl.*15.
26. The word *viśeṣaḥ*, which is frequently used in the ordinary sense of 'particular', can also have the meaning of 'esoteric' and so contrasts with *sāmānya*, 'exoteric', 'basic'. Padoux, *Vāc*, p.55.
27. Sacrifice 3 is the Primordial Sacrifice. Sacrifice 4 is the Subsequent Sacrifice.

Jr.16d.2 'In due order, the one is placed over the other': the cloth ['rises'] from the ground, the skull ['rises'] from the [cloth]. 'Prepared from ghee': because of the preeminence [of ghee]. Therefore [the 'lamp'] may also be prepared from sesamum oil. As has been said:

> Qt.16d.2 "Let him prepare lamps [furnished] with red wicks, filled with ghee or sesamum oil."

Jr.16d.3 And the reason [given] in the [*śloka* 16a] for the clear preeminence [of ghee over sesamum oil] is that 'the cows that move upon the earth are said to be goddesses'. As has been said:

> Qt.16d.3 "In order to bring grace to the world, Brāhmī and the other goddesses move upon the earth using the form of cows. He should, therefore, procure the product of the [cow]."

Jr.16d.4 'Diligent': he should be unhesitating in collecting the [product]. There must be absolutely no doubt.

śl. 17 **c. Conclusion: The Absence of Doubt**

Jr.16d.5 In our teaching the 'vessel' [viz. the sexual fluid] enjoys preeminence [viz. with respect to the other two, namely the sacred place and the 'lamp']. Parameśvara taught that other ingredients [viz. the 'lamp'] also are quite suitable for [being combined with] the ['vessel']. One should not, therefore, entertain doubts regarding the ['vessel'] or regarding the [other ingredients]. It has often been said before that mere doubt is a serious fault. Accordingly he says:

> *Therefore, having understood the supremacy of the 'vessel', he is unhesitating with regard to the ingredients which have been named here [viz.* śl.*14] by Śambhu. In this matter hesitation is a defect.* ||17||

Jr.17d.1 'The ingredients': the five jewels etc. Therefore it is said:

> Qt.17d.1 "Male semen, male urine, and menstrual blood, faeces and phlegm; human flesh, beef, goat's flesh, fish,

fowl; onion and indeed garlic[28] : these are the beautiful set of twelve ingredients."

Jr.17d.2 'Here' refers to the statement [viz.in *śl.*14] about the ingredients.

The Opening Ritual

A. Preparation

śl. 18ab **1. He enters**

śl. 18cd-19 **2. He purifies himself with the Mantras**

Jr.17d.3 Having thus explained the setting for the Kula sacrifice, he begins to describe the procedure itself of the [Kula sacrifice].

> *After entering[29] the hall of sacrifice rich with perfume and incense, facing north-east he should, by means of Parā or Mālinī, upwards and downwards,[30]* ||18|| *perform the cleansing which consists of 'fire' and 'growth', 'burning' and 'cooling' respectively, in due order. Or else [he may do this], with the mantra Mātṛsadbhāva.* ||19||

Jr.19d.1 'After entering': after first making an act of worship just to the threshold.[31] 'Upwards': from the feet to the top of the head, in the direction of reabsorption. 'Downwards': from the head to the feet, in the direction of emanation. 'Burning' goes with 'fire', 'growth' goes with 'cooling', for which reason it is said: 'in due order'.

---

28. The use of onion and garlic is specifically forbidden in *Manusmṛti* 5.5.
29. *TĀ* 15 gives the tantric ritual procedure. Whereas the placing of the mantra occurs outside the hall of sacrifice, *TĀ* 15.115cd ff., the cleansing occurs within the hall, *TĀ* 15.232cd ff. In *TĀ* 29.18 they constitute one act and both take place within the hall.
30. *TĀ* 15.121-125ab gives the procedure in detail, from the tuft of hair to the feet, in the direction of emanation. See also *Tantrasāra* p.199.
31. *TĀ* 15.187ab states '... at the threshold he should worship Ananteśa and Ādhāraśakti.'

śl. 20ab **On Occasion he may Initiate**

śl. 20cd **3. He Purifies the Instruments**

Jr.19d.2 On the other hand, when an occasional ritual is [to be performed], there is a variation from the daily [worship]. He says.

> *If he wishes to perform an initiation,*[31b] *[the mantra] is then ritually installed on the pathway to be purified. Next, by means of śakti alone*[32] *he should bestow immortality on the articles to be purified.* ||20||

Jr.20d.1 'The pathway to be purified' is any one [of the pathways], starting with 'worlds' etc. 'Then': immediately after the purification of the body etc. 'To be purified': if the materials of the sacrifice, i.e. 'vessel', flower etc., are not purified, they are not suitable for the sacrifice. 'By means of a 'śakti' alone': not, by contrast, as before, through sprinkling a droplet from the vessel etc. [33]

śl. 21 **A Comment on the Three *Mantras***

Jr.20d.2 In [śl.18-19] three mantras are mentioned, but how are they applied? To this question he says:

> *[Mālinī] enclosed by Parā; or [Mālinī] enclosed even by Mātṛ[sadbhāva]; or Mālinī by itself: these are the [distributions of Mālinī] in all ritual actions.* ||21||

Jr.21d.1 In all ritual actions, Mālinī is distributed as follows: [Mālinī alone] is to be used for success; if the aim is for liberation, [Mālinī] is enclosed by Mātṛsadbhāva; if the aim is for both [success and liberation], [Mālinī] is enclosed by Parā. For these same purposes Parā and Mātṛsadbhāva can be used individually also. Therefore it is said:

31b. The tantric initiation has a shorted form which is described in *TĀ* 18 and which is reminiscent of *TĀ* 29.20ab.

32. Is the term *śakti* to be understood as *rudraśakti*?

33. Jayaratha is referring to *TĀ* 15.292b.

Qt.21d.1 "In all ritual actions, O Beloved, let him who knows the ceremonial use Mālinī in the centre enclosed by Parā or use Parā alone."

Jr.21d.2 In that quote, the author specifies Mātṛsadbhāva as well along with the word 'Parā' since [Mātṛsadbhāva] is a higher form of Parā.[34]

śl. 22ab **4. He Prepares the Vessel**

Jr.21d.3 [It is said that]

Qt.21d.2 "After making himself ready with whatever is pleasing and with whatever is gladdening, let him worship the god without ceasing" -

Jr.21d.4 —therefore [let him make himself ready] with any blissful range of ingredients. It is said everywhere that [any blissful range of ingredients] may be used as material for worship. But in this [ritual] why was mention made [viz. in *śl.* 10] of that which is disgusting [in comparison with the blissful range]? To this question he says:

Let him fill the vessel with ingredients which are
the fruit and the causes of joy.

Jr.22b.1 'Of joy' means 'of bliss'; 'with the causes' means 'with alcohol etc.'; and 'with the fruits' means 'with sexual fluid etc.'. Therefore it is said:

Qt.22b. 1"The [sacred oral tradition], whose essences, on the occasion of the Ceremony of the Cord, cause the finest bliss, is reflected upon and committed to memory. [Such is the practice] in the tradition [revealed] by Bhairava who cuts [the thread of] existence."

Jr.22b.2 'The', in the above quote, means 'the sacred oral tradition for filling the [vessel]'. Due to its secrecy and out of fear of break-

34. Jayaratha is commenting on Qt.21d.1 which is taken from *Mālinīvijayottaratantra* 11.7.

ing the rule we do not teach it here. The [manner of filling the vessel] is to be learned directly from the guru's 'mouth'. Therefore it is said:

> Qt.22b.2 "The 'oblation' and the sacred oral tradition, the discriminating knowledge and the mating and the ceremonial of worship are located in the 'mouth' of the yoginīs."[35]

B. Sacrifice

śl. 22cd **5. He becomes Bhairava**

> Qt.22b.3 "Whatever ceremonial of worship, whatever recitation he may perform with an undeified body—all of it will be fruitless."

Jr.22b.3 According to that statement, the sacrifice etc. which is performed with an undeified body will not produce fruit. For that reason the Adept should, at this point, contemplate in himself the state of Bhairava. He says;

> *At that point, through an identity with the mantra*
> *that has been mentioned, he should bring himself*
> *to the state of Bhairava.* ||22||

Jr.22d.1 [The mantras] that have been mentioned are Mātṛsadbhāva etc. On this matter he will say:

> Qt.22d.1 " 'I am not, nor am I another; I am only energies.' He should, at every instant, simply through recollection, maintain that attitude of mind."

35. On the understanding that the word 'oblation' (*carukaḥ*) can also refer to the ejaculated form (*abhyuditaṃ rūpam*) in *TĀ* 29.127d, these five elements are found in close association in *TĀ* 29.125cd-132 and investigation, in the rituals more particularly associated with the use of the sexual fluid. 'Oblation' is identified with 'ejaculated form' in *śl.* 128cd, and sexual fluid in Jr.128b.1. The sacred oral tradition associated with the 'mouth of the yoginī' is mentioned in śl.125ab. Discriminating knowledge is mentioned in *śl.* 129cd-130ab. The mating is referred to by the word 'union' in Jr.126b.3. The ceremonial of worship performed on the sexual organ is set out in śl.130cd-132.

Śl. 23 6. He Satiates the Self and the Goddesses

Jr.22d.2 And so, because of this sort of contemplation, [the goddesses draw close] to the body etc.: -

> Qt.22d.2 "The goddesses who have no physical form, turning to him who does have physical form, abide within the body. They play with diverse attitudes since they long for the finest ingredients."

Jr.22d.3 according to this statement, all the goddesses of the faculties etc., because of a lust for worship, draw close [to the body etc.]. So much for the [goddesses].

> Qt.22d.3 "If he does not satiate the mantra which has come to him, it will cut off half his body."

Jr.22d.4 according to this statement, satiation must necessarily be given. He says:

> *Consequently, he should satiate the self with its multitude [of goddesses] in the circle and sub-circle, externally by sprinkling drops upwards and downwards, and internally by drinking.*||23||[36]

Jr.23d.1 'Consequently': since he has brought himself to the state of Bhairava, in a causal sense. 'Upwards and downwards' means right and left as well. Therefore it is said:

> Qt.23d.1 "The droplets, therefore, O Beloved, are to be sprinkled upwards and horizontally."

Jr.23d.2 Therefore he should, externally in every direction with droplets and internally by means of drink, satiate the self followed by the varied circles of goddesses.

Śl. 24 7. He Externalises

Jr.23d.3 [Performed] in just this way, the Kula sacrifice is successfully completed. What else is left? To this question he says:

---

36. In Qt.109b.1, Jayaratha quotes this *śloka* with a slight change. Thus 'circle', 'sub-circles' and 'satiate' can also mean 'the sexual organ', 'the sexual zones' and 'sexual activity' but Abhinava intends that all faculties and centres be included.

In that way the stream of his rays [viz. of his faculties] is replete. Wishing, as a result of a surging drive towards activity, to see his self externally [replete], he should perform the ritual externally. ||24||

Jr.24d.1 In that way, i.e. by means of the process just mentioned,[37] the circle of goddesses, i.e. the goddesses of his faculties etc., is fully satisfied. He too is reposing simply in his own self. When the Adept.

> Qt.24d.1 "After entering the blissful temple of his own sacred place which, being like a she-ass or a mare, is contracting and expanding, he exults in his heart."

Jr.24d.2 —according to this roundabout manner of speaking, [when the Adept], the functioning of his senses being fully operative, wishing to see his self outwardly quite replete as well, focusses on the fact that consciousness, Parā herself, by a process of original and reflection, shines forth[38] with an external form also, then he should perform the rite externally. In that case too, the procedure of adoration is according to custom. As our original gurus etc. have said:

> Qt.24d.2 "O Lord, when the whole outer world consists of your directly perceptible being, what place is not a sacred region for the devotees, where would their mantra be without success?"

Sacrifice 1 External (*bahiḥ*)

śl. 25-27ab **1. The External Setting**

Jr.24d.3 And where is the [external setting]? To this question he says:

> *On a beautiful red cloth measuring twelve* (arka) *finger-widths, or two or three times larger; on a*

37. That is, *śl.*23.
38. The word *avabhāsa*, 'shines forth', refers to the second stage of the fourfold Krama process.

circle which is made with a lovely vermilion or which is indigo-coloured; ||25|| *in a 'skull' consisting of a coconut, i.e. in a receptacle filled with wine*[39]*; in other words on the assemblage, which moreover is placed on the maṇḍala : on such [an arrangement]* ||26|| *the wise man should perform the sacrifice. The [ritual] procedure on this [external setting] is described [as follows].*

Jr.27b.1 '*arka*' [viz. sun of twelve rays]: twelve. 'On a circle': on the ground. And it is said:

> Qt.27b.1 "Let him make a dot with indigo powder. Let him then trace a reddish circular line [around it] with vermilion. [Another] circular line should be done, either in the contrary direction or in white."[40]

Jr.27b.2 Thus, 'the sacred place which is said to be the earth, the cloth and the skull' is not only an assortment but also a combination, for which reason he says: 'In other words, on the assemblage'. Accordingly, the red cloth is [placed] on the surface of the ground and on top of it is [placed] the skull which is designated by the expression 'the sacred site of the body', or its equivalent: a Viśvamitra-bowl. 'On such [an arrangement]', simply means 'on the assemblage'; but what is [the meaning of the phrase] 'on the place where the *maṇḍala*' is [drawn]? The *maṇḍala* is the diagram drawn on the ground, and there, i.e. anywhere, as on a support, the red cloth is [placed] and of top of the [cloth] is [placed] the skull.

---

39. The term *madya* refers to any kind of strong liquor. Prakash, *Food and drinks*, p.299. However, in his investigation of *TĀ* 15.69b, Jayaratha explains that *madya* is made from grapes (*mṛdvīka*). *Tantrāloka* vol.6, p.2478 line15. Given the importance attached to 'the produce of the grape' in *śl.*12c, the word 'wine' will mostly be used.
40. The diagram seems to refer to the Krama cycle. For details on its symbolism see Sanderson, 'Maṇḍala', p.198 and 'Meaning', p.56.

2. The Ritual:

A. Reabsorption into the Centre:

śl. 27cd-29ab 1. Personages on the Square

Jr.27b.3 He describes that ritual procedure:

> *On the northern side, starting from the north-east corner and finishing at the north-west, he should honour Gaṇeśvara,*||27|| *Vaṭuka,*[41] *the three gurus, the Perfected Beings, the yoginīs and the sacred site. On the east side, starting from below Gaṇeśa,*||28|| *he should then honour the circle of the Perfected Beings at the four cardinal points, finishing at the spot below Gaṇeśa.*[42]

Jr.29b.1 'On the north [side]': by proceeding from 'Prajāpati'.[43] [He should honour] 'Gaṇeśvara': in order to ward off obstacles.[44] It is implied that [Gaṇeśvara] is with his favourite [consort].[45] Vaṭuka likewise. 'The three gurus': his guru, his grand-guru and great grand-guru.[46] 'The Perfected Beings': the eternal Perfected Beings etc. The *yoginīs*': the eternal *yoginīs* etc. 'The sacred site': Jālandhara,

---

41. Of the two, only Gaṇeśa is invoked at the beginning of the *Tantrāloka*, in *TĀ* 1.6. Jayaratha, in *Tantrāloka* vol.2, p.23 lines 7-9, corrects the omission and mentions both since he considers that a tantra must mention both. The protective deities are mentioned at the beginning of the Kula ritual, *TĀ* 29.27d-28a, and at its end, *śl.*288b.
42. The same arrangement is found in the *Netratantra*. Brunner, 'Un tantra du nord', p.154.
43. In the first instance the name Prajāpati refers to the creator. Daniélou, *Hindu polytheism* p.238. In a second sense it comes to mean one of the spirants, *Ś, Ṣ, S*. Padoux, *Vāc*, p.17. This is taken up by Abhinava who interprets *S* to mean the objective universe, *TĀ* 3.165cd, while *S*, in *SAUḤ* in its direction of reabsorption, refers to the categories which extend from earth to *māyā*. Therefore, in worshipping upon the cloth, the celebrant starts from the outermost layer, *S*, and moves through the three energies of knowledge, will and action symbolised by *AU*, to reach the centre, *Ḥ*.
44. *Parātriṃśikāvivaraṇa* p.277 lines 13-14 defines *vighna* as 'the stains of the waves of differentiation in a sea of limitation and fragmentation within the supreme self'.
45. The phrase *sa-vallabhaḥ* can mean 'with Vallabhā' or 'with his favourite [consort]'. In Bühneman, p.358, 'Vallabhā' is the personal name of the consort of Gaṇeśa but the term *savallabhaḥ* more probably means 'with his favourite [consort]' since, in Jr.29b.1, Vaṭuka is described as being 'likewise'.
46. Rastogi uses this nomenclature. Rastogi, p.96. Pandey uses the term 'great-grand-teacher'. *Īśvarapratyabhijñāvimarśinī*, vol.3, p.17.

from which the doctrine was propagated by the lineage of the [eternal] Perfected Beings and the [eternal] *yoginīs*. Therefore, on the outer square of the *maṇḍala*, at the north-east corner he should honour Gaṇeśa. Likewise [he should honour] Vaṭuka, the three gurus, the sacred site, the eternal Perfected Being and the eternal *yoginī* so that, going on down in a line to finish at the north-west corner, [he honours] the class of gurus divided three ways according to the divine stream, the stream of the Perfect Beings and the human stream. Therefore it is said:

> Qt.29b.1 "After worshipping Gaṇeśa at the door so as to remove obstacles, he should then, beginning with his own guru, worship the series of gurus."

Jr.29b.2 Similarly:

> Qt.29b.2 "[He should worship] Gaṇeśa, Vaṭuka, the Perfected Beings and the line of gurus."

Jr.29b.3 And the above [set of personages] is mentioned with regard to the Adept when he is facing east such that the [set of personages] is worshipped on his left. But when he is facing north, the [set of personages] is interpreted with respect just to his own self, such that [the set of personages] is worshipped only on his left. Furthermore, Gaṇeśa and Vaṭuka, who are at the door, are to be worshipped firstly in the outer square, at the corners proper to the [north-east and] north-west winds. That is understood from the context since [Gaṇeśa and Vaṭuka] should be at the right and left sides of the sacrifice. As the gurus [say]:

> Qt.29b.3 "On the outer [square] are Gaṇeśa and Vaṭuka, traditionally at both the right and the left-hand corners."

Jr.29b.4 Then, immediately after worshipping the [three] gurus, [he should,] commencing on the eastern side from the spot below Gaṇeśa who is at the north-east corner on the outer square; starting from the second square which is one space immediately next; moving by a circular movement from the east etc. to the place exactly below Gaṇeśa who is in the north; he should then, in the four directions, namely in the four squares adjacent to the [Gaṇeśa's] square, honour the set of the four Perfected Beings who descend successively from the Golden Age etc., i.e. he should worship in a way that will be described.[47]

> Qt.29b.4 "Then, beneath Gaṇeśa, he should sacrifice to the whole multitude of 'mantras'.[48] Then, at the same spot, he should worship the set of their wives'."

Insertion of the Kula Hierarchy

śl. 29cd-32ab **a. The 4 Perfected Beings and Wives**
śl. 32cd-34 **b. The 6 Qualified Gurus**

Jr.29b.5 For that reason he says:

> *Khagendra with Vijjāmbā, Vaktaṣṭi with Illāīambā,* (||29||) *Vimala with Ananta-mekhalāmbā are in front. Kūrma together with Maṅgalā the śakti, Jaitra with Illāīambā,* (||30||) *and Avijata with Ānandamekhalā are in the south. Meṣa with Kāmamaṅgalā, Vindhya with Kullāīambā* (||31||) *and Ajita with the ever youthful Mekhalā are further on. Macchanda and Kuṅkuṇāmbā [and] the group of the six who are qualified* (||32||) *are in the north. From the north-west to the north-east there is a second such series. The set of six are, in due order, Amara, Varadeva, Citra, Ali, Vindhya and Guḍikā.* ||33||[49]

Jr.33d.1 'In front': in the east. 'In the south': on the right. 'With the ever youthful Mekhalā': with Ajaramekhalā. 'Further on': on the

47. In *śl.*29cd ff.
48. The word 'mantra' can refer to the person who embodies it so that in this present context the mantras are the Perfected Beings, Khagendra and his sons.
49. Elements of *śl.*29-32 are found in *TĀ* 4.267ab where Abhinava starts his listing with Kūrma instead of Khagendra and finishes with Mīna instead of Macchanda. The names Mīnanātha and Matsyanātha are aliases of Macchandanātha. Gnoli, *Luce*, p.877 footnote 1. In his investigation of *TĀ* 4.266-267ab, Jayaratha squares that listing with *TĀ* 29.29-32.

west side. Thus the order is that there are, in three directions starting with the east, a Perfected Being, his wife and two sons. By contrast, there is that particular feature in the north, so that he says there is 'the group of the six', i.e. the group consisting of the six sons [of Macchanda] and their wives, with the result that there is a set of twelve. [The word] 'second' refers to a series of gurus. And thus it is pointed out that worship is to be performed in the four directions as well, in sequential fashion.

śl. 33 **i. Their śaktis**

Jr.33d.2 He then describes the set of twelve:

> *The six śaktis are Sillāī along with Eruṇā, and Kumārī and Bodhāī and Mahālacchī along with Aparamekhalā.* ||34||

Jr.34d.1 Eruṇā [third case ending] and Aparamekhalā [third case ending]': means 'along with' [Eruṇā and Aparamekhalā].

śl. 35 **ii. The Identifying Marks of the Lineages**

a. Definition

Jr.34d.2 He explains their qualification.

> *Those qualified [gurus] are to be worshipped to whom the multiple lineage belongs, a lineage which is unbroken, varied and which consists of disciples and granddisciples.* ||35||

śl. 36-39 **b. Examination**

Jr.35d.1 That variety of [lineage] is explained.

> *Those dynasties*[50] *terminate with the words 'ānanda', 'āvali', 'bodhi', 'prabhu', 'pāda',*[51] *and*

---

50. Earlier, in his investigation of *TĀ* 4.274d, Jayaratha had explained word 'dynasty' as 'schools of knowledge'.
51. *TĀ* 4.265ab states that the Śaivasiddhāntins bear the names 'Śiva' or 'śakti' which, Jayaratha explains, they acquire by the ritual of dropping the flower. Abhinava goes on to state that the followers of Kula are named 'differently' (*anyathā*) which Jayaratha explains by quoting a text which lists the same name-endings as in *TĀ* 29.36ab.

'yogi'.[52] *There is a set of six gestures. It starts respectively* ||36|| *from the thumb of the right hand and ends with the little finger [of the right hand] and the little finger of the left hand. The codes are: 'end-of-twelve', 'upper kuṇḍali', 'pertaining to bindu', 'heart', 'navel' and 'bulb'.* ||37|| *Śavara, Aḍabilla, Paṭṭilla, Karabilla, Ambi, Śarabilla; Aḍabī, Ḍombi, Dakṣiṇā, Billa, Kumbhārikā and what is called 'Akṣara';* ||38|| *Devikoṭṭa, Kulādri, Tripurī, what is called 'Kāma' and Aṭṭahāsa and Dakṣiṇapīṭha: that is the set of six hermitages,*[53] *begging-places*[54] *and sacred sites,*[55] *respectively.* ||39||[56]

Jr.39d.1 'Dynasties': streams of knowledge. '[The word] respectively' applies to the gestures and to the codes. The [word] *baindava* which derives from *'bindu'* is the place known as 'the eye-brow centre'. 'Śavara': what is known as 'Pulinda'. 'Ambi': Ambilla. 'Dakṣiṇā': Dakṣiṇāvarta. 'Kulādri': Kaulagiri. 'Tripurī': Tripurottara. 'Kāma': Kāmarūpa. Therefore it is said in the illustrious *Kulakriḍāvatāra* :

Qt.39d.1 "Their gestures and codes and begging-places and dynastics, their order of sacred sites and their very hermitages are apportioned by the father."

52. Gnoli, *Luce*, for reasons unexplained, alters the order of the dynasties, hermitages, begging-places and sacred sites both in his translation and in his Appendix X, p.879. Furthermore, he prefers Jayaratha's equivalents of the names of the hermitages etc.
53. In his investigation of *TĀ* 4.237c, Jayaratha glosses *ghara* as 'hermitage' or 'ashram' (*āśramasthānam*). In *Luce*, Gnoli translates it as 'place of ascesis'. The word 'house' may also be a possibility. Padoux, *Le coeur*, p.37 and von Stietencron, 'Bhairava', p.867 footnote 16.
54. In his investigation of *TĀ* 4.237c, Jayaratha glosses palli as 'begging-place' (*bhikṣāsthānam*). Padoux translates the word as 'village'. Padoux, *Le coeur*, p.37.
55. *TĀ* 4.267cd lists hermitages, begging-places and sacred sites in the same order and adds 'minor sacred site'.
56. In his investigation of *TĀ* 4.265-268ab, Jayaratha quotes *ślokas* 35-39 exactly, with the puzzling exception of *śl.* 38 into which he inserts some minor variations.

Jr.39d.2 Having said which, [the text continues]:

Qt.39d.2 "And a [dynasty which ends with] 'bodhi' belongs to the revered Amara and [one ending with] 'prabhu' relates to Varadevaka; Citra and [a dynasty ending with] 'pāda' are mentioned together; [one ending with] 'ānanda' is recognised as [belonging to] Ali, while the venerable Vindhya and [a dynasty ending with] 'yogī' go together; Guḍikā and [a dynasty with the suffix] 'āvali' go together."

Qt.39d.3 "Listen in detail to the six gestures starting from the thumb of the right hand and going as far as the little finger of the left hand. The thumb belongs to the first son while the index finger belongs to the second, the middle finger to the third and the ring finger to the fourth, the little finger belongs to the fifth and the [other] little finger to the sixth."

Qt.39d.4 "I will explain the codes as they apply to the Kula sacred textual tradition. 'Transcendent' is [code] for the first [son] while '*kuṇḍalī*' is [code] for the second. ['The *bindu*] in the eye-brow centre' is [code] for the third and 'union' refers to the fourth. 'Navel' is [code] for the fifth whilst 'the generative organ' refers to the sixth."

Qt.39d.5 "Listen to the series of hermitages and begging places of the six princes: Amara has Paṭṭilla [as his hermitage], Dakṣiṇāvarta as his begging-place. As regards Varadeva: [his hermit-age] is Karabilla; his begging-place is Kumbhārikā. And Citra has Ambilla itself [as his hermitage], Billa as his begging-place, O You whose waist is beautiful! In the case of Alinātha, [his hermitage] is called 'Pulinda', Aḍabī is called [his] begging-place. In the case of Vindhyanātha: [his hermitage] is Śarabilla and his begging-place is known 'Akṣara'. The hermitage of the revered Guḍikānātha is Aḍabilla, O Beloved, and Ḍombī is pointed out as his begging-place ..."

Qt.39d.6 "The wise man says: The house and Amara's place of supernatural power is in Tripurottara. O You whose hips are lovely, Kāmarū is [the sacred site] of Varadeva. Aṭṭahāsa is [the sacred site] of Citra and Devikoṭṭa is [the sacred site] of Ali and Dakṣiṇā itself is [the sacred site] of Vindhya, Guḍikā is associated with Kaulagir."

śl. 40 **iii. The Advantage of These Marks**

Jr.39d.3 What is the value of such a teaching concerning the dynasties etc.? To this question he says:

> *Being conversant with such signs, if he tours around the sacred sites in search of supernatural powers, he will quickly acquire what ever is to be obtained from the 'mouth of the* yoginī'. ||40||

Jr.40d.1 When the Adept knows the usage of such gestures etc., if he tours the sacred sites out of a desire for various supernatural powers, because he displays the various gestures etc., the *yoginīs*, having recognised their respective lineage, quickly grant every supernatural power. As has been said:

> Qt.40d.1 "The lineage a *nātha* belongs to: its gesture is said to be his. After he has extended his hand, after he has displayed [the gestures] connected with the word which is his title, the [*yoginīs*], by this procedure, recognise their own *kula* lineage. He who points upwards [for example] points to his particular [*kula*]. He who points to all [the signals] such as *kauṇḍiḷī* etc. [of the kula to which he belongs]: by this means [the *yoginīs*], who indeed recognise [their own lineage], recognise their own *kula* [member] as well."

śl. 41 **c. The 6 Non-qualified Gurus**

Jr.40d.2 Having thus explained the set of six princes who are qualified, he also explains the [set of six] who are not qualified.

> *Bhaṭṭa, Indra, Valkala, Ahīndra, Gajendra and Mahīdhara, having raised their seed, are separated from the rank of the six who are qualified.* ||41||

śl. 42 Difference of Qualified and Non-qualified

Jr.41d.1 Who is 'qualified'? To this question he says:

> *The one who is qualified: in his case there is a pouring of seed within the kula path. [In the case of those who are not qualified:] because there is no pouring [of seed] they are the aforementioned*[57] *who have raised their seed.* ||42||

Jr.42d.1 'The one who is qualified': in his case there is a pouring, i.e. a transference, of seed, i.e. of pulsation and of semen which is connected with mantra and *mudrā* [viz. copulation]. [This pouring takes place] 'within the *kula* path': i.e. within the primordial support, i.e. in the central channel etc. of the disciple and in the vagina of the śakti. The same [pouring] does not occur in the case of those [who are not qualified], for which reason the aforementioned who have raised their seed naturally repose in their own self alone.

śl. 43-45ab **d. The Bodiless Gurus**
End of the Kula Hierarchy

śl. 45cd-46ab **2. The Mantras in the Circle: Mālinī and Mātṛkā**
3. The Goddesses in the Triangle: Parā, Parāparā and Aparā

Jr.42d.2 It is said in the illustrious *Devīpañcaśatika* etc.:

> Qt.42d.1 "And Niṣkriyānandanātha, together with Jñānadīptī, is in first place. Both Vidyānanda and Raktā are second as you have declared. Śaktyānanda [and] Mahānandā are rightly worshipped in third place. Śivānanda and she who is known as Samayā are fourth."

Jr.42d.3 According to that teaching, other gurus too and their wives are mentioned. Why then are they not mentioned here as well? To

57. In *śl.*41.

this question he says:

> *Other gurus and their wives are cited in the illustrious* Kālīkula. *Having no bodies, they amuse themselves fearlessly with various bodies.* ||43|| *Since they have desired [the particular amusement]* (tathā) [58] *of enlightenment, the kaula shines forth in their offspring. Because they have taken on a form of that sort, guruhood is acknowledged in their case.* || 44|| [59] *These [gurus and their wives] are not to be worshipped especially, they are only to be called to mind. Next, between north-west and south-east, along with Mātṛkā* ||45|| *Mālinī is to be worshipped—in due order. Then, further in, the group of mantras*[60] *[is to be worshipped].*[61]

Jr.46b.1 These and other gurus with their wives who are cited in the scripture are bodiless in the sense that they do not possess their own body. For that reason they are without fear of being recognised by someone else. Because they desire the particular amusement of enlightenment by using the trick of 'entering into another's city',[62] they play with various female and male bodies, i.e. they experience the game of carnal pleasure. The effect is that, as a result of such mating, *kaula* knowledge shines forth in the offspring, i.e. in the foetus itself through the process of transferring

58. In Jr.46b.1, the word *tathā* is interpreted by Jayaratha as 'particular amusement'.
59. *Śloka* 43-44ab are quoted by Kṣemarāja in his *Spandasaṃdoha*. He states: '*The Khecarīs*, disembodied, wander in the sky. He who is conceived by the practice of sexual union presided over by (their) pure desire and within whom takes place the dawning of pure awakened knowledge is (an enlightened) being issued from the womb of a *yoginī*.' Dyczkowski, *The stanzas*, p.70.
60. The group of mantras are Parā, Parāparā and Aparā as Jayaratha explains in Jr.46b.2.
61. Though it seems awkward, Jayaratha makes the break correctly at this point. Abhinava has arrived at the moment of transition when the Trika, the three goddesses Parā, Parāparā and Aparā who are 'the group of mantras' (*śl*.46b) are transcended by Kuleśvarī and become her emanation.
62. The military reference is also a pun because *pura* can mean 'body'. The phrase *parapura-praveśa* reflects the phrases *para-kāya-praveśa* and *kaya-praveśa*,'... which are the art of entering another's body', Minoru Hara, 'La bhakti, p.212, and which are a yogic supernatural power.

[seed] or at the very moment of birth or at a later time. Consequently their guruhood is just of that kind. Such is the agreed teaching of the scriptures.

The [*kaula*] knowledge which is is seen by the favour of Svabhāva and Bhagavatī is received in embodied form, i.e. it is transmitted by the illustrious Rahasyarājikā Yoginīs to a pregnant woman in the same *kula* as themselves; is seen by them while still in the womb; is seen by other [*yoginīs*] when just born; is seen by others at the end of twenty-seven years.

Since the [bodiless gurus and their wives] have no physical form, they are only to be called to mind. They are not to be worshipped in particular: there is no command from our ancient gurus to do so. Or else they are to be identified by [the terms] 'viśva', 'yoni' etc. As is said by that same text:

> Qt.46b.1 "The set of five gurus mentioned above finishes with the words: -viśvam, -jagad and -bhavam and -prajāpatikulam and -yoni. The śaktis are called 'Vīryam', 'Kṣobha', 'Bījam', 'Sṛṣṭi', 'Sarga'.[63] [The stages are] 'beyond-energy', 'śakti', [their] 'enduring union', 'surge' and 'emanation'. All these śaktis, in keeping with the pulsations of their own gurus, seize any external body anywhere. In no way does it happen automatically. [It happens] by virtue of their will alone. When they sit in pairs, so it is said, then, as they delight in their play, knowledge at the highest level truly results."

Jr.46b.2 'Next': [moving inwards] from the second square. 'Between': in the space. 'In due order': starting from the north-west corner and going as far as the south-east corner, so that Mātṛkā is to be worshipped with an ascending sequence [of phonemes] while Mālinī [is to be worshipped] from the south-east to the north-west with a descending sequence [of phonemes]. 'Then': immediately after the worship of Mātṛkā and Mālinī. 'Further in': at the centre

63. These various names or suffixes imitate Qt.42d.1 and are given in the masculine, feminine or neuter genders since the *khecarī* divinities do not have male and female bodies but only play with them.

point of sacrifice in the pericarp of the lotus[64] within the triangle. There, at the front, right and left corners [of the triangle] are the three goddesses Parā etc. together with their bhairavas and, at the centre, Kuleśvara. As he will say:

> Qt.46b.2 "Having worshipped the couple, Kuleśa [and Kuleśī], in the central path, the goddesses on the three beams of light ..."

śl. 46cd-48 **4. Kuleśvarī in the Centre**

Jr.46b.3 And even as he explains the significance [of Kuleśvarī] in relation to [the goddesses etc.], he describes [her] role in the worship, given that Kuleśvarī has the primacy.[65]

> *She who dwells within the kula which consists of a circle, i.e. of the mantras, the Perfected Beings, the subtle-breath and the instrument of consciousness,* ||46|| *she who is consciousness, she who has been called Prabhvī: she, in this context, is Kuleśvarī. She [dwells] at the centre as Śrī Parā, as Devī, as the form of Mātṛsadbhāva.* ||47|| *She is then to be worshipped as Aparā and Parāparā. Furthermore, [Kuleśvarī] is to be worshipped as a single heroine or rather with Kuleśvara.* ||48||

Jr.48d.1 She who dwells within the *kula* which consists of a circle comprising Parā etc., the mantras [viz. Mālinī, Mātṛkā], the Perfected Beings and comprising the subtle-breath and the instruments of intelligence [viz. of the practitioner], she who is Prabhvī because she is the sacred place of repose within the multitude of

64. The pericarp of the lotus is a symbol of the female sex-organ. Silburn, *Hymnes de Abhinavagupta*, p.93 footnote 1.

65. Jayaratha is considering a problem. The Perfected Beings and Mālinī, Mātṛkā, Parā etc. lead the worshipper to Kuleśvarī who rules all. What then is the value of the lineage into which the worshipper has been initiated? Should he simply not abandon its worship in favour of Kuleśvarī? The answer is that the goddess of his *kula* is to be worshipped in association with Kuleśvarī, since the lesser goddess is the legitimate expression of the greater. Jr.48d.1 will elaborate. The same situation is described in Jr.223d.1.

divinities to be worshipped and within the body of the worshipper, she who is truly nothing other than the complete throbbing, she who has been called consciousness: she alone, in this context, is to be designated by the name [Kuleśvarī] due to the fact that she is governor over the kula. 'Then': i.e. [she is to be worshipped as Aparā and Parāparā] individually. Therefore, the [goddess] who, during the [initiatory] practice of dropping the flower etc., is chosen for someone to venerate, should be worshipped by him in the same way [i.e. as forms of Kuleśvarī]. This is the meaning.

B. Emanation from the Centre:

śl. 49-50 **1. Śakti and Bhairava at the Centre**

Jr.48d.2 What difference is there in worship between the ritual of the single hero [Kuleśvara] and the ritual of the pair [viz. Kuleśvara and Kuleśvarī]? To this question he says:

> *The swollen śakti pours forth. Bhairava, for his part, is overjoyed. By reposing in the bliss of [their] union [the practitioner] fully worships such a couple. A stream of rays flows like sparks of fire from consciousness which has the form of a great splendour. He should worship that same [stream] within [consciousness] as a group of deities.* ||50||

Jr.50d.1 When śakti, facing Bhairava, pours forth and when Bhairava, for his part, faces śakti: at that point, [the practitioner] fully worships such a couple - ['such'] meaning that they are facing each other. [He does so] by reposing in the bliss, i.e. in the amazement at one's own self, which arises because of their union, i.e. their coming together.

> Qt.50d.1 "When he is brought to perfection by means of bliss alone, the state of brahman arises spontaneously."

Jr.50d.2 According to that statement, one should focus on the pair as the inner reality simply of one's own nature which is *parabrahman*, i.e. the single mass of consciousness and bliss. 'That same [stream]' is not, however, separate from [consciousness].

śl. 51 2. Deities in the Triangle: 12, 64, 4, etc.

Jr.50d.3 For that very reason he says:

> *Within [the triangle] the set of twelve is to be worshipped and then the set of sixty-four or the set of four or whatever one desires. What number do they assign to the rays [of light]?* ||51||

Jr.51d.1 'The set of twelve': the goddess of emanation etc. or [the set of twelve] which will be explained in the synoptic chapter.[66] 'Set of four': Siddhā etc. or Jayā etc.[67] 'Whatever is desired': in keeping with one's own religious practice.

sl. 52-54c 3. The 8 Goddesses and their Consorts on the Lotus Outside the Triangle

śl. 54d 4. The 'lamps' :
a. According to the 64 Masters

Jr.51d.2 It is said that the rays of light are endless. And this description of them is given in the scriptures in many ways. Therefore, given the fact that there is no limitation whatever [to the number of rays of light], the celebration of the [above-mentioned] religious practice should definitely not be performed because there is no mention of the totality [of the rays]. So what is the reason for that phrase which is without scriptural injunction: 'Within [the triangle] the set of twelve [goddesses] is to be worshipped' etc? Point

66. In Jr.51d.1, Jayaratha gives two interpretations of 'twelve'. First, he interprets it as the twelve stages of the Krama. Secondly he refers the reader to *TĀ* 33 which, in *TĀ* 33.1b, is called *ekī-kāra*, synoptic, and gives various lists of goddesses, of beams of light, of phonemes etc. In particular, *TĀ* 33.3ab-4ab lists twelve śaktis: the eight goddesses Māheśī etc. plus the consorts (*mātṛbhir*) of Agni, Nirṛti, Vāyu and Īśāna. This listing, which repeats some of the names given in *TĀ* 29.52, will help provoke the objection raised in Jr.51d.2.

67. Jayaratha identifies the 'four' of *TĀ* 29.51c as referring to the four goddesses of either the Dakṣiṇa or the Vāma schools. The four goddesses of the Dakṣiṇa school are Śuṣkā, Siddhā, Utpalā, Raktā / Caṇḍikā. The four goddesses of the Vāma school are Jayā, Vijayā, Jayantī and Aparājitā.

taken! But this is the opinion of other gurus. That is why the matter was presented in that way.[68] Consequently, it is just the two sets of eight,which he himself mentions, that are principally to be worshipped, in pairs. He says:

> *Māheśī, Vairiñcī, Kaumārī, Vaiṣṇavī are at the four cardinal points, while Aindrī, Yāmyā, Muṇḍā, Yogeśī are at the corners, starting from the north-east.* ||52|| *The set of eight [goddesses is each with a bhairava] starting with Aghora and finishing with Pavana.*[69] *Then, as regards this set of eight [couples], [each of them] is to be worshipped in turn in a paired state by contemp-lating the bliss of their union.* ||53|| *As regards the sixty-four [Masters] also, who are often listed in the ritual under various names, that same ritual procedure is enjoined [viz. of worshipping them in a paired state]. The row of 'lamps' should number [sixty-four].* ||54||

Jr.54d.1 'In turn': he should, outside the triangle, on a lotus of eight petals, on the east, south, west and north petals, worship the set of four [goddesses] starting with Māheśī, accompanied by Aghora etc.; and on the other [four petals] starting from the north-east and finishing at the south-east he should worship the set of four [goddesses] starting with Aindrī along with Bhīma etc. As has been said:

> Qt.54d.1 "In the east, south and following directions, there is the set of four [goddesses] starting with Māheśī. [The

68. That is, with the rhetorical question in *śl.*51d.
69. These are not listed in *Mālinīvijayottaratantra* 11 but *ibid.* 1.19cd-21ab lists the eight lords as Aghora, Paramaghora, Ghorarūpa, Ghorānana, Bhīma, Bhīṣaṇa, Vamana, Pivana [sic]. Gnoli, referring to *Mālinīvijayottaratantra* 11.15cd and agreeing with Jr.54d.1, notes that Aghora, Paramāghora, Ghorarūpa, Ghorānana are on the east, south, west and north petals while Bhīma, Bhīṣaṇa, Vamana, Pibana [*sic*] are on the north-east, north-west, south-west, south-east petals. Gnoli, *Luce*, p.834 footnote 11.

set of four goddesses] starting with Indrāṇī is located within the petals starting from the north-east and finishing at the south-east."

Qt.54d.2 "Then he should sacrifice to the set of eight heroes starting from the left according to the order indicated by the śaktis."

Jr.54d.2 On this matter:

Qt.54d.3 "On the sacred region which is divided into eight; in the middle, within a circle consisting of two portions, he should draw a triangle. After that, on one portion in the [remaining sacred region] which is divided on every side into three, [he should draw] an eight-petalled lotus. Then there is a space for one portion and four squares. Then the [remaining] portions extend[70] in a square, in the [four] directions, as far as the diagonals on both sides. Thus, the *maṇḍala*, in the Kula tradition, is square."

Jr.54d.3 Such is the overview of the *maṇḍala*. 'Often listed under various names': because of the endless number of Kula scriptures and because of the variety of their names. The [names] of the earlier Masters are not indicated by the order of worship at this point [viz. *śl.*54a] since traditionally, i.e. by established custom, no mention of their names is made by the [Kula scriptures]. But in order to demonstrate the unbroken succession, their names may be mentioned according to one's inclination. As has been stated in this same sense in another text:

Qt.54d.4 "The names of the set of fifty-six [Masters] which are taken, according to one's inclination, from other Kula scriptures..."

Jr.54d.4 And from the statement 'fifty-six' [viz. 8x7 Masters made] in that [quote] it is implied that the sixty-four [viz. 8x8 Masters

70. The word *bhāgāḥ*, 'portions', is masculine whereas *gāminyaḥ*, 'extend', is feminine. Nevertheless I have taken these as agreeing with each other.

referred to] in [*śloka* 54] are approved for worship. Thus there is no need to worship the set of eight [couples] by proceeding around the encircling [Masters] individually. If it were [were necessary to do so] there would be an inconsistency in the scripture. Enough on that subject! 'This same [ritual procedure]': [worshipping them in] the paired state. In this matter:

> Qt.54d.5 "When the group of mantra[-deities] has been invoked, satiation, arising out of the strength of [the practitioner's] faith and devotion, should be made with flowers, liquor and offerings of food and with incense. Satiation should be given to the radiant mantras of the śakti and of the Lord etc., first of all with [offerings of] liquor, meat and menstrual blood. Afterwards there should be a quantity of flowers, incense etc."

Jr.54d.5 Accordingly, in the Kula tradition, satiation must necessarily be done. And in that tradition the preeminence of the oblation of the 'lamp' alone [viz. as compared to flowers, incense etc.] is due to the fact that [the 'lamp'] is a substitute for human flesh. [71] Consequently, because there is an offering just of the ['lamp'], he first of all uses [the phrase] 'the row of 'lamps' should number [sixty-four]'. [The phrase] 'should number [sixty-four]' means that the line of succession of the sixty-four [Masters mentioned] in [*śl*.54a] is celebrated. And that [line of succession] is an aspect of [the ceremony of] consecration.[72]

śl. 55 **b. According to One's *Vidyā***

Jr.54d.6 He gives another procedure as regards the ['lamps'].

> *On the other hand, according to the illustrious* Ratnamālā-śāstra, *the 'lamps' should be as many as the phonemes. He who is very wise will calculate*

71. Sanderson translates the word *mahāpaśu* as 'human flesh'.Sanderson, 'Meaning',p.82.
72. In *śl*.228d-229a, the consecration of the Master involves 64 lamps.

the phonemes according to the vidyā *which is the principal object of worship.* || 55 ||[73]

Jr.55d.1 It is said in the [*Ratnamālā-śāstra*]:

Qt.55d.1 "Once the first watch of the night is over, the practitioner of mantra should set out the 'lamps', O You whose face is beautiful! He should place them down, equivalent to the number of the phonemes [in his *vidyā*], in the four directions, O You whose hips are lovely!"

Qt.55d.2 "I will now describe the supreme sacrifice [performed] with Mālinī."

Jr.55d.2 According to that statement, Mālinī is the principal object of worship. Therefore, the lamps are said to be fifty in number since the figure is derived from the phonemes of [Mālinī]. Consequently, the root *vidyā* [which was referred to] in [*śl.*55cd] is equivalent to the syllables [of Mālinī]. An equivalent number of 'lamps' should be set out. That is the correct meaning.

73. Jayaratha argues that the *vidyā* of *śl.*55d is Mālinī. However, it is not sure that Abhinava intends to be quite so specific.

SUB-TOPIC 3 The Ritual of Adoration
Sacrifice 2 Based on the Śakti.

śl. 56 Enunciation of the Sub-topic

Jr.55d.3 Having in this way explained the Kula procedure concerning the Perfected Beings and their wives ... Wishing to explain yet another text involving a sequence of modes of adoration, [a text] which corresponds to that [same Kula procedure concerning the Perfected Beings and their wives], he says:

> *Or else he may worship the kula by means of 'sacred sites', 'sacred region' etc., as declared by Parameśa in the illustrious* Mādhavakula. ||56||

Jr.56d.1 'In the illustrious *Mādhavakula*': in one section of the book [called] the illustrious *Tantrarājabhaṭṭāraka*. In the [*Tantrarājabhaṭṭāraka*] the sacred oral tradition of a number of gurus has been brought together by combining the substance of the illustrious *Devyāyāmala* and of the illustrious *Mādhavakula*. Consequently, the [ritual] called 'the sacred sites' etc. or the worship of the kula according to the Krama tradition is to be performed according to the following procedure as given in the *Mādhavakula*. Such is the implication [of the *śloka*].

śl. 57 Definition of the Sub-topic : The Four Stages of the Krama Cycle

Jr.56d.2 For that reason he says:

> *'Emanation', 'permanence', 'reabsorption' and 'the nameless'*[74] *constitute the set of four in the Krama [tradition]. He should worship [the set of four] in connection with 'sacred sites' and 'cremation ground' with a view to enjoyment and liberation.* ||57||

---

74. The term *anāma*, 'nameless', is synonymous with the Krama system. Gnoli, *Luce*, p.380 footnote 26. In Qt.57d.1, the more usual word *anākhyā*, 'the ineffable', is used.

Jr.57d.1 'With a view to enjoyment and liberation': indicates the reason for the [worship]. Therefore it is said in that text:

> Qt.57d.1"The process of emanation is first. Continuation is second. reabsorption is third. The ineffable is fourth."

Jr.57d.2 Having said which, [the text continues]:

> Qt.57d.2 "Born into the family of Kālī, he should definitely engage in contemplation."

> Qt.57d.3 "The sacred textual tradition [performed] according to the ritual of 'the sacred sites' is governed by Saṅkarṣaṇī. Without the ['sacred sites'] he will not become a Perfected Being. I will give you the teaching on this matter."

Jr.57d.3 According to the illustrious *Devyāyāmala* the three goddesses and the illustrious Saṅkarṣaṇī constitute the set of four.

Examinations:

A. Cycle I Object of Knowledge

śl. 58 **Definition of the Ritual**

Jr.57d.4 Regarding the ritual, he explains the location of the sacred sites within the body.

> *[This ritual] concerns one's self and the circle of the śakti [viz. Cakriṇī]. He should, by means of recollection, perform this ritual through installation upon the body which is called the 'sacred site'. [The ritual] which is called the 'sacred site' comes from Parameśvara.* ||58||

Jr.58d.1 'This': as is about to be described.

Examination

śl. 59-63 **1. Emanation**

a. 24 Sacred Sites Installed on One's Body

Jr.58d.2 He describes that [ritual]:

> *He should ritually install] Aṭṭahāsa on the tuft of hair and Caritra on the aperture of 'Ka'; Kaulagiri*

on the ears and Jayantikā on the nostrils;||59|| *Ujjayinī on the eye-brows, Prayāga on the mouth. Furthermore, [he should ritually install] Vārāṇasī on the heart, Śrīpīṭha on the two shoulders, Viraja on the throat;*||60|| *Eḍābhī on the stomach, Hālā on the navel and Gośruti on the 'bulb'.[He should install] Marukośa on the generative organ, Nagara, Pauṇḍravardhana,*||61|| *Elāpura and Purastīra on the right [and left] buttocks and thighs, Kuḍyākeśī and Sopāna, Māyāpū and Kṣīrakam* ||62|| *on the knees and calves while Āmrāta and Nṛpasadmanī are on the two ankles, but [he should install] Vairiñcī on the soles of the feet, she who supports the full extent of Kālāgni.* ||63||

Jr.63d.1 'Aṭṭahāsa': the previously mentioned phrase: 'he should recall ... by means of installation' is added. The same applies to the later [sacred sites] as well. 'On the tuft of hair': on the 'end-of-twelve', i.e. at the place where the energy of the subtle-breath reposes. 'On the mouth': on the face. 'Hālā': Alipura. As has been said:

> Qt.63d.1 "Alipura is in the region of the navel, above the 'bulb', O Parameśvarī".

Jr.63d.2 'Gośruti': Gokarṇa. 'On the buttocks and thighs', 'on the knees and calves' and 'on the two ankles': everywhere 'on the right' is used implies 'on either side'. Therefore, on the right buttock is Nagara; on the left [buttock] is Pauṇḍravardhana; on the right thigh, Elāpura; on the left [thigh], Purastīra; on the right knee, Kuḍyākeśī; on the left [knee], Sopāna; on the right calf, Māyāpurī; on the left [calf] Kṣīrakam; on the right ankle Āmrātakeśvara; on the left [ankle], Rājagṛha." Therefore it is said in that [text]:

> Qt.63d.2 "On the right buttock is Nagara, on the left, Pauṇḍravardhana, on the left thigh Purastīra, Elāpura on the right; Kuḍyākeśī is on the right knee and Sopāna is said to be on the other [knee]; Kṣīraka is on the left calf

and Vāmapurī on the right, Āmrātakeśvara is on the [right] ankle, on the left, Rājagṛha the beautiful."

Jr.63d.3 'Vairiñcī': Brahmāṇī. Śrīśaila is her sacred site. Therefore it is said in the illustrious *Kulakramodaya*:

Qt.63d. 3 "Brāhmī dwells on Śrīśaila."

Jr.63d.4 Having said which, [the text continues]:

Qt.63d. 4 "Brāhmī stands on the soles of [her] feet."

śl. 64 Note: i. 'I' am not

Jr.63d.5 One should not remain limited by the [sacred sites] existing in [one's body]. Rather, one should focus on the statement: 'I am the sacred site and its presiding śaktis'. As a result supernatural power will be given. He says:

> *'I am not, neither does another exist; I am only energies.' He should, in every circumstance, as a result simply of recollection, maintain that attitude of mind.* ||64||

Jr.64d.1 Therefore it is said in that [text]:

Qt.64d.1 " 'I am not, neither does another exist; energies alone exist'. If he meditates on that [thought], that place of repose, that true nature, even for a moment, then, having become a sky-traveller, he will enter the company of *yoginīs*."[75]

śl. 65 Note: ii. All is done by Recollection

Jr.64d.2 It said everywhere that supernatural power occurs by means of restraints such as those associated with place, time, vow etc. Therefore, how can [supernatural power] come about quite simply by focusing on that [thought]? To this question he says:

75. In *TĀ* 32.20cd-24ab, this quote is explained according to the practice of *khecarīmudrā* as given in the *Yogasaṃcāra*.

No lunar day nor asterism, no fasting is prescribed. He who is engrossed in every day life becomes a Perfected Being by means of continual recollection. ॥ 65॥

Jr.65d.1 'He who is engrossed in every day life': he who is involved in the activity of [every day life]. And this subject matter was mentioned in the very first chapter,[76] to which, therefore, reference should be made.

śl. 66 **b. The Śakti-circle of the 9 Wives**

Jr.65d.2 What exactly is the circle of the [śakti, viz. of Cakriṇī]? By performing its ritual installation as well, the intended ritual called 'the sacred sites' takes place. To this question he says:

The husbands are an outcaste, a kṛṣṇa, *a bowman, a butcher, a tanner, an eunuch, a bone-splitter, a fisherman, a potter: their wives are [involved] in the nine-fold sacrifice which is performed in nine ways.* ॥ 66 ॥

Jr.66d.1 A *kṛṣṇa* is a black, a washerman (*ḍomba*).[77] An eunuch is a liquor merchant, a vendor or distiller of spirits. A bone-splitter is a bone-breaker, one who deals in skulls.[78] Therefore it is said in that text:

> Qt.66d.1 "The wife of an outcaste, of a black, of a bowman, of a butcher, of a tanner and of a liquor merchant, of a bone-breaker, of a fisherman, of a potter, O Beloved!"

---

76. *TĀ* 1.82 ff.
77. The precise meaning of *ḍomba* is uncertain: 'untouchable', 'cremator', White, p.305; 'a man of low caste, living by dancing and singing', Monier-Williams, *Sanskrit English dictionary*, p.431.1; 'a low caste woman', i.e. of the washer men's caste ...', Agehananda Bharati, p.175. In Marglin p.231, where she quotes Mircea Eliade's translation of *ḍombī* [*sic*] as 'washer-woman', the author makes the observation that the 'washer man is the one who washes the clothes soiled by menstrual blood.'
78. The meaning of the word *kāpālika* is not clear. Does it refer to the sectarian, the *kāpālika*, feared and despised for his impure practices, a fitting person for this 'unclean' group, an ascetic who yet has a wife? Does it refer to a person of mixed caste, *kapālin*, the child of a Brāhman mother and fisherman father? Does it refer simply to the person who provides the skull for the ritual?

Jr.66d.2 'In the nine-fold sacrifice': in the sacrifice involving nine circles. Therefore it is said in that text:

> Qt.66d.2 "Just as the goddesses, who are engrossed in the sacrifice of the nine [circles], worship Īśvara, so too the worship should be undertaken in nine ways in nine circles."

śl. 67 **Their 9 (8+1) Sacred Sites**

Jr.66d.3 And their own homes, since they are the agreed meeting places, are 'sacred sites'. He says:

> *[Their sacred sites are] Saṅgama, Varuṇā, Kulagiri, Aṭṭahāsa, Jayantī, Caritraka, Āmraka, Koṭṭam; Haimapura is the ninth and in the midst of these [wives] is the potter's wife* (cakriṇī), *the principal [śakti].* ‖67‖

Jr.67d.1 As it is said in that [text]:

> Qt.67d.1 "The house of the outcaste's wife, O Most Lovely One, is called Prayāga, while [that of] the black's wife is called Varuṇā; [that of] the bowman's wife is Kulagiri, O Beloved, and [the house of] the butcher's wife is Aṭṭahāsa and [that of] the tanner's wife is Jayantī. Caritra is said above to be [the house of] the castrate's wife, Ekāmra [that of] the bone-breaker's wife, while Devīkoṭṭa is [the house of] thc fisherman's wife and Hiraṇyapura itself, the ninth, is the sacred site of the potter's wife, difficult to attain, even for the gods."

Jr.67d.2 'Of these': of the wives of the outcaste etc.

śl. 68 **2. Maintenance: Cakrinī i.e. Kuṇḍalinī**

śl. 69ab **3. Reabsorption: Kuleśvarī**

śl. 69cd **4. "Nameless": Saṅkarṣiṇī**

śl. 70ab **Alone or Paired**

Jr.67d.3 He explains the reason why [Cakriṇī] is the principal [śakti]:

> *She brings pressure to bear on the seed in order to separate the oil from the husk, she who, in the [midst of these wives], is Kuṇḍalinī. As mistress of the 'three-and-a-half' tradition, she, while standing on the 'bulb', circulates everywhere.* ||68|| *After [the practitioner] has made sacrifice to the arising of the circle in this way,*[79] *Kuleśvarī is to be worshipped during the middle [stage of the contraction of the circle]. At the final end of the [contraction of the circle], Saṅkarṣiṇī, she who resorbs and produces growth, [is to be worshipped]* ||69|| *either as a single heroine accompanied by the circle or even paired [with a consort] within the circle.*

Jr.70b.1 [Cakriṇī, the principal śakti,] who is located in the [midst of these wives], is located on the 'bulb' which is the source of the origin of the whole world. She proceeds with her attention directed to the splendour itself, i.e. the supreme knowing subject. Therefore, because the universe is placed within her womb she has the form of Kuṇḍalinī, she is the śakti of Parā. When, out of her own freedom, she wishes to display the extent of duality, she, the mistress of the 'three-and-a-half' tradition, assuming the [limited] subjectivity of the body etc., circulates everywhere, i.e. she irradiates in every direction by means of whatever is blue, pleasant etc. Then again, intending to bring the universe to rest in the self alone, she brings pressure to bear on the seed in order to separate the oil from the husk, i.e. by a process of reducing the subjectivity which derives from the body etc., she draws out the essence of supreme consciousness, she veils *māyā* which is the cause of the universe.

Then again, standing on the 'bulb' as her support, she, who has the form of the *kuṇḍalinī* of subtle-breath, transforms the seed—which is the cause of the menstrual fluid etc., which is enjoyed, which is food etc.—into a secretion of essence etc.. As a result, she, who impels the support of the body, circulates everywhere,

79. In *śl.*59-67.

i.e. because she is by nature the subtle-breath she dwells every where, i.e. in channel, circle etc.

And so, she, who in an external sense is the oil-presser, who impels the circle which amounts to the quantity 'three-and-a-half',[80] who abides in the centre of the [circle], circulates everywhere, i.e. in no [particular] direction. The result is that, through just circulating everywhere, i.e. in no [particular] direction, she, Kuṇḍalinī, brings pressure to bear on the seed, i.e. sesamum etc., in order to separate the oil from the husk, i.e. she brings firm pressure to bear until she produces the separation of sesamum oil and fodder.

Therefore it is said:

> Qt.70b.1 "She who is the ninth [śakti], Cakriṇī, circulates while remaining at the centre of the universe. She brings pressure to bear on every seed inorder to separate the oil from the husk. Moreover, she who is called 'Kuṇḍalinī' moves out from the confines of the 'bulb'."

Jr.70b.2 'The arising of the circle': the circle which has [already] arisen [viz. in śl.68]. Saṅkarṣiṇī has seventeen syllables. As has been said in the illustrious *Devyāyāmala* :

> Qt.70b.2 "The phoneme for nose [*Ī*] and buttock [*M*] and subtle-breath [*H*] are joined to the half-prong [*R*]. [=*ḤRĪM*] Having extracted the subtle-breath [*H*], it is joined to the buttock [*M*] along with the phoneme for breast-milk [*Ā*]. [=*MAHĀ*]. 'Three-eyed' [*C*] and the phoneme for the ears [*Ṇ*] is joined to the right arm [*Ḍ*]. [=*CAṆḌA*] The left [shoulder] [*Y*] is joined to the right shank [*O*]. The phoneme for tooth—having extracted the third [one] [*G*]—is placed on the right knee [*E*]. [=*YOGE*] The staff of the trident [*R*] should be on the [generative organ] [*Ś*] and throat [*V*] and on the two tongues [*I*]. [=*ŚVARI*] By contrast, the second

80. The term *hasta* can mean 'hand' or 'quantity'. Monier-Williams, *Sanskrit English Dictionary*, p.1294c. The term *sa-ardha-tri-hasta* echoes the phrase 'the 'three-and-a-half' tradition'.

phoneme of the garland around the head [*Ṝ*] is joined to the hands [*ṬH*] [=*ṬHṜ*]. The same [*Ṝ*] is then [joined] to the eye [*DH*] [=*DHṜ*]. And the same [*Ṝ*] [is joined] to the head [*TH*] [=*THṜ*]. Then let him join the skull [*Ṭ*] to the left foot [*PH*] five times [=*PHAṬ, PHAṬ, PHAṬ, PHAṬ, PHAṬ*]. The vidyā of seventeen syllables is to be fully worshipped, even by the gods,[81] with the title 'Kālasaṅkarṣiṇī'."[82]

Jr.70b.3 And this same *vidyā* is found in the illustrious *Mādhava-kula* as well.

Qt.70b.3"He should use [the phrase] 'deluding' [=*HRĪṂ*], 'time' [=*MAHĀ*], 'self' [=*CAṆḌA*], and 'O Lord of heroes' [=*YOGEŚVARI*]."

Jr.70b.4 Starting with that [it goes on]:

Qt.70b.4 "He should extract - joined with my adornments [*ṬHṜ, DHṜ, THṜ*] - the stream of five [PHAṬ, PHAṬ, PHAṬ, PHAṬ, PHAṬ]."

Jr.70b.5 The [vidyā viz. *HRĪṂ, MAHĀ, CAṆḌA, YOGEŚVARI*] is pronounced together with this last [part, viz. *ṬHṜ, DHṜ, THṜ, PHAṬ, PHAṬ, PHAṬ, PHAṬ, PHAṬ*] since that is the sacred textual tradition of the gurus. [83] 'At final end of the [contraction of the circle]': the end of [the contraction of] the circle is composed mostly of beams of light; and 'at the final [end of the contraction of the circle]' means in the sacred place of repose, i.e. in the creative awareness of complete 'I am'. Therefore it is said:

Qt.70b.5 "After knowing the arising of the circle in this way, Kālakṛntanī,[84] she who knows, [stands] at the centre [of the circle]. However, she who abides at the final end

81. 'by the gods' : Literally 'by the thirty', i.e. by the deities who actually number thirty-three. *ibid.* p.458.3.
82. The code for this *vidyā* is to be found at *Mālinīvijayottaratantra* 3.37-41ab and is paraphrased in *TĀ* 15.121-125ab.
83. These are presumably the gurus mentioned in Jr.56d.1.
84. Kālakṛntanī, literally 'she who cuts time short', transcends *māyā* and dwells within *śuddhavidyā*, true knowledge, therefore 'she knows'.

of the [contraction of the circle], she, by contrast, is called Saṅkarṣiṇī."

Jr.70b.6 'Paired [with a consort] within the circle': since the pairing takes place within the circle; i.e. being part of a pair, she is accompanied by the circle in a paired fashion.

Cycle II: Means of Knowledge

śl. 70cd-71ab 1. Emanation: The 24 Sacred Sites in 8 Directions

Jr.70b.7 How are these sacred sites to be worshipped in combination in the [circle]? To this question he says:

> *In the north-east, east, south-east, south, [south-west, west],*[85] *north-west and north directions, starting with Aṭṭahāsa,*[86] ||70|| *he should sacrifice to the [sacred sites] in sets of three. [Each sacred site] should be placed in its triad, as will be [explained].*

Jr.71b.1 Thus, in the north-east corner he should sacrifice to the triad 'Aṭṭahāsa, Caritra and Kulagiri', just as, in the north, he should [sacrifice to] the triad 'Āmrātakeśvara, Rājagṛha and Śrīparvata'.[87] Moreover, he should not sacrifice to each sacred site just on its own, for which reason he says: '[Each sacred site] should be placed in its triad, as will be [explained] ...'. 'Will be [explained] ...' means 'will be described'.

śl. 71cd-72ab The Triads—Their Code

Jr.71b.2 For that reason he says:

> *'Heart', 'kuṇḍalī', 'eye-brow-centre' are a triad in due order.* ||71|| *These [mean], respectively,*

85. The phrase *kravyātka* must mean 'south-west, west', but I do not know how it is construed.
86. See Gnoli, *Luce*, p.688.
87. Jayaratha gives the triads not according to the list given in *śl.*59-63 but according to Qt.63d.2 and Qt.63d.3. Furthermore he identifies the Śrīśaila of Qt.63d.3 with the Śrīparvata of Jr.71b.1.

'cremation grounds', 'that which arises from the sacred region', 'the group of true yoginīs'.|

Jr.72b.1 [The phrase] 'he should make sacrifice to....' is applied to [*śl.*71cd-72ab] in keeping with the earlier [*śl.*71a]. 'That which originates in the sacred region' is equivalent to 'the set of sacred sites which develop out of the [sacred region]'[88] Therefore it is said:

> Qt.72b.1 "... [the directions] starting in due order from the north-east corner etc. and the directions east, south, west andnorth, O Beloved ..."

> Qt.72b.2 " 'The cremation ground' is the region of the heart, while 'the tree of plenty' is *kuṇḍalī*. The 'eye-brow centre', which is to be considered as the sacred region of the *yoginīs*, refers to the family of *yoginīs*."

śl. 72cd-73ab **2. Maintenance: 'Lamps' are Placed There**

Jr.72b.2 When worship is performed, [the sacrifice] must necessarily be done with an offering of food.[89] He says:

> *He should place 'lamps' which are eight finger-widths tall, round on top, set in the middle of the [sacrificial] ground, [* ||72|| *] furnished with redwicks, traditional [in number] and fed with clarified butter.*|

88. *TĀ* 15.84 notes that 'the will of [Parameśvara] is the basis of the sacred sites' and that this will corresponds externally to Kāmarūpa. He goes on to note that the two other sacred sites, Pūrṇagiri and Uḍḍīyāna, develop out of Kāmarūpa. This is glossed by Jayaratha in a quote, *Tantrāloka* vol.6, p.2488 line 4, which reads: *tataḥ pīṭhadvayaṃ jātaṃ*, 'two sacred sites develop out of [Kāmarūpa]'. Accordingly, the phrase *kṣetra-bhava* refers simply to the sacred site which emerges from the sacred region. The code is clearly explained in *śl.*71cd-72ab. A second explanation of the code is given in Qt.72b.2 while Jr.72b.1 harmonises these two versions.

89. The 'lamps' are edible and a cup of wine is used in *śl.*76ab. One may suppose they form part of the hero's meal in *śl.*77a.

Jr.73b.1 Traditional [in number']: twenty-four. Therefore it is said:

> Qt.73b.1 "And he should set out twenty-four 'lamps' in the four directions. And they are made of paste, set on the ground in the middle of the supporting [sacrificial ground], quite circular, measuring eight finger-widths in height, beautiful, four finger-widths [in diameter],[90] supplied with ghee flame and furnished on top with red wicks.

śl. 73cd-75ab **Insertion of One's Private Ritual**

Jr.73b.2 Some other ritual action may take place during that [ceremony]. He says:

> *On the other hand, he may perform in the middle [of the ceremony] any religious practice of his own. ||73|| 'Non-dual only, not dual' is Parameśitā's command. The mantras given by the Siddhāntas and the Vaiṣṇavas etc. are therefore impure. ||74|| Because they cannot bear so much splendour they are lifeless, according to the non-dual tradition.*[91]

Jr.75b.1 'Any' means 'his chosen [ritual]'. Therefore it is said:

> Qt.75b.1 "The person who is established in the tantric ritual tradition by virtue of a mantra ..."

Jr.75b.2 Having said which, [the text continues]:

> Qt.75b.2 "... may sacrifice according to his own ritual in the middle [of the ceremony] but he must avoid the dualist tradition."

Jr.75b.3 Having said which, [the text goes on]:

> Qt.75b.3 "The Siddhāntas, the Vaiṣṇavas, the Buddhists, the Vedāntins and those who follow Smārta teachings are to be avoided diligently indeed since they are said to be 'bonded animals'. They avoid the [divine] presence which

---

90. '[in diameter]': The translation is uncertain.

91. Sanderson has traced *śl.*73cd-75ab to the *Jayadrathayāmala* 4 folio 127v2-6. Sanderson, 'Meaning', p.17 note 2.

comes from contact with the non-dual drink [viz. wine]. They turn away from it. They are lifeless, deprived of life.

śl. 75cd-76ab 3. Reabsorption: Setting aside the Instruments

4. 'Nameless': The Goddess Kṛśā

śl. 76cd-77 Aside: Hymn of the Sacred Site

Jr.75b.4 And then, putting aside the set of materials, [the practitioner] should focus just on the item which is directly in front of him. As a result supernatural power is acquired without effort. He says:

> *When he has set aside the jar, the blindfold etc., the* maṇḍala*, the large and small sacrificial ladles, the fire,* ||75|| *at that point supernatural power occurs. He should sacrifice to Kṛśā in the wine in the vessel placed in the centre [of the sacrificial surface]. And when he has performed this sacrifice for a day and a night,*[92] *on the following day,* ||76|| *when the hero's meal has been taken, the mantras inevitably succeed without effort. During the sacrifice he should recite 'The Hymn of the Sacred Site' in order to invoke good fortune.* ||77||

Jr.77d.1 'On the following day': when night has turned into day. Therefore it is said:

> Qt.77d.1 "He should leave aside the jar and the blindfold, the *maṇḍala* etc. Supernatural power comes about when he is without those things, without the fire, the large and small ladles etc. O Gaṇāmbikā, in the aforementioned cups which are filled with wine, which are said to contain the revitalising fluid, [93] she is to be adored at the centre [of

92. The details given in *TĀ* 28.44cd ff. and in *TĀ* 28.53-56ab which reads 'after performing the ceremonial, after having, in the middle of the night, meditated and having recited [the mantra], he—when he has gone out—receives a prediction, so too [during the month of] ... friendship, wealth, union [with a desired woman], the destruction of an enemy ...' would suggest that the rite being described in *śl.*75c-77 is in some sense a *kāmya* ritual.

93. The use of the word 'revitalising fluid' in Qt.129b.1 would indicate that the substance mentioned in Qt.77d.1 is sexual fluid.

the sacrificial surface], she whose waist is emaciated."

Jr.77d.2 Having said which, [the text continues]:

> Qt.77d.2 "Either in the forenoon or in the afternoon, or else for a day and a night, he should recite the 'The Hymn of the Sacred Site'. At night he should perform the recitation attentively[94] whilst in the clear light of dawn he should have the aforementioned hero's meal. Great good fortune will arise in the kingdom and in the end he will become a sky-traveller."

Cycle III: Subject of Knowledge

Śl. 78 1. Emanation: The Śaktis by Themselves

Jr.77d.3 Or else he should worship the same circle [of śaktis] without the *maṇḍala* etc. He says:

> *Or else, the enlightened man should worship, in turn, just the images [of the śaktis], as coupled [or] as their own female versions of the hero. [He should worship them] as independent, not bound to ạny ritual.* ||78||

Jr.78d.1 'Just the images [of the śaktis]': because of [the word] 'just' the śaktis are [being described as] by themselves. 'As their own female versions of the hero': as heroines just by themselves. 'Pure': without differentiated thought.

Śl. 79 2. Maintenance: Pairing with the Śaktis

Jr.78d.2 In the case of the śaktis by themselves, how is the worship performed? To this question he says:

> *Moreover, having by his own nature become the sole lord of the* kula, *he should satiate the many śaktis by pairing [with ṭhem], he who possesses every form.* ||79||

94. It is not clear whether the 'Praise of the Sacred Site' and 'recitation' are the same or, if they are not, how they are both recited at night.

Jr.79d.1 Then, the guru, having by his own nature become the sole [lord], he is, through his identity with Kuleśvara, the lord of the *kula*. In consequence, having every form so to speak, he should satiate the many, i.e. the numerous, śaktis by pairing [with them]; i.e., by means of the perfect fusion which is found in the bliss of union, he should make [the śaktis] truly repose in his own self alone.

śl. 80 **3. Reabsorption**

a. No Time

Jr.79d.2 On this subject -

> Qt.79d.1 "During the first half of the year, on an auspicious day of the week, at an asterism, the preliminary purification ritual should take place."

Jr.79d.3 —accordingly, why is there no mention of a specific calendar in the Kula sacrifice? To this question he says:

> *There is no succession of any sort in consciousness which consists of splendour. Consciousness is in no way absent. Therefore the act of satiation is timeless.* ||80||

Jr.80d.1 On this subject:

> Qt.80d.1 "The Self shines forth eternally."[95]

Jr.80d.2 accordingly, consciousness, which consists of great splendour, which is eternally active, shines ceaselessly. It is not like the gleam of lighting, in the sense of occurring intermittently, fragmentedly. No succession of any sort exists in [consciousness] - because [succession] depends on distinction. And since time too, which depends simply on [succession], does not exist in [consciousness], the act of satiation is said to be altogether timeless. How can [time] which does not encroach on [consciousness] produce the divisions [of a specific calendar] within [consciousness]?

95. Jayaratha uses this half line again in his investigation of *TĀ* 4.178cd.

That is the meaning.

śl. 81ab **b. No Throne**

śl. 81cd **4. The 'nameless': His Śakti (*sva-śakti*)**

Jr.80d.3 Therefore, even spatial order does not exist [in consciousness]. He says:

> *As regards [spatial] order [in consciousness]: due to the total uprooting of the tree of difference, a discussion regarding the throne*[96] *is not especially enjoined, for Parameśvara works vigorously* (viśaṁśramīti)*,*[97] *above all within the sacred place of his śakti.* ॥81॥

Jr.81d.1 'In the sacred place of his śakti':-

> Qt.81d.1 "His śaktis are the whole universe ..."[98]

Jr.81d.2 —according to this teaching, he alone is the whole. What place is there, different from [the whole], which might become his throne?

B Recitation

śl. 82 **Enunciation and Definition**

Jr.81d.3 Having explained the the ritual of adoration in this way he investigates the nature of the recitation which is closely associated with it.

---

96. *TĀ* 15.313-323ab discusses the throne (āsana) in detail.

97. The root *ŚRAM* means to make an effort, to be weary, to exert oneself especially in performing acts of austerity. Monier-Williams, *Sanskrit English dictionary*, p.1096.1. The form *viśaṃśramīti* is the intensive form, present 3d person sing. Communication of Raffaele Torella, 27-07-99.

98. In *TĀ* 5.40, Abhinava gives the whole quote and its source: ' 'His śaktis are the whole universe and the one who possesses śakti is Maheśvarah', as the illustrious Śrīkaṇṭha said in the *Māṅgalaśāstra*.' He quotes the first whole line again in *Parātriṃśikāvivaraṇa* p.199 line 22. Jayaratha quotes the first half-line in his investigation after *TĀ* 3.67, after *TĀ* 3.206ab, after *TĀ* 8.174, before *TĀ* 9.155cd and before *TĀ* 13.266. He quotes the first whole line in his investigation after *TĀ* 3.100ab and again after *TĀ* 3.191ab. In his investigation after *TĀ* 5.40, he quotes a two-lined variant.

Recitation is then to be performed, divided into sets of three hundred thousand repetitions and so on. It is said in the illustrious Yogasañcāra*: 'And [recitation] is of various kinds.'* ||82||

Jr.82d.1 What is the evidence for its being divided into sets of three hundred thousand repetitions and so on? To this question, he stated: 'It is said in the illustrious *Yogasañcāra*'. [Quoting] from that same text he declares: 'And [recitation] is of various kinds.'

śl. 83-88 **1. The Objects of Focus**

Jr.82d.2 He explains those various kinds of [recitation]:

In relation to the 'rising', to the 'joining' and to the 'resting', recitation is performed three hundred thousand times. With regard to the face, to the exhalation and inhalation, to the thread, to what is called 'haṁsa'*, to the Śaiva couple [viz. Śiva and śakti],* ||83|| *five hundred thousand recitations are performed, as mentioned above. For every set of ten [recitations] he should offer [one] oblation into the fire. The eyes, the exhalation and inhalation, with reference to the mouth and to the* 'haṁsa'*, to the 'rosary',* ||84|| *to the union of Śiva and śakti, recitation is done six hundred thousand times. The eyes, the exhalation and inhalation, with reference to the ear, to the* 'haṁsa' *and to the mouth, O Splendid Lady,* ||85|| *and to the hand and to the couple itself, [viz. Śiva and śakti], recitation numbering seven sets [of one hundred thousand] is made. The eyes, the exhalation and inhalation, the ears, the face, the 'private place'*[99] *and the [top of the head],* ||86|| *the centre point*

99. In Jr.88d.1, Jayaratha explains *guhyam*, 'private place' as 'mouth of the *yoginī*' *(yoginī-vaktra)* and 'generative organ' *(janma-ādhāra)*. See also Padoux, *Le coeur*, p.305. It can also refer to the perineum or to the base of the body in general. *ibid.* p.313.

within the hundred beams of light and within the thousand beams of light, O Splendid Lady: that recitation amounts to eight hundred thousand times. Here too, [one] oblation [should be made], for every set of ten [recitations]. ‖ 87‖ *The eyes, the exhalation and inhalation, the ears, the face, near the pit-of-Brahmā, the breasts, the hands and feet, with reference to the pair comprising the 'private place' [and the top of the head] he should perform the practice twice.* ‖ 88 ‖

Jr.88d.1 'In relation to the 'arising' ': in relation to the generative organ, to the place where the energy of subtle-breath arises. 'In relation to the 'joining' ': with regard to the heart which is the place where the various channels divide. 'In relation to the 'resting' ': with regard to the state of deep attentiveness which at the same time conduces to the restraint of the subtle-breath. 'With regard to the exhalation and inhalation': with reference to the flow of *prāṇa* and *apāna*. 'In respect of the 'thread' ': with regard to the source of the threads of the sense-organs, channels and circles. 'With regard to what is called '*haṁsa*' ': as regards the heart which manifests the self. 'With regard to the couple': with respect to the union of Śiva and śakti at the generative organ or at the 'end-of-twelve'. 'The 'private place' is the generative organ. 'The [top of the head]': the private aperture which is found within the 'cavern'. [It] designates Ka, i.e. the aperture of Ka, the pit-of-Brahmā. 'Within the hundred beams of light', 'within the thousand beams of light': within the countless many channels starting with [the hundred and the thousand beams of light]. 'The central point' is the heart and the navel. 'Here too, [one] oblation [should be made]': by the word 'too' it is understood that in every case 'one oblation for every ten' [recitations] should be made. 'With reference to the pair comprising the 'private place' [and the 'top of the head']': the generative organ and the 'end-of-twelve' are synonymous with the 'mouth of the *yoginī*' and 'the mouth of Aja'. 'That recitation amounts to sixteen hundred thousand repetitions': it is to be performed according to the same procedure as above. It follows that, in all such locations,[100] the subtle-breath should circulate twice. End of topic.

100. These locations are mentioned in *śl*.83-88.

2. The *Haṁsa*

śl. 89 **a. Enunciation of *Haṁsa***

Jr.88d.2 He himself explains the [phrase 'should perform the practice twice'].

> *Wherever the eye goes, wherever the mind goes,*
> *there* 'haṁsa', *which consists of expansion and*
> *contraction, is twice to be exercised.* ||89||

Jr.89d.1 Wherever, referring to a place such as the face etc., wherever the eye or mind goes, i.e. wheresoever the *yogī* concentrates his attention: at that very spot *haṁsa*, whose nature is a 'giving' and 'taking', i.e. the subtle-breath, is twice to be exercised in the sense that it consists of expansion and contraction, i.e. it consists simply of externalisation and absorption. Therefore he should focus on restraining the lesser outlets of the [subtle-breath], such as the face etc. as mentioned above, so that, being restrained on every side, i.e. in the absence of any other avenue, the [subtle-breath] enters into the central sacred place itself. The *yogī*, arousing the mantra by identifying it with [the subtle-breath] which has entered into the [central sacred place], acquires any supernatural power [he wishes]. As it is said in another place.

> Qt.89d.1 "He should perform the recitation in harmony with the subtle-breath. As a result, a supernatural power manifestly occurs."

Jr.89d.2 It is said that 'In order just to achieve [success], sixteen hundred thousand recitations are to be made', and so on. Mention has been made [in *śl.*83-88] of the gradual reduction of the hundreds of thousands. The reason for this is the *yogīs*' relative level of concentration.

śl. 90ab **b. Definition of *Haṁsa***

Jr.89d.3 The subtle-breath, which has taken on the expansiveness which occurs within the central sacred place itself as a result of restraining the lesser outlets in the manner mentioned above [viz. Jr.89d.1], acquires, through an outpouring of consciousness, a universal nature. Therefore he says:

> *The* [haṁsa] *is the [individual] self, is the goddess Mātṛkā, is Śiva abiding in the body.*

Jr.90b.1 The *haṁsa*, which abides in the body as well, which has become identical with the mantra-goddess, is the [universal] self in the contracted form of an individual.

> Qt.90b.1 "But śakti is to be known as Mātṛkā and she [Mātṛkā] is to be known as consisting of Śiva."

Jr.90b.2 According to this statement, the goddess Mātṛkā is the śakti of Parameśvara. And Śiva, since he is essentially *nara-śakti-śiva*,[101a] alone shines forth.

śl. 90cd-91 **Note: No Distinctions**

Jr.90b.3 Therefore, one should not make the slightest distinction between the practitioner of the mantra [and] the mantra [viz. Śiva], the *prāṇa* which is identical with the [mantra-goddess] and the [limited] self. He says:

> *'The [*haṁṣa, *viz. the subtle-breath] is one thing, I am another': one must not entertain such a thought.* ‖ 90 ‖ *For the person who differentiates, supernatural power and liberation are far distant. [This principle applies], therefore, to the performance of sixteen hundred thousand etc. subtle-breaths as mentioned above.* ‖91‖

> Qt.91d.1 "If the practitioner of the mantra is one thing, the mantra another, perfection is never attained. All is based on knowledge [viz. non-dual consciousness]. Without such [knowledge] perfection is in no way attained."

101a. The triad *nara-śakti-Śiva* is a technical phrase. It refers to levels of being variously classed as: object of knowledge, means of knowledge and subject of knowledge; Aparā, Parāparā, Parā; the inert, śakti, Śiva; it, you, I; etc. The triad is discussed, for example, in *Parātriṃśikāvivaraṇa* p.211 line 21 - p.214 line 16.

Jr.91d.1 In keeping with just such a teaching, it is said in all the scriptures:

> Qt.91d.2 "One should perform the recitation in solitude."

Jr.91d.2 and so on.

śl. 92-95ab **3. Oblation into the Fire of Consciousness**

śl. 95cd **Bridge: In Praise of Śambhunātha**

Jr.91d.3 The principal meaning of the word 'solitude' is said to be just the absence of differentiated thought. Therefore he says:

> *The abandonment of the categories 'pure' and 'impure' is said to be solitude. Established in that [solitude], he both makes oblation and performs the recitation by himself alone.* || 92 || *Recitation and the practice of murmuring are a form of the awareness of sound. The dissolution of the awareness of [sound] in the fire of consciousness is said to be the oblation.* || 93 || *And the above mentioned awareness [of sound] consists of the set of twelve goddesses. The last two [stages] of consciousness amongst these [twelve goddesses] are an act of oblation in the form of dissolution.* || 94 || *The other ten [goddesses] are the means of arriving at the [two last stages]. That is the reason why there is [one] oblation into the fire for every ten [recitations].*
> *The illustrious Śambhu-nātha is the moon shining on the ocean of Trika knowledge.* || 95 ||

> Qt.95d.1 "[The supreme knowing subject] (*sa*) is twelve-fold, so that all reality is comprised within [him]."[101b]

Jr.95d.1 'Amongst these': from amongst the twelve. 'The last two [stages] of consciousness': the "supreme knowing subject and the

101b. This is an exact quote of *TĀ* 4.123cd where the pronoun *sa*, according to Jayaratha's comment, refers to *pramātṛrūpa*, the knowing subject, or to *parāmarśa*, creative awareness. *TĀ* 4.123cd text forms part of the introduction to the twelve stages of the Krama.

power of freedom".[102] These same two—according to what is stated in our teaching: 'The ultimate state is autonomous consciousness' —are the place of repose. For that reason it is said that [the other ten] are 'the means of arriving at [those last two stages]', in this sense they repose in the supreme knowing subject by a gradual progression through objects of knowledge and means of knowledge etc. And that point is made in detail in the chapter on the śakti-method,[103] for which reason [that chapter] should be referred to. Therein lies the meaning of '[one] oblation into the fire for every ten [repetitions]'. So [say] our gurus.

---

102. Jayaratha quotes the same phrase in *Tantrāloka* vol.3, p.337 line 10.
103. *TĀ* 4.

SUB-TOPIC 4 The Ritual with the Sexual Partner
Sacrifice 3 Based on the Pair

śl. 96 Enunciation of the Sub-topic

Jr.95d.2 Having thus explained the ritual of adoration which finishes with the recitation and the oblation into the fire, he begins to explain the ritual with a sexual partner.

> *If, however, he would perform the ceremony with an external śakti, then this secret ritual, which has been given by Parameśa, shall be described [for him].* ‖ 96 ‖

> Qt.96d.1 "Parā, the śakti, is always present. But even if she [is always present], the *kaula* ritual is unachievable if there is no external activity."[104]

Jr.96d.1 According to this teaching [the *kaula* ritual] must necessarily be done by means of external activity. Even if [external activity is undertaken], the [*kaula* ritual] can in no way be successfully performed without a sexual partner, for which reason he says: 'with an external śakti'. As has been said:

> Qt.96d.2 "A sexual partner should be used in every case. He receives no supernatural power if he has no sexual partner."

Jr.96d.2 Similarly:

> Qt.96d.3 "Just as [in the case of] a brahman's wife, he [the brahman] should worship with her at the sacred festival, so the sexual partner should be seen at the *kula* Master's side when the *kula* [group] is assembled."

---

104. Jayaratha also uses this quote to introduce *TĀ* 12.16cd.

Introduction

1. The Participants:

śl. 97ab **a. Enunciation of Brahmacarya**

Jr.96d.3 Everywhere, without any exception, the description of a person devoted to god is given in these terms:

> Qt.96d.4 "Free from arrogance, devoted to the guru, celibate, in control of his faculties, committed to the worship of Śiva, silent, abstaining from meat and wine ...."

Jr.96d.4 How then is it said here: '... he would perform the ceremony with an external śakti'? Dismissing such a doubt by means of Parameśvara's own teaching, he prepares the setting for that procedure.

> *It is said in the illustrious* Yogasañcāra[105a] *: "He should observe* brahmacarya*".*

śl. 97cd-98ab **i. Definition of *Brahman***

Jr.97b.1 What exactly is *brahman* if [the practitioner] should observe [its] use also? To this question he says:

> *Bliss is the supreme* brahman *and it resides in the body in three ways.*|| 97 || *Of these, two are aids, the other is the result, [all three] consisting of [bliss]* (tad).

> Qt.98b.1"Bliss is the form of *brahman* ..."[105b]

Jr.98b.1 [The word] 'supreme' implies that [*brahman*] must necessarily be served. And [*brahman*]—which is defined as *parabrahman* etc.—resides not only in the self but also in a form which is 'not

---

105a. At the beginning of *Tantrasāra* ch.22 which is a summary of *TĀ* 29, Abhinava quotes several lines from the *Yogasañcāra* which show that *TĀ* 29.97cd and 98cd-100ab are a paraphrase from the same work.

105b. Jayaratha quotes this passage once after *TĀ* 1.242, *TĀ* 4.139, and *TĀ* 28.331cd and twice in *TĀ* 29, i.e. in Qt.98b.1 and Qt.128b.1. According to his understanding of these quotes, he interprets 'bliss' to mean both the highest experience and the fluid that pours out.

self', even in the external body etc., for which reason he says: 'in the body'. 'Of these': from amongst the three. 'Two': wine and meat. 'The other': intercourse. When the [physical] element is nourished by the drinking of wine and the eating of meat, the person who is enjoying [these things] arrives at bliss. For that reason it is said: 'aids' and 'result'. Therefore, [the phrase]: 'consisting of [bliss]' is to be added to each one. And in this [*śloka*] the word *tat* refers to bliss.

śl. 98cd **ii. Definition of *Brahmacarya***

Jr.98b.2 Since such things consist of brahman, their practitioner is called a *brahmacārī*. He says:

> *He who observes the three last-of-the-labials [viz. M] is called a* brahmacārī. ǁ 98 ǁ

Jr.98d.1 'The labial' is the 'P' class of phonemes. The 'last' of the ['P' class] is 'M'. The three [M's] refer to wine, meat and intercourse.

śl. 99-100ab **iii. Contrast of 'bonded animal'**

Jr.98d.2 [But]

> Qt.98d.1 "There is no sin in eating meat nor in wine nor in intercourse. The use [of those things] is proper to human beings. Abstinence, however, is highly beneficial."

Jr.98d.3 According to this teaching, the scripture is to be invoked as regards abstinence from meat etc. It is not [to be invoked] as regards their use since the [use of these things] is natural. In this connection no scripture whatever is quoted [as saying] 'a dirty person should wash', 'a hungry person should eat' etc. Therefore why is that [statement, viz. *śl.*98cd] made? To this question he says:

> *Those who [always] abstain from the [three M's, viz. even during the Circle Sacrifice] are 'bonded animals', abstaining from bliss. [There are others] who [outside the Circle Sacrifice] consume the three M's which cause bliss [but] abstain from them whilst partaking in the circle-sacrifice.*ǁ99ǁ
> *For a double reason these will go to the two hells, the Terrifying*[106] *and the Frightful.*

106. The hell called Raurava, 'Terrifying', is mentioned in *TĀ* 13.355 as the destiny of apostates. Even so, those condemned can be rescued by means of the initiation described in *TĀ* 24.

Jr.100b.1 Whosoever, even though they have entered on the Kula ritual procedure, do not, because of confusion or uncertainty, offer [the three M's] during the 'Circle Sacrifice' etc., to themselves or to others, even though it is prescribed therein, are truly 'bonded animals'. As a result, abstaining from the bliss which is produced by [*parabrahman*] and which consists essentially of *parabrahman*, their conceit is fixated on the body etc. alone. Therefore it is said:

> Qt.100b.1 "Those who, belonging to the Kula sacred textual traditions, are deprived of these ingredients, are called 'bonded animals'. There should be no association with them."

Jr.100b.2 Those also who, independently [of the Circle Sacrifice], avidly consume the three M's which cause bliss, i.e. who enjoy the three M's; who sacrifice to the circle while abstaining out of confusion etc. from the [three M's]: they too are simply 'bonded animals'. That is the meaning of the aforesaid [*śloka* 99cd]. Therefore it is said:

> Qt.100b.2 "Without a guru, without a deity, like dullards, O Parameśvarī, forever consuming wine and meat, they are 'bonded animals'. There is no doubt about it."

Jr.100b.3 Thus, for a double reason, i.e. for not doing what is prescribed and for doing what is not prescribed, they will go to the two hells, the Frightful and the Terrifying. There they will experience thousands of hellish tortures. Therefore the [set of three M's] is to be utilised by the person who has entered upon the Kula path for the reason that he is in every way committed simply to manifesting his own bliss. [The set of 3 M's] is not [to be utilised] out of greed. If that were the case, how would [the use of the 3 M's] differ from worldly usages? As they have said:

> Qt.100b.3 "The form known as 'the bliss of *brahman*'[107]

107. The terms 'bliss of *brahman*' and 'particular object' can be understood at various levels. The 'bliss of *brahman*' refers either to the experience of transcendental bliss or to the 3 M's which are intimately associated with it. The 'bliss of *brahman*' can also refer to all at once or especially to the sexual fluid alone. The term 'particular object' can refer to the 3 M's either as used by the true Kula practitioner or as debased by those who act under delusion.

which is obtained only through an ardent desire for repose: this he should consume in its entirely without avidity for that particular object. Whatever 'bliss' flows from an excessive emotion deriving from the particular object which itself is due to the delusion arising from desire: that is the support of 'bonded animals'. The particular object which is found in consciousness alone and in the external substance [and] which is indicative of perception, is experienced in the very being of him who is equivalently ever *yogī* and enjoyer. The [above-] mentioned particular object is divided [into two kinds] and [each sort] leads to non-differentiation equally."

Qt.100b.4 "The perception obtained by means of the particular object is not essentially different from that [perception which is obtained] by its undifferentiated forms. [The particular object is] truly enjoyed. Those who have taken the hero's vow, are involved in the great ritual procedure.

He who performs a hundred thousand [recitations], who is committed to restraint, who is at ease regarding *brahmacarya* [viz. the 3 M's] and who, even while involved in sexual union, is perfectly mindful, his body utterly tranquil, who is fully acquainted with the rules of unlawful behaviour mentioned in the Atimārga [tradition], who is fully enlightened as well, who indeed is composed of consciousness, is autonomous at all times, who comes in contact with the particular object in order to acquire the supernatural power of experiencing his own consciousness and not because of an attitude of greed, who is free of the attitude of the 'bonded animal': he is certainly committed to the great path.

He whose conduct shows an attentiveness to his own self both in the midst of worldly affairs and during the performance of the ritual of the left, always retains his

> seed[108] during the observance [of the ritual of intercourse]. He, whose mind, at the moment of emitting semen, i.e. within the split-second of time, has spontaneously settled in respect of all the fluctuations of thought, all at once there arises in his mind the consciousness of bliss. The resulting form is perfectly described as 'pertaining to *brahman*'."

śl. 100cd-101ab **b. Definition of the Term Śakti**

Jr.100b.4 "In that case, the use of wine and meat is easy"! Let that remain the case! However, the other ['M', viz. intercourse] is difficult even for immortals. How much more [difficult] it is for unfortunate mortals! It is said:

> Qt.100b.5 "Let him, then, bring a sexual partner to the place [of ritual], her eyes reeling with desire; her lips are red as *bimba* fruit, her teeth are lovely, her face is furrowed at the brow, she is beautiful; her eyes are like those of a trembling fawn; pleasantly she smiles; her abundant hair is like a glittering swarm of large black bees; her eyes are tremulous because of the furrowing of her brows which are shaped like cupid's bow; her complexion is the colour of liquid gold; she is tranquil; she is made very beautiful in a hundred ways by the varied beauty of her ear-ornaments; she is adorned with a lovely necklace on her lovely conch-like throat; she is bent down by the weight of her breasts which are as haughty as the frontal lobes of an elephant in rut; she is adorned with *kandali* flowers on her well-rounded arms; the fingers of her hand flare like cobra's hood; she is adorned with a finger-ring streaming with the variegated flames of a glittering jewel; her face, with the lovely charm of the full moon, ravishes the heart; her slim lovely waist resembles a noble lion or a rainbow; the languid movement of her loins reveals the

108. The word *skhalana* can also refer to the emission of semen. The *yogī* who holds his seed could be described as 'unfaltering'.

triple row of folds [over her navel]; her lovely thighs are like a plantain tree and her lovely calves are like the trunk of an elephant; she is most beautiful, with feet and ankles like cupid's chariot wheel; she is adorned with a string of beautiful [pearls] which tinkle like ghee falling [into the sacrificial fire]; she makes a clinking sound with her trembling anklet and jingling girdle; she makes a murmuring hum with her bracelet and jingling armlet; her gait is like that of a huge elephant in rut, her navel is deep; her speech is beautiful like the many stammering cries of the goose; she is adorned with a garland of fragrant flowers on the thread of her armlet; she is perfectly eager for the gift of harmless betel-nut from 'the huge cobra'; she dances, she sings and makes cries of pleasure (*sīt*), she plays and pretends to repulse a lover's caress; she is untroubled and she retains her composure, her mind is devoted to the goddess alone; greed and folly having disappeared from her mind, she is consciousness itself; her one attitude is that of savouring the unique wonder of Bhairava: she is the sexual partner, the enchantress, the *mudrā* in this world of the movable-and-immovable."

Jr.100b.5 in the illustrious *Tantrarājabhaṭṭāraka*;

Qt.100b.6 "She is very distinguished and virtuous, obedient to her teacher's command; her speech is agreeable, her form is pleasing, she is placid, free from attachment; she is accomplished in the Bhairava ceremony and eager for the nectars; she is unfailingly committed to the non-dual, devoted to practice, firm in her vow; she looks on everyone as a son, she abhors nothing, she is clearly wise; she is born of a family which always performs the [Kula] ceremony; she is childless,[109] she has beautiful hair, she is delicately formed since she is not addicted to wine, she is

109. In *Yonitantra* as in *Samyācāratantra* the sexual partner must be childless. Schoterman, *Yonitantra*, pp.18-19.

radiant with light,[110] her smile is beautiful; very affectionate and modest, she always attends to the well-being of guests; and in herself she is devoted to the mantra,[111] she is unsullied, without ego; she is committed to the traditional [Kula] sequence [of rituals], yet she observes popular custom; she observes the daily ritual as well as the occasional rites which occur at the junctures of the cycle; she is devoted to the traditional (*tantra*) ritual of pleasure, she knows the ritual of satiation of the god; she is truly content in all circumstances ... "

Jr.100b.6 and in the illustrious *Triśirobhairava.* In the light of [the contrasting description (*tasmāt*, Jr.100b.4)] an external śakti with the aforementioned characteristic qualities is simply unobtainable! All the qualities listed in that way have not been seen, anywhere, at any time, assembled in one person. As they have said:

> Qt.100b.7 " ... but where can all the qualities of every sort be found?"

Jr.100b.7 Yet a sexual partner who does not have [the qualities] listed in that way is to be avoided! As it is said:

> Qt.100b.8 "Better a sacrifice without a sexual partner than [a sacrifice] which has been contaminated by an inadequate sexual partner."

Jr.100b.8 The statement in that quote [viz. Qt.100b.8] about 'eating poison' is not an argument in favour of [performing the sacrifice] without a sexual partner.[112] It means that the sacrifice should not be performed if it is without a sexual partner. In addition, a sexual partner with [the qualities] listed in that way is

110. The word *śukra*, 'light', also means semen.
111. The word 'mantra' can refer to the phonic form etc. or to the divinity which it expresses so that the translation can refer to her fidelity to recitation or to her devotion to her Lord.
112. Jayaratha insisted, at the beginning of his investigation of Sacrifice 3, that an external sexual partner is absolutely necessary for the performance of the Sacrifice. He now adduces Qt.100b.8 to clinch his argument but realises that the quote can be misconstrued to mean that Sacrifice 3 can be performed without a sexual partner. He now clarifies the matter.

unobtainable. Therefore this religious practice is impossible! To this question he says:

> *The characteristic quality of a śakti is that she is in no way separated from him who possesses her.* ॥100॥ *Let him, therefore, bring [a śakti] of this sort, but without regard to castes etc.*

Jr.101b.1 Many a supernatural power is acquired even from a deficient śakti. Therefore it is said:

> Qt.101b.1"Even though she is without [some of] the characteristics, for the Adepts she is still the sexual partner. With her mind set solely on the hero, unflinching, she is approached in all the rituals."

Jr.101b.2 The castes are 'outcaste' and so on. The word 'etc.' implies all the characteristics such as youth and so on.[113] 'The characteristic quality of a śakti' ... non-separation from him who possesses her. Thus age, caste etc. is irrelevant.[114] Having, therefore, devoted [herself] solely to identity with him [who possesses her], it is said she can assume all forms.

śl. 101cd-102 **Examination of the Term Śakti**

Jr.101b.3 For that reason he says:

> *In the teaching of the guru [the śakti] is said to be three-fold. She is 'caused', 'cause' and 'co-caused'. This is because she has an excellence which derives from her identity [with him who possesses her, an identity] which surpasses the dualistic association of worldly and non-worldly.* ॥101॥ *She is like that*[115a] *directly as well as indirectly. Thus she is three-fold in two ways.* ॥102॥

---

113. These are listed more fully at *TĀ* 15.552cd-553ab.

114. Jayaratha has woven into his investigation an almost exact quotation of some lines from the *Yogasañcāra* which are found at the beginning of *Tantrasāra* ch.22 which is a summary of TĀ 29. *Tantrasāra* p.201 lines 15-16 reads as *śakterlakṣaṇam-etattadvadabhedas tato 'napekṣyaṃ vayaḥ* | *jātyādīṃścāsaṅgāt* ...\

115a. The phrase 'like that' refers to 'caused', 'cause' and 'co-caused'.

Jr.102d.1 Now, in the teaching of the guru, i.e. in our teaching; the śakti who has [the characteristic quality] listed in that way [viz. not separated from him who possesses her] is 'born', 'bearing' and 'co-born' such that she is said in the first instance to be threefold. This is because her identity [with him who possesses her] surpasses the combination of worldly, i.e. what pertains to the womb, and non-wordly, i.e. what pertains to knowledge. If, on the other hand, the association were only a matter of knowledge, there would be no such [surpassing] identity with [the one who possesses her]. And since that śakti is [three-fold] in two ways, i.e. directly or indirectly, there is a six-fold classification. Therefore it is said:

> Qt.102d.1 "The three-fold classification which results from being 'caused' 'cause' and 'co-caused' [applies] directly and [indirectly]."

Jr.102d.2 The use of [the word] 'indirectly' means that there can be the 'result even of a result', the 'cause even of a cause' and the 'result even of a co-caused'. For that reason, the [phrase] 'like that' was used in [*śloka* 102d] with reference to these [three types].[115b]

The Wife

Jr.102d.3 [It is said that]

> Qt.102d.2 "One's wife, sister, mother or daughter can be the beautiful mistress."

Jr.102d.4 According to that teaching, why is one's wife also not included in this [ritual], given that the two-fold combination of the worldly and the non-worldly may exist in [her case] as well? Consequently, how is it maintained that the [śakti] is classified only in six ways? That is true! In this [ritual], however, the activity is not undertaken because of a desire for sexual pleasure in a

115b. The phrase '[three types]' refers to 'cause', 'caused' and 'co-caused'.

worldly sense. Rather, [the activity is undertaken]—in keeping with a later instruction[116]—because of the intensity of the absorption into the very nature of undivided supreme consciousness. For that reason the [activity] is said to be supreme. If one's wife were indeed involved, there would be a danger of focussing on sexual pleasure. As has been said:

> Qt.102d.3 "The person who wishes to perform a religious act should bring a sexual partner, but not if he is deluded by desire."
>
> Qt.102d.4 "He should enjoy a beautiful woman for the sake of achieving steadiness, never because of lust."
>
> Qt.102d.5 "And let him contemplate each in turn as having the form of Śiva and śakti. Let him not entertain a human mentality, full of anger and delusion etc. The whole ritual is to be performed by the finest Adepts by means of contemplating knowledge."[117]

Jr.102d.5 In this [ritual], even an offence against the scripture is avoided. Indeed, even in the [scripture], such a practice is observed because of the wish to perform a religious act—whilst avoiding sexual pleasure. As the tradition [says]:

> Qt.102d.6 "After smearing his limbs with ghee or even with sesamum oil, avoiding the kiss, shunning the embrace; with regard to the family and its offspring, for the sake of the family line, not out of desire; he who is appointed by

116. See in particular, *śl.*117cd-119ab, *śl.*124cd-125ab.
117. The opening hymn of the *Tantrāloka* contains the term *bharitanuḥ*, 'complete body'. This phrase, Jayaratha says, refers to Śiva and śakti joined together in total absorption, but since the hymn can also be applied to the parents of Abhinava, the term *bharitanuḥ* can also be applied to the parents who, joined together in mutual absorption (*samāveśamaya*) are Śiva and śakti. In this context, Jayaratha, at *Tantrāloka* p.14 lines 7-9, quotes Qt.102d.5 and shortly afterwards adds *TĀ* 29.162cd-163ab concerning the *yoginī*-born. In other words, Abhinava's parents are perfect examples of the ritual described in Jr.102d.4.

the gurus, should approach the wife of a [deceased] younger brother."[118]

Jr.102d.6 And so the person who is qualified for this [ritual] belongs amongst those great-hearted knowledgeable persons whose thought is undifferentiated. By putting aside their own fluctuating mental states, they attend to just one consideration: is the mind centred just on the non-duality of consciousness or not? As been said in this very connection:

> Qt.102d.7 "The aforementioned perfect expression of sexual desire, as it is called, is not to be performed for the sake of enjoyment. [It is to be performed] for the sake of considering one's own consciousness: is the mind steady or fluctuating?"[119]

Jr.102d.7 And so on.

Śl. 103 Concluding Bibliography and Effect

Jr.102d.8 And that [teaching] is not just an invention of ours. He says:

> *That very point is summarised in the illustrious* Sarvācārahṛdaya. *Those six śaktis mentioned above*[120] *bestow enjoyment and liberation.* || 103||

---

118. Compare *Ṛgvidhāna* III.43-44: 'With the verse beginning with *Udīrṣva* [*RV*.10.18.8], a brother-in-law should prohibit the wife of [his] issueless brother, for the sake of progeny, from ascending [the funeral pyre] when [her] husband is dead. And smearing himself with ghee and controlling his speech, [the brother-in-law] should at the proper time after menses beget one son, but on no account a second [son].' M.S. Bhat, *Vedic tantrism, a study of Ṛgvidhāna of Śaunaka with text and translation* Delhi, Motilal Banarsidass, 1987, p.356.
119. The question is important. In *TĀ* 28.303 ff., Abhinava distinguishes between two types of person, according to the stability of their discriminating knowledge. In the first type, differentiated thought has not been uprooted and their discriminating knowledge is therefore not stable and they become Śiva only at the end of their life. The second type, 'by contrast, those whose discriminating knowledge is well exercised, are identified with Śiva at all times: they are liberated-while-alive'. Jayaratha quoted this text earlier in his investigation of *TĀ* 4.243cd which states: 'The ascetics (*munayo*) too, who were occupied with undifferentiated thought, held this opinion.'
120. In *śl.* 102d.

Qt.103d.1"Vegavatī and Saṁhārī and Trailokyakṣobhaṇī and Ardhavīrāsanā and Vaktrakaulā: a set of five."[121]

Jr.103d.1 and so on. Even though each [of the six śaktis] has a further subdivision [the sub-division] is not listed here because it is interminable.

2. The Ritual

śl. 104ab **a. i. Definition of the Ritual as**
1. Emanation,
2. Reabsorption and
3. Blending.

Jr.103d.2 Let that [topic] be!
Why was it said: '[If ...] he would perform the ceremony with an external śakti'? To this question he says:

From the two come emanation and reabsorption.
Therefore their union is the ultimate reality.

Jr.104b.1 From the two, i.e. from śakti and from the one who possesses śakti, who are the causes, in the context of their union, come emanation in the sense that they are intent on each other; and reabsorption, principally in the sense that they repose each in their own form. As result there is a pause which involves both of them and then there is a welling-up [known] as 'the Fourth' since it arises just from their own essence in that way. As a result there is the union which is the ultimate reality. [That is], through granting access to the supreme level, it produces identity.

śl. 104cd-105ab **ii. Brief Examination of the Ritual**
Jr.104b.2 And how is this to be done? He says:

After drawing her close, after reverencing each other, having satiated each other, || 104 || *worship*

121. The set of five is not an attempt to name the six śaktis but is an example of a subdivision of just one of the six śaktis. The five personified goddesses are emanations of the six aspects of the one śakti who is inseparate from her lord. Thus Qt.103d.1 is a preparation for Jr.103d.1 rather than a comment on *śl.*103.

of the principal circle takes place by a process involving 'the inner part' (antaraṅga).[122]

Jr.105b.1 After reverencing [each other]': at the level of śakti and the one who possesses śakti. 'Worship': the [sexual] act which is to be performed.

śl. 105cd-106ab **b. i. Definition of 'principal circle' and 'Sub circle'**

Jr.105b.2 What is this 'inner' 'process' and what then is 'the principal circle'? With this question in mind he says:

> *That alone which produces bliss is the 'inner part' of consciousness.*||105|| *For that reason it is the preeminent circle. The rest, therefore, is the sub-circle.*

Jr.106b.1 'The rest, therefore': it does not produce bliss to the same extent.

śl. 106cd-107ab **ii. Etymology of *Cakra* (circle)**

Jr.106b.2 And what is the reason for the use of the word 'circle'? To this question he says:

> *Due to 'expansion', 'satiation', 'cutting of bonds' and 'energy of action',* ||106|| 'cakra' *is said to derive from* 'kasi' *[shining],* 'caki' *[satisfying],* 'kṛtyā' *[cutting] and* 'karoti' *[it does].*[123]

Jr.107b.1 '*kasi*' in the sense of 'expansion'; '*caki*' in the sense of 'satiation'; '*kṛtya*' in the sense of 'division'; *ḍukṛñ* in the sense of

122. *Anuttarāṣṭikā* 4 line 1 uses the term *aṅganā* to refer to a women with beautiful limbs. The term *antaraṅga*, however, has a wider connotation.

123. In his commentary on the *Nāṭyaśāstra* VI.3.5.14, '... Abhinavagupta distinguishes four modes of *nirukta* [traditional etymology]: by the noun, by the verb, by both of them at a time, lastly by convention, taken from the 'worldly' (*laukika*) usage, from Vedic usage or from the technical language (*pratiśāstrapārṣada*).' Louis Renou and Lilian Silburn, L. 'Nirukta and anirukta in Vedic', in *Sarupa Bharati*, [the Lakshman Sarup Memorial Volume], Hoshiarpur (India), Vishveshvaranand Institute,1954, p.71 footnote 5. The first line, *śl.*106cd, gives the derivation of the word *cakra* on the basis of the noun. The second line, *śl.*107ab, gives the phonological derivation. The 'worldly' and Vedic usages are not given in *śl.*106cd-107ab.

'instrument'. Accordingly, in that text [viz. *śl.*106cd-107ab], the word '*cakra*' is derived from the logical connection of the fourfold meaning of the verbal roots. Because 'it shines, satisfies, cuts, makes', it is a *cakra*.

Examination of the ritual

The First Emission : Emanation (*sṛṣṭi*);
The 'arisen' (*udita*);

Trajectory 1. Emphasis on Action,

śl. 107cd **Definition: Satiation (*tarpaṇa*)**
—Expansion (*vikāsa*)

Jr.107b.2 [It is said:] -

> Qt.107b.1 "That which produces bliss should be used in worship since it ravishes the heart."

Jr.107b.3 - according to this teaching, the characteristic quality of the range of ingredients suitable for use in worship is everywhere said to be the fact that it produces bliss. But how does that relate to the principal circle etc. which is to be worshipped? To this question he says:

> *And the sacrifice, viewed externally, is called 'satiation'; and as a result there is an expansion.*||107||

Jr.107d.1 The external sacrifice is specifically called 'satiation'. And as a result, i.e. as a result of bringing about an absence of desire, there is an expansion of consciousness, a welling.

Examination
Level of Bliss 3: *Parānanda*
śl. 108-109ab **i. Satiating Subcircle with 3 M's etc.**

Jr.107d.2 Where does that same external satiation—from which also an expansion of consciousness develops—come from? To this question he says:

> *Resulting from what is done by the one who possesses śakti in the circle and sub-circle and in*

the 'subtle-breath'; resulting from taking the food which pours forth bliss ||108|| *and from external sources such as perfume, incense, garlands etc., there is a welling up of consciousness.*

Jr.109b.1 Thus, 'from what is done by the one who possesses śakti':

> Qt.109b.1 "Consequently, he should satiate the self with its multitude [of goddesses] in the circle and sub-circle, externally by sprinkling drops upwards and downwards, and internally by drinking."

Jr.109b.2 according to this instruction, [from what is done by the one who possesses śakti] in the circle and the sub-circle, i.e. as result of kissing[124] etc.;

> Qt.109b.2 "The 'air' comes from the womb[125]. There is an erection of the penis. From the union of 'air' and penis ...." -

Jr.109b.3 —according to this teaching, [from what is done by the one who possesses śakti] within the 'subtle-breath', i.e. from driving [the penis within the 'air']; and from external sources such as perfume, incense, garlands etc.; from taking the food which pours forth bliss: - [from all these] there is a welling of consciousness, an expansion.

śl. 109cd-110ab ii. Satiating Sub-circle in other Ways

Jr.109b.4 In order to reach unity with the principal circle in this way, satiation must be made in the sub-circles. He says:

With measures which are suitable to themselves in that way, the [śakti and the one who possesses śakti] should bring about a satiation in the sub-circles ||109|| *so that oneness with the principal circle is mutually achieved.* |

124. The word *pāna* can refer both to drinking and to kissing and so allows Jayaratha to link the word *pītyā*, drinking, mentioned in *śl.*23d above with the kissing mentioned in *śl.*155a below and so to show how the Opening Ritual is observed in Sacrifice 3.

125. Jayaratha uses the term 'void' to mean womb, which is an acceptable usage. White, p.517 footnote 16.

Jr.110b.1 'Something suitable to themselves' means any form etc. 'In the sub-circles': in the faculties such as sight etc. And so 'something suitable to themselves' implies 'embracing', 'passionate kissing', etc. Therefore it is said:

> Qt.110b.1 "What is to be worshipped, who is the worshipper, what sort of invocation should there be? What flower, incense and oblation, which mantra and recitation? What is the sacrificial pit, [what is] the fire and what is the stick or what is the ghee? What is the divine rapture? Tell, O Three-Eyed One!"

Jr.110b.2 Having said which, [the text continues]:

> Qt.110b.2 "The young women themselves are worshipped, and the man himself is the worshipper; their joy is the invocation and the scratch caused by their finger-nails is the flower. The embrace mentioned above is the incense; the 'oblation' is produced from [their] bodies. The confused language of the beloved woman is the mantra and the 'lower nectar' is the recitation. The vulva is the sacrificial pit, the penis is the ladle and the clitoris is the fire itself and the seed is called 'ghee'. So it is said in the Bhairava tradition. Word and touch, form and essence and smell are a set of five. When bliss is aroused, the five-fold universe[126] [appears]. That is the rapture, O Maheśanī. Knowing this, let him reach Śiva."

śl. 110cd-111ab **Summary Quotation for Levels 4-7**

Jr.110b.3 How, as a result of satiating the sub-circle, does unity with the principal circle occur? Having raised that question, he now quotes the authority of the *āgama* itself on the matter.

> *And it is said in the* Triśirastantra: *"He whose interior faculties are set on an unsullied foundation* ||110|| *while in the midst of the set of*

126. The thirty-six categories are mostly divided into sets of five, as shown in Appendix 1. Only in love-making are all the categories present so that nothing is missing which might limit the rapture.

> *six senses*[127] *becomes fully absorbed into the abode of Rudra."*

Jr.111b.1 While there is an agitation within all the circles and their sub-circles, i.e. even as he enjoys the range of suitable objects, he remains firmly based on a foundation, i.e. a condition which is unsullied, i.e. which is without the stain of lack of self-control because it is without attachment [to the range of suitable objects]; as a result of resorbing the agitation of the [sub-circles etc.] by reposing in his own true nature, he becomes fully absorbed into the abode of Rudra, i.e. he becomes absorbed in the state of the supreme knowing subject which is the principal circle.

śl. 111cd-112ab **Level of Bliss 4: *Brahmānanda***

Jr.111b.2 He explains the [reabsorption into the principal circle]:

> *When the awareness of one's own nature becomes evident through the enjoyment of the respective*[129] *pleasures,* || 111 || *one by one the goddesses of the sub-circles enter the central circle of consciousness.*

Jr.112b.1 Because of the enjoyment of the respective pleasures such as the contemplation of one or other form etc., i.e. because of the external upsurge, there is an awareness of one's own nature, i.e. of one's own nature as a knowing subject which has become innately evident. [The awareness is] a welling of amazement at one's own self. [When this happens], one by one the goddesses of the sub-circles such as sight etc. [enter] the central [circle which is] the principal [circle] because it is the resting place of universal consciousness. That is, they enter into the circle of consciousness

127. These six are the five faculties of knowledge (*jñānendriya*) and their organising principle, the mind (*manas*).
Footnote 128 has been eliminated.

129. The term *nija-nija*, 'respective', is used in a distributive sense. In the context of the preceding *śloka*, it refers to the various circles and sub-circles which are being satiated in various suitable ways. It contrasts with the unicity of *nija* in the phrase *nija-sva-rūpa*, 'one's own nature', for although consciousness has many forms, in itself it is one.

which is essentially the knowing subject composed of supreme bliss, i.e. they repose in that very place.

śl. 112cd-113ab Contrasting Example: The Egoist

Jr.112b.2 In that case, at the moment of perceiving various objects, identity with the principal circle is obtained in a manner which is not at all different from the common-place! What is the point of such a teaching? To this question he says:

> *However, the [goddesses] of another person who is self-sufficient, since they abandon their governance of his body, stop still.* ||112|| *As a consequence his sense of self is not complete nor is it expansive.*

Jr.113b.1 On the other hand, [the goddesses] of a person different to the [one under consideration in the previous *ślokas*], i.e. a person who is self-sufficient; [these goddesses] stand aloof because such a person is without creative awareness; i.e. the goddesses of the sub-circles such as sight etc., since they abandon the governance of his body, stop still, i.e. they assume indifference towards the [body of that person]. Consequently, the self-image, which is perceived in the [person's] very body as a sense of self, is not complete. That is, because all desire has disappeared [in the goddesses], the faculties stop their movement [towards identity with the central circle]. Nor is [his sense of self] expansive, i.e. even when there is desire [viz. for a lesser enjoyment, the sense of self], due to an indifference towards the functioning of the sense-organs such as sight etc., is not outward looking. [The sense of self] is indeed deprived of both [completeness and expansiveness].

śl. 113cd-114ab Level of Bliss 5: *Mahānanda* i. Sub-circles Lead to Principal Circle

Jr.113b.2 What effect follows with regard to those two [viz. śakti and the one who possesses śakti] when the goddesses of those sub-circles repose in the principal circle? To this question he says:

> *Potency is acquired through a replenishment caused by the sparks of light, i.e. by the goddesses*

of the subcircles.||113|| *Because of this [replenishment] the couple, śakti and the one who possesses śakti, face each other.*

Jr.114b.1 'By means of the sparks of light', i.e. by the forms of the goddesses of sight etc.-

> Qt.114b.1 "Any object may appear by means of any faculty. The *yogī* who enters into the [object] by virtue of an attentiveness to the self becomes the [object]."[130]

Jr.114b.2 - according to this teaching, there is, in consequence [of the rays], a replenishment. Because of this [replenishment], [the pair, śakti and the one who possesses śakti] are attentive to the self which has become evident. As a result, the form that has been described in that way, i.e. the pair, śakti and the one who possesses śakti, become intent on each other, i.e. they arrive at union.

śl. 114cd-115ab **ii. Principal Circle affects Sub-circle**

Jr.114b.3 In this case too, what is the result of the [union]? To this question he says:

> *As a result, the pair [viz. śakti and the one who possesses śakti], who are intensely agitated by the contact which occurs through being absorbed into the upper sacred place,* ||114|| *agitates the sub-circles as well. The [sub-circles], in this case, are integrated with the [sacred place], they are not separate from it.*

---

130. In *Tantrāloka* vol.1, p.11, Jayaratha quotes this same text with reference to the phrase 'the light hidden by the five mouths', which occurs in the opening stotra of the *Tantrāloka*. He interprets 'light' as the supreme knowing subject and 'mouths' as the faculties such as sight etc. That light is 'hidden by the reabsorption into various objects'. His interpretation accords with the general principle that to emit is to be concealed, so that Śiva in his emitting of the universe and Abhinavagupta's father in his procreating and the *yogī* in his knowing, all become their effect.

Jr.115b.1 At the moment of union, [an agitation occurs] within the upper sacred place which consists of supreme bliss, i.e. [the agitation occurs] in the 'mouth of the *yoginī*', in the principal channel. The agitation, which occurs relative to the degree of absorption, involves a corresponding sub-ordination of conceit as regards the body etc. [It is an agitation] whose fullest definition is 'a preeminent sense of amazement at one's self'. The pair, so described, i.e. who are characterised as śakti and the one who possesses śakti, agitates the sub-circles also, i.e. [the pair] impacts on [the sub-circles] since the [sub-circles] are one with the [sacred place].

Jr.115b.2 When [the pair] has become fully absorbed in the [supreme sacred place] by subordinating the conceit as regards the body etc., what possible role is there for the sub-circles? Having this question in mind he had said: 'The [sub-circles], at this point, are integrated with the [sacred place], they are not separate from it'. And so, in that situation, the agitation is characterised as mutual slapping, embracing, passionate kissing etc.

śl. 115cd-117ab **Levels of Bliss 6: *Cidānanda* and 7: *Jagadānanda***

Jr.115b.3 In such an situation, the arising of truly supreme consciousness should occur! To this question he says:

> *The expression of differentiated thought subsides for the pair who are in that state. For that reason alone,* || 115 || *consciousness itself, i.e. their uniting [form of]*[131] *emission, gradually [appears]. The unalterable*[132] *sacred place [of their uniting form of emission] is the*

131. *TĀ* 29.140b mentions the three emissions: 'uniting', fully risen' and 'rested'. The first is the highest and is the source of the other two.

132. Gnoli, *Luce*, p.145 footnote 103 notes that the word *dhruva* 'unalterable', can also mean *anuttara*, 'the unsurpassable'. Therefore, the phrase could be translated as '... the sacred place of the Unsurpassable [Śiva].'

> *Unsurpassable. It is the universal, generous bliss which is composed of both [śakti and the one who possesses śakti].* || 116 || *The supreme kaula*[133] *is neither 'rested' nor 'risen'; it is the cause which produces the 'rested' and the 'risen'.*

Jr.117b.1 'The uniting [form of] emission': the emission which has the form 'uniting'. 'Composed of both': the universal bliss which consists of the perfect fusion of Śiva and śakti. 'Rested': transcending the universe. 'Risen': immanent to the universe. 'Supreme *kaula*': through not using the attribution 'rested' and 'risen' etc., the 'highly secret form' is meant. And so, when there is no expansion, [the supreme *kaula*] is not 'rested' and because it reposes in its own form, it is not 'risen'. Rather, as the cause of those two states, its reality is that of simple undivided consciousness.

Trajectory 2. Emphasis on Knowledge

śl. 117cd-118ab **Enunciation: Self and the Goddess 'consciousness'**

Jr.117b.2 And attention must necessarily be paid to absorption into the [reality of simple undivided consciousness]. He says:

> *He who aims at that undivided state should always draw consciousness to himself.* || 117 || *The nature of consciousness, i.e. of the goddess, is in the highest meaning of the word undivided.*[134]

śl. 118cd-119ab **Summary Examination**

Jr.118b.1 And how is entry to that [state] achieved? To this question he says:

---

133. The *kaula* is Kula and Akula, śakti and Śiva.

134. Supreme consciousness is called 'the goddess'.' *Parātriṃśikāvivaraṇa* p.198 line 1.

By carefully considering how objects chiefly described as 'like this' and 'like that' begin and finish to cease and to arise, || 118 || *the very fortunate man will enter the undivided sacred place which is the source of the emission.*

Jr.119b.1 [By extending his awareness, Jr.119b.2] to the beginning and finishing, i.e. the starting and ending of the ceasing and arising, i.e. of the forms 'rested' and 'risen', i.e. of objects which, since they result from the unique form simply of the experience of the self, cannot therefore be determined, i.e.which are chiefly [described as] 'this' and 'that'—on this subject:

> Qt.119b.1 "When an object[135] has been set aside, the mind which is restrained simply does not attend to another object. Then, by means of what lies between the [objects], highest realisation bursts forth."

Jr.119b.2 —in other words, by extending his awareness, in every direction, on every side, the very fortunate man will enter the undivided sacred place which is the source of emission. The direct experience of consciousness, i.e. of complete, supreme consciousness, will come to perfection in him.

Examination in Detail

śl. 119cd i. The Differentiation

Jr.119b.3 So be it! But how does the emergence of the two forms 'rested' and 'risen' occur? Does [the emergence] come about simply with reference to śakti or simply with reference to the one who possesses śakti? With these questions in mind he says:

Well then, the two, i.e. the 'rested' and the 'risen', emerge simultaneously in śakti and the one who possesses śakti. || 119 ||

135. The word *bhāva* can mean object, mood, attitude etc. The sentence could thus read, 'when one mood is set aside ....'

Jr.119d.1 The phrase 'well then' is used in reply.[136]

śl. 120ab **ii. The Merging**

Jr.119d.2 On the other hand, there is a difference between the ['rested' and 'risen' forms]. He says:

> *The 'risen' state is a focussing on the other's sacred place. The 'rested' form is a focussing just on the self.*

Jr.120b.1 The 'risen' state becomes evident by the coupling of their respective 'sacred places' [viz. sexual organs] which are called 'the principal circles'. [This 'risen' state] occurs while śakti and the one who possesses śakti continue to be intent on each other. The 'rested' [form], on the other hand, is located just in the self. In this [latter] case, i.e. when [the 'rested' form] is just in its self, the repose 'emerges' in a supreme fashion.

śl. 120cd **iii. The Identity**

Jr.120b.2 If that be the case, how does the identity, which is predicated in regard to śakti and the one who possesses śakti, not become lost? To this question he says:

> *In point of fact, the two [viz. śakti and the one who possesses śakti] are said to be a pair. Thus the 'risen' is the 'rested.* ||120||

Jr.120d.1 In point of fact, their identity is not discarded. The two, i.e. śakti and the one who possesses śakti, repose in the 'rested' state, i.e. in the self, but without attention being given to their mutual difference. Therefore, with reference to the self, the 'rested' form is said to be the 'risen' [form].

śl. 121 **iv. The Emission**

Jr.120d.2 Even so, this [following] difference exists between both of them. He says:

---

136. In Jr.119b.3, Jayaratha provides the questions to which the word *atha*, 'well then', is supposedly given in reply.

Even though there is a parity of creative awareness in the two forms, the 'rested' and the 'risen', śakti displays an emanation which is in keeping with the one who possesses her. The one who possesses her does not [do this]. || 121 ||

Jr.121d.1 The double form, 'rested' and 'risen', has a [double] creative awareness. Even though there is a parity in [creative awareness], by contrast it is śakti alone who displays an emanation which is in keeping with the one who possesses her, i.e. which becomes apparent in a manner which is congenial to the one who possesses śakti. It is the śakti who gives birth. The one who possesses śakti does not. For that reason she has the particularity.

Trajectory 3. Emphasis on the Śakti
1. Descriptions of the Śakti :

śl. 122ab **i. Her Nature**

Jr.121d.2 And therefore, precisely because she is endowed with a womb, her fully opening and closing central sacred place is mentioned everywhere in the scripture. He says:

In the scripture therefore, the śakti is described as 'the fully opening and closing central path'. |

Jr.122b.1 As is said in this same connection:

Qt.122b.1 "An Adept may remain bound to his vow for a whole year. The supernatural power which is his, young women acquire in one day."

Jr.122b.2 This statement has been made in another text.

śl. 122cd-123ab **ii. Her Ritual Preparation**

Jr.122b.3 And for this reason she alone is to be involved in the transference of knowledge. He says:

To her alone, because [of the fact that her central path is fully opening and closing], the guru properly transmits the substance of the Kula. || 122 || *And by means of the [mouth of the śakti], he transmits [the substance of the Kula] to men, in the manner which has been described.*[137]

Jr.123b.1 'Because': because of the fact that her centre is fully opening and closing—in a causal sense.'By means of the': by means of the 'mouth' of the śakti. In the case of men there is no opening of a central path. That is the meaning. As is said in this same connection:

> Qt.123b.1 "The wise man installs [his teaching] in the mouth of a woman. From the mouth of a woman [the disciple] takes [it], O Beloved."[138]
>
> Qt.123b.2 "And supernatural power comes from the 'mouth' of women. In their case, their 'path' is full of supernatural power."

Jr.123b.2 And so on.

śl. 123cd-124ab **Quote: The Śakti as *Bhāvā* and *Bhāvitā***

Jr.123b.3 And the same is said by the guru as well. He says:

> *"[The guru] should ritually prepare [the śakti] because by her very being*[139] *she is superior to his own body."* ||123|| *The illustrious Kallaṭanātha, in order to give the whole meaning of what has been said above, spoke that sentence.*

---

137. The manner is union (*saṃghaṭṭa*) and it is explicitly mentioned in the equivalent phrase from *Tantrasāra* p.203 lines 11-12: 'To her the Kula rite is communicated and from her, due to the above-mentioned process of uniting (*saṃghaṭṭāt*), it is communicated to men.' The phrase 'has been described' refers to the first and second Trajectories.

138. In *TĀ*.1.16, Abhinava praises Baṭṭanāthā and Bhaṭṭārikā, i.e. his guru Śambhunātha and his guru's *dūti*. In his investigation of that text Jayaratha uses this same quotation, Qt.123b.1. The first man, the one who 'places', is the guru. The second man, the one who 'receives', is the disciple.

139. The term *sad-bhāva* is translated here as 'by her very being'. The terms *kaula-sad-bhāva* and *kaulāmṛta* can be used to designate the *yoginī*'s sexual emission. White, p.138.

Jr.124b.1 The illustrious Kallaṭanātha, in order to sum up the whole meaning of what has just been said—starting from the characteristic quality of the śakti[140] —uttered the sentence. That is, because her central sacred space is spontaneously fully opening and closing, [the śakti is superior even to the [guru's] own body. For this reason, i.e. because of her own nature, the guru should ritually prepare the śakti, i.e. should purify her [for the ritual]. This is the meaning of the sentence.

2. Summary Description of the Ritual

śl. 124cd-125ab **i. At the Mouth of the *Yoginī***

Jr.124b.2 Having quoted the [sentence] in that way because the opportunity presented itself, he resumes the main topic.

> *Because of that [superiority], the 'mouth of the* yoginī' *is said by Maheśī to be the principal circle.* ||124|| *At that place this sacred oral [ritual] tradition [is celebrated]. From it, knowledge is obtained.*

Jr.125b.1 'Because of that [superiority]', i.e. because of the [superior] nature [of the śakti] which has been mentioned, the 'mouth of the *yoginī*' alone, which is synonymous with other ['mouths'] such as the Picu-mouth[141] etc., is said by the Lord Maheśvara to be the principal circle. At that very place this sacred oral [ritual] tradition—as stated or about to be described[142] —is to be celebrated. As a result knowledge is received from it, i.e. the [disciple's] entire absorption into supreme consciousness takes place.

---

140. That is, from *śl.*100c, 'the characteristic quality of the śakti' (*śakter-lakṣaṇam*) up to *śl.*123ab.

141. Śiva has six faces (*mukha*) of which the Picu-mouth, the lower face, is here identified with the female sex organ.

142. The whole of Sacrifice 3 is concerned with reaching consciousness by means of the 'mouth of the *yoginī*'. However, Jayaratha is referring particularly to *śl.*107cd-117ab and to *śl.*122 ff.

śl. 125cd-126ab **ii. The Result: Consciousness etc.**

Jr.125b.2 Therefore, please tell what sort of knowledge is received? To this question he says:

> *The [knowledge] which comes from that [place] cannot be put into writing. It is 'stated'. It comes from 'mouth' to mouth and by means of what is 'said'.*|| 125 || *The 'mouth' is the preeminent circle. Moreover, how could consciousness, which is unique to oneself, be put into writing?*

Jr.126b.1 'It cannot be put into writing': it is impossible to have it expressed in terms of differentiated thought.
Jr.126b.2 That [knowledge] '... goes from 'mouth' to mouth'. How then is it said: '[The knowledge] cannot be put into writing'. To this question he says: ['by means of] what is 'said' '. And the 'mouth' -

> Qt.126b.1 "The 'mouth' is said by Maheśī to be the principal mouth. The 'mouth of the yoginī' ..."

Jr.126b.3 according to that teaching, is said to be the preeminent circle. [Consciousness,] therefore, which arises during the union of both [their 'mouths'], consciousness which is unique to oneself, i.e. which is essentially pure experience, how could it [be put] into writing?

Examination of the Ritual:

1. For the Person who Seeks Liberation

śl. 126cd-127ab **Focus on the Ejaculating**

Jr.126b.4 How is this [knowledge] 'spoken'? To this question he says:

> *Well then, those who, whilst they are involved in this two fold, i.e. in this 'rested' and 'risen' sacred place which has been emanated,*

SUB-TOPIC 5 The Ritual of the Secret Teaching

Sacrifice 4 Based on the Body *(dehe)*

śl. 166cd-168 **1. Installation of *Vidyā* and Mantra**

Jr.166b.2 The scripture has a four-fold base: *vidyā*, mantra, *mudrā* and *maṇḍala.* The oral tradition concerning the two bases —mantra and *mudrā*—has been given above. Now, in what immediately follows, he outlines the oral tradition concerning the remaining [two bases], *vidyā* and *maṇḍala*, as well.

> *Thanks to this couple [of bases], he is free from having to perform vows and yoga.* ॥ 166 ॥ *Being constantly recollected he is committed to the Primordial Sacrifice alone. He should install the* vidyā *on the śakti's body and* kṣa *on his own [body], in proper order.* ॥ 167 ॥ *Having meditated on her lotus as the moon and on himself as the light of the sun, he should mate the two bases—*vidyā *and mantra—at the same spot.* ॥ 168 ॥

Jr.168d.1 Thanks to these couple of bases described [above], i.e. *mantra* and *mudrā*, the guru, by means simply of concentration, i.e. disregarding vow and *yoga* etc., is at all times committed to the Primordial Sacrifice. After meditating on the lotus of the śakti which, due to its mass of bliss, is like the moon, [and after meditating] on himself as the light of the sun since [the sun] induces [the lotus] to open; he should install, in due order, on the body of the śakti the chosen *vidyā* which is preeminently 'śakti', and on his own body *KṢA* which is preeminently 'Śiva', in order that, in the same spot, according to the degree of attentiveness to the practice just mentioned, the two bases—mantra and *vidyā*—might be brought together.

since it is a most pure substance because of its proximity to consciousness.[145]

Jr.128b.1 Those who desire to acquire a supernatural power such as immortality etc., should consume the [body's] ejaculated form which is designated by the term 'sexual fluid' etc. Then, with it alone, i.e. with the ejaculated form -

Qt.128b.1 "Bliss is the form of *brahman* ..."

Jr.128b.2 —since, according to the sacred text, [the ejaculated form] consists of bliss through its proximity to consciousness -

Qt.128b.2 "Therefore, let him consume the pure [substance] when it is not far removed from consciousness."

Jr.128b.3 —according to this instruction, they should worship with the most pure substance, i.e. they should satiate the circle of goddess.

śl. 128cd-129ab i. For the Knowledgeable Person —Consuming the Ejaculate

Jr.128b.4 And in this case how does the consumption etc. take place? To this question he says:

And the [ejaculated form], since it is stated to go especially from mouth to mouth, in reciprocal fashion, || 128 || *being intent on bestowing eternal youth and immortality, is designated as* kula. *It is supreme.*

Jr.129b.1 'And the' ejaculated form, since-

Qt.129b.1 "The ingredient that is located in one's own body is utterly revitalising [and] auspicious."[146]

Jr.129b.2 —i.e. according to this view, because it resides in the

145. This viewpoint is elaborated in *TĀ* 15.164cd-167ab.

146. This same quote is given by Jayaratha after *TĀ* 15.166ab which deals with the same subject.

body itself, the ingredient is designated as *kula*. For that reason it is supreme. Accordingly:

> Qt.129b.2 "Śiva is praised each day. That which is called 'the worship' [viz. the ejaculated form] is honoured by the thirty [gods], since, just by consuming it, a man becomes immortal. Alternatively, if someone who is forever human should drink it blended,[147] O Goddess, being without wrinkles and grey hair he becomes attractive to the *yoginīs*."

Jr.129b.3 —according to this principle, that which is intent on bestowing eternal youth and immortality is stated, i.e. is said in all the scriptures, to go above all from the mouth, i.e. from the 'mouth of the *yoginī*', to the mouth [of the hero] reciprocally, i.e. mutually. That [ejaculated form goes] from the 'mouth of the *yoginī*' to his own mouth, then to the mouth of the śakti, then to his own mouth and then he places it in the vessel etc., say the gurus. As the *āgama* also says:

> Qt.129b.3 "After liquefying the *golaka* and the *kuṇḍa*[148] at that spot, O Slim-waisted Lady, after taking with his mouth the auspicious ingredient located there, O Slim-waisted Lady, then after placing it in [her] mouth and after placing it in his own mouth, he should, with it, fill the vessel which contains a blend of wine and water. With it he should prepare the vessel which gives every supernatural power as a result."

> Qt.129b.4 "Having, by the procedure of 'from mouth to mouth', extracted the noble essence he should use it

147. That is, probably, with wine and water as in Qt.129b.3

148. The quote seems to imply two substances. *Kuṇḍa* means bowl, fire-pit, spring, etc. and also the vulva, as in Qt.110b.2. *Golaka* has a number of meanings: a ball or globe, glans penis, myrrh etc. Monier-Williams, *Sanskrit English dictionary,* p.368.3. The following quotes, Qt.129b.5 and Qt.129b.6, seem to imply both male and female sexual fluids. However, since the practitioner also placed the substance in his mouth, removed it and then placed it in the vessel, it could also be said to come from him.

to fully satiate the circle[149] comprising the goddesses and heroes."

Qt.129b.5 "Then after agitating the sexual partner, he whose 'desire' has become evident-should feed [himself and her] a quantity of the ingredient which issues from [her]."

Qt.129b.6 "He should sacrifice to the gods and goddesses with the semen that issues from both of them."

ii. For an Officiant —Anointing the Organ

śl. 129cd-130ab **Definition of the Ritual**

Jr.129b.4 Having thus explained the [ritual] which is particular to the knowledgeable person, he also gives [the ritual]which is particular to the officiant.

> *Even those who have not received enlightenment, are firmly established [at the highest level] by a sacrifice which is enhanced with the ejaculate.* ||129|| *The deities of the circle who are delineated [by the ejaculate] acquire discriminating knowledge.*[150]

---

149. The word *cakra* can mean 'circle' or 'pair'. If it means a circle in the sense of a group, the sentence reads as given. If only one couple is involved, the sentence reads: 'the pair comprising the goddess and the hero'.

150. The knowledgeable person has discriminating knowledge; the officiant does not. Even though the officiant himself does not acquire this discriminating knowledge—he remains an officiant—at least the deities who are present do. They are brought to the centre, as described in *śl.*131-132. and will therefore grant him the boons he desires. The deities are satiated in the same way as in the Opening Ritual and as in Sacrifice 4, *śl.*174cd-175.

Jr.130b.1 'Who have not received enlightenment': their knowledge is not fully established, they are on the path of ritual action.[151]

śl. 130cd -132 Examination

a. On Her Sex Organ

Jr.130b.2 He explains the delineation of the deities of the circle which is at that spot [viz. 'the mouth of the *yoginī*'].

> *They [who have not received enlightenment perform the ritual] at that spot, i.e. on the circle of the śakti, with the same [ejaculate] which consists of the essence of bliss.* ‖ 130 ‖ *[Having worshipped], on the outside [of the 'mouth'], in the four directions, according to the order given above,*[152] *the whole [group of divinities] starting with Gaṇanātha; having worshipped the couple, Kuleśa [and Kuleśī], in the central path, the goddesses on the three beams of light,* ‖ 131 ‖

---

151. How strong is the privative *a* in *a-prāpta-vibodhās*, 'those who have not (*a*-) received enlightenment', of *śl.*129c? What does the term *vibodhās* mean? Does the phrase mean a total absence of enlightenment? In Jr.130b.1, Jayaratha softens the rigour of the statement and does so with some justification. In *TĀ* 13, Abhinava discusses the degrees of descent of energy. In his description of the person who has received an 'intense' descent of energy, in *TĀ* 13.136-7, Abhinava distinguishes between one person whose intuition is sure (*dārḍhya*) and another whose intuition is vacillating (*kampa*). For the latter type he recommends the use of reasoning, the scripture, a guru, conversation [with the wise], practice, etc. Thus even the recipient of an 'intense' descent of energy may be insecure, his intuition not 'fully established'. Later in *TĀ* 13.163ab, while still discussing the intense descent of energy, he quotes the *Kiraṇatantra* which makes the following distinction: 'Some are suited to knowledge (*jñāna*) and others are suited to ritual action (*caryā*)'. Thus, two pairs of distinction are being made: the intuition may be sure or vacillating; the intuition may be expressed through knowledge or ritual action.
In short, the phrase 'who have not received enlightenment' refers to a person who is not without intuition but who is not secure in the knowledge of his intuition and who expresses his intuition in action. The privative '*a*' does not mean total exclusion.
152. The phrase 'the order given above' refers to *TĀ* 29.27-29ab, 46cd-51. Footnote 153 has been eliminated.

the subsidiary set of beams of light outside of them, then the 'set of four', as they say: the sage should worship, in turn, the circle of rays, i.e. the twelve beams of light, the eight, the sixty-four and the myriad. ||132||

Jr.132d.1 'On the circle of the śakti': on the 'mouth of the *yoginī*' itself which belongs to the śakti, i.e. on the principal circle. 'With the same': with the ejaculated form. 'Given above': in the relevant section connected with the daily ceremony. [The phrase] *arka-aram* means the twelve beams of light.

śl. 133ab **b. On his Own Body**

Jr.132d.2 That [set of divinities] is to be worshipped not only on the śakti's circle itself but also on oneself. He says:

He should repeat the worship [of the set of divinities] in exactly the same way on the sacred place within his own body.

The Second Emission: Reabsorption (*saṃhāra*)

the 'rested' (*śānta*)

śl. 133cd-134ab **Level 1: The 'rested' State**

Jr.133b.1 It was stated [viz. in *śl.*129cd-130ab] that those who focus on the double emission ejaculated during the union arrive at the undivided level and acquire discriminating knowledge. What is the course of events for those, by contrast, who are fully established in the emission which is essentially 'rested'? To this question he says:

Any 'rested' form, because it is developed with heart-felt attention, arrives at the 'rested' state of Śiva. It is called 'the sea of subsiding billows'. ||133||

Jr.133d.1 'Arrives at': the 'rested' form, which has been developed, [arrives at ...]. The 'rested' state [of Śiva] is explained as 'the sea of subsiding billows'.'

śl. 134cd-135ab **Level 2: Non-bliss (*nirānanda*)**

a. The Principal Circle Stops,

Jr.133d.2 And what is the effect of that sort of [state of rest]? To this question he says:

> *Then, as a result of settling down in the state of 'rest', the whole group of divinities which is located upon the [central] circle* ||134|| *stops still. It ceases to function. It is poised over the void, without bliss.*

Jr.135b.1 'It ceases to function': because all things have completely disappeared. For that reason it is said: '[the group of divinities] is poised over the void'. So:

> Qt.135b.1 "Supreme Śiva is without support."

Jr.135b.2 - according to this teaching, [the whole group of divinities] is without bliss because it reposes at the level of Śiva.

śl. 135cd-136ab **b. The Sub-circles Stop**

Jr.135b.3 Not only does the group of divinities of the central circle itself halt in this way, but [the group] located on the sub-circle does so as well. He says:

> *Any [group of deities] which has the nature of a sub-circle such as sight etc., since it depends on the [group of divinities of the central circle]* ||135|| *is therefore plunged in non-bliss. It stops still, longing for bliss.*

Jr.136b.1 'Which has the nature of a sub-circle such as sight etc.': a group of deities. 'Depends on the [central circle]': is subject to the group of deities on the principal circle. 'Therefore': by the fact of depending on the [principal circle].

śl. 136cd-137ab **c. The Desire for Bliss**

Jr.136b.2 Even the particular group of divinities of the sub-circle such [as has been mentioned] reposes at the level simply of non-bliss. So be it! What is the result of the fact that it longs for bliss? To this question he says:

> *Since it is not united with the supreme reality [of consciousness], this group of rays of the faculties* ||136|| *halts. It is deprived of its nature and is intent on regaining its nature.*

Jr.137b.1 This group of divinities of the faculties, i.e. sight etc., is without repose in the supreme, i.e. in what is superior to everything because of the plenitude of its bliss. [The group is without repose] in that reality just mentioned, i.e. in the knowing subject which has the form of consciousness. [The group] is deprived of its own nature, i.e. it is unable to absorb etc. its own respective objects etc. and it is intent on regaining its own nature. It halts, it longs for bliss.

śl. 137cd-138ab **Levels 3, 4, 5, 6 or the Krama**

Jr.137b.2 And, so described, what will this group of rays of the faculties undertake? To this question he says.

> *As the result of an intense longing [which is felt in the group of faculties], there comes into being an external reality which is full of the essence of the [group]. Because of a powerful wish to savour [that external reality]*[154a] ||137|| *[the group of rays of the faculties], after reaching the indefinable sacred place of re-pose, offers the object to its self.*

Jr.138b.1 As a result of a craving and an attachment [which is

---

154a. The very dense lines of *śl.*137cd-138ab make use of the Krama cycle when described in four stages. The stage of *udyoga* is indicated by the words *rasān* and *abhiṣvaṅgāt* in *śl.*137d and Jr.138b.1. The second term *avabhāsa* is found only in the word *avabhāsitānāṃ* of Jr.138b.1, but the phrase 'an external reality which is full of the essence of the [group]', *śl.*137cd, refers to this second moment. The word *carvaṇa* occurs in both *śl.*137d and Jr.138b.1. The word *viśrānti* occurs in both

felt in the group of faculties], there come into being realities which are full of [the group's] own essence, i.e. which are externally manifested because they consist of [the group's] own consciousness. Because of a powerful wish to savour, i.e. to taste, those realities, this group of rays of the faculties after, i.e. immediately after, reaching the indefinable sacred place of repose, i.e. the form of self-perception, offers what is relished, i.e. all these realities, to itself, i.e.—

> Qt.138b.1 "When the awareness of one's own nature becomes evident through the enjoyment of the respective pleasures, one by one the goddesses of the sub-circles enter the central circle of consciousness."

Jr.138b.2 —according to this teaching, [the group of faculties] finds repose in the knowing subject itself, i.e. in the principal circle of consciousness.

śl. 138cd-139 **Level 7: The Surging**

Jr.138b.3 What happens to the [group of deities] when it reposes in the [principal circle of consciousness] in this way? To this question he says:

> *As a result of [the group of faculties] offering their own objects to [the self], there is an outpouring of fully surging consciousness.* ||138||
> *There is an agitation of the potency which is due to the utter repleteness of the group of deities of the sub-circles. The lord of the circles himself, according to what was said earlier,*[154b] *surges vigorously.* ||139||

Jr.139d.1 The lord, [who is lord of the circles] because he is the sacred place of repose, i.e. the knowing subject himself, — As a result of the wish to offer their respective objects to the self an utter repleteness is thereby [acquired] by the group of

154b. That is, in *śl.*113cd-114ab which Jayaratha quotes in Qt.139d.1.

deities of the sub-circles. [That repleteness] is the reason for the agitation of the potency whilst the stability of the self [remains] ever present. As a result there is an outpouring of fully surging consciousness. As was said earlier, [namely]

> Qt.139d.1 "Potency is acquired through a replenishment caused by the sparks of light, i.e. by the goddesses of the sub-circles. Because of this [potency] the couple, śakti and the one who possesses śakti, face each other." —

Jr.139d.2 he, [the lord of the circles], surges vigorously, i.e. he quite suddenly turns his attention outwards.

The Third Emission: Union (*saṅghaṭṭa*), Blending (*melaka*)

Transition and introduction

śl. 140 **1. Enunciation**

a. The Three Emissions (*visarga*)

b. Etymology of *Visarga*

Jr.139d.3 He summarises the present topic:

> *The emission is three fold in the following ways:*
> *union, 'risen' and 'rested'.* |

Jr.140b.1 He explains the reason for the use of the word 'emission' in three ways:

> *Emission means: that which emits; that from*
> *which the varied emission comes; and the place*
> *to which it returns.* ||140||

Jr.140d.1 [The phrase] 'that from which' refers to the cause.

śl. 141-142ab **2. Definition of the Three Emissions**

Jr.140d.2 That is not just an invention of ours. He says:

> *That point has been stated in the illustrious Tattvarakṣaṇa,*

in the illustrious Nigama[155] *and in the Triśiromata.*

Jr.141b.1 With regard to that [half line, viz. *śl.*141ab, Abhinava has already said that]:

> Qt.141b.1 "The threefold emission is mentioned, moreover, in the *Tattvarakṣāvidhāna.*"

Jr.141b.2 Because he had earlier explicitly quoted from the *Tattvarakṣāvidhāna* with those words, he does not [now] quote that book. He explicitly quotes the illustrious *Gama-śāstra*:

> *Śakti is the fire-pit; Śiva is the liṅga; [their] blending is the supreme plane.* ||141||
> *Emanation, reabsorption [and] 'that' (tad)*[156] *derive from those two. The emission is threefold, according to the* Gama.

Jr.142b.1 The fire-pit, i.e. the female śakti, is the 'risen'form. Śiva is the 'rested' form. [Their] blending is the union. With regard to [those three]: the emergence of the emanation, in the sense of being 'risen', is because of the śakti; [the emergence] of reabsorption, in the sense of being 'rested', is because of Śiva; and [the emergence] of 'the ineffable' (*anākhya*), in the sense of 'absence of all division', is because of the union, i.e. because of what is called 'the supreme plane'. Such is the threefold emission according to the *Gama-śāstra.*

The Ritual

1. The 'mantra', i.e. The Practitioner:

śl. 142cd-146ab **a. i. The Coupling of all Diversity**

Jr.142b.2 After quoting the *Gama-śāstra* in this way, he

155. The title *Nigama* could give rise to confusion. Does it refer to the Veda which is also called the *Nigama*? Jean Filliozat, 'Les agamas sivaites', in Bhatt, N.R., ed. *Rauravāgama.* Pondichéry, Institut Français d'Indologie, 1961, (Publications de l'Institut Français d'Indologie, no.18) Vol.1, p.vi. In order to avoid any confusion, Jr.141b.2 specifies that the text in question is the *Gamaśāstra* mentioned in *śl.*142b.

156. In Jr.142b.1, Jayaratha explains that the pronoun 'that' (*tad*) refers to *anākhya*, 'the ineffable'

explicitly quotes the illustrious *Triśirobhairava* as well:

> *There is the final stopping of the two streams, the awakening [to consciousness] of the upper and lower circles,* ||142 || *the quietening of the veins and the entire absorption of the winds and the absence of division into diagrams, joints and vital parts.* ||143|| *Being steadily without*[157] *the exhalation and inhalation [of the subtle-breaths] at the level of the seventy-two thousand [channels] within the body, he, as Śiva, unites the two existences.* ||144|| *He should always stay diligently within the union, at the level of Bhairava. As a result, the formless state which these two attain* ||145|| *is characterised as being devoid of time and space. It is the splendour of perfectly evident reality.*

Jr.146b.1 He permanently eliminates the divisions into the upper and lower circles, the veins, diagrams, joints, vital parts and winds. He therefore [brings about] a final stopping of the two streams, i.e. the right and left currents, which ends with repose in the central sacred place, i.e. [he brings about] the awakening [to consciousness], the quietening and the entire absorption [of all of these]. [After this] there is, at the level of the seventy-two thousand [channels], within the body -

> Qt.146b.1 "There are seventy-two thousand channels in the navel centre."

Jr.146b.2 —i.e., according to this teaching, by putting an end, within the region of the navel which is divided into that many channels, to the *prāṇa* and *apāna*, i.e. being without [*prāṇa* and *apāna*], he is absorbed into Śiva. Since he unites the two existences consisting of the 'rested' and the 'risen', he becomes

157. Gnoli, following Jayaratha, interprets *antarā* as 'without'. Gnoli, *Luce*, p.697 footnote 84.

intent on the reality which is the blending etc. of those two. He should therefore at all times stay diligently at the level of the union which is the form of complete consciousness, i.e. he should become attentive to that same level [of union]. As a result there is, at either level of its two forms which are described as 'rested' and 'risen', a reality which originally is without shape in the sense that it is without division into composite shapes etc. Therefore [the reality] is without time or distinction since it is without parts. As a result there occurs the splendour, the revelation, of the quite evident reality, whose unique form is simply one's own experience.

śl. 146cd-147ab **ii. Constant Perception**

Jr.146.3 And constancy is required in this. He says:

> *He should focus [his] perception on Being -*
> *through withdrawing from all beings,* ||146||
> *after restraining both 'sun' and 'moon' from*
> *the paths of dissolution and dissemination.*

Jr.147b.1 After withdrawing from all beings such as the circles etc., after restraining out-going and in-coming subtle-breaths from the right and left sides, he should focus [his] perception on the central sacred place. [That perception] is the form of the knowing subject, it is connected to all beings [and] it consists of their union. That is, he should be simply committed to the awareness of [the perception]. In this teaching [the term] 'existences' (*vittī*)[158] is to be explained simply as 'rested' and 'risen'.

śl. 147cd-149ab **iii. Creative Awareness Appears (*parāmarśa*)**

Jr.147b.2 As a result therefore [of focussing on the perception

158. The word *vittī* can mean existence or consciousness. In order to eliminate the ambiguity, Jayaratha notes that *vittī*, as used in *śl.* 144b, means existences, i.e. the 'rested' and the 'risen' and is not to be confused with *saṃvittiṃ*, consciousness, which is used in *śl.*146.

of Being], there is an [emission] which is also three-fold.[159] It shines forth as an indefinable spontaneous creative awareness for those who are entirely absorbed in the [unitive] emission. That same [creative awareness] is the supreme potency of the mantra. He says:

> *That which, as a result [of focussing on the perception of Being], arises in the three-fold sacred place consisting of awareness, absorption and becoming is the resonance. It is essentially the creative awareness of consciousness. For that very reason [the resonance] is the potency of the mantra.*[160] *The person who is eager to receive such fruit as arises in that same [resonance], if, after continually concentrating on his own mantra, he perseveres [therein]; will truly know the arising of the mantra.*| 149ab|

Jr.149b.1 Whoever, as a result [of focussing on the perception of Being], is absorbed in the [uniting form of] emission, who is eager to receive the fruit which arises during the uniting [form of emission, namely the fruit which is called] 'such' because it derives from the unique inner knowledge of simple experience, i.e. which cannot be described since it is full of bliss; if, after focussing continually and not intermittently on his chosen mantra in relation to the same spot, i.e. in relation to the creative awareness of consciousness which consists of amazement at 'I am', i.e. in relation to the resonance: if he perseveres, he will, within [the resonance], know the arising of the mantra, i.e. his mantra will arise.

---

159. Śl.142b reads: *visargas-tri-vidho game,* 'emission is three-fold, according to the *Gama*'. In the present context the word *trividha,* three-fold, is short for 'triple emission'.

160. Śl.147cd-148ab as well as *śl.*182 are quoted, with a slight variation, by Jayaratha in his investigation after *TĀ* 5.130cd-131ab.

śl. 149cd-150ab **b. Recitation**

Jr.149b.2 And [this practice] must increasingly be performed in relation to that same [resonance] with a commitment to contemplation so that one-pointedness in the central circle alone might be achieved. He says:

> *He should perform the recitation in relation to that same [procedure, viz.* śl.*142cd-149ab], i.e. even as the sub-circles jointly assemble together within consciousness.* ||149|| *[The recitation] is arranged in sets of hundred thousands. It is [performed] in keeping with the modalities of sound.*

> Qt.150b.1 "One by one the goddesses of the sub-circles enter the central circle of consciousness."

Jr.150b.1 According to this teaching, the joint assembling of the goddesses of the sub-circles within the principle circle, i.e. within consciousness, brings about repose. In connection with that same [assembling of the goddesses], i.e. while the mantra which is the creative awareness of consciousness is arising, he should, in keeping with what is simply the awareness of sound—

> Qt.150b.2 "In relation to the 'rising', to the 'joining' and to the 'resting', recitation is performed three hundred thousand times."

Jr.150b.2 —perform the recitation which, according to that quote, is arranged by sets of hundred thousands, i.e. he should increasingly focus his attention.

2. The Six Rayed *Mudrā*, i.e. Intercourse:

śl. 150cd-153ab **a. i. Intercourse**

Jr.150b.3 And it is said in another [text] that the *mudrās* too have this same supreme potency. He says:

> *And according to the illustrious* Yogasañcāra *as well this* mudrā, *which is favoured by the yoginīs, is* supreme. ||150|| *There is a lotus*

covering the circle which is ever upward-looking and which is supported within the triangle. Permanently attached [to that lotus] there is a stalk whose root is adorned with a lotus of sixteen petals. ||151|| *Within the fire which results from the process of rubbing the pair of lotuses attached to the stalk which is shared between them; which results from uniting the torrent of portions of the full and lovely moon and sun which are shared between them;* || 152 || *which results from associating the portions of semen and of the 'blood' of the three petals, i.e. at the centre [of the three petalled lotus], there is a sprout, an emanation.*

Jr.153b.1 Within the triangle [there is a circle] which is always facing upwards since it is forever fully opening and closing.

> Qt.153b.1 "The lotus of the sex organ has three petals."[161]

Jr.153b.2 —according to this teaching, the three-petalled lotus of the sexual organ—which is male or female—covers the circle. [The stalk] is always attached to this [lotus], since it has the function of producing growth.

> Qt.153b.2 "Moon' is male semen ....."

Jr.153b.3 —according to this teaching, [the stalk] is adorned with the sixteen petalled lotus of the moon—meaning, therefore, that it is full of bliss. It is, therefore, the sacred place of origin, the source of the emanation whose form will be described later.[162] The stalk has the form of the central channel.

> Qt.153b.3 "[The channel] on the left carries urine; [the channel] in the centre carries semen; and [the channel]

161. In the first instance the 'three petals' refers to the femal sex organ as in Qt.153b.1, Jr.153b.5. It also refers to both the male and the female sex organs, as in Jr.153b.2. In Jr.154b.1 and Jr.156b.1, Jayaratha refers to the union of the male and female sex organs as the six rayed shape.

162. This would seem to refer, in particular, to the *yoginī-bhū*, *śl.*163a.

on the right carries menstrual blood ..."[163]

Jr.153b.4 According to this teaching, by the process of mutually rubbing the pair of lotuses, i.e. the male and female [lotuses], which are attached, i.e. joined, by means of the stalk which is shared between them; as a result of uniting the portions of the full, i.e. without parts—therefore lovely in the sense that they are composed of bliss—male and female semen, i.e. of sun and moon which are shared between them;

> Qt.153b.4 "The fire that is born from uniting sun and moon is called 'The Pure'."[164]

Jr.153b.5 - according to this teaching, whatever, as a result of associating the portions of female and male semen, pours forth within the fire, which is explained as the knowing subject alone, i.e. at the centre of the three-petalled lotus, is the sprout, which is able to produce the universe. The emanation, in an external sense as well, becomes visible by the same means. Therefore it is said:

> Qt.153b.5 "The 'fire' is located within the vulva and the *liṅga*; the 'sun' is located within; the 'moon', i.e. *soma,* is located above. From the uniting [of these] comes the essence."[165]

> Qt.153b.6 "The 'sacred site' refers to the circle of the *śākinī*; the 'emanation' refers to the world of the moving

---

163. The meaning of this text is uncertain. Jayaratha uses Qt.153b.3 in his investigation of *TĀ* 4.137cd but even so its meaning is unclear. Whatever about its meaning, it is quoted principally for the phrase: '[the channel] in the centre carries semen', which introduces the discussion in Jr.153b.4 on the meaning of the phrase: 'the stalk which is shared between them'.

164. Jayaratha uses this quote in his investigation of *TĀ* 3.122ab, and understands the fire, moon and sun to refer to subject, object and means of knowledge respectively. He uses it again after *TĀ* 5.72 where Abhinava says that: 'As a result of the mutual friction of the various portions of moon and sun the bliss of emission shines forth in the sacred place of fire and moon.' In this context Jayaratha again gives the quote under discussion and notes the various meanings of Abhinava's words. In particular he notes that the bliss of emission is in its primary sense an emission of semen but in an associated sense is the entry into supreme consciousness.

165. Neither the translation nor the meaning of the quotation is clear.

and non-moving. The 'sacred region' is [code] for the best type of seed and for the menstrual discharge of the monthly period; it is [code] for the enjoyment of female semen and menstrual blood, it is [code] for just Kula and Akula. [One should adore] the golden Lord Hāṭakeśvara located within the pericarp of the lotus, him who is merged within the lotus of the śakti, the non-dual, the supreme Śiva."

śl. 153cd-154ab **ii. Stability at the Fourth**

Jr.153b.6 What advantage is there to the [practitioner] by being involved with the *mudrā* in that way? To this question he says:

> *The practitioner], by means of the* mudrā *which unites moon, sun and fire (*citragu*)*[166] *in this way will all at once,* ||153|| *even as he generates interiorly the sequence comprising emanation etc.,*[167] *becomes settled at the Fourth.*

Jr.154b.1 'Which unites': the [*mudrā*] is said to have the shape of six beams of light[168]

śl. 154cd-156ab **iii. Awareness Appears (*vimarṣa*)**

Jr.154b.2 Having thus explained the nature of the *mudrā* as a means of giving potency to the mantra; wishing to describe the [sexual] interplay of one [partner] with the other, and wishing to giving to the mantras the potency of [that interplay] as well, he says:

> *The awareness which occurs at the moment of*

166. '*Citragu*', which means 'possessing brindled cows', is the name of a son of Kṛṣṇa. Monier-Williams, *Sanskrit English dictionary*, p.396.2. The dictionary gives no other meaning to this word. However, in *TĀ* 3.122cd, Abhinava states: '... because the nature of consciousness is fiery, it is called 'variously gleaming' (*citrabhānuḥ*)'. See also *TĀ* 3.123cd-125ab.
167. This refers to the twelve stages of the Krama cycle.
168. The double triangle represents the phoneme of six rays, *AI*, or the unity of Śiva and Śakti or of seed and womb.

> *absorption into that* khecara-mudrā *during the mutual kissing, pleasure, play, laughter and so on of the śakti and the one who possesses śakti is the potency of the mantra. It has the [following] forms: 'inarticulate', 'resonance', 'roaring', 'bursting', 'heard sound', 'sound', 'end-of-sound','unbroken unstruck'.*[169] ‖ 156ab ‖

Jr.156b.1 The awareness, i.e. the experience, which arises at the moment of absorption in that *khecarī-mudrā* which is characterised as a *mudrā* of six beams of light, i.e. during the mutual kissing, pleasure etc. of the śakti and the the one who possesses śakti, is the potency of the mantra which is essentially the awareness of the supreme sound divided into eight sections, starting with 'inarticulate' etc.

śl. 156cd-157ab **b. The Natural Recitation: Enunciation:**

Jr.156b.2 As a result of contemplating again and again the [events of *śl.*154cd-156ab], he acquires the [potency of the mantra]. He says:

> *Having in this way reached stability with respect to the set of eight circles,*[170] *he practices a natural*[171] *recitation within the supreme sacred place.* ‖156 ‖ *He attains the plane of the eight bhairavas which is divided into eight phases.*

---

169. In *Luce,* p.698 footnote 97, these eight forms are identified by Gnoli - who states that he is following Jayaratha - with the eight stages of sound as listed in the 'arousing' of *OṂ* given in Appendix 3.However, according to *śl.*158d the first stage, 'inarticulate' is audible, whereas 'half-moon' (*ardhacandra*) normally the first of the set of eight, is inaudible. It would seem, therefore, that the eight stages correspond to a certain way of combining the twelve stages of the 'arousing' but it is not clear how. The eight forms are not mentioned again but their place is taken by the eight phases of sound in their normal order.
170. The set of eight circles are listed in *śl.*157cd-158ab.
171. The term *sahaja,*'natural', may also refer to *haṃsa,* see Bagchi, *Kaulajñānanirṇaya,* p.ix, or to the phonemes *SA* and *HA* and all their meanings.

Jr.157b.1 'Eight phases': [the plane] is split, divided, into eight phases starting with 'half-moon' etc. and ending with 'transmental'.

Examination

śl. 157cd-158ab **i. The 8 Circles (*cakra*)**

Jr.157b.2 What exactly is the set of eight circles, reaching which he should perform the recitation? To this question he says:

> *The double coming and going, the two understandings, the two ears, the two eyes, the double contact of the* liṅgas, || 157 || *their two matings and the two 'ends-of-body': [these are] the pairings, i.e. the circles.*

Jr.158b.1 'The double coming and going' means 'the double *prāṇa* and *apāna*'. 'The two understandings' refers to the apprehension and the intellect.[172] 'Contact' means 'just touching'. 'Their two matings' means 'the mating of their two *liṅgas*', at the moment of union. 'The two 'ends-of-body' means the two 'ends-of-twelve'. [The phrase] 'the pairings, i.e. the circles' is to be applied to each [of the terms].

śl. 158cd-160ab **ii. The 8 Phases (*uccāra*)**

Jr.158b.2 What exactly is the level of the eight bhairavas, [mentioned] there in [*śloka* 157ab], which, furthermore, is split into eight phases starting with 'half-moon' etc.? To this question he says:

> *The inarticulate [sound, viz.* HĀ-HĀ*] which comes from the region of the heart between the breasts and ends at the lips, is [uttered] in*

172. It is not clear, from *śl.*157cd-158ab, how there are eight circles. In Jr.158b.1, Jayaratha seems to count the phrase 'the two understandings' twice, as two apprehensions and two intellects. If that is so, the eight are: [1] the coming and going of the subtle breath; [2] apprehension; [3] intellect; [4] the two ears; [5] the two eyes; [6] the contact of the two sexual organs; [7] the mating; [8] the two 'ends-of-body'. They are different from the eight locations listed in *śl.*86cd-87ab.

the throat.||158|| *After hearing [the inarticulate sound] between the two circles [viz. in the throat] ... when the agitation ceases, at that moment [all the audible forms of sound] vanish. And at that moment,*[173] *Bhairava as sound [appears], which is divided into eight [phases] in that way.*[174] *It is supreme.*|| 159 || *It is set over 'light', 'resonance' and 'air'.*[175] *It is called the supreme pervasion*[176] *of the mantra.*

Jr.160b.1 [The sound *HĀ-HĀ*], starting from the region of the heart between the breasts, finishing at the lips, is [uttered] in the throat of the śakti.

> Qt.160b.1 "Any syllable which is unagitated, which arises in the throat of the beloved, which is supreme,[177] natural, which is called 'sound', which is the [supreme] category, which is ever-present, is recitation."

> Qt.160b.2 "As a result of savouring everlasting bliss, the [sound] '*HĀ-HĀ*' occurs in the throat. Coming into being of its own accord, it is a pleasurable utterance which perceives the category of sexual desire."

---

173. The 'arousing' of *OṂ* according to the *Svacchandatantra*, for which see Appendix 3, has twelve stages. The first four are audible. The next eight are inaudible. *TĀ* 29.158 deals with the audible sound. *Śl.*159ab deals with the transition from the audible sound to the inaudible and *śl.*160ab explicitly deals with some of the eight stages of inaudible sound.

174. That is, according to the list given in *śl.*155cd-156a which, as Jayaratha notes in Jr.160b.2, is equivalent to the list of eight referred to in Jr.157b.1 and Jr.158b.2, namely the list starting with 'half-moon' and finishing with 'transmental'.

175. The same trio, 'light', 'resonance' and 'air' (*jyotir-dhvani-samira*) listed and named slightly differently as *dhvani-jyotir-marud*, appears again in *TĀ* 32.12a. In his investigation of that text, Jayaratha interprets *dhvanir* as 'sound' (*nāda*); *jyotir* as *bindu* and *marut* as *śakti*. In Jr.160b.2 he interprets *jyotir* as *ardha-candra*. The difference is not significant since *ardhacandra* is the next step after *bindu*.

176. The 'pervasion' of *śl.*160b is not the antepenultimate stage of sound but all eight stages of inaudible sound, as indicated in *śl.*161ab.

177. *Param* has a double meaning. It means 'supreme', 'supremely', but can also refer to the phoneme *A*. The phrase could be translated as 'Any unagitated syllable which occurs in the throat of the beloved as *A*'.

Jr.160b.2 The reality so described, which is mostly inarticulate, arises as the double phoneme '*HĀ-HĀ*'. [The practitioner] adverts to the [the double phoneme] which reposes within the 'mouth of the *yoginī*', i.e. within the principal circle, as soon as the agitation resulting from the mutual uniting ceases. At that moment all [forms of sound] vanish, i.e. come to repose. At that very point, i.e. at the level of the extinction, Bhairava as sound appears. It is divided into eight according to the forms 'inarticulate' etc. as given above; it therefore appears as a set of eight phases starting with *ardhacandra* etc. It is therefore supreme: it is said everywhere to be the supreme pervasion of the mantra. Such is the meaning of [Abhinava's] statement. 'Light' is *ardhacandra*; 'resonance' is sound; 'joining together', i.e. touching, is *śakti*.[178] However, [the stages of sound that are] below[179] ['light', 'resonance' and 'air'] are pervaded by the ['half-]moon'. That is the implied meaning.

śl. 160cd-161ab **iii. The 8 Bhairavas (*unmanā*)**

Jr.160b.3 And what is the set of eight bhairavas [mentioned] in [*śl.*157a] and what is the pervasion of the mantra? With these questions in mind he says:

> *[The eight Bhairavas are:] Sakalam, Akaleśam, Śūnyam, Kalāḍhyam and Kha-malam and Kṣapaṇakam,* || 160 || *Antaḥstham, Kaṇṭhyoṣṭhyam.*[180] *This pervasion, therefore, extends*

178. *Sparśa*, 'touching', is an alternative name for the term *śakti*. Silburn, *Le Vijñāna Bhairava*, p.50.

179. 'Below' refers to the audible stages of sound.

180. In *TĀ* 6.70cd, Abhinava mentions them in the masculine gender: '... the eight bhairavas starting from Sakala and finishing with Kaṇṭhyoṣṭhya', and places them among many sets of eight: asterisms, 'serpents', directions of the compass etc. Jayaratha gives no comment on those eight bhairavas and those meanings are quite absent from our list. These names, with variations, are also listed in *Svacchandatantra* 10.1194 which Abhinava copies to some extent in *TĀ* 8.368. They refer to the members of the cortege of Sadāśiva who are the sources of the scriptures. In his interpretation, Jayaratha reconciles the two listings. Some of the names can also refer to phonemes or classes of phonemes.

from '[half-] moon' and finishes with 'transmental'.

Jr.161b.1 The neuter gender alone is suited to the [eight bhairavas] as a result of the absence of any other designation for 'that' which arises at the moment of the perfect fusion of Śiva and śakti. For that reason the presentation is in the [neuter] gender.

Results:

śl. 161cd-162ab **1. Liberated-while-living, Bhairavī**

Jr.161b.2 Through contemplating the pervasion [of the mantra] in this way, he becomes, in every respect, supreme Bhairava. He says:

> *Recalling, in every action and in every place, the pervasion [of the mantra] in this fashion,* ||161|| *being ever unattached, liberated-while-living, he becomes the supreme Bhairava.*

śl. 162cd-163 **2. The *Yoginī*-child**

Jr.162b.1 And the offspring which is conceived at the time of a mating performed in that way is supremely distinguished. He says:

> *Any body conceived during such a mating, which develops in the womb,* || 162 || *is called* 'yoginī-*born'. Of himself alone the* [yoginī-*born*] *is the repository of knowledge, a Rudra.*[181] *According to the illustrious* Vīrāvali-

For example, the word *antasthā* refers to the semi-vowels while the word *kaṇṭhya* can refer to the first class of consonants and can also refer to the vowels *A* and *Ā*. Padoux, *Vāc*, p.297 footnote 204. The word *oṣṭhya* can refer to the fifth class or to the vowels *U* and *Ū*. *ibid.* p.298 In short it would seem that the names refer in general to emanations from the primordial sound and can be understood in particular either as the scriptural traditions or some combination of the phonemes or the eight levels of sound.

181. In *Tantrāloka* vol.2. p.14 lines 13-16, Jayaratha quotes *śl.*162cd-163ab, with two slight changes, with reference to Abhinavagupta himself whom he considers to be *yoginī-bhū*.

śāstra, *even as a child in the womb he has the form of Śiva.* || 163||

Conclusion:

śl. 164-166ab **1. Etymology of *Ādi-yāga*, (Primordial Sacrifice)**

2. Concluding Bibliography

Jr.163d.1 [It is said:]

Qt.163d.1 "In this way, O Devadeveśi, you have presented the Primordial Sacrifice."

Jr.163d.2 Accordingly, what is the reason for the use, in that [quote], of the expression 'Primordial Sacrifice'? To this question he says:

And this [sacrifice] pertains to the principal [circle] from which the essence is extracted, with the result that it is also the principal sacrifice [of the Kula ritual]. For that reason it is called the 'Primordial Sacrifice'. || 164 || *And in various places in the scripture, Vibhu has praised its nature, i.e. in parts of the illustrious* Vīrāvali, Hārdeśa, Khamata, Arṇava, || 165 || *in the illustrious* Siddha,[182] Utphulla, Maryādāhīna, Caryākula *etc.*

Jr.166b.1 'Essence': it consists of the 'substance' of consciousness and it appears as 'nectar'. And for that reason, this sacrifice [performed with the nectar] is the primary [sacrifice of the Kula ritual]. Moreover, the sacrifice pertains to the primordial, the principal circle. Therefore, in all the *āgamas* the [sacrifice] has the utmost superiority, for which reason he says: 'in many places'. '*Hārdeśa*': the *Hṛdayabhaṭṭāraka*. '*Khemata*': 'the *Khecarīmata*'. '*Arṇava*': the *Yonyarṇava*. 'In parts' [of those]:

---

182. Gnoli, *Luce*, p.699 identifies this as *Siddhayogeśvarīmata*.

in certain passages of the books.'*Utphulla*': the *Utphullakamata*'. '*Maryādāhīna*': the *Nirmaryāda-śāstra.* As it is said:

> Qt.166b.1 "This Kula sacrifice immediately gives you the superhuman powers of *yoga*. It is called the supreme, secret [sacrifice], utterly perplexing to the dualists. To the heroes it gives pain and pleasure, playfully bestowing enjoyment and liberation. According to the usage of yogic intentional language [the Kula sacrifice] is, with reference to the day of worship, called 'oblation into the fire'. However, to those who remain on the path of 'bonded animals', to the foolish, to the evil-doers, it should remain forever undisclosed, O Goddess, like some great treasure. For them it is certainly not the supreme sacrifice which derives from its own nature [and] confers great prosperity. There is no fire-pit, no act of sacrifice into the fire, no cycle of acts of oblation, neither is there an invocation [of the god] to this [sacrifice], nor a dismissal [of the god] from this [sacrifice]. There is no sacrifice to the image [of the deity], no sacred site other [than his own]. [This sacrifice] is without vow or ritual action, without ingredients derived from external sources. It is perfectly accomplished by virtue of the nectar of its own bliss, giving the supernatural power of great bliss.
>
> Accordingly the great *yogī* should contemplate Śiva alone in his own reality or as composed of all the śaktis; as having every form, as having no form; as his own source, as the supreme-non-supreme. He should worship the Lord of the circle and his secret, supreme generative organ which is united to the Highest One. The *kaula* sacred textual tradition is utterly radiant. Out of affection towards you, it is bestowed today. [The *yogī*] should keep it forever quite concealed. It should not be given, O Beloved of the hero, to the dualists, to the narrow-minded, to those whose mind is afflicted

with greed, to the deceptive, to the cruel nor indeed to the curious. And after bestowing the whole world, [the *yogī*] should dwell like a dumb person on the surface of the earth. Then the knower of the mantra will be made perfect. He will be admitted to the company of the Perfected Beings. Free of all disease, he is made perfect during this life-time, by means of this yogic path. I speak no lie."

SUB-TOPIC 5 The Ritual of the Secret Teaching

Sacrifice 4 Based on the Body *(dehe)*

śl. 166cd-168 1. Installation of *Vidyā* and Mantra

Jr.166b.2 The scripture has a four-fold base: *vidyā*, mantra, *mudrā* and *maṇḍala*. The oral tradition concerning the two bases —mantra and *mudrā*—has been given above. Now, in what immediately follows, he outlines the oral tradition concerning the remaining [two bases], *vidyā* and *maṇḍala*, as well.

> *Thanks to this couple [of bases], he is free from having to perform vows and yoga.* ǁ 166 ǁ *Being constantly recollected he is committed to the Primordial Sacrifice alone. He should install the* vidyā *on the śakti's body and* kṣa *on his own [body], in proper order.* ǁ 167 ǁ *Having meditated on her lotus as the moon and on himself as the light of the sun, he should mate the two bases—*vidyā *and mantra—at the same spot.* ǁ 168 ǁ

Jr.168d.1 Thanks to these couple of bases described [above], i.e. *mantra* and *mudrā*, the guru, by means simply of concentration, i.e. disregarding vow and *yoga* etc., is at all times committed to the Primordial Sacrifice. After meditating on the lotus of the śakti which, due to its mass of bliss, is like the moon, [and after meditating] on himself as the light of the sun since [the sun] induces [the lotus] to open; he should install, in due order, on the body of the śakti the chosen *vidyā* which is preeminently 'śakti', and on his own body *KṢA* which is preeminently 'Śiva', in order that, in the same spot, according to the degree of attentiveness to the practice just mentioned, the two bases—mantra and *vidyā*—might be brought together.

śl. 169 Note: There is Secrecy on this Matter

Jr.168d.2 And, since [Abhinava] has excluded [the reader] from participation in what is extremely secret, we do not speak of that matter. A person must find out simply for himself. He says:

> *On the other hand, because of its secrecy, I do not speak in plain words. Nevertheless, the interested person will find it out just by reading the scriptures that have been mentioned.* || 169 ||

śl. 170-173 2. The *Maṇḍala*

Jr.169d.1 In order to expound the very essence of the *maṇḍala* which is located at that same spot, he says:

> *That which all always enjoy, in the same way as the god and the goddess do, is the supreme circle. It causes the [divinities] to draw near* ||170|| *to the goddess-sacrifice etc. The supreme* liṅga, *which is found within the body it self, is composed of all the categories. It is auspicious. When it is surrounded by the circle of the goddess it is the finest sacred place of worship.* ||171|| *That same* maṇḍala, *the principal* [maṇḍala] *is a triple trident con-sisting of lotus, circle and space. At that same spot one should always sacrifice, externally and internally, to the circle of the goddess.* ||172|| *[Arousing], first of all, the creative awareness of his own mantra, he should perform the sprinkling with the essences produced by [the circle], rich with bliss, according to the rite of emanation and reabsorption.*[183] ||173||

---

183. Upwards and downwards, as in *śl.*18d and *śl.*23c.

Jr.173d.1 'In the same way as': [the god] possesses the primary identifying mark.[184] The phrase: 'and the goddess', means that she possesses the [primary identifying mark]. 'The [supreme] circle': the principal circle. For that reason, it is called the 'supreme [circle]' whose form, namely 'the triple trident, lotus, circle and space'—

> Qt.173d.1 "Regarding the triple trident: a set of seven lotuses, circles or spaces springs together from the centre on seven beams of light."

Jr.173d.2 —will be given in a later instruction.[185] 'Of his own [mantra]': of his chosen [mantra]. '[With the essences] produced by the [circle]': with the sexual fluid etc. issuing from the principal circle. 'According to the rite of emanation and reabsorption': according to the process [described as] 'rested' and 'risen'.

Śl. 174-175 **3. Satiation of the Self and Deities**

Jr.173d.3 And what is the effect of such [a procedure]? To this question he says:

> *The circle of consciousness is vigorously aroused by the touch of the [sexual fluid]. The lord of the [circle of consciousness] reaches the supreme sacred place, due to all the deities being satiated.* ||174|| *He should fully satiate [all the deities] with the ingredients which ravish the heart, in the sense of the ritual called the 'Subsequent Sacrifice'. He should do exactly the same internally through awareness of his own self.* ||175||

Jr.175d.1 According to the ritual called 'Subsequent Sacrifice': as was said earlier—

184. That is, the sexual organ.
185. In *TĀ* 31.10-42ab.

Qt.175d.1 "'Whatever causes his mind to open, by that same means he should worship.' Such is Śambhu's decree."

Jr.175d.2 —having said which, [the text continues]:

Qt.175d.2 "The range of moods which derives in full measure from the non-duality of Śiva spills forth the essence. That same [essence] the awakened man should offer in worship at the supreme sacred place."

śl. 176 **Aside: A Hymn**

Jr.175d.3 And then, in order to show the preeminence of his respect, he quotes a certain passage from one of his hymns which he had also quoted earlier.

After taking as a support[186] *the earth which is forever cleansed by a sprinkling with the essence of amazement, [I worship you] with the flowers which arise spontaneously from the mind, which pour forth their own fragrance; [I worship you] according as the priceless vessel of my heart brims with the nectar of bliss; I worship you, O god, together with the goddess, in the temple of the body, night and day.* ||176||

śl. 177 **Concluding Bibliography**

Jr.176d.1 And we do not state this as though it were just our own invention. He says:

In the collection of scriptures starting with the illustrious Vīrāvali, Amaryāda *and so on, this supreme sacrifice is praised by Śītāṃśum-aulī.* ||177 ||

---

186. The full *stotra* of three stanzas is given in *TĀ* 26.63-65. In his investigation of *śl.*64, Jayaratha comments only on the word *ādhāra*, 'support', equiparating it with *janmādhāra*, 'organ of generation'.

Jr.177d.1 'This... [sacrifice]': refers to the particular [sacrifice] which is performed in the body. With this very point in mind, it is said in another place [*ity-ādi anyatra uktam*]:

> Qt.177d.1 "The temple is found in one's very own body. One should not go to a temple in some other place."

Jr.177d.2 *ity-ādi anyatra uktam* ||177||

Sacrifice 5 Based on the Subtle-breath (*prāṇa*)

śl. 178 **1. Definition**

Jr.177d.3 And that [ritual] should be performed in the subtle-breath as well, in the same way as in the body. He says:

> *Or else the guru should see the whole group of goddesses located within the modalities of the subtle-breath. He should perform the ceremony in that same place by the same means as given earlier.* ||178||

śl. 179 **2. Examination**

Jr.178d.1 And how should worship be performed in the [subtle-breath]? He says:

> *The satiation of the goddesses who dwell in the prāṇa [is achieved] by the 'circle of the moon', i.e. the* apāna, *penetrating through openings such as the 'Brahmā', the nose etc., i.e. through the apertures of Ka.* ||179||

Jr.179d.1 'Brahmā': the 'aperture of Brahmā'.

śl. 180 **3. Effect: Powers of Knowledge**

Jr.179d.2 And what is the result of such [a procedure]? To this question he says:

> *By means simply of the procedure performed in that way with the subtle-breath he should satiate the group of goddesses. In a short time,*

by their favour, he will certainly acquire the supernatural powers of knowledge. ||180||

Sacrifice 6 Based on the Mind (*matau*)

śl. 181 **1. Definition**

Jr.180d.1 On the other hand, given that she simply dwells in consciousness alone, how should he satiate the circle of the goddess with corporeal forms such as the body etc.? He says:

> *Or else, the circle of the goddess, which stands on consciousness alone, is to be satiated through an offering to consciousness which the wise man makes by utilising every form of enjoyment.* ||181||

Jr.181d.1 The phrase 'through an offering to consciousness' is elucidated by the phrase '... by utilising every form of enjoyment'. For that reason it is said 'the wise man'.

śl. 182 **2. Examination:**
i. In Brief

Jr.181d.2 How should the circle of the goddess, which stands upon consciousness alone, be satiated in the living body etc. even of a wise man? He says:

> *Where all are dissolved, where the multitudes of categories are consumed, see the funeral pyre which is located within the body, radiant as the Fire of Time!* ||182|| [187]

Jr.182d.1 Where all knowing subjects, i.e. those who are composite etc. and objects of knowledge, i.e. those which consist of elements and beings etc., come to an essential unity: see the funeral pyre which is located within the body, as radiant as the Fire of Time because [the Fire] is the agent of total, universal reabsorption. Consciousness itself alone shines on every side in the body etc. even while it exists.

187. This *śloka* is quoted by Jayaratha in his investigation of *TĀ* 5.130cd-131ab.

śl. 183-185c **ii. In Detail**

śl. 185d **3. Effect: Perfection**

Jr.182d.2 He clarifies that same [teaching]:

> *In this cremation ground which has the form of the void, which is frequented by* yoginīs *and the Perfected Beings, in this place of play which is highly fearsome, which is the passing bodily form of all things,* ||183|| *which is filled with its own circle of rays, where the spread of darkness is destroyed, which is free of all differentiated thoughts, where the state of bliss alone remains,* ||184|| *which is filled with countless funeral pyres, in this cremation ground which is dreadful because of consciousness: who entering in this support of all the deities will not be brought to perfection?* ||185||

Jr.185d.1 In this [body], which is filled with countless funeral pyres consisting of what is pleasant and unpleasant etc.; which is therefore highly fearsome in the sense that it causes the pain of transient existence; in the body, therefore, which is substantially a cremation ground in the sense that it is to be abandoned etc.: who, after entering [in this body], i.e. turning inwards, will not be brought to perfection? This is the meaning.

And to what sort of reality does 'in this [body]' refer? 'In that [body]', in the sense simply of turning inwards, refers to the form of the void which results from the disappearance of the ego. ['In that [body]'] refers, therefore, to the passing bodily form of all things starting with those which are composite etc.; [the phrase] refers, therefore, to the place where the expanse of darkness is destroyed, i.e. where the darkness of duality is completely destroyed. ['In that [body]'] refers, therefore, to what is free of all differentiated thoughts; it therefore refers to what is filled with the circle of rays—belonging just to [the body] itself, not to something external—i.e. with the group of deities of the faculties such as sight etc.; it refers, therefore, to what is frequented by the *yoginīs* and the Perfected Beings, to the support of all the deities; it refers, therefore, -

> Qt.185d.1 "The goddesses who abide within the body play with diverse moods"

Jr.185d.2 —to their place of play; it refers, therefore, to the cremation ground in the sense that it is the agreed meeting place of all the deities. ['In that [body]'] refers, therefore, to the place which is dreadful, in the sense that consciousness, i.e. the single form of the knowing subject, causes reabsorption; it refers, therefore, to where the state of bliss alone remains, i.e. to the place of repose in one's self alone.

śl. 186ab **Concluding Bibliography**

Jr.185d.3 And that is not just an invention of ours. He says:

> *Bhairava, in the illustrious* Vīrāvalī-śāstra,
> *speaks in those terms.*

Jr.186b.1 The progression of consciousness in its ritual form [which was adumbrated] in that [text, viz. *śl.*183-185], which [Abhinava] has excluded even allusively [from consideration] is not given in detail. The scholars should not therefore vent their anger on us!

PART II: THE RITUALS OF INITIATION

SUB-TOPIC 6 Initiation

śl. 186cd-187ab **Enunciation of the Sub-topic**

Jr.186b.2 Concluding in that way the ritual of the secret teaching which is closely connected to the ritual with the sexual partner, he discloses the ritual of initiation.

> *After first of all performing the sacrifice in that manner, he should initiate his own disciple—one among a hundred thousand who possesses the suitability for such things—into such a procedure.* ||187 ab||

Jr.187b.1 'One among a hundred thousand' : means one who has been found to be suitable by examination on many occasions—which is the reason for the expression 'his own disciple'—i.e. he possesses the suitability for such things. 'Into such [a procedure]': into the [procedure] whose nature has been described above.

I. Ordinary Initiation

śl. 187cd-192ab **1. In the *Mālinīvijayottaratantra* —By Means of Mantra and Flower**

Jr.187b.2 Therefore he says:

> *After sprinkling the [disciple] with* rudraśakti, *[the guru] should bring him before the god.* ||187|| *After looking at the arms of the [disciple], [the guru] should set them on fire with rudraśakti. With the same* [rudraśakti] *he should place a flower in the hands of the [disciple] which have been smeared with sandal-paste.* ||188|| *Having ensured that [his disciple's hands] are unsupported, [the guru] should reflect on them as being pulled by rudraśakti*

> *which is a flame with the form of a hook.* ||189|| *Then, after the [disciple] has spontaneously taken the cloth, he is blind-folded and he spontaneously drops the flower. From its fall [the guru] ascertains the* kula *to which the disciple belongs].* ||190|| *Then, after [the disciple] has uncovered his face, [the* rudraśakti*] makes [him] fall prostrate at the feet [viz. of the goddess into whose kula he has been initiated].*[188] *[The guru] honours the 'circle of the goddess' on the hands and also on the head of the [disciple],* ||191||

Jr.191d.1 *Rudraśakti* is Mālinī enclosed by Parā or enclosed by Mātṛsadbhāva. 'He should set [the arms] on fire': he should make [the arms] splendid by a process of pulling back [into the disciple's arms] the quantity of energy in the heart which has been dissipated through the fingers. 'With the same': with the *rudraśakti.* 'Unsupported': they are almost lifeless since the [disciple's] energy, which is transitory and artificial, has ebbed away. 'With the form of a hook': because of its capacity to pull. 'Then': because of the pull of *rudraśakti* in his arms, which derives from the [guru's] reflection—in a causal sense. '[The guru] should ascertain': he should easily ascertain in this way the [disciple's] own *kula.* 'Makes [him] fall prostrate': the [*rudra-*]*śakti* itself [makes him fall prostrate].

Jr.191d.2 And how should [the guru] honour the circle of the goddess on the [hands and the head]? To this question he says:

> *by the fact that [the circle] is pulled and is pulling, is impelled and is impelling.*

Jr.192b.1 [The guru] honours the 'circle of the goddess' in the hands [of the disciple] with the result that [the circle] is impelled [therein by the guru's meditation] and [he honours the

188. At whose feet? At the feet of the god before whom the disciple has been brought, *śl.*187d? At the feet of the goddess, as suggested perhaps by Jr.197b.1? In his translation of *Mālinīvijayottaratantra* 11.21b, Gnoli, *Luce*, p.834 interprets the phrase to mean 'at the feet of the guru'.

'circle'] on the [disciple's] head with the result that the ['circle'] impels [the disciple's hands to go to the head to put on the blind-fold]. Just as the ['circle'] is pulled [by the guru's meditation] so too [the 'circle'] pulls [the hands of the disciple to drop the flower]. Similarly, the two hands [of the disciple] are pulled to [his] head by the power of the 'circle of the goddess' which has been worshipped. [The act described] in that [last sentence] concerning the fall [of the hands on the head] is [the ritual of] the 'hand of Śiva'. As has been said:

> Qt.192b.1 "Then, after honouring the 'circle' on the head and hands of the [disciple], the knower of *yoga* should impel the [disciple's] hands with [*rudra*-]*śakti* in such a way that they go to the top of the head. The aforementioned[189] ritual of the 'hand of Śiva' immediately causes conviction."

Śl. 192cd-195 **2. In the *Ratnamālā***
—By Mantra and 'Oblation' etc.

Jr.192b.2 On the other hand, if the ritual of the 'hand of Śiva', performed in that way, is not successful, he should in that case perform the procedure as given in another scripture.
He says:

> *It is said in the illustrious Ratnamālā: The 'navel'* [KṢ] *is enclosed by the 'staff'* [R].
> ||192|| *It is adorned with the 'left ornament'* [Ū] *and 'left shank'* [AU] *and with the 'buttock'* [M].[190] *He should place the 'driving force' on the disciple's hand which is carrying the flower.*
> ||193|| *At the moment the ['hand of Śiva']*(sa)[191] *is released,*[192] *it falls spontaneously on [the*

189. *TĀ* 15.456cd-474ab describes the ritual in detail.
190. The code is given in *Mālinīvijayottaratantra* 3.37-41ab.
191. Gnoli interprets the pronoun *sa* as referring to the the disciple's hand. However, Jayaratha, in Jr.195d.1, interprets *sa* as the 'hand of Śiva.' In fact, the two are the same.
192. The word *stobha* has the two contrasting meanings of 'pause' and 'praise'. Gnoli generally uses the first meaning, 'paralysis', the negation of the effect of the bonds which hold a person prisoner. However, the English phrase 'paralysis of the bonds' is not clear whereas the word 'release' gives the double meaning, as when the restraining force of a brake is negated and the vehicle begins to move freely.

disciple's] head. The 'hand of Śiva', acting spontaneously, itself immediately causes conviction. ||194|| *In the very same way the guru should make [him] eat the 'oblation'. And [as regards the dropping of] the tooth-stick by the disciple: its fall [is treated] exactly as above.* ||195||

Jr.195d.1 'Navel': *KṢ*. 'Staff': *R*. [*KṢ* is] enclosed by the [phoneme *R*], i.e. is intersected [by two *R*'s] above and below.[193] 'Left ornament': *Ū*. 'Left shank': *AU*. 'Buttock': *M*. The [phoneme *M*] means the *bindu* form [*Ṃ*]. Therefore: *RKṢRŪAUṂ*. 'The' (*sa*): the 'hand of Śiva'. It is said in that text:[194]

> Qt.195d.1 "After extracting the 'base of the staff' [*R*], he should extract the phoneme of the 'navel' [*KṢ*]. To the 'tip of the staff' [*R*], which is the seat, the 'left ornament' [*Ū*] is joined. To the'left shank' [*AU*] the 'adornment of the buttock' [*Ṃ*] is joined, O Beloved. That divine weapon is supreme. He who is without fault openly takes hold of it."

Jr.195d.2 Having said which, [the text continues]:

> Qt.195d.2 "He should, O Maheśānī, place the cluster [of phonemes] on the 'hand of Śiva'. At the moment when [the 'hand of Śiva'] is released, O Goddess, it moves quite spontaneously."

Jr.195d.3 'Immediately causes conviction': [it causes conviction] at the very spot in the circle of the body where the 'hand' suddenly falls. To that same spot [the disciple] should direct his practice, say the gurus. 'In the very same way': by being pulled and by pulling. 'Oblation': after first offering it to the

193. In the *śāradā* script, the letter *R* prior to a phoneme is written immediately above and *R* following a phoneme is written immediately underneath. See Slaje, pp.36-37.

194. In the *Ratnamālā*.

goddesses. [The phrase] 'by the disciple' refers to the one who casts [the tooth-stick]—instrumental case. 'Exactly as above': as mentioned in chapter fifteen.[195]

Transition

śl. 196-197ab a. Assessing Degree of Absorption

Jr.195d.4 His absorption into śakti is discerned merely by the single release of the hand which means essentially the grasping of the blindfold etc. But what is inferred by that statement? To this question he says:

> *The release of the hand, starting with grasping the blindfold and ending with taking the tooth-stick, as they say: in that [movement the guru] ascertains* || 196 || *the descent of energy which is classified according to the categories 'strong', 'weak' etc.*

Jr.197b.1 'In that [movement]': i.e. in the release of the hand which has been outlined in that way. 'Classified in that way': the categorisation into 'intense', 'weak' etc. This is the meaning of that [sentence]: — if, on the very spot in the circle where the flower has fallen, a prostration is made [by the disciple]; if on that same spot the 'oblation' is offered [by him to the goddess]; if immediately after that [the 'oblation'] is taken [by him] etc.: in that case, the descent of energy is to be discerned as 'intense', but otherwise it is weak. Therefore it is said:

> Qt.197b.1 "The wise man should examine the descent of energy according to their movement. In keeping with the categorisations 'weak', 'intense' etc., the intelligent man [should ascertain the descent of energy as] weak, intense etc."

195. In *TĀ* 15.446cd-447.

śl. 197cd-198ab **b. The Ordinary Initiate and the Son**

Jr.197b.2 Being done in that way [the initiation] is called, in our tradition, 'ordinary initiation'. He says:

> *For this reason he has been called an ordinary initiate, according to the illustrious* Pūrva—*because of the trembling of the hand.*[196] ||197||

Jr.197d.1 That is not been said out of sense of novelty.[197] He says:

> *He is an ordinary initiate because of a releasing of the hand, according to the illustrious* Bhogahastaka.

Jr.198b.1 As the illustrious *Pañcāśikā* says:

> Qt.198b.1 "He is an ordinary initiate due to a releasing of the hand. He is a Son because of the position of the hand."

Jr.198b.2 And so on.

śl. 198cd-199ab **3. In the *Ānandeśvara* —By Means of the 'oblation' Alone**

śl. 199cd-200 **Result: The Way of Life for an Ordinary Initiate**

---

196. *Mālinīvijayottaratantra* 11.27cd reads as follows: *ityayaṃ samayī proktaḥ saṃsthitoktena vartmanā* The phrase *saṃsthitoktena vartmanā*, 'by means of the stated method', refers to the ritual of *ibid.* 11.17-26 to which *TĀ* 29.187cd-192ab and196-197ab correspond. According to the *Mālinīvijayottaratantra*, therefore, the ritual of dropping the flower etc., i.e. the release of the hand (kara-*stobha*) initiates a person as an ordinary initiate (*samayī*). Abhinava replaces the phrase, *saṃsthitoktena vartmanā*, with the phrase *kara-kampataḥ*. By doing so he prepares the reader for *śl.*199c which reads: 'if, however, he should tremble' (*sakampas-tv*). According to Abhinava, therefore, hesitation at receiving the 'oblation', i.e. the trembling of the hand (*kara-kampa*) means that the person remains an ordinary initiate since he has failed the test. By contrast, as Qt.198b.1 notes, the steadiness of the Son's hand is like a significant gesture (*mudrā*).

197. The word *apūrvatayā*, 'out of sense of novelty', could also be translated as 'in a way that is contrary to the *Pūrva*', viz. the *Mālinīvijayottaratantra*.

Jr.198b.3 On the same subject he mentions another ritual procedure. He says:

> *Or else the guru should give [him] just the 'oblation' immersed in 'nectar-of-the-left'.* ||198||
> *As a result of taking it unhesitatingly he becomes a member of the śakti's clan, free of* māyā. *If, however, he should tremble, vacillating, he is an ordinary initiate, [bound] to the recitation [of the scriptures] etc.* ||199||
> *At a later time, after faithful observance of the rule, he will, by a complete cleansing of the pathways, be fit for supernatural powers. So it is said in the illustrious* Ānandeśvara. ||200||

Jr.200d.1 ' 'Oblation' ': consisting of the five jewels etc. As it is said:

> Qt.200d.1. "I will speak of the 'oblation' located within the body, which is difficult to obtain even for the gods: male urine, male semen and menstrual blood, phlegm, faeces.[198] Hence, when he has performed the ritual, he should obtain the 'oblation' which is located in the body."

Jr.200d.2 'A member of the śakti's clan': belonging to a branch of Brāhmī etc. Therefore, as a result of taking [the 'oblation'] unhesitatingly, he is free of *māyā*, i.e. he reaches the category of consciousness which is without the method of differentiated thought because it is caused by direct perception. For that reason, the eating of 'oblation' etc. was earlier[199] said to be an indirect method of the 'non-means'. The hesitant person, on

198. This translation is indebted to Sanderson, 'Meaning', p.82.

199. In *TĀ* 2, which deals with the 'non-means', Abhinava states that '... the teaching occurs once only' (*śl.*2c) since nothing more is needed to come to full consciousness. In *Tantrāloka* vol.2, p.312 line 13, in his investigation of that phrase, Jayaratha quotes a source which states: 'The eating of the 'oblation' (*carubhojanam*) is a revelation to the *siddhas* and *yoginīs*.' The quote goes on to say that nothing else is needed to come to full consciousness.

the other hand, who vacillates as regards the ['oblation'], is an 'ordinary initiate' bound to reciting and hearing [the scriptures] etc. Consequently later on, after receiving a descent of energy which is shown to be intense through a complete fidelity to the rule as given in various scriptures, he will, by means of a cleansing of the six-fold pathway, i.e. by a proper process of initiation as a Son, receive the supernatural power of liberation and wealth. And that is not said as just an invention of ours. Therefore he declares: 'It is said in the illustrious *Ānandeśvara*'.

II Initiation as a Son

śl. 201ab **Enunciation**

Jr.200d.3 Having explained ordinary initiation in this way, he goes on to speak of initiation as a Son.

> *If, however, [the guru] wants to make a Son,*
> *he should celebrate the initiation.*

Jr.201b.1 In this regard:

> Qt.201b.1 "He who performs 'initiation-by penetration' for someone without [first performing] initiation [as a Son], O Beloved: they both go to hell. This is the established view of the Śākta school."

Jr.201b.2 According to this statement, the initiation[-by-penetration] of the disciple must not be performed without [him first experiencing] absorption. Accordingly, absorption itself must first be generated so that when his suitability for initiation[-by-penetration] is recognised, the guru may celebrate the ritual procedure [of initiation-by-penetration] for him. On the other hand, if [absorption] has not happened, because he is unworthy of initiation[-by-penetration], he is simply to be excluded. As will be said:

> Qt.201b.2 "If, however, even in this instance [absorption] does not happen to him, [the guru] should, at that point, abandon him like a stone."

1. According to the *Ratnamālā*

śl. 201cd-202ab a. Definition of the Ṛitual

Jr.201b.3 Full absorption is mentioned in all the scriptures without exception. In order to explain it, he now describes how it is done, as stated in the *Ratnamālā,* as well as its significance.

> *It is said in the illustrious* Ratnamālā: *[the guru] should install Nādiphānta, which has a fiery splendour,* || 201 || *as far as the end of the tuft of hair. [The disciple] falls [to the ground]. Because of that, the [ritual] procedure relates to the topic in question [viz. initiation as a Son].*

Jr.202b.1 'Because of that': because of the ritual placing which has been described in those terms—in a causal sense. 'Falls': because he ceases to interpret the body etc. as the self, he is absorbed simply into *rudraśakti*. Therefore it is said in that [text]:

> Qt.202b.1 "He should, then, install Mālinī, the mother of the world, she who has the appearance of a fiery flame, from the disciple's foot to the very end of his tuft of hair. As a result of fully arousing Nādiphānta, he causes [the disciple], whose faculties have been overpowered, to fall. This initiation is [known as] 'the great goddess', according to the *Mālinīvijaya*, O Beloved."

Jr.202b.2 [The phrase] 'because of that' is to be taken in two senses. Accordingly, [the phrase] 'because of that' means 'because of falling'—in a causal sense. 'Relates to the topic in question': to initiation as Son. Such a [ritual] procedure will [now] be described.

śl. 202cd-206 b. Examination of the Ritual

Jr.202b.3 He describes that [procedure]:

> *[The disciple] has been sprinkled [and] the above-stated ritual for the cleansing of the*

pathways has been applied to him. He stands upright before [the guru]. The guru who is composed of the śakti should [then] reflect on the śakti, which is all blazing, as going from the foot to the top of the head of the [disciple], burning his bonds. ||202-203|| *After that, when the [disciple] has sat down, [the guru] should reflect, step-by-step, on the [śakti] as burning [the bonds], starting right from the cleansing of the base [and] terminating with the final cleansing of the top [of his head].* ||204|| *Having thus burnt, in the manner stated above,*[200] *all the categories etc. that are to be cleansed, he should meditate [on the śakti] as merged in Śiva, whether in his simple or his composite form.* ||205|| *[The śakti,] which the yogī joins to the path, nourishes that which is of the same nature [as herself and] burns up anything else that belongs to a different class.* ||206||

Jr.206d.1 'Of which he is composed': composed of the blazing śakti. 'After that': immediately after [the disciple has been] in the standing position. 'The cleansing of the base' is the cleansing of the beginning, for example *nivṛttiḥ* in the pathway of the *kalā*. 'The cleansing of the top [of the head]': for example *śāntyatītā* in the same [pathway of the *kalā*]. 'Thus': beginning from the cleansing of the base and finishing with the cleansing of the top [of the head]. '[In the manner stated] above': in the section dealing with initiation into the categories.[201] 'Simple' refers to the Son etc. 'Composite' refers to the Adept. 'To the path': to the central sacred place. 'Same nature' means consciousness. [The things that] 'belong to a different class' means the stains etc.

200. In *śl.*203-204.
201. In *TĀ* 16.97-163ab.

śl. 207-208 **c. Result:**

i. 5 Possible Effects

Jr.206d.2 What is the result of the [ritual performed] in this way? To this question he says:

> *Entering—as a result of a descent of energy classified as intense etc.—into the mind, space, subtle-breath, internal and external bodies of the student who is being cleansed by her,* ||207||
> *the* rudraśakti *produces the following respective results: bliss, lightness, trembling, sleep and a reeling in the body.* ||208||

Jr.208d.1 The *rudraśakti* which enters as a result of a very intense descent of energy into the mind, i.e. into the immediately perceptible self, of the disciple whose bond has been burnt in this way, produces bliss, just as [the *rudraśakti*] which enters into the body as the result of a very weak descent of energy [produces] a reeling. It follows that, as regards consciousness, because its form is bliss, the appropriate effect is bliss. As regards the void, i.e. the space, because of its expansiveness [the effect is] lightness. As regards the subtle-breath, i.e. the 'wind', because of its active quality [the effect] is trembling. As regards the inner body, i.e. the eightfold subtle body starting with intelligence, as a result of restraining the various modalities of *māyā* [the appropriate effect] is sleep. As regards the external body, because there is a turning away from reliance on the ego [the effect is] a reeling. The initiation of the [disciple] which occurs perceptibly in these ways gives satisfaction to the guru.

śl. 209 **ii. Enjoyment**

Jr.208d.2 Union is effected at [the level of] Śiva himself by the fact that the [initiate's] bond has been released in this way. At that very moment, death should be the logical consequence! To this question he says:

> *When the bond is released in this way, when [the disciple's] self is joined to Śiva, [the guru] should produce an emanation consisting of quite pure categories in order that he might enjoy the 'remainder'.* ||209||

Jr.209d.1 'The remainder' is the *karma* which causes his body to function. 'Emanation': in his same body.

śl. 210-211ab **2. Another Method: A Surrounding Fire**

Jr.209d.2 If even in such [an initiatory procedure]—since none of those signs has appeared because there has been a weak descent of energy—this sort of absorption does not occur for a [disciple], then in that case [the guru] should use a different purifying ritual for him. He says:

> *Or else, no such absorption has occurred for a [disciple]. In that case, the [guru] should burn him, outside and inside, with the* [rudra-]śakti *that has been mentioned. He will thus fall to the ground.* ||210|| *If, however, even in this instance [absorption] does not happen to him, [the guru] should, at that point, abandon him like a stone.*

Jr.211b.1 The [guru] should simultaneously burn him, outside and inside, with the [*rudra-*]*śakti* which is composed of a bundle of flames: i.e. should burn the disciple who is surrounded on every side by *R*, who is seated within an upward pointing triangle which is a blaze of fire shooting out upwards and downwards. Such is the teaching of the gurus. 'If ... does not happen': if absorption [does not happen]. 'Like a stone': since no descent of energy has occurred, he is dense, inert and arrogant.

śl. 211cd-212ab **3. According to the *Sadbhāva***

Jr.211b.2 [The guru] knows that the disciple who is abandoned in this way continues plunging into and emerging from a merely transient existence. He wishes [therefore]—out of a commitment to showing him grace—to describe another initiation which is effective, irresistible [and] which derives from the guru and from the scripture. He says:

> *I will now describe an initiation which brings conviction. It was taught by the contented*[202] *[and] wise* ||211|| *Śambhunātha [and] occurs in the text of the* Sadbhāva.

Jr.212b.1 'In the text of the *Sadbhāva*': in the illustrious *Tantrasadbhāva*.

śl. 212cd-213 **a. Enunciation: 3 Masses of Phonemes**

Jr.212b.2 He describes that same [initiation]:

> *'Elixir', 'fire', 'wind'; 'weak', 'after [weak]', 'Kālāgni', 'fire' (agni), 'wind';* || 212 || *'fire', 'elixir', 'breath', 'peak', 'fire', 'wind'. All have the sixth* [*vowel, viz.* Ū]. *Each one of those three masses [of phonemes] is said to release [the bonds].* || 213 ||

Jr.213d.1 'Elixir' is *S*. 'Fire' is *R*. 'Wind' is *Y*. Thus: *SRYŪṀ*. 'Weak': the phoneme *Ḍ*. 'After [weak]', designated by the term 'bearer of the cobra's hood', is the phoneme *ḌH*. 'Quietening of the subtle-breath', 'death', is *M*. 'Fire' is *R*. 'Wind' is *Y*. Thus: *ḌḌHMRYŪṁ*. 'Fire' is *R*. '*Soma*' is *S*. 'Breath', 'subtle-breath', is *H*. 'Peak' is *KṢ*. 'Fire' is *R*. 'Wind' is *Y*. Thus: *RSHKṢRYŪṂ*. In [each] collection [of phonemes given] in [*śl.*212cd-213ab] there is a *dvandva*. 'All': the three masses [of phonemes]. '[All] have the sixth vowel': [all] are 'seated' on the phoneme *Ū* and are furnished with *bindu* etc. 'Each one': [each one] separately. Therefore is said in that [text]:

> Qt.213d.1 "Furthermore, if, even in such [a procedure of initiation], absorption does not occur for someone

202. In Jr.208d.1, Jayaratha speaks of the guru who satisfied at the visible manifestation of absorption. Śambhunātha is contented because the initiation he has taught is effective, as hinted in Jr.211b.2.

who is faint-hearted, the [guru] should, by means of one of the three masses [of phonemes], lead him to desire the awakened state. In the first place, he should extract one mass [of phonemes] made up of '*soma*' [*S*], 'flame' [*R*], 'air' [*Y*]. Next, 'cobra's hood' [*ḌH*], 'quietening of the subtle-breath' [*M*], 'flame' [*R*], 'wind' [*Y*] are joined.[203] The third [aggregate] is made up of 'flame' [*R*], '*ṣoma*' [*S*], 'breath' [*H*], 'peak' [*KṢ*], 'fire' [*R*] and 'air' [*Y*]. O Beautiful One, all [the masses] seated on the sixth [vowel] [*Ū*] are adorned with the dot [*Ṃ*]. By means of these three, applied separately, bodily absorption into śakti occurs."

śl. 214-216 **b. Examination of the Ritual**

Jr.213d.2 He describes the [procedure] to be followed in the same [initiation].

> *And he should install what is known as 'śakti-bīja' [viz.* ĪṂ*] on all the limbs [of the disciple]. The mantra [viz.* HA*], adorned with the twelve vowels, is installed on the heart circle.*||214|| *Consciousness, resembling a china rose, [arises] from the centre of the [mantra* HA *adorned with the twelve vowels arranged in circular fashion]. And he should meditate on the group [of mantras] as impelled by the wind* [Y] *and inflamed by the fire* [R]. ||215|| *He should recite the mantra [viz. the mass of phonemes] with the insertion of the [initiand's] name. All at once a releasing of the disciple will undoubtedly occur.* ||216||

Jr.216d.1 '*Śakti-bījam*' is the combination of the triangular *bīja*, *Ī*, and *māyā* which is referred to by the word 'multitude'. 'He

203. This line is supposed to give the code for *ḌḌHMRYŪṁ*. It seems, however, that the code for *Ḍ*, namely *maṇḍa*, is missing.

should install ...on all the limbs': he should reflect on the initiand at the centre of that double *bīja* [*ĪṂ*]. 'Mantra': the phoneme *HA* which is essentially equivalent to all the mantras. 'Of the [mantra]': of the mantra which is arranged in circular fashion between the twelve vowels excluding the neuter phonemes. 'The group [of mantras]': the whole multitude of mantras deriving from speech etc.[204] is reflected upon as present outside and inside the initiand. He should, therefore, meditate upon that [multitude of mantras] as surrounded externally on every side by 'wind', i.e. by the phoneme *Y*, and by 'fire', i.e. the phoneme *R*, so that the [multitude of mantras] which is inflamed in this way will lead to a distinctive manifestation of release. 'Mantra': one or other of the three masses of phonemes. 'With the insertion of the [initiand's] name': at first the mantra, then the name of the initiand, [then] the mantra again.

> Qt.216d.1 "He should install the triangular [*bīja Ī*] and the multitude [*Ṃ*], as appropriate, on all the limbs. [He should install] on the heart circle the leading mantra which is distributed between the twelve vowels. It resembles the rising sun. And with it he should quicken the [limited] living being. He should inflame [the mantra] with 'fire' [*R*] and arouse [it] with 'wind' [*Y*]. He should, O Splendid One, repeat the disciple's name which is placed within the mantra. After that [the disciple], who is eagerly engaged in the [mantra], enters into absorption immediately.

Śl. 217-218ab **Results: a. He is Bhairava**

Jr.216d.2 And [when he does become absorbed], what sort of experience does the [disciple] have? He says:

> *While he is attached to a [particular] category,*
> *O Goddess, he notices his self within that*

204. The meaning is not clear. The term *vāg-bhava* may refer to *vāk*, 'word', or *parāvāk*, 'supreme word'.

category. On the other hand, when he has reached the supreme category, 'he does not see'.||217|| *By the same procedure he sees the whole pathway.*

Jr.218b.1 'He notices': [he notices] only one [category] at a time. 'He does not see': his one true nature is that of the perceiver.

śl. 218cd **b. He is a Guru**

Jr.218b.2 An experience of that sort gives rise to sure knowledge, not just with reference to himself, but also with reference to himself and other things. He says:

Or he comprehends all the scriptures as well, in an instant.|| 218 ||

Jr.218d.1 'All the scriptures': those he has not seen or heard.

III Regarding the Son Who Desires Enjoyments

śl. 219-220 **1. a. Enjoyment in a Category**
b. Enjoyment in All Categories
c. Enunciation of the Kula Sacrifice

Jr.218d.2 And if anyone desires specific enjoyments, then the [practitioner] should perform the appropriate initiation for him. He says:

In the case where the [disciple] has the aptitude, the accomplished yogī *should celebrate [his] initiation into a particular category with a ritual of practice which is appropriate to that category.* ||219|| *As regards the life-long [ritual] conduct of the person who seeks liberation and who has been fully initiated in [as a Son], the Kula tradition of sacrifice should be taught in connection with the five states [viz. of consciousness].* ||220||

Jr.220d.1 'Aptitude' is the wish someone has for mastery over a world within the category 'earth'; [or the wish], by contrast, of someone with regard to the state of Sadāśiva. 'With a ritual of practice which is appropriate to that category': by means of the various objects of concentration etc. 'As regards the life-long [ritual] conduct': indicates the rule of conduct [to be practised] for the rest of his life.

Śl. 221 **2. Definition of the Kula Sacrifice**

Jr.220d.2 He explains the connection with the five states:

> *Consciousness abides without varying in the [five states] starting with wakefulness etc. For that reason, the Kula sacrifice, which takes place in the 'mouth of the* yoginī', *is to be taught in those same terms [viz. in the five states].* ||221||

Jr.221d.1 'Abides without varying':

> Qt.221d.1 "... there is no state which is not Śiva."[205]

Jr.221d.2 In other words, [consciousness] is unceasingly active.

Śl. 222-223 **3. Examination of the Sacrifice**

Jr.221d.3 Therefore he says:

> *In tne wakened state, the whole [range of mantras] is to be worshipped. In dreaming sleep, [the range of mantras is absorbed] into a specific mantra. In deep sleep, after leaving aside [the specific mantra], what is known as 'the source [of the range of mantras' is to be worshipped] encircled by his śaktis.* || 222 || *At the Fourth, however, there is just the single [śakti, viz. Kuleśvarī] who is called 'the sexual*

205. This is quoted exactly from the *Spandakārikā* 2.4b. In quoting the final half-line, Jayaratha implies the two whole ślokas, i.e. 3-4 which include most of the five states. Jayaratha quotes the same half-line in his commentary on *TĀ* 10.214-215ab.

partner'. Kuleśitā is at the 'Beyond[-Fourth]'. The worship is presented in this way for the benefit of those who are completely involved with their own śakti. ||223||

Jr.223d.1 In the various states starting with wakefulness there is a gradual abating of duality and a manifestation of non-duality. Thus, in the state of wakefulness the whole range of mantras is to be used in worship. In the state of dreaming sleep too [the whole range is to be used for worship], but the specific [mantra] which is preferred for worship, i.e. just a single [mantra], is used with reference to the mantra Parā etc. In the state of deep sleep, however, after discarding the attendant range of mantras, the three bhairavas joined to the three śaktis Parā etc., as well as Kuleśvara and Kuleśvarī, are to be worshipped. And at the Fourth just the single [goddess] Kuleśvarī [is to be worshipped] and at Beyond-Fourth Kuleśvara alone [is to be worshipped].

śl. 224 **4. Further Instruction on the Five States**

Jr.223d.2 He indicates the same in another passage as well.

And the [guru] should explain to him the set of five states divided in the aforesaid manner, starting from the corporeal and ending with the Beyond-All, as mentioned earlier. ||224||

Jr.224d.1 '[As mentioned] earlier': in the tenth chapter[206] 'Divided in the aforesaid manner': according to the types '*yogī*' and 'knowledgeable person'. 'To him': to the fully initiated person who seeks liberation.

206. *TĀ* 10 describes the five states of consciousness in general. *TĀ* 10.242-281 describes the fives states as they variously occur in the yogī or the knowledgeable person.

SUB-TOPIC 7 Consecration

1. In the *Mālinīvijayottara*—An External Ritual

Śl. 225-227 **a. The Ritual i. Anointing the Adept**

Śl. 228-229 **ii. Anointing the Master**

Jr.224d.2 He also describes the consecration of the Adept and of the Master which is now presented immediately after the initiation.

> *The correct consecration*[207] *into yoga of the Adept who desires enjoyments [is as follows]. In this [ceremony], after sacrificing to the god according to [the disciple's financial] means,*[208] *[the guru] should light eight flawless lamps made of a gold etc., after furnishing them with red wicks and with ghee.* ॥ 226ab ॥ *The [eight lamps] are to be worshipped according to the set of eight kula [goddesses]. Kuleśvara and Kuleśvarī are also [to be worshipped] in the 'conch-shell'* ॥ 226 ॥ *full of the nectar of bliss. By using the aforesaid process of the 'hand of Śiva' [the guru] consecrates [the disciple] by using the ['conch-shell']. Afterwards, the [Adept]* (sa) *should undertake mantra practice.*॥ 227॥
>
> *This is the consecration of the Master. The [guru] who is qualified should set out for him sixty-four 'lamps' made with paste etc.* ॥ 228 ॥

207. The word 'consecration' is often used to translate *abhiṣeca*. It describes the effect but not the manner. 'Anointing' expresses the manner but is associated with unguents. 'Sprinkling' sounds banal.

208. Even if the means be only some water and *dūrvā* grass. *TĀ* 15.37ab.

> *The ['lamps'] are to be worshipped according to the sixty-four [*kula *goddesses]. Kuleśvara and Kuleśvarī are [to be wor-shipped] in the centre as before. [The guru] also consecrates him as guru simply by means of what is called the 'hand of Śiva'.* ||229||

Jr.229d.1 'Into *yoga*': indicates the particular emphasis of the [consecration]. 'In this [ceremony]': in the consecration into *yoga*. 'In the conch-shell': in the skull. 'By using the aforesaid process of the 'hand of Śiva' ': by the process of pulling the śakti. 'By using the': by using the 'conch-shell'. 'The' (*sa*): the Adept who desires enjoyments. 'Made with paste etc.': the word 'etc.' means the earth of an anthill etc.[209] 'As before': by means of what is in the 'conch-shell'.

śl. 230 **b. Acclaim by the Group of *Yogīs***

Jr.229d.2 What benefit accrues to these two by way of such a consecration? Wishing to resolve that question he quotes the *āgama* itself.[210]

> *These two, who have been consecrated, are acknowledged [as Adept and Master] by the whole group of* yogīs. *Their guru is the one who grants liberation.* || 230 ||

śl. 231 **c. After the Ritual i. Their Respective Roles**

śl. 232 **ii. Further Instruction**

Jr.230d.1 In order to explain the intended meaning of the fourth half-line in [*śl.*230d] he says:

> *The intended meaning of the half-line is [as follows]: the guru who is an Adept in the first instance [viz. and who is not subsequently consecrated as Master] dispenses supernatural*

209. The earth of an anthill, since it comes from the mouth of a living being, is considered to be particularly pure.
210. That is, the *Mālinīvijayottaratantra*.

powers; the other [viz. the Master] bestows liberation in an appropriate manner. ||231|| *To both [Adept and Master the consecrating guru] should explain the entire threefold knowledge in an appropriate manner and should grant his own authority in respect of performing his own ritual.* ||232||

Jr.232d.1 This is the intended meaning of [*śl*.230d]: — From amongst the two, the one who is an Adept in the first place [viz. and who has not subsequently been consecrated as Master and] in this sense is a guru, dispenses only supernatural powers to others; the other [viz. the Master] who has been a guru from the very start [viz. without being consecrated as an Adept], after first bestowing supernatural powers bountifully, i.e. outstandingly, [grants] liberation as well. The position of a Master is transmitted just to the person who seeks liberation [viz. and not to the one who only seeks enjoyments] even if he has been initiated with *sa-bīja* initiation. Likewise also, the particular [position] of officiant is [transmitted] to the [person who seeks liberation]; similarly the particular [position] of a knowledgeable person is [transmitted to him]. There is no inconsistency whatever in this arrangement. 'The threefold [knowledge]' is the 'individual', 'śakti' and 'Śaṃbhu' methods. 'His ritual' means initiation etc.

2. In the *Vīrāvalibhairava*—An Internal Ritual

Jr.232d.2 He describes that same [consecration] according to an internal procedure as well.

The set of six causes as they are called and Parama Śiva || 233|| *along with Bhairava-nātha are designated as 'the set of eight'. Viewing each of that [set] as identical with all, the guru should transfer the modality which is in himself to the eye etc., i.e. to any sense-organ [of the disciple].* || 234|| *This consecration with 'full jars' is called 'the supreme [consecration]'. Indeed [it is performed] without external [jars]. Thus it is said in the illustrious* Vīrāvalibhairava. || 235 ||

Jr.235d.1 Brahmā, Viṣṇu, Rudra, Īśvara, Sadāśiva and Anāśriśiva, [constitute the set of six]. 'Paramaśiva' is the thirty-sixth. 'Bhairavanātha' is the totality, designated by the term 'Thirty-Seventh' etc. Therefore, because each one of that set of eight is identical with all, a set of sixty-four modalities is present. Having established the [set] in himself, the guru should transfer [it], by means of the outlet of his own faculty, to any faculty such as the eye etc. of the person to be consecrated, i.e. he brings about the identity [of the consecrand with the set of sixty-four modalities]. The [consecration] is [performed] without external [jars]; i.e. [it is performed] with full, internal 'jars' since the [the guru] is full of the essence of consciousness. Because it is quite different from [consecration performed] with external [jars] our gurus call it 'the supreme [consecration]' which is approved for ritual practice.

SUB-TOPIC 8 Penetration

Śl. 236 Enunciation of the Sub-topic

Jr.235d.2 After explaining the ritual of consecration in this way; desiring, then, to investigate the nature of 'penetration mentioned above,[211] he begins to speak of that initiation.

> *When, however, there is a desire for an immediate enjoyment, the guru, who is most accomplished in yoga, should immediately perform initiation-by-penetration which gives the chosen result in the matter [of enjoyment].* ‖236 ‖

Jr.236d.1 'Most accomplished in *yoga*': [the guru] who is well-practised with respect to *yoga* is qualified [to perform this form of initiation]. As he will say:

> Qt.236d.1 "And [initiation-by-penetration] is to be celebrated by a person who is practised ...."

Jr.236d.2 'Penetration' is a piercing of the support of the circles etc., in an ever-ascending order, by using the energy of the central breath. As he will say:

> Qt.236d.2 "... so that, through being absorbed into ever higher levels, the disciple's conviction, because of the complete piercing of the circles, becomes firm."

Jr.236d..3 As it is said with that very point in mind:

> Qt.236d.3 "After joining the 'self' [viz. *haṃsa*][212a] to the *maṇi*[*-pura* circle], he should bring the energy as

211. In Qt.201b.1.

212a. The *ātmānaṃ*, 'self', in Qt.236d.3 refers to the subtle-breath in its contracted form. By leading the contracted form upwards, the individual self acquires the state of Heruka. The name 'Heruka' refers to Śiva. Farrow and Menon, *The concealed essence*, p.xliv.

far as 'Heruka'. The instrument for loosening the bonds is known as 'penetration'."

Jr.236d.4 And so on.

śl. 237-239ab Definition of Initiation-by-penetration

Jr.236d.5 Therefore he says:

> *And initiation-by-penetration is described by many methods and in various places. And it is to be celebrated by a person who is practised, so that through being absorbed into ever higher levels,* ||237|| *the disciple's conviction, because of the piercing of the circles, becomes firm*[212b]...

Jr.238b.1 'So that': by virtue of the fact that [the guru] is practised.

Jr.238b.2 What does [the initiand] gain by such a piercing? To this question he says:

> *with the result that there is a supernatural power such as minuteness etc.* ||238c||

Jr.238c.1 On the other hand, if such is not the case, i.e. if there is no absorption into ever higher circles, an obstacle etc. will result, as the *āgama* states in this regard:

> *By contrast, [the following 'supernatural power'] is enjoined in the illustrious* [Ratna-]mālā: || 238 || *when the region of a higher circle is not reached, [the 'supernatural power'] is simply absorption by a Piśāca.*[213]

212b.The word *dhruvaḥ*, 'firm' is linked with *anuttara*, 'unsurpassable'. Likewise, the word *pratyayaḥ*, according to Jr.271d.1, can mean absorption, *aveśaḥ*. The sentence could be translated as: ' the disciple's absorption ... reaches the highest level.'

213. The *Agni-Purāṇa* lists three classes of monsters: Piśāca whose body is emaciated; Vetāla whose face is hideous and Preta who is thin but has a large belly. de Mallmann, *Les enseignements*, p.305. The *Śilparatna* states that the Piśāca are skin, bone and tendons. ibid. p.201. See also Wendy Doniger O'Flaherty, *Hindu myths*, Harmondsworth, England, Penguin Books,1975, p.45.

Jr.239b.1 As it is said in that [text]:

> Qt.239b.1 "When the lower states move to a higher level, O You whose face is beautiful, the [supernatural power] is a state of liberation, it is an acquisition of knowledge. And the states which are in the higher circle, if they go to a lower level, then there is possession by a Piśāca which certainly produces an obstacle."

Examination

I Penetration According to the *Gahvara*

śl. 239cd-240ab **Enunciation of the 6 Forms**

Jr.239b.2 He explains the statement 'by many methods':

> *Initiation-by-penetration, which is of six kinds, is described by Parameśī in the illustrious* Gahvara.
> *It consists of 'mantra', 'sound', 'bindu', 'energy', 'cobra', 'supreme'.* (||239cd-240ab||)

Jr.240b.1 It is stated in that [text]:

> Qt.240b.1 "There is penetration by mantra [and penetration] which is called 'sound'. Then penetration by *bindu* is next. There is [penetration] relating to śakti [and] penetration by 'cobra'. The supreme [penetration] is listed as sixth."

Jr.240b.2 And as regards the fact that [the penetration] is of six kinds, the reason for it is the cleansing of the pathways. As it is said:

> Qt.240b.2 "O Beloved, since consciousness occurs by means of penetrating in six ways, he should bring about the cleansing of the pathway."

Examination:

śl. 240cd-241ab **1. Mantra**

a. From the *Gahvara*

Jr.240b.3 He cites the text which is before him[214] both literally

214. That is, the *Gahvara*.

and according to its meaning."

> *[1a.] He [first] meditates on the bundle of flames which is described in his own scripture, a circle of eight beams of light etc.,* ||240|| *Because he [then] penetrates the circle of [his disciple's] heart with it, this is 'penetration by mantra'.*

Jr.241b.1 'In his own': according to [his own] ritual practice. 'With it': with the [circle of] eight beams of light etc. 'Circle of ... heart': [the disciple's] self is characterised as reduced to the condition of an object of perception through something that is before him. As it is said:

> Qt.241b.1 "He [first] meditates on the bundle of flames, i.e. the upmost circle which consists of eight beams of light, or even on [the circle of] twelve beams of light, in keeping with the ritual given in his own scripture. [Then] the other person's mind is to be penetrated. It is called 'penetration by mantra'."

śl. 241cd-247 **b. From the *Dīkṣottara***

2. Sound

3. *Bindu*

4. Śakti

Jr.241b.2 He gives the same [penetration by mantra] according to another procedure as well.

> *[1b.] After placing the phoneme Ā*[215] *in [his own] body in nine ways,*[216] *[the guru] should then, by the act of ritual placing, transfer [the phoneme Ā],*[217] || 241|| *which is shining [and] powerfully resplendent, across to the disciple.*

---

215. The word *ākāra* can means both 'the phoneme Ā' and 'shape'.
216. These are the nine openings of the body. Silburn, *La kuṇḍalinī*, p.114. These are the eyes, ears, nostrils, mouth, sex-organ and anus.
217. Silburn translates this as 'makes it penetrate by means of yogic projection'. *ibid.* p.114.

Then, as a result of the bond being released, he is joined to the supreme category. ||242|| *Such a procedure, presented in the* Dīkṣottara, *was explained to me by Śambhu. [2] It is called 'sound' because sound is pronounced. It occurs with regard to 'emanation' [viz. Mālinī].* ||243|| *[The guru] should penetrate the [disciple's] mind with sound. It is called 'penetration by sound'.[3] The [disciple's] mind is located in the position of the* bindu *which is placed either between the eyebrows* ||244|| *or in the target of the heart, O Great Goddess. [After visualising] the bindu as possessing the splendour of a bundle of flames, the [guru] should, by means of it, fully awaken [the mind which is] the subject [of the penetration]. This is called '[penetration] by* bindu'.||245|| *[4] By arousing the base of the body*[218] *[the guru] arouses that which pertains to śakti* [*viz.* Ḥ] *as far as the one who possesses śakti, O Beautiful One.* [Ḥ] *is seated in the triangle, it is curved, ear-ring shaped.* ||246|| *Having silently aroused* [Ḥ], *he should penetrate the whole universe. Because it is a circulating penetration of this sort, it is called 'the penetration which pertains to śakti'* [*viz. to* Ḥ]. ||247||

---

218. In his book, *Vāc*, p.413 footnote 89, Padoux translates *matta-gandha-sthāna* as 'the place of the exciting smell' and notes that '... this expression often indicates the sexual organs, - thus *TĀ* 29.246 ...'. He notes that it may sometimes also refer to the 'bulb', *kanda*. Silburn states that *matta-gandha* refers to the muscles of the rectum. Silburn, *La kuṇḍalinī*, p.117. The anatomical location of *gandha* or *matta-gandha*, like that of *kanda* is imprecise. In *TĀ* 5.54, Abhinava speaks of 'applying the staff to the subtle-breath'. This arouses the energy located at the base of the spine, which then rises like a serpent. In glossing this text, Jayaratha uses the phrase *matta-gandha-saṃkoca- ādi-krameṇa* and gives a quote which has the guru performing this act.

Jr.247d.1 'In nine ways': through the different apertures. 'In the body: in his own [body]. The [phoneme *Ā*] shines in those nine ways [viz. through the nine apertures] because it is being placed, i.e. because it is being given over. 'Powerfully resplendent': the capacity of the [phoneme *Ā*] to release the bond is highlighted by this [phrase]. 'Because sound is pronounced': the word 'sound' refers to the prolonged sound-seed. 'Emanation' means Nādiphānta [viz. Mālinī]. 'With sound': with the *Ḥ* which arises spontaneously. It is said in that respect:

> Qt.247d.1 "After pronouncing a prolonged sound, he should merge that sound into the [higher levels of] sound. After pronouncing Nādiphānta (viz. Mālinī], he should purify the pathway of the phonemes. O Goddess, he should penetrate by means of sound. It is called 'penetration by sound'."

Jr.247d.2 The phrase 'in the position of the *bindu*' is explained by the phrase 'between the eyebrows' and so on. 'Mind': the disciple's [mind]; and the [disciples' mind] is possessed by *bindu*. The word *bindu* implies [the phrase] 'after visualising' [the *bindu*]. Therefore it is said:

> Qt.247d.2 "Having entered [the disciple] as a resulting of visualising the *bindu* between the eye-brows or in the heart or in the 'bulb', he should penetrate the mind of the disciple by means of one or other *bindu*."

Jr.247d.3 And as it [is said]: "As a result of the guru contracting the excited base of the body, the highly ferocious one jumps up." [?][219] According to this teaching, [the guru] strongly applies the device of firmly pressing etc. the base of the body, i.e. the excited base of the body. By this upward impetus, he powerfully secures a perfect fusion of the impetus of the central śakti within the one who possesses śakti, i.e. within Śiva

219. The editors add a question mark to the text at this point and so ask whether this is actually a quotation.

himself, who is located at the 'end-of-twelve'. That is, he silently arouses the *anacka* [*Ḥ*].[220] The *anacka* [*Ḥ*] which is located in the generative organ is seated in the 'triangle' in the sense that it is ever present. It is ear-ring shaped, curved, meaning that it is undifferentiated from the energy of subtle-breath. He attends to this arousal which is quite spontaneous both as regards itself and anything else in the sense that it occurs irrespective of any effort at arousal, i.e. it is self-arousing. Having done this, he should penetrate the whole world. The [guru] makes [*Ḥ*] circulate by going round the different locations. It is said to be 'the penetration which pertains to śakti' [viz. *Ḥ*].

śl. 248 **5. Cobra**

a. In Brief

Jr.247d.4 Then, in order to explain 'cobra penetration' which is closely connected with the [penetration which belongs to śakti], he says:

> *[5] And the same supreme śakti, she who manifests bliss, goes from the womb to the supreme level, she who is adorned with the five cobra-hoods.* || 248 ||

Jr.248d.1 'Supreme level': to the one who possesses śakti who is located at the 'end-of-twelve'. Therefore it is said:

> Qt.248d.1 "Thus the goddess who has five cobra-hoods comes from the *maṇḍala* of the generative organ;

Jr.248d.2 Having said which, [the text continues]:

> Qt.248d.2."she goes to the supreme space, to the supreme *maṇḍala* of extinction."

---

220. In Pāṇini's grammar the term '*ac*', signifies a vowel. Padoux, *Vāc*, p.294 footnote 193. The term *anacka* means 'possessing no '*ac*' ', a consonant without a following vowel. In *Parātrīśikālaghuvṛtti* p.62, Abhinava himself defines it: 'Therefore he should meditate, in his heart and in his body, on the seed which, being without vowel (*svara*) or *visarga*, is in a state of *anacka* and which therefore is at the centre of the limited *prāṇa* and *apāna*' and being at the centre, it governs and rises as *uccāra*.

śl. 249-252 **b. In Detail**

Jr.248d.3 He explains the fact that she is adorned with five cobra-hoods.

> *The* kalā, *the categories, the* nanda *etc. and the spaces and the* kulas, *the causal deities starting with Brahmā, the sense-organs: she consists of [that] set of five.* ||249|| *She who five-fold in this way, leaves the 'place of Brahmā' [and] comes to rest in the 'abode of Brahmā'. She flashes like lightning as she merges.* ||250|| *When she has entered [the 'abode of Brahmā'], she penetrates the body [and] pierces right through to the self. The 'penetration by cobra' is thus described in the* Bhairavāgama. ||251|| *One should contemplate the mind until the mind has faded away. Once the mind has faded away, O Sureśānī, there is what is called 'supreme bliss'.* ||252||

Jr.252d.1 The '*kalā*' are five, i.e. *śāntyatītā* etc. The 'categories' are earth etc. '*Nanda* etc.' are the lunar days. The 'spaces' are the locations of the generative organ, navel, heart, *bindu* [and space]. The '*kula*' are called *mahākaula*, *kaula*, *akula*, *kula*, *kula-akula*. 'The causes', starting with Brahmā etc., finish with Sadāśiva. The sense-organs are the faculties of intellect and the faculties of action. 'From the abode of Brahmā': from the generative organ. 'To the abode of Brahmā': to the 'end-of-twelve', which means that both of these [places] are the principal abode of [Brahmā]. 'Body': the support etc. of the circles. Given the penetration of the body, what happens to the self? For that reason it is said: 'she pierces right through to the self'. And it is said:

> Qt.252d.1 "She who has the coiled appearance of a cobra is located below the navel. When aroused she moves like a cobra, she who is adorned with five hoods. [The penetration consists of] five sets of five sets, so that the penetration is known as 'cobra [penetration]'."

Jr.252d.2 'Once [the mind has] faded away': as a result of abandoning the form of differentiated thought. 'Supreme bliss': undifferentiated wonder itself.

śl. 253-254ab **6. Supreme**

Jr.252d.3 For that reason, the duality of the [mind] melts away from every side. He says:

> *[6] There are no faculties, no subtle-breaths, nothing known by the internal faculties, no mind, neither object nor subject of thought nor act of thinking.* ||253|| *The waning of all beings is called the'supreme penetration'.*

II Penetration According to Some Gurus

śl. 254cd-255ab **Enunciation of the 9 Forms**

Jr.254b.1 He explains the [statement] 'many methods' [of initiation-by-penetration] by another set.

> *By distinguishing between 'mantra', 'śakti', 'world', 'form', '[discriminating] knowledge', 'mass', 'place', 'channel' and 'supreme',* ||254|| *other gurus who know the secret present the knowledge in nine ways.*

śl. 255cd-27 **Examination:**

1. Mantra
2. Śakti
3. World
4. Form
5. Discriminating Knowledge
6. Mass
7. Place
8. Channel
9. Supreme

Jr.255b.1 He describes the [nine forms] in turn.

[1] After meditating [on the disciple who is] inside the triangular maṇḍala *which is inundated with the phonemes for fire [R] of* māyā [HRĪṂ], ||255|| *he should pierce the knots with this excellent flame. He should strike [him] with droplets of menstrual blood*[221] *and should unite him to the supreme. The procedure is named mantra[-penetration].* ||256||

[2] [The guru], after entering by any one of the [disciple's] channels, after forming his consciousness into a ball in the sacred place of [the disciple's] 'bulb', after forcefully circulating with the 'flame' [which consists] of the 'five' and of the 'eight', should join [his mind] ||257|| *which has been placed at the summit of the śakti spike, to any circle. Since it is done by means of śakti, it is the penetration which belongs to śakti. It immediately causes conviction.* ||258||

[3] The flame, bright as moonlight, emerges vigorously from the support. Moving progressively from the toe or from the perineum, [the flame] merges in the 'space' of the disciple. [By means of this flame the guru] makes the body [of the disciple] crystal clear. ||259|| *Recalling the multitudes of fore-mentioned worlds from KṢA to A, [the guru] mirrors them [in the disciple's body] through meditating on his own maṇḍala.*[222] *It is the 'penetration by worlds'.* ||260||

[4] He should meditate in the sense of identifying with any desired shape within the bindu's *sacred*

---

221. The word *puṣpa* can refer to a flower or to menstrual blood or an emotion or faculty etc. The present context would suggests droplets of menstrual blood.

222. The *maṇḍala* is his own body.

place between the eye-brows. And afterwards he should make [the disciple] consist of the [shape]. ||261|| *That is called 'piercing by form'. And the shape then becomes visible [to the disciple]. In the end, when the disciple becomes composed of it, he enters into union with it.* ||262||

[5] Discriminating knowledge is eightfold since it comprises the faculties of smell etc. and the interior (antaḥ) *faculties known as 'intellect' [etc.] By means of the thread of his own channels, he should transmit the [discriminating knowledge] to the disciple.* ||263|| *Because of the attitude of firm and constant conviction the penetration is known as '[penetration by] discriminating knowledge'. It immediately causes the sun of divine knowledge to arise in the space of the heart.* ||264||

[6] Mass [viz. body]: the supreme [body] is the 'kalās'*; the subtle [body] is the 'eightfold subtle body'; the gross [body] is the external [body]. The self [which is seen] in the reflection is [in fact] invisible. But it is thought to be visible when it is [seen] in the mirror etc.* ||265|| *Accordingly, [the guru] vigorously melds the different sorts of mass one into the next. When they variously ebb away, the highest level gradually [appears] because of the 'penetration of the mass'.* ||266||

[7] Having settled on the various circles in the pupil's body, [the guru] should illuminate each circle in turn. It is called 'penetration by place'. The [penetration] confers [illumination]. ||267||

[8] The preeminent channels are three in number, whilst the other [channels] contained in them are innumerable. 'Penetration by channel' uses the channels to bring about unity. It produces that result in these [innumerable channels]. || 268 || *[The guru] who is floating along a desired channel will reach consciousness by means of the principal [channels] which are associated with the eye etc. Penetration by channel has many different forms.* || 269 || *Like a powerful, tail-shaped animal, the great* yogī *, after shaking someone else's channel which has been enclosed by his own channel, forcefully makes him fall to the ground, even though he is a perfected being.* ||270 ||
[9] The supreme penetration: reflecting on the non-dual in all the circles, the guru, who is the dispenser of the state of Śiva, should transform [the disciple] into supreme Śiva. || 271 ||

Jr.271d.1 *Māyā* is *māyā-bīja* [*HRĪṂ*]. 'The phonemes for fire': *R*"s. 'Inside the triangular ...': inside a [triangle] which is pointing upwards. 'After meditating': on the disciple who is seated inside the [triangle]. 'With this [excellent flame]': with the triangular *maṇḍala*. 'By any one of the ...': by one of the three channels, *suṣumṇa* etc. 'After forming ... into a ball': after resorbing in every respect. 'After circulating': in that same ['bulb'], in a clockwise direction, with great velocity. 'The five' are the faculties of action. 'The eight' are the five faculties of intellect and the three internal faculties. '*Śakti*' implies *śakti*, pervasion and *samanā*. 'To any [circle]': to any chosen [circle]. 'Conviction' means absorption. 'The flame': the śakti in the shape of a [flame]. 'Bright as moonlight': this [phrase] indicates the splendour and unsullied nature of the [flame]. And because of the sheer capacity of the [flame] it is said: 'he makes the body [of the disciple] crystal clear'. 'In the space':

at the 'end-of-twelve'. And the merging into that [space] is to be considered [as coming] from the toe or from the perineum. 'Moving progressively from the toe or from the perineum': moving progressively from *KṢA* to *A*, therefore in the direction of reabsorption. 'Fore[-mentioned]': in chapter eight etc.[223] 'His own *maṇḍala*' is his own body. 'Mirrors': he structures the disciple in exactly the same way also. 'Any [desired shape]': the form of his chosen deity. And what is the result in this case? To this question he says: 'and the [shape then becomes visible]. He elucidates the phrase 'the [discriminating knowledge] is eightfold' by [the phrase] 'smell' etc. '*Antaḥ*'[224] : the three internal faculties. '[In the space of] the heart': because it is the place where all the channels become evident. 'The mass' is the body. '*Kalā*': the five coverings. 'The [different sorts of mass]': the three types [of mass]. 'One into the next': the gross into the subtle and the subtle into the supreme. 'Gradually': one after the other, according to their durability. And at this point in the [text] an image [is used]:

> Qt.271d.1 "The self [which is seen] in the reflection is [in fact] invisible. But it is thought to be visible when it is [seen] in the mirror etc."

Jr.271d.2 That half-[*śloka*] is to be regarded as largely superfluous because it is out of context. But if it does fit the context for those who are determined on an exposition of the text as given, so be it! Our outlook, however, is not like that. 'Circle': the generative organ and the other circles are implied. 'In turn': starting from the circle of the channels etc. 'He should illuminate': [the guru] should inflame [the circle] by making [the disciple] intent on consciousness. 'Confers': [the penetration] causes illumination. 'Contained in [the preeminent channels]': since [the other channels are] generally a reflection of the

223. The whole of *TĀ* 8 describes the divine geography through which the initiate passes in the pathway of space (*deśa-adhva*).

224. The word *antaḥ* can mean either 'end' or 'interior'. To prevent misunderstanding, Jayaratha explains that *antaḥ* means 'internal'.

[preeminent channels]. 'By using the [channels]': by using the innumerable other channels. 'That result': it produces unity. There is no question of asking: 'Which [channel] then?', for which reason he says: 'the desire [channel]' etc. 'Tail-shaped': just as an animal with great bodily strength can, by agitating its tail, fell a tree etc., so can he as well. [The word] 'supreme' is implied [as an epithet of the title 'perfected being'].[225] 'Great *yogī*': a guru who dispenses the state of Śiva. This is the final thing to be known.

III Supreme Penetration in *Vīrāvalibhairava*

śl. 272ab **Enunciation**

Jr.271d.3 And that [supreme initiation-by-penetration] is mentioned in the *āgama* too as follows. He says:

> *And the [supreme initiation-by-penetration] is described in the illustrious* Vīrāvalikula *as follows:*

śl. 272cd-273ab **Examination**

i. The Guru

Jr.272b.1 Therefore he says:

> *Having come to know the centre which is indivisible [and] in every respect knowable, he is undefiled.*||272|| *The guru, who is accomplished as regards the subsidiary divisions of the [centre], should liberate the 'bonded animal'.*

Jr.273b.1 [The guru] has come to know the centre, i.e. the energy of the central subtle-breath, which is incapable of being penetrated by non-*yogī*s, and therefore must necessarily be

225. The word *siddha*, 'perfect', can be applied to persons of greater or lesser excellence but it is a perfected being of highest excellence whom the great *yogī* is felling in *śl.*270cd. Therefore Jayaratha needs to explain that the word 'supreme' (*param*) is implied.

known by the practice of *yoga* etc. [That is] he has experienced [the energy of the central subtle-breath] flowing freely through the divisions of the various circles etc. [Having done this] he remains undefiled and he is not immersed in the movement of both the *prāṇa* and the *apāna*. He has, therefore, an enduring experience of the subsidiary divisions of the mantra etc. which are located there, i.e. in the central subtle-breath just mentioned. He, the one who teaches the supreme reality, should liberate the 'bonded animals', i.e. should have [them] emerge from the support etc. of the various circles.

śl. 273cd-274ab **ii. How to Penetrate the Disciple**

Jr.273b.2 And how should the guru do that? He says:

> *The disciple should sit before the guru. The [guru] should penetrate [him] 'mouth' to 'mouth',* ||273|| *form to form, in various particular ways until [the disciple] becomes perfectly fused.*

Jr.274b.1 The guru [should insert his 'mouth'] into the 'mouth' of the disciple seated before him -

> Qt.274b.1 "... the consort of Śiva [viz. śakti] is, in this instance, called 'mouth'."

Jr.274b.2 - according to this teaching, he should insert his central śakti into the central śakti of the [disciple], he should insert his form of the faculty of sight into the [disciple's] form, i.e. into [the disciple's] faculty of perception, his faculty of sight; he should insert his internal sense-organs into the internal sense-organs of the [disciple] which are implied in the [external sense-organs such as sight etc.]. [That is,] he should focus his attention on the cause [of the sense organs]. [This is done] until, by means of these particular activities, [the disciple] becomes fused, i.e. until he achieves identity with the [centre] (*tat*).[226]

śl. 274cd-275 **iii. The Result: Disciple is one with Centre**

Jr.274b.3 And in that case, what is the result? To this question he says:

> *[Their] minds become perfectly fused. Both acquire the transmental state,* ||274|| *and by their arrival at the transmental, at that moment, [the disciple] is initiated. When 'moon' and 'sun' are united, he, while alive becomes composed of the [centre].* ||275||

Jr.275d.1 'Is initiated': the disciple. As a result [of his being initiated] his [limited] self becomes composed of the [centre]. This happens when there is union, i.e. when there is the perfect fusion of 'moon' and 'sun', i.e. of the *prāṇa* and *apāna*. [This perfect fusion happens] through appropriately putting an end to the respective forms [of the *prāṇa* and *apāna*] within the central śakti. [That is] he becomes one with [the centre].

IV Initiation to Śivahood of all Living Beings

śl. 276ab **Enunciation**

Jr.275d.2 And that [centre] is what even the causal agents desire. He says:

> *As regards the [centre], the gods, Brahmā etc. long for the liberation which leads to liberation.*

226. The indefinite terms *tat*, *etat* and *atra* appear several times in the present context: *etac*, Jr.271d.3; *tad*, Jr.274b.2; *tad*, *tan*, Jr.275d.1; *etac*, Jr.275d.2; *atra*, *śl.*276a; *tan*, 275d. Do they refer to the centre mentioned in *śl.*272d or to 'the ineffable' (*anākhya*) as in *śl.*142a and Jr.142b.1? Do they refer to the supreme penetration, as in Jr.271d.3, or to the state of Śiva which is the result of the initiation? Do all these things in fact coincide? The guru has come to know the centre and he sets about bringing the disciple to this highest state. Accordingly the word *tat* etc. will be translated to mean 'centre'.

śl. 276cd-277ab **Definition**

Jr.276b.1 How does that happen? To this question he says:

> *After restraining his circle of rays, when he 'devours'*[227] *both enjoyment and liberation:* ||276|| *the initiation which results is proclaimed as 'belonging to Śarva'.*

Jr.277b.1 When the guru etc.,[228] who has been described in that way,[229] after restraining his circle of rays beginning with the mind, 'devours' enjoyment and liberation, which are both mutually incompatible, i.e. when he is liberated even in enjoyment: the [initiation] which results is called 'the initiation which belongs to Parameśvara', i.e. it is so named because it gives liberation in life.

śl. 277cd-278ab **Examination**

i. In Brief

Jr.277b.2 Therefore he says:

> *This liberation is said to be 'motionless' in the midst of all living beings.* ||277|| *By striking and hammering the phases of 'fire' and 'moon', he eliminates the vibration.*

Jr.278b.1'Motionless': unwavering in all circumstances. Initiated according to [Śarva initiation], he should—as a result of repeatedly striking the phases of 'fire' and 'moon', i.e. of *prāṇa* and *apāna* which consist of the means of knowledge and the objects of knowledge, i.e. by denying their nature, by reposing in the form of the knowing subject alone—eliminate the vibration, i.e. should bring an end to the dominance of external things.

---

227. The term 'devours' links up with the term 'relish' which is the third stage in the fourfold presentation of the Krama cycle. He 'devours' in the sense that he reaches a state which is higher than both liberation or enjoyment and from which both emanate.
228. The term 'etc.' refers to the disciple.
229. Namely, in *śl.*272cd-275cd.

śl. 278cd-281 **ii In Detail**

iii Result: All acquire Śivahood

Jr.278b.2 And how does such a thing take place? To this question he says:

> *The external subtle-breath which goes outside, which, taking on the form of darkness,* || 278 || *has left through the pores, circulates through all the causal deities. After he has aimlessly made the [external subtle-breath] arrive at a centre, he causes it to [continue to] circulate. Then he 'emits'.* ||279|| *By increasing the union [of* prāṇa *and* apāna*] he penetrates the five knots. He reflects on the central sacred place which is the pairing of the modalities of the coupling [of* prāṇa *and* apāna*].* ||280|| *He does not focus on the combination of self, space, external reality, mind or body. This initiation grants the acquisition of the state of Śiva to all living creatures.* ||281||

Jr.281d.1 The 'pouring out' is the external *apāna* and *prāṇa*, in the sense that it consists of objectivity. When these [*apāna* and *prāṇa*] become intent on repose, [the pouring] is the central [subtle-breath]. Therefore, the form which pours out through the pores, i.e. through the channels in every direction -

> Qt.281d.1 "There is no sadness prior to duality. Darkness is not due to the state of non-duality."

Jr.281d.2 —assumes, according to this quote, the appearance of darkness, i.e. the form of the [limited] knowing subject. And, as a result of arresting the upwards movement, [the subtle-breath] circulates in the regions governed by the causal deities such as Brahmā etc., i.e. [the limited knowing subject] causes [the subtle-breath] to circulate in those [regions] by abandoning and approaching an object of meditation. And, immediately after [the subtle-breath] circulates in this way, he 'emits'.

Then, by means of an upward movement of the union of *prāṇa* and *apāna*, he pierces the set of five knots which govern the various causes. Then he reflects on the central sacred place, i.e. on the couple, *prāṇa* and *apāna*, which have become fused, i.e. he becomes closely attentive to that same [central sacred place]. Then he ceases to focus on the combination [of the following aspects] which pertain to the limited self; space, i.e. void; external reality, i.e. external objects such as blue etc.; mind which, since it is the basis of the mirroring [of objects], is a hidden speech; and the body. He experiences the directly self-evident within the self alone. This initiation, therefore, is said to grant the acquisition of the state of Śiva.

RITES TO CONCLUDE THE INITIATION

śl. 282-283 The First Ritual: With Masters and Adepts —Oblation

Jr.281d.3 Having explained in this way the many kinds of initiation-by-penetration, he also says what remains to be done in that connection.

> *At the end of the initiation, having cooked the 'lamps', the 'oblation' is to be eaten by the* kula *Masters along with all the Adepts. It destroys great sins.* || 282 || *Such is said in the illustrious* Ratnamālā. *The ritual which is 'defective' or 'excessive' is indeed a sin. This [ritual of eating the oblation] is said to be 'the ceasing of [sin]'.* ||283||

Jr.283d.1 And the [ritual] is not declared on the basis of his own judgment [alone], for which reason it is stated: 'such is said in the illustrious *Ratnamālā*'. As it is said in that [text]:

> Qt.283d.1 "At the end of the initiation, 'lamps' should be made. After cooking, the 'oblation' is to be eaten by the *kula* Masters along with the Adepts. It destroys great sins."

Jr.283d.2 [It is said:]

> Qt.283d.2 "If not all are persons who know reality, he should not present the 'lamp'."

Jr.283d.3 According to this teaching, when there are people present who do not know reality, then an 'oblation' meal is forbidden. And for those who do know reality, even the fear of contact with sin is absent. Therefore, what does the phrase 'destroys great sins' mean in that [text, viz. *śl.*282d]? To this question he says: 'defective etc.'.

The Second Ritual: With all the Heroes —Wine

śl. 284-285ab **Enunciation**

Jr.283d.4 He says what else must be done in the [ritual of initiation] to complete it:

> *On the next day, the sacrifice is to be celebrated in honour of the guru. Since the ritual is not complete without it, [the initiate] should then do it with energy.* ||284|| *He should offer to the guru whatever pleases him.*

Jr.285b.1 [The phrase] 'the ritual is not complete' refers to an ancillary aspect of the sacrifice in honour of the [guru]. It is not done for the [guru's personal] pleasure.

Examination

śl. 285cd-287ab **1. The Ritual**
a. The Guru and the Initiate Partake

Jr.285b.2 And what is the ritual mentioned in [*śl*.284ab] which will complete the [initiation]? He says:

> *The ritual of [initiation] which occurs during the ceremony of the circle[-sacrifice] is called 'the transmission'.* || 285|| *The cup of liquor, filled to the top, is held in the hand of the Vīrendra. After looking upon it as the supreme brahman, [the initiate] should drink from it at the guru's command.* ||286|| *Then, having satiated the spirits, he should offer it to the guru.*

Jr.287b.1'Of ... ': of initiation. 'The Virendra' is the Master.

śl. 287cd-289ab **b. All the Heroes Partake**

Jr.287b.2 Regarding the same matter as mentioned in [*śl*.284ab], he teaches [the following]:

> *After making [a prostration] on the ground and having made obeisance to the guru, having fully*

> *satiated the sky-travellers* ||287|| *and after bowing to his 'mantra' and to the [cup of liquor]* (tac-ca), *to the sexual partner, to Gaṇapati, to the gurus, to the guardian deity of the region, to the assembly of heroes in due order starting with the gurus etc.,* ||288|| *[the initiate] should, of his own accord, drink the ingredient which has been touched by the heroes. It should never be done in any other way.*

Jr.289b.1'After making [a prostration] on the ground' means that [he makes] himself [fall prostrate]. Therefore, [the phrase] means: after falling to the ground, a prostration is to be made to the guru. [The phrase] '*tac-ca*' is to be construed as 'and after bowing to the cup of liquor'. 'Touched by the heroes': all of them, starting with the guru, in due order [consume] what is left of the drink.

śl. 289cd-290 **2. Notes:**

a. Exclusion Text

Jr.289b.2 And that [ceremony] is to be performed just by those who know reality together with the ordinary initiates. It is not to be done with other persons. He says:

> *Those who have no knowledge of the* para-brahman, *who are without the* āgama *of Agama,*[230] ||289|| *and who are given over to greed, folly, conceit, anger, attachment and* māyā: *with them that [ceremony]*[231] *is not to be performed, if one desires one's own good.* ||290||

230. Firstly, the term *agama* means 'inaccessible', 'unattainable' and is similar to *anuttera*, 'unsurpassable' which is a epithet of Śiva. Secondly, the ordinary initiate is bound to the recitation of the scriptures. Thus the phrase 'those who are without the *āgama* of Agama' can be understood to mean 'those who are without commitment to the Śaiva scriptures', in other words, those who are not ordinary initiates.

231. The ceremony described in *śl.*284-289ab.

Śl. 291 **b. The Timing of the Second Ritual**

Jr.290d.1 And when is that [Second Ritual] to be done? To this question he says:

> *At the beginning of the sacrifice and in the middle of the sacrifice, at the end of the sacrifice, during the worship of the guru, during the occasional rites mentioned above,*[232] *the disciple should perform that ritual.* ||291||

Jr.291d.1 'Mentioned above': in chapter twenty-eight.

Śl. 292ab **Summation of the Whole Chapter.**

Jr.291d.2 He sums up the meaning of the chapter with a half-*śloka*.

> *Thus has the secret ritual been thoroughly discussed. It has been described in very clear terms by means of the experiences obtained from the mouth of the guru.* ||292ab||

Jr.292b.1 Let [this work] be auspicious!

Jr.292b.2 The *kaula* experience has been transmitted in proper order by the teaching of the illustrious guru. Jayaratha has explained this twenty-ninth chapter.

Jr.292b.3 Such is the elucidation of the secret ritual as contained within the investigation of the illustrious *Tantrāloka*—the twenty-ninth chapter.

232. In *TĀ* 28.6-9, Abhinava lists 23 occasional rites.

APPENDICES

APPENDIX 1

The 36 categories (*tattva*),
the 5 *kalā*,
the 4 spheres (*aṇḍa*)

Categories :

36	śiva	consciousness	*cit*

***kalā* of *śāntātītā*,** 'beyond rest' = categories 36-35
sphere of *śakti* = categories 35-32

35	śakti	bliss	*ānanda*

***kalā* of *śāntā*,** 'rest' = categories 34-32

34	Sadāśiva	will	*icchā*
33	Īśvara	knowledge	*jñāna*
32	Śuddhāvidyā	action	*kriyā*

sphere of *māyā*, 'illusion' = categories 31-25
***kalā* of *vidyā*,** (impure) 'knowledge' = categories 31-25
6 coverings (*kañcuka*, *āvaraṇa*) = categories 31-26

31	illusion	*māyā*
	3 levels	i. supreme
		ii. subtle
		iii. gross = knot (*granthi*)

5 *kalā* = categories 30 - 25

30	force	*kalā*
29	knowledge	*vidyā*
28	attachment	*rāga*
27	necessity	*niyati*
26	time	*kāla*
25	individual	*puruṣa*

sphere of *prakṛti*, 'matter' = categories 24-2
***kalā* of *pratiṣṭhā*,** 'foundation' = categories 24-2

24	matter	*prakṛti*

3 interior faculties (*antaḥ-karaṇa*)

23	intelligence	*buddhi*
22	ego	*ahamkāra*
21	mind	*manas*

5 faculties of knowledge (*jñānendriya*) **or of intellect** (*buddhendriya*)

20	hearing	*śrotra*
19	touching	*tvac*
18	seeing	*cakṣus*
17	tasting	*rasana*
16	smelling	*ghrāṇa*

5 faculties of action (*karmendriya*)

15	speaking	*vāc*
14	grasping	*pāṇi*
13	excreting	*pāyu*
12	procreating	*upastha*
11	walking	*pāda*

5 subtle elements (*tanmātra*)

10	sound	*śabda*
9	touch	*sparśa*
8	form	*rūpa*
7	taste	*rasa*
6	smell	*gandha*

5 gross elements (*mahābhūta*)

5	space	*ākāśa*
4	air	*vāyu*
3	fire	*tejas*
2	water	*jala*

sphere of *pṛthivī*, 'earth' = category 1
***kalā* of *nivṛtti*, 'inaction'** = category 1

1	earth	*pṛthivī*

APPENDIX 2

The Phonemes of Śabdarāśī, Mātṛkā and Mālinī together with their Corresponding Categories.

Note: The following is adapted from Gnoli, *Il commento*, p.82 and from Padoux, *Vāc,* pp.318-319 which is more detailed on the listing of the categories in Śabdarāśi.

	Parāvāc **Parā** **Śabdarāśi**	**Paśyantī** **Parāparā** **Mātṛkā**	**Madhyamā** **Aparā** **Mālinī**	**Categories** (*tattva*)		
1.	A	A	N	36+35 Śiva / Śakti		
2.	Ā	Ā	Ṝ	"		
3.	I	I	Ṛ	"		
4.	Ī	Ī	Ḷ	"		
5.	U	U	Ḹ	"		
6.	Ū	Ū	TH	"		
7.	Ṛ	Ṛ	C	"		
8.	Ṝ	Ṝ	DH	"		
9.	Ḷ	Ḷ	Ī	"		
10.	Ḹ	Ḹ	Ṅ	"		
11.	E	E	U	"		
12.	AI	AI	Ū	"		
13.	O	O	B	"		
14.	AU	AU	K	"		
15.	Ṃ	Ṃ	KH	"		
16.	Ḥ	Ḥ	G	"		
17.	K	KṢ	GH	34	*sadāśiva*	
18.	KH	H	Ṅ	33	*īśvara*	
19.	G	S	I	32	*śuddhāvidyā*	
20.	GH	Ṣ	A	31	*māyā*	illusion
21.	Ṅ	Ś	V	30	*kalā*	force
22.	C	V	BH	29	*vidyā*	knowledge
23.	CH	L	Y	28	*rāga*	attachment
24.	J	R	Ḍ	27	*niyati*	necessity
25.	JH	Y	ḌH	26	*kāla*	time
26.	Ñ	M	ṬH	25	*puruṣa,*	*aṇu,* individual

27.	Ṭ	BH	JH	24	*prakṛti*	matter
28.	ṬH	B	Ñ	23	*buddhi*	intelligence
29.	Ḍ	PH	J	22	*ahaṃkāra*	ego
30.	ḌH	P	R	21	*manas*	mind
31.	Ṇ	N	Ṭ	20	*śrotra*	hearing
32.	T	DH	P	19	*tvac*	touching
33.	TH	D	CH	18	*cakṣus*	seeing
34.	D	TH	L	17	*rasana*	tasting
35.	DH	T	Ā	16	*ghrāṇa*	smelling
36.	N	Ṇ	S	15	*vāc*	speaking
37.	P	ḌH	Ḥ	14	*pāṇi*	grasping
38.	PH	Ḍ	H	13	*pāyu*	excreting
39.	B	ṬH	Ṣ	12	*upastha*	rocreating
40.	BH	Ṭ	KṢ	11	*pāda*	walking
41.	M	Ñ	M	10	*śabda*	sound
42.	Y	JH	Ś	9	*sparśa*	touch
43.	R	J	Ṃ	8	*rūpa*	form
44.	L	CH	T	7	*rasa*	taste
45.	V	C	E	6	*gandha*	smell
46.	Ś	Ṅ	AI	5	*ākāśa*	space
47.	Ṣ	GH	O	4	*vāyu*	air
48.	S	G	AU	3	*tejas*	fire
49.	H	KH	D	2	*jala*	water
50.	KṢ	K	PH	1	*pṛthivī*	earth

APPENDIX 3

The *Uccāra* of OṂ According to the *Svacchandatantra*, Adapted from Padoux, *Vāc*, p.408.

Number		Phase	Deity	Category	Caḱra
1.	1.	*unmanā*	Paramaśiva		'end-of-twelve'
2.	2.	*samanā*	Śiva /	*śiva*	
3.	3.	*vyāpinī*	/śakti		tuft of hair
4.	4.	*śakti* [1]	śakti	*śakti*	pit-of-Brahmā
5.	5.	*nādānta*			
6.	6.	*nāda*	Sadāśiva	*sadāśiva*	from forehead to crown
7.	7.	*nirodhinī*			
8.	8.	*ardhacandra*			forehead region
9.		*bindu*	Īśvara	*īśvara*	eyebrows
10.		*MA*	Rudra	*māyā*	palate
11.		*U*	Viṣṇu	6 *tattvas* (*kalā* to *puruṣa*)	throat
12.		*A*	Brahmā	24 *tattvas* (*prakṛti* to earth)	heart

1. *śakti* is also called *sparśa*. Silburn, *Le Vijñāna Bhairava*, p.50.

APPENDIX 4

The Mantras Referred to in *TĀ 29* and in Jayaratha's Investigation.

	DEITY	NAME	PHONIC FORM	FIRST REFERENCE
1.	Mālinī	Nādiphānta	*NA-PHA*	śl.18c
2.	Parā		*SAUḤ*	śl.18c
3.	Parāparā			śl.48b
4.	Aparā			śl.48b
5.	Mātṛsadbhāva			śl.19d
	= Saṅkarṣinī			śl.69c
	= Kālāntakī			Qt.13d.8
	= Kālasaṅkarṣiṇī		see below	Qt.70b.2
6.	Mātṛkā	Kṣādyānta	*A-KṢA*	śl.45d
7.		*hapsa*	*HAṀSA*	*Ḍl.*83d
8.			*HÀ-HÀ*	Qt.160b.2
9.		*akṣara*	*Oṁ*	Qt.160b.1
10.		*kūṭa*	*KṢA*	śl.167d
11.		*rudra-śakti*	Mālinī enclosed by either Parā or Mātṛsadbhāva	śl.187c
12.			*RKṢRŪAUṂ*	Jr.195d.1
13.			*SRYŪṁ*	Jr.213d.1
14.			*ḌḌHMRYŪṁ*	Jr.213d.1
15.			*RSHKṢRYŪṂ*	Jr.213d.1
16.		*śakti-bīja*	*ĪṂ or HRĪṂ*	śl.214a
17.			*HA*	Jr.216d.1
18		*māyā-bīja*	*ĪṂ or HRĪṂ*	Jr.271d.1

The 17 syllables of Kālasaṅkarṣiṇī are as follows:
hrīṃ mahācaṇḍayogeśvarī ṭhr̄ dhr̄ thr̄ phaṭ phaṭ phaṭ phaṭ phaṭ

Further references to some of these mantras are given in Appendix 5.

APPENDIX 5

The Deities Named in *TĀ* 29 and in Jayaratha's Investigation.

Akula	Jr.0.1, Jr.252d.1 bis; Qt.153b.6;
Agama	*śl.*289c;
Aghora	*śl.*53a; Jr.54d.1;
Aja	Jr.88d.1
Anaśriśiva	Jr.235d.1;
Aparā	*śl.*48b;
Ānandabhairava	Qt.13d.6,
Īśvara	Qt.66d.2; Jr.235d.1;
Aindrī	*śl.*52c, Jr.54d.1;
Ka	*ka-randhraka śl.*59b;
	*ka-randhra śl.*179c; Jr.88d.1;
Kālasaṅkarṣiṇī	Qt.70b.2;
Kālāntakī	Qt.13d.8;
Kālī	Qt.57d.2;
Kula	*passim*
Kuleśa	*kuleśa-yugma śl.*131cd, Qt.46b.2;
Kuleśitā	*śl.*223b
Kuleśvara	*śl.*48d, *śl.*226d, *śl.*229b; Jr.46b.2, Jr.79d.1,
	Jr.223d.1 bis.
Kuleśvarī	*śl.*47b, *śl.*69b, *śl.*48d, *śl.*226d, *śl.*229b;
	Jr.46b.3, Jr.48d.1, Jr.223d.1 bis;
Kṛśā	*śl.*76b; Qt.77d.1 (*kṛśa-udarī*);
Kaumārī	*śl.*52a;
Jayā	Jr.51d.1;
Gaṇāmbikā	Qt.77d.1;
Gaṇeśa	*śl.*28c, *śl.*29b; Jr.29b.1, Jr.29b.3, Jr.29b.4 bis;
	Qt.29b.1, Qt.29b.2, Qt.29b.3, Qt.29b.4;
Gaṇeśvara	*śl.*27d; Jr.29b.1;
Gaṇapati	*śl.*288b;
Trilocana	Qt.70b.2, Qt.110b.1;
Devadeveśi	Qt.163d.1;
Parameśa	*śl.*2c, śl.4a, *śl.*56d, *śl.*96c,
Parameśvara	*śl.*58d (*pārameśvara*), *śl.*81c; Jr.16d.5,
	Jr.90b.2 (*pārameśvarī*), Jr.96d.4, Jr.277b.1;

	rudra-koṇa *śl.*27c; Jr.29b.4;
Vaṭuka	*śl.*28a; Jr.29b.1 bis, Jr.29b.3; Qt.29b.2, Qt.29b.3;
Vibhu	*śl.*165b; Qt.4d.4, Qt.13d.5;
Viṣṇu	Jr.235d.1;
Vairiñcī	*śl.*52a, *śl.*63c; Jr.63d.3;
Vaiṣṇavī	*śl.*52b;
Śaṅkara	Qt.13d.17 (*śāṅkara*);
Śambhu	*śl.*17b; Jr.232d.1 (*śāṃbhava*); Qt.175d.1;
Śarva	*śl.*277b (*śārvī*);
Śiva	*passim*
śaiva	*śl.*83d;
Śaivī	Qt.274b.1;
Śākta	Qt.201b.1;
Śītāṃśumaulī	*śl.*177d;
Śuci	Qt.9d.2, Qt.153b.4;
Saṅkarṣaṇī	Jr.57d.3; Qt.57d.3;
Saṅkarṣiṇī	*śl.*69c; Jr.70b.2; Qt.70b.2, Qt.70b.5;
Sadāśiva	Jr.220d.1, Jr.235d.1, Jr.252d.1;
Sureśānī	*śl.*252c;
Śrī-rahasya-rājikā-yoginī	Jr.46b.1;
Svayaṃbhū	Qt.13d.25;
Hāṭakeśvara	Qt.153b.6;
Heruka	Qt.236d.3.

APPENDIX 6

The Perfected Beings etc. and the Marks of their Lineages.

1. The Perfected Beings (*siddha*)

The Kṛta Age:	East:	Khagendra+Vijjāmbā, their sons and wives: Vaktaṣṭi + Illāīambā Vimala + Anantamekhalāmbā
The Dvāpara Age:	South:	Kūrma + Maṅgalā the śakti, their sons and wives: Jaitra + Illāīambā Avijata + Ānandamekhalā
The Tretā Age:	West:	Meṣa + Kāmamaṅgalā, their sons and wives: Vindhya + Kullāīambā Ajita+Ever-youthful-Mekhalā
The Kali Age:	North:	Macchanda + Kuñkuṇāmbā and the group of six who are qualified:

2. The row of six 'who are qualified' (*adhikāra*) śl.36d;
princes' (*rājaputra*) Jr.40d.2, Qt.39d.5;
and their wives:

Amara	Varadeva	Citra	Ali	Vindhya	Guḍikā
+	+	+	+	+	+
Sillāī	Erūṇā	Kumārī	Bodhāī	Mahālacchī	Aparamekhalā

3. Their lineages have the following identifying marks:

	Amara:	**Varadeva:**	**Citra:**
dynasty (*ovalli*)			
*śl.*36ab	-ananda	-āvali	-bodhi
Jr.	-	-	-
Qt.39d.2	-bodhi	-prabhu	-pāda
gesture (*mudrā*)			
*śl.*37ab	thumb	index finger	middle finger
Jr.	-	-	-
Qt.39d.3	-	-	-

code (*chumma*)			
*śl.*37cd	end-of-twelve	upper kuṇḍali	bindu
Jr.	-	-	-
Qt.39d.4	Transcendent	-	eye-brow centre
hermitage (*ghara*)			
*śl.*38ab	Śavara	Aḍabilla	Paṭṭilla
Jr.39d.1	Pulinda	-	-
Qt.39d.5	Paṭṭilla	Karabilla	Ambilla
begging-place (*palli*)			
*śl.*38cd	Aḍabī	Ḍombi	Dakṣiṇā
Jr.39d.1	-	-	Dakṣiṇāvarta
Qt.39d.5	Dakṣiṇāvarta	Kumbhārikā	Billa
sacred site (*pīṭha*)			
*śl.*39abc	Devikoṭṭa	Kulādri	Tripurī
Jr.39d.1	-	Kaulagiri	Tripurottara
Qt.39d.6	Tripurottara	Kāmarū [sic]	Aṭṭahāsa

	Ali:	**Vindhya:**	**Guḍikā:**
dynasty (*ovalli*)			
*śl.*36ab	-prabhu	-pāda	-yogī
Jr.	-	-	-
Qt.39d.2	-ānanda	-yogī	-āvali
gesture (*mudrā*)			
*śl.*37ab	ring f.	little f.	left little f.
Jr.	-	-	-
Qt.39d.3	-	-	-
code (*chumma*)			
*śl.*37cd	heart	navel	bulb
Jr.	-	-	-
Qt.39d.4	'union'	-	organ of generation
hermitage (*ghara*)			
*śl.*38ab	Karabilla	Ambi	Śarabilla
Jr.39d.1	-	Ambilla	-
Qt.39d.5	Pulinda	Śarabillaṃ	Aḍabilla
begging-place (*palli*)			
*śl.*38cd	Billa	Kumbhārika	Akṣara
Jr.39d.1		-	-

Qt.39d.5	Aḍabī	Akṣara	Aḍabilla
sacred site (*pīṭha*)			
śl.39abc	Kāmākhya	Aṭṭahāsa	Dakṣiṇapīṭha
Jr.39d.1	Kāmarūpa	-	-
Qt.39d.6	Devikoṭṭa	Dakṣiṇā	Kaulagir

4. The row of six who have no qualification (*niradhikāra*)

Bhaṭṭa	Indra	Valkala	Ahīndra	Gajendra	Mahīdhara

APPENDIX 7

The Installation of Sacred Sites on the Body

1. According to *TĀ* 29.59-63.

Head:

1	Aṭṭahāsa			tuft of hair	
2	Caritra			fontanelle	
3	Kaulagiri			ears	
4	Jayantikā			nostrils	
5	Ujjayinī			eye-brows	
6	Prayāga			face	

Torso:

7	Vārāṇasī			heart	
8	Śrīpīṭha			two shoulders	
9	Viraja			throat	
10	Eḍābhī			stomach	
11	Hālā			navel	
12	Gośruti			testicles	

Legs:

13	Marukośa			generative organ	
14-15	Nagara	+	Pauṇḍravardhana	right	+ left buttocks
16-17	Elāpura	+	Purastīra	right	+ left thighs
18-19	Kuḍyākeśī	+	Sopāna	right	+ left knees
20-21	Māyāpū	+	Kṣīraka	right	+ left calves
22-23	Āmrāta	+	Nṛpasadmanī	right	+ left ankles
24	Vairiñcī			soles of the feet	

2. There are variations in the quoted texts and a further variation in Jayaratha's investigation:

for	Hālā	Qt.63d.1	reads	Alipura
for	Gośruti	Jr.63d.2	reads	Gokarṇa
for	Māyāpura	Qt.63d.2	reads	Vāmapurī
for	Āmrāta	Qt.63d.2	reads	Āmrātakeśvara
for	Nṛpasadmanī	Qt.63d.2	reads	Rājagṛha
for	Vairiñcī ... soles	Qt.63d.3 + 4	read	Brahmī: her sacred site is Śrīśaila

APPENDIX 8

The Schools and Systems Named in *TĀ* 29 and in Jayaratha's Investigation.

Advaita	*śl.*74a; perhaps Qt.75b.3, perhaps Qt.100b.6;
Atimārga	Qt.100b.4;
Bauddha	Qt.75b.3;
Dvaita	*śl.*74a; Qt.75b.2, Qt.166b.1 bis;
Krama	*śl.*57b; Jr.56d.1, *passim*;
Kula	*passim;*
Śākta	Qt.201b.1;
Siddhānta	*śl.*74c; Qt.3d. Qt.75b.3;
Smārta	Jr.102d.5; Qt.75b.3;
Trika	*śl.*95d;
Tantra	Jr.7d.2; Qt.75b.1, Qt.100b.6;
Vaiṣṇava	Qt.75b.3;
Vāma	perhaps Qt.100b.4;
Vedānta	Qt.75b.3;

APPENDIX 9

The Texts Named in *TĀ* 29 and in Jayaratha's Investigation[1]

Arṇava	*śl.*165d; Jr.166b.1;
=Yonyārṇava	Jr.166b.1;
Ānandeśvara	*śl.*200d; Jr.200d.2;
Utphulla	*śl.*166a; Jr.166b.1;
=Utphullakamata	Jr.166b.1;
Kālīkula[2]	*śl.*43b;
Kulakriḍāvatāra	Jr. 39d.1, Jr. 39d.1, Jr. 39d.2, Jr. 39d.3, Jr. 39d.1, Jr. 39d.1, Jr. 39d.6;
Kulakramodaya[3]	Jr.63d.3;
Kramarahasya	*śl.*14a;
Khamata	*śl.*165d;
=Khemata	Jr.166b.1;
=Khecarīmata	Jr.166b.1;
Gama-śāstra	*śl.*142b; Jr.141b.2, Jr.142b.1, Jr.142b.2;
=Nigama	*śl.*141a;
Gahvara[4]	*śl.*240a;

1. The references which follow only refer to the places where Abhinava and Jayaratha name texts. They make further quotations with or without attribution. They also quote from texts which they have not named at all in *TĀ* 29 and its investigation, such as the *Uccuṣmabhairavatantra*, the *Jayadrathayāma*, the *Vijñānabhairava*, the *Spandakārikā* and the *Manusmṛti* or quote from sources which other texts also use, such as the *Kaulāvalī*. See Appendix 10.
2. In Rastogi, p.255 footnote 15, the author says that the MSS of this text are available in the Darbar Library, Nepal, Tantra Catalogue, Vol. I, pp.37-42. For other references to that text see New Catalogue, Vol.IV, pp.48-49, 72-73 (*Upodghāta*. p.26.) He considers that the *Kālīkula* may be identical with the *Kālikākulakramasadbhāva* or the *Kālikākulasadbhāva* of which he also gives manuscript details, *loc.cit.* and *op.cit.* p.309 footnote 3. The *Kālikākulakramasadbhāva* is listed in Darbar Library, Nepal, Tantra Catalogue, Vol.I, pp.37. Rastogi, p.310 footnote 5.
3. 'Kramodaya ... a text of the Krama school known only through a few quotations.' Padoux, *Le coeur*, p.329 footnote 200.
4. Rastogi asks whether *Gahvara* is the same as the *Matagahvarapañcāśītikā* of which he gives the MS details. Rastogi, p.255 footnote 11. A *Kulagahvara* is mentioned in *TĀ* 24.16d.

Caryākula	*śl.* 166b;
Tattvarakṣaṇa	*śl.* 141a;
=Tattvarakṣā	Jr.141b.2; Qt.141b.1;
Tantrarājabhaṭṭāraka[5]	Jr.56d.1, Jr.100b.5;
Tantrasadbhāva[6]	Jr.212b.1;
=Sadbhāva	*śl.*212b; Jr.212b.1;
Triśirastantra	*śl.* 110c;
Triśirobhairava	Jr.100b.6; Jr.142b.2;
Triśiromata[7]	*śl.* 141b;
Traiśirasa	*śl.*9d; Qt.9d.1;
Thohakāsa[8]	Qt.13d.25;
Dīkṣottara	*śl.*243a;
Devīpañcaśatika[9]	Jr.42d.2;
Devyāmyāmala[10]	
Maryādāhīna	*śl.* 166a; Jr.166b.1;
=Nirmaryāda	Jr.166b.1;

5. The *Jayadrathayāmala* is one of the four basic scriptures of Kashmir Śaivism along with the *Siddhayogeśvarīmata*, the *Tantrasadbhāva* and the *Brahmayāmala*. Alexis Sanderson, 'Vajrayāna: origin and function', in *Buddhism into the year 2000. International conference proceedings*, Bangkok, Dhammakaya Foundation, 1994, p.94. More specifically, it is an *āgama* of the Krama tradition. Sanderson, 'Maṇḍala', p.197. The work is also known as the *Tantrarājabhaṭṭaraka*. ibid. p.199 footnote 141. For details concerning the manuscript, see ibid. p.205. Further details concerning the manuscript and comments on the place of this work in the canon are also given in Prabodh Chandra Bagchi, *Studies in the tantras*, Part I, Calcutta, Calcutta University Press, 1939, pp.1-15 and pp.109-114.
6. The *Tantrasadbhāva* belongs to the Trika tradition and is one of the four basic scriptures of Kashmir Śaivism. Sanderson, 'Vajrayāna', p.94. Sanderson gives the manuscript details in 'Maṇḍala', p.206. Śambhunātha and the *Tantrasadbhāva* are linked in *TĀ* 29.212ab and *TĀ* 30.99. K.C. Pandey and R.C. Dwivedi hold that Śambhunātha is its author. Rastogi, p.52.
7. *Triśiromata* appears as a work of the Kula tradition. Padoux, *Vāc*, p.281 and *ibid.* footnote 166.
8. Is *Thohakāsa* a text? It is not listed in Gnoli, *Luce*. It is not included in the list of Kubjikāmata tantras of the *paścimāmnāya* or Western Transmission given in Dyczkowski, *The canon* pp.127-133, or in the index of some 800 titles given in *ibid.* pp.216-226.
9. The *Devīpañcaśatika* is an *āgama* of the Krama tradition. Sanderson, 'Maṇḍala', p.197. For the manuscript details, see ibid. p.206.
10. The *Devyāyāmala* belongs to the Trika but shows its allegiance to the Kālī-cult by enthroning Kālsamkarṣiṇī, the highest of the Kālīs, as a fourth goddess above the three godesses of the Trika, Parā, Parāparā and Aparā. *ibid.* p.194. Padoux, *Vāc* p.203. Sanderson, 'The visulisation', pp.558-59.

=Amaryāda	*śl.*177a;
Pañcāśikā	Jr.198b.1;
Pūrva see Mālinīvijayottaratantra	
Brahmayāmala11 śl.[11];	
Bhogahastaka	*śl.*198b;
Mādhavakula[12]	*śl.*56; Jr.56d.1 bis, Jr.70b.3;
Mālinīvijayottaratantra	
=Pūrva	*śl.*197d
Yogasañcāra	*śl.*82c, *śl.*97a, *śl.*150c; Jr.82d.1;
Ratnamālā[13]	*śl.*55a, *śl.*192c, *śl.*201c, *śl.*238d, *śl.*283a;
	Jr.201b.3, Jr.283d.1;
Vīrāvali	*śl.*165c, *śl.*177a;
= Vīrāvali-kula	*śl.*272a;
= Vīrāvali-bhairava	*śl.*235d;
= Vīrāvali-śāstra	*śl.*163c;
= Vīrāvalī-śāstra	*śl.*186a;
Siddha[14]	*śl.*166a;
Sarvācārahṛdaya	*śl.*103a;
Hārdeśa	*śl.*165c; Jr.166b.1;
Hṛdayabhaṭṭāraka	Jr.166b.1.

---

11. The *Brahmayāmala*, alias the *Picumata*, is one of the four basic scriptures of Kashmir Śaivism. Sanderson, 'Vajrayāna', p.94. It is the basic Tantra of the cult of Kapālīśabhairava and his consort Caṇḍā Kāpālinī and is applicable to all the systems of the Vidyāpīṭha.' ibid. p.94. Seven MSS all incomplete - are listed in Rastogi, p.254 footnote 8. Details concerning the manuscript and comments on the place of this work in the canon are given in Prabodh Chandra Bagchi, *Studies*, pp.1-15 and pp.102-105.
12. The *Mādhavakula* is the fourth section of the *Jayadrathayāmala* which is also known as the *Tantrarājabhaṭṭaraka*. Sanderson, 'Maṇḍala', p.199 footnote 141. Sanderson notes that it 'teaches the cult of a Kālī Madhaveśvarī to be worshipped as the consort of [a form of] Viṣṇu ...', Sanderson, 'Saivism', p.686, and goes on to to connect her with the third form of the Northern Transmission, the cult of Guhyakālī.
13. In *TĀ* 28.128ab, Abhinava states that the *Ratnamālā* is an *āgama* of the Kula tradition. In *Tantrāloka* vol.2, p.281 line 16, Jayaratha identifies it with the *Kularatnamālā*.
14. Gnoli identifies this text with the *Siddhayogeśvarīmata*, Gnoli, *Luce*, p.699, which is one of the four basic scriptures of Kashmir Śaivism. Sanderson, 'Vajrayāna', p.94. Also called *Siddhāmata* and *Siddhātantra*, it 'is probably the earliest and most fundamental of the Trika's scriptures. This work survives, but in what is certainly a much shorter redaction than that known to the Kashmirians.' ibid. p.94. For the manuscript details, see Sanderson, 'Maṇḍala', p.207 and Rastogi, p.260 footnote 47.

APPENDIX 10

Index of Quotations and their Source

Qt.23d.1	*ata ūrdhvaṃ tathā tiryag*	
Qt.55d.2	*athātaḥ saṃpravakṣyāmi*	*Ratnamālā*
Qt.213d.1	*athaivamapi yasya syānnāveśaḥ*	*Tantrasadbhāva*
Qt.96d.4	*adāmbhiko gurau bhakto*	
Qt.100b.8	*adūtiko varaṃ yāgo*	
Qt.239b.1	*adho 'vasthā yadā ūrdhvaṃ*	*Ratnamālā*
Qt.139d.1	*anucakradevatātmakamarīci*	*TĀ* 29.113cd-14ab
Qt.100b.4	*aparicyutasvarūpair*	
Qt.22d.2	*amūrtā mūrtimāśritya*[1]	
Qt.153b.3	*ambuvāhā bhavedvāmā*	
Qt.13d.10	*ayaṣṭvā bhairavaṃ devam*	See *Kaulāvalī* [2]
Qt.13d.22	*arghaṃ puṣpaṃ tathā dhūpaṃ*	
Qt.13d.24	*alinā rahitaṃ yastu*	
Qt.54d.4	*aṣṭakasaptakasya tu*	
Qt.22d.3	*āgatasya tu mantrasya*	*TĀ* 26.51cd-53ab [3]
Qt.236d.3	*ātmānaṃ maṇimāśritya*	
Qt.107b.1	*ānandajananaṃ pūjā*	

1. This is quoted again as Qt.185d.1, in the context of Sacrifice 6 which describes the cremation ground of consciousness.
2. The *Kaulāvalī* 8.70cd-71ab reads almost identically: *ayaṣṭvā bhairavaṃ devam-akṛtvā guru-tarpaṇam\ paśu-pāna-vidhau pītvā vīro 'pi narakaṃ vrajet*| *Arthur* Avalon ed. Delhi, Bharatiya Vidya Prakashan, 1985.
3. The full text, found in *TĀ* 26.51cd-54ab, reads as follows: *āvāhite mantra-gaṇe puṣpa-āsava-niveditaiḥ\ dhūpaiś-ca tarpaṇaṃ kāryaṃ śraddhā-bhakti-bala-uditam*| *dīptānāṃ śakti-nāda-ādi-mantrāṇām-āsavaiḥ palaiḥ* | *raktaiḥ-prāk-tarpaṇaṃ paścāt-puṣpa-dhūpa-ādi-vistaraḥ*| *āgatasya tu mantrasya na kuryāt-tarpaṇaṃ yadi* | *haraty-ardha-śarīraṃ sa ityuktaṃ kila śambhunā*| Jayaratha quotes the first four lines in Qt.54d.5 with a slight change, reading *śakti-nātha-ādi* for *śakti-nāda-ādi*. The first four lines speak of meat and menstrual blood as well as of flowers etc. He quotes the last two lines here in Qt.22d.3 to hint at the contents of the vessel and to stress the need to use them. The same last two lines, with a very slight change, have already been used by Abhinava in *TĀ* 15.562. The word mantra, in the phrase *āgatasya tu mantrasya*, refers to one of the mantra-deities of the phrase *śakti-nāda-ādi-mantrāṇām* or of the phrase *āvāhite mantra-gaṇe*.

Qt.50d.1	*ānandenaiva sampanne*	
Qt.98b.1	*ānando brahmaṇo rūpaṃ*	
Qt.128b.1	*ānando brahmaṇo rūpaṃ*	
Qt.54d.5	*āvāhite mantragaṇe*	*TĀ* 26.51cd 53ab[4]
Qt.163d.1	*ityevaṃ devadeveśi*	
Qt.72b.1	.... *īśakoṇāditaḥ kramāt*	
Qt.13d.14	*uttamaṃ tu sadā pānaṃ*	
Qt.79d.1	*udagayane śubhavāre sthiralagne*	
Qt.150b.2	*udaye saṅgame śāntau*	*TĀ* 29.83ab
Qt.129b.6	*ubhayotthena vīryeṇa*	
Qt.13d.18	*ekataścaravaḥ sarve*	
Qt.91d.2	.....*ekānte japamārabhet*[5]	
Qt.197b.1	*eteṣāṃ calanānmantrī*	*Mālinīvijaya* 11.26cd-27ab
Qt.70b.5	*evaṃ cakrodayaṃjñātvā*	
Qt.248d.1	*evaṃ pañcaphaṇā devī*	
Qt.166b.1	*eṣa te kauliko yāgaḥ*	
Qt.13d.19	*eṣāmabhāve dravyāṇāṃ*	
Qt.96d.2	*kartavyā sarvato dūtir*	
Qt.77d.1	*kalaśaṃ netrabandhaṃ ca*	
Qt.102d.1	*kāryahetusahotthatvāt*	*Tantrasāra* p.201 line18
Qt.110b.1	*kiṃ pūjyaṃ pūjakaḥ ko 'sāv*	
Qt.13d.21	*kimanyairdravyasaṅghātair*	
Qt.4d.9	*kulaṃ śarīramityuktam*	
Qt.4d.7	*kulaṃ sa paramānandaḥ*	
Qt.4d.1	*kulaṃ hi paramā śaktiḥ*	
Qt.4d.8	*kulamātmasvarūpaṃ tu*	
Qt.13d.11	*kulācārasamāyukto*	
Qt.100b.1	*kulāmnāyeṣu ye saktā*	*Mādhavakula*[6]
Qt.150b.1	*kramaśo 'nucakradevyaḥ saṃvic*	*TĀ* 29.112ab
Qt.185d.1	*krīḍanti vividhairbhāvair*	
Qt.100b.7	.... *kva nu punaḥ sarvatra sarve guṇāḥ*	
Qt.54d.3	*kṣetre 'ṣṭadhā vibhakte madhye*	
Qt.29b.1	*gaṇeśaṃ pūjayitvā tu*	*Mālinīvijaya* 11.8
Qt.29b.2	*gaṇeśaṃ vaṭukaṃ siddhān*	
Qt.29b.4	*gaṇeśādhastataḥ sarvaṃ*	*Mālinīvijaya* 11.9[7]

4. From *TĀ* 26.51cd-53ab, for which see footnote to Qt.22d.3 above.
5. This phrase is a common expression. Gnoli, *Luce*, p.690 footnote 53.
6. In *TĀ* 15.532, Abhinava makes a similar quote from the *Mādhavakulatantra*.
7. An almost exact quote from *Mālinīvijayottaratantra* 11.9 which reads: *gaṇeśādhastataḥ sarvaṃ yajenmantrakadambakam| tatpatīnāṃ tato 'rdhaṃ ca tatraiva paripūjayet*

Qt.248d.2	*gatā sā paramākāśaṃ*	
Qt.13d.6	*gauḍī mādhvī tathā paiṣṭī*	
Qt.102d.6	*ghṛtenābhyajya gātrāṇi*	
Qt.13d.7	*caturastrastvayaṃ dharmaś*	
Qt.73b.1	*caturviṃśatidīpāṃśca*	*Jayadrathayāmala*[8]
Qt.22b.2	*carukaḥ sampradāyaśca*	
Qt.271d.1	*chāyātmā sa parāñmukha*	*TĀ* 29.265cd
Qt.39d.4	*chummakāḥ sampravakṣyāmi*	*Kulakriḍāvatāra*
Qt.89d.1	*japettu prāṇasāmyena*	
Qt.241b.1	*jvālākulaṃ tato dhyātvā*	*Gahvara (?)*
Qt.100b.5	*tatastatrānayeddūtīṃ*	
	Tantrarājabhaṭṭāraka	
Qt.129b.5	*tato dūtīṃ kṣobhayitvā*	
Qt.202b.1	*tato nyasyettu śiṣyasya*	*Ratnamālā*
Qt.54d.2	*tato vīrāṣṭakaṃ paścāc*	*Mālinīvijaya* 11.25cd
Qt.192b.1	*tato 'sya mastake cakraṃ*	*Mālinīvijaya*11.21cd-22
Qt.141b.1	*tattvarakṣāvidhāne 'to*	*TĀ* 3.215ab
Qt.153b.6	*tatpīṭhaṃ śākinīcakre*	
Qt.128b.2	*tasmādyatsaṃvido nātidūre*	
Qt.122b.1	*tiṣṭhetsaṃvatsaraṃ pūrṇaṃ*	
Qt.109b.1	*tena nirbharamātmānaṃ*	*TĀ 29.23*
Qt.39d.1	*teṣāṃ mudrāśca chummāśca*	*Kulakriḍāvatāra*
Qt.216d.1	*trikoṇakaṃ ḍambaraṃ ca*	
Qt.173d.1	*tritriśūle 'tra saptāre*	*TĀ 31.28*
Qt.153b.1	*tridalaṃ bhagapadmaṃ tu*	
Qt.39d.6	*tripurottare niketaṃ*	*Kulakriḍāvatāra*
Qt.39d.3	*dakṣahastasya cāṅguṣṭhād*	*Kulakriḍāvatāra*
Qt.63d.2	*dakṣiṇe sakthni nagaraṃ*	*Mādhavakula*
Qt.13d.13	*dinamekaṃ dinārdhaṃ vā*	
Qt.13d.16	*dīkṣākāle tu viprasya*	
Qt.283d.1	*dīkṣānte dīpakāḥ kāryāḥ*	*Ratnamālā*
Qt.16d.2	*dīpānkuryādraktavartīn*	
Qt.102d.3	*dūtīṃ kuryāttu kāryārthī*	
Qt.200d.1	*dehasthaṃ tu caruṃ vakṣye*	
Qt.10d.1	*dravyaiśca lokavidviṣṭaih*	
Qt.146b.1	*dvāsaptatisahasrāṇi*	
Qt.102d.7	*na caryā bhogataḥ proktā*	

8. Sanderson notes, in 'Meaning', p.83 footnote 231, that this quote is from the *Jayadrathayāmala-tantra* 4 folio 125v1-3.

Qt.22b.3	*nanvadivyena dehena*	
Qt.98d.1	*na māṃsabhakṣaṇe doṣo*	*Manusmṛti* 5.56 [9]
Qt.70b.1	*navamī cakriṇī yā sā bhramantī*	*Jayadrathayāmala* [10]
Qt.66d.2	*navayāgaratā devyaḥ*	*Mādhavakula* (?)
Qt.221d.1	*...na sāvasthā na yā śivaḥ*	*Spandakārikā* 2.4b
Qt.281d.1	*nahi bhedātparaṃ duḥkhaṃ*	
Qt.247d.1	*nādaṃ dīrghaṃ samuccārya*	
Qt.160b.2	*nityānandarasāsvādād*	*Kulaguhvara (?)*
Qt.96d.1	*nityoditā parā śaktir*	
Qt.13d.2	*nānena rahito mokṣo*	
Qt.63d.1	*nābhideśe tvalipuraṃ*	
Qt.70b.2	*nāśārṇaṃ ca nitambaṃ ca*	*Devyāyāmala*
Qt.8d.1	*nāsyāṃ maṇḍalakuṇḍādi*	*Mālinīvijaya* 11.2
Qt.64d.1	*nāhamasmi nacānyo 'sti*	*Mādhavakula* (?)
Qt.22d.1	*nāhamasmi nacānyo 'smi*	*TĀ* 29.64 [11]
Qt.138b.1	*nijanijabhogābhogapravikāsi*	*TĀ* 29.111cd-112ab
Qt.135b.1	*...nirālambaḥ paraḥ śivaḥ*	
Qt.42d.1	*niṣkriyānandanāthaśca*	*Devīpañcaśatika*
Qt.21d.1	*parāsampuṭamadhyasthāṃ*	*Mālinīvijaya* 11.7
Qt.63d.4	*pādādhārasthitā brāhmī*	*Kulakramodaya*
Qt.57d.3	*pīṭhakrameṇa cāmnāyaṃ*	*Mādhavakula*
Qt.13d.20	*puṣpadhūpopahārādi*	
Qt.54d.1	*pūrvayāmyāparādikṣu*	*Mālinīvijaya* 11.11 [12]
Qt.77d.2	*pūrvāhṇe vāparāhṇe vā*	
Qt.91d.1	*pṛthaṅmantraḥ pṛthaṅmantrī*	*Śrīkaṇṭhī-saṃhitā* [13]
Qt.13d.4	*paiṣṭī gauḍī tathā mādhvī*	
Qt.55d.1	*pradoṣe vilīne mantrī*	*Ratnamālā*
Qt.29b.3	*bāhye gaṇeśavaṭukau śrutipūrva*	
Qt.39d.2	*bodhiścāmarapādānāṃ*	*Kulakrīḍāvatāra*
Qt.100b.3	*brahmaṇyānandākhyaṃ rūpam*	
Qt.96d.3	*brāhmaṇasya yathā patnī*	
Qt.153b.5	*bhage liṅge sthito vahnir*	

9. An exact quote of *Manusmṛti* 5.56.
10. Taken from the *Jayadrathayāmala*. André Padoux, 'The *Ṣaṭsāhasrasaṃhitā:* Chapters 1-5 edited, translated and annotated, by J.A. Schoterman' [review] *Indo-Iranian Journal* vol.28:140-145, 1985, p.141.
11. Qt.22d.1 is an almost exact quote of *TĀ* 29.64.
12. An almost exact quote from *Mālinīvijayottaratantra* 11.11.
13. In his commentary on *Śivasūtra* 2.1, Kṣemarāja attributes this quote to the *Śrīkaṇṭhī-saṃhitā*. Jaideva Singh, *Śiva Sūtras*, Delhi, Motilal Banarsidass, 1979. p.84.

Qt.119b.1	*bhāve tyakte niruddhā cin*	*Vijñānabhairava* 62
Qt.252d.1	*bhujaṅgakuṭilākārā*	
Qt.13d.9	*bhairavasya priyaṃ nityaṃ*	
Qt.247d.2	*bhrūmadhye hṛdaye vātha*	
Qt.70b.4	*madīyabhūṣaṇairyuktaṃ*	*Mādhavakula*
Qt.13d.12	*madyamāṃsādhivāsena*	
Qt.13d.25	*madyariktāstu ye devi*	
Qt.13d.23	*madyenaikatamenaiva*	
Qt.240b.1	*mantravedhaṃ tu nādākhyaṃ*	*Gahvara*
Qt.13d.15	*malayena tu viprāṇāṃ*	
Qt.66d.1	*mātaṅgī kajjalī saunī*	*Mādhavakula* (?)
Qt.67d.1	*mātaṅgīveśma subhage*	*Mādhavakula* (?)
Qt.13d.5	*mārdvīkaḥ sahajastvekas*	
Q.195d.1	*mūladaṇḍaṃ samuddhṛtya*	*Ratnamālā*
Qt.70b.3	*mohinī kāla ātmā ca*	*Mādhavakula*
Qt.13d.17	*yataḥ prabhṛti kālācca*	
Qt.21d.2	*yatkiñcinmānasāhlādi*	
Qt.160b.1	*yattadakṣaramakṣobhyaṃ*	*Kulaguhvara* (?)
Qt.13d.8	*yathā bhairavacakreṣu*	*Brahmayāmala*[14]
Qt.101b.1	*yadi lakṣaṇahīnā syāt*	
Qt.175d.1	*yadyadevāsya manasi*	*TĀ* 26.54cd-55ab
Qt.153b.2	*yadretaḥ sa bhaveccandraḥ*	
Qt.201b.2	*yasya tvevamapi syānna*	*TĀ* 29.211ab
Qt.22b.1	*yasya sārāḥ pavitratve*	
Qt.9d.2	*yāvanna vedakā ete*	*Uccuṣmabhairavatantra*[15]
Qt.283d.2	*yāvanna sarve tattvajñās*	
Qt.114b.1	*yena yenākṣamārgeṇa*	
Qt.13d.3	*yenāghrātaṃ śrutaṃ dṛṣṭaṃ*	
Qt.236d.2	... *yenordhvordhvapraveśatah*	*TĀ* 29.237d
Qt.75b.1	*yo yasminmantrayogena*	*Jayadrathayāmala* (?)[16]
Qt.40d.1	*yo yasyāḥ santaternāthaḥ*	
Qt.110b.2	*yoṣitaś caiva pūjyante*	

14. Gnoli, *Luce*, p.681 footnote 10.
15. Sanderson, 'The category', p.212 footnote 74.
16. Sanderson notes, in 'Meaning' p.17 footnote 2, that Qt.75b.1, Qt.75b.2 and Qt.75b.3 come from the *Jayadrathayāmala* 4 folio 127v2-6.

Qt.27b.1	*rājavartena rajasā*	*Devipañcaśatika* 5.50 51b[17]
Qt.24d.1	*rāsabhī vaḍavā yadvat*	*TĀ* 5.58cd-59ab [18]
Qt.17d.1	*reto harāmbu puṣpaṃ ca*	
Qt.4d.2	*layodayaścitsvarūpas*	
Qt.16d.3	*lokānugrahahetvarthaṃ*	
Qt.126b.1	*vaktraṃ hi nāma tatmukhyaṃ*	
Qt.129b.4	*vaktrādvaktraprayogeṇa*	
Qt.129b.3	*vidrāvyam golakaṃ tatra*	*Jayadrathayāmala*[19]
Qt.100b.2	*vinā guruṃ vinā devaṃ*	
Qt.46b.1	*viśvaṃ jagadbhāvamatho*	*Devīpañcaśatika*
Qt.103d.1	*vegavatyatha saṃhārī*	
Qt.201b.1	*vedhadīkṣāṃ vinā dīkṣāṃ*	
Qt.81d.1	*śaktayo 'sya jagatkṛtsnaṃ*	*Māñgalaśāstra*
Qt.4d.6	*śaktigocaragaṃ vīryaṃ*	
Qt.90b.1	*śaktistu mātṛkā jñeyā*	*Tantrasadbhāva*[20]
Qt.127b.2	... *śāntoditasūtikāraṇaṃ*	*TĀ* 29.117ab
Qt.129b.2	*śivaḥ praśasyate nityaṃ*	
Qt.102d.5	*śivaśaktyātmakaṃ rūpaṃ*	
Qt.195d.2	*śivahaste maheśāni*	*Ratnamālā*

17. The first two lines come from the *Devipañcaśatika* 5.50-51b which reads as follows:
rājavartena rajasā vyomabimbaṃ tu kārayet|
bimbadvādaṣakaṃ bāhye tadrūpam avatārayet
lohitām vyomarekhāṃ tu dadyātsindūrakeṇa tu|
Sanderson, 'Maṇḍala', p.198 footnote 134. The quote goes on to describe the *maṇḍala* wherein the worshipper venerates *Mahākālī* in the central circle and twelve *Kālīs* in the ring of circles (*bimbadvādaṣakaṃ*) around her. It belongs to the Krama ritual. *ibid.* p.197-198.

18. In the *Parātriṃśikāvivaraṇa* p.280 lines 8-9, quotes a variant form : *rāsabhī vaḍavā vāpi svaṃ jagaj janmadhāma yat| samakālaṃ vikāsyaiva saṃkocya hṛdi hṛṣyati* The same idea is found in the image of the belly of a fish (*matsyodarī*) which '... keeps throbbing inwardly without any external movement. So the I-consciousness keeps throbbing without movement.' Singh, *Parātriṃśikāvivaraṇa*, p.30 note 16 to the text which is also found in the *Parātriṃśikāvivaraṇa* p.195 line 27 where the belly of the fish is connected with 'full awareness of wonder at one's own self', *svātmavimarśasaṃrambhamayī...*

19. '... equals JY [*Jayadrathayāmalatantra*] 3, foll.76v8-77r2 ....'. Sanderson, 'The category', p.213 footnote 97.

20. Kṣemarāja in his commntary on the *Śivasūtra* 2.3 attributes this quote to the *Tantrasadbhāva*.

Qt.175d.2	*śivābhedabharādbhāva*	*TĀ* 26.61cd-62ab[21]
Qt.153b.4	*śucirnāmāgnirudbhūtaḥ*	
Qt.109b.2	*śūnyodbhavo bhavedvāyur*	
Qt.274b.1	*... śaivī mukhamihocyate*	*Vijñānabhairava* 20d
Qt.72b.2	*śmaśānaṃ hṛtpradeśaḥ syāt*	
Qt.63d.3	*śrīśaile saṃsthitā brāhmī*	*Kulakramodaya*
Qt.9d.1	*ṣaḍcakreśvaratā nāthasya*	*TĀ* 1.114bcd
Qt.39d.5	*ṣaṇṇāṃ vai rājaputrāṇāṃ*	*Kulakriḍāvatāra*
Qt.240b.2	*ṣoḍhā vai vedhabodhena*	
Qt.57d.2	*sa kālīkulasambhūto*	*Mādhavakula*
Qt.80d.1	*sakṛdvibhāto 'yamātmā*|	
Qt.95d.1	*saca dvādaśadhā tatra*	*TĀ* 4.123cd
Qt.198b.1	*samayī tu karastobhān*	*Pañcāśikā*
Qt.46b.2	*sampūjya madhyamapade*	*TĀ* 29.131cd[22]
Qt.4d.4	*sarvakartṛ vibhu sūkṣmaṃ*	
Qt.16d.1	*sarvāsāṃ devatānāṃ tu*	
Qt.4d.5	*sarveśaṃ tu kulaṃ devi*	
Qt.236d.1	*sā cābhyāsavatā kāryā ...*	*TĀ* 29.237c
Qt.24d.2	*sākṣānbhavanmaye nātha*	*Śivastotrāvalī* 1.4
Qt.75b.3	*siddhāntavaiṣṇavabauddhā*	*Jayadratha-āmala*(?)[23]
Qt.3d.1	*siddhāntādiṣu tantreṣu*	
Qt.100b.6	*subhagā satyaśīlā ca*	*Triśirobhairava*
Qt.13d.1	*surā ca paramā śaktir*	
Qt.57d.1	*sṛṣṭikramaṃ tu prathamam*	*Mādhavakula*
Qt.123b.2	*strīmukhācca bhavetsiddhiḥ*	
Qt.123b.1	*strīmukhe nikṣipetprājñaḥ*	
Qt.102d.4	*sthityarthaṃ ramayetkāntāṃ*	
Qt.75b.2	*svakramaṃ tu yajenmadhye*	*Jayadrathayāmala*(?)[24]
Jr.95d.1	*svatantro bodhaḥ paramārthaḥ*	

21. An almost exact quote of *TĀ* 26.61cd-62ab which introduces three stanzas, *TĀ* 26.63-65, given in the context of 'the daily ceremony on the sacrificial surface'. In *Tantrasāra* p.180 line11- p.181 line 6, Abhinava quotes both *TĀ* 26.63 and 64 in the same context of the daily ceremony. In *TĀ* 29.176, he quotes śl.64 only.
22. An almost exact quote of *śl.*131cd - not of śl.126 as printed in *Tantrāloka* vol.7, p.3324.
23. Sanderson notes, in 'Meaning' p.17 footnote 2, that Qt.75b.1, Qt.75b.2 and Qt.75b.3 come from *Jayadrathayāmala* 4 folio 127v2-6.
24. Sanderson notes, in 'Meaning' p.17 footnote 2, that Qt.75b.1, Qt.75b.2 and Qt.75b.3 come from *Jayadrathayāmala* 4 folio 127v2-6.

Qt.177d.1	*svadeha evāyatanaṃ*	*TĀ* 15.605ab[25]
Qt.129b.1	*svadehāvasthitaṃ dravyaṃ*	
Qt.102d.2	*svapatnī bhaginī mātā*	
Qt.4d.3	*svabhāve bodhamamalam*	
Qt.127b.1	*svātantryāmuktamātmanaṃ*	*Īśvarapratyabhijñā kārikā* 1.5.16 [26]

25. An almost exact quote of *TĀ* 15.605ab.
26. From *Īśvarapratyabhijñākārikā* 1.5.16 which reads as follows: 'The Lord having, from his unrivalled autonomy, veiled (*nirmāya*) his self, when it is without autonomy, with the images of Īśa and the other gods, has himself invoked by means of [these same images].' *svātantryāmuktam ātmānaṃ svātantryād advayātmanaḥ| prabhur īśādisaṃkalpair nirmāyavyavahārayet* In *TĀ* 10.28, Abhinava concludes his discussion on the thirty-seventh and thirty-eighth categories by stressing the freedom of Śiva. In his long investigation of that *śloka*, Jayaratha quotes the whole of *Īśvarapratyabhijñākārikā* 1.5.16. The same *śloka* 16 is quoted by Abhinava in *Parātriṃśikāvivaraṇa* p.278 lines 20-21.

APPENDIX 11

The Places Mentioned in *TĀ* 29 and in Jayaratha's Investigation[1]

Akṣarākhya	*śl.*38d; Qt.39d.5;
Aṭṭahāsa [2]	*śl.*39b, *śl.*59a, *śl.*67a, *śl.*70d;
	Jr.63d.1, Jr.71b.1;
	Qt.39d.6, Qt.67d.1;
Aḍabilla	*śl.*38a; Qt.39d.5;
Aḍabī	*śl.*38c; Qt.39d.5;
Alipura	Jr.63d.1; Qt.63d.1;
Ambi	Jr.39d.1;
Ambilla	Jr.39d.1;
Āmrāta	*śl.*63b;
Āmrātakeśvara[3]	Jr.63d.2, 71b.1; Qt.63d.2;
Āmraka	*śl.*67b.
Ujjayinī [4]	*śl.*60a;
Ekāmra [5]	Qt.67d.1;
Eḍābhī	*śl.*61a;

1. Many of the places named in *TĀ* 29 and its investigation are also listed in *TĀ* 15.
2. Aṭṭahāsa: '... near Labhpur in the Birbhum district, Bengal ...' Sircar, *The śākta pīṭhas*, p.82. It is still an active place of pilgrimage. E. Alan Morinis, *Pilgrimage in the Hindu tradition*, Delhi, Oxford University Press, 1984, p.17.
3. This place is named without further detail in Sircar, *The śākta pīṭhas*, p.81.
4. '*Ujjayinī* (modern Ujjain in Central India) was one of the centres of the *Kāpālika* cult.' Gyula Wojtilla, 'Notes on popular Śaivism and Tantra in eleventh century Kashmir, (A study of Kṣemendra's *Samayamātṛkā*)'. In L. Ligati, ed. *Tibetan and Buddhist studies, commemorating the 200th anniversary of the birth of Alexander Csoma de Körös*. Budapest, Akadémia Kiadó, 1984. (Bibliotheca Orientalis Hungarica Vol.XXIX/2) Vol.2, p.384. '... modern Ujjain in the Gwalior State; but see also Ujānī ...' Sircar, *The śākta pīṭhas*, p.98. 'Ujānī (v.l. Ujjayinī, Urjanī, Ujjanī) ... modern Kogram in the Burdwan District, Bengal.' ibid. p.97.
5. Ekāmra: '... modern Bhubaneśvara in Orissa.' *ibid.* p.84. It is, in particular, the Liṅgarāja Temple. Anncharlott Eschmann, 'Hinduization of tribal deities in Orissa: the Śākta and Śaiva typology', in Anncharlott Eschmann, Herman Kulke, Gaya Charan Tripathi, eds. *The cult of Jagannath and the regional tradition of Orissa*, New Delhi, Manohar Publications, 1978, p.97.

Elāpura[6]	*śl*.62a; Jr.63d.2; Qt.63d.2;
Karabilla	*śl*.38b; Qt.39d.5;
Kāma[7]	*śl*.39b;
=Kāmākhya	
=Kāmārūpa	Jr.39d.1;
Kuḍyākeśī	*śl*.62c; Jr.63d.2; Qt.63d.2;
Kumbhārika	*śl*.38d; Qt.39d.5;
Kulagiri	*śl*.67a; Jr.71b.1; Qt.67d.1;
Kulādri[8]	*śl*.39a; Jr.39d.1;
Koṭṭam	*śl*.67b; see Devīkoṭṭa;
Kaulagiri	*śl*.59c; Jr.39d.1; Qt.39d.6;
Kṣīraka[10]	*śl*.62d; Jr.63d.2; Qt.63d.2;
Gośruti	*śl*.61b;
= Gokarṇa[11]	Jr.63d.2;
Caritra[12]	*śl*.59b; Jr.71b.1; Qt.67d.1;
= Caritraka	*śl*.67b;
Jayantī[13]	*śl*.67b; Qt.67d.1;
= Jayantikā	*śl*.59d;
Jālandhara[14]	Jr.29b.1;
Tripurī	*śl*.39a; Jr.39d.1;

6. Elāpura : '... modern Ellora in the Hyderabad State.' Sircar, *The śākta pīṭhas*, p.84.
7. Kāma = Kāmākhya = Kāmārūpa : 'The temple of Kāmākhyā stands on the Nīlakūṭa or Nīlaparvata, called the Kāmarūpa-parvata by Rājaśekhara in the *Kāvyamīmaṃsā*. This blue hill is the same as Kāmagiri.' *ibid*. p.87. The Kāmarūpa country corresponds to the Gauhati District of Assam and the adjoining region. *ibid*.
8. In *TĀ* 8.69, the word *kulādri* is used to refer to the seven mountain ranges of the continent Ketumāla.
   Footnote 9 has been eliminated.
10. 'Kṣiragrāma ... Kṣirikā ... modern Khirgram near Katwa in the Burdwan District, Bengal.' Sircar, *The śākta pīṭhas*, p.89.
11. 'Gokarṇa ... modern Gendia about 30 miles from Goa.' *ibid*. p.85.
12. 'Caritrā [*sic*] is Caritrapura ... in the district of Puri, Orissa.' Bagchi, *Kaulajñānanirṇaya*, p.71
13. Jayantī is 'in the Sylhet District, Assam ...' Sircar, *The śākta pīṭhas*, p.86.
14. Jālandhara is a city of the Punjab located on the Sutlej and may be the modern day Jullundur. Padoux, *La Parātrīśikālaghuvṛtti*, p.4 footnote 3. '... in the Punjab ... The Jālandhara Pīṭha is now located near Jvālāmukhī.' Sircar, *The śākta pīṭhas*, p.86.

Tripurottara[15]	Jr.39d.1; Qt.39d.6;
Ḍombi	*śl*.38c;
Dakṣiṇā	*śl*.38c; Qt.39d.6;
Dakṣiṇāvarta	Qt.39d.5;
Dakṣiṇapīṭha	*śl*.39c;
Devīkoṭṭa	Qt.16d.1; Qt.67d.1;
Devikoṭṭa[16]	Qt.39d.6;
Nagara[17]	*śl*.61d; Jr.63d.2; Qt.63d.2;
Nṛpasadmanī	*śl*.63b;
Paṭṭilla	*śl*.38a; Qt.39d.5;
Purastīra[18]	*śl*.62a; Qt.63d.2;
Pulinda[19]	Jr.39d.1; Qt.39d.5;
Pauṇḍravardhana[20]	*śl*.61d; Jr.63d.2; Qt.63d.2;
Prayāga[21]	*śl*.60b; Qt.67d.1;
Billa	*śl*.38c; Qt.39d.5;
Marukośa	*śl*.61c;
Māyāpura[22]	Jr.63d.2;
= Māyāpū	*śl*.62d;

15. Tripurottara : 'Tripurā ... the Tripurā (Hill Tipperah) State in Bengal.' *ibid.* p.97.
16. Devikoṭṭa : Sircar lists it as '... modern Bangarh in the Dinajpur District, Bengal. Same as Devakoṭṭa Devakoṭa, Devakūṭa, Devīkoṭa, Devīkūṭa, Devidaikoṭha.' *ibid.* p.83.
17. Nagara : This common word for 'city' is described as the 'ancient site of Nagar', P.K. Majumdar, 'Śakti worship in Rajasthan', in D.C. Sircar, ed. *The śākti cult and Tārā*, Calcutta, Calcutta University Press, 1967, p. 93; 'near Jaipur', *ibid.* footnote 93, in Rajasthan. By contrast, the *Yogaratnamālā* says : '... nagaraṃ: Refers to the city of Pāṭalīputra.' G.W. Farrow and I. Menon, *The Concealed Essence*, p. 77. Sircar notes that 'Pāṭaliputra [is] near modern Patna ...' *The śākta pīṭhas*, p.93.
18. Purastīra : Sircar mentions a 'Purasthira...' *ibid.* p.94.
19. Pulinda : '... the oft-quotes verses of the Āryā-stava (*Harivaṃśa*, II.3.6-8.) : "O Mahādevī, ... you are well worshipped by the Śavaras, Barbaras and Pulindas. ... These verses are significant ... for the reference to the well-known Nonaryan tribes [of the Vindhya mountain] as worshippers of the goddess Mahādevī, ...' A.K. Bhattacharya, 'A nonaryan aspect of the devī', in Sircar, *The śākti cult*, p.57.
20. 'Puṇḍravardhana ... same as Puṇḍra, Pauṇḍravardhana; identified with modern Mahasthan in the Bogra District, Bengal. 'Sircar,*The śākta pīṭhas*, p.94.
21. Prayāga : '... modern Allahabad in U.P.' *ibid.* p.93.
22. 'See Māyā, Māyāpurī, Māyāvatī; the Haridvāra (Hardwar) region.' *ibid.* p.91.

Rājagṛha[23]	Jr.63d.2; 71b.1; Qt.63d.2;
Vāmapurī	Qt.63d.2;
Varuṇā	*śl*.67a; Qt.67d.1;
Vārāṇasī[24]	*śl*.60c;
Viraja[25]	*śl*.60d;
Śarabilla	*śl*.38b; Qt.39d.5;
Śavara	*śl*.38a; Jr.39d.1; see Pulinda;
Śrīparvata[26]	Jr.63d.3, Jr.71b.1; Qt.63d.3;
Śrīśaila[27]	Jr.63d.3; Qt.63d.3;
Śrīpīṭha[28]	*śl*.60b;
Saṅgama	*śl*.67a;
Sopāna	*śl*.62c; Jr.63d.2; Qt.63d.2;
Hālā	*śl*.61a; Jr.63d.1;
Hiraṇyapura[29]	Qt.67d.1;
Haimapura	*śl*.67c.

23. Rājagṛha : '... modern Rajgir in the Gaya Distrcit, Bihar.' *ibid.* p.94.
24. This is the well-known Vārāṇasī or Benares in Uttar Pradesh.
25. Viraja : '... modern Jājpur on the Vaitaraṇī in the Cuttack District, Orissa.' *ibid.* p.99.
26. '... Śrīparvata (also called Śrīśailam) is located in the Kurnool District of Andhra Pradesh.' Lorenzen, *The Kāpālikas*, p.51. '... [it] was already famous as a center of tantric worship by the first half of the seventh century,' *ibid.* '... see Śrīśaila'. Sircar, *The śākta pīṭhas*, p.96.
27. 'Srisailam [sic], ... has been identified with at least three peaks ... ' White, p.422 footnote 81. It was '... an important center for such sects as the Kāpālikas, Nāth Siddhas and Rasa Siddhas.' *ibid.* p. 238 . However, Lorenzen identifies it with Śrīparvata and locates it 'in the Kurnool District of Andhra Pradesh.' Lorenzen, *The Kāpālikas*, p.51.
28. Śrīpīṭha : '... possibly the same as Śrīhaṭṭa.' Sircar, *The śākta pīṭhas*, p.97. 'Śrīhaṭṭa ... modern Sylhet in Assam'. *ibid.*
29. Hiraṇyapura : '... modern Herdoun or Hindaun in the Jaipur State, about 70 miles from Agra.' *ibid.* p.85.

APPENDIX 12

The *Maṇḍala* of the Kula Tradition and its Construction According to Qt.54d.3

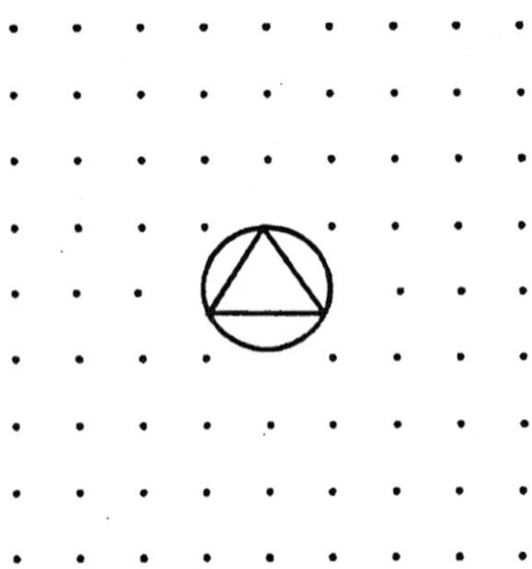

'On the sacred region which is divided into eight; in the middle, within a circle consisting of two portions, he should draw a triangle.

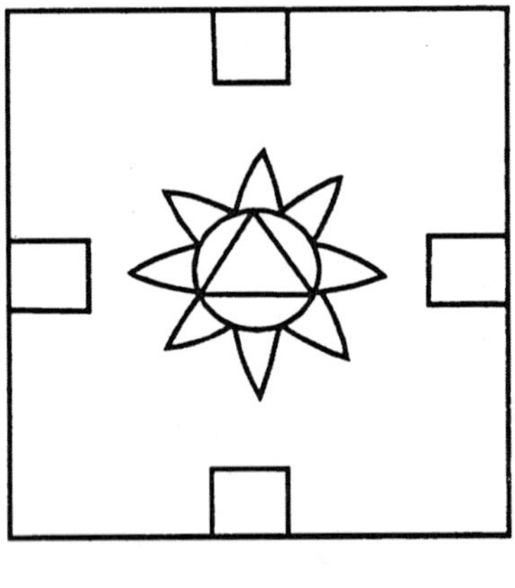

After that, on one portion in the [remaining sacred region] which is divided on every side into three, [he should draw] an eight-petalled lotus. Then there is a a space for one portion and four squares. Then the [remaining] portions extend in a square, as far as the diagonals on both sides. Thus the *maṇḍala*, in the Kula tradition, is square.'

APPENDIX 13

The Sanskrit Text of *Tantrāloka* 29 and of Jayaratha's Investigation.

Note: The following text has been Romanised exactly from the 1987 edition of the *Tantrāloka* and includes the commas etc. which have been added by the editors. The footnotes draw attention to typographical errors.

3291 *atha śrī-tantrāloke śrī-man-mahāmāheśvara-ācārya-abhinavagupta-viracite śrī-jayaratha-kṛta-viveka-ākhya-ṭīka-upete eka-ūna-triṃśam-āhnikam*|[1]

Jr.0.1 *bhadrāṇi bhadra-kālaḥ kalayatu vaḥ sarva-kālam-atula-gatiḥ*|
akula-pada-stho 'pi hi muhuḥ kula-padam-abhidhāvati-iha prasabham||

Jr.0.2 *idānīṃ dvitīya-ardhena rahasya-carcā-vidhim-abhidhātuṃ pratijānīte*

AG. *atha samucita-adhikāriṇa uddiśya rahasya ucyate 'tra vidhiḥ*|

Jr.1b.1 *rahasya iti kula-prakriyāyām*|
vidhir-iti yāgaḥ||

Jr.1b.2 *etad-eva vibhajati*

AG. *atha sarvā-apy-upāsā-iyaṃ kula-prakriyayā-ucyate*|| **1** ||

3292 *tathā dhārā-adhirūḍheṣu guru-śiṣyeṣu yā-ucitā*

Jr.2b.1 *kula-prakriyayā upāsā-iti kula-yāga ity-arthaḥ*|
tathā dhāra-adhirūḍheṣv-iti anena para-kāṣṭhā-prāpta-nirvikalpaka-daśa-adhiśāyitayā rūḍha-prāyatām-abhidadhatā adhikāri-bhedo 'pi upakṣiptaḥ|
atra ca sva-kṛta-pratijñā-sūtra-vārtika[1b] *-prāyatām-abhidyotayitum-atha-śabdasya upādānam*||

Jr.2b.2 *nanu kula-prakriyāyāḥ prakriyā-antarebhyaḥ kiṃ nāma vailakṣaṇyaṃ yad-evam-adhikāri-bhedo 'pi vivakṣita ity-āśaṅkya āha*

---

1. This sentence is found in somewhat similar terms at the start of every chapter. It seems to be an addition by the editors.

1b. For *vārtika* read *vārttika*.

AG. *uktaṃ ca parameśena sāratvaṃ krama-pūjane*|| **2** ||

Jr.2d.1 *tad-eva āha*

AG. *siddha-krama-niyuktasya māsena-ekena yad-bhavet*|
na tad-varṣa-sahasraiḥ syān-mantra-oghair-vividhair-iti|| **3** ||

Jr.3d.1 *siddha-krama-iti siddhānāṃ kṛta-yuga-ādi-krameṇa*
3293 *avatīrṇānāṃ śrī-khagendranātha-ādīnāṃ krame tat-paramparа-agatāyāṃ kula-prakriyām-ity-arthaḥ*|
vividhair-iti tat-tat-prakriyā-antara-uditair-ity-arthaḥ|
tad-uktaṃ

Qt.3d.1 *siddhānta-ādiṣu tantreṣu ye mantrāh samudāhṛtāḥ*|
vīrya-hīnās-tu te sarve śakti-teja-ujjhitā yataḥ||
kaulikās-tu mahā-mantrāḥ sva-bhāvād-dīpta-tejasaḥ|
sphuranti divya-tejaskāḥ sadyaḥ-pratyaya-kārakāḥ||

Jr.3d.2 *tatra kula-prakriyayā-ity-atra uktaṃ kula-śabdaṃ tāvad-vyācaṣṭe*

AG. *kulaṃ ca parameśasya śaktiḥ sāmarthyam-ūrdhvatā*|
svātantryam-ojo vīryaṃ ca piṇḍaḥ saṃvic-charīrakam|| **4** ||

Jr.4d.1 *sāmarthyam-iti laya-udaya-kāritvam*|
ūrdhvatā-iti sarveṣāṃ kāraṇatayā upari-vartitvam|
svātantryam-iti sarva-kartṛtva-ādy-ātmakam|
piṇḍa iti viśvasya atra sāmarasyena avasthānāt|
saṃvid-iti ātmā|
tad-uktaṃ

Qt.4d.1 *kulaṃ hi paramā śaktiḥ* ...|
3294 *iti*

Qt.4d.2 *laya-udayaś-cit-sva-rūpas-tena tat-kulam-ucyate*|
iti

Qt.4d.3 *sva-bhāve bodham-amalaṃ kulaṃ sarvatra kāraṇam*|
iti

Qt.4d.4 *sarva-kartṛ vibhu*[2] *sūkṣmaṃ tat-kulaṃ varavarṇini*|
iti

Qt.4d.5 *sarva-īśaṃ tu kulaṃ devi sarvaṃ sarva-vyavasthitam*|
tat-tejaḥ paraṃ ghoraṃ ...||
iti

Qt.4d.6 *śakti-gocara-gaṃ vīryaṃ tat-kulaṃ viddhi sarva-gam*|
iti

---

2. For *sarva-kartṛ vibhu*, read *sarva-kartṛ-vibhu*.

Qt.4d.7 *kulaṃ sa parama-ānandaḥ* .... ।
iti

Qt.4d.8 *kulam-ātma-sva-rūpaṃ tu* .... ।
iti

Qt.4d.9 *kulaṃ śarīram-ity-uktam* .... ।
iti ॥ 4 ॥

Jr.4d.2 *evaṃ kula-śabdaṃ vyākhyāya*
vidhy-upāsā-ādi-śabda-unnītaṃ yāga-śabdam-api
vyākhyātum-āha

AG. *tathātvena samastāni bhāva-jātāni paśyataḥ*।
3295 *dhvasta-śaṅkā-samūhasya yāgas-tādṛśa eva saḥ* ॥ **5** ॥

Jr.5d.1 *tathātvena-iti śiva-śakti-sphāra-sāratayā* ॥ 5 ॥

Jr.5d.2 *tathā paśyatas-tasya yāgo' pi tādṛśa eva-iti kiṃ-artham-*
uktam-ity-āśaṅkya āha

AG. *tādṛg-rūpa-nirūḍhy-arthaṃ mano-vāk-kāya-vartmanā*।
yad-yat-samācared-vīraḥ kula-yāgaḥ sa sa smṛtaḥ॥ **6** ॥

Jr.6d.1 *evam-ukta-satattvaś-ca-ayaṃ yāgaḥ kiṃ-ādhāra ity-āśaṅkya*
āha

AG. *bahiḥ śaktau yāmale ca dehe prāṇa-pathe matau*।
iti ṣoḍhā kula-ijyā syāt-pratibhedaṃ vibhedinī ॥ **7** ॥

Jr.7d.1 *yāmale iti ādya-yāga-adhirūḍhe mithune*।
prāṇa-pathe iti madhya-nāḍyām।
matāv-iti buddhau
tat-tad-adhyavasāya-dvārikā-api tat-sampattir-bhaved-iti
3296 *bhāvaḥ*।
pratibhedaṃ vibhedinī-iti
yathā bahir-eva bhū-vastra-ādyā vibhedāḥ ॥ 7 ॥

Jr.7d.2 *nanu evam-ādhāra-bhedavad-iti-kartavyatā-api*
atra kiṃ tantra-prakriyātaḥ kiñcid-vibhidyate navā-ity-
aśaṅkya āha

AG. *snāna-maṇḍala-kuṇḍa-ādi ṣoḍhā-nyāsa-ādi yan-na tat*।
kiñcid-atra-upayujyeta kṛtaṃ vā khaṇḍanāya no ॥ **8** ॥[3]

Jr. 8d.1 *tena yathā-iccham-etat-kuryād-ity-arthaḥ*।
yad-uktaṃ

---

3. *TĀ* 29.8 is a paraphrase of *Mālinīvijayottaratantra* 11.2. The words quoted from that source are underlined. The same procedure will be followed whenever Abhinava quotes from that text. Jayaratha gives the exact quote at Qt.8d.1

Qt.8d.1 na-asyāṃ maṇḍala-kuṇḍa-ādi kiñcid-apy-upayujyate
na-ca nyāsa-ādikaṃ pūrvaṃ snāna-ādi ca yathā-icchayā
iti || 8 ||
Jr.8d.2 nanu atra bāhya-snāna-ādāv-anavaklṛptau kiṃ nimittam
-ity-āśaṅkya āha
AG. ṣaṇ-maṇḍala-vinirmuktaṃ sarva-āvaraṇa-varjitam|
jñāna-jñeya-mayaṃ kaulaṃ proktaṃ traiśirase mate || **9** ||
3297
Jr.9d.1 iha śiva-śakti-sāmarasya-ātmakaṃ kula-jñānaṃ
ṣaḍbhir-maṇḍalaiḥ
Qt.9d.1 ṣaḍ-cakra-īśvaratā nāthasya-uktā traiśirase mate|
Jr.9d.2 ity-ādau nirūpitais-tatra-tyaiś-cakrair-vinirmuktaṃ
niṣprapañcam, ata eva sarva-āvaraṇa-varjitam-
ata eva jñānaṃ bahir-mukhaṃ pramāṇa-ātma vedanaṃ,
jñeyaṃ nīla-sukha-ādi vedyaṃ tan-mayam|
tat-sphāra-sāram-eva idaṃ sarvaṃ vedya-vedaka-ādi,
na-tu tad-atiriktaṃ kiñcid-ity-arthaḥ|
tad-uktaṃ
Qt.9d.2 yāvan-na vedakā ete tāvad-vedyāḥ kathaṃ priye|
434 The Kula Ritual
vedakaṃ vedyam-ekaṃ tu tattvaṃ na-asty-aśucis-tataḥ|
iti || 9 ||
Jr.9d.3 ataś-ca saṃvin-mātra-sāratvāt sarvasya
śuddhy-aśuddhī api vāstave na sta
iti kaṭākṣayituṃ tad-vibhāgo 'pi na-iha abhimata ity-āha
AG. atra yāge ca yad-dravyaṃ niṣiddhaṃ śāstra-santatau|
tad-eva yojayed-dhīmān-vāma-amṛta-pariplutam || **10** ||
3298
Jr.10d.1 tad-uktaṃ
Qt.10d.1 dravyaiś-ca loka-vidviṣṭaih śāstra-arthāc-ca bahiṣ-kṛtaiḥ|
vijugupsyaiś-ca nindyaiś-ca pūjanīyas-tv-ayaṃ kramaḥ|
iti || 10 ||
Jr.10d.2 nanu bhavatu nāma atra śāstra-ādi-bahiṣ-kṛtaṃ dravyaṃ
madya-saṃsparśanena punar-asya ko 'rtha ity-āśaṅkya āha
AG. śrī-brahmayāmale 'py-uktaṃ surā śiva-raso bahiḥ|
tāṃ vinā bhukti-muktī no piṣṭa-kṣaudra-guḍais-tu sā || **11** ||
strī-napuṃsaka-puṃ-rūpā tu pūrva-apara-bhoga-dā

drākṣā-utthaṃ tu paraṃ tejo bhairavaṃ kalpana-ujjhitam || **12** ||
etat-svayaṃ rasaḥ śuddhaḥ prakāśa-ānanda-cin-mayaḥ |
devatānāṃ priyaṃ nityaṃ tasmād-etat-pivet-sadā || **13** ||

3299

Jr.13d.1 *śiva-rasa iti tad-uktaṃ*
Qt.13d.1 *surā ca paramā śaktir-madyaṃ bhairava ucyate* |
ātmā kṛto drava-rūpo bhairaveṇa mahā-ātmanā |
iti |
Jr.13d.2 *tāṃ vinā no bahir-bhukti-muktī iti* |
tad-uktaṃ
Qt.13d.2 *na-anena rahito mokṣo na-anena rahitā gatiḥ* |
na-anena rahitā siddhir-viśeṣād-bhairava-āgame |
iti |
Qt.13d.3 *yena-āghrātaṃ śrutaṃ dṛṣṭaṃ pītaṃ spṛṣṭaṃ maheśvari* |
bhoga-mokṣa-pradaṃ tasya ..... ||
iti ca |
Jr.13d.3 *sā ca dvi-dhā kṛtrimā sahajā ca* |
tatra kṛtrimā tri-vidhā paiṣṭī kṣaudrī gauḍī ca-iti,
sahajas-tu eka eva drākṣā-uttho
bhairava-ādi-śabda-vyapadeśyaḥ
param-utkarṣa-bhāg
-ity-āha piṣṭa-ity-ādi |
pum-apekṣayā ca strī-napuṃsakayor-bhogyatvam-eva
-ity-uktaṃ pūrva-apara-bhoga-dā-iti |
kalpana-ujjhitam-iti
strī-napuṃsaka-ādi rūpayā pratiniyatayā kalpanayā
ujjhitaṃ para-pramātr-eka-rūpam-ity-arthaḥ |
tad-uktaṃ
Qt.13d.4 *paiṣṭī gauḍī tathā mādhvī kṛtrimā tu surā smṛtā* |
strī-puṃ-napuṃsakatayā sādhake bhoga-dāyikā |
3300 *iti*
Qt.13d.5 *mārdvīkaḥ sahajas-tv-ekas-tat-tejo bhairava-ātmakam* |
na strī napuṃsakaṃ vā-api na pumān paramo vibhuḥ |
iti
Qt.13d.6 *gauḍī mādhvī tathā paiṣṭī ūrdhve ānanda-bhairavaḥ* |
iti

Qt.13d.7 *catur-astras-tv-ayaṃ dharmaś-catur-yuga-samo nayaḥ*|
caturṇāṃ ca-eva madyānām-ānandaḥ śānti-tat-paraḥ||
iti|

Jr.13d.4 *para-tejastvād-eva ca etat svayaṃ pāratīyo rasas*
-tat-samāna-māhātmya ity-arthaḥ|
śuddha iti tat-tad-upādhibhūta-dravya-antarā-saṃbhinnaḥ,
tathātve hi asya niyata eva prabhāvo bhaved-iti bhāvaḥ|
ata eva uktaṃ prakāśa-ānanda-cin-maya iti|
tad-uktaṃ

Qt.13d.8 *yathā bhairava-cakreṣu nāyakaḥ śiva-bhairavaḥ*|
devatā-cakra-sandohe yathā kālāntakī parā||
tathā sarva-rasa-indrāṇāṃ nāyakau dvāv-udāhṛtau|
madya-bhairava-nāthas-tu rasa-indraḥ pāratīyakaḥ||
iti|

Jr.13d.5 *devatānāṃ priyam-iti*|
yad-uktaṃ

Qt.13d.9 *bhairavasya priyaṃ nityaṃ bahu mātṛ-gaṇasya ca*|
iti|

Jr.13d.6 *tasmād-iti evaṃ-māhātmyavattvāt,*
natu paśuvat laulya-ādinā|
yad-uktaṃ

3301

Qt.13d.10 *ayaṣṭvā bhairavaṃ devam-akṛtvā mantra-tarpaṇam*|
paśu-pāna-vidhau pītvā vīro 'pi narakaṃ vrajet|
iti|

Jr.13d.7 *pived-iti vidhiḥ*|
ata eva apānāt-pratyavāyopi[4] *syāt*|
yad-uktaṃ

Qt.13d.11 *kula-ācāra-samāyukto brāhmaṇaḥ kṣatriyo'pi vā*|
yadā madyena na spṛṣṭaḥ prāyaścittaṃ tadā caret||
iti

Qt.13d.12 *madya-māṃsa-ādhivāsena mukhaṃ śūnyaṃ yadā bhavet*|
tadā paśutvam-āyāti prāyaścittaṃ samācaret ||
iti ca|

Jr.13d.8 *sadā-iti yāga-avasare,*

---

4. For *pratyavāyopi* read *pratyavāyo 'pi.*

anyathā hi kṣaṇam-api madya-pāna-viratau pratyavāyaḥ prasajet |
tena
Qt.13d.13 *dinam-ekaṃ dina-ardhaṃ vā tad-ardhaṃ ca-ardham-eva ca* |
nivṛtter-ali-pānasya prāyaścittī bhaven-naraḥ |
iti
Jr.13d.9 *yāga-kāla-apekṣya-eva yojyam* |
yat punaḥ
Qt.13d.14 *uttamaṃ tu sadā pānaṃ bhavet-parvasu madhyamam* |
adhamaṃ māsa-mātreṇa māsād-ūrdhvaṃ paśur-bhavet |
Jr.13d.10 *ity-ādi,*
tad-āpad-viṣayatayā uktam |
yat-tu
Qt.13d.15 *malayena tu viprāṇāṃ kṣatrāṇāṃ kuṅkumena ca* |
karpūra-vāri vaiśyānāṃ śūdrāṇām-alinā priye ||
iti
Qt.13d.16 *dīkṣā-kāle tu viprasya kṣatriyasya raṇa-āruhe* |
vaiśyasya kṣiti-māṅgalye śūdrasya-antyeṣṭi-karmaṇi ||
3302
Jr.13d.11 *ity-ādy-uktaṃ,*
tad-adīkṣita-viṣayam;
kintu pūrvatra
asmad-ukta-arcā-tarpaṇa-śraddhā-alu-viṣayatvam-adhikam-anyathā jāti-bhedo durvacaḥ syāt |
dīkṣā-kāle iti sautrāmaṇy-ādau |
ata eva
Qt.13d.17 *yataḥ prabhṛti kālāc-ca daitya-ācāryeṇa dūṣitam* |
tataḥ prabhṛti varṇānāṃ nāma-bhedaḥ pradarśitaḥ ||
sautrāmaṇyāṃ brāhmaṇānāṃ pāna-arthaṃ smṛtam-adhvare |
mahā-āhave kṣatriyāṇāṃ vaiśyānāṃ kṣiti-karmaṇi ||
mahā-utsave tu bandhūnāṃ mitrāṇāṃ ca samāgame |
śmaśāna-ante ca śūdrāṇāṃ vivāhe putra-janmani ||
pāna-bhedam-idaṃ bhadre jantūnāṃ mūḍha-cetasām |
ye punaḥ śāṅkare tantre devī-tantre ca dīkṣitāḥ ||
gurv-ājñā-niratā guptā japa-pūjā-parāyaṇāḥ |

jñāna-vijñāna-kuśalā laulyān-na mahita-āśayāḥ|
teṣāṃ punar-dvi-jānāṃ tu na viruddhaṃ sadā priye||
Jr.13d.12 *ity-ādi uktam,*
—ity-alam-avāntareṇa|
evam-iyad-anena upakṣiptaṃ —
yad-evaṃ-śāstra-ādi-bahiṣ-kṛtaṃ dravya-jātaṃ
sambhṛtam-api vinā madyaṃ
na yāga-sampattau nimittaṃ,
madyaṃ-punar-ekakam-eva vinā-api evaṃ dravya-jātaṃ
tatra nimittam-iti,
yena-uktaṃ vāma-amṛta-pariplutaṃ tad-yojayed-iti|
yad-āgamaḥ
Qt.13d.18 *ekataś-caravaḥ sarve madyam-eva-ekam-ekataḥ*|
caru-hīno 'pi kurvīta madya-hīnaṃ na jātucit|
3303 *iti*
Qt.13d.19 *eṣām-abhāve dravyāṇāṃ nityaṃ pūjā vidhīyate*|
ekena madya-nāthena vinā tena-api niṣphalā ||
iti
Qt.13d.20 *puṣpa-dhūpa-upahāra-ādi yadi na syāt-sulocane*|
alinā tarpayen-mantraṃ ....
iti
Qt.13d.21 *kim-anyair-dravya-saṅghātair-devi yāga-upayogibhiḥ*|
vāma-amṛtena ca-ekena kalāṃ na-arghanti ṣoḍaśīm ||
iti
Qt.13d.22 *arghaṃ puṣpaṃ tathā dhūpaṃ dīpaṃ naivedyam-eva ca*|
vīra-dravya-ādi yat-kiñcit-sarvaṃ madye pratiṣṭhitam ||
iti
Qt.13d.23 *madyena-ekatamena-eva śakti-īśaṃ śaktibhir-yutam*|
yajet-sānnidhya-kāmas-tu sarvadā sarvathā priye ||
iti
Qt.13d.24 *alinā rahitaṃ yas-tu pūjayet-pādukā-kramam*|
yoginyas-tasya sīdanti bhakṣayanti rasa-āmiṣam||
iti
Qt.13d.25 *madya-riktās-tu ye devi na te siddhyanti paścime*
thohakāsa-mate nityaṃ kula-bhraṣṭāḥ svayaṃbhuvaḥ
iti ca|
Jr.13d.13 *iha madya-ādhīnam-eva sarveṣām-anuṣṭhānam-iti*

3304 *atra āgama-saṃvāde bharo 'smābhiḥ kṛta*
iti na asmabhyam-abhyasūyayitavyam ǁ 13 ǁ

Jr.13d.14 *evam-asya prādhānye 'pi*
avāntara-vastv-apekṣayā
śāstra-antare 'nyad-api kiñcit-pradhānatayā-uktam-ity-āha

AG. *śrīmat-kramarahasye ca nyarūpi parameśinā* ǀ
argha-pātraṃ yāga-dhāma dīpa ity-ucyate trayam ǁ **14** ǁ
rahasyaṃ kaulike yāge tatra-arghaḥ śakti-saṃgamāt ǀ
bhū-vastra-kāya-pīṭha-ākhyaṃ dhāma ca-utkarṣa-bhāk
kramāt ǁ **15** ǁ
dīpā ghṛta-utthā gāvo hi bhū-caryo devatāḥ smṛtāḥ ǀ
iti jñātvā traye 'muṣmin-yatnavān-kauliko bhavet ǁ **16** ǁ

Jr.16d.1 *tatra-iti traya-nirdhāraṇe* ǀ
argha iti kuṇḍa-golaka-ākhyo dravya-viśeṣaḥ ǀ
śakti-saṅgamād-iti

3305 *ādya-yāgatayā vakṣyamāṇāt* ǀ
kāya-pīṭhaṃ svaṃ parakīyaṃ vā śiraḥ ǀ
tad-uktaṃ

Qt.16d.1 *sarvāsāṃ devatānāṃ tu ādhāraḥ śira iṣyate* ǀ
devīkoṭṭaṃ tu tat-sthānaṃ nityaṃ tatra prapūjayet ǁ
iti

Jr.16d.2 *kramād-utkarṣa-bhāg-iti yathā bhuvo vastraṃ,*
tasmān-muṇḍam-iti ǀ
ghṛta-utthā iti prādhānyāt,
tena taila-utthā api ǀ
yad-uktaṃ

Qt.16d.2 *dīpān-kuryād-rakta-vartīn-ghṛta-taila-prapūritān* ǀ
iti ǀ

Jr.16d.3 *prādhānya eva ca atra hetur-gāvo bhū-caryo devatāḥ smṛtā*
iti ǀ
yad-uktaṃ

Qt.16d.3 *loka-anugraha-hetv-arthaṃ brāhmy-ādyā devatā bhuvi* ǀ
caranty-āsthāya go-rūpaṃ tena tad-dravyam-āharet ǁ
iti ǀ

Jr.16d.4 *yatnavān-iti tat-sambharaṇe śraddhāvān-bhavet,*
nā-no vicikitsitavyam-ity-arthaḥ ǁ 16 ǁ

Jr.16d.5 *asmad-darśane hi arghasya-eva prādhānyam-iti*

tad-ucitāny-eva dravya-antarāṇy-api parameśvaraḥ samādikṣat,
tat tatas-tebhyo vā na śaṅkitavyam।
śaṅkā-eva hi mahad-dūṣaṇam-ity-uktaṃ prāg-bahuśaḥ।
tad-āha

AG. *tena-argha-pātra-prādhānyaṃ-jñātvā dravyāṇi śambhunā*।
3306 *yāny-uktāny-aviśaṅko 'tra bhavec-chaṅkā hi dūṣikā* ।। **17** ।।

Jr.17d.1 *yāni dravyāṇi-iti ratna-pañcaka-ādīni*।
tad-uktaṃ

Qt.17d.1 *reto hara-ambu puṣpaṃ ca kṣāraṃ nāla-ājyakaṃ tathā*।
pauruṣaṃ kṣmā-bhavaṃ chāgaṃ mīna-jaṃ śākunīyakam ।।
palāṇḍuṃ laśunaṃ ca-eva dravya-dvā-daśakaṃ śubham।
iti।

Jr.17d.2 *atra-iti dravya-vacane* ।।17 ।।

Jr.17d.3 *evaṃ kula-yāge pīṭhikā-bandhaṃ vidhāya*
tat-kramam-eva nirūpayitum-upakramate

AG. *yāga-oko gandha-dhūpa-āḍhyaṃ praviśya prāg-udaṅ-mukhaḥ*।
parayā vā 'tha mālinyā vilomāc-ca-anulomataḥ ।।**18** ।।[5]
dāha-āpyāya-mayīṃ śuddhiṃ dīpta-saumya-vibhedataḥ।
krameṇa kuryād-atha-vā mātṛsadbhāva-mantra-taḥ ।। **19** ।।

Jr.19d.1 *praviśya-iti-dehalī-mātra-pūjana-pūrvam*।
vilomād-iti saṃhāra-krameṇa pādābhyāṃ śirontam।
3307 *anulomata iti sṛṣṭi-krameṇa śirastaḥ pāda-antam*।
dāhe dīptā āpyāyane saumyā-ity-uktaṃ krameṇa-iti ।।19 ।।

Jr.19d.2 *naimittike punar-nityād-viśeṣo 'sti-ity-āha*

AG. *dīkṣāṃ cet-pracikīrṣus-tac-chodhya-adhva-nyāsa-kalpanam*।
tataḥ saṃśodhya-vastūni śaktyā-eva-amṛtatāṃ nayet ।। **20** ।।

Jr.20d.1 *śodhyo 'dhvā bhuvana-ādy-anyatamaḥ*।
tata iti deha-śuddhy-ādy-anantaram।
saṃśodhya-iti
yāga-upakaraṇa-bhūtānām
-argha-puṣpa-ādy-ātmanām-asaṃśodhitatve

5. *TĀ* 29.18ab is paraphrase of *Mālinīvijayottaratantra* 11.3; śl.18cd is a paraphrase of *Mālinīvijayottaratantra* 11.5ab. The words in common are underlined.

hi yāga-yogyatvaṃ na bhaved-iti bhāvaḥ|
śaktyā-eva-iti
na punaḥ prāgvad-argha-pātra-vipruṭ-prokṣaṇa-ādinā
|| 20 ||

Jr.20d.2 *nanu atra mantra-trayam-uddiṣṭaṃ,*
tasya punaḥ kathaṃ viniyoga ity-āṣaṅkya āha

AG. *parā-sampuṭa-gā yad-vā mātṛ-sampuṭa-gā-apy-atho*|
kevalā mālinī yad-vā tāḥ samasteṣu karmasu || **21** ||[6]

3308

Jr.21d.1 *samasteṣu karmasu evaṃ-vidhā mālinī*
arthād-yojanīyā
mukty-arthinā mātṛsadbhāvena sampuṭitā
tad-ubhaya-arthinā parayā|
kevalayor-api parā-matṛsadbhāvayor-evam-eva yojanam-iti|
tad-uktaṃ

Qt.21d.1 *parā-sampuṭa-madhya-sthāṃ mālinīṃ sarva-karmasu*|
yojayet vidhāna-jñaḥ parāṃ vā kevalāṃ priye ||

Jr.21d.2 *iti atra grantha-kṛtā parā-śabdena-eva mātṛsadbhāvo 'pi*
vyākṛto yat parāyā eva asau parataraṃ rūpam-iti ||21||

Jr.21d.3 *nanu*

Qt.21d.2 *yat-kiñcin-mānas-āhlādi yac-ca saubhāgya-vardhanam*|
tena-ātmānam-alaṅkṛtya devam-abhyarcayet-sadā ||

Jr.21d.4 *ity-ādinā*
yat-kiñcid-ānanda-mayaṃ dravya-jātaṃ,
tat pūja-upakaraṇatayā yojyam-iti sarvatra-uktam-iti|
iha punas-taj-jugupsyaṃ kasmād-abhihitam-iti-āśaṅkya āha

AG. *nanda-hetu-phalair-dravyair-argha-pātraṃ prapūrayet*|

Jr.22b.1 *nandasya ānandasya hetubhiḥ surā-ādibhiḥ,*
phalaiś-ca kuṇḍa-golaka-ādibhiḥ|
ata eva uktaṃ

Qt.22b.1 *yasya sārāḥ pavitratve kuryanty-ānandam-uttamam*|
so 'nudhyāta-smṛtas-tantre bhairaveṇa bhavac-chidā

3309 *iti*|

6. *Śloka* 21 is a paraphrase of *Mālinīvijayottaratantra* 11.7. The words found in 11.7 are underlined. Jayaratha gives the complete text in Qt.21d.1.

Jr.22b.2 *yaś-ca atra etat-pūraṇe sampradāyaḥ,*
sa rahasyatvāt samaya-bhaṅga-bhayāc-ca
na iha asmābhiḥ pradarśita iti।
etad-guru-mukhād-eva boddhavyam।
tad-uktaṃ

Qt.22b.2 *carukaḥ sampradāyaś-ca vijñānaṃ melakaṃ tathā*।
pūjā-krama-vidhānaṃ ca yoginīnāṃ mukhe sthitam ॥
iti ॥

Qt.22b.3 *nanv-adivyena dehena yad-yat-pūjā-kramaṃ japam*।
kiñcit-kuryāt-tu tat-tasya sarvaṃ bhavati niṣphalam ॥

Jr.22b.3 *ity-ādy-ukter*
-adivya-vapuṣā kriyamāṇaṃ yāga-ādi phala-dāyi na syād
ity-atra sādhakena sva-ātmani bhairavī-bhāvo
bhāvayitavya ity-āha

AG. *tatra-ukta-mantra-tādātmyād-bhairava-ātmatvam-*
ānayet ॥ **22** ॥

Jr.22d.1 *uktā mātṛsadbhāva-ādayaḥ*। *vakṣyati hi*

Qt.22d.1 *na-aham-asmi naca-anyo 'sti kevalāḥ śaktayas-tv-aham*।
ity-evaṃ-vāsanāṃ kuryāt-sarvadā smṛti-mātrataḥ ॥
iti ॥ 22 ॥

Jr.22d.2 *ittham-evaṃ-bhāvanayā ca deha-ādau*

Qt.22d.2 *amūrtā mūrtim-āśritya devyaḥ piṇḍa-antare sthitāḥ*।
krīḍanti vividhair-bhāvair-uttama-dravya-lipsayā॥

3310

Jr.22d.3 *ity-ādy-uktyā*
pūjā-lāmpaṭyena sarvā eva karaṇeśvary-ādyā devatāḥ
saṃnidadhate iti āsām।

Qt.22d.3 *āgatasya tu mantrasya na kuryāt-tarpaṇaṃ yadi*।
haraty-ardha-śarīraṃ ...... ॥

Jr.22d.4 *ity-ādy-uktyā tarpaṇam-avaśyaṃ kāryam-ity-āha*

AG. *tena nirbharam-ātmānaṃ bahiś-cakra-anucakragam*।
vipruḍbhir-ūrdhva-adharayor-antaḥ-pītyā ca tarpayet ॥ **23** ॥

Jr.23d.1 *tena-iti bhairava-ātmatva-ānayanena hetunā*।
ūrdhva-adharayor-iti arthāt-tiryag-api।
tad-uktam

Qt.23d.1 *ata ūrdhvaṃ tathā tiryag-dātavyā vipruṣaḥ priye*।
iti।

Jr.23d.2 tad-bahiḥ sarvato vipruḍbhir-antaś-ca pānena
nānā-devatā-cakra-anuyātam-ātmānaṃ tarpayed-ity-arthaḥ || 23 ||
Jr.23d.3 nanu evam-iyatā-eva siddhaḥ kula-yāgaḥ,
kim-anyad-avaśiṣyate ity-āśaṅkya āha
AG. tathā pūrṇa-sva-raśmy-oghaḥ procchalad-vṛttitā-vaśāt|
bahis-tādṛśam-ātmānaṃ didṛkṣur-bahir-arcayet || **24** ||
3311
Jr.24d.1 tathā samanantara-ukta-krameṇa
pūrita-nija-karaṇeśvary-ādi-devatā-cakraḥ san
sva-ātma-mātra-viśrānto 'pi
yadā sādhakaḥ
Qt.24d.1 rāsabhī vaḍavā yadvat-sva-dhāma-ānanda-mandiram|
vikāsa-saṅkoca-mayaṃ praviśya hṛdi hṛṣyati ||
Jr.24d.2 ity-ādy-ukta-bhaṅgyā
vikasita-indriya-vṛttir-
bahir-api pūrṇam-eva ātmānaṃ didṛkṣur-
bahī-rūpatayā-api bimba-pratibimba-nyāyena
parā-eva saṃvid-avabhāsata ity-anusandhatte,
tadā bahir-arcayet|
tatra-api arcā-kramo nyāyya ity-arthaḥ|
yad-āhur-asmad-ādi-guravaḥ
Qt.24d.2 sākṣān-bhavan-maye nātha sarvasmin-bhuvana-antare|
kiṃ na bhaktimatāṃ kṣetraṃ mantraḥ kva-eṣāṃ na
siddhyati ||
iti || 24 ||
Jr.24d.3 tac-ca kutra-ity-āśaṅkya āha
AG. arka-aṅgule 'tha tad-dvi-tri-guṇe rakta-paṭe śubhe|
vyomni sindūra-subhage rāja-varttabhṛte 'tha-vā || **25** ||
nārikel-ātmake kādye madya-pūrṇe 'tha bhājane|
3312 yad-vā samudite rūpe maṇḍala-sthe ca tādṛśi || **26** ||
yāgaṃ kurvīta matimāṃs-tatra-ayaṃ krama ucyate|
Jr.27b.1 arka-iti dvā-daśa|
vyomni-iti arthād-bhū-gate|
uktaṃ ca
Qt.27b.1 rājavartena rajasā vyoma-bimbaṃ tu kārayet|
lohitāṃ vyoma-rekhāṃ tu dadyāt-sindūrakeṇa tu ||

viparyayeṇa vā kāryā śuklā vā vyoma-rekhikā।
iti।
Jr.27b.2 *evaṃ na kevalaṃ vyastam-eva*
bhū-vastra-kāya-pīṭha-ākhyaṃ dhāma bhavet
yāvat-samastam-api
-ity-āha yad-vā samudite rūpe iti।
tena bhū-pṛṣṭhe rakta-vastraṃ,
tad-upari ca kāya-pīṭha-śabda-abhidheyaṃ kādyaṃ
tad-anukalpa-ātmakaṃ viśvāmitra-kapālaṃ vā-iti।
tādṛśi iti samudite eva
kin-tu maṇḍala-sthe iti
bhūlāv-uhyamāna-sanniveśaṃ maṇḍalaṃ
tatra ca kvacid-api ādhāre rakta-vastraṃ,
tad-upari ca kādyam-iti ।।
Jr.27b.3 *tam-eva kramam-āha*
AG. *diśy-udīcyāṃ rudra-koṇād-vāyavy-antaṃ gaṇeśvaram* ।। **27**।।
3313 *vaṭukaṃ trīn gurun-siddhān-yoginīḥ pīṭham-arcayet*।
prācyāṃ diśi gaṇeśa-adha ārabhya-abhyarcayet-tataḥ ।। **28**।।
siddha-cakraṃ dik-catuṣke gaṇeśa-adhastana-antakam।
Jr.29b.1 *udīcyām-iti prājāpatya-krameṇa*।
gaṇeśvaram-iti nairvighnyāya,
saca arthāt savallabhaḥ।
evaṃ vaṭuko 'pi।
trīn gurun-iti guru-paramaguru-parameṣṭhinaḥ।
siddhān-iti anādi-siddha-ādīn।
yoginīr-iti anādi-yoginy-ādyāḥ।
pīṭham-iti jālandharaṃ
yatas-tat-siddha-yoginī-krameṇa asya darśanasya avatāraḥ।
tena maṇḍalasya bahiś-catur-astre īśāna-koṇe gaṇeśam-arcayet,
tato vaṭukaṃ guru-trayaṃ pīṭham-anādi-siddham-anādi-yoginīṃ yāvad-adho 'dhaḥ paṅkti-krameṇa vāyavya-koṇa-antaṃ divya-augha-siddha-augha-mānava-augha-bhedena tri-vidham-api guru-vargam-iti।
tad-uktaṃ

Qt.29b.1 *gaṇeśaṃ pūjayitvā tu dvāri vighna-praśāntaye*|
tataḥ sva-gurum-ārabhya pūjayed-guru-paddhatim ||

3314 *iti*|

Jr.29b.2 *tathā*

Qt.29b.2 *gaṇeśaṃ vaṭukaṃ siddhān guru-paṅktiṃ tathā-eva ca*|
iti|

Jr.29b.3 *idaṃ ca prāṅ-mukhaṃ sādhakam-adhikṛtya uktaṃ*
yena etat tasya vāme pūjitaṃ bhaved-iti|
udaṅ-mukhasya punar-etat-sva-apekṣayā-eva yojyaṃ
yena tad-vāma eva pūjitaṃ bhaved-iti|
dvāre punar-gaṇeśa-vaṭukau
bahiś-catur-astra eva prathamato vāyavy-anair-ṛta-koṇayoḥ
pūjyāv-iti artha-siddhaṃ yena yāgasya dakṣa-vāma-bhāga-
āgatau syātām|
yad-guravaḥ

Qt.29b.3 *bāhye gaṇeśa-vaṭukau śruti-pūrva-koṇa-dakṣa-itara-dvaya-*
gatau
iti|

Jr.29b.4 *tato guru-pūjā-anantaraṃ*
pūrvasyāṃ diśi
bahiś-catur-astre rudra-koṇa-avasthitasya gaṇeśasya
adhastanād-eka-bhāga-anantara-bhāvino dvitīyasmāt
catur-astrād-ārabhya pūrva-ādi-krameṇa āvarta bhaṅgyā
saumya-diśi gaṇeśasya adhastanam-eva sthānaṃ
yāvat dik-catuṣṭaye
arthād-etac-catur-astra-saṃlagna-catuṣkikā-catuṣṭaye
kṛta-ādi-yuga-krama-avatīrṇaṃ siddha-catuṣkam-
abhyarcayed-vakṣyamāṇa-krameṇa pūjayed-ity-arthaḥ
taduktaṁ

Qt.29b.4 *gaṇeśa-adhas-tataḥ sarvaṃ yajen-mantra-kadambakam*|
tat-patīnāṃ tato vargaṃ tatra-eva paripūjayet ||

3315 *iti* ||

Jr.29b.5 *tad-eva āha*

AG. *khagendraḥ saha-vijjāmba illāīambayā saha* || **29** ||
vaktaṣṭir-vimalo 'nantamekhalāmbā-yutaḥ purā|
śaktyā maṅgalayā kūrma illāīambayā saha || **30** ||
jaitro yāmye hy-avijitas-tathā sa-ānandamekhalaḥ|

kāmamaṅgalayā meṣaḥ kullāīambayā saha || **31** ||
vindhyo 'jito 'py-ajarayā saha mekhalayā pare |
macchandaḥ kuṅkuṇāmbā ca ṣaḍ-yugmaṃ sa-adhikārakam || **32** ||
saumye marutta īśa-antaṃ dvitīyā paṅktir-īdṛśī |
3316 *amara-varadeva-citra-ali-vindhya-guḍikā iti kramāt-ṣaḍamī* || **33** ||

Jr.33d.1 *purā-iti pūrvasyām* |
yāmye iti dakṣiṇe |
ajarayā saha mekhalayā-iti ajaramekhalayā saha-ity-arthaḥ |
pare iti paścime |
evaṃ pūrva-ādi-dik-traye
siddhas-tat-patnī suta-dvayaṃ ca-iti kramaḥ |
uttarasyāṃ punar-ayaṃ viśeṣa ity-āha ṣaḍ-yugmam-iti
ṣaṇṇāṃ putra-tat-patnīnāṃ sambandhi yugmaṃ
tad-dvā-daśakam-ity-arthaḥ |
dvitīyā-iti guru-paṅkty-apekṣayā |
anena ca dik-catuṣke 'pi paṅkti-krameṇa-eva pūjā kāryā-iti sūcitam ||

Jr.33d.2 *tad-eva dvā-daśakam-āha*
AG. *sillāī eruṇayā tathā kumārī ca bodhāī* |
sa-mahālacchī ca-aparamekhalayā śaktayaḥ ṣaḍimāḥ || **34** ||

Jr.34d.1 *eruṇayā aparamekhalayā ca saha-ity-arthaḥ* || 34 ||

Jr.34d.2 *sa-adhikāratvam-eva eṣāṃ vyanakti*
AG. *ete hi sa-adhikārāḥ pujyā yeṣām-iyaṃ bahu-vibhedā* |
3317 *santatir-anavacchinnā citrā śiṣya-praśiṣya-mayī* || **35** ||

Jr.35d.1 *citratvam-eva asyā darṣyati*
AG. *ānanda-āvali-bodhi-prabhu-pāda-antā-atha yogi-śabda-antā* |
etā ovallyaḥ syur-mudrā-ṣaṭkaṃ kramāt-tv-etat || **36** ||
dakṣa-aṅguṣṭha-ādi-kaniṣṭhikā-antam-atha sā kanīyasī vāmāt |
dvi-daśa-anta-ūrdhva-ga-kuṇḍali-baindava-hṛn-nābhi-kandam-iti chummāḥ || **37** ||
śavara-aḍabilla-paṭṭillāḥ karabilla-ambi-śarabillāḥ |
aḍabī-ḍombī-dakṣiṇa-billāḥ kumbhārikā-akṣara-ākhyā -ca || **38** ||

devikoṭṭa-kulādri-tripurī-kāma-ākhyam-aṭṭahāsaś-ca |
3318 *dakṣiṇapīṭhaṃ ca-etat-ṣaṭkaṃ ghara-palli-pīṭha-gaṃ*
kramaśaḥ || **39** ||
Jr.39d.1 *ovallyo jñāna-pravāhāḥ* |
kramād-iti mudrā-chummā-viṣayam |
bindor-idaṃ baindavaṃ bhrū-madhya-saṃjñaṃ sthānam |
śavara-iti pulinda-ākhyam |
ambi-iti ambillam |
dakṣiṇā-iti dakṣiṇāvartam |
kulādri-iti kaulagiriḥ |
tripurī-iti tripurottaram |
kāma-iti kāmarūpam |
tad-uktaṃ śrī-kulakriḍāvatāre
Qt.39d.1 *teṣāṃ mudrāś-ca chummāś-ca pallī ovallayas-tathā* |
pīṭha-kramo gharāś-ca-eva pitrā vibhajatā[7] *tathā* ||
Jr.39d.2 *ity-upakramya*
Qt.39d.2 *bodhiś-ca-amara-pādānāṃ prabhuś-ca varadevake* |
citraḥ pādaś-ca saṃprokto hy-alir-ānanda-saṃjñitaḥ ||
vindhya-pādaś-ca yogī tu guḍikā-āvalir-eva ca | *iti*
Qt.39d.3 *dakṣa-hastasya ca-aṅguṣṭhād-ārabhya ca kaniṣṭhakām* |
vāmasya yāvan-mudrā vai ṣaṭsu vistarataḥ śṛṇu ||
aṅguṣṭho jyeṣṭha-putrasya dvitīyasya tu tarjanī |
madhyamā vai tṛtīyasya caturthasya-apy anāmikā ||
pañcamasya kaniṣṭhā vai ṣaṣṭhasya ca kaniṣṭhikā |
iti
Qt.39d.4 *chummakāḥ saṃpravakṣyāmi kula-āmnāye yathā sthitāḥ* |
atītaṃ prathamasya-api dvitīyasya tu kuṇḍalī ||
3319 *bhrū-madhye vai tṛtīyasya saṅghaṭṭaś-ca caturthake* |
nābhis-tu pañcamasya-eva janma-ādhāras-tu ṣaṣṭhake ||
iti
Qt.39d.5 *ṣaṇṇāṃ vai rāja-putrāṇāṃ ghara-palli-kramaṃ śṛṇu* |
amarasya tu paṭṭillaḥ dakṣiṇāvarta-pallikā ||
varadeve karabillaṃ pallī kumbhārikā bhavet |
ambillaṃ ca-eva citrasya billaṃ pallī sumadhyame ||
alināthe pulinda-iti aḍabī pallir-ucyate |

---

7. For *vibhajatā* should one read *vibhajyās* or *vibhājitās*?

śarabillaṃ vindhyanāthe pallī ca-akṣara-saṃjñitā ||
guḍikānātha-pādānām-aḍabillaṃ gharaṃ priye|
ḍombī pallī ca nirdiṣṭā ...||
iti

Qt.39d.6 *tripurottare niketaṃ siddhi-sthānaṃ ca tad-viduḥ*|
amarasya vara-ārohe varadevasya kāmarū ||
citrasya aṭṭahāsaṃ vai devikoṭṭam-ales-tathā|
dakṣiṇaṃ ca-eva vindhyasya guḍikā kaulagir-yatā ||
iti || 39 ||

Jr.39d.3 *nanu kim-evam-ovally-ādy-upadeśena-ity-āśaṅkya āha*

AG. *iti saṅketa-abhijño bhramate pīṭheṣu yadi sa siddhi-īpsuḥ*|
acirāl-labhate tat-tat-prāpyaṃ yad-yoginī-vadanāt || **40** ||

3320

Jr.40d.1 *evaṃ mudrā-ādi-vṛttaṃ jānānasya hi sādhakasya*
tat-tat-siddhi-kāmatayā pīṭheṣu paribhrāmyatas-
-tat-tan-mudrā-ādi-pradarśana-krameṇa
yoginyo nijāṃ nijāṃ santatiṃ jñātvā
kṣipram-eva nikhila-siddhi-pradā bhavanti-ity-arthaḥ|
yad-uktaṃ

Qt.40d.1 *yo yasyāḥ santater-nāthaḥ sā mudrā tasya kīrtitā*|
prasārya hastaṃ sandarśya nāma-akṣara-samanvitāḥ ||
krameṇa tena jñāsyanti svakīyāṃ kula-santatim|
ūrdhvaṃ pradarśayed-yas-tu tasya svaṃ tu pradarśayet ||
kauṇḍily-ādiṣu sarveṣu yo yasya ca nidarśayet|
anena santati-jñā vai jñasyanti ca nijaṃ kulam ||
iti || 40 ||

Jr.40d.2 *evaṃ sa-adhikāraṃ rājaputra-ṣaṭkam-abhidhāya*
niradhikāram-api abhidhatte

AG. *bhaṭṭa-indra-valkala-ahīndra-gajendrāḥ samahīdharāḥ*|
ūrdhva-retasa ete ṣaḍ-adhikāra-pada-ujjhitāḥ || **41** ||

Jr.41d.1 *nanu adhikāra eva ka ity-āśaṅkya āha*

AG. *adhikāro hi vīryasya prasaraḥ kula-vartmani*|
3321 *tad-aprasara-yogena te proktā ūrdhva-retasaḥ* || **42** ||

Jr.42d.1 *adhikāro hi nāma vīryasya*
mantra-mudrā-sambandhinaḥ sphārasya carama-dhātoś-ca
kula-vartmani
śaiṣye madhya-nāḍy-ādau deha-mārge śākte ca ādya-ādhāre
prasaraḥ saṅkramaṇaṃ,
sa eva eṣāṃ na-asti

-iti ete ūrdhva-retasaḥ proktāḥ sva-ātma-mātra-viśrānti-
satattvā eva-ity-arthaḥ || 42 ||
Jr.42d.2 *nanu śrī-devīpañcaśatika-ādau*
Qt.42d.1 *niṣkriya-ānanda-nāthaś-ca jñāna-dīptyā saha-ekataḥ* |
vidyā-ānandaś-ca raktā ca dvitīyaṃ kathitaṃ tava ||
śaktyānando mahā-ānandā tṛtīyaṃ siddha-pūjitam |
śiva-ānandas-tathā jñeyā samayā tac-caturthakam ||
Jr.42d.3 *ity-ādy-uktyā anye 'pi sapatnīkā gurava uktās*
-tadvad-iha-api kathaṃ na-ucyanta ity-āśaṅkya āha
AG. *anyāś-ca guru-tat-patnyaḥ śrīmat-kālīkula-uditāḥ* |
anātta-dehāḥ krīḍanti tais-tair-dehair-aśaṅkitāḥ || **43** ||
3322 *prabodhita-tathā-icchākais-taj-je kaulaṃ prakāśate* |
tathā-rūpatayā tatra gurutvaṃ paribhāṣitam || **44** ||
te viśeṣān-na saṃpūjyāḥ smartavyā eva kevalam |
tato 'bhyantarato vāyu-vahnyor-mātṛkayā saha || **45** ||
mālinī kramaśaḥ pūjyā tato 'ntar-mantra-cakrakam |
Jr.46b.1 *ye ca anye śāstra-antara-uditāḥ sapatnīkā guravaḥ*
pratiniyata-deha-anupagrahād-anātta-dehā
ata eva ananya-saṃviditatvād-aśaṅkitāḥ
para-pura-praveśa-yuktyā
prabodhita-krīḍā-viṣaya-icchāvadbhis
-tais-taiḥ strī-puṃsa-sambandhibhir-dehaiḥ krīḍanti
sambhoga-līlām-anubhavanti,
yena tādṛśa-melakāt jāte
saṅktamaṇa[8] *-krameṇa garbha eva*
niḥsaraṇa-kāla eva vā tad-uttara-kālaṃ vā
kaula jñānaṃ prakāśate
yata evaṃ-vidham-eva eṣāṃ gurutva-
3323 *- m-iti*
śāstrīyaḥ samayo 'yaṃ
—śrī-rahasya-rājikā-yoginībhiḥ,
sva-bhāvād-bhagavatyāḥ prasādena dṛṣṭaṃ
vigrahāj-jnānaṃ labdham,
tābhiḥ sva-kule garbha-sthānāṃ saṅkrāmitam,
tābhir-garbhāt dṛṣṭam,

---

8. For *saṅktamana* read *saṅkramaṇa.*

jāta-mātrābhiś-ca anyābhir-dṛṣṭam,
anyābhiḥ saptaviṃśateḥ samānām-ante dṛṣṭam-iti।
tad-amūrtatvād-iha te kevalaṃ smartavyā eva,
natu viśeṣāt sampūjyāḥ pūrva-gurubhis-tathā na-upadiṣṭā
ity-arthaḥ।
yadvā viśva-yony-ādyā vyākhyeyāḥ।
yad-uktam-anena-eva
Qt.46b.1 *viśvaṃ jagad-bhāvam-atho prajāpati-kulaṃ tataḥ*।
yoni-śabda-antakaṃ proktaṃ guruṇāṃ pañcakaṃ tv-idam॥
vīryaṃ kṣobho bījaṃ sṛṣṭiḥ sarga iti-imāḥ śaktaya uktāḥ।
atyutsāhaḥ śaktiś-ca kṣama-saṅgatir-ucchalā praklptiḥ ॥
tā etāḥ kila śaktayo nija-guru-sphāraiḥ samaṃ bāhyakaṃ
dehaṃ kaṃcid-api kvacij-jagṛhire na-eva sva-tantra-
udayaḥ।
icchā-mātra-balena yat-kila yadā dvandvaṃ samadhyāsate
tatra krīḍita-lālasāḥ parapada-jñānaṃ phalaṃ tattvataḥ ॥
iti।
Jr.46b.2 *tata iti dvitīyasmāt catur-astrāt*।
abhyantarata iti vyomni।
kramaśa iti tena vāyu-koṇa-ādārabhya vahni-koṇaṃ
yāvad-upary-upari krameṇa mātṛkā pūjyā,
mālinī tu vahner-vāyv-antam-adho 'dhaḥ
3324 *krameṇa-iti siddham*।
tata iti mātṛkā-mālinī-pūjā-anantaram।
antar-iti yāga-madhya-vartini karṇikā-sthānīye tri-koṇe।
tatra pūrva-dakṣiṇa-vāma-koṇeṣu
sa-bhairavaṃ parā-ādi-devī-trayam,
madhye ca kuleśvaram-iti।
yad-vakṣyati
Qt.46b.2 *sampūjya madhyama-pade kuleśa-yugmaṃ tv-arā-traye*
devīḥ।
iti ॥
Jr.46b.3 *evaṃ ca atra anvarthatām-abhidhāsyan*
-kuleśvaryā mukhyatayā pūjāyāṃ viniyogam-āha
AG. *mantra-siddha-prāṇa-saṃvit-karaṇa-ātmani yā kule* ॥ **46** ॥
cakra-ātmake citiḥ prabhvī proktā sā-iha kuleśvarī।
sā madhye śrī-parā devī mātṛsadbhāva-rūpiṇī ॥ **47** ॥
pūjyā-atha tat-samāropād-aparā-atha parāparā।
eka-vīrā ca sā pūjyā yadi-vā sakuleśvarā ॥ **48** ॥

3325

Jr.48d.1 *yā nāma parā-ādi-mantra-siddha-ādy-ātmatayā*
prāṇa-buddhi-karaṇa-ātmatayā ca
cakra-ātmake kule
pūjya-samūhe pūjaka-śarīre ca viśrānti-dhāmatvāt prabhvī
pūrṇa-sphurattā-mātra-satattvā citiḥ proktā,
sā-eva iha kula-īśvarītvāt tac-chabda-vyapadeśyā-ity-arthaḥ।
tat-samāropād-iti pratyekam-abhisambandhaḥ।
tena puṣpa-pāta-ādy-anusāraṃ
yā yasya ārādhayitum-iṣṭā,
sā tena tathā pūjyā-ity-abhiprāyaḥ ॥ 48 ॥

Jr.48d.2 *nanu eka-vīra-kramāt yāmala-krameṇa pūjāyāṃ ko viśeṣa ity-āśaṅkya āha*

AG. *prasarec-chaktir-ucchūnā sa-ullāso bhairavaḥ punaḥ*।
saṅghaṭṭa-ānanda-viśrāntyā yugmam-itthaṃ prapūjayet ॥**49**॥
mahā-prakāśa-rūpāyāḥ saṃvido visphuliṅgavat।
yo raśmy-oghas-tam-eva-atra pūjayed-devatā-gaṇam ॥**50**॥

3326

Jr.50d.1 *yadā hi bhairava-unmukhī śaktih prasaret*
bhairavaś-ca punaḥ śakty-unmukhaḥ,
tadā itthaṃ paraspara-unmukhyāt
tayoḥ saṅghaṭṭena samāpattyā
yo 'yam-ānandaḥ sva-ātma-camat-kāras
-tad-viśrāntyā yugmaṃ prapūjayet।

Qt.50d.1 *ānandena-eva sampanne brahma-avasthaḥ svayaṃ sthitaḥ*।

Jr.50d.2 *ity-ādy-uktyā*
cid-ānanda-eka-ghana-para-brahma-sva-rūpa-mātra-satattvaṃ yāmalam-anusandadhyād-ity-arthaḥ।
tam-eva-iti natu tato 'tiriktam-ity-arthaḥ ॥ 50 ॥

Jr.50d.3 *tad-eva āha*

AG. *antar-dvā-daśakaṃ pūjyaṃ tato 'ṣṭa-aṣṭakam-eva ca*।
catuṣkaṃ vā yathecchaṃ vā kā saṅkhyā kila raśmiṣu ॥ **51** ॥

Jr.51d.1 *dvā-daśakam-iti sṛṣṭi-devy-ādi,*
ekī-kāra-āhnike vakṣyamāṇaṃ vā।
catuṣkam-iti siddhā-ādi,

jayā-ādi vā |
yatheṣṭam-iti nija-anuṣṭhāna-avasthitam || 51 ||
Jr.51d.2 *nanu raśmayas-tāvad-anantā ity-uktam* |
tāsāṃ ca śāstra-antareṣu bahu-prakāraṃ nirdeśa
iti nirnibandhanam-eva upekṣāyāṃ
sarvasya tathā-abhāva-prasaṅgād
-anava-
3327 *-sthitam-eva tad-anuṣṭhānaṃ syād*
-iti kim-etac-chāstra-avihitam-antar-dvā-daśakaṃ pūjyam-
ity-ādi uktam |
satyam-evaṃ,
kintu gurv-antarāṇām-ayam-āśaya
ity-evam-etat sandarśitam |
tasmāt mukhyayā vṛttyā sva-kaṇṭha-uktam-aṣṭaka-dvayam-
eva yāmala-krameṇa sampūjyam-ity-āha
AG. *māheśī vairiñcī kaumārī vaiṣṇavī catur-dikkam* |
aindrī yāmyā muṇḍā yogeśīr-īśatas-tu koṇeṣu || **52** ||
pavana-antam-aghora-ādikam-aṣṭakam
-asminn-atha-aṣṭake kramaśaḥ |
saṅghaṭṭa-ānanda-dṛśā sampūjyaṃ yāmalī-bhūtam || **53** ||
aṣṭa-aṣṭake 'pi hi vidhau nānā-nāma-prapañcite bahu-dhā |
vidhir-eṣa eva vidhitas-tat-saṃkhyā dīpa-mālā syāt || **54** ||
Jr.54d.1 *kramaśa iti try-astrād-bahir-aṣṭa-dale padme*
pūrva-da-
3328 *-kṣiṇa-paścima-uttareṣu daleṣu*
aghora-ādi-sahitaṃ māheśy-ādi-catuṣkaṃ
tad-itareṣu api īśāt vahny-antaṃ
sa-bhīma-ādikam-aindry-ādi-catuṣkaṃ pūjayet |
yad-uktaṃ
Qt.54d.1 *pūrva-yāmya-aparā-dikṣu māheśy-ādi-catuṣṭayam* |
indrāṇī-pūrvakaṃ tadvad-aiśād-agni-dala-antagam ||
iti,
Qt.54d.2 *tato vīra-aṣṭakaṃ paścāc-chakty-ukta-vidhinā yajet* |
iti ca |
Jr.54d.2 *atra*
Qt.54d.3 *kṣetre 'ṣṭa-dhā vibhakte madhye bhāga-dvayād-bhramasya-*
antaḥ |

try-astraṃ kuryāt-tad-anu tridhā vibhakte samantato
bhāge ||
vasu-dalam-ambhojam-atho bhāgena nabhaś-
catuṣkikāś-ca catuḥ |
veda-astre dikṣu tato bhāgāḥ śruti-bhāva-gāminyaḥ ||
pārśvābhyām-evam-idaṃ kula-krame maṇḍalaṃ sacatur-
astram |

Jr.54d.3 *iti maṇḍala-saṃgrahaḥ* |
bahu-dhā nānā-nāma-prapañcite iti
kula-śāstrāṇām-ānantyāt tan-nāmnām-api nānātvāt |
na-hi pūrva-ācāryāṇām-etad-iha pūjyatvena abhihitaṃ
yena paramparayā naiyatyena tair-nāmnām-aparigrahaḥ
syāt,
kin-tu vyāpti-mātra-pradarśana-āśayena-iti
yathā-ruci tan-nāmāni grāhyāṇi-iti |
yad-uktam-anena-eva anyatra

Qt.54d.4 *aṣṭaka-saptakasya tu yathā-ruci-itara-kula-śāstrebhyaḥ* |
nāmāni-iti tat-ta...ni ||

3329 *iti* |

Jr.54d.4 *atra ca aṣṭaka-saptaka-ity-abhidhānād*
-aṣṭa-aṣṭakam-iha pūjyatayā sammatam-ity-eva
saṃlakṣitam |
evaṃ hi aṣṭakasya pṛthag-āvaraṇa-krameṇa pūjanīyatvaṃ
na syāt tathātve ca śruti-virodha ity-alaṃ bahunā |
eṣa eva-iti yāmala-lakṣaṇaḥ |
iha tāvat |

Qt.54d.5 *āvāhite mantra-gaṇe puṣpa-āsava-niveditaiḥ* |
dhūpaiś-ca tarpaṇaṃ kāryaṃ śraddhā-bhakti-bala-uditam ||
dīptānāṃ śakti-nātha-ādi-mantrāṇām-āsavaiḥ palaiḥ |
raktaiḥ prāk-tarpaṇaṃ paścāt-puṣpa-dhūpa-ādi-vistaraḥ ||

Jr.54d.5 *ity-ādy-uktyā avaśya-kāryaṃ kula-krame tarpaṇam* |
tatra ca mahā-paśu-pratinidhitvāt dīpa-caror-eva
prādhānyam-iti prathamaṃ tad-eva upahartavyatayā
abhidhatte tat-saṃkhyā dīpa-mālā syād-iti |
tat-saṅkhyā-ity-anena aṣṭa-aṣṭa-vyāpter-atra āsūtraṇaṃ
kṛtam |
etac-ca abhiṣeka-viṣayam-iti || 54 ||

Jr.54d.6 *atra prakāra-antaram-āha*
AG. *śrī-ratnamālā-śāstre tu varṇa-saṃkhyāḥ pradīpakāḥ* ।
varṇāṃś-ca mukhya-pūjyāyā vidyāyā gaṇayet-sudhīḥ ॥ **55**॥
3330
Jr.55d.1 *tad-uktaṃ tatra*
Qt.55d.1 *pradoṣe vilīne mantrī dīpān-dadyād-vara-ānane* ।
varṇa-saṅkhyān-vara-ārohe catur-dikṣu gatān-nyaset ॥ *iti* ।
Qt.55d.2 *athātaḥ saṃpravakṣyāmi mālinyā yajanaṃ param* ।
Jr.55d.2 *ity-upakrāntatvāt mukhya-pūjyā mālinī*
-iti tad-varṇa-saṅkhyāyāḥ pañcāśad-dīpā uktāḥ ।
tena yāvad-akṣarā mūla-vidyā tatra,
tāvat-saṃkhyā dīpāḥ kāryā iti siddham ॥ 55 ॥
Jr.55d.3 *evam-iyatā siddha-patnī-kula-kramam-abhidhāya,*
arcā-prakārā-sūtraṇāya
atra sasaṃvādaṃ mata-antaram-api abhidhātum-āha
AG. *pīṭha-kṣetra-ādibhiḥ sākaṃ kuryād-vā kula-pūjanam* ।
yathā śrī-mādhavakule parameśena bhāṣitam ॥ **56** ॥
Jr.56d.1 *śrī-mādhavakule iti śrī-tantrarājabhaṭṭāraka-grantha-eka-deśa-bhūte ity-arthaḥ* ।
atra hi keṣāṃcana gurūṇāṃ
srī-devyāyāmala-śrī-mādhavakula-artha-sammelanayā
sampradāyaḥ samasti-iti śrī-mādhavakula-ukta-
3331 *vakṣyamāṇa-krameṇa*
pīṭha-ādy-uktaṃ vā kula-krama-pūjanaṃ kāryam-ity-upakṣiptam ।
Jr.56d.2 *tad-eva āha*
AG. *sṛṣṭi-saṃsthita-saṃhāra-anāma-krama-catuṣṭayam* ।
pīṭha-śmaśāna-sahitaṃ pūjayed-bhoga-mokṣayoḥ ॥ **57** ॥
Jr.57d.1 *bhoga-mokṣayor-iti tan-nimittam-ity-arthaḥ* ।
tad-uktaṃ tatra
Qt.57d.1 *sṛṣṭi-kramaṃ tu prathamam-avatāraṃ dvitīyakam* ।
saṃhāraṃ tu tṛtīyaṃ syād-anākhyā-iyaṃ caturthakam ॥
iti
Jr.57d.2 *upakramya*
Qt.57d.2 *sa kālī-kula-sambhūto bhāvanāṃ bhāvayet-sphuṭam* ।
iti

Qt.57d.3 *pīṭha-krameṇa ca-āmnāyaṃ saṅkarṣaṇyā tv-adhiṣṭhitam*।
tair-vinā na bhavet-siddhas-tat-padaṃ kathayāmi te।
iti ca।
Jr.57d.3 *śrī-devyāyāmale hi devī-trayaṃ śri-saṅkarṣaṇī ca-iti catuṣṭayam* ॥ 57 ॥
Jr.57d.4 *tatra dehe pīṭhānāṃ padam-abhidhatte*
AG. *ātmano vā-atha-vā śakteś-cakrasya-atha smared-imam*।
3332 *nyasyatvena vidhiṃ dehe pīṭha-ākhye*[9] *pārameśvaram* ॥ **58**॥
Jr.58d.1 *imam-iti vakṣyamānam* ॥ 58 ॥
Jr.58d.2 *tam-eva āha*
AG. *aṭṭahāsaṃ śikhā-sthāne caritraṃ ca ka-randhrake*।
śrutyoḥ kaulagiriṃ nāsā-randhrayoś-ca jayantikām ॥ **59** ॥
bhruvor-ujjayinīṃ vaktre prayāgaṃ hṛdaye punaḥ।
vārāṇasīṃ skandha-yuge śrīpīṭhaṃ virajaṃ gale ॥ **60** ॥
eḍābhīm-udare hālāṃ nābhau kande tu gośrutim।
upasthe marukośaṃ ca nagaraṃ pauṇḍravardhanam ॥ **61** ॥
elāpuraṃ purastīraṃ sakthy-ūrvor-dakṣiṇa-āditaḥ।
3333 *kuḍyākeśīṃ ca sopānaṃ māyāpū-kṣīrake tathā* ॥ **62** ॥
jānu-jaṅghe gulpha-yugme tv-āmrāta-nṛpasadmanī।
pāda-ādhāre tu vairiñcīṃ kāla-agny-avadhi-dhārikām ॥ **63**॥
Jr.63d.1 *aṭṭahāsam-iti nyasyatvena smared-iti pūrveṇa sambandhaḥ*।
evam-uttaratra-api।
śikhā-sthāne iti prāṇa-śakti-viśrānty-avasthity-ātmani dvā-daśa-ante ity-arthaḥ।
vaktre iti āsye।
hālām-iti alipuram।
yad-uktaṃ
Qt.63d.1 *nābhi-deśe tv-alipuraṃ kanda-ūrdhve parameśvari*।
iti।
Jr.63d.2 *gośrutim-iti gokarṇam*।
sakthy-ūrvor-iti jānu-jaṅghe iti gulpha-yugme iti ca sarvatra dakṣiṇata iti sambandhanīyam।
tena dakṣiṇe sakthni nagaraṃ,

9. Gnoli, *Luce*, p.687 footnote 36 suggests that *pīṭha-ākhye*, which agrees with body, should read *pīṭha-ākhyaṃ* to agree with *vidhiṃ*.

vāme pauṇḍravardhanaṃ,
dakṣiṇe ūrāv-elāpuraṃ,
vāme purastīraṃ,
dakṣiṇe jānuni kuḍyākeśīṃ,
vāme sopānaṃ,
dakṣiṇa-jaṅghāyāṃ māyāpurīṃ,
vāmāyāṃ
3334 *tu kṣīrakaṃ,*
dakṣiṇe gulphe āmrātakeśvaraṃ,
vāme tu rājagṛham-iti |
tad-uktaṃ tatra
Qt.63d.2 *dakṣiṇe sakthni nagaraṃ vāme syāt pauṇḍravardhanam* |
vāma-ūrau tu purastīram-elāpuraṃ tu dakṣiṇe ||
kuḍyākeśī dakṣa-jānau sopānaṃ ca-uttare smṛtam |
kṣīrakaṃ vāma-jaṅghāyāṃ vāmapury-api dakṣiṇe |
āmrātakeśvaraṃ gulphe vāme rājagṛhaṃ śubham || *iti* |
Jr.63d.3 *vairiñcīm-iti brahmāṇīṃ,*
śrīśaila-ākhyaṃ tu tat-pīṭham-ity-arthaḥ |
tad-uktaṃ śrī-kulakramodaye
Qt.63d.3 *śrīśaile saṃsthitā brāhmī ....* |
Jr.63d.4 *ity-ādi upakramya*
Qt.63d.4 *pāda-ādhāra-sthitā brāhmī........* |
iti || 63 ||
Jr.63d.5 *naca atra tātsthyena avasthātavyaṃ,*
kintu aham-eva pīṭhas-tad-adhiṣṭhātryaḥ śaktayaś-ca-iti
anusandhātavyaṃ yena siddhiḥ syād-ity-āha
AG. *na-aham-asmi naca-anyo 'sti kevalāḥ śaktayas-tv-aham* |
ity-evaṃ-vāsanāṃ kuryāt-sarvadā smṛti-mātrataḥ || **64** ||
3335
Jr.64d.1 *tad-uktaṃ tatra*
Qt.64d.1 *na-aham-asmi naca-anyo 'sti kevalāḥ śaktayas-tv-iti* |
kṣaṇam-apy-atra viśrāmaṃ sahajaṃ yadi bhāvayet |
tadā sa khecaro bhūtvā yoginī-melanaṃ labhet ||
iti || 64 ||
Jr.64d.2 *nanu deśa-kāla-vrata-ādi-niyantraṇayā siddhir-bhaved-iti*
sarvatra uktam |
tat katham-atra anusandhi-mātreṇa-eva evaṃ syād-ity-
āśaṅkya āha

AG. *na tithir-na ca nakṣatraṃ na-upavāso vidhīyate*। [10]
grāmya-dharma-rataḥ siddhyet-sarvadā smaraṇena hi ।। **65** ।।

Jr.65d.1 *grāmya-dharma-rataḥ iti tad-vṛttir-ity-arthaḥ*।
etac-ca prathama-āhnike eva uktam-iti tata eva-avadhāryam ।। 65 ।।

Jr.65d.2 *nanu kiṃ nāma tac-cakraṃ*
yasya-api nyasyatvena pīṭha-ākhyo 'yaṃ vidhir-vivakṣita ity-āśaṅkya āha

AG. *mātaṅga-kṛṣṇa-saunika-kārmuka-cārmika-vikoṣi-dhātu-vibhedāḥ*।
mātsyaka-cākrika-dayitās-teṣāṃ patnyo nava-atra nava-yāge ।। **66** ।।

3336

Jr.66d.1 *kṛṣṇaḥ kajjalo ḍomba iti yāvat*।
vikoṣi dhvajī kalyapāla।
dhātu-vibhedo 'sthi-bhettā kāpālikaḥ।
tad-uktaṃ tatra

Qt.66d.1 *mātaṅgī kajjalī saunī kārmukī carmakāriṇī*।
dhvajinī ca-asthidalanī dhīvarī cakriṇī priye ।।
iti।

Jr.66d.2 *nava-yāge iti navānāṃ cakrāṇāṃ yajane ity-arthaḥ*।
tad-uktaṃ tatra

Qt.66d.2 *nava-yāga-ratā devyaḥ pūjayanti yathāśīśvaram*।
tadvat-pūjā prakartavyā nava-dhā nava-cakra-gā ।।
iti ।। 66 ।।

Jr.66d.3 *tad-gṛhāṇy-eva ca saṅketa-sthānatayā pīṭhāni-ity-āha*

AG. *saṅgama-varuṇā-kulagiry-aṭṭahāsa-jayantī-*
-caritraka-āmraka-koṭṭam।
haimapuraṃ navamaṃ syān-madhye tāsāṃ ca cakriṇī mukhyā ।। **67** ।।

Jr.67d.1 *yad-uktaṃ tatra*

Qt.67d.1 *mātaṅgī-veśma subhage prayāgaṃ parikīrtitam*।
kajjalī varuṇā-ākhyaṃ tu saunī kulagiriḥ priye ।।

---

10. The *Kaulajñānanirṇaya* 21.9 reads: *na tithir-na ca nakṣatraṃ na-upavāsaṃ vidhīyate*।

kārmukī ca-aṭṭahāsaṃ ca jayantī carmakāriṇī |
caritraṃ dhvajinī proktam-ekāmra-asthi-vidāraṇī ||
3337 *devīkoṭṭaṃ dhivarī tu hiraṇyapuram-eva ca* |
navamaṃ cakriṇī-pīṭhaṃ yat-surair-api durlabham ||*iti*|
Jr.67d.2 *tāsām-iti mātaṅgy-ādīnām* || 67 ||
Jr.67d.3 *mukhyatvam-eva asyā darśayati*
AG. *bījaṃ sā pīḍayate rasa-śalka-vibhāgato 'tra kuṇḍalinī* |
adhyuṣṭa-pīṭha-netrī kanda-sthā viśvato bhramati || **68** ||
iṣṭvā cakra-udayaṃ tv-itthaṃ madhye pūjyā kuleśvarī |
saṅkarṣiṇī tad-anta-ante saṃhāra-āpyāya-kāriṇī || **69** ||
eka-vīrā cakra-yuktā cakra-yāmala-gā-api vā |
Jr.70b.1 *atra hi sā kande nikhila-jagad-utpatti-mūla-bhūte*
prakāśa-ātmani para-pramātari
ābhimukhyena vartamānā,
ata eva garbhī-kṛta-viśvatvāt kuṇḍalinī-rūpā parā-śaktir
-yadā sva-svātantryāt
bheda-prathā-
3338 *-m-avabibhāsayiṣur*
-adhyuṣṭa-pīṭhe netrī
deha-ādi-pramātṛtām-avalambamānā
viśvato bhramati
tat-tan-nīla-sukha-ādy-ātmatayā paritaḥ sphurati,
tadā punar-api ātmany-eva viśvaṃ viśramayitum-
udyacchantī rasa-śalka-vibhāgato bījaṃ pīḍayate
deha-ādi-pramātṛtā-nyak-kāra-krameṇa
para-saṃvid-rasam-utkarṣayantī
viśva-kāraṇaṃ māyāṃ tiras-karoti-ity-arthaḥ |
anyac-ca sā-eva kanda-ādhāra-sthā prāṇa-kuṇḍalinī-rūpā
bījaṃ puṣpa-ādi-nimittam-upabhuktam-āhāra-ādi
rasa-kiṭṭa-ādi-rūpatayā pariṇāmayati
yena deha-ādhāraṃ prerayantī
viśvato bhramati
sarvato nāḍī-cakra-ādau prāṇana-ātmatayā avatiṣṭhate ity-arthaḥ |
athaca bahiḥ sā cākrikī
sa-ardha-tri-hasta-prāya-parimāṇaṃ cakraṃ prerayantī
tan-madhya-sthā viśvataḥ sarvataḥ-adikkaṃ bhramati

yena sarvataḥ-adikkaṃ bhramaṇād-eva kuṇḍalinī
bījaṃ tila-ādi rasa-śalka-vibhāgataḥ pīḍayate
taila-piṇyāka-vibhāga-āsādana-paryantaṃ niṣpīḍayati-ity-arthaḥ |
tad-uktaṃ

Qt.70b.1 *navamī cakriṇī yā sā bhramantī viśva-madhya-gā* |
sarvaṃ bījaṃ pīḍayantī rasa-śalka-vibhāgataḥ ||
sā ca kuṇḍalinī nāma kanda-veṣṭa-vinirgatā |

3339 *iti* |

Jr.70b.2 *cakra-udayam-iti uditaṃ cakram-ity-arthaḥ* |
saṅkarṣiṇī sapta-daśa-akṣarā |
yad-uktaṃ śrī-devyāyāmale

Qt.70b.2 *nāśa-arṇaṃ*[11] *ca nitambaṃ ca prāṇaṃ śūla-ardha-yojitam* |
nitambaṃ prāṇam-uddhṛtya kṣīra-varṇena saṃyutam ||
tri-locanaṃ karṇa-varṇaṃ bāhu-dakṣiṇa-yojitam |
bāhu-skandhaṃ tu tad-vāmaṃ dakṣa-jaṅghā-niyojitam ||
danta-arṇaṃ tṛtīya-uddhṛtya dakṣa-jānusu-saṃsthitam |
guhya-kaṇṭhe niveśyeta śūla-daṇḍaṃ tu jihvayoḥ ||
śiro-māla-arṇa-dvitīyaṃ hastayor-yojitaṃ punaḥ |
netraṃ tathā-eva parata uttama-aṅgaṃ tathā-evaca ||
vāma-pādaṃ kapāla-sthaṃ pañca-dhā yojayet-tataḥ |
tri-daśair-api sampujyā vidyā sapta-daśa-akṣarā ||
kālasaṅkarṣiṇī nāmnā .... |
iti |

Jr.70b.3 *iyam-eva ca vidyā śrī-mādhavakule 'pi*

Qt.70b.3 *mohinī kūla ātmā ca vīra-nātha-iti yojayet* |

Jr.70b.4 *ity-ādinā*

Qt.70b.4 *madīya-bhūṣaṇair-yuktaṃ pañca-dhārārdham-uddharet* |

Jr.70b.5 *ity-antena uktā yena-ayam-eva gurv-āmnāyaḥ* |
tad-anta-ante iti tasya cakrasya antaḥ arā-prāyaḥ, tasya-api ante
pūrṇa-ahaṃ-parāmarśa-ātmani viśrānti-dhāmani-ity-

---

11. For *nāśa-arṇaṃ*, read *nāsa-arṇaṃ*. Sanderson,'The visualisation', p.59 footnote 120.

arthaḥ |
tad-uktam
Qt.70b.5 *evaṃ cakra-udayaṃ-jñātvā madhye jñā kālakṛntanī* |
tasya-anta-ante tu yā āste sā tu saṅkarṣiṇī smṛtā ||
3340 *iti* |
Jr.70b.6 *cakra-yāmala-gā-iti cakre yat yāmalaṃ,*
tad-gatā yāmala-krameṇa cakra-yuktā-ity-arthaḥ ||
Jr.70b.7 *atra kathaṃ pīṭhāni sāhityena pūjyāni-ity-āśaṅkya āha*
AG. *īśa-indra-agni-yama-kravyātka-vāyu-udakṣu hāsataḥ* ||**70** ||
trikaṃ trikaṃ yajed-etad-bhāvi-sva-trika-saṃyutam |
Jr.71b.1 *evam-īśāna-koṇe aṭṭahāsaś-caritraṃ kulagiriś-ca-iti trayaṃ*
yajed-yāvad-udīcyām-āmrātakeśvaro
rājagṛhaṃ śrīparvataś-ca-iti trayam
-iti |
naca etad-ekaikaṃ pīṭhaṃ kevalam-eva yajed-ity-āha
bhāvi-sva-trika-saṃyutam-iti,
bhāvi-iti vakṣyamāṇam ||
Jr.71b.2 *tad-eva āha*
AG. *hṛt-kuṇḍalī bhruvor-madhyam-etad-eva kramāt-trayam*
|| **71** ||
śmaśānāni kramāt-kṣetra-bhavaṃ sad-yoginī-gaṇam |
3341
Jr.72b.1 *yajed-iti pūrveṇa atra sambandhaḥ* |
kṣetra-bhavam-iyat-tat-pīṭha-jātam-ity-arthaḥ |
tad-uktam
Qt.72b.1 .... *īśa-koṇa-āditaḥ kramāt* |
pūrva-dakṣiṇa-vāruṇyaḥ saumyā yāś-ca diśaḥ priye ||
iti,
Qt.72b.2 *śmaśānaṃ hṛt-pradeśaḥ syāt-kalpa-vṛkṣas-tu kuṇḍalī* |
bhrū-madhyaṃ yoginī-kṣetraṃ jñātavyaṃ yoginī-kule ||
iti ca ||
Jr.72b.2 *kṛtāyāṃ pūjāyāṃ naivedyena-eva avaśya-bhāvyam-ity-āha*
AG. *vasv-aṅgula-unnatān-ūrdhva-vartulān kṣāma-madhyakān*
|| **72** ||
rakta-vartīñ-śruti-dṛśo dīpān-kurvīta sarpiṣā |
Jr.73b.1 *śruti-dṛśa iti catur-viṃśatiḥ* |
tad-uktaṃ

Qt.73b.1 *catur-viṃśati-dīpāṃś-ca catur-dikṣu pradāpayet* ।
piṣṭa-ātmakāś-ca ādhāra [12] *-madhya-kṣāmāḥ suvartulāḥ* ॥
aṣṭa-aṅgula-pramāṇa-sthāḥ śobhanāś-catur-aṅgulāḥ ।
ghṛta-dīpena saṃyuktā rakta-varty-upari-sthitāḥ ॥
iti ॥

3342
Jr.73b.2 *atra-eva pakṣa-antaram-āha*
AG. *yat-kiñcid-atha-vā madhye sva-anuṣṭhānaṃ prap-*
ūjayet ॥**73** ॥
advaitam-eva na dvaitam-ity-ājñā parameśituḥ ।
siddhānta-vaiṣṇava-ādy-uktā mantrā mala-yutās-ta-
taḥ ॥ **74** ॥
tāvat-tejo 'sahiṣṇutvān-nirjīvāḥ syur-iha-advaye ।
Jr.75b.1 *yat-kiñcid-ity-abhīṣṭam* ।
tad-uktaṃ
Qt.75b.1 *yo yasmin-mantra-yogena tantra-ācāra-pade sthitaḥ* ।
Jr.75b.2 *ity-upakramya*
Qt.75b.2 *sva-kramaṃ tu yajen-madhye dvaita-ācāraṃ tu varjayet* ॥
Jr.75b.3 *ity-uktvā*
Qt.75b.3 *siddhānta-vaiṣṇava-bauddhā vedāntāḥ smārta-darśanāḥ* ।
te prayatnena vā varjyā yasmāt-te paśavaḥ smṛtāḥ ॥
advaita-drava-saṃparkāt-sannidhānaṃ tyajanti te ।
parāṅ-mukhatvam-āyānti nirjīvā jīva-varjitāḥ ॥ *iti*

3343
Jr.75b.4 *ataś-ca tad-upakaraṇa-jātam-apahāya*
ihatyam-eva tad-āśrayaṇīyaṃ
yena vinā-āyāsaṃ siddhiḥ syād-ity-āha
AG. *kalaśaṃ netra-bandha-ādi maṇḍalaṃ sruk-sruva-ana-*
lam ॥ **75** ॥
hitvā-atra siddhiḥ san-madye pātre madhye kṛśāṃ yajet ।
aho-rātram-imaṃ yāgaṃ kurvataś-ca-apare 'hani ॥ **76** ॥
vīra-bhojye kṛte 'vaśyaṃ mantrāḥ siddhyanty-ayatnataḥ ।
pīṭha-stotraṃ paṭhed-atra yāge bhāgya-āvaha-āhv-
aye ॥ **77** ॥

---

12. For *ādhāra* Sanderson reads *ādhāre*. Sanderson,'Meaning',p.83 footnote 231.

Jr.77d.1 *apare 'hani-iti prabhātāyāṃ rātrāv-ity-arthaḥ*।
tad-uktaṃ

Qt.77d.1 *kalaśaṃ netra-bandhaṃ ca maṇḍala-ādi vivarjayet*।
tair-vihīne bhavet-siddhir-agninā sruk-sruva-ādibhiḥ ॥
madya-pūrṇeṣu bhāṇḍeṣu pūrva-ukteṣu gaṇāmbike।
rasāyana-maya-ukteṣu madhye pūjyā kṛśa-udarī ॥

3344

Jr.77d.2 *ity-ādi upakramya*

Qt.77d.2 *pūrva-ahṇe vā-apara-ahṇe vā aho-rātraṃ viyogataḥ*।
pīṭha-stotraṃ paṭhed-rātrau japaṃ kuryāt-samāhitaḥ ॥
prabhāte vimale proktaṃ vīra-bhojyaṃ tu kārayet।
mahā-bhāgya-udayo jāyed-rājye 'nte khecaro bhavet ॥
iti ॥ 77 ॥

Jr.77d.3 *yad-vā maṇḍala-ādi-parihāreṇa cakram-eva pūjayed-ity-āha*

AG. *mūrtīr-eva-athavā yugma-rūpā vīra-sva-rūpiṇīḥ*।
avadhūtā nirācārāḥ pūjayet-kramaśo budhaḥ ॥ **78** ॥

Jr.78d.1 *mūrtīr-eva-iti eva-kāreṇa kevalāḥ śaktīḥ*।
vīra-sva-rūpiṇī-iti kevalā eva vīrāḥ।
avadhūtā nirvikalpāḥ ॥ 78 ॥

Jr.78d.2 *nanu kevala-śakti-pakṣe pūjā kathaṅkāraṃ paripūrtim-iyād-ity-āśaṅkya āha*

AG. *eka eva-atha kauleśaḥ svayaṃ bhūtvā-api tāvatīḥ*।

3345 *śaktīr-yāmala-yogena tarpayed-viśva-rūpavat* ॥ **79** ॥

Jr.79d.1 *atha svayam-eka eva bhūtvā guruḥ kuleśvara-aikātmyāt kauleśaḥ,*
ata eva viśva-rūpa iva
tāvatīr-bahvīr-api śaktīr-yāmala-yogena tarpayet,
saṅghaṭṭa-ānanda-sāmarasya-mayatayā
sva-ātma-viśrānti-mātra-satattvāḥ kuryād-ity-arthaḥ ॥ 79॥

Jr.79d.2 *nanu iha kasmāt*

Qt.79d.1 *udag-ayane śubha-vāre sthira-lagne sthāpana-adhivāsaḥ syāt*।

Jr.79d.3 *ity-ādivat pratiniyataḥ kālaḥ kula-yāge na-ukta ity-āśaṅkya āha*

AG. *kramo nāma na kaścit-syāt-prakāśa-maya-saṃvidi*।
cid-abhāvo hi na-asty-eva tena-akālaṃ tu tarpaṇam ॥ **80** ॥

Jr.80d.1 *iha*
Qt.80d.1 *sakṛd-vibhāto 'yam-ātmā* ǀ
Jr.80d.2 *iti nyāyena mahā-prakāśa-mayī saṃvid*
-an-idaṃ-prathamatayā pravṛttā
anuparatena rūpeṇa ābhāsate,
3346 *na-tu vidyud-uddyota-vad-antarā-antarā vicchedena-iti*
na atra kramo nāma kaścid-vidyate bheda-āśrayatvāt-tasya ǀ
ataś-ca tad-eka-jīvitaḥ kālo 'pi atra na-asti-iti
akālam-eva tarpaṇam-uktam ǀ
yo hi yatra na prapatati,
sa kathaṃ tatra avacchedakatām-iyād-ity-āśayaḥ ǁ 80 ǁ
Jr.80d.3 *ata eva deśa-kramo 'pi atra na-asti-ity-āha*
AG. *atra krame bheda-taroḥ samūlam-unmūlanād-āsana-pakṣa-carcā* ǀ
pṛthaṅ-na yuktā
parameśvaro hi sva-śakti-dhāmni-iva viśaṃśramīti ǁ **81** ǁ
Jr.81d.1 *sva-śakti-dhāmni-iti*
Qt.81d.1 *śaktayo 'sya jagat-kṛtsnaṃ ....* ǀ
Jr.81d.2 *ity-ādy-uktyā hi sarvaṃ sa eva-iti*
ko nāma tad-atirikto deśo 'sti yo 'pi asya āsanatāṃ gacchet ǁ
Jr.81d.3 *evam-arcā-vidhim-abhidhāya,*
tat-saṅgatam-eva japa-sva-rūpaṃ nirṇayati
AG. *tato japaḥ prakartavyas-tri-lakṣa-ādi-vibhedataḥ* ǀ
3347 *uktaṃ śrī-yogasañcāre sa ca citra-sva-rūpakaḥ* ǁ **82** ǁ
Jr.82d.1 *tri-lakṣa-ādi vibhedavattve asya kiṃ pramāṇam-*
-ity-āśaṅkya uktam-uktaṃ śrī-yogasañcāre iti ǀ
tad-eva paṭhati sa ca citra-sva-rūpakaḥ ǁ 82 ǁ
Jr.82d.2 *citra-sva-rūpatvam-eva asya darśayati*
AG. *udaye saṅgame śāntau tri-lakṣo japa ucyate* ǀ
āsye gama-agame sūtre haṃsa-ākhye śaiva-yugmake ǁ **83** ǁ
pañca-lakṣā ime proktā daśa-aṃśaṃ homam-ācaret ǀ
netre gama-agame vaktre haṃse ca-eva-akṣa-sūtrake ǁ **84** ǁ
śiva-śakti-samāyoge ṣaḍ-lakṣo japa ucyate ǀ
netre gama-agame karṇe haṃse vaktre ca bhāmini ǁ **85** ǁ
3348 *haste ca yugmake ca-eva japaḥ sapta-vidhaḥ smṛtaḥ* ǀ

netre gama-agame karṇāv-āsyaṃ guhyaṃ ca guhya-
kam ||**86**||
śata-areṣu ca madhya-sthaṃ sahasra-areṣu bhāmini|
japa eṣa rudra-lakṣo homo 'py-atra daśa-aṃśataḥ || **87** ||
netre gama-agame karṇau mukhaṃ brahma-bila-antaraṃ|
stanau hastau ca pādau ca guhya-cakre dvir-abhy-
aset || **88**||

Jr.88d.1 *udaye iti prāṇa-śakty-udaya-sthāne janma-ādhāre*|
saṅgame iti nānā-nāḍi-saṃbheda-bhāji hṛdaye|
śāntāv-iti prāṇa-nirodhāya yugapad-gāḍha-avadhāna-
ātmake ity-arthaḥ|
gama-agame iti prāṇa-āpāna-pravāha-rūpe|
sūtre iti akṣa-nāḍī-cakra-sūtrāṇāṃ bhuvi|
haṃsa-ākhye iti ātma-avabhāsake hṛdaye|
3349 *yugmake iti śiva-śakti-samāyoga-ātmani*
janma-ādhāre, dvā-daśa-ante vā|
guhyaṃ janma-ādhāraḥ|
guhyakam-iti guhāyāṃ bhavaṃ guhyaṃ randhraṃ,
tena upalakṣitaṃ kaṃ ka-randhraṃ brahma-bilam-iti
yāvat|
śata-areṣv-iti sahasra-areṣv-iti
evam-ādikāsu asaṅkhyāsu bahvīṣu nāḍīṣu|
madhyaṃ sthānaṃ hṛdayaṃ nābhiś-ca-ity-arthaḥ|
atra-api homa iti api-śabdena sarvatra daśa-aṃśo homaḥ
kārya iti āveditaṃ|
guhya-cakre iti yoginī-vaktra-aja-vaktra-apara-paryāyau
janma-ādhāra-dvā-daśa-antau|
japa eṣa ṣoḍaśa-lakṣa iti prāg-rītyā kalpanīyam|
yata evam-ādiṣu sthāneṣu prāṇo dvir-bhramed-iti
sarva-śeṣaḥ || 88 ||

Jr.88d.2 *etat svayam-eva vyācaṣṭe*

AG. *yatra yatra gataṃ cakṣur-yatra yatra gataṃ manaḥ*|
haṃsas-tatra dvir-abhyasyo vikāsa-ākuñcana-ātma-
kaḥ || **89** ||

Jr.89d.1 *yatra yatra vaktra-ādau sthāne cakṣur-mano vā gataṃ,*
yatra-eva asāv-anusandhatte yogī;
tatra-eva haṃso hāna-

3350 *samādāna-dharmā prāṇo*
vikāsa-ākuñcana-ātmakatvāt dvir-abhyasyo
nirgama-praveśa-para eva-ity-arthaḥ।
tena asya evam-uktānām-āsya-ādīnām-apamārgāṇāṃ
nirodhe anusandhātavyaṃ
yena sarvato rūddhaḥ san
gaty-antara-abhāvān
-madhya-dhāma-eva asāv-anupraviśati-iti।
atra hi praviṣṭasya aikātmyena mantram-uccārayan-yogī
tāṃ tām-āsādayet siddhim।
yad-uktam-anyatra
Qt.89d.1 *japet-tu prāṇa-sāmyena tataḥ siddhy-araho bhavet*। *iti*।
Jr.89d.2 *etad-adhigamāya-eva ca ṣoḍaśa-lakṣo japaḥ kāryaḥ*
ity-evam-ādi uktam।
yat-tu lakṣāṇāṃ yathāyathaṃ nyūnatvam-uktaṃ,
tatra yoginām-anusandhāna-tāratamyaṃ nimittam ॥ 89 ॥
Jr.89d.3 *evam-apamārga-nirodhāt*
madhya-dhāmani eva prarohaṃ prāptaḥ prāṇaḥ
saṃvid-rūpa-udrekāt viśva-ātmakatām-eva yāyāt।
tad-āha
AG. *sa ātmā mātṛkā devī śivo deha-vyavasthitaḥ*।
Jr.90b.1 *sa deha-vyavasthito 'pi haṃsaḥ*
prāpta-mantra-devatā-aikātmyaḥ san
ātmā saṅkucita-aṇu-rūpaḥ।
Qt.90b.1 *śaktis-tu mātṛkā jñeyā sā ca jñeyā śiva-ātmikā*।
3351
Jr.90b.2 *ity-ādy-uktyā mātṛkā devī pārameśvarī śaktiḥ*
śivaś-ca nara-śakti-śiva-ātmatayā sa eva parisphured-ity-arthaḥ ॥
Jr.90b.3 *ata eva mantrasya prāpta-tad-aikātmyasya prāṇasya*
ātmanaś-ca mantrayitur-na na kaṃcid-api bhedam-
anusandadhyād-ity-āha
AG. *anyaḥ so 'nyo 'ham-ity-evaṃ vikalpaṃ na-ācared-yataḥ*॥ **90** ॥
yo vikalpayate tasya siddhi-muktī sudūrataḥ।
atha ṣoḍaśa-lakṣa-ādi-prāṇa-cāre purā-uktavat ॥ **91** ॥
Qt.91d.1 *pṛthaṅ-mantraḥ pṛthaṅ-mantrī na siddhyati kadācana*।

jñāna-mūlam-idaṃ sarvam-anyathā na-eva siddhyati ||
Jr.91d.1 *ity-anena-eva abhiprāyeṇa sarva-śāstreṣu*
Qt.91d.2 *............ekānte japam-ārabhet* ||
Jr.91d.2 *ity-ādi uktam* || 91 ||
Jr.91d.3 *mukhyayā vṛttyā hi vikalpa-vigama eva ekānta ucyate* |
tad-āha

3352
AG. *śuddha-aśuddha-vikalpānāṃ tyāga ekānta ucyate* |
tatra-sthaḥ svayam-eva-eṣa juhoti ca japaty-api || **92** ||
japaḥ sañjalpa-vṛttiś-ca nāda-āmarśa-sva-rūpiṇī |
tad-āmṛṣṭasya cid-vahnau layo homaḥ prakīrtitaḥ || **93** ||
āmarśaś-ca purā prokto devī-dvā-daśaka-ātmakaḥ |
dve antye saṃvidau tatra laya-rūpa-ahuti-kriyā || **94** ||
daśa-anyās-tad-upāyāya-ity-evaṃ home daśa-aṃśatām |
śrī-śambhunātha ādikṣan-trika-artha-ambhodhi-candr-amāḥ || **95** ||
Qt.95d.1 *sa-ca dvā-daśa-dhā tatra sarvam-antar-bhaved-yataḥ iti* |

3353
Jr.95d.1 *tatra-iti dvā-daśaka-madhyāt* |
dve antye saṃvidāv-iti para-pramātṛ-svātantrya-śakti-rūpe |
ete eva ca asmad-darśane
'sva-tantro bodhaḥ parama-arthaḥ'
ity-ādy-uktyā viśrānti-sthānam-ity
-evam-uktaṃ tad-upāyāya-iti
meya-māna-ādi-sopāna-krameṇa parapramātari viśrānter-uktatvāt |
etac-ca śākta-upāya-ahnika eva vibhajya uktam-iti
tata eva avadhāryam |
evam-atra homasya daśa-aṃśatāyām-ayam-abhiprāyaḥ
ity-asmad-guravaḥ || 95 ||
Jr.95d.2 *evaṃ japa-homa-paryantam-arcā-vidhim-abhidhāya*
dautaṃ vidhim-abhidhātum-upakramate
AG. *sākaṃ bāhya-sthayā śaktyā yadā tv-eṣa samarcayet* |
tadā-ayaṃ parameśa-ukto rahasyo bhaṇyate vidhiḥ || **96** ||
Qt.96d.1 *nitya-uditā parā śaktir-yady-apy-eṣā tathā-api-tu* |
bāhya-caryā-vihīnasya duṣprāpaḥ kauliko vidhih ||
Jr.96d.1 *ity-ādy-uktyā bāhya-caryayā tāvad-avaśya-bhāvyam* |

tatra-api-ca dūtīm-antareṇa na kācit-tat-sampattir
-ity-āha bāhya-sthayā śaktyā sākam-iti।
yad-uktaṃ
Qt.96d.2 *kartavyā sarvato dūtir-dūti-hīno na siddhi-bhāk*।
3354 *iti,*
Jr.96d.2 *tathā*
Qt.96d.3 *brāhmaṇasya yathā patnī tayā saha yajen-makhe*।
evaṃ dūtiḥ kula-ācārye jñeyā nitya-udite kule ॥
iti ॥ 96 ॥
Jr.96d.3 *nanu sarvatra aviśeṣeṇa-eva bhagavad-ārādhakasya*
Qt.96d.4 *adāmbhiko gurau bhakto brahmacārī jita-indriyaḥ*।
śiva-pūjā-paro maunī madya-māṃsa-parāṅ-mukhaḥ ॥
Jr.96d.4 *ity-ādi lakṣaṇam-uktam*।
tat-katham-iha bāhya-sthayā śaktyā saha samarcayed-ity-uktam-ity-āśaṅkāṃ parameśvara-uktyā-eva niravakāśayann -amuṣya vidheḥ pīṭhikā-bandhaṃ karoti
AG. *uktaṃ śrī-yogasañcāre brahmacarye sthitiṃ bhajet*।
Jr.97b.1 *nanu brahma-eva nāma kiṃ yadā-caraṇe 'pi sthitiṃ bhajed -ity-āśaṅkya āha*
AG. *ānando brahma paramaṃ tac-ca dehe tri-dhā sthitam* ॥ **97**॥
upakāri dvayaṃ tatra phalam-anyat-tad-ātmakam।
Qt.98b.1 *ānando brahmaṇo rūpaṃ* .... ।
3355 *iti*।
Jr.98b.1 *paramam-ity-anena asya avaśya-sevyatvam-uktam*।
tac-ca na kevalaṃ para-brahma-ādi-vibhedam-ātmani eva sthitaṃ,
yāvad-anātma-rūpe bāhya-śarīra-ādāv-api-ity-āha dehe iti।
tatra-iti trayāṇāṃ madhyāt।
dvayam-iti madya-māṃsa-lakṣaṇam।
anyad-iti maithunam।
madya-māṃsa-pāna-aśana-pravardhita-dhātur-hi ramamāṇa ānandam-iyād-ity-uktam-upakāri-iti phalam-iti ca।
ata eva tad-ātmakam-iti sarva-śeṣatvena uktam।
tac-chabdena ca atra ānanda-parāmarśaḥ ॥
Jr.98b.2 *evam-eṣāṃ brahma-mayatvād-etad-anuṣṭhātā brahmacārī-ity-ucyate ity-āha*

AG. *oṣṭhya-antya-tritayā-sevī brahmacārī sa ucyate* || **98** ||
Jr.98d.1 *oṣṭhyaḥ pa-vargaḥ,*
tasya antyo ma-kāras-tan-tritayaṃ madya-māṃsa-
maithuna-lakṣaṇam || 98 ||
Jr.98d.2 *nanu*
Qt.98d.1 *na māṃsa-bhakṣaṇe doṣo na madye naca maithune*|
pravṛttir-eṣā bhūtānāṃ nivṛttis-tu mahā-phalā ||
Jr.98d.3 *ity-ādy-uktyā māṃsa-ādi-nivṛttau śāstraṃ prayojakaṃ,*
na tat-pravṛttau tasyāḥ svā-rasikatvāt|
na-hi malinaḥ
3356 *snāyāt bubhukṣito 'śnīyād-ity-ādau kvacic-chāstram-*
upayuktam|
tat-kim-etad-uktam-ity-āśaṅkya āha
AG. *tad-varjitā ye paśava ānanda-parivarjitāḥ*|
ānanda-kṛt-tri-mā-āhārās-tad-varjaṃ cakra-yājakāḥ || **99**||
dvaye 'pi niraye yānti raurave bhīṣaṇe tv-iti|
Jr.100b.1 *iha ye kecana kula-prakriyām-anupraviṣṭā api*
tatra vihitam-api
etat lobhena vicikitsayā vā
cakra-yāga-ādau svasmai parasmai vā na dadati,
te paśava eva
yataḥ para-brahma-ātma-bhūtena tad-udbhūtena ānandena
parivarjitā deha-ādāv-eva gṛhīta-ātma-abhimānā ity-
arthaḥ|
tad-uktaṃ
Qt.100b.1 *kula-āmnāyeṣu ye saktā ebhir-dravyair-bahiṣ-kṛtāḥ*|
paśavas-te samuddiṣṭā na tais-tu saha vartanam ||
iti|
Jr.100b.2 *ye 'pi svayaṃ gardha-vaśād-ānanda-kṛtas-trīn mān-*
āharanti ma-kāra-trayam-upabhuñjate,
cakraṃ punar-lo-
3357 *-bha-ādinā tad-varjaṃ yajante;*
te 'pi paśava eva-iti prācyena sambandhaḥ|
tad-uktaṃ
Qt.100b.2 *vinā guruṃ vinā devaṃ mūḍhavat-parameśvari*|
madya-māṃsa-aśino nityaṃ paśavas-te na saṃśayaḥ || *iti*|
Jr.100b.3 *evaṃ dvaye 'pi te vihitasya akaraṇād-avihitasya ca karaṇād*

-bhīṣaṇe raurave narake yānti
tatra yātanā-sahasrāṇi anubhavanti-ity-arthaḥ |
evam-etat kula-mārga-anupraviṣṭena
sarvathā sva-ātma-ānanda-vyañjakatā-mātra-paratayā
sevyaṃ,
na-tu tad-gardhena |
tathātve hi asya laukikebhyaḥ ko viśeṣaḥ syāt |
yad-āhuḥ
Qt.100b.3 *brahmaṇya-ānanda-ākhyaṃ rūpam-ato yat-samāśraya-vaśena* |
labhyata eva tad-akhilaṃ samāhared-viṣaya-gardha-nirmuktaḥ ||
kāmān-mohād-viṣayād-vyatirikta-bhāva-saṃrūḍhāt |
prasaraty-ānando yaḥ so 'pi paśūnām-api-iha sa-ādhāraḥ ||
cin-mātra-ātma-paratve saṃvitter-vyañjako hi yo viṣayaḥ |
yogy-ātmanā vibhāti ca bhoktuḥ sva-ātmany-abhedataḥ satatam |
uktaḥ sa eva viṣayo bhinnaś-ca-abheditāṃ samāyātaḥ | *iti,*
Qt.100b.4 *aparicyuta-sva-rūpair-apṛthag-bhūtā-api viṣaya-saṃvittiḥ* |
bhujyata eva ta ete vīra-vratino mahā-krama-ārūḍhāḥ |
lakṣa-stho niyama-rato brahmacarya-śānta-manāḥ |
saṅghaṭṭe 'pi ca rūḍho mahā-manasvī suśānta-vapuḥ ||
3358 *atimārga-vinaya-kathitaiḥ samaya-adharmaiś-ca saṃgraho yasya* |
yo 'pi mahā-saṃbuddhaḥ saṃvin-maya eva sarvadā sva-sthaḥ ||
sva-ātma-anubhūti-siddhyai viṣaya-sparśī na laulya-bhāvanayā |
paśu-bhāvanā-vimuktaḥ sa hy-abhiyukto mahā-mārge ||
yaḥ sa-avadhāna-vṛttiḥ sva-ātmani madhye 'pi lokayātrāyām |
vāma-ācāra-vidhāv-api bhavaty-asau pālane sadā-askhalitaḥ ||
yaś-carama-dhātu-sarge samaya-lavasya-antare sva-saṃvṛttyā |
sarvāsāṃ vṛttīnāṃ pratyasta-manāś-cetaso jhaṭiti ||
ānanda-saṃvid-udayo rūpaṃ tad-brahmaṇaḥ

samākhyātam|
iti ca|
Jr.100b.4 nanu atra madya-māṃsa-āsevanaṃ sukaram-iti āstām-etat|
itarat tu amartyānām-api duṣkaraṃ
kiṃ punar-daurbhāgya-bhājāṃ martyānām|
tasmāt
Qt.100b.5 tatas-tatra-ānayed-dūtīṃ mada-ghūrṇita-locanām|
bimba-oṣṭhīṃ cāru-daśanāṃ sabhrū-bhaṅga-ānanāṃ śubhām ||
trasta-bāla-mṛga-ābhāsa-nayanāṃ cāru-hāsinīm|
sphurad-bhramara-saṅghāta-nibha-sat-keśa-pāśikām ||
kāma-kārmuka-saṅkāśa-bhrū-bhaṅga-tarala-īkṣaṇām|
dravac-cāmīkara-ākāra-savarṇāṃ nistaraṅgiṇīm ||
karṇa-ābharaṇa-sac-citra-śobhā-śata-suśobhanām|
sat-kambu-nibha-sat-kaṇṭha-vara-bhūṣaṇa-bhūṣitām ||
gaja-kumbha-nibha-uddāma-stana-bhāra-avanāmitām|
suvṛtta-upacita-ākāra-bāhu-kandali-māṇḍitām
3359 sat-pañca-phaṇa-saṅkāśa-kara-śākhā-virājitām|
sphurad-ratna-śikhā-citraka-ūrmikā-aṅguli-śobhitām ||
pūrṇa-indu-vara-lāvaṇya-vadanāṃ citta-hāriṇīm|
hari-heti-mahā-siṃha-pipīla-vara-madhya-gām|
trivali-śreṇi-sad-bimba-jaghana-alasa-gāminīm|
rambhā-kari-kara-ākāra-vara-uru-vara-jaṅghikām|
sat-kāma-ratha-cakra-ābha-gulpha-pāda-suśobhanām ||
pralamba-homa-ābha-raṇa-hāra-āvali-virājitām|
sphuran-mañjīra-jhāṅkāra-raśanā-mukhara-svanām ||
pārihārya-jhaṇatkāra-valaya-dhvāna-mantharām|
matta-nāgendra-saṅkāśa-gatiṃ gambhīra-nābhikām ||
haṃsa-gadgada-vāg-vaṃśa-sadṛśāṃ śubha-bhāṣiṇīm|
keyūra-sūtrika-āmodi-puṣpa-sragdāma-bhūṣitām ||
mahā-pañca-phaṇa-apīḍa-tāmbūla-vara-lālasām|
nṛtta-gīta-sa-sīt-kāra-līlā-kuṭṭamita-āvṛtā ṃ||
nistaraṅgāṃ savarṇāṃ ca devy-ekā-arpita-mānasām|
lobha-moha-parikṣīṇa-cetasaṃ cit-sva-bhāvikām ||
bhairava-eka-camat-kāra-carvaṇa-eka-sva-rūpiṇīm|
sā dūtir-mohanī mudrā jagaty-asmiṃś-carācare ||
Jr.100b.5 iti śrī-tantrarājabhaṭṭārake

Qt.100b.6 *subhagā satya-śīlā ca daiśika-ājñā-anuvartinī*।
priya-vādinī sukha-rūpā sāttvikā saṅga-varjitā ॥
bhairava-ācāra-sampannā amṛtānāṃ ca saspṛhā।
sadā-eva-advaita-niratā abhyāsa-sthā dṛḍha-vratā ॥
3360 *putravat-paśyate sarvān-na jugupset-prasanna-dhīḥ*।
sadā-ācāra-kula-utpannā aprasūtā sukeśinī ॥
madyaka-amatta-mṛdv-aṅgī śukra-āḍhyā cāru-hāsinī।
susnigdhā ca vinītā ca sadā-atithy-asu-bhāvitā ॥
mantra-arpita-sva-rūpā ca nirmalā nirahaṅkṛtiḥ।
pāramparya-krama-sthā tu loka-ācāra-anuvartinī ॥
nitye naimittike ca-eva krama-parvasu vārtinī।
kāma-tantra-kriyā-niṣṭhā jānānā deva-tarpaṇam ॥
san-tuṣṭā sarva-bhāveṣu .... ।
Jr.100b.6 *iti śrī-triśirobhairave ca*
prokta-lakṣaṇā bāhyā śaktir-aprāpyā-eva।
nahi evaṃ-vidhāḥ sarve guṇā
ekatra saṅghaṭamānāḥ kvacit kadācit dṛṣṭāḥ।
yad-āhuḥ
Qt.100b.7 .... *kva nu punaḥ sarvatra sarve guṇāḥ*। *iti*।
Jr.100b.7 *an-evaṃ-vidhā ca dūtiḥ pariharaṇīyā*।
yad-uktam
Qt.100b.8 *adūtiko varaṃ yāgo natu durdūti-dūṣitaḥ*। *iti*।
Jr.100b.8 *naca atra viṣa-bhakṣaṇa-vākyavad-adūtikatve tātparyam*।
tad-adūtiko yāgo na-kāryaḥ,
dūtiś-ca evaṃ-vidhā na prāpyā
-ity-aśakya-anuṣṭhānam-etad
-ity-āśaṅkya āha
AG. *śakter-lakṣaṇam-etāvat-tadvato hy-avibheditā* ॥ **100** ॥
3361 *tādṛśīṃ tena tāṃ kuryān-natu varṇā-ādy-apekṣaṇam*।
Jr.101b.1 *hīnāyā api śakter-anekā siddhiḥ syāt*।
tad-uktaṃ
Qt.101b.1 *yadi lakṣaṇa-hīnā syāt dūtī vai sādhaka-ātmanām*।
vīra-eka-cittā niṣkampā sarva-karmasu gamyate ॥ *iti*।
Jr.101b.2 *varṇā mātaṅga-ādyāḥ*।
ādi-śabdāt vayaḥ-prabhṛti lakṣaṇa-jātam।
śakter-lakṣaṇam-etat --- [13] *tadvad-abhedaḥ*।

13. It would seem that a section of text is missing here.

tato 'napekṣyaṃ vayo-jāty-ādi|
ata eva tat-tādātmyam-eva avalambya
asyāḥ sarvatra tat-tad-bheda-bhinnatvam-uktam ||

Jr.101b.3 *tad-āha*

AG. *laukika-alaukika-dvaya-ātma-saṅgāt-tādātmyato*
'dhikāt || **101** ||
kārya-hetu-saha-utthā sā tri-dhā-uktā śāsane guroḥ|
sākṣāt-paramparā-yogāt-tat-tulyā-iti tri-dhā punaḥ || **102** ||

3362

Jr.102d.1 *iha khalu guroḥ śāsane asmad-darśane*
sā evaṃ-vidhā śaktir-janyā janikā saha-jā ca
-iti mukhyayā vṛttyā tri-vidhā uktā
yato 'tra asyā laukikāt yaunād-alaukikāt jñānīyāc-ca
sambandhād-adhikaṃ tādātmyam|
anyatra hi jñānīya eva saṅga iti
tatra tathā na tādātmyam-iti|
evaṃ-ca asyāḥ śakteḥ sākṣāt pāramparyeṇa vā dvaidhe
ṣaḍ-vidhatvam| *tad-uktaṃ*

Qt.102d.1 *kārya-hetu-saha-utthatvāt-traidhaṃ sākṣād-atha-any-*
athā| *iti*|

Jr.102d.2 *pāramparya-yogo*
yathā kāryāyā api kāryā hetor-api hetuḥ saha-utthāyā api
kāryā ca-iti|
ata eva atra āsāṃ tat-tulyatvam-uktaṃ|

Jr.102d.3 *nanu*

Qt.102d.2 *sva-patnī bhaginī mātā duhitā vā śubhā sakhī*|

Jr.102d.4 *ity-ādy-uktyā sva-patny-api atra kasmāt na parigaṇitā*
yat tatra-api asti laukika-alaukikatayā dvy-ātma-saṅgaḥ|
tat katham-iha asyāḥ ṣaḍ-vidhatvam-eva uktaṃ|
satyaṃ,
kin-tu atra laukikavat riraṃsayā na pravṛttiḥ,
api-tu vakṣyamāṇa-dṛśā
anavacchinna-para-saṃvit-sva-rūpa-āveśa-samutkatayā
-ity-evaṃ-param-

3363 *eta-d-uktam*|
sva-patnyāṃ hi riraṃsā-sambhāvanāyā api avakāśaḥ syāt|
yad-uktaṃ

Qt.102d.3 *dūtīṃ kuryāt-tu kārya-arthī na punaḥ kāma-mohitaḥ*।
iti,

Qt.102d.4 *sthity-arthaṃ ramayet-kāntāṃ na laulyena kadācana* ॥
iti,

Qt.102d.5 *śiva-śakty-ātmakaṃ rūpaṃ bhāvayec-ca parasparam*।
na kuryān-mānavīṃ buddhiṃ rāga-moha-ādi-saṃyutām ॥
jñāna-bhāvanayā sarvaṃ kartavyaṃ sādhaka-uttamaiḥ।
iti ca।

Jr.102d.5 *atra-eva śāstra-antara-virodho 'pi parihṛtaḥ*।
tatra-api hi riraṃsā-parihāreṇa kārya-arthitayā evam-āmnātam।
yat-smṛtiḥ

Qt.102d.6 *ghṛtena-abhyajya gātrāṇi tailena-api ghṛtena vā*।
mukhān-mukhaṃ pariharan gātrair-gātrāṇy-asaṃspṛśan ॥
kule tad-avaśeṣe ca santāna-arthaṃ na kāmataḥ।
niyukto gurubhir-gacched-bhrātur-bhāryāṃ yavīyasaḥ ॥ *iti*।

Jr.102d.6 *evaṃ-ca atra nirvikalpa-vṛttīnāṃ mahā-ātmanāṃ jñāninām-eva adhikāro,*
yeṣāṃ sva-vṛtti-pratikṣepeṇa

3364 *saṃvid-advaite eva kim-ekāgrī-bhūtaṃ ceto na vā-iti*
pratyavekṣā-mātre eva anusandhānam।
yad-abhiprāyeṇa-eva

Qt.102d.7 *na caryā bhogataḥ proktā khyātā kāma-surūpiṇī*।
sva-citta-pratyavekṣātaḥ sthiraṃ kiṃ vā calaṃ manaḥ ॥

Jr.102d.7 *ity-ādi uktam* ॥ 102 ॥

Jr.102d.8 *naca etad-asmad-upajñam-eva-ity-āha*

AG. *śrī-sarvācārahṛdaye tad-etad-upasaṃhṛtam*।
ṣaḍ-etāḥ śaktayaḥ proktā bhukti-mukti-phala-pradāḥ ॥ **103**॥

Qt.103d.1 *vegavaty-atha saṃhārī trailokyakṣobhaṇī tathā*।
ardhavīrāsanā ca-eva vaktrakaulā tu pañcamī ॥

Jr.103d.1 *ity-ādi tu avāntara-bheda-prāyaṃ pratyekaṃ sambhavad api ānantyād-iha na pariganitam* ॥ 103 ॥

Jr.103d.2 *nanu etad-āstām,*
'bāhya-sthayā śaktyā sākaṃ samarcayet' ity-eva kasmād-uktam-ity-āśaṅkya āha

AG. *dvābhayāṃ tu sṛṣṭi-saṃhārau tasmān-melakam-uttamam*।

3365

Jr.104b.1 *dvābhyāṃ śakti-śaktimadbhyāṃ hetu-bhūtābhyāṃ*
hi saṅghaṭṭa-velāyāṃ paraspara-aunmukhyena
mukhyena sva-sva-rūpa-viśrāṇtyā
sṛṣṭi-saṃhārau |
tasmād-ubhaya-mayī sthitis
-tad-ullāsas-tu
turya-aṃśo iti evaṃ tat-sva-rasata eva yad-udeti,
tata idaṃ melakam-uttamaṃ
para-pada-āpatti-dāyitvāt tādātmya-karam-ity-arthaḥ ||

Jr.104b.2 *kathaṃ ca etat kāryam-ity-āha*

AG. *tām-āhṛtya mitho 'bhyarcya tarpayitvā parasparam* || **104** ||
antar-aṅga-krameṇa-eva mukhya-cakrasya pūjanam |

Jr.105b.1 *abhyarcya-iti arthāt śakti-śaktimat-pade* |
pūjanam-iti arthāt kāryam ||

Jr.105b.2 *nanu ko 'sāv-āntaraḥ kramaḥ,*
kiṃ-ca tat mukhyaṃ cakram-ity-āśaṅkya āha

AG. *yad-eva-ānanda-sandohi saṃvido hy-antar-aṅgakam* || **105** ||

3366 *tat-pradhānaṃ bhavec-cakram-anucakram-ato 'param* |

Jr.106b.1 *ato 'param-iti tathā na ānanda-sandohi-ity-arthaḥ* ||

Jr.106b.2 *cakra-śabdasya ca pravṛttau kiṃ nimittam-ity-āśaṅkya āha*

AG. *vikāsāt-tṛptitaḥ pāśa-utkartanāt-kṛti-śaktitaḥ* || **106** ||
cakraṃ kaseś-cakeḥ kṛtyā [14] *karoteś-ca kila-uditam* |

Jr.107b.1 *kasī vikāse,*
caka tṛptau,
kṛtī cchedane,
ḍukṛñ [15] *karaṇe,*
—iti dhātu-catuṣṭaya-artha-anvayād-atra cakra-śabdaḥ |
tena vikasati, cakati, kṛntati, karoti-iti cakram ||

Jr.107b.2 *nanu*

Qt.107b.1 *ānanda-jananaṃ pūjā-yogyaṃ hṛdaya-hāri yat* |

Jr.107b.3 *ity-ādi-nītyā pūjā-upayogino dravya-jātasya*
ānanda-sandohitvaṃ lakṣaṇaṃ sarvatra uktam | *iha*

3367 *punar-mukhya-cakra-ādeḥ pūjyasya-eva kathaṃ tad-ucyate*

---

14. For *kṛtyā* read *kṛtyāḥ*.
15. For *ḍukṛñ*, read *dukṛñ*. Pandey, p.525.

ity-āśaṅkya āha

AG. *yāgaś-ca tarpaṇaṃ bāhye vikāsas-tac-ca kīrtyate* || **107** ||

Jr.107d.1 *bahir-api yāgo nāma tarpaṇam-ucyate*|
tac-ca cito nairākāṅkṣya-utpādāt vikāsaḥ samucchalad-rūpatvam-ity-arthaḥ || 107 ||

Jr.107d.2 *nanu bahis-tarpaṇam-eva kutaḥ syād-*
-yato 'pi cito vikāsaḥ samudiyād-ity-āsaṅkya āha

AG. *cakra-anucakra-antara-gāc-chaktimat-parikalpitāt*|
prāṇa-gād-apy-atha-ānanda-syandino 'bhyavahār-ataḥ || **108** ||
gandha-dhūpa-sraga-ādeś-ca bāhyād-ucchalanaṃ citaḥ|

Jr.109b.1 *tena śaktimat-parikalpitāt*

Qt.109b.1 *tena nirbharam-ātmānaṃ bahiś-cakra-anucakra-gam*|
vipruḍbhir-ūrdhva-adharayor-antaḥ prītyā [16] *ca tarpayet* ||

3368

Jr.109b.2 *ity-ādi-nītyā cakra-anucakra-antaragāt-pāna-ādy-ātmanaḥ*

Qt.109b.2 *śūnya-udbhavo bhaved-vāyur-meḍhrasya-utthāpanaṃ bhavet*|
vāyu-meḍhra-samāyogāt .... ||

Jr.109b.3 *ity-ādi-dṛśā prāṇa-gāt tat-preraṇa-ātmano*
gandha-dhūpa-sraga-āder-bāhyāt ca
ānanda-syandino 'bhyavahārāt
cita ucchalanaṃ vikāsaḥ syād ity arthaḥ ||

Jr.109b.4 *evaṃ mukhya-cakra-ekātmyam-āptum*
-anucakreṣu tarpaṇaṃ kāryam-ity-āha

AG. *itthaṃ sva-ucita-vastv-aṃśair-anucakreṣu tarpaṇam* || **109** ||
kurvīyātām-iha-anyonyaṃ mukhya-cakra-ekatā-kṛte|

Jr.110b.1 *sva-ucitaṃ vastu rūpa-ādy-anyatamam,*
anucakreṣv-iti cakṣur-ādi-indriya-rūpeṣu;
athaca sva-ucitaṃ vastu āliṅgana-paricumbana-ādi|
tad-uktaṃ

Qt.110b.1 *kiṃ pūjyaṃ pūjakaḥ ko 'sāv-āhvānaṃ kīdṛśaṃ bhavet*|
kiṃ puṣpaṃ dhūpa-carukaṃ ko mantro japa eva ca ||

---

16. This is a quotation of *TĀ* 29.23 which for *prītyā*, 'joyfully', reads *pītyā*.

kim kuṇḍaṃ bhavati hy-agniḥ kāṣṭhaṃ kiṃ ca-ājyam-eva vā I
kaḥ samādhiḥ mahā-īśāna iti brūhi tri-locana II

3369
Jr.110b.2 *iti upakramya*
Qt.110b.2 *yoṣitaś ca-eva pūjyante puruṣaś-ca-eva pūjakaḥ* I
āhvānaṃ tu tayoḥ prītiḥ puṣpaṃ ca kara-ja-kṣatam II
dhūpam-āliṅganaṃ proktaṃ caru tanu-kṛtaṃ bhavet I
mantraḥ priyāyā vāg-jālaṃ japaś-ca-apy-adhara-amṛtam II
bhagaṃ kuṇḍaṃ sruvaṃ liṅgam-agniś-ca-eva bhaga-aṅkuraḥ I
ājyaṃ ca bhajate bījam-ity-uktaṃ bhairava-āgame II
śabdaḥ sparśaś-ca rūpaṃ ca raso gandhaś-ca pañcamaḥ I
utkṣepa-ānanda-kāle tu pañca-dhā vastu-santatiḥ II
sa samādhiḥ mahā-īśāni jñātvā śivam-avāpnuyāt I *iti* II

Jr.110b.3 *nanu anucakra-tarpaṇāt kathaṃ mukhya-cakra-ekātmyaṃ syād-ity-āśaṅkāṃ garbhī-kṛtya āgamam-eva atra saṃvādayati*

AG. *uktaṃ ca triśirastantre vimala-āsana-gocaraḥ* II **110** II
akṣa-ṣaṭkasya madhye tu rudra-sthānaṃ samāviśet I

Jr.111b.1 *iha anucakra-ātmanāṃ nikhilānāṃ cakrāṇāṃ madhye tat-saṃkṣobhe yathā-ucitam-artha-jātam-āharann-api vimalaṃ*
3370 *tad-āsaṅga-abhāvāt vaivaśya-kalaṃka-unmuktaṃ yad-āsanam-avasthāna*[17] *tan-niṣṭhaḥ san sva-sva-rūpa-viśrāntyā tat-kṣobha-upasaṃhārāt rudra-sthānaṃ samāviśet mukhya-cakra-ātmaka-parapramātṛ-daśā-āveśa-bhāg-bhaved-ity-arthaḥ* II

Jr.111b.2 *etad-eva prapañcayati*

AG. *nija-nija-bhoga-ābhoga-pravikāsi-nija-sva-rūpa-parim-arśe* II **111** II
kramaśo 'nucakra-devyaḥ saṃvic-cakraṃ hi madhyamaṃ yānti I

17. For *avasthāna* read *avasthānaṃ*.

Jr.112b.1 *yat nija-nijena rūpa-ādy-anyatama-ālocana-ātmanā bhoga-ābhogena bahir-ucchalad-rūpatayā*
pravikāsana-śīlasya nijasya pramātṛ-rūpasya sva-rūpasya parimarśe
sva-ātma-camat-kāra-ullāse sati
yathāyathaṃ dṛg-ādy-anucakra-devyo
madhyamaṃ
sarva-saṃvid-viśrānti-sthānatayā mukhyaṃ
parama-ānanda-maya-pramātṛ-satattvaṃ
saṃvic-cakraṃ-yānti
tatra-eva viśrāntim-āsādayanti-ity-arthaḥ ||

Jr.112b.2 *nanu evaṃ tat-tad-artha-grahaṇa-kāle*
sarveṣām-aviśeṣe-
3371 *-ṇa-eva*
mukhya-cakra-ekātmyaṃ setsyati-iti
kim-etad-upadeśena-ity-āśaṅkya āha

AG. *sva-stha-tanor-aparasya tu tā deha-adhiṣṭhitaṃ vihāya yataḥ* || **112** ||
āsata iti tad-ahaṃyur-no pūrṇo na-api ca-ucchalati|

Jr.113b.1 *tad-itarasya punaḥ sva-stha-tanor*
-evaṃ-parāmarśa-śūnyatayā taṭastha-prāyatā
dṛg-ādy-anucakra-devyo
yato deha-adhiṣṭhitaṃ vihāya āsate
tatra udāsīnatvam-ālambante,
tatas-tatra dehe eva ahaṃyur-gṛhīta-abhimāno no pūrṇaḥ
sarva-ākāṅkṣā-saṃkṣayād-uparata-indriya-vṛttiḥ,
na-api ca ucchalati
sa-ākāṅkṣatve 'pi
dṛg-ādī-indriya-vṛtty-audāsīnyāt bahir-unmukhyo na bhaved-
-ubhaya-bhraṣṭa eva asāv-ity-arthaḥ ||

Jr.113b.2 *nanu evam-anucakra-devīnāṃ mukhya-cakra-viśrāntyā*
anayoḥ kiṃ syād-ity-āśaṅkya āha

AG. *anucakra-devatā-ātmaka-marīci-paripūraṇa-adhigata-vīryam* || **113** ||
3372 *tac-chakti-śaktimad-yugam-anyonya-samunmukhaṃ bhavati*|

Jr.114b.1 *dṛg-ādi-devī-rūpābhir-marīcibhiḥ*
Qt.114b.1 *yena yena-akṣa-mārgeṇa yo yo 'rthaḥ pratibhāsate*।
sva-avaṣṭambha-balād-yogī tad-gatas-tan-mayo bhavet ॥
Jr.114b.2 *ity-ādi-nītyā yat paripūraṇaṃ,*
tena labdha-nija-avaṣṭambhaṃ sat
tad-evam-ukta-rūpaṃ śakti-śaktimad-yugalam-
-anyonya-saṃmukhaṃ bhavati
saṅghaṭṭam-āsādayed-ity-arthaḥ ॥
Jr.114b.3 *nanu evam-api asya kiṃ syād-ity-āśaṅkya āha*
AG. *tad-yugalam-ūrdhva-dhāma-praveśa*
-saṃsparśa-jāta-saṅkṣobham ॥ **114** ॥
kṣubhnāty-anucakrāṇy-api tāni tadā tan-mayāni -na pṛth-
ak tu।
Jr.115b.1 *saṃghaṭṭa-velāyāṃ*
hi ūrdhva-dhāmani para-ānanda-maye
yoginī-vaktra-ātmani mukhya-cakre
samāveśa-tāratamyāt jātaḥ
samyak deha-ādy-abhimāna-nyag-bhāvena kṣobhaḥ
pūrṇatā-lakṣaṇaḥ sva-ātma-camat-kāra-atiśayo yasya,
evaṃ-vidhaṃ tat śakti-śaktimal-lakṣaṇaṃ yugala-
3373 *-m-*
-anucakrāṇy-api kṣubhnāti
tad-eka-mayatayā-eva parāmṛśed-ity-arthaḥ ॥
Jr.115b.2 *nanu deha-ādy-abhimāna-nyag-bhāvena tatra samāviṣṭasya*
ka iva anucakra-arthaḥ
ity-āśaṅkya uktaṃ tāni tadā tan-mayāni na pṛthak tu iti।
athaca atra paraspara-āhanana-āliṅgana-paricumbana-ādi
-lakṣaṇaḥ kṣobhaḥ ॥
Jr.115b.3 *evam-atra parasyā eva saṃvidaḥ samudayaḥ syād-ity-*
āśaṅkya āha
AG. *itthaṃ yāmalam-etad-galita-bhidā-saṃkathaṃ yad-*
eva syāt ॥ **115** ॥
krama-tāratamya-yogāt-sā-eva hi saṃvid-visarga-
saṅghaṭṭaḥ।
tad-dhruva-dhāmā-anuttaram-ubhaya-ātmaka-jagad-
udāra-
-sa-ānandam ॥ **116** ॥

no śāntaṃ na-apy-uditaṃ śānta-udita-sūti-kāraṇaṃ paraṃ kaulam |

Jr.117b.1 *visarga-saṃghaṭṭa iti saṅghaṭṭa-rūpo visarga*

3374 *ity-arthaḥ* |

ubhaya-ātmaka-iti śiva-śakti-sāmarasya-maya-jagad-ānanda-rūpam -ity-arthaḥ |

śāntam-iti viśva-uttīrṇam |

uditam-iti viśva-mayam |

paraṃ kaulam-iti śānta-udita-ādi-śabda-vyapadeśyatva-ayogād

-atīva rahasya-rūpam-ity-arthaḥ |

athaca kṣepasya asampatter-na śāntaṃ

sva-sva-rūpa-viśrāntyā ca na uditaṃ,

kintu etad-avasthā-dvaya-hetu-bhūtam-

-anavacchinna-saṃvin-mātra-satattvam-ity-arthaḥ ||

Jr.117b.2 *etad-āveśe ca avaśyam-avadhātavyam-ity-āha*

AG. *anavacchinna-pada-īpsus*

-tāṃ saṃvidam-ātma-sāt-sadā kuryāt || **117** ||

anavacchinnaṃ parama-arthato hi rūpaṃ cito devyāḥ |

Jr.118b.1 *kathaṃ-ca atra āveśaḥ siddhyed-ity-āśaṅkya āha*

AG. *īdṛk-tādṛk-prāya-praśama-udaya-bhāva-vilaya-pari kathayā* || **118** ||

anavacchinnaṃ dhāma praviśed-vaisargikaṃ subhagaḥ |

3375

Jr.119b.1 *īdṛk-tādṛk-prāyayoḥ*

sva-anubhava-mātra-eka-rūpatvāt tathā vyapadeṣṭum-aśakyayoḥ

praśama-udayayoḥ śānta-uditayoḥ rūpayor

-yau bhāva-vilayāv-utpatty-anutpattī,

tatra

Qt.119b.1 *bhāve tyakte niruddhā cin-na-eva bhāva-antaraṃ vrajet* |

tadā tan-madhya-bhāvena vikasaty-ati-bhāvanā ||

Jr.119b.2 *iti bhaṅgyā paritaḥ samantād-āmarśanena*

vaisargikam-anavacchinnaṃ dhāma subhagaḥ praviśet

pūrṇa-para-saṃvid-ātma-saṃvit-sākṣāt-kāro 'sya siddhyed

-ity-arthaḥ ||

Jr.119b.3 *nanu bhavatu evaṃ,*

śānta-uditayos-tu rūpayor-udaya eva kathaṃ bhavet;
kiṃ śakti-gatatvena-eva,
kim-uta śaktimad-gatatvena-eva-ity-āśaṅkya āha
AG. *śānta-udita-ātmakaṃ dvayam-atha*
yugapad-udeti śakti-śaktimatoḥ ॥ **119** ॥
Jr.119d.1 *atha-śabdaḥ prativacane* ॥ 119 ॥
Jr.119d.2 *iyān-punar-atra viśeṣa ity-āha*
AG. *rūpam-uditaṃ paraspara-dhāma-gataṃ śāntam-ātma-*
gatam-eva ॥
Jr.120b.1 *uditaṃ hi rūpaṃ*
śakti-śaktimator-anyonyam-au-
3376 *-nmukhya-anativṛtteḥ*
sva-sva-mukhya-cakra-ākhya-dhāma-aikya-kroḍī-karaṇena
parisphuret ।
śāntaṃ punar-ātma-gatam-eva,
tathātve hi sva-ātmany-eva paraṃ viśrāntir-udiyāt ॥
Jr.120b.2 *nanu evaṃ śakti-śaktimator-uktam-aikātmyaṃ kiṃ na hīyeta*
-ity-āśaṅkya āha
AG. *ubhayam-api vastutaḥ kila yāmalam-iti tathā-uditaṃ*
śāntam ॥ **120** ॥
Jr.120d.1 *vastuto hi aparityakta-aikātmyam-api*
idaṃ śakti-śaktimal-lakṣaṇam-ubhayaṃ śāntatāyām-ātmani
viśrāmyet,
natu parasparasya bheda-abhisandhānena-iti ।
tathā ātma-gatatvena śāntaṃ rūpam-uditam-uktam-ity-
arthaḥ ॥ 120 ॥
Jr.120d.2 *evam-api anayor-ayaṃ viśeṣa ity-āha*
AG. *śaktis-tadvad-ucitāṃ sṛṣṭiṃ puṣṇāti no tadvān* ।
śānta-udita-ātmaka-ubhaya-rūpa-parāmarśa-sāmya-yoge
'pi ॥ **121** ॥
Jr.121d.1 *śānta-udita-ātmano rūpa-dvayasya ya evaṃ parā-*
3377 *-marśaḥ,*
tatra sāmya-yoge 'pi
śaktir-eva punas-tadvad-ucitāṃ śaktimad-ānuguṇyena
ullasitāṃ sṛṣṭiṃ puṣṇāti garbhaṃ janayet,
na śaktimān-iti tato 'syā viśeṣa ity-arthaḥ ॥ 121 ॥
Jr.121d.2 *tataś-ca garbha-dhāraṇād-eva*

asyāḥ sarvatra śāstre pravikas-vara-madhya-dhāmatvam-uktam-ity-āha

AG. *pravikas-vara-madhya-padā śaktiḥ śāstre tataḥ kathitā* |

Jr.122b.1 *yad-abhiprāyeṇa-eva*

Qt.122b.1 *tiṣṭhet-saṃvatsaraṃ pūrṇaṃ sādhako niyata-vrataḥ* |
siddhir-bhavati yā tasya sā dina-ekena yoṣitām ||

Jr.122b.2 *ity-ādi anyatra uktam* ||

Jr.122b.3 *ataś-ca iyam-eva jñāna-saṅkramaṇe yogyā-ity-āḥa*

AG. *tasyām-eva kula-arthaṃ samyak saṃcārayed-gurus-tena* || **122** ||
tad-dvāreṇa ca kathita-krameṇa saṃcārayeta nṛṣu |

Jr.123b.1 *tena-iti pravikas-vara-madhyatvena hetunā-ity-arthaḥ* |

3378 *tad-dvāreṇa-iti śakti-mukhena* |
nṛṇāṃ hi madhya-pada-pravikāso na-asti-ity-āśayaḥ |
yad-abhiprāyeṇa-eva

Qt.123b.1 *strī-mukhe nikṣipet-prājñaḥ strī-mukhād-grāhayet-priye* | *iti*

Qt.123b.2 *strī-mukhāc-ca bhavet-siddhiḥ susiddhaṃ tāsu tat-padam* |

Jr.123b.2 *iti ca uktam* ||

Jr.123b.3 *etac-ca gurubhir-api uktam-ity-āha*

AG. *sva-śarīra-adhika-sad-bhāva-bhāvitām-iti tataḥ prāha* || **123** ||
śrīmat-kallaṭa-nāthaḥ prokta-samasta-artha-labdhaye vākyam |

Jr.124b.1 *śrī-kallaṭanātho hi*
samanantaram-eva proktaṃ
śakti-lakṣaṇāt-prabhṛti samastam-arthaṃ saṃgrahītuṃ
sva-śarīrād-api
svā-rasika-madhya-dhāma-pravikas-varatayā adhikena,
ata eva satā bhāvena
bhāvitāṃ saṃskṛtāṃ śaktiṃ guruḥ kuryād-iti
vākyaṃ prāha-iti vākya-arthaḥ ||

Jr.124b.2 *evam-etat prasaṅgād-abhidhāya prakṛtam-eva āha*

AG. *tan-mukhya-cakram-uktaṃ maheśinā yoginī-vaktram* || **124** ||

3379 *tatra-eṣa sampradāyas-tasmāt-saṃprāpyate jñānam* |

Jr.125b.1 *tat uktena prakāreṇa*
bhagavatā maheśvareṇa
picu-vaktra-ādy-apara-paryāyaṃ

yoginī-vaktram-eva mukhya-cakram-uktam।
tatra-eva eṣa ukto vakṣyamāṇo vā sampradāyo 'nuṣṭheyo
yatas-tasmāt jñānaṃ saṃprāpyate
para-saṃvit-samāveśo 'sya jāyate ity-arthaḥ ॥

Jr.125b.2 *nanu ataḥ kīdṛk jñānam-āpyate ity-ucyatām-ity-āśaṅkya āha*

AG. *tad-idam-alekhyaṃ bhaṇitaṃ*
vaktrād-vaktra-stham-ukta-yuktyā ca ॥ **125** ॥
vaktraṃ pradhāna-cakraṃ svā saṃvil-likhyatāṃ ca katham।

Jr.126b.1 *alekhyam-iti vikalpayitum-aśakyam-ity-arthaḥ* ॥

Jr.126b.2 *nanu etat vaktrād-vaktra-sthaṃ,*
tat katham-alekhyam-ity-uktam-ity-āśaṅkya āha ukta-ity-ādi।
vaktra ca

Qt.126b.1 *vaktraṃ hi nāma tat-mukhyaṃ vaktram-uktaṃ maheśinā*।
yoginī-vaktraṃ .... ॥

3380

Jr.126b.3 *ity-ādy-ukta-yuktyā pradhāna-cakram-ucyate*
iti tad-ubhaya-saṃghaṭṭe jāyamānā
svā anubhūti-mātra-sva-bhāvā saṃvit
kathaṃ likhyatām-iti ॥

Jr.126b.4 *katham-etad-uktam-ity-āśaṅkya āha*

AG. *atha sṛṣṭe dvitaye 'smin śānta-udita-dhāmni ye 'nusaṃdadhate* ॥ **126** ॥
prācyāṃ visarga-sattām-anavacchidi te pade rūḍhāḥ।

Jr.127b.1 *atha-śabdaḥ prativacane*।
tena śānta-uditatvena dvi-prakāre asmin samanantara-ukta-satattve

Qt.127b.1 *svātantryā-muktam-ātmanaṃ* .... ।

Jr.127b.2 *ity-ādi-dṛṣṭyā sṛṣṭe sva-samullāsite dhāmni ye prācyāṃ*

Qt.127b.2 .... *śānta-udita-sūti-kāraṇaṃ paraṃ kaulam*।

Jr.127b.3 *ity-ādy-uktyā etad-avasthā-dvaya-udaya-hetu-bhūtāṃ*
tat-saṃghaṭṭa-mayīṃ visarga-sattām-anusandadhate
tat-sphāra-sāram-eva-idaṃ sarvam-ity-āmṛśānti,
te anavacchinne pade rūḍhāḥ pūrṇe pade viśrāntā ity-arthaḥ ॥

3381

Jr.127b.4 *evam-etat mumukṣu-viṣayam-abhidhāya,*
bubhukṣu-viṣayam-api āha

AG. *ye siddhim-āptu-kāmās-te 'bhyuditaṃ rūpam-āhareyur-*
atho || **127** ||
tena-eva pūjayeyuḥ saṃvin-naikaṭya-śuddhatama-vapuṣā|

Jr.128b.1 *ye piṇḍa-sthairya-ādi-rūpāṃ siddhim-āptu-kāmāḥ,*
te tad-abhyuditaṃ rūpaṃ
kuṇḍa-golaka-ādi-śabda-vyapadeśyam-āhareyuḥ|
atha tena-eva abhyuditena rūpeṇa

Qt.128b.1 *ānando brahmaṇo rūpaṃ* ... | *iti*

Jr.128b.2 *śruter-ānanda-mayatayā saṃvin-naikaṭyāt*

Qt.128b.2 *tasmād-yat-saṃvido nātidūre tac-chuddham-āharet* ||

Jr.128b.3 *iti nītyā śuddhatama-vapuṣā pūjayeyur-devī-cakraṃ*
tarpayeyur-ity-arthaḥ|

Jr.128b.4 *kathaṃ-ca atra āharaṇa-ādi syād-ity-āśaṅkya āha*

AG. *tad-api-ca*
mitho hi vaktrāt pradhānato vaktragaṃ yato
bhaṇitam ||**128** ||
ajara-amara-pada-dāna-pravaṇaṃ kula-saṃjñitaṃ
paramam|

3382

Jr.129b.1 *tad-api-ca abhyuditaṃ rūpaṃ yataḥ*

Qt.129b.1 *sva-deha-avasthitaṃ dravyaṃ rasāyana-varaṃ śubham*|

Jr.129b.2 *ity-ādi-dṛśā dehe eva avasthānāt kula-saṃjñitam-ata eva*
paramam,
ata eva

Qt.129b.2 *śivaḥ praśasyate nityaṃ pūjā-ākhyaṃ tri-daśa-arcitam*|
yena prāśita-mātreṇa-amaro bhavati mānavaḥ ||
athavā miśritaṃ devi bhuṅkte yaḥ satataṃ naraḥ|
valīpalita-nirmukto yoginīnāṃ priyo bhavet ||

Jr.129b.3 *ity-ādi-nayena ajara-amara-pada-dāna-pravaṇaṃ*
pradhānato vaktrāt yoginī-vaktrāt mithaḥ parasparasya
vaktragaṃ bhaṇitaṃ sarva-śāstreṣu uktam-ity-arthaḥ|
etad-dhi yoginī-vaktrāt sva-vaktre,
tataḥ śakti-vaktre,
tataḥ sva-vaktre,
tato 'pi argha-pātra-ādau nikṣiped-iti guravaḥ|
yad-āgamo 'pi

Qt.129b.3 *vidrāvya golakaṃ tatra kuṇḍaṃ ca tanu-madhyame*|
tat-sthaṃ gṛhya mahā-dravyaṃ mukhena tanu-madhyame ||

tad-vaktragaṃ tataḥ kṛtvā punaḥ kṛtvā sva-vaktragam।
pātraṃ prapūrayet-tena mahā-aly-ambu-vimiśritam ॥
tena-argha-pātraṃ kurvīta sarva-siddhi-phala-pradam ॥
iti,

3383
Qt.129b.4 *vaktrād-vaktra-prayogeṇa samāhṛtya mahā-rasam*।
tena santarpayec-cakraṃ devatā-vīra-saṃyutam ॥ *iti,*
Qt.129b.5 *tato dūtīṃ kṣobhayitvā yasya-icchā saṃpravartate*।
tad-utthaṃ dravya-nicayaṃ prāśayec-ca parasparam ॥ *iti,*
Qt.129b.6 *ubhaya-utthena vīryeṇa mantra-vidyā yajet-tathā*। *iti* ॥
Jr.129b.4 *evam-etat jñāni-viṣayam-abhidhāya,*
karmi-viṣayam-api āha
AG. *ye 'py-aprāpta-vibodhās-te*
'bhyudita-utphulla-yāga-saṃrūḍhāḥ ॥ **129** ॥
tat-parikalpita-cakra-stha-devatāḥ prāpnuvanti vijñānam।
Jr.130b.1 *aprāpta-vibodhā iti aprarūḍha-jñānāś-caryā-mārga-niṣṭhā*
ity-arthaḥ ॥
Jr.130b.2 *atra-eva cakra-sthānāṃ devatānāṃ parikalpanāṃ darśayati*
3384
AG. *te tatra śakti-cakre tena-eva-ānanda-rasa-mayena bahiḥ*
॥ **130** ॥
dikṣu catasṛṣu prokta-krameṇa gaṇa-nātha-taḥ prabhṛti
sarvam।
saṃpūjya madhyama-pade kuleśa-yugmaṃ tv-arā-traye
devīḥ ॥ **131** ॥
bāhye pratyaram-atha kila catuṣkam-iti raśmi-cakram-arka-
aram।
aṣṭakam-aṣṭa-aṣṭakam-atha vividhaṃ
saṃpūjayet-krameṇa muniḥ ॥ **132** ॥
Jr.132d.1 *śakti-cakre iti*
śakteḥ saṃbandhini yoginī-vaktra-ātmani mukhya-cakre ity-
arthaḥ।
tena-eva-iti abhyuditena rūpeṇa।
prokta-iti nitya-arcā-abhidhāna-avasare।
arka-aram-iti dvā-daśa-aram ॥ 132 ॥
Jr.132d.2 *na kevalam-etat śakti-cakre eva pūjyaṃ,*
yāvat-svasminn-api-ity-āha

AG. nija-deha-gate dhāmani tathā-eva pūjyaṃ samabhyasyet|
3385
Jr.133b.1 nanu
saṅghaṭṭa-abhyudita-ubhaya-ātmakaṃ visargam-anusandadhatām-anavacchidi pade praroho vijñāna-prāptiś-ca bhaved-ity-uktaṃ,
śānta-ātmani visarge punaḥ prarūḍhānāṃ kā gatir-ity-āśaṅkya āha
AG. yat-tac-chāntaṃ rūpaṃ tena-abhyastena hṛdaya-saṃvittyā || **133** ||
śāntaṃ śiva-padam-eti hi galita-taraṅga-arṇava-prakhyam|
Jr.133d.1 eti-iti abhyasta-śānta-rūpaḥ|
śāntatvam-eva sphuṭī-kṛtaṃ galita-taraṅga-arṇava-prakhyam-iti ||
Jr.133d.2 nanu evaṃ ca asya kiṃ syād-ity-āśaṅkya āha
AG. tac-chānta-pada-adhyāsāc-cakra-stho devatā-gaṇaḥ sarvaḥ || **134** ||
tiṣṭhaty-uparata-vṛttiḥ śūnya-ālambī nirānandaḥ|
Jr.135b.1 uparata-vṛttir-iti sarva-bhāva-saṃkṣayāt,
ata eva uktaṃ śūnya-ālambī-iti,
ata eva
Qt.135b.1 .... nirālambaḥ paraḥ śivaḥ|
3386
Jr.135b.2 iti dṛśā śiva-pada-viśrāntyā nirānandaḥ ||
Jr.135b.3 na kevalaṃ madhya-cakrasya eva devatā-gaṇa evam-āste, yāvad-anucakra-stho 'pi-ity-āha
AG. yo 'py-anucakra-dṛg-ādi-sva-rūpa-bhāk so 'pi yat-tad-āyattaḥ || **135** ||
tena-anande[18] magnas-tiṣṭhaty-ānanda-sākāṅkṣaḥ|
Jr.136b.1 anucakra-dṛg-ādi-sva-rūpa-bhāg-iti arthāt devatā-gaṇaḥ|
tad-āyatta iti mukhya-cakra-stha-devatā-gaṇa-vaśaḥ|
tena-iti tad-āyattatvena ||
Jr.136b.2 nanu evam-anucakra-devatā-gaṇo' pi nirānande eva pade viśrānto 'stu,

18. Gnoli replaces with *tenānande* with *nirānande*. Gnoli, *Luce*, p.696 footnote 76 . If *anande* is understood to be equivalent to *nirānande*, as Jr.136b.1 implies, the correction is unnecessary.

kim-asya ānanda-sākāṅkṣatvena-ity-āśaṅkya āha
AG. *para-tat-sva-rūpa-saṅghaṭṭam-antareṇa*
-eṣa karaṇa-raśmi-gaṇaḥ || **136** ||
āste hi niḥ-sva-rūpaḥ sva-rūpa-lābhāya ca-unmukhitaḥ ||
Jr.137b.1 *eṣa dṛg-ādy-ātmā karaṇa-devatā-gaṇo hi*
pare sva-ā-
3387 *-nanda-nirbharatayā sarva-utkṛṣṭe*
tasmin samanantara-ukta-satattve pramātṛ-ātmani saṃvid-rūpe viśrāntiṃ vinā
niḥ-sva-rūpo nija-nija-artha-āharaṇa-ādāv-akṣamaḥ
sva-rūpaṃ labdhum-unmukhitaś-ca
āste ānanda-sākāṅkṣo bhaved-ity-arthaḥ ||
Jr.137b.2 *evaṃ-vidhaś-ca ayaṃ karaṇa-raśmi-gaṇaḥ kiṃ kuryād -ity-āśaṅkya āha*
AG. *raṇaraṇaka-rasān-*
nija-rasa-bharita-bahir-bhāva-carvaṇa-vaśena || **137** ||
viśrānti-dhāma kiñcil-labdhvā sva-ātmany-artha-arpayate|
Jr.138b.1 *eṣa karaṇa-raśmi-gaṇo hi*
abhilāṣa-abhiṣvaṅgāt
nija-rasa-bharitānāṃ
sva-saṃvin-mayatayā-eva bahir-avabhāsitānāṃ
bhāvānāṃ yat carvaṇaṃ raktis-tad-vaśena
sva-avamarśa-rūpaṃ-kiñcit viśrānti-dhāma labdhvā
anantaram-arthāt
carvitam-eva bhāva-jātaṃ sva-ātmani arpayet
Qt.138b.1 *nija-nija-bhoga-ābhoga-pravikāsi-nija-sva-rūpaparimarśe*|
kramaśo 'nucakra-devyaḥ saṃvic-cakraṃ hi madhyamaṃ yānti ||
3388
Jr.138b.2 *ity-ādi-dṛśā pramātṛ-ātmani mukhye saṃvic-cakre viśrāntiṃ bhajate ity-arthaḥ* ||
Jr.138b.3 *nanu evaṃ tad-viśrāntyā asya kiṃ syād-ity-āśaṅkya āha*
AG. *tan-nija-viṣaya-arpaṇa-taḥ*
pūrṇa-samucchalita-saṃvid-āsāraḥ || **138** ||
anucakra-devatā-gaṇa-paripūraṇa-jāta-vīrya-vikṣobhaḥ|
cakra-īśvaro 'pi pūrva-ukta-yuktitaḥ procchaled-rabhasāt || **139** ||

Jr.139d.1 *cakrāṇāṃ hi viśrānti-dhāmatvād-īśvaraḥ pramātā-api*
nija-nija-viṣaya-arpaṇa-vaśād-
-anucakra-devatā-gaṇena yat paripūraṇaṃ,
tena jāta-vīrya-vikṣobho
vyakta-nija-avaṣṭambhaḥ,
ata eva pūrṇa-samucchalita-saṃvid-āsāraḥ
pūrvam

Qt.139d.1 *anucakra-devatā-ātmaka-marīci-paripūraṇa-adhigata-vīryam* |
tac-chakti-śaktimad-yugam-anyonya-samunmukhaṃ
bhavati ||

Jr.139d.2 *ity-ādy-ukta-yuktito rabhasāt procchalet*
sahasā-eva bahir-unmukhaḥ syād-ity-arthaḥ || 139 ||

3389

Jr.139d.3 *prakṛtam-eva upasaṃharati*

AG. *trividho visarga itthaṃ saṅghaṭṭaḥ proditas-tathā śāntaḥ* |

Jr.140b.1 *triṣu prakāreṣu visarga-śabdasya pravṛttau nimittaṃ*
darśayati

AG. *visṛjati yato vicitraḥ sargo vigataś-ca yatra sarga iti* || **140** ||

Jr.140d.1 *yata iti hetau* || 140 ||

Jr.140d.2 *naca etad-asmad-upajñam-eva-ity-āha*

AG. *śrī-tattvarakṣaṇe śrī-nigame triśiromate ca tat-proktam* |

Jr.141b.1 *tatra*

Qt.141b.1 *tattvarakṣāvidhāne 'to visarga-traidham-ucyate* |

Jr.141b.2 *ity-ādinā tattvarakṣāvidhānasya prāk-saṃvāditatvāt*
tad-grantham-anuktvā-eva,
śrī-gama-śāstraṃ saṃvādayati

AG. *kuṇḍaṃ śaktiḥ śivo liṅgaṃ melakaṃ paramaṃ padaṃ* || **141** ||

3390 *dvābhyāṃ sṛṣṭiḥ saṃhṛtis-tad-visargas-tri-vidho game* |

Jr.142b.1 *kuṇḍaṃ bhaga-vac-chaktir-uditaṃ rūpam,*
śivaḥ śāntaṃ,
melakaṃ saṅghaṭṭaḥ |
tatra-uditatvād-eva śaktyā sṛṣṭeh,
śāntatvād-eva śivena saṃhārasya,
paramaṃ padam-ity-uktyā saṅghaṭṭena
sarva-avaccheda-virahād-anākhyasya ca udaya
ity-ayaṃ gama-śāstre tri-vidho visargaḥ ||

Jr.142b.2 *evaṃ gama-śāstraṃ saṃvādayitvā śrī-triśirobhairavam-api*
saṃvādayati
AG. *sroto-dvayasya niṣṭha-antam-ūrdhva-adhaś-cakra-*
bodhanam ॥ **142** ॥
viśrāmaṃ ca samāveśaṃ suṣīṇāṃ marutāṃ tathā।
gata-bhedaṃ ca yantrāṇāṃ sandhīnāṃ marmaṇām-api
॥ **143** ॥
dvā-saptati-pade dehe sahasrāre ca nityaśaḥ।
3391 *gaty-āgaty-antarā vittī saṅghaṭṭayati yac-chivaḥ* ॥ **144** ॥
tat-prayatnāt-sadā tiṣṭhet-saṅghaṭṭe bhairave pade।
ubhayos-tan-nirākāra-bhāva-saṃprāpti-lakṣaṇam ॥ **145** ॥
mātrā-vibhāga-rahitaṃ susphuṭa-artha-prakāśakam।
Jr.146b.1 *iha nityam-ūrdhva-adho-vartināṃ cakrāṇāṃ*
suṣīṇāṃ yantrāṇāṃ sandhīnāṃ marmaṇāṃ marutāṃ ca
gata-bhedam-
-ata eva dakṣa-vāma-vāha-ātmanaḥ sroto-dvyasaya niṣṭha-
antaṃ madhya-dhāma-viśrānti-paryantaṃ
bodhanaṃ viśrāmaṃ samāveśaṃ ca vidhāya,
dvā-saptati-pade sahasrāre dehe
Qt.146b.1 *dvā-saptati-sahasrāṇi nāḍīnāṃ nābhi-cakrake*।
Jr.146b.2 *ity-ādy-uktyā tāvan-nāḍi-sambhinne nābhi-deśe*
prāṇa-apāna-troṭanena antarā
gṛhīta-śiva-āveśaḥ
śānta-udita-ātmike vittī yat saṅghaṭṭayati
tad-ubhaya-melana-ādi-sva-rūpe pronmukho bhavet,
tataḥ pūrṇa-saṃvid-rūpe saṅghaṭṭe pade
sarva-kālaṃ prayatnatas-tiṣṭhet
tatra-eva sa-ava-
3392 *-dhāno bhaved-ity-arthah*।
yatas-tad-ubhayoḥ śānta-udita-lakṣaṇayo rūpayoḥ
pratiniyata-pade sakala-ākāra-ādy-avaccheda-śūnyatvāt
nirākāratva-āpatti-satattvam-
-ata eva niraṃśatvāt mātrā-vibhāga-rahitam
-ata eva susphuṭasya sva-anubhava-mātra-eka-rūpasya
arthasya prakāśakam-abhivyañjakam-ity-arthaḥ ॥
Jr.146b.3 *atra-eva ca dārḍhyaṃ kāryam-ity-āha*
AG. *abhyasyed-bhāva-saṃvittiṃ sarva-bhāva-nivartanāt* ॥**146**॥

sūrya-somau tu saṃrudhya laya-vikṣepa-mārga-taḥ।
Jr.147b.1 *sarvebhyaś-cakra-ādibhyo bhāvebhyo nivartya*
dakṣa-vāma-mārgābhyāṃ prāṇa-apānau nirudhya
madhya-dhāmni
sarva-bhāva-anusyūtāṃ tat-saṃghaṭṭa-mayīṃ
pramātṛ-rūpāṃ saṃvittim-abhyasyet
tad-āmarśa-para eva syād-ity-arthaḥ।
vittīr-iti pāṭhe tu śānta-udita-ātmikā eva-iti vyākhyeyam ॥
Jr.147b.2 *tad-evam-atra tri-vidho 'pi*
visarge samāveśa-bhājāṃ
yaḥ kaścana svā-rasikaḥ parāmarśaḥ parisphurati,
3393 *tad-eva paraṃ mantra-vīryam-ity-āha*
AG. *evaṃ tri-vidha-vimarśa-āveśa-samāpatti-dhāmni ya*
udeti ॥ **147** ॥
saṃvit-parimarśa-ātmā dhvanis
-tad-eva-iha mantra-vīryaṃ syāt।
tatra-eva-udita-tādṛśa-phala-lābha-samutsukaḥ
svakaṃ mantram ॥ **148** ॥
anusandhāya sadā ced-āste mantra-udayaṃ sa vai vetti।
Jr.149b.1 *yaḥ kaścid-evaṃ visarga-āveśa-śālī*
saṅghaṭṭa-velāyām-uditam
-anubhava-mātra-eka-gocaratvāt-tādṛśaṃ
vaktum-aśakyaṃ yad-ānanda nirbharaṃ
phalaṃ tal-lābhe samutsukaḥ sann
-abhīṣṭaṃ mantraṃ sadā, natu kṣaṇa-mātraṃ,
tatra-eva saṃvit-parāmarśa-ātmani ahaṃ-camat-kāra-maye
dhvanāv-anusandhāya ced-āste,
sa tatra mantra-udayaṃ vetti udito 'sya mantraḥ syād-ity-
arthaḥ ॥
Jr.149b.2 *bhūyo-bhūyaś-ca atra-eva bhāvanā-pareṇa bhāvyaṃ*
yena madhya-cakre eva aikāgryaṃ siddhyed-ity-āha
3394
AG. *atra-eva japaṃ kuryād-anucakra-ekatva-saṃvid-*
āgamane ॥ **149** ॥
yugapal-lakṣa-vibheda-prapañcitaṃ nāda-vṛttyā-eva।
Qt.150b.1 *kramaśo 'nucakra-devyaḥ saṃvic-cakraṃ hi madhyamaṃ*
yānti।

Jr.150b.1 ity-ādy-dṛśā yugapad-anucakra-devīnām
ekatvena mukhya-cakra-rūpāyāṃ saṃvidi yad-āgamanaṃ
viśrāntis-tan-nimittam
-atra-eva saṃvit-parāmarśa-ātmani udīyamāne mantre
nāda-āmarśa-mātra-mayatayā
Qt.150b.2 udaye saṅgame śāntau tri-lakṣo japa ucyate।
Jr.150b.2 ity-ādy-uktena lakṣa-vibhedena prapañcitaṃ japaṃ kuryāt
bhūyo bhūyo 'nusandhānaṃ vidadhyād-ity-arthaḥ ॥
Jr.150b.3 idam-eva ca mudrāṇām-api-paraṃ vīryam-iti anyatra
uktam-ity-āha
AG. śrī-yogasañcare 'pi-ca mudrā-iyaṃ yoginī-priyā
paramā ॥ **150** ॥
koṇa-traya-antarā-āśrita-nitya-unmukha-maṇḍala-cchade
kamale।
3395 satata-aviyutaṃ nālaṃ ṣoḍaśa-dala-kamala-kalita-san-
mūlam ॥ **151** ॥
madhya-stha-nāla-gumphita-saroja-yuga-ghaṭṭana-kramād-
agnau।
madhya-stha-pūrṇa-sundara-śaśa-dhara-dina-kara
-kalā-augha-saṅghaṭṭāt ॥ **152** ॥
tri-dala-aruṇa-vīrya-kalā-saṅgān-madhye 'ṅkuraḥ sṛṣṭiḥ।
Jr.153b.1 koṇa-traya-antar-varti
nitya-unmukhaṃ sadā-eva pravikas-varaṃ yat
Qt.153b.1 tridalaṃ bhaga-padmaṃ tu .... ।
Jr.153b.2 ity-ādy-uktyā maṇḍala-cchadaṃ
tridalaṃ pauṃsnaṃ straiṇaṃ vā bhaga-kamalaṃ
tatra āpyāya-kāritayā satatam-aviyutaṃ
Qt.153b.2 yad-retaḥ sa bhavec-candraḥ .... ।
Jr.153b.3 ity-ādy-uktyā ṣoḍaśa-dalena cāndramasena kamalena
kalitam,
ata eva ānanda-nirbharatvāt sat,
ata eva vakṣyamāṇa-rūpayāyāḥ sṛṣṭer-mūlam-utpatti-dhāma
yat madhya-nāḍī-rūpaṃ nālam,
3396
Qt.153b.3 ambu-vāhā bhaved-vāmā madhyamā śukra-vāhinī।
dakṣa-sthā rakta-vāhā ca .... ॥
Jr.153b.4 ity-uktyā madhya-sthena tena nālena gumphitam-umbhitaṃ

yat strī-puṃsa-saṃbandhi saroja-yugaṃ
tasya paraspara-saṅgharṣa-krameṇa,
tan-madhya-sthayoḥ pūrṇayor-avikalayoḥ,
ata eva ānanda-mayatayā sundarayo [19]
reto-rajo-rūpayoḥ śaśa-dhara-dina-karayoḥ
kalānāṃ saṅghaṭṭāt
Qt.153b.4 *śucir-nāma-agnir-udbhūtaḥ saṅghaṭṭāt-sūrya-somayoḥ*।
Jr.153b.5 *ity-uktyā agnau pramātr-eka-rūpe samullasite*
tri-dalasya kamakalasya madhye
rajo-retaḥ-kalānāṃ saṅgāt
yaścit-prasara-ātmā viśva-garbhī-kāra-sahiṣṇur-aṅkuraḥ,
sā sṛṣṭir-bahir-api tathā-avabhāsate ity-arthaḥ।
tad-uktaṃ
Qt.153b.5 *bhage liṅge sthito vahnir-antare bhāskaraḥ sthitaḥ*।
ūrdhve vipraḥ sthitaḥ somaḥ saṅghaṭṭān-niṣkramed-rasaḥ॥
iti,
Qt.153b.6 *tat-pīṭhaṃ śākinī-cakre sā sṛṣṭiḥ sa-cara-acare*।
tat-kṣetraṃ bīja-rājasya ṛtu-kāla-udbhavasya tu ॥
rajaḥ-puṣpa-upabhogasya kulasya-eva-akulasya ca।
karṇikā-madhya-vartinaṃ hāṭakaṃ hāṭaka-īśvaram ॥
śakti-padma-antare līnam-advaitaṃ paramaṃ śivam।
iti ca ॥

3397
Jr.153b.6 *nanu evaṃ mudrayā baddhayā asya kiṃ syād-ity-āśaṅkya*
āha
AG. *iti śaśa-dhara-vāsara-pati-citragu*
-saṃghaṭṭa-mudrayā jhaṭiti ॥ **153** ॥
sṛṣṭy-adi-kramam-antaḥ kurvaṃs-turye sthitiṃ labhate।
Jr.154b.1 *saṅghaṭṭa-ity-anena asyāḥ ṣaḍ-ara-saṃniveśa-bhāktvam-*
uktam ॥
Jr.154b.2 *evaṃ mantra-vīrya-atideśa-dvārakaṃ mudrā-sva-rūpam-*
abhidhāya,
parasparasya lolī-bhāvaṃ darśayituṃ
punas-tad-vīryam-api mantreṣu atideṣṭum-āha
AG. *etat-khecara-mudrā-āveśe 'nyonyasya śakti-śaktim-*
atoḥ ॥ **154** ॥

19. For *sundarayo* read *sundarayoḥ*.

pāna-upabhoga-līlā-hāsa-ādiṣu yo bhaved-vimarśa-mayaḥ ।
avyakta-dhvani-rāva-sphoṭa-śruti-nāda-nāda-ant-
aiḥ ।। **155** ।।

3398 *avyucchinna-anāhata-rūpais-tan-mantra-vīryaṃ syāt* ।

Jr.156b.1 *etasyāṃ ṣaḍ-ara-mudrā-lakṣaṇāyāṃ khecarī-mudrāyām-āveśe śakti-śaktimator-anyonyasya pāna-upabhoga-ādau yo vimarśa-ātmā anubhavaḥ samudiyāt, tad-avyakta-ādy-aṣṭa-bheda-bhinna-para-nāda-āmarśa-sva-bhāvaṃ māntraṃ vīryaṃ syāt* ।।

Jr.156b.2 *atra-eva paunaḥ-punyena bhāvanātas-tal-lābho bhaved-ity-āha*

AG. *iti cakra-aṣṭaka-rūḍhaḥ sahajaṃ japam-ācaran pare dhāmni* ।। **156** ।।
yad-bhairava-aṣṭaka-padaṃ tal-labhate 'ṣṭaka-kalā-bhinnam ।

Jr.157b.1 *aṣṭaka-kalā-iti aṣṭabhir-ardhacandra-ādibhir-unmanā-antābhiḥ kalābhir-bhinnaṃ bheditam-ity-arthaḥ* ।।

Jr.157b.2 *nanu kiṃ nāma cakra-aṣṭakaṃ, yad-ārūḍho 'pi japam-ācared-ity-āṣaṅkya āha*

AG. *gamana-agamane 'vasitau karṇe nayane dvi-liṅga-saṃparke* ।। **157** ।।

3399 *tat-saṃmelana-yoge deha-anta-ākhye ca yāmale cakre* ।

Jr.158b.1 *gamana-āgamane prāṇa-sahite apāne ity-arthaḥ* ।
avasitāv-adhyavasāye buddhāv-iti yāvat ।
saṃparkaḥ sparśa-mātram ।
tat-saṃmelana-yoge iti tayor-dvayor-liṅgayoḥ saṃmelana-yoge saṅghaṭṭa-avasare ity-arthaḥ ।
deha-anta-ākhye iti dvā-daśa-ante ।
yāmale cakre iti sarva-śeṣaḥ ।।

Jr.158b.2 *nanu atra kiṃ nāma bhairava-aṣṭakasya padaṃ yad-api ardhacandra-ādibhir-aṣṭābhiḥ kalābhir-bhinnaṃ syād-ity-āśaṅkya āha*

AG. *kuca-madhya-hṛdaya-deśād-oṣṭha-antaṃ kaṇṭha-gaṃ yad-avyaktam* ।। **158** ।।
tac-cakra-dvaya-madhya-gam-ākarṇya kṣobha-vigama-samaye yat ।
nirvānti

tatra ca-evaṃ yo 'ṣṭa-vidho nāda-bhairavaḥ
paramaḥ || **159** ||
3400 *jyotir-dhvani-samira-kṛtaḥ sā māntrī vyāptir-ucyate*
paramā |
Jr.160b.1 *kuca-madhya-hṛdaya-deśād-ārabhya oṣṭha-puṭa-paryantaṃ*
śakteḥ kaṇṭha-antaḥ
Qt.160b.1 *yat-tad-akṣaram-akṣobhyaṃ priyā-kaṇṭha-uditaṃ param* |
sahajaṃ nāda ity-uktaṃ tattvaṃ nitya-uditaṃ japaḥ || *iti*
Qt.160b.2 *nitya-ānanda-rasāsvādād-dhā hā-iti gala-koṭare* |
svayaṃ-bhūḥ sukha-da-uccāraḥ kāma-tattvasya vedakaḥ ||
Jr.160b.2 *ity-ādi-nirūpita-sva-rūpaṃ yad-avyakta-prāyaṃ*
hā-hā-ity-akṣara-dvayam-udeti,
tat paraspara-saṃghaṭṭa-ātmanaḥ kṣobhasya vigama-
samaye yoginī-vaktra-ātma-mukhya-cakra-antar-viśrāntaṃ
parāmṛśya yat sarve nirvānti viśrāntiṃ bhajante,
tatra-eva nirvāṇa-ātmani pade
ya evam-avyakta-ādi-rūpatayā aṣṭa-vidhaḥ,
ata eva ardhacandra-ādi-kalā-aṣṭaka-ullasitaḥ,
ata eva paramo nāda-bhairavaḥ;
sā paramā māntrī vyāptiḥ sarvatra ucyate iti vākya-arthaḥ |
jyotir-ardhacandraḥ,
dhvanir-nādaḥ,
samīraḥ sparśa-atmā śaktiḥ,
adhas-tu candreṇa-eva vyāptam-iti artha-siddham ||
3401
Jr.160b.3 *atra ca kiṃ tat bhairava-aṣṭakaṃ,*
kā ca māntrī vyāptir-ity-āśaṅkya āha
AG. *sakala-akaleśa-śūnyaṃ kalāḍhya-khamale tathā*
kṣapaṇakaṃ ca || **160** ||
antaḥ-sthaṃ kaṇṭhy-oṣṭhyaṃ
candrād-vyāptis-tathā-unmanā-antā-iyam |
Jr.161b.1 *eṣāṃ ca śakti-śaktimat-sāmarasya-velāyām-udayāt*
tad-anyatara-vyapadeśa-ayogāt
napuṃsakatvam-eva ucitam
-iti tal-liṅgena nirdeśaḥ ||
Jr.161b.2 *evaṃ-vyāpti-bhāvanād-asya sarvatra-eva para-bhairavī-*
bhāvo bhaved-ity-āha

AG. *evaṃ karmaṇi karmaṇi yatra kva-api smaran*
vyāptim || **161**||
satatam-alepo jīvan-muktaḥ para-bhairavī-bhavati|
Jr.162b.1 *evaṃ-vidhe ca melaka-avasare gṛhīta-janmā param-utkṛṣṭa*
ity-āha
AG. *tādṛṅ-melaka-kalikā-kalita-tanuḥ ko 'pi yo bhaved-*
garbhe || **162** ||
3402 *uktaḥ sa yoginī-bhūḥ svayam-eva jñāna-bhājanaṃ rudraḥ*|
śrī-vīrāvali-śāstre bālo 'pi ca garbha-go hi śiva-
rūpaḥ || **163** ||
Jr.163d.1 *nanu*
Qt.163d.1 *ity-evaṃ deva-deva-īśi ādi-yāgas-tavaśuditaḥ*|
Jr.163d.2 *iti-dṛśā ādi-yāga-śabdasya atra pravṛttau kiṃ nimittam*
-ity-āśaṅkya āha
AG. *ādīyate yataḥ sāraṃ tasya mukhyasya ca-eṣa yat*|
mukhyaś-ca yāgas-tena-ayam-ādi-yāga iti smṛtaḥ || **164** ||
tatra tatra ca śāstre 'sya sva-rūpaṃ stutavān vibhuḥ|
śrī-vīrāvali-hārdeśa-khamata-arṇava-vartiṣu || **165** ||
śrī-siddha-utphulla-maryādāhīna-caryākula-ādiṣu|
3403
Jr.166b.1 *sāram-iti saṃvit-tattva-ātmakam-amṛta-lakṣaṇaṃ ca*|
tena ādiś-ca asau yāga iti,
āder-mukhya-cakrasya yāga iti ca|
ata eva asya sarva-āgameṣu param-utkarṣa ity-āha tatra-
ity-ādi|
hārdeśo hṛdayabhaṭṭārakaḥ,
khemataṃ khecarīmatam,
arṇavo yonyarṇavaḥ,
tad-vartiṣu arthāt grantha-eka-deśeṣu|
utphulla-iti utphullakamatam|
maryādāhīnaṃ nirmaryāda-śāstram|
yatha-uktam
Qt.166b.1 *eṣa te kauliko yāgaḥ sadyo yoga-vibhūti-daḥ*|
ākhyātaḥ paramo guhyo dvaitināṃ mohanaḥ param ||
vīrāṇāṃ duḥkha-sukha-daṃ līlayā bhukti-mukti-dam|
yoga-sandhā-prayogeṇa pūjā-ahni havanaṃ smṛtam ||
paśu-mārga-sthitānāṃ-tu mūḍhānāṃ pāpa-karmaṇām|

aprakāśyaṃ sadā devi yathā kiñcin-mahā-dhanam ||
na ca-atra paramo yāgaḥ sva-bhāva-stho mahā-udayaḥ|
na kuṇḍaṃ na-agni-yajanaṃ na-āhuty-ācāra-maṇḍalam ||
āvāhanaṃ na ca-eva-atra na ca-eva-atra visarjanam|
na mūrti-yāga-karaṇaṃ na-anyad-āsanam-eva ca ||
vrata-caryā-vinirmuktaṃ bahir-dravya-vivarjitam|
sva-ānanda-amṛta-saṃpūrṇaṃ mahad-ānanda-siddhi-dam||
kevalaṃ vā-ātma-sattāyāṃ sarva-śakti-mayaṃ śivaṃ|
sarva-ākāraṃ nirākāram-ātma-yoniṃ parāparam ||
3404 *bhāvayet-tan-mahā-yogī pūjayec-cakra-nāyakam*|
etad-rahasyaṃ paramaṃ guhyaṃ ca-uttama-yojitam ||
saṃsphurat-kaulika-āmnāyaṃ tvat-snehād-adya yojitam|
suguptaṃ kārayen-nityaṃ na deyaṃ vīra-vatsale ||
dvaitināṃ svalpa-buddhīnāṃ lobha-upahata-cetasām|
māyināṃ krūra-sattvānāṃ jijñāsūnāṃ na ca-eva hi ||
pṛthivīm-api yo dattvā mūkavat-kṣmā-tale vaset|
tadā siddhyati mantra-jñaḥ siddha-melāpakaṃ labhet ||
sarva-āmaya-vinirmukto dehena-anena siddhyati|
anena yoga-mārgeṇa na-ānṛtaṃ pravadāmy-aham || *iti* ||
Jr.166b.2 *iha vidyā-mantra-mudrā-maṇḍala-ātmatayā catuṣ-pīṭhaṃ*
tāvac-chāstram|
tatra mantra-mudrā-ātmanaḥ pīṭha-dvayasya saṃpradāya
uktaḥ|
idānīm-atra-eva avaśiṣṭasya vidyā-maṇḍala-ātmano 'pi
asya saṃpradāyaṃ nirūpayati
AG. *yugmasya-asya prasādena vrata-yoga-vivarjitaḥ* || **166** ||
sarvadā smaraṇaṃ kṛtvā ādi-yāga-eka-tat-paraḥ|
śakti-dehe nije nyasyed-vidyāṃ kūṭam-anukramāt || **167** ||
3405 *dhyātvā candra-nibhaṃ padmam-ātmānaṃ bhāskara-*
dyutim|
vidyā-mantra-ātmakaṃ pīṭha-dvayam-atra-eva mela-
yet ||**168**||
Jr.168d.1 *asya uktasya mantra-mudrā-ātmanaḥ pīṭha-yugmasya*
prasādād-anusandhāna-mātreṇa-eva
vrata-yoga-ādi-nirapekṣaḥ
sarva-kālam-ādi-yāga-parāyaṇo guruḥ
śāktaṃ padmam-ānanda-nirbharatvāt candra-nibham-

-ātmānaṃ vikāsa-ādhāyakatayā bhāskara-dyutim-nudhyāya
śākte nije dehe kramād-abhīpsitāṃ śakti-pradhānāṃ vidyāṃ,
śiva-pradhānaṃ kūṭaṃ mantraṃ ca nyasyet
yena atra-evȧ samanantara-ukta-yukty-anusandhāna-tāratamyāt vidyā-mantra-ātmakam-api
pīṭha-dvayaṃ mīlitaṃ syāt ॥ 168 ॥

Jr.168d.2 *etac-ca asmābhir-atirahasyatvāt nirbhajya na-uktam-ity*
svayam-eva avadhāryam-ity-āha

AG. *na paṭhyate rahasyatvāt-spaṣṭaih śabdair-mayā punaḥ*।
kutūhalī tu-ukta-śāstra-saṃpāṭhād-eva lakṣayet ॥ **169** ॥

3406

Jr.169d.1 *atra-eva maṇḍala-ātmatām-api abhidhātum-āha*

AG. *yad-bhajante sadā sarve yadvān devaś-ca devatā*।
tac-cakraṃ paramaṃ devī-yāga-ādau saṃnidhāp-akam ॥ **170** ॥
deha eva paraṃ liṅgaṃ-sarva-tattva-ātmakaṃ śivam।
devatā-cakra-saṃjuṣṭaṃ pūjā-dhāma tad-uttamam ॥ **171** ॥
tad-eva maṇḍalaṃ mukhyaṃ tri-tri-śūla-abja-cakra-kham।
tatra-eva devatā-cakraṃ bahir-antaḥ sadā yajet ॥ **172** ॥
sva-sva-mantra-parāmarśa-pūrvaṃ taj-janmabhī rasaiḥ।
ānanda-bahulaiḥ sṛṣṭi-saṃhāra-vidhinā spṛśet ॥ **173** ॥

3407

Jr.173d.1 *yadvān-iti ādya-ādhāra-vān*।
devatā ca-iti arthāt tadvatī।
cakram-iti mukhyaṃ cakram।
ata eva uktaṃ paramam-iti
tri-tri-śūla-abja-cakra-kham-
-iti

Qt.173d.1 *tri-tri-śūle 'tra sapta-are śliṣṭa-mātreṇa madhyataḥ*।
padmānām-atha cakrāṇāṃ vyomnāṃ vā saptakaṃ bhavet ॥ *iti*

Jr.173d.2 *vakṣyamāṇa-nītyā tad-rūpam-ity-arthaḥ*।
sva-sva-iti abhīpsitasya।
taj-janmabhir-iti mukhya-cakra-udgataiḥ kuṇḍa-golaka-ādibhiḥ।
sṛṣṭi-saṃhāra-vidhinā-iti śānta-udita-krameṇa-ity-arthaḥ ॥ 173 ॥

Jr.173d.3 *evaṃ-ca asya kiṃ syād-ity-āśaṅkya āha*
AG. *tat-sparśa-rabhasa-udbuddha-saṃvic-cakraṃ tad-īśvaraḥ*|
labhate paramaṃ dhāma tarpita-aśeṣa-daivataḥ || **174** ||
anuyāga-ukta-vidhinā dravyair-hṛdaya-hāribhiḥ|
tathā-eva sva-svaka-āmarśa-yogād-antaḥ
pratarpayet || **175** ||
3408
Jr.175d.1 *anuyāga-ukta-vidhinā-iti*
yad-uktaṃ prāk
Qt.175d.1 *yad-yad-eva-asya manasi vikāsitvaṃ prayacchati*|
tena-eva kuryāt pūjāṃ sa iti śambhor-viniścayaḥ ||
Jr.175d.2 *ity-ādi upakramya*
Qt.175d.2 *śiva-abheda-bharād-bhāva-vargaś-cyotati yaṃ rasam*|
tam-eva parame dhāmni pūjanāya-arpayed-budhaḥ ||
iti || 175 ||
Jr.175d.3 *etac-ca ādara-atiśayam-avadyotayituṃ*
prāk-saṃvāditena-api nija-stotra-eka-deśena saṃvādayati
AG. *kṛtvā-ādhāra-dharāṃ camat-kṛti-rasa-prokṣa-akṣaṇa-*
kṣālitām-āttair-mānasataḥ sva-bhāva-kusumaiḥ sva-āmoda-
sandohibhiḥ|
ānanda-amṛta-nirbhara-sva-hṛdaya-anargha-argha-pātra-
kramāt tvāṃ devyā saha deha-deva-sadane deva-arcaye
'har-niśam || **176** ||
Jr.176d.1 *naca evam-asmābhiḥ sva-upajñam-eva-uktam-ity-āha*
3409
AG. *śrī-vīrāvaly-amaryāda-prabhṛtau śāstra-sañcaye*|
sa eṣa puramo yāgaḥ stutaḥ śītā-aṃśu-maulinā || **177** ||
Jr.177d.1 *eṣa iti deha-viṣayaḥ,*
yad-abhiprāyeṇa-eva
Qt.177d.1 *sva-deha eva-āyatanaṃ na-anyadā-āyatanaṃ vrajet*|
Jr.177d.2 *ity-ādi anyatra uktam* || 177 ||
Jr.177d.3 *etac-ca dehe iva prāṇe 'pi kāryam-ity-āha*
AG. *athavā prāṇa-vṛtti-sthaṃ samastaṃ devatā-gaṇam*|
paśyet-pūrva-ukta-yuktyā-eva tatra-eva-abhyarcayed-
guruḥ || **178** ||
Jr.178d.1 *kathaṃ-ca atra pūjanaṃ kāryam-ity-āha*
AG. *prāṇa-āśritānāṃ devīnāṃ brahma-nāsa-ādi-bhedibhiḥ*|
ka-randhrair-viśata-apāna-cāndra-cakreṇa
tarpaṇam || **179** ||
Jr.179d.1 *brahma-iti brahma-randhram* || 179 ||

3410
Jr.179d.2 *evaṃ-ca asya kiṃ syād-ity-āśaṅkya-āha*
AG. *evaṃ prāṇa-krameṇa-eva tarpayed-devatā-gaṇam*।
acirāt-tat-prasādena jhāna-siddhīr-atha-aśnute ।। **180** ।।
Jr.180d.1 *yadvā kim-anātma-rūpair-deha-ādibhiḥ*
saṃvin-niṣṭhatayā-eva devī-cakraṃ tarpayed-ity-āha
AG. *saṃvin-mātra-sthitaṃ devī-cakraṃ vā saṃvid-arpaṇāt*।
viśva-ābhoga-prayogeṇa tarpaṇīyaṃ vipaścitā ।। **181** ।।
Jr.181d.1 *saṃvid-arpaṇād-iti vyākhyātaṃ viśva-ābhoga-prayogeṇa-iti,*
ata eva vipaścitā-iti uktam ।। 181 ।।
Jr.181d.2 *nanu vipaścito 'pi sati deha-ādau*
saṃvin-mātra-sthitaṃ devī-cakraṃ kathaṃ tarpaṇīyam-ity-āha
AG. *yatra sarve layaṃ yānti dahyante tattva-sañcayāḥ*।
3411 *tāṃ citiṃ paśya kāya-sthāṃ kāla-anala-samaprabhām* ।। **182** ।।
Jr.182d.1 *yatra sarve sakala-ādyāḥ pramātāro*
bhūta-bhāva-ādy-ātmakāni prameyāṇi ca
tad-eka-sād-bhāvaṃ yānti
tām-aśeṣa-viśva-saṃhāra-kāritvāt kāla-anala-samaprabhāṃ
kāya-sthāṃ citiṃ paśya,
saty-api deha-ādau vid-eva ekā sarvataḥ parisphurati -ity-arthaḥ ।। 182 ।।
Jr.182d.2 *etad-eva sphuṭayati*
AG. *śūnya-rūpe śmaśāne 'smin yoginī-siddha-sevite*।
krīḍā-sthāne mahā-raudre sarva-astamita-vigrahe ।। **183** ।।
sva-raśmi-maṇḍala-ākīrṇe dhvaṃsita-dhvānta-santatau।
sarvair-vikalpair-nirmukte ānanda-pada-kevale ।। **184** ।।
asaṃkhya-citi-saṃpūrṇe śmaśāne citi-bhīṣaṇe।
3412 *samasta-devatā-ādhāre praviṣṭaḥ ko na siddhyati* ।। **185** ।।
Jr.185d.1 *asminn-asaṅkyābhiḥ sukha-duḥkha-ādy-ātmikābhiś-citibhiḥ saṃpūrṇe,*
ata eva saṃsāra-yātanā-dāyitayā mahā-raudre,
ata eva pariharaṇīyatva-ādinā śmaśāna-prāye śarīre
praviṣṭo 'ntar-mukhī-bhūtaḥ
ko na siddhyati-iti saṃbandhaḥ।
kīdṛśe ca asmin।
antar-mukhī-bhāvād-eva tatra ahantā-vigalanāt śūnya-rūpe,
ata eva sarveṣāṃ sakala-ādīnām-astamita-vigrahe,

ata eva dhvaṃsita-dhvānta-santatau pradhvasta-bheda-
andha-kāre,
ata eva sarvair-vikalpair-nirmukte,
ata eva svasminn-eva,
natu bāhye,
raśmi-maṇḍalena cakṣur-ādi-indriya-devatā-vargeṇa
ākīrṇe,
ata eva yoginī-siddha-sevite samasta-devatā-ādhāre,
ata eva
Qt.185d.1 krīḍanti vividhair-bhāvair-devyaḥ piṇḍa-antara-sthitāḥ|
iti
Jr.185d.2 āsām-eva krīḍā-sthāne,
ata eva sarva-devatā-saṅketa-sthānatayā śmaśāne,
ata eva saṃhāra-kāriṇyā pramātr-eka-rūpayā cityā bhīṣaṇe,
3413 ata eva ānanda-pada-kevale
sva-ātma-mātra-viśrānte ity-arthaḥ || 185 ||
Jr.185d.3 naca etad-asmad-upajñam-eva-ity-āha
AG. śrī-mad-vīrāvalī-śāstre itthaṃ provāca bhairavī|
Jr.186b.1 atra saṃvit-kramaś-caryā-mayaḥ
kaṭākṣito 'pi atirahasyatvāt nirbhajya
bhedena na-ukta
iti na vid-vadbhir-asmabhyam-abhyasūyitavyam ||
Jr.186b.2 evaṃ dauta-vidhy-anuṣaktaṃ
rahasya-upaniṣat-kramam-upasaṃharan
dīkṣā-vidhim-avatārayati
AG. itthaṃ yāgaṃ vidhāya-ādau tādṛśa-aucitya-bhāg-
inam || **186** ||
lakṣa-ekīyaṃ sva-śiṣyaṃ taṃ dīkṣayet-tādṛśi krame|
Jr.187b.1 lakṣa-ekīyam iti bahuśaḥ parīkṣā-aucitya-labdham,
ata eva-uktaṃ sva-śiṣyam-iti,
tādṛśa-aucitya-bhāginam-iti|
tādṛśi-iti evaṃ-nirūpita-sva-rūpe ||
3414
Jr.187b.2 tad-eva āha
AG. rudra-śaktyā tu taṃ prokṣya deva-abhyāśe niveśayet || **187** ||
bhujau tasya samālokya rudra-śaktyā pradīpayet|
tayā-eva-asya-arpayet-puṣpaṃ karayor-gandha-digd-
hayoḥ || **188** ||
nirālambau tu tau tasya sthāpayitvā vicintayet|
rudra-śakty-ākṛṣyamāṇau dīptayā aṅkuśa-rūpayā || **189** ||

tataḥ sa svayam-ādāya vastraṃ baddha-dṛśir-bhavet।
svayaṃ ca pātayet-puṣpaṃ tat-pātāl-lakṣayet-kulam ॥ **190**॥
tato 'sya mukham-udghāṭya pādayoḥ praṇipātayet।
3415 *hastayor-mūrdhni ca-apy-asya devī-cakraṃ sama-*
rcayet ॥ **191** ॥

Jr.191d.1 *rudra-śaktiḥ parayā mātṛsadbhāvena vā saṃpuṭitā mālinī*।
pradīpayed-iti hṛd-gata-śakti-puñjasya aṅguli-dvāra-
niḥsṛtasya ākarṣaṇa-krameṇa uttejayed-ity-arthaḥ।
tayā-eva-iti rudra-śaktyā।
nirālambāv-iti vigalita-sāṃsārika-kṛtrima-nija-śaktikatvāt
nirjīva-prāyāv-ity-arthaḥ।
aṅkuśa-rūpayā-iti ākarṣaṇa-aucityāt।
tata iti bhujayoḥ rudraśakty-ākṛṣyamāṇatvena cintanāt
hetoḥ।
lakṣayed-iti evaṃ hi asya sva-kulam-anāyāsena
siddhyed iti।
praṇipātayed-iti śaktir-eva ॥ 191 ॥

Jr.191d.2 *devī-cakraṃ ca atra katham-arcayed-ity-āśaṅkya āha*
AG. *ākṛṣya-ākarṣakatvena prerya-preraka-bhāvataḥ*।

Jr.192b.1 *hastayor-hi preryatvena devī-cakram-abhyarcayet*
mūrdhni ca prerakatvena।
yatas-tad-ākārṣaṇīyaṃ,
tac-ca ākarṣakam।
evaṃ hi mūrdhni pūjitasya devī-cakrasya
3416 *sāmarthyena ākṛṣṭaṃ hasta-dvayam*।
tatra-eva pātataḥ śiva-hastatāṃ yāyād-iti।
yad-uktaṃ

Qt.192b.1 *tato 'sya mastake cakraṃ hastayoś-ca-arcya yogavit*।
tad-dhastau prerayec-chaktyā yāvan-mūrdha-antam-
āgatau ॥
śiva-hasta-vidhiḥ proktaḥ sadyaḥ-pratyaya-kārakaḥ। *iti* ॥

Jr.192b.2 *yadā punar-evaṃ śiva-hasta-vidhir-na siddhyate,*
tadā śāstra-antarīyaṃ kramam-anutiṣṭhed-ity-āha
AG. *uktaṃ śrī-ratnamālāyāṃ nābhiṃ daṇḍena saṃpuṭam* ॥ **192**॥
vāma-bhūṣaṇa-jaṅghābhyāṃ nitambena-apy-alaṅkṛtam।
śiṣya-haste puṣpa-bhṛte codana-astraṃ tu yojayet ॥ **193** ॥
yāvat-sa stobham-āyātaḥ svayaṃ patati mūrdhani।
śiva-hastaḥ svayaṃ so 'yaṃ sadyaḥ-pratyaya-kārakaḥ ॥**194**॥
3417 *anena-eva prayogeṇa carukaṃ grāhayed-guruḥ*।
śiṣyeṇa danta-kāṣṭhaṃ ca tat-pātaḥ prāgvad-eva tu ॥ **195** ॥

Jr.195d.1 *nābhiḥ kṣaḥ* |
daṇḍo rephaḥ,
tena sampuṭam-ūrdhva-adhaḥ-saṃbhinnam-ity-arthaḥ |
vāma-bhūṣaṇam ū |
vāma-jaṅghā au |
nitambaṃ m |
saca arthād-bindu-rūpaḥ |
tena rkṣrūauṃ |
sa iti śiva-hastaḥ |
tad-uktaṃ tatra
Qt.195d.1 *mūla-daṇḍaṃ samuddhṛtya nābhi-sthaṃ varṇam-uddharet* |
śūla-daṇḍa-āsana-sthaṃ tu vāma-bhūṣaṇa-saṃyutam ||
vāma-jaṅghā-samāyuktaṃ nitamba-alaṃkṛtaṃ priye |
divya-astram-etat-paramaṃ na-apuṇyo labhate sphuṭam ||
Jr.195d.2 *iti upakramya*
Qt.195d.2 *śiva-haste mahā-īśāni idaṃ kūṭaṃ tu yojayet* |
yāvat stubhyaty-asau devi svayam-eva calaty-asau || *iti* |
Jr.195d.3 *sadyaḥ-pratyaya-kāraka iti*
yatra-eva śarīra-cakre jhaṭati hastaḥ patati,
tatra-eva abhyāsa-paro bhaved-iti guravaḥ |
anena-eva-iti ākarṣya-ākarṣaka-bhāva-lakṣaṇena |
carukam-iti arthāt devībhyo 'gre
3418 *dāpayitvā* |
śiṣyeṇa-iti prayojya-kartari tṛtīyā |
prāg-vad-eva-iti pañca-daśa-āhnika-uktavat || **195** ||
Jr.195d.4 *nanu ekena-eva netra-paṭa-graha-ādy-ātmanā kara-stobhena asya śakty-āveśo lakṣita iti*
kiṃ punas-tad-vacanena-ity-āśaṅkya āha
AG. *kara-stobho netra-paṭa-grahāt prabhṛti yaḥ kila* |
danta-kāṣṭha-samādāna-paryantas-tatra lakṣayet || **196** ||
tīvra-manda-ādi-bhedena śakti-pātaṃ tathā-vidham |[20]
Jr.197b.1 *tatra-iti evaṃ-vidhe kara-stobhe* |
tathā-vidham-iti tīvra-manda-ādi-bhedam |
ayam-atra āśayaḥ—
yadā-hi
yatra-eva cakre puṣpa-pāto vṛttas-
tatra-eva praṇāmaḥ,
tatra-eva caru-dānaṃ,

---

20. The underlined words are from *Mālinīvijayottaratantra* 11.27c. The full quote is given in Qt.197b.1.

tata eva tad-grahaṇam-ity-ādi;
tadā tīvraḥ śakti-pāto lakṣaṇīyaḥ,
anyathā tu mandaḥ iti।
tad-uktam

Qt.197b.1 *eteṣāṃ calanān-mantrī śakti-pātaṃ parīkṣayet*।
manda-tīvra-ādi-bhedena manda-tīvra-ādikaṃ budhaḥ
॥ *iti* ॥

3419
Jr.197b.2 *evam-iyatā asmad-darśane samayi-dīkṣā-uktā-ity-āha*
AG. *ity-eṣa samayī proktaḥ śrī-pūrve kara-kampa-taḥ* ॥ **197** ॥
Jr.197d.1 *naca etad-iha apūrvatayā uktam-ity-āha*
AG. *samayī tu kara-stobhād-iti śrī-bhogahastake*।
Jr.198b.1 *yac-chrī pañcāśikā*
Qt.198b.1 *samayī tu kara-stobhān-mudrayā putrako bhavet*।
Jr.198b.2 *ity-ādi* ॥
Jr.198b.3 *atra-eva prakriya-antaram-āha*
AG. *carv-eva vā gurur-dadyād-vāma-amṛta-pariplutam* ॥ **198** ॥
niḥśaṅkaṃ grahaṇāc-chakti-gotro māyā-ujjhito bhavet।
sa-kampas-tv-āda-dānaḥ syāt samayī vācana-ādiṣu ॥ **199** ॥
3420 *kāla-antare 'dhva-saṃśuddhyā pālanāt-samaya-sthiteḥ*।
siddhi-pātram-iti śrī-mad-ānandeśvara ucyate ॥ **200** ॥
Jr.200d.1 *carv-iti ratna-pañca-ādy-ātmakam*।
yad-uktaṃ
Qt.200d.1 *deha-sthaṃ tu caruṃ vakṣye yat-surair-api durlabham*।
śiva-ambu reto raktaṃ ca nāla-ājyaṃ viśva-nirgamaḥ ॥
ato vidhāna-pūrvaṃ tu deha-sthaṃ grāhayec-carum। *iti*।
Jr.200d.2 *śakti-gotra-iti brāhmy-ādy-aṃśaka-rūpa ity-arthaḥ*।
ata eva niḥśaṅkaṃ grahaṇāt māyā-ujjhitaḥ
sākṣāt-kṛtā-vikalpa-nirupāya-saṃvit-tattvo bhaved-ity-arthaḥ।
ata eva caru-bhojana-āder-anupāya-parikaratvaṃ prāk saṃvāditam।
saśaṅkaḥ punar-etad-āda-dāno
vācana-śravaṇa-ādau samayī yogyaḥ syād-
-yena uttara-kālaṃ
tat-tac-chāstriya-samaya-paripālana-sūcita-tīvra-śakti-pātaḥ
ṣaḍ-vidhasya adhvanaḥ samyak putraka-dīkṣā-krameṇa
śuddhyā mokṣa-lakṣmī-lakṣaṇāyāḥ
siddher-bhājanaṃ bhavet।

naca etat sva-upajñam-eva uktam-ity-āha
śrī-mad-ānandeśvara ucyate iti || 200 ||

3421
Jr.200d.3 *evaṃ samayi-dīkṣām-abhidhāya,*
putraka-dīkṣāṃ vaktum-upakramate
AG. *yadā tu putrakaṃ kuryāt-tadā dīkṣāṃ samācaret*|
Jr.201b.1 *iha tāvat*
Qt.201b.1 *vedha-dīkṣāṃ vinā dīkṣāṃ yo yasya kurute priye*|
dvāv-etau narakaṃ yāta iti śāktasya niścayaḥ ||
Jr.201b.2 *ity-ādy-uktyā vinā āveśaṃ śiṣyasya dīkṣā na kāryā*
-iti prathamam-āveśa eva utpādanīyo
yena asya dīkṣā-yogyatve jñāte gurus-tat-prakriyām-
anutiṣṭhet,
anyathā punar-dīkṣā-arhatva-abhāvāt sa tyājya eva|
yad-vakṣyate
Qt.201b.2 *yasya tv-evam-api syān-na tam-atra-upalavat-tyajet*| *iti*
Jr.201b.3 *samāveśaḥ sarva-śāstreṣu avigānena ukta*
iti darśayituṃ śrī-ratnamālāyām-uktaṃ tal-lakṣaṇaṃ
tāvad-artha-gatyā abhidhatte
AG. *uktam śrī-ratnamālāyāṃ na-ādi-pha-antāṃ jvalat-*
prabhām || **201** ||
3422 *nyasyec-chikhā-antaṃ patati tena-atra-īdṛk kramo bhavet*|
Jr.202b.1 *tena-iti evaṃ-vidhena nyāsena hetunā*|
patati-iti deha-ādy-ātma-graha-parihāreṇa
rudra-śaktim-eva āviśati-ity-arthaḥ|
tad-uktaṃ tatra
Qt.202b.1 *tato nyasyet-tu śiṣyasya mālinīṃ jagad-ambikām*|
jvalaj-jvalana-saṅkāśāṃ pādād-yāvac-chikhā-antakam ||
na-ādi-pha-anta-samuccārāt pātayed-vihvala-indriyam|
eṣā dīkṣā mahā-devī mālinīvijaye priye ||*iti*||
Jr.202b.2 *tena-iti kākākṣivad-yojyam,*
tat tena-iti pātena hetunā|
atra-iti putra-dīkṣāyām|
īdṛk vakṣyamāṇaḥ ||
Jr.202b.3 *tam-eva āha*
AG. *prokṣitasya śiśor-nyasta-prokta-śodhya-adhva-*
paddhateḥ ||**202** ||
ṛju-deha-juṣaḥ śaktiṃ pādān-mūrdha-antam-āgatām|
pāśān-dahantīṃ saṃdīptāṃ cintayet-tan-mayo guruḥ || **203**||
3423 *upaviśya tatas-tasya mūla-śodhyāt prabhṛty-alam*|

anta-śodhya-avasāna-antāṃ dahantīṃ cintayet-
kramāt || **204** ||
evaṃ sarvāṇi śodhyāni tattva-ādīni purā-uktavat|
dagdhvā līnāṃ śive dhyāyen-niṣkale sakale 'thavā || **205** ||
yoginā yojitā mārge sajātīyasya poṣaṇam|
kurute nirdahaty-anyad-bhinna-jāti-kadambakam || **206** ||
Jr.206d.1 *tan-maya iti dīpta-śakti-mayaḥ*|
tata iti utthāna-anantaram|
mūla-śodhyam-ādi-śodhyaṃ yathā kalā-adhvani nivṛttiḥ,
anta-śodhyaṃ yathā atra-eva śānty-atītā|
evam-iti mūla-śodhyād-ārabhya anta-śodhya-avasānam|
purā-iti tattva-dikṣā-prakaraṇe|
niṣkale iti putraka-ādy-apekṣayā|
sakale iti sādhaka-uddeśena|
3424 *mārge iti madhya-dhāmni*|
sajātīyaṃ caitanyam|
bhinna-jātīyā mala-ādyāḥ || 206 ||
Jr.206d.2 *nanu evam-asya kiṃ phalam-ity-āśaṅkya āha*
AG. *anayā śodhyamānasya śiśos-tīvra-ādi-bhedataḥ*|
śakti-pātāc-citi-vyoma-prāṇana-antar-bahis-tanūḥ || **207** ||
āviśantī rudra-śaktiḥ kramāt-sūte phalaṃ tv-idam|
ānandam-udbhavaṃ kampaṃ nidrāṃ ghūrṇim ca deha-
gām || **208** ||
Jr.208d.1 *evam-asya dagdha-pāśasya śiṣyasya*
tīvra-tīvrāt śakti-pātāt citiṃ sākṣād-ātmānam-āviśantī
rudra-śaktir-ānandaṃ sūte
yāvat manda-mandāt śakti-pātāt deham-āviśantī ghūrṇim|
yataḥ citāv-ānanda-rūpatvād-ānandasya aucityaṃ,
śūnya-ātmani vyomni avakāśavatvād-udbhavasya,
prāṇa-ātmanī vāyau tat-kāritvāt kampasya,
antas-tanau buddhi-puryaṣṭake tat-tan-māyīya-vṛtti-
nirodhāt nidrāyāḥ,
bahis-tanā-
3425 *-v-ahantā-avaṣṭambha-bhaṅgāt ghūrṇer-iti*|
evaṃ hi sākṣād-asya dīkṣā vṛttā-iti guror-āśvāso bhaved
-iti bhāvaḥ || 208 ||
Jr.208d.2 *evam-asya stobhita-pāśatayā śive eva yojanikā jātā-iti*
tadā-eva deha-pātaḥ prasajed-ity-āśaṅkya āha
AG. *evaṃ stobhita-pāśasya yojitasya-ātmanaḥ śive*|
śeṣa-bhogāya kurvīta sṛṣṭiṃ saṃśuddha-tattva-gām || **209** ||

Jr.209d.1 *śeṣasya etad-deha-arambhakasya karmaṇaḥ* |
sṛṣṭim-iti arthād-etad-deha-gatām-eva || 209 ||

Jr.209d.2 *evam-api yadi*
etac-cihna-anudayāt manda-śakti-pātavataḥ
kasya-cit na ayam-evam-āveśo jāyate,
tadā evam-asya saṃskāra-antaraṃ kuryād-ity-āha

AG. *athavā kasyacin-na-evam-āveśas-tad-dahed-imam* |
bahir-antaś-ca-ukta-śaktyā pated-itthaṃ sa bhūtale || **210** ||

3426 *yasya tv-evam-api syān-na tam-atra-upalavat-tyajet* |

Jr.211b.1 *yugapad-eva*
ūrdhva-adho-vamad-agni-puñjasya
ūrdhva-mukhasya tri-koṇasya antar-upaveśitaṃ
sarvato repha-valitaṃ
jvālā-kalāpa-mayyā śaktyā bahir-antaś-ca dahed-iti guravaḥ |
syān-na-iti āveśaḥ |
upalavad-iti anāyāta-śakti-pātatvāt nibiḍa-jaḍi-mānam-ity-arthaḥ ||

Jr.211b.2 *evaṃ parityakto hi śiṣyaḥ saṃsāre eva majjana-unmajjanāni kurute iti tad-anujighṛkṣā-paratayā*
gurutaḥ śāstrataś-ca
siddham-apratihataṃ dīkṣā-antaraṃ vaktum-āha

AG. *atha sapratyayāṃ dīkṣāṃ vakṣye tuṣṭena dhīmatā* || **211** ||
śambhunāthena-upadiṣṭāṃ dṛṣṭāṃ sadbhāva-śāsane |

Jr.212b.1 *sadbhāva-śāsane iti śrī-tantrasadbhāve* ||

Jr.212b.2 *tām-eva āha*

AG. *sudhā-agni-maruto manda-para-kāla-agni-vāyavaḥ* || **212** ||

3427 *vahni-saudha-asu-kūṭa-agni-vāyuḥ sarve sa-ṣaṣṭhakāḥ* |
etat-piṇḍa-trayaṃ stobha-kāri pratyekam-ucyate || **213** ||

Jr.213d.1 *sudhā saḥ,*
agniḥ raḥ,
marut yaḥ,
evaṃ sryūṛ;
mando ḍa-kāraḥ,
tat-paraḥ phaṇa-bhṛc-chabda-vācyo ḍha-kāraḥ,

prāṇa-śamano 'ntako maḥ,
agniḥ raḥ,
vāyur-yaḥ,
evaṃ ḍḍhmryūṛ;
vahniḥ raḥ,
somaḥ saḥ,
asuḥ prāṇo haḥ,
kūṭaṃ kṣaḥ,
agniḥ raḥ,
vāyur-yaḥ,
evaṃ rshkṣryūṃ|
atra samāhāre dvandvaḥ|
sarve iti trayo 'pi piṇḍāḥ|
sa-ṣaṣṭhakā iti ū-kāra-āsana-sthā arthāt bindv-ādi-lāñchitāś-ca|
pratyekam-iti vyastam-ity-arthaḥ|
tad-uktaṃ tatra

Qt.213d.1 *atha-evam-api yasya syān-na-āveśaḥ kaśmala-ātmanaḥ|*
taṃ piṇḍa-tritayād-ekena-udbodha-padavīṃ nayet ||
soma-anala-anilair-ekaṃ piṇḍam-ādau samuddharet|
phaṇa-bhṛt-prāṇa-śamana-śikhi-vāyu-yutaṃ param ||
śikhi-soma-asu-kūṭa-agni-samīraiś-ca tṛtīyakam|
ṣaṣṭha-āsanāni sarvāṇi tilaka-aṅkāni sundari ||
tribhir-ebhir-bhaved-vyastaiḥ śakty-āveśaḥ śarīra-gaḥ
|| *iti* || 213 ||

3428

Jr.213d.2 *atra-eva iti-kartavyatām-āha*

AG. *śakti-bījaṃ smṛtaṃ yac-ca nyasyet-sārva-aṅgikaṃ tu tat|*
hṛc-cakre nyasyate mantro dvā-daśa-svara-bhūṣitaḥ || **214**||
japā-kusuma-saṃkāśaṃ caitanyaṃ tasya madhyataḥ|
vāpunā preritaṃ cakraṃ vahninā paridīpitam || **215** ||
tad-dhyāyec-ca japen-mantraṃ nāma-antarita-yogataḥ|
nimeṣa-ardhāt-tu śiṣyasya bhavet-stobho na saṃś-ayaḥ || **216** ||

Jr.216d.1 *śakti-bījaṃ śliṣṭatayā tri-koṇa-bījam-ī-kāro*

ḍambara-śabda-vācyā māyā ca|
sārva-aṅgikaṃ nyasyed-iti
etad-bīja-dvaya-madhye dīkṣyaṃ cintayed-ity-arthaḥ|
mantra iti sarva-mantra-sāmānya-ātmā ha-kāraḥ|
tasya-iti ṣaṇṭha-varjaṃ svara-dvā-daśaka-saṃbhinnatvāt
cakra-ākāratayā
3429 *avasthitasya mantrasya*|
tac-cakram-iti dīkṣyasya bahir-antaś-ca cintitaṃ
vāg-bhava-ādi-nikhila-mantra-kadambakam-ity-arthaḥ|
tena etat vāyunā ya-kāreṇa vahninā repheṇa ca
bahiḥ sarvato veṣṭitaṃ dhyāyet
yena evam-uddīpitaṃ sat stobha-āvir-bhāvana-
prāgalbhyam-iyāt|
mantram-iti piṇḍa-traya-madhyād-ekatamam|
nāma-antarita-yogataḥ iti tena ādau mantraḥ,
tato dīkṣya-nāma,
punar-mantra iti|
Qt.216d.1 *tri-koṇakaṃ ḍambaraṃ ca nyasyet-sarva-aṅga-saṅgatam*|
dvā-daśa-svara-saṃbhinnam hṛc-cakre mantra-nāyakam ||
udaya-āditya-saṅkāśaṃ jīvaṃ tena ca cālayet|
dīpayed-analena-eva vāyunā-api prabodhayet ||
mantreṇa-antaritaṃ nāma japec-chiṣyasya bhāmini|
āveśam-āyāti tatas-tat-kṣaṇād-eva tat-paraḥ ||
iti || 216 ||
Jr.216d.2 *evaṃ-ca asya kīdṛg-anubhava ity-āha*
AG. *ātmānaṃ prekṣate devi tattve tattve niyojitaḥ*|
yāvat-prāptaḥ paraṃ tattvaṃ tadā tv-eṣa na paśyati || **217**||
3430 *anena krama-yogena sarva-adhvānaṃ sa paśyati*
Jr.218b.1 *prekṣate iti arthāt yathāyathaṃ śuddham*|
na paśyati-iti draṣṭṛ-eka-sva-bhāva eva bhaved-ity-arthaḥ|
Jr.218b.2 *na kevalam-asya sva-ātmani eva pratyaya-nimittam*
-evam-anubhavo jāyate,
yāvat sva-parayor-api-ity-āha
AG. *atha-vā sarva-śāstrāṇy-apy-udgrāhayati tat-kṣaṇāt* ||**218**||
Jr.218d.1 *sarva-śāstrāṇi-iti arthād-adṛṣṭa-śrutāni* ||218||
Jr.218d.2 *yadi nāma ca pratiniyata-bhoga-icchuḥ ko 'pi syāt,*
tadā asya tādṛśīm-eva dīkṣāṃ kuryād-ity-āha
AG. *pṛthak-tattva-vidhau dīkṣāṃ yogyatā-vaśa-vartinaḥ*|
tattva-abhyāsa-vidhānena siddha-yogī samācaret ||**219**||

iti saṃdīkṣitasya-asya mumukṣoḥ śeṣa-vartane।
3431 *kula-krama-iṣṭir-ādeśyā pañca-avasthā-samanvitā* ॥ **220** ॥
Jr.220d.1 *yogyatā kasyacit pṛthvī-tattve eva bhuvana-īśatve vāñchā, kasyacit tu sadāśivatve*।
tattva-abhyāsa-vidhānena-iti tat-tad-dhāraṇa-ādy-ātmanā-ity-arthaḥ।
śeṣa-vartane iti śeṣa-vṛtti-nimittam-ity-arthaḥ ॥ 220 ॥
Jr.220d.2 *pañca-avasthā-samanvitam-eva vyācaṣṭe*
AG. *jāgrad-ādiṣu saṃvittir-yathā syād-anapāyinī*।
kula-yāgas-tathā-ādeśyo yoginī-mukha-saṃsthitaḥ ॥ **221** ॥
Jr.221d.1 *anapāyinī-iti*
Qt.221d.1 .... *na sā-avasthā na yā śivaḥ*
Jr.221d.2 *iti bhaṅgyā pravṛttā avirata-rūpā-ity-arthaḥ* ॥ 221 ॥
Jr.221d.3 *tad-eva āha*
AG. *sarvaṃ jāgrati kartavyaṃ svapne pratyeka-mantra-gam*।
nivārya supte mūla-ākhyaḥ sva-śakti-paribṛṃhitaḥ ॥ **222** ॥
3432 *turye tv-ekā-eva dūty-ākhyā tad-atīte kuleśitā*।
sva-śakti-paripūrṇānām-itthaṃ pūjā pravartate ॥ **223** ॥
Jr.223d.1 *iha khalu jāgrad-ādy-avasthāsu*
yathāyathaṃ bhedasya hānir-abhedasya ca udaya iti
jāgrad-avasthāyāṃ nikhilam-eva mantra-jātaṃ
pūjanīyatayā yojyam;
svapna-avasthāyām-api evaṃ,
kintu pratyekam-ārirādhayiṣitam-ekam-eva
parā-ādi-mantram-adhikṛtya-ity-arthaḥ।
suṣupta-avasthāyāṃ tu
sarvaṃ parivāra-bhūtaṃ mantra-jātam-apāsya
parā-ādi-śakti-traya-yogi-bhairava-trayaṃ kuleśvarau ca ity-eva pūjyam,
evaṃ turye 'pi ekā-eva kuleśvarī,
turya-atīte ca kuleśvara eva-iti ॥ 223 ॥
Jr.223d.2 *etad-eva anyatra-api atidiśati*
AG. *piṇḍa-stha-ādi ca pūrva-uktaṃ sarva-atīta-avasānakam*।
avasthā-pañcakaṃ prokta-bhedaṃ tasmai nirū-payet ॥ **224** ॥

3433
Jr.224d.1 *pūrva-iti daśam-āhnike*। *prokta-bhedam-iti yogi-jñāni-*

viṣayatayā। *tasmai-iti evaṃ saṃdīkṣitāya mum-*
ukṣave ॥ 224 ॥
Jr.224d.2 *idanīṃ dīkṣā-anantara-uddiṣṭaṃ sādhaka-ācāryayor-*
abhiṣekam-api āha
AG. *sādhakasya bubhukṣos-tu samyag-yoga-abhiṣecanam*।
tatra-iṣṭvā vibhavair-devaṃ hema-ādi-mayam-
avraṇam ॥ **225** ॥
dīpa-aṣṭakaṃ rakta-varti-sarpiṣā-pūrya bodhayet।
kula-aṣṭakena tat-pūjyaṃ śaṅkhe ca-api kuleśvarau ॥ **226** ॥
ānanda-amṛta-saṃpūrṇe śiva-hasta-ukta-vartmanā।
tena-abhiṣiñcet-taṃ paścāt sa kuryān-mantra-sād-
hanam ॥ **227** ॥
3434 *ācāryasya-abhiṣeko 'yam-adhikāra-anvitaḥ sa tu*।
kuryāt-piṣṭa-ādibhiś-ca-asya catuṣ-ṣaṣṭiṃ pradī-
pakān ॥ **228** ॥
aśṭa-aśṭakena pūjyās-te madhye prāgvat kuleśvarau।
śiva-hasta-ukta-yuktyā-eva gurum-apy-abhiṣecayet ॥ **229** ॥
Jr.229d.1 *yoga-iti tat-pradhānam-ity-arthaḥ*।
tatra-iti yoga-abhiṣecane।
śaṅkhe iti mahā-śaṅkhe।
śiva-hasta-ukta-vartmanā-iti śakty-ākarṣaṇa-ātmanā
krameṇa।
tena-iti śaṅkhena।
sa iti bubhukṣuḥ sādhakaḥ।
piṣṭa-ādibhir-iti ādi-śabdāt valmīka-mṛd-ādi।
prāgvad-iti śaṅkha-gatatvena ॥ 229 ॥
Jr.229d.2 *evam-abhiṣekeṇa anayoḥ kiṃ syād*
-ity-āśaṅkāṃ nirācikīrṣur-āgamam-eva paṭhati
AG. *abhiṣiktāv-imāv-evaṃ sarva-yogi-gaṇena tu*।
3435 *viditau bhavatas-tatra gurur-mokṣa-prado bhavet* ॥ **230** ॥
Jr.230d.1 *atra-eva turya-pādasya tātparyato 'rthaṃ vyākhyātum-āha*
AG. *tātparyaṁ-asya pādasya sa siddhīḥ saṃprayacchati*।
gurur-yaḥ sādhakaḥ prāk-syād-anyo mokṣaṃ dadāty
-alam ॥ **231** ॥
anayoḥ kathayej-jñānaṃ tri-vidhaṃ sarvam-apy-alam।
svakīya-ājñāṃ ca vitaret sva-kriyā-karaṇaṃ prati ॥ **232** ॥
Jr.232d.1 *idam-atra tātparyam —*

yad-anayor-madhyāt yaḥ pūrvaṃ sādhakaḥ san guruḥ,
sa parebhyaḥ siddhīr-eva dadāti;
anyaḥ prathamam-eva yo guruḥ,
so 'tyarthaṃ prakarṣeṇa siddhi-dāna-puraḥ-sarī-kāreṇa
mokṣam-api-ity-arthaḥ |
yady-api sa-bīja-dīkṣā-dikṣitasya
mumukṣor-eva ācāryatvam-āmnātaṃ,
tathā-api tat karmi-viṣayam;
idaṃ tu
3436 *jñāni-viṣayam*
-iti na kaścid-virodhaḥ |
tri-vidham-āṇava-śākta-śāṃbhava-rūpam |
sva-kriyā dīkṣā-ādikā ||
Jr.232d.2 *etad-eva āntareṇa krameṇa-api abhidhatte*
AG. *ṣaṭkaṃ kāraṇa-saṃjñaṃ yat-tathā yaḥ paramaḥ śivaḥ* |
sākaṃ bhairava-nāthena tad-aṣṭakam-udāhṛtam || **233** ||
pratyekaṃ tasya sārva-ātmyaṃ paśyaṃs-tāṃ vṛttim-ātma-gām |
cakṣur-ādau saṃkramayed-yatra yatra-indriye guruḥ || **234** ||
sa eva pūrṇaiḥ kalaśair-abhiṣekaḥ paraḥ smṛtaḥ |
vinā bāhyair-api-ity-uktaṃ śrī-vīrāvalibhairave || **235** ||
Jr.235d.1 *brahmā viṣṇuḥ rudra īśvaraḥ sadāśivo 'nāśriśivaś-ca-iti* |
paramaśiva iti ṣaṭ-triṃśaḥ |
bhairava-nāthaḥ
3437 *sapta-triṃśa-ādi-śabda-vyavahāryaṃ pūrṇaṃ rūpam* |
tat yad-etasya aṣṭakasya pratyekaṃ sārva-ātmyena
catuṣ-ṣaṣṭikā vṛttir-avabhāsate,
tām-ātma-gāṃ vidhāya
yatra yatra cakṣur-ādāv-indriye
sva-indriya-praṇālikayā abhiṣecyasya guruḥ saṃkramayet
tad-aikya-āpattiṃ kuryāt;
sa eva vinā bāhyaṃ
saṃvid-rasā-pūritatvāt pūrṇair-āntaraiḥ kalaśair
-bāhya-vailakṣaṇyāt paro 'bhiṣeko 'smad-gurubhiḥ smṛto
'nuṣṭheyatayā abhisaṃhita ity-arthaḥ ||
Jr.235d.2 *evam-abhiṣeka-vidhim-abhidhāya,*

tat purā-uddiṣṭaṃ vedha-sva-rūpaṃ nirṇetu-kāmas
-tad-dīkṣāṃ vaktum-upakramate

AG. *sadya eva tu bhoga-ipsor-yogāt-siddhatamo guruḥ* |
kuryāt-sadyas-tathā-abhīṣṭa-phala-daṃ vedha-dīkṣ-aṇam || **236** ||

Jr.236d.1 *yogāt-siddhatama iti svabhyasta-yogo 'tra adhikṛta ity-arthaḥ* |
yad-vakṣyati

Qt.236d.1 *sā ca-abhyāsavatā kāryā ... iti* |

Jr.236d.2 *vedha-iti madhyama-prāṇa-śaktyā ūrdhva-ūrdhva-kram-*
3438 *ṇena cakra-ādhāra-ādināṃ bhedanam* |
yad-vakṣyati

Qt.236d.2 ... *yena-ūrdhva-ūrdhva-praveśataḥ* |
śiṣyasya cakra-saṃbheda-pratyayo jāyate dhruvaḥ || *iti* |

Jr.236d..3 *yad-abhiprāyeṇa-eva*

Qt.236d.3 *ātmānaṃ maṇim-āśritya śaktiṃ nyasyet-tu herukam* |
pāśa-viśleṣa-karaṇaṃ vedha ity-abhisaṃjñitam ||

Jr.236d.4 *ity-ādi uktam* || 236 ||

Jr.236d.5 *tad-eva āha*

AG. *vedha-dīkṣā ca bahu-dhā tatra tatra nirūpitā* |
sā ca-abhyāsavatā kāryā yena-ūrdhva-ūrdhva-praveśataḥ || **237** ||
śiṣyasya cakra-saṃbheda-pratyayo jāyate dhruvaḥ |

Jr.238b.1 *yena-iti abhyāsavattvena* ||

Jr.238b.2 *evaṃ-vidhena asya kiṃ syād-ity-āśaṅkya āha*

AG. *yena-aṇimā-ādikā siddhiḥ ...*

Jr.238c.1 *anyathā punar-ūrdhva-ūrdhva-praveśa-abhāve*
vighna-ādi-bhājanatvaṃ bhavet
yad-āgama ity-āha

3439

AG. ... *śrī-mālāyāṃ ca coditā* || **238** ||
ūrdhva-cakra-daśa-alābhe piśāca-āveśa eva sā |

Jr.239b.1 *yad-uktaṃ tatra*

Qt.239b.1 *adho 'vasthā yadā ūrdhvaṃ saṅkramanti varānane* |
sā-eva mokṣa-pada-avasthā sā-eva jñānasya bhājanam ||
ūrdhva-cakra-gata-avasthā yadā-adhaḥ saṃbhavanti ca |
tadā paiśāca āveśaḥ sa vai vighnasya kāraṇam ||
iti ||

Jr.239b.2 *bahu-dhā-ity-uktaṃ nirūpayati*

AG. *mantra-nāda-bindu-śakti-bhujaṅgama-para-ātmikā* ||**239**||
ṣoḍhā śrī-gahvare vedha-dīkṣā-uktā parameśinā|

Jr.240b.1 *tad-uktaṃ tatra*

Qt.240b.1 *mantra-vedhaṃ tu nāda-ākhyaṃ bindu-vedham-ataḥ param*|
śāktaṃ bhujaṅga-vedhaṃ tu paraṃ ṣaṣṭham-udāhṛtam\iti

Jr.240b.2 *ṣoḍhātve ca atra adhva-śuddhi-garbhī-kāraḥ kāraṇam*|
yad-uktaṃ

Qt.240b.2 *ṣoḍhā vai vedha-bodhena adhvānaṃ śodhayet-priye*|
iti ||

3440

Jr.240b.3 *tatratyam-eva grantham-arthataḥ śabdataś-ca paṭhati*

AG. *jvālā-kulaṃ sva-śāstra-uktaṃ cakram-aṣṭa-araka-ādikam* || **240** ||
dhyātvā tena-asya hṛc-cakra-vedhanān-mantra-vedhanam|

Jr.241b.1 *sva-iti anuṣṭheyatayā*|
tena-iti aṣṭa-araka-ādinā|
hṛc-cakra-iti tātsthyāt cetya-saṃkocita ātmā lakṣyate|
yad-uktaṃ

Qt.241b.1 *jvālā-kulaṃ tato dhyātvā aṣṭa-araṃ cakram-uttamam*|
dvā-daśa-aram-atho vā-api sva-śāstra-vidhi-yogataḥ ||
para-cittaṃ vedhanīyaṃ mantra-vedha udāhṛtaḥ| *iti* ||

Jr.241b.2 *etad-eva krama-antareṇa-api āha*

AG. *ā-kāraṃ nava-dhā dehe nyasya saṃkramayet-tataḥ*|| **241** ||
nyāsa-yogena śiṣyāya dīpyamānaṃ mahā-arciṣam|
pāśa-stobhāt-tatas-tasya para-tattve tu yoganam || **242** ||

3441 *iti dīkṣottare dṛṣṭo vidhir-me śaṃbhunā-uditaḥ*|
nāda-uccāreṇa nāda-ākhyaḥ sṛṣṭi-krama-niyogataḥ|| **243**||
nādena vedhayec-cittaṃ nāda-vedha udīritaḥ|
bindu-sthāna-gataṃ-cittaṃbhrū-madhya-patha-saṃs-thitam || **244** ||
hṛl-lakṣye vā maheśāni binduṃ jvālā-kula-prabham|
tena saṃbodhayet [21] *-sādhyaṃ*
-bindv-ākhyo 'yaṃ prakīrtitaḥ || **245** ||

---

21 Gnoli, *Luce*, p.708 footnote 155 reads: *saṃvedhayet* for *saṃbodhayet*. The change seems unnecessary.

śāktaṃ śaktimad-uccārād-gandha-uccāreṇa sundari ।
śṛṅgāṭaka-āsana-sthaṃ tu kuṭilaṃ kuṇḍala-ākṛtim ॥ **246** ॥
anuccāreṇa ca-uccārya vedhayen-nikhilaṃ jagat ।
3442 *evaṃ bhramara-vedhena śākta-vedha udāhṛtaḥ* ॥ **247** ॥
Jr.247d.1 *nava-dhā-iti randhra-bhedāt* ।
dehe iti arthāt svakīye ।
nyāsa-yogena tyaktāt nava-dhā-eva dīpyamānam ।
mahā-arciṣam-ity-anena asya pāśa-stobhena sāmarthyaṃ darśitam ।
nāda-uccāreṇa-iti nāda-śabdena dīrgha-ātma-nāda-bījam ।
sṛṣṭi-iti na-ādi-pha-anta-lakṣaṇā ।
nādena-iti anacka-kalā-ātmanā svayam-uccarad-rūpeṇa ।
tad-uktaṃ
Qt.247d.1 *nādaṃ dīrghaṃ samuccārya nādaṃ nāde samākramet* ।
na-ādi-pha-antaṃ samuccārya varṇa-adhvānaṃ viśodhayet ॥
nādena vedhayed-devi nāda-vedha udāhṛtaḥ । *iti*
Jr.247d.2 *bindu-sthāna-gatatvam-eva bhrū-madhya-ity-ādinā vyākhyātam* ।
cittam-iti śiṣyasya saṃbandhi,
tac-ca arthāt bindv-āviṣṭam ।
bindum-iti arthāt bhāvayitvā ।
tad-uktaṃ
Qt.247d.2 *bhrū-madhye hṛdaye vā-atha kande vā bindu-bhāvanāt* ।
āviśya śiṣya-cittaṃ tu bindu-bhedena vedhayet ॥ *iti*
Jr.247d.3 *yac-ca*
'guru-matta-gandha-saṅkocanād-utplavate 'tibhīmaḥ'? [sic]
ity-ādi-dṛśā
-gandhasya matta-gandhasya niṣpīḍana-ādi-yukti-bala-upanatena ūrdhvaṃ cāreṇa madhya-śakte-
3443 *-r-dvā-daśa-anta-avasthite śiva-ātmani śaktimati uccaiś-caraṇa-sāmarasyam-āsādya*
janma-ādhāre satata-uditatvāt śṛṅgāṭaka-āsana-sthaṃ prāṇa-śakty-abheditayā kuṇḍala-ākṛtiṃ kuṭilam
-anackam-anuccāreṇa uccārya
vayam-uccarad-rūpatvād-uccāra-prayatna-nirapekṣatayā
sva-parayoḥ svā-rasike eva uccāre 'vadhāya

nikhilam-api jagad-vedhayet,
asau tat-tat-sthāna-gatyā bhramaṃ dadhānaḥ śākto vedhaḥ
uktaḥ || 247 ||
Jr.247d.4 atha etad-anuṣaktaṃ bhujaṅga-vedham-abhidhātum-āha
AG. sā ca-eva paramā śaktir-ānanda-pravikāsinī |
janma-sthānāt-paraṃ yāti phaṇa-pañcaka-bhūṣitā || **248** ||
Jr.248d.1 param-iti dvā-daśa-anta-avasthitaṃ śaktimantam |
tad-uktam
Qt.248d.1 evaṃ pañca-phaṇā devī nirgatā-ādhara [22] -maṇḍalāt
Jr.248d.2 ity-upakramya
Qt.248d.2 gatā sā parama-akāśaṃ paraṃ nirvāṇa-maṇḍalam ||
iti || 248 ||

3444

Jr.248d.3 phaṇa-pañcaka-bhūṣitatvam-eva prapañcayati
AG. kalās-tattvāni nanda-ādyā vyomāni ca kulāni ca |
brahma-ādi-kāraṇāny-akṣāṇy-eva sā pañcaka-
ātmikā || **249** ||
evaṃ pañca-prakārā sā brahma-sthāna-vinirgatā |
brahma-sthāne viśantī tu taḍil-līnā virājate || **250** ||
praviṣṭā vedhayet-kāyam-ātmānaṃ pratibhedayet |
evaṃ bhujaṅga-vedhas-tu kathito bhairava-āgame || **251** ||
tāvad-bhāvayate cittaṃ yāvac-cittaṃ kṣayaṃ gatam |
kṣīṇe citte sureśāni para-ānanda udāhṛtaḥ || **252** ||
Jr.252d.1 kalāḥ śānty-atītā-ādyāḥ pañca |
tattvāni pṛthi-
3445 -vy-ādīni |
nanda-ādyās-tithayaḥ |
vyomāni janma-nābhi-hṛd-bindu-sthānāni |
kulāni mahākaula-kaula-akula-kula-akula-ākhyāni |
brahma-ādi-kāraṇāni sadāśiva-antāni |
akṣāṇi buddhi-indriyāṇi karma-indriyāṇi ca |
brahma-sthāna-iti janma-ādhārāt,
brahma-sthāne iti dvā-daśa-ante,
etad-ubhayam-api hi asya mukhyam-adhiṣṭhānam-ity-
abhiprāyaḥ |

22. For *ādhara* read *ādhāra*.

kāyam-iti cakra-ādhāra-ādi-rūpam।
nanu kāya-vedhena ātmanaḥ kiṃ syād
-ity-uktam-ātmānaṃ pratibhedayed-iti।
uktaṃ ca
Qt.252d.1 *bhujaṅga-kuṭila-ākārā adho nābher-vyavasthitā*।
prabuddhā phaṇi-vad-gacchet phaṇā-pañcaka-bhūṣitā ॥
pañcakāt pañcakaṃ yāvad-vedhaṃ bhujaṅga-saṃjñitam। *iti*।
Jr.252d.2 *kṣīṇe iti vikalpa-rūpatā-parityāgāt*।
para-ānanda iti nirvikalpaka-camat-kāra-ātmā ॥ 252 ॥
Jr.252d.3 *ata eva asya sarvato bheda-vigalanam-ity-āha*
AG. *na-indriyāṇi na vai prāṇā na-antaḥ-karaṇa-gocaraḥ*।
na mano na-api mantavyaṃ na mantā na mani-
kriyā ॥ **253** ॥
3446 *sarva-bhāva-parikṣīṇaḥ para-vedha udāhṛtaḥ*।
Jr.254b.1 *prakāra-antareṇa-api asya bahu-dhātvaṃ darśayati*
AG. *manu-śakti-bhuvana-rūpa-jñā-piṇḍa-sthāna-nāḍi-para-*
bhedāt ॥ **254** ॥
nava-dhā kalayanty-anye vedaṃ [23] *guravo rahasya-vidaḥ*।
Jr.255b.1 *etad-eva krameṇa lakṣayati*
AG. *māyā-garbha-agni-varṇā-augha-yukte try-aśriṇi maṇ-*
ḍale ॥ **255** ॥
dhyātvā jvālā-kara-ālena tena granthīn vibhedayet।
puṣpair-hanyād-yojayec-ca pare mantra abhidho
vidhiḥ ॥ **256** ॥
nāḍy-āviśya-anyatarayā caitanyaṃ kanda-dhāmani।
piṇḍī-kṛtya paribhramya pañca-aṣṭa-śikhayā haṭhāt
॥ **257** ॥
3447 *śakti-śūla-agra-gamitaṃ kva-api cakre niyojayet*।
śaktyā-iti śākto vedho 'yaṃ sadyaḥ-pratyaya-kār
akaḥ ॥ **258** ॥
ādhārān-nirgatayā śikhayā jyotsna-avadātayā rabhasāt।
aṅguṣṭha-mūla-pīṭha-krameṇa śiṣyasya līnayā
vyomni ॥ **259**॥
dehaṃ svacchī-kṛtya
kṣa-ādinā-a-antān smaran-purā-ukta-pury-oghān।

---

23. Rastogi, p.163, suggests that this should read *vedhaṃ* but even so it means much the same..

nija-maṇḍala-nirdhyānāt-pratibimbayate bhuvana-vedhaḥ || **260** ||
bhrū-madhya-udita-baindava-dhāma-antaḥ kāṃcid-ākṛtiṃ rucirām|
tādātmyena dhyāyec-chiṣyaṃ paścāc-ca tan-mayī-kuryāt || **261** ||
iti rūpa-vedha uktaḥ sā ca-iha-ākṛtir-upaiti dṛśyatvam|
3448 *ante tat-sāyujyaṃ śiṣyaś-ca-āyāti tan-mayī-bhūtaḥ* || **262** ||
vijñānam-aṣṭa-dhā yad-ghrāṇa-ādika-buddhi-saṃjña-karaṇa-antaḥ|
tat sva-sva-nāḍi-sūtra-krameṇa saṃcārayec-chiṣye || **263** ||
abhimāna-dārḍhya-bandha-krameṇa vijñāna-saṃjñako vedhaḥ|
hṛdaya-vyomani sadyo divya-jñāna-arka-samudayaṃ dhatte || **264** ||
piṇḍaḥ paraḥ kalā-ātmā sūkṣmaḥ puryaṣṭako bahiḥ sthūlaḥ|
—chāyā-ātmā sa parāṅ-mukha
ādarśa-ādau ca saṃmukho jñeyaḥ || **265** ||—
iti yaḥ piṇḍa-vibhedas-taṃ rabhasād-uttara-uttare śamayet|
tat-tad-galane kramaśaḥ parama-padaṃ piṇḍa-vedhena || **266** ||
3449 *yad-yad-dehe cakraṃ tatra śiśor-etya viśramaṃ kramaśaḥ*|
ujjvalayet-tac-cakraṃ sthāna-ākhyas-tat-phala-prado vedhaḥ || **267** ||
nāḍyaḥ pradhāna-bhūtās-tisro 'nyās-tad-gatās-tv-asaṃkhyeyāḥ|
ekī-kāras-tābhir-nāḍī-vedho 'tra tat-phala-kṛt || **268** ||
abhilaṣita-nāḍi-vāho mukhyābhiś-cakṣur-ādi-niṣṭhābhiḥ|
tad-bodha-prāptiḥ syān-nāḍī-vedhe vicitra-bahu-rūpā || **269** ||
lāṅgūla-ākṛti-bala-vat sva-nāḍi-saṃveṣṭitām-apara-nāḍīm āsphoṭya siddham-api bhuvi pātayati haṭhān-mahā-yogī || **270** ||
3450 *para-vedhaṃ samasteṣu cakreṣv-advaitam-āmṛśan*|
paraṃ śivaṃ prakurvīta śivatā-āpatti-do guruḥ ||**271**||

Jr.271d.1 *māyā*।
māyā-bījam।
agni-varṇā rephāḥ।
try-aśriṇi-iti arthād-ūrdhva-mukhe।
dhyātvā-iti arthāt tad-antar-upaviṣṭaṃ śiṣyam।
tena-iti try-aśreṇa maṇḍalena।
anyatarayā-iti suṣumṇa-ādi-nāḍi-traya-madhyād-ekayā।
piṇḍī-kṛtya-iti sarvata upasaṃhṛtya।
paribhramya-iti tatra-eva dakṣiṇāvarta-krameṇa mahatā vegena।
pañca karma-indriyāṇi,
aṣṭau buddhi-indriya-pañcakam-antaḥ-karaṇa-trayaṃ ca।
śakti-iti śakti-vyāpinī-samanā-lakṣaṇam।
kva-api-iti yathā-abhīṣṭe।
pratyayaḥ āveśa-lakṣaṇaḥ।
śikhayā-iti tad-rūpayā śaktyā।
jyotsna-avadātayā-ity-anena asyāḥ prakāśakatvaṃ nairmalyaṃ ca āveditam।
etad-aucityād-eva ca dehaṃ svacchī-kṛtya-iti uktam।
vyomni-iti dvā-daśa-ante।
tac-ca līnatvam-aṅguṣṭhān-mūla-pīṭhād-vā anusandhātavyam।
aṅguṣṭha-mūla-krameṇa-iti kṣa-ādi-na-antān-iti saṃhāra-krameṇa।

3451 *purā-iti aṣṭam-āhnika-ādau*।
nija-maṇḍalaṃ sva-śarīram।
pratibimbayate iti śiṣyam-api tathā-vidham-eva kuryād-ity-arthaḥ।
kāṃcid-iti yathā-iṣṭa-devatā-rūpām।
kiṃ-ca atra phalam-ity-āśaṅkya āha sā ca-ity-ādi।
aṣṭa-dhātvam-eva sphuṭayati ghrāṇa-ity-ādinā।
antar-iti antaḥ-karaṇa-trayam।
hṛdaya-iti sarva-nāḍīnām-abhivyakti-sthānatvāt।
piṇḍaḥ śarīram।
kalā-iti kañcuka-pañcaka-upalakṣaṇam।
ya iti tri-vidha-uddiṣṭaḥ।
uttara-uttare iti sthūlaḥ sūkṣme, sūkṣmaś-ca pare iti।

kramaśa iti yathāyathaṃ dārḍhyena-ity-arthaḥ।
atra ca antarā parikalpitaṃ
Qt.271d.1 chāyā-ātmā sa parāṅ-mukha ādarśa-ādau ca saṃmukho
jñeyaḥ।
Jr.271d.2 iti ardham-asaṅgatatvād-antar-gaḍu-prāyam-iti upekṣyam।
yathā-sthita-vyākhyāna-hevākinām-etat-tu saṅgatiṃ yadi
upeyāt,
tad-āstām;
asmākaṃ punar-iyatī na-asti dṛṣṭiḥ।
cakram-iti ādhāra-ādīnām-upalakṣaṇam।
kramaśa iti nāḍī-cakra-āder-ārabhya।
ujjvalayed-iti saṃvid-unmukhatayā dīptī-kuryād-ity-arthaḥ।
tat-phala-iti
3452 ujjvalī-karaṇa-ātmā।
tad-gatā iti tac-chāyā-prāyatvāt।
tābhir-iti anyābhir-asaṅkhyeyābhir-nāḍībhiḥ।
tat-phalam-ekī-kāra-lakṣaṇam।
kim-ata iti na mantavyam-ity-āha abhilaṣita-ity-ādi।
lāṅgūla-ākṛti-ity-anena
yathā kaścin-mahā-prāṇī sva-puccha-āsphoṭanena tarv-ādi
pātayati,
tathā ayam-api।
param-iti kaṭākṣitam।
mahā-yogī-iti śivatā-patti-do gurur-iti ca
sarva-śeṣatvena jñeyam ॥ 271 ॥
Jr.271d.3 etac-ca āgame 'pi evam-uktam-ity-āha
AG. śrī-mad-vīrāvalikule tathā ca-itthaṃ nirūpitam।
Jr.272b.1 tad-eva āha
AG. abhedyaṃ sarvathā jñeyaṃ madhyaṃ jñātvā na
lipyate ॥ **272** ॥
tad-vibhāga-krame siddhaḥ sa gurur-mocayet paśun।
Jr.273b.1 iha ayogibhiḥ bhettum-aśakyam, ata eva yoga-abhyāsa-ādi-
krameṇa avaśya-jñātavyaṃ,madhyaṃ ma-
3453 dhya-prāṇa-śaktiṃ jñātvā tat-tac-cakra-ādi-bhedanena
nirargalaṃ pravahantīm-anubhūya yo na lipyate prāṇa-
apāna-ubhaya-vāhani-magno na bhavet
ata eva tatra madhya-śaktāv-anantara-ukte

mantra-ādy-ātmani vibhāga-krame
dārḍhyena labdha-anubhavaḥ;
sa tāttvika-artha-upadeṣṭā paśūn mocayet
tat-tac-cakra-ādhāra-ādibhya unmajjayed-ity-arthaḥ ||
Jr.273b.2 *katham-ca etat guruḥ kuryād-ity-āha*
AG. *guror-agre viśec-chiṣyo vaktraṃ vaktre tu vedhayet* || **273** ||
rūpaṃ rūpe tu viṣayair-yāvat-samarasī-bhavet |
Jr.274b.1 *sva-agra-upaviṣṭasya hi śiṣyasya gurur-vaktre*
Qt.274b.1 ... *śaivī mukham-iha-ucyate* |
Jr.274b.2 *ity-ādy-uktyā tan-madhya-śaktau svāṃ madhya-śaktiṃ*
tadīya-rūpe tad-grāhake cakṣur-indriye
svaṃ cakṣur-indriya-rūpam-
-etad-upalakṣiteṣu
tad-indriya-antareṣv-api sva-i-
3454 *ndriya-antarāṇi vedhayet*
tan-nimittaṃ prayuñjīta,
yāvad-viṣayī-krīyamāṇair-ebhiḥ samarasī-bhavet
tad-aikātmyam-āsādayed-ity-arthaḥ ||
Jr.274b.3 *nanu evam-api kiṃ syād-ity-āśaṅkya āha*
AG. *citte samarasī-bhūte dvayor-aunmanasī sthitiḥ* || **274** ||
ubhayoś-ca-unmano-gatyā tat-kāle dīkṣito bhavet |
śaśi-bhāskara-saṃyoge jīvas-tan-mayatāṃ vrajet || **275** ||
Jr.275d.1 *dīkṣita iti arthāt śiṣyaḥ* |
yatas
-tad-ātmā
śaśi-bhāskarayoḥ prāṇa-apānayoḥ
madhya-śaktau samyak sva-sva-rūpa-troṭanena
sāmarasya-ātmani yoge sati
tan-mayatāṃ vrajet
tad-aikadhyam-āsādayed-ity-arthaḥ || 275 ||
Jr.275d.2 *etac-ca kāraṇānām-api āśaṃsā-āspadam-ity-āha*
AG. *atra brahma-ādayo devā muktaye mokṣa-kāṅkṣiṇaḥ* |
3455
Jr.276b.1 *nanu evaṃ kasmād-iti-āśaṅkya āha*
AG. *nirudhya raśmi-cakraṃ svaṃ bhoga-mokṣāv-ubhāv*
-api || **276** ||
grasate yadi tad-dīkṣā śārvī-iyaṃ parikīrtitā |

Jr.277b.1 *yadi nāma ayam-evaṃ-vidho gurv-ādiḥ*
svaṃ manaḥ-prabhṛti raśmi-cakraṃ nirudhya
ubhau paraspara-vyāvṛttau bhoga-mokṣāv-api grasate
bhoge 'pi muktas-
-tad-iyaṃ pārameśvarī dīkṣā parikīrtitā
jīvan-mukti-pradatvena prakhyātā-ity-arthaḥ ||
Jr.277b.2 *ata eva āha*
AG. *sa eṣa mokṣaḥ kathito niḥspandaḥ sarva-jantuṣu* || **277** ||
agnī-ṣoma-kalā-āghāta-saṅghātāt spandanaṃ haret|
Jr.278b.1 *niḥspanda iti sarva-daśāsv-api avicalad-rūpa ity-arthaḥ*|
evaṃ dīkṣito hi
pramāṇa-prameya-maya-prā-
3456 *-ṇa-apāna-ātmanor-agnī-somayoḥ kalānāṃ paunaḥ-*
punyena āghātāt sva-rūpa-apohanena pramātṛ-rūpe eva
viśrāntyā spandanaṃ haret
bahir-mukhatāṃ śamayed-ity-arthaḥ ||
Jr.278b.2 *evam-ca asya kathaṃ syād-ity-āśaṅkya āha*
AG. *bāhyaṃ prāṇaṃ bāhya-gataṃ timira-ākāra-yogataḥ* || **278**||
niryātaṃ romakūpais-tu bhramantaṃ sarva-kāraṇaiḥ|
madhyaṃ nirlakṣyam-āsthāya bhramayed-visṛjet-tat-
aḥ || **279** ||
saṃghaṭṭa-utpāṭa-yogena vedhayed-granthi-pañcakam|
saṃghaṭṭa-vṛtti-yugalaṃ madhya-dhāma vicintayet || **280** ||
na-ātma-vyoma-bahir-mantra-deha-saṃdhānam-ācaret|
3457 *dīkṣā-iyaṃ sarva-jantūnāṃ śivatā-āpatti-dāyikā* || **281** ||
Jr.281d.1 *iha bahiḥ-prasaraṇa-śīlam-api*
prameya-ātmakatvāt bāhyam-apānaṃ prāṇaṃ ca
tad-viśrānty-unmukhatvāt madhyam,
ata eva romakūpa-ātma-nāḍi-dvāraiḥ sarvataḥ prasarad-
rūpaṃ
Qt.281d.1 *nahi bhedāt-paraṃ duḥkhaṃ tamo na-advaya-saṃvṛtteḥ*|
Jr.281d.2 *ity-ādy-uktyā timira-ākāraṃ pramātṛ-rūpam-avalambya*
brahma-ādibhih kāraṇair-adhiṣṭhiteṣu sthāneṣu
ūrdhvaṃ gati-rodhāt bhramantam-api
dhyeya-antara-parityāga-āśrayaṇena tatra-eva bhramayet;
tathā bhramaṇa-anantaraṃ ca visṛjet
yena prāṇa-apānayoḥ saṃghaṭṭasya ūrdhva-gati-yogena
tat-tat-kāraṇa-adhiṣṭhitaṃ granthi-pañcakaṃ vedhayet

yathā samarasī-bhūta-prāṇa-apāna-yugmaṃ
madhya-dhāma vicintayet
tatra-eva baddha-avadhāno bhavet
yena parimita-ātmano vyomnaḥ śūnyasya
bahir-bāhyasya nīla-ādeh
pratibimba-dhāraṇāt gupta-bhāṣiṇyā buddher-dehasya ca
sandhānaṃ na ācared-
-ātmany-eva sākṣā-
3458 -t-kāram-anubhavet
yena asyā dīkṣāyāḥ śivatā-āpatti-dāyitvam-uktam || 281 ||
Jr.281d.3 evaṃ bahu-vidhāṃ vedha-dīkṣām-abhidhāya
tad-iti-kartavyatā-śeṣam-api āha
AG. dīkṣā-ante dīpakān paktvā samastaiḥ sādhakaiḥ saha ||
caruḥ prāśyaḥ kula-ācāryair-mahā-pātaka-nāśanaḥ || **282**||
iti śrī-ratnamālāyām-ūna-adhika-vidhis-tu yaḥ|
sa eva pātakaṃ tasya praśamo 'yaṃ prakīrtitaḥ || **283** ||
Jr.283d.1 na-ca etat sva-manīṣikayā abhihitam
-ity-uktam-iti śrī-ratnamālāyām-iti|
yad-uktaṃ tatra
Qt.283d.1 dīkṣā-ante dīpakāḥ kāryāḥ pacitvā sādhakaiḥ saha|
caruḥ prāśyaḥ kula-ācāryair-mahā-pātaka-nāśanaḥ || iti|
Jr.283d.2 nanu
Qt.283d.2 yāvan-na sarve tattva-jñās-tāvad-dīpaṃ na darśayet|
3459
Jr.283d.3 ity-ukta-nayena atattva-vidūṃ tāvad-evaṃ caru prāśanaṃ
niṣiddhaṃ,
tattva-vidāṃ ca pāpa-sparśa-āśaṅkā-api na-asti;
tat kim-abhipretya atra mahā-pātaka-naśana iti uktam
-ity-āśaṅkya āha ūna-ity-ādi || 283 ||
Jr.283d.4 atra-eva pūrṇatā-nimittam-iti-kartavyatā-antaram-api āha
AG. pare 'hani guroḥ kāryo yāgas-tena vinā yataḥ|
na vidhiḥ pūrṇatāṃ yāti kuryād-yatnena taṃ tataḥ || **284** ||
yena yena gurus-tuṣyet-tat-tad-asmai nivedayet|
Jr.285b.1 na vidhiḥ pūrṇatāṃ yāti-ity-anena asya yāga-aṅgatvam-
uktaṃ,
na-tu tat-tuṣṭi-kāritvam ||
Jr.285b.2 kaś-ca atra vidhir-vivakṣito yasya anena pūrṇatā syād-ity-
āha
AG. cakra-caryā-antarāle 'syā vidhiḥ saṃcāra ucyate || **285** ||
3460 ali-pātraṃ susaṃpūrṇaṃ vīra-indra-kara-saṃsthitam|

avalokya paraṃ brahma tat-pived-ājñayā guroḥ || **286** ||
tarpayitvā tu bhūtāni gurave vinivedayet|
Jr.287b.1 *asyā iti dīkṣāyāḥ*|
vīra-indra ācāryaḥ ||
Jr.287b.2 *etad-eva atra śikṣayati*
AG. *kṛtvā bhuvi guruṃ natvā-ādāya saṃtarpya khecarīḥ*
|| **287** ||
svaṃ mantraṃ tac-ca vanditvā dūtīṃ gaṇapatiṃ gurūn|
kṣetra-paṃ vīra-saṅghātaṃ gurv-ādi-kramaśas-tat-
aḥ || **288**||
vīra-spṛṣṭaṃ svayaṃ dravyaṃ piven-na-eva-anyathā kvacit|
Jr.289b.1 *kṛtvā bhuti-iti arthād-ātmānam,*
tena bhuvi pa-
3461 *-titvā guroḥ praṇāmaḥ kārya ity-arthaḥ*|
tac-ca ali-pātraṃ vanditvā ādāya-iti yojyam|
vīra-spṛṣṭam-iti gurv-ādi-krameṇa sarveṣāṃ pīta-śeṣam-ity-
arthaḥ ||
Jr.289b.2 *etac-ca tattva-jñair-eva sāmayikaiḥ saha kāryaṃ,*
na anyair-ity-āha
AG. *para-brahmaṇy-avettāro 'gama-āgama-vivarjitāḥ* || **289** ||
lobha-moha-mada-krodha-rāga-māyā-juṣaś-ca ye|
taiḥ sākaṃ na ca kartavyam-etac-chreyorthin-
ātmani || **290** ||
Jr.290d.1 *kadā-ca etat-kāryam-ity-āśaṅkya āha*
AG. *yāga-ādau yāga-madhye ca yāga-ante guru-pūjane*|
naimittikeṣu prokteṣu śiṣyaḥ kuryād-imaṃ vidhim || **291** ||
Jr.291d.1 *prokteṣv-iti aṣṭāviṃś-āhnike* || 291 ||
Jr.291d.2 *āhnika-artham-eva śloka-ardhena upasaṃharati*
3462
AG. *iti rahasya-vidhiḥ paricarcito*
guru-mukha-anubhavaiḥ suparisphuṭaḥ ||**292ab**||
Jr.292b.1 *iti śivam* ||
Jr.292b.2 *śrī-mad-guru-upadeśa-prakrama-saṅkrānta-kaulika-*
anubhavaḥ|
ekān-na-triṃśam-idaṃ jayaratha-nāma-āhnikaṃ vyavṛṇot ||
Jr.292b.3 *iti śrī-tantrāloka-viveke rahasya-vidhi-prakāśanaṃ*
nāma ekona-triṃśam-āhnikam || 292 ||

APPENDIX 14

Glossary of Terms and their Location within the Text

Note: *śl.* refers to a passage in *TĀ* 29.
Jr. refers to an intervention of Jayaratha
Qt. refers to one of the quotations he gives;
bis means that the word occurs twice in the location;
ter means that the word occurs three times there;

akāla — **timeless,** *śl.*80d, Jr.80d.2; see **kāla;**

akula — **non-Kula,** Jr.0.1;
Akula, Jr.0.1, Jr.252d.1 bis, Qt.153b.6;

akṣara — **Akṣara,** *śl.*38d; Qt.39d.5;
syllable, Jr.55d.2, Jr.70b.2, Jr.160b.1, Jr.160b.2 = double syllable *HĀ-HĀ*; Qt.40d.1, Qt.160b.1;

akṣa-sūtraka — **rosary,** *śl.*84d; see **sūtra;**

aṅkura — **sprout,** Jr.153b.5; see **bhaga-aṅkura;**

aṅga — **part, limb,** Qt.70b.2, Qt.100b.2, Qt.216d.1;

aṅgatva — **ancillary aspect,** Jr.285b.1;

aṅgika — **part, limb,** *śl.*214b; Jr.216d.1;

aṅgula — **finger width,** *śl.*25a, *śl.*72c; Qt.73b.1 bis;

  aṅguli — **finger,** Jr.191d.1; Qt.100b.5;

  aṅguṣṭha — **thumb,** *śl.*37a, Qt.39d.3 bis;
big toe, *śl.*259c, Jr.271d.1;

agni — **south-east,** *śl.*70c; Qt.54d.1;
fire = the phoneme *R*, *śl.*212c, *śl.*212d, *śl.*213a, *śl.*255c, Jr.211b.1, Jr.271d.1, Qt.213d.1;
(sacrificial) fire , Qt.77d.1, Qt.110b.1, Qt.110b.2, Qt.166b.1;
fire = subject of knowledge, *śl.*152b;Jr.153b.5; Qt.153b.4;

  agnī — **fire = means of knowledge,** ***prāṇa*,** *śl.*278a; Jr.278b.1;

aṇimā — **minuteness,** *śl.*238c;

aṇu — **individual,** Jr.90b.1; see **āṇava;**

advaita **non-dual,** *śl.*74a, *śl.*271b; Jr.102d.6; Qt.75b.3, Qt.100b.6, Qt.153b.6;

adhikāra **qualified,** *śl.*35a, *śl.*41d, *śl.*42a, *śl.*228b; Jr.40d.2, Jr.41d.1, Jr.42d.1, Jr.102d.6;

  adhikāraka **qualified,** *śl.*32d;

  adhikāratva **qualification,** Jr.34d.2;

  adhikāri **qualified,** *śl.*1a, Jr.2b.1, Jr.2b.2;

adhirūḍha **advanced, sublimated,** *śl.*2a; Jr.2b.1, Jr.7d.1;

adhiṣṭhita **governance,** *śl.*112d, Jr.113b.1; **governed,** Jr.281d.2 bis; Qt.57d.3;

adhvan **pathway,** *śl.*20b, *śl.*202d, *śl.*218b, Jr.200d.2, Jr.240b.2; Qt.240b.2, Qt.247d.1;

anacka ***anacka*,** Jr.247d.1, Jr.247d.3; see phoneme *Ḥ*;

ananda **non-bliss,** *śl.*136a; see **nirānanda;**

anapāyinī **abides without varying,** *śl.*221b; Jr.221d.1;

anavacchinna **undivided, unbroken,** *śl.*35c, *śl.*117c, *śl.*118a, *śl.*119a; Jr.102d.1, Jr.117b.1, Jr.119b.2, Jr.127b.3;

anākhya **ineffable,** Jr.142b.1, Qt.57d.1;

anātman **'not self',** Jr.98b.1; **corporeal,** Jr.180d.1; see **ātman, sva-ātman;**

anāman **the 'nameless',** *śl.*57b;

anāhata **unstruck,** *śl.*156a;

anugraha **grace,** Qt.16d.3;

anucakra **sub-circle,** *śl.*23b = Qt.109b.1, *śl.*106b, *śl.*112a = Qt.138b.1 = Qt.150b.1, *śl.*108a, *śl.*109d, *śl.*113c, *śl.*115a, *śl.*139a, *śl.*135c, *śl.*149c; Jr.109b.2, Jr.109b.4, Jr.110b.1, Jr.110b.3, Jr.111b.1, Jr.112b.1, Jr.113b.1, Jr.113b.2, Jr.115b.1, Jr.115b.2, Jr.135b.3, Jr.136b.1, Jr.136b.2, Jr.139d.1, Jr.150b.1; Qt.139d.1;

anuccāra **silence,** *śl.*247a; Jr.247d.3; see **uccāra;**

anuttara **unsurpassable,** *śl.*116a;

anudhyāya **having meditated,** Jr.168d.1; see **dhyāyet;**

anupāya **'non-means',** Jr.200d.2; see **upāya, nirupāya;**

anubhava **experience,** *śl.*292b; Jr.46b.1, Jr.100b.3, Jr.119b.1, Jr.146b.2, Jr.149b.1, Jr.156b.1, Jr.216d.2, Jr.218b.2, Jr.273a.1, Jr.281d.2, Jr.292b.2;

anuyāga **Subsequent Sacrifice,** *śl.*175a; Jr.175d.1; see **ādi-yāga, yāga;**

anuloma **downwards,** *śl.*18d; Jr.19d.1;
anusandadhate **those who focus,** Jr.127b.3;
  anusandadhan **one who focusses,** Jr.133b.1;
  anusandadhyād **should focus, should attend to,** Jr.50d.2, Jr.90b.3;
  anusandhatte **focusses on, concentrates on,** Jr.24d.2, Jr.89d.1;
  anusandhātavya **to be focussed on,** Jr.63d.5, Jr.89d.1, Jr.271d.1;
  anusandhāna **concentration,** Jr.89d.2, Jr.102d.6, Jr.168d.1;
  ansusandhi **focussing,** Jr.64d.2;
  anusandhāya **after concentrating,** *śl.*149a, *śl.*148.84; Jr.149b.1;
anuṣṭhāna **religious practice,** *śl.*73d; Jr.13d.3, Jr.51d.1, Jr.51d.2, Jr.100b.8;
antar-aṅga **inner-limb,** *śl.*105a;
  antar-aṅgaka **inner-limb,** *śl.*105d,
antaḥ-karaṇa **internal faculties,** *śl.*253d; Jr.271d.1 *bis*; see **upakaraṇa, karaṇa;**
anyonyam **mutually,** *śl.*110a;
mutual, *śl.*154d; Jr.156b.1;
on each other, *śl.*114b = Qt.139d.1, Jr.114b.2, Jr.120b.1;
apamārga **lesser outlets,** Jr.89d.1, Jr.89d.3; see **mārga;**
aparicyuta **transcendental,** Qt.100b.4;
apāna ***apāna,*** Jr.88d.1, Jr.146b.2, Jr.147b.1, Jr.158b.1, Jr.273a.1, Jr.275d.1, Jr.278b.1, Jr.281d.1, Jr.281d.2 bis; *śl.*179c;
aprakāśya **undisclosed,** Qt.166b.1; see **prakāśa etc.;**
abhimāna **conviction,** *śl.*264a;
conceit, Jr.115b.1, Jr.115b.2;
abhilāṣa **craving,** Jr.138b.1;
abhiṣikta **consecrated,** *śl.*230a;
  abhiṣiñcet **he should consecrate,** *śl.*227c;
  abhiṣeka **consecration,** *śl.*228a, *śl.*235b; Jr.54d.5, Jr.224d.2, Jr.229d.2, Jr.235d.1, Jr.235d.2;
  abhiṣecana **consecration,** *śl.*225b, Jr:229d.1;
  abhiṣecayet **he should consecrate** *śl.*229d;
  abhiṣecya **the person to be consecrated,** Jr.235d.1;

abhīṣṭa	**chosen,** *śl.*236c, Jr.75b.1, Jr.149b.1, Jr.271d.1;
abhedya	**indivisible,** *śl.*272c;
abhyāsa	**practice,** *śl.*219c; Jr.195d.3, Jr.220d.1, Jr.273a.1; Qt.100b.6;
abhyāsavat	**the person who is practised,** *śl.*237c =Qt.236d.1;
abhyāsavattva	**the fact of being practised,** Jr.238b.1;
abhyudita	**ejaculate, ejaculated,** *śl.*127d, *śl.*129d; Jr.128b.1 *bis*, Jr.129b.1, Jr.132d.1, Jr.133b.1; see **udita, nitya-udita;**
amūrta	**without physical form,** Qt.22d.2; see **mūrti;**
amūrtatva	**being without physical form,** Jr.46b.1;
amṛta	**nectar,** *śl.*176; Jr.166b.1, Qt.100b.6, Qt.110b.2, Qt.166b.1; see **vāma-amṛta;**
amṛtatā	**immortality,** *śl.*20d;
ara	**beam of light,** *śl.*87a, *śl.*87b, *śl.*131d = Qt.46b.2, *śl.*132a, *śl.*132b; Jr.70b.5, Jr.88d.1, Jr.132d.1, Jr.154b.1, Jr.156b.1; Qt.173d.1, Qt.241b.1 *bis*;
araka	**beam of light,** *śl.*240d, Jr.241b.1;
aruṇa	**'blood',** *śl.*153a;
arka	**sun, twelve,** *śl.*25a , *śl.*132b, *śl.*264d; Jr.27b.1, Jr.132d.1; see **dvādaśa, dvidaśa;**
argha	**vessel** or **'vessel',** *śl.*15b, *śl.*176; Jr.16d.1, Jr.16d.5, Jr.20d.1; Qt.13d.22;
argha-pātra	**vessel** or **'vessel',** *śl.*17a, *śl.*22b; Jr.129b.3; Qt.129b.3;
arcā	**adoration, ceremony,** Jr.13d.11, Jr.24d.2, Jr.55d.3, Jr.81d.3, Jr.95d.2;
ardhacandra	**half-moon,** *śl.*161a; Jr.157b.1, Jr.158b.2, Jr.160b.2 *ter*;
arpaṇa	**offering,** *śl.*138c, *śl.*181b; Jr.139d.1, Jr.181d.1;
ali	**liquor, spoiled liquor,** *śl.*286a; Jr.289b.1; Qt.13d.13, Qt.13d.20, Qt.13d.24;
alekhya	**cannot be put into writing,** *śl.*125c; Jr.126b.1, Jr.126b.2;
alaukika	**'non-worldly',** *śl.*101c; Jr.102d.1, Jr.102d.4; see **laukika**;

avatāra **disclosure, continuation,** Jr.29b.1;Qt.57d.1;
  avatārayati **discloses,** Jr.186b.2;
avadhūta **pure,** *śl.*78c; Jr.78d.1;
avabhāsa Jr.24d.2, Jr.88d.1, Jr.138b.1, Jr.153b.5, Jr.235d.1;
avyakta **inarticulate,** *śl.*155c, *śl.*158d; Jr.156b.1, Jr.160b.2 *bis*;
aṣṭa **eight,** *śl.*159c, *śl.*257d, *śl.*263a, *śl.*240d; Jr.54d.1, Jr.156b.1, Jr.157b.1, Jr.158b.2, Jr.160b.2, Jr.241b.1, Jr.271d.1 *ter*; Qt.54d.3, Qt.73b.1, Qt.241b.1;
  aṣṭaka **eight,** *śl.*53b *bis*, *śl.*132c, *śl.*156c, *śl.*157a, *śl.*157b, *śl.*226a, *śl.*226c, *śl.*233d; Jr.51d.2, Jr.54d.4, Jr.157b.1, Jr.157b.2, Jr.158b.2, Jr.160b.2, Jr.160b.3, Jr.235d.1; Qt.54d.2; see **puryaṣṭaka,**
aṣṭa-aṣṭa **sixty-four,** Jr.54d.5;
  aṣṭa-aṣṭaka **sixty-four,** *śl.*54a, *śl.*132c; Jr.54d.4; see **catuṣ-ṣaṣti, catuṣ-ṣaṣtika;**
ahaṃ **'I am',** Jr.70b.5, Jr.149b.1;
ahaṃyu **sense of self, self-image, haughtiness,** *śl.*113a; Jr.113b.1;
ākāra **the phoneme *Ā*, shape,** *śl.*241c;
ākarṣaka **pulling,** Jr.192b.1, Jr.195d.3;
  ākarṣakatva **the pulling,** *śl.*192a;
  ākarṣaṇa **pulling,** Jr.191d.1 *bis*; Jr.229d.1;
  ākarṣya **pulled,** Jr.195d.3;
  ākārṣanīya **pulled,** Jr.192b.1;
  ākṛṣya **pulled,** *śl.*192a;
  ākṛṣyamāna **pulled,** *śl.*189c;
  ākṛṣyamānatva **the being pulled** Jr.191d.1;
  ākṛṣṭa **pulled,** Jr.192b.1;
ākuñcana **contraction,** *śl.*89d; Jr.89d.1;
ākṛti **shape,** *śl.*246d, *śl.*261b, *śl.*270a; Jr.247d.3, Jr.271d.1;
āgama ***āgama***, *passim*; see **tantra;**
āghāta **striking,** *śl.*278a; Jr.278b.1; see **saṅghāta;**
ācārya **Master,** *śl.*228a, *śl.*282c; Jr.0.1, Jr.54d.3,

Jr.224d.2, Jr.287b.1; Qt.13d.17, Qt.96d.3, Qt.283d.1;

ājñā — **command, authority,** *śl.*74b, *śl.*232c, *śl.*286d; Qt.13d.17, Qt.100b.6;

āṇava — **individual,** Jr.232d.1; see **aṇu;**

ātman — **self,** the word can refer to the universal self or to the limited self. It can just mean 'is' or is used as an emphatic etc. It is found *passim*. Some of the more important uses are listed as follows: *śl.*23a = Qt.109b.1, *śl.*24c, *śl.*90a, *śl.*217a, *śl.*251b, *śl.*265c = Qt.271d.1, *śl.*281a; Jr.4d.1, Jr.23d.2, Jr.24d.2, Jr.88d.1, Jr.90b.1, Jr.98d.3, Jr.100b.3, Jr.112b.1, Jr.241b.1, Jr.252d.1, Jr.275d.1; Qt.13d.1, Qt.80d.1, Qt.100b.4, Qt.166b.1, Qt.236d.3;
see also **anātman, sva-ātman;**

ādi-yāga — **Primordial Sacrifice,** *śl.*164c, *śl.*167b; Jr.163d.2,
Jr.168d.1; Qt.163d.1; see **anuyāga, yāga;**

  ādya-yāga — **Primordial Sacrifice,** Jr.7d.1, Jr.16d.1;

ādhāra — **support, base,** *śl.*63c, *śl.*17c, *śl.*176, *śl.*185c, *śl.*259a; Jr.6d.1, Jr.7d.2, Jr.27b.2, Jr.70b.1 *bis*, Jr.185d.1, Jr.236d.2, Jr.252d.1, Jr.271d.2, Jr.273b.1, Qt.16d.1, Qt.63d.4, Qt.73b.1, Qt.100b.3; see **ādya-ādhāra** and **janma-ādhāra;**

ādya-ādhāra — **primordial support, primary identifying mark,** Jr.42d.1, Jr.173d.1;

ānanda — **bliss, sexual fluid,** *śl.*13b, *śl.*49c, *śl.*53c, *śl.*97c, *śl.*99b, *śl.*99c, *śl.*105c, *śl.*108c, *śl.*130d, *śl.*136b, *śl.*173c, *śl.*176, *śl.*184d, *śl.*208c, *śl.*227a, *śl.*248b, *śl.*252d; Jr.13d.4, Jr.21d.4, Jr.22b.1, Jr.50d.1, Jr.50d.2, Jr.79d.1, Jr.98b.1 *bis*, Jr.100b.1, Jr.100b.2, Jr.100b.3, Jr.106b.1, Jr.107b.3, Jr.109b.3, Jr.112b.1, Jr.115b.1, Jr.128b.2, Jr.136b.2, Jr.137b.1, Jr.149b.1, Jr.153b.3, Jr.153b.4, Jr.168d.1, Jr.185d.2, Jr.208d.1 *ter*, Jr.252d.2; Qt.4d.7, Qt.13d.6, Qt.13d.7, Qt.22b.1; Qt.24d.1, Qt.50d.1, Qt.98b.1

	= Qt.128b.1, Qt.100b.3 *bis*, Qt.100b.4, Qt.107b.1, Qt.110b.2, Qt.160b.2, Qt.166b.1 *bis*; see **jagad-ānanda, nanda, wine,** Qt.13d.7;
āpyāya	**growth,** *śl.*19a, *śl.*69d; Jr.19d.1, Jr.153b.2;
ābhoga	**enjoyment,** *śl.*111c = Qt.138b.1, *śl.*181c; Jr.181d.1; see **bhoga;**
āmarśa	**awareness,** *śl.*93b, *śl.*175c, Jr.119b.2, Jr.147b.1, Jr.150b.1, Jr.156b.1; see **parāmarśa, parimarśa, vimarśa;**
āmnāya	**sacred textual tradition,** Jr.70b.5; Qt.39d.4, Qt.57d.3, Qt.100b.1, Qt.166b.1;
āvaraṇa	**delimitation, surrounding,** *śl.*9b; Jr.8d.2, Jr.54d.4
āveśa	**absorption,** *śl.*147c, *śl.*154c, *śl.*210b, *śl.*239b; Jr.102d.4, Jr.111b.1, Jr.117b.2, Jr.118b.1, Jr.146b.2, Jr.149b.1, Jr.156b.1, Jr.195d.4, Jr.201b.2 *bis*, Jr.209d.2, Jr.211b.1, Jr.271d.1; Qt.213d.1 *bis*, Qt.216d.1, Qt.239b.; see **samāveśa, praveśa;**
āsaṅga	**attachment,** Jr.111b.1; see **saṅga;**
āsana	**throne, seat, foundation,** *śl.*81b, *śl.*110d, *śl.*246c; Jr.81d.2, Jr.111b.1, Jr.213d.1,Jr.247d.3; Qt.166b.1, Qt.195d.1, Qt.213d.1;
āsanatā	**seat,** Jr.81d.2;
āsāra	**outpouring,** *śl.*138d; Jr.139d.1; see **sāra, sāratā, sāratva;**
āsava	**liquor,** Qt.54d.5 *bis*;
āsūtraṇa	**line,** Jr.54d.5; see **sūtra, sūtraka, sūtraṇa, sūtrika;**
icchā	**desire, will,** Qt.46b.1, Qt.129b.5;
icchāka	**desire,** *śl.*44a;
icchāvat	**desire,** Jr.46b.1;
indriya	**faculty,** *śl.*234d, *śl.*253a; Jr.110b.1, Jr.113b.1, Jr.185d.1, Jr.235d.1 *bis*, Jr.252d.1 *bis*, Jr.271d.1 *bis*, Jr.274b.2 *ter*; Qt.96d.4,Qt.202b.1;
Ī	**the phoneme *Ī*,** Jr.216d.1;
ucita	**suitable, in keeping with, appropriate,** *śl.*1a, *śl.*2b, *śl.*109b, *śl.*121a; Jr.16d.5, Jr.110b.1 *bis*, Jr.111b.1, Jr.121d.1, Jr.161b.1; see **aucitya;**

ucchalati	**wells up, is expansive** *śl.*113b; Jr.113b.1; see **procchalad;**
ucchalad	**surging, expansive,** Jr.112b.1, Jr.107d.1;
ucchalā	**surge,** Qt.46b.1;
ucchalana	**welling up,** *śl.*109b, Jr.109b.3;
ucchalita	**surging,** *śl.*138d, Jr.139d.1;
uccāra	**arousing, utterance** *śl.*243c, *śl.*246a, *śl.*246b, *śl.*247a *bis*; Jr.247d.1, Jr.247d.3 *ter*; Qt.160b.2, Qt.202b.1, Qt.247d.1 *bis*; see **anuccāra;**
uccārayan	**arousing,** Jr.89d.1;
uccarad	**arousing,** Jr.247d.3;
uttama	**finest, upmost, highest,** *śl.*104b, *śl.*171d; Jr.104b.1; Qt.13d.14, Qt.22b.1, Qt.22d.2, Qt.70b.2, Qt.102d.5, Qt.166b.1, Qt.241b.1;
udaya	**arising, emergence, happening, prosperity, manifestation** *śl.*69a, *śl.*83a, *śl.*118c, *śl.*264d; Jr.4d.1, Jr.70b.2, Jr.88d.1, Jr.115b.3, Jr.119b.1, Jr.119b.3, Jr.127b.3, Jr.142b.1, Jr.223d.1; Qt.4d.2, Qt.46b.1, Qt.70b.2, Qt.70b.5, Qt.77d.2, Qt.100b.4, Qt.110b.4, Qt.166b.1, Qt.216d.1; see **mantra-udaya;**
udita	**risen, emerged, presented, explained, manifest, derives,** *śl.*26c, *śl.*43b, *śl.*107b, *śl.*117a *bis*, *śl.*119c, *śl.*120a, *śl.*120d, *śl.*121c, *śl.*126d, *śl.*140b, *śl.*148c, *śl.*243b, *śl.*261a; Jr.3d.1, Jr.27b.2 *bis*, Jr.46b.1, Jr.70b.2, Jr.117b.1 *ter*, Jr.119b.1, Jr.119b.3, Jr.120b.1, Jr.120d.1, Jr.121d.1, Jr.127b.1, Jr.142b.1, Jr.147b.1, Jr.146b.2 *bis*, Jr.149b.1, Jr.173d.2, Jr.247d.3; Qt.54d.5, Qt.127b.2, Qt.160b.1, Qt.163d.1; see **abhyudita, nitya-udita;**
udeti	**arises, emerges,** *śl.*119d, *śl.*147d; Jr.104b.1, Jr.160b.2;
uddīpita	**inflamed,** Jr.216d.1; see **dīpita, paridīpita**;
udbodha	**awakened,** Qt.213d.1; see **prabodhayet, bodha, saṃbodhayet;**
udbhava	**lightness,** *śl.*208c; Jr.208d.1;

	menstrual discharge, Jr.153b.6; Qt.109b.2, Qt.153b.6;
unmanā	**transmental,** *śl*.161b; Jr.157b.1; see **aunmanasī;**
unmanaḥ	**transmental,** *śl*.275a;
unmukha	**facing, upwards facing, turning one's attention to,** *śl*.114b = Qt.139d.1, *śl*.151b; Jr.50d.1 *bis*; Jr.139d.2, Jr.153b.1; see **aunmukhya;**
unmukhatā	**intentness,** Jr.271d.2;
unmukhatva	**intentness,** Jr.281d.1;
unmukhita	**intent on,** *śl*.137b; Jr.137b.1;
unmukhī	**facing,** Jr.50d.1;
unmukhya	**facing, intent upon,** Jr.50d.1, Jr.113b.1;
unmūlana	**uprooting,** *śl*.81b; see **mūla;**
upakaraṇa	**materials,** Jr.20d.1, Jr.75b.4; see **karaṇa;**
upakaraṇatā	**materials,** Jr.21d.4;
upasaṃhāra	**resorbing,** Jr.111b.1; see **saṃhāra;**
upāya	**means, method,** *śl*.95a; Jr.95d.1 *bis*; see **anupāya, nirupāya;**
ullāsa	**overjoyed, welling up, expansiveness,** *śl*.49b; Jr.104b.1, Jr.112b.1;
ullāsita	**apparent, manifested,** Jr.121d.1, Jr.127b.2;
Ū	**the phoneme *Ū*,** see **ṣaṣṭha, ṣaṣṭhaka;**
ūrdhvaga-kuṇḍali	**'upper *kuṇḍali*',** *śl*.37c; see **kuṇḍalī, kuṇḍalinī;**
ūrdhva-dhāman	**upper sacred place,** *śl*.114c; Jr.115b.1; see **dhāman, madhya-dhāman;**
ūrdhva-retasaḥ	**those who have raised their seed,** *śl*.41c, *śl*.42d, Jr.42d.1; see **retas;**
Ṛ	**the phoneme *Ṛ*,** Jr.216d.1;
Ṝ	**the phoneme *Ṝ*,** Jr.216d.1;
Ḷ	**the phoneme *Ḷ*,** Jr.216d.1;
Ḹ	**the phoneme *Ḹ*,** Jr.216d.1;
eka	**one, single, alone, unique, only,** *śl*.79a, *śl*.167b; Jr.29b.4, Jr.50d.2, Jr.56d.1, Jr.79d.1, Jr.80d.2, Jr.115b.1, Jr.119b.1, Jr.146b.2, Jr.149b.1, Jr.153b.5, Jr.166b.1, Jr.175d.3, Jr.182d.1, Jr.185d.2, Jr.218b.1, Jr.223d.1, Jr.271d.1; Qt.9d.2, Jr.13d.3 *bis*, Qt.13d.5,

	Qt.13d.13, Qt.13d.18, Qt.100b.5 *bis*, Qt.101b.1, Qt.213d.1;
ekaka	**by itself,** Jr.13d.12;
ekataḥ	**by itself, in the first place, on one side,** Qt.13d.18 *bis*, Qt.42d.1;
ekatama	**alone, one or other** Jr.216d.1; Qt.13d.23;
ekatā	**oneness,** *śl*.110b;
ekatra	**in one [person],** Jr.100b.6;
eka-vīra	**single-heroine,** *śl*.48c, *śl*.70a; Jr.48d.2, Jr.78d.1; see **vīra;**
eka-agrī	**centred,** Jr.102d.6;
ekānta	**solitude,** *śl*.92b; Jr.91d.3; Qt.91d.2;
ekaika	**on its own,** Jr.71b.1;
ojas	**vitality,** *śl*.4c;
ovallī	**dynasty,** *śl*.36c; Jr.39d.1, Jr.39d.3; Qt.39d.1;
aucitya	**suitable, capacity, appropriate effect,** *śl*.186d; Jr.187b.1 *bis*, Jr.191d.1, Jr.208d.1, Jr.271d.1; see **ucita;**
aunmanasī	**transmental,** *śl*.274d; see **unmanaḥ, unmanā;**
aunmukhya	**intent,** Jr.104b.1; see **unmukha etc.;**
Ṃ	**the phoneme *Ṃ*,** see **bindu, baindava, māyā;**
Ḥ	**the phoneme *Ḥ*, emission, *visarga*;** see **visarga, vaisargika, sarga;** *anacka Ḥ*, Jr.247.d1;
ka	**Ka,** Jr.88d.1; see **ka-randhra**
kañcuka	**covering,** Jr.271d.1; see **kalā,** force**; kalā,** all five *kañcuka*;
kanda	**'bulb',** *śl*.37d, *śl*.61b, *śl*.68c, *śl*.257b; Jr.70b.1 *bis*; Qt.63d.1, Qt.70b.1, Qt.247d.2;
kampa	**trembling, flinching,** *śl*.197d, *śl*.199c, *śl*.208c; Jr.208d.1; Qt.101b.1;
karaṇa	**faculty, instrument, action,** *śl*.46d, *śl*.136d, *śl*.232d, *śl*.263b; Jr.22d.3, Jr.24d.1, Jr.48d.1, Jr.100b.3 *bis*, Jr.120b.1, Jr.107b.1, Jr.137b.1, Jr.137b.2, Jr.138b.1, Jr.271d.2; Qt.166b.1, Qt.236d.3; see **upakaraṇa, antaḥ-karaṇa;**
kāraṇa	**cause, causal deity, reason,** *śl*.117b, *śl*.233a, *śl*.249c, *śl*.279b; Jr.4d.1, Jr.70b.1, Jr.240b.2, Jr.252d.1, Jr.275d.2, Jr.281d.2 *bis*;

	Qt.4d.3, Qt.127b.2, Qt.239b.1;
ka-randhra	**aperture of Ka,** *śl*.179c; Jr.88d.1; see **Ka, brahma-bila, randhra;**
ka-randhraka	*śl*.59b;
karṇikā	**'the pericarp of the lotus', the vulva,** Jr.46b.2; Qt.153b.6;
karma	**action, ritual action,** ***karma,*** *śl*.21d, *śl*.161c; Jr.21d.1, Jr.209d.1, Jr.252d.1, Jr.271d.1; Qt.13d.16, Qt.13d.17, Qt.21d.1, Qt.101b.1, Qt.166b.1;
karmī	***karmī,*** **officiant,** Jr.129b.4, Jr.232d.1;
kalā	**force, division, portion, section, phase;** see **niṣkala, sakala.** In *TĀ* 29 and its investigation, the term *kalā* is used with a variety of meanings as follows:
kalā	**force,** i.e. category *śl*.30, one of the *kañcuka*; see **kañcuka,**
kalā	**all five** ***kañcuka,*** *śl*.265a; Jr.271d.1;
kalā	**the 5 divisions of reality,** *śl*.249a; Jr.206d.1, Jr.252d.1;
kalā	one of the six pathways, *adhvan*;
kalā	**a section** of the moon, especially the sixteenth section, Qt.13d.21;
kalā	the16th **lunar day;** 17th **lunar day;** 18th **lunar day;**
kalā	one or other of the 16 **vowels**;
kalā	**part of,** as in *anacka-kalā,* a phoneme without the accompanying vowel (*ac*), for example *Ḥ*, Jr.247d.1;
kalā	**phase** of sound, *śl*.157b; Jr.157b.1 *bis*, Jr.158b.2, Jr.160b.2;
kalā	**portion** of 'moon' and 'sun', i.e. of male sexual fluid and female sexual fluid, *śl*.153a, *śl*.152d; Jr.153b.4. Jr.153b.5;
kalā	**portion** of 'sun' and 'moon', i.e. of means of knowledge and object of knowledge, or of *prāṇa* and *apāna*; *śl*.278c; Jr.278b.1;
kalpana	**restriction, ritual act,** *śl*.12d, *śl*.20b; Jr.13d.3; see **nirvikalpa, parikalpita, vikalpa;**
kalpanā	**restriction,** Jr.13d.3;

kalpanīya	**to be performed,** Jr.88d.1;
kalpa-vṛkṣa	**tree of plenty,** Jr.72b.2;
kāma	**desire, cupid,** *śl.*127c; Jr.128b.1, Jr.235d.2; Qt.13d.23, Qt.100b.3, Qt.100b.5 *bis*, Qt.100b.6, Qt.102d.3, Qt.102d.6, Qt.102d.7, Qt.160b.2;
kāmatā	**desire,** Jr.40d.1;
kāla	**time,** *śl.*200a, *śl.*275b; Jr.0.1 *bis*, Jr.13d.9, Jr.13d.11, Jr.46b.1 *bis*, Jr.64d.2, Jr.79d.3, Jr.80d.2, Jr.112b.2, Jr.146b.2, Jr.168d.1, Jr.200d.2; Qt.13d.16, Qt.13d.17, Qt.70b.3, Qt.110b.2, Qt.153b.6; see **akāla;**
kāla-anala	**Fire of Time,** *śl.*182d; Jr.182d.1;
kāla-agni	**Kālāgni, Fire of Time,** *śl.*63d, *śl.*212d;
kādya	**skull,** *śl.*26a; Jr.27b.2 *bis*; see **kāya-pīṭha, śiras;**
kāya	**body,** *śl.*6b, *śl.*182c, *śl.*251a; Jr.182d.1, Jr.252d.1 *bis*;
kāya-pīṭha	**skull,** *śl.*15c; Jr.16d.1, Jr.27b.2 *bis*; see **kādya, śiras;**
kuṇḍa	**sacrificial pit, fire-pit, vulva,** *śl.*8a, *śl.*141c; Qt.8d.1, Qt.110b.1, Qt.110b.2, Qt.166b.1;
kuṇḍa-golaka	***kuṇḍa-golaka,*** Jr.16d.1, Jr.22b.1, Jr.128b.1, Jr.173d.2; Qt.129b.3;
kuṇḍala	**ring,** *śl.*246d, Jr.247d.3;
kuṇḍalinī	***kuṇḍalinī,*** *śl.*68b; Jr.70b.1 *bis*; Qt.70b.1;
kuṇḍalī	***kuṇḍalī,*** 71c; Qt.39d.4, Qt.72b.2; see **ūrdhvaga-kuṇḍalī**
kula	*passim*; see **kaula, kaulika;**
kusuma	**flower, menstrual blood,** *śl.*176, *śl.*215a;
kūṭa	***KṢA*, cluster,** Qt.195d.2;
kṛta-yuga	**golden age,** Jr.3d.1;
koṇa-traya	**triangle,** *śl.*151a; Jr.153b.1; see **tri-koṇa;**
kaula	**pertaining to the Kula, Kula and Akula,** see **kula**;
kaulika	**pertaining to the Kula,** *śl.*15a, *śl.*16d; Jr.292b.2; Qt.3d.1, Qt.96d.1, Qt.166b.1 *bis*;
krama	**procedure, process, Krama, etc.,** *passim*;
kriyā	**ritual, act,** *śl.*94d, *śl.*232d; Jr.232d.1;Qt.100b.6; see **prakriyā;**
kriyamāṇa	**performed,** Jr.22b.3;
krīḍa	**play, amusement,** *śl.*43c, *śl.*183c; Jr.46b.1;

krīḍanti	**they play, amuse themselves,** Jr.46b.1; Qt.22d.2 = Qt.185d.1;
krīḍita	**play, amusement,** Qt.46b.1;
kṣaya	**disappearance, fading away,** *śl.*252b; Jr.113b.1, Jr.135b.1;
kṣetra	**sacred region, sexual union,** *śl.*56a, *śl.*72a, *śl.*288c; Jr.72b.1; Qt.24d.2, Qt.54d.3, Qt.72b.2, Qt.153b.6;
kṣobha	**agitation,** *śl.*159b; Jr.111b.1, Jr.115b.1, Jr.115b.2, Jr.160b.2; Qt.46b.1, Qt.160b.1; see **vikṣobha, saṅkṣobha, saṃkṣobha;**
kṣobhayitvā	**having agitated,** Qt.129b.5;
kṣaudra	**honey,** *śl.*11d;
kṣaudrī	**mead,** Jr.13d.3;
kha	**space,** *śl.*172b; Jr.173d.1;
khecara	**sky-traveller, transcendental,** Qt.64d.1, Qt.77d.2;
khecara-mudrā	***khecara-mudrā,*** *śl.*154c; see **mudrā;**
khecarī	**sky-traveller,** *śl.*287d;
khecarī-mudrā	***khecarī-mudrā,*** Jr.156b.1;
gandha	**perfume, sandal-paste, smell,** *śl.*18a, *śl.*109a, *śl.*188d; Jr.109b.3; Qt.110b.2; **base of the body,** *śl.*246b; Jr.247d.3 *ter*;
galita	**subsiding, ebbing,** *śl.*115c, *śl.*134b; Jr.133d.1, Jr.191d.1;
guḍa	**treacle,** *śl.*11d; see **gauḍī;**
guru	**guru,** *passim*;
guru-pūjana	**worship of the guru,** *śl.*291b;
guhya	**private, genera etc.,** sl. 86d, sl88d, Jr. 88d. 1 *ter*, Qt. 70b.2, Qt. 166b. 1 *bis*
guhyaka	**[top of the head],** *sl.* 86d; Jr/ 88d.1;
gocara	**internal faculties,** *sl.* 110d; *sl.* 253b; Qt. 4d.6
gocaratva	**inner knowledge,** Jr. 149b.1;
gotra	**clan,** *śl.*199b; Jr.200d.2;
gauḍī	**rum,** Jr.13d.3; Qt.13d.4, Qt.13d.6; see **guḍa;**
grāmya-dharma	**engrossed in every day life,** *śl.*65c; Jr.64d.2;
grasate	**'devours',** *śl.*277a; Jr.277b.1;
ghaṭṭana	**rubbing,** *śl.*152b; see **saṃghaṭṭa, saṅghaṭṭa, saṅghaṭṭayati;**
ghara	**hermitage,** *śl.*39d; Qt.39d.1, Qt.39d.5 *bis*;

ghūrṇi	**reeling,** *śl.*208d; Jr.208d.1 *bis*;
ghūrṇita	**reeling,** Qt.100b.5;
ghṛta	**ghee,** *śl.*16a; Jr.16d.2; Qt.16d.2, Qt.73b.1, Qt.102d.6 *bis*;
cakra	**circle, pair,** *passim*, see especially *śl.*105 ff.;
cakra-yājaka	**the one who takes part in a Circle Sacrifice,** *śl.*99d;
catur-astra	**square, four,** Jr.29b.1, Jr.29b.4 *ter*, Jr.46b.2; Qt.13d.7, Qt.54d.3;
catuṣ-pīṭha	**four-fold base,** Jr.166b.2; see **pīṭha;**
catuṣ-ṣaṣṭi	**sixty-four,** *śl.*228d; see **aṣṭa-aṣṭa;**
catuṣ-ṣaṣṭika	**sixty-four,** Jr.235d.1;
candra	**moon, semen, female sex organ,** *śl.*168a; Jr.168d.1; Qt.153b.2;
candrama	**moon,** *śl.*95d; see **cāndra, cāndramasa;**
camat-kāra	**amazement, wonder,** Jr.50d.1, Jr.112b.1, Jr.115b.1, Jr.149b.1, Jr.252d.2; Qt.100b.5;
camat-kṛti	**amazement, wonder,** *śl.*176;
caru	**'oblation',** *śl.*198c, *śl.*282c; Jr.54d.5, Jr.197b.1, Jr.200d.1, Jr.200d.2, Jr.283d.3; Qt.13d.18 *bis*, Qt.200d.1 *bis*, Qt.283d.1;
caruka	**'oblation',** *śl.*195c; Jr.195d.3; Qt.22b.2, Qt.110b.1, Qt.110b.2;
caryā	**ceremony, activity, ritual action,** *śl.*285c; Jr.96d.1, Jr.130b.1, Jr.186b.1; Qt.96d.1, Qt.102d.7, Qt.166b.1;
carvaṇā	**savouring,** *śl.*137d; Jr.138b.1; Qt.100b.5;
cāndra	**moon,** *śl.*179d; see **candra, candrama;**
cāndramasa	**moon,** Jr.153b.3;
cit	**consciousness,** *passim,* see especially *śl.*13b, *śl.*80c, *śl.*93c, *śl.*109b, *śl.*118b; Jr.50d.2, Jr.107d.1; see **citi, citta, caitanya, bodha, saṃvit** etc.;
citi	**consciousness,** *śl.*47a;
citi	**funeral pyre,** *śl.*182c, *śl.*185b; Jr.182d.1, Jr.185d.1;
citta	**mind, heart,** *śl.*244a, *śl.*244c, *śl.*252a, *śl.*252b, *śl.*252c, *śl.*274c; Jr.247d.2; Qt.100b.5, Qt.101b.1, Qt.102d.7, Qt.241b.1, Qt.247d.2; see **cit, citi, caitanya, bodha, saṃvit** etc.;

caitanya — **consciousness,** *śl.*215b, *śl.*257b; Jr.206d.1; see **cit, citi, citta, bodha, saṃvit** etc.;

codana-astra — **'driving force',** *śl.*193d;

chāyā — **reflection,** *śl.*265c = Qt.271d.1; Jr.271d.1;

chumma — **code,** *śl.*37d; Jr.39d.1; Qt.39d.1;

  chummaka — **code,** Jr.39d.4;

jagat — **world, universe,** *śl.*247b; Jr.70b.1, Jr.247d.3; Qt.81d.1, Qt.100b.5, Qt.202b.1;

  jagad-ānanda — **universal bliss,** *śl.*116d, Jr.117b.1; see **ānanda, nanda;**

jaḍi — **inert,** Jr.211b.1;

janma — **source, womb, offspring,** *śl.*173b, *śl.*248c; Jr.162b.1, Jr.173d.2, Jr.252d.1; Qt.13d.17;

  janma-ādhāra — **generative organ,** Jr.88d.1 - four times, Jr.247d.3, Jr.252d.1; Qt.39d.4; see **ādhāra, ādya-ādhāra;**

  janma-sthāna — **generative organ,** *sl.*248c;

japa — **recitation,** *śl.*82a = Qt.150b.2, *śl.*83b, *śl.*85b, *śl.*86b, *śl.*87c, *śl.*92d, *śl.*93a, *śl.*149c, *śl.*156d, *śl.*216a; Jr.81d.3, Jr.88d.1, Jr.89d.2, Jr.95d.2, Jr.150b.2, Jr.157b.2; Qt.13d.17, Qt.22b.3, Qt.77d.2, Qt.89d.1, Qt.91d.2, Qt.110b.1, Qt.110b.2, Qt.160b.1, Qt.216d.1;

jāgrat — **wakened state, wakefulness,** *śl.*221a, *śl.*222a; Jr.223d.1 *bis*;

jīvan-mukta — **liberated-while-living,** *śl.*162;

  jīvan-mukti — **liberation in life,** Jr.277b.1; see **muktī, mokṣa;**

jñāna — **knowledge,** *śl.*9c, *śl.*125b, *śl.*135b, *śl.*163b, *śl.*232a, *śl.*264d; Jr.9d.1, Jr.9d.2, Jr.39d.1, Jr.46b.1, Jr.122b.3, Jr.125b.1, Jr.125b.2, Jr.130b.1; Qt.13d.17, Qt.46b.1, Qt.91d.1, Qt.102d.5, Qt.239b.1; see **vijñāna;**

  jñānī — **knowledgeable person,** Jr.102d.6, Jr.129b.4, Jr.224d.1, Jr.232d.1;

  jñānīya — **what pertains to knowledge,** Jr.102d.1 *bis*;

tattva — **category, substance,** *passim*,

  tattva-jña — **a person who knows reality,** Jr.289b.2; Qt.283d.2;

tādātmya — **identity,** *śl.*22c, *śl.*101d, *śl.*261c; Jr.101b.2,

	śl.237a, *śl*.239d, *śl*.277a, *śl*.281c, *śl*.282a; Jr.13d.11, Jr.186b.2, Jr.197b.2, Jr.200d.2, Jr.200d.3 *bis*, Jr.201b.2 *ter*, Jr.202b.2, Jr.208d.1, Jr.211b.2, Jr.216d.1, Jr.218d.2, Jr.224d.2, Jr.232d.1, Jr.235d.2, Jr.281d.2, Jr.287b.1; Qt.13d.16, Qt.201b.1 *bis*, Qt.202b.1, Qt.283d.1; see **sa-bīja-dīkṣā, samayī-dīkṣā;**
dīkṣaṇa	**initiation,** *śl*.236d;
dīkṣya	**to be initiated,** Jr.216d.1 *bis*;
dīkṣayed	**he should initiate,** *śl*.187b;
dīkṣita	**initiated,** *śl*.220a, *śl*.275b; Jr.13d.11, Jr.224d.1, Jr.232d.1, Jr.275d.1, Jr.278b.1; Qt.13d.17;
dīpa	**lamp, 'lamp',** *śl*.14d, *śl*.16a, *śl*.15d, *śl*.73b, *śl*.226a; Jr.54d.5 *bis,* Jr.55d.2 *bis*; Qt.13d.22, Qt.16d.2, Qt.55d.1, Qt.73b.1 *bis*, Qt.283d.2;
dīpaka	**lamp,** *śl*.282a; Qt.283d.1; see **pradīpaka;**
dīpayet	**should set on fire,** Qt.216d.1; see **paridīpayet;**
dīpta	**blazing, burning, radiant, fire,** *śl*.19b, *śl*.203c; Jr.19d.1, Jr.206d.1; Qt.3d.1, Qt.54d.5; see **uddīpita, paridīpita;**
dīptī	**flame,** *śl*.189d; Jr.271d.2;
dīpyamāna	**shining,** *śl*.242b; Jr.247d.1;
dūti	**sexual partner,** Jr.100b.7, Jr.100b.8; Qt.96d.2 *bis*, Qt.96d.3, Qt.100b.5, Qt.100b.8;
dūtika	**with a sexual partner,** Jr.100b.8 *bis*, Qt.100b.8;
dūtī	**sexual partner,** *śl*.223a, *śl*.288b; Jr.96d.1; Qt.100b.5, Qt.101b.1, Qt.102d.3, Qt.129b.5; see **dauta;**
deha	**body,** *śl*.7b, *śl*.43c, *śl*.43d, *śl*.58c, *śl*.90b, *śl*.97d, *śl*.112d, *śl*.133a, *śl*.144a, *śl*.167c, *śl*.171a, *śl*.176, *śl*.203a, *śl*.208d, *śl*.241c, *śl*.260a, *śl*.267a, *śl*.281b; Jr.20d.1, Jr.22d.2, Jr.42d.1, Jr.46b.1 *ter*, Jr.57d.4, Jr.70b.1 *ter*, Jr.90b.1, Jr.98b.1, Jr.100b.1, Jr.113b.1 *bis*, Jr.115b.1, Jr.115b.2, Jr.129b.2, Jr.146b.1, Jr.168d.1, Jr.177d.1, Jr.177d.3, Jr.180d.1, Jr.181d.2, Jr.182d.1, Jr.202b.1, Jr.208d.1, Jr.208d.2, Jr.209d.1 *bis*, Jr.247d.1, Jr.271d.1, Jr.281d.2; Qt.22b.3, Qt.46b.1, Qt.129b.1, Qt.166b.1, Qt.177d.1, Qt.200d.1 *bis*;

see **tanuḥ, piṇḍa, vapuḥ, śarīra;**

deha-anta **end of the body, viz. top of the head,** *śl.*158a; Jr.158b.1;

dauta **pertaining to the sexual partner,** Jr.95d.2, Jr.186b.2; see **dūti etc;**

dravya **ingredient, product,** *śl.*10a, *śl.*17b, *śl.*22a, *śl.*175b, *śl.*289a; Jr.10d.2, Jr.13d.4, Jr.13d.12 *bis*, Jr.16d.1, Jr.16d.5, Jr.17d.1, Jr.17d.2, Jr.21d.4, Jr.107b.3; Qt.10d.1, Qt.13d.19, Qt.13d.21, Qt.13d.22, Qt.16d.3, Qt.17d.1, Qt.22d.2, Qt.100b.1, Qt.129b.1, Qt.129b.3, Qt.129b.5, Qt.166b.1;

drākṣā **grape,** *śl.*12c; Jr.13d.3;

dvādaśa **twelve,** *śl.*51a, *śl.*94b, *śl.*214d; Jr.27b.1, Jr.33d.1, Jr.33d.2, Jr.51d.1, Jr.51d.2, Jr.95d.1, Jr.216d.1; Qt.17d.1, Qt.95d.1, Qt.216d.1, Qt.241b.1;
see **arka;**
twelve goddesses, see **krama;**
twelve vowels, *śl.*214d;
twelve levels of sound Qt.241b.1;
the 'end-of-twelve', see **dvādaśa-anta, dvidaśa-anta;**

dvādaśa-anta **'end-of-twelve',** Jr.63d.1; Jr.88d.1 *bis*, Jr.158b.1, Jr.247d.3, Jr.248d.1, Jr.252d.1, Jr.271d.1;
see **dvidaśa-anta;**

dvidaśa-anta **'end-of-twelve',** *śl.*37c;

dvaita **dualist,** *śl.*74a; Qt.75b.2, Qt.166b.1 *bis*;

dhāman **sacred place, sex organ,** *śl.*14c, *śl.*15d, *śl.*81d, *śl.*116c, *śl.*119a, *śl.*120a, *śl.*126d, *śl.*133a, *śl.*138a, *śl.*147d, *śl.*156d, *śl.*171d, *śl.*174c, *śl.*257b, *śl.*261a; Jr.27b.2, Jr.81d.1, Jr.119b.2, Jr.120b.1, Jr.127b.2, Jr.138b.1, Jr.139d.1, Jr.153b.3; Qt.24d.1, Qt.70b.5, Qt.175d.2;
see **ūrdhva-dhāman, madhya-dhāman;**

dhāmatva **sacred place,** Jr.488d.1;

dhūpa **incense,** *śl.*19a, *śl.*109a; Jr.109b.3; Qt.13d.20, Qt.13d.22, Qt.54d.5 *bis*, Qt.110b.1, Qt.110b.2;

dhyāyet **should meditate,** *śl.*205c, *śl.*216a, *śl.*261c; Jr.216d.1; see **anudhyāya;**

dhyātvā	**having meditated,** *śl.*169a, *śl.*241a, *śl.*256a; Jr.271d.1; Qt.241b.1; see **nirdhyāna;**
dhvani	**resonance,** *śl.*148a, *śl.*155c, *śl.*160a; Jr.149b.1, Jr.160b.2;
napuṃsaka	**neuter,** *śl.*12a; Jr.13d.3 *bis*, Jr.161b.1; Qt.13d.4, Qt.13d.5;
nanda	**joy,** *śl.*22a; Jr.22b.1; see **ānanda, jagad-ānanda;**
	an auspicious lunar day, *śl.*249a; Jr.252d.1;
nava	**nine,** *śl.*66d *bis*, *śl.*67c, *śl.*241c, *śl.*255a; Jr.66d.2 *bis*, Jr.247d.1 *bis*; Qt.66d.2 *ter*, Qt.67d.1, Qt.70b.1;
nāḍī	**channel,** *śl.*254d, *śl.*257a, *śl.*263c, *śl.*268a, *śl.*268c, *śl.*269a, *śl.*269c, *śl.*270a, *śl.*270b; Jr.70b.1, Jr.88d.1 *ter*, Jr.146b.2, Jr.271d.1 *bis*, Jr.271d.2 *bis*, Jr.281d.1; Qt.146b.1; see **madhya-nāḍī;**
nātha	**Lord,** ***nātha***, Qt.9d.1, Qt.13d.8, Qt.13d.19, Qt.24d.2, Qt.40d.1, Qt.54d.5, Qt.70b.3;
nāda	**sound,** *śl.*93b, *śl.*150b, *śl.*155d, *śl.*239c, *śl.*243c, *śl.*244a, *śl.*244b; Jr.150b.1, Jr.156b.1, Jr.160b.2, Jr.247.1 - four times; Qt.160b.1, Qt.240b.1, Qt.247d.1 - five times;
nāda-anta	**'end-of-sound',** *śl.*155d;
nādā-bhairava	**Bhairava as sound,** *śl.*159d; Jr.160b.2;
nābhi	**navel,** *śl.*37d, *śl.*61b; Jr.88d.1, Jr.146b.2, Jr.252d.1; Qt.39d.4, Qt.63d.1, Qt.100b.5, Qt.146b.1, Qt.252d.1;
	'navel' = *KṢ*, *śl.*192d; Jr.195d.1, Jr.252d.1; Qt.195d.1;
nāla	**stalk,** *śl.*151c, *śl.*152a; Jr.153b.3, Jr.153b.4;
nāla-ājya	**phlegm,** Qt.17d.1, Qt.200d.1;
nitya	**always, daily, daily rite,** *śl.*13d, *śl.*144b, *śl.*151a; Jr.19d.2, Jr.132d.1, Jr.146b.1, Jr.153b.1; Qt.13d.9, Qt.13d.19, Qt.13d.25, Qt.16d.1, Qt.100b.2, Qt.100b.6, Qt.129b.2, Qt.160b.2, Qt.166b.1;
nitya-udita	**always present,** Qt.96d.1, Qt.96d.3, Qt.160b.1; see **abhyudita, udita;**
nidrā	**sleep,** *śl.*208d; Jr.208d.1;

nirācāra	**not bound to any ritual,** *śl*.78c;
nirānanda	**non-bliss,** *śl*.135b; Jr.135b.2, Jr.136b.2; see **ananda;**
nirudhya	**after restraining,** *śl*.276c; Jr.147b.1, Jr.277b.1; see **nirodha, rūddha;**
nirupāya	**non-means,** Jr.200d.2; see **anupāya, upāya;**
nivṛtti	**abstinence, cessation,** ***nivṛtti*,** Jr.98d.3, Jr.206d.1; Qt.13d.13, Qt.98d.1;
nirodha	**restraint,** Jr.88d.1, Jr.89d.1, Jr.89d.3, Jr.208d.1; see **nirudhya, rūddha;**
nirvāṇa	**extinction,** Jr.160b.2; Qt.248d.2;
nirvānti	**vanish,** *śl*.159b; Jr.160b.2;
nirvikalpa	**undifferentiated thought,** Jr.2b.1, Jr.78d.1, Jr.102d.6; see **kalpana, parikalpita, vikalpa;**
nirdhyāna	**meditation,** *śl*.260c; see **dhyāyet;**
niṣiddha	**forbidden,** *śl*.10b; Jr.283d.3;
niṣkala	**simple,** *śl*.205d; Jr.206d.1; see **kalā, sakala;**
niṣpīḍāna	**firm pressure,** Jr.247d.3; see **pīḍayate;**
niḥspanda	**non-vibrating,** *śl*.277; Jr.278b.1; see **spandana;**
naimittika	**occasional rite,** *śl*.291c; Jr.19d.2; Qt.100b.6;
nyasyatva	**installation,** *śl*.58c; Jr.63d.1, Jr.65d.2;
nyāsa	**installation,** *śl*.8b, *śl*.20b, *śl*.242a; Jr.202b.1, Jr.247d.1; Qt.8d.1;
patnī	**wife,** *śl*.43a, *śl*.66d; Jr.33d.1 *bis*, Jr.42d.3, Jr.46b.1, Jr.55d.3, Jr.102d.4 *bis*; Qt.96d.3, Qt.102d.2;
pañca	**five,** *śl*.84a, *śl*.220d, *śl*.250a, *śl*.257d; Jr.200d.1, Jr.220d.2, Jr.252d.1, Jr.271d.1; Qt.70b.4, Qt.100b.5 *bis*, Qt.248d.1;
pañcaka	**five,** 224c, *śl*.249d, *śl*.248d, *śl*.280b; Jr.17d.1, Jr.248d.3, Jr.271d.1 *bis*, Jr.281d.2; Qt.46b.1, Qt.252d.1 *ter*;
pañca-daśa	**fifteen,** Jr.195d.3;
pañca-dhā	**five-fold,** Qt.70b.2, Qt.110b.2;
pañcama	**fifth, five-fold,** Qt.39d.3, Qt.39d.4, Qt.110b.2;
pañcamī	**set of five**; Qt.103d.1;
pañcāśad	**fifty,** Jr.55d.2;
para	**supreme,** *passim*
parama	**supreme,** *passim*
parampara	**tradition,** *śl*.102; Jr.3d.1, Jr.54d.3;

paraspara	**mutual,** *śl.*104d, *śl.*120a; Jr.50d.1, Jr.104b.1, Jr.115b.2, Jr.120d.1, Jr.129b.3, Jr.153b.4, Jr.154b.2, Jr.160b.2, Jr.277b.1; Qt.102d.5, Qt.277d.1; see **mithaḥ;**
parabrahman	***parabrahman*,** *śl.*289c; Jr.50d.2, Jr.98b.1, Jr.100b.1; see **brahman**
parāmarśa	**creative awareness,** *śl.*121d, *śl.*173a; Jr.70b.5, Jr.98b.1, Jr.113b.1, Jr.147b.2, Jr.149b.1, Jr.150b.1; see **āmarśa, parimarśa, vimarśa;**
parikalpita	**done, performed, delineated, enacted, imagined,** *śl.*108b, *śl.*130a; Jr.109b.1, Jr.130b.2, Jr.271d.1; see **kalpana, nirvikalpa, vikalpa;**
paridīpayet	**should set on fire,** *śl.*188b; Jr.191d.1; see **dīpa etc.;**
paridīpita	**inflamed,** *śl.*215d; see **uddīpita, dīpita;**
paribhramya	**after circulating,** *śl.*257c; Jr.271d.1; see **bhrama;**
parimarśa	**awareness,** *śl.*111d = Qt.138b.1, *śl.*148a; Jr.112.1; see **āmarśa, parāmarśa, vimarśa;**
parva	**juncture,** Qt.13d.14, Qt.100b.6;
palli	**begging-place,** *śl.*39d; Qt.39d.1 - seven times;
pavitratva	**Ceremony of the Cord,** Qt.22b.1;
paśu	**'bonded animal',** *śl.*99a, *śl.*273b; Jr.13d.6, Jr.100b.1, Jr.100b.2, Jr.273b.1; Qt.13d.10, Qt.13d.14, Qt.75b.3, Qt.100b.1, Qt.100b.2, Qt.100b.3, Qt.100b.4, Qt.166b.1; see **mahā-paśu;**
paśutva	**the condition of being a bonded animal,** Qt.13d.12;
paśyet etc.	**he should see, as a result of seeing, viewing etc.,** *śl.*5b, *śl.*178c, *śl.*182c, *śl.*217d, *śl.*218b, *śl.*234b; Jr.5d.2, Jr.182d.1, Jr.218b.1; Qt.100b.6;
pātaka	**sin,** *śl.*282d, *śl.*283c; Jr.283d.3; Qt.283d.1;
pāratīya	**mercurial,** Jr.13d.4; Qt.13d.8;
picu-vaktra	**the Picu-mouth,** Jr.125b.1; see ***yoginī*-vaktra;**
piṣṭa	**flour, paste,** *śl.*11d, *śl.*228c; Jr.13d.3, Jr.229d.1; Qt.73b.1; see **paiṣṭī;**
piṇḍa	**mass, body,** *śl.*4d, *śl.*254d, *śl.*257c, *śl.*224a,

pūjita	**worshipped,** Jr.29b.3 *bis*, Jr.192b.1; Qt.42d.1;
pūjya	**to be worshipped,** *śl*.45a, *śl*.46a, *śl*.48a, *śl*.48c, *śl*.51a, *śl*.53d, *śl*.69b, *śl*.133b, *śl*.226c, *śl*.229a; Jr.29b.3, Jr.46b.1, Jr.46b.2, Jr.48d.1 *bis*, Jr.51d.2 *bis*, Jr.55d.2, Jr.70b.7, Jr.107b.3, Jr.132d.2, Jr.223d.1; Qt.46b.2, Qt.77d.1, Qt.110b.1;
pūjyatā	**worship,** Jr.54d.3;
pūjyatva	**worship,** Jr.54d.4;
pūrṇa	**complete, replete, filled, total,** *śl*.24a, *śl*.26b, *śl*.113b, *śl*.138c, *śl*.152c, *śl*.185a, *śl*.223c, *śl*.227a, *śl*.235a, *śḷ*.286a; Jr.24d.2, Jr.48d.1, Jr.70b.5, Jr.113b.1, Jr.119b.2, Jr.127b.3, Jr.139d.1, Jr.146b.2, Jr.153b.4, Jr.185d.1, Jr.235d.1; Qt.77d.1, Qt.100b.5, Qt.122b.1, Qt.166b.1;
pūrnatā	**completeness, repletion, fullness,** *śl*.284c; Jr.115b.1, Jr.283d.4, Jr.285b.1, Jr.285b.2;
pṛthivī	**earth, world,** Qt.166b.1;
paiṣṭī	**grain alcohol,** Jr.13d.3; Qt.13d.6; see **piṣṭa;**
prakāśa	**splendour, light,** *śl*.13b, *śl*.50a, *śl*.80b; Jr.13d.4, Jr.70b.1, Jr.80d.2;
prakāśaka	**splendour, light,** *śl*.146b; Jr.146b.2;
prakāśate	**shines forth,** *śl*.44b; Jr.46b.1;
prakāśatva	**splendour, llght,** Jr.271d.1;
prakāśana	**elucidation,** Jr.292b.3; see **aprakāśya;**
prakriyā	**ritual procedure,** *śl*.1d; Jr.1b.1, Jr.2b.1, Jr.2b.2 *bis*, Jr.3d.1 *bis*, Jr.3d.2, Jr.7d.2, Jr.100b.1, Jr.198b.3, Jr.201b.2; see **kriyā;**
pratibimba	**reflection,** *śl*.260d; Jr.24.2, Jr.271d.1;
pratyaya	**conviction,** *śl*.194d, *śl*.211c, *śl*.238b, *śl*.258d; Jr.195d.3, Jr.218b.2, Jr.271d.1; Qt.3d.1, Qt.192b.1, Qt.236d.2;
pradīpaka	**lamp,** *śl*.55b, *śl*.228d; see **dīpa;**
prabodhayet	**should arouse,** Qt.216d.1; see **udbodha, bodha, saṃbodhayet;**
prabodhita	**enlightenment,** Jr.46b.1;
pramātṛ	**knowing subjct;** Jr.13d.3, Jr.70b.1 *bis*, Jr.95d.1 *bis*, Jr.111b.1, Jr.112b.1 *bis*, Jr.137b.1,

Jr.138b.2, Jr.139d.1, Jr.147b.1, Jr.153b.5, Jr.182d.1, Jr.185d.2, Jr.278b.1, Jr.281d.2;

pravikāsa **opening,** Jr.123b.1; see **vikāsa;**

  pravikāsi **evident,** *śl.*111d; Jr.112b.1; Qt.138b.1;

  pravikāsinī **manifesting,** *śl.*248b;

  pravikas-vara **fully opening and closing,** *śl.*122a; Jr.121d.2, Jr.123b.1, Jr.124b.1, Jr.153b.1;

pravṛtta **active,** Jr.80d.2, Jr.221d.2;

  pravṛtti **use, activity,** Jr.98d.3, Jr.102d.4, Jr.106b.2, Jr.140b.1, Jr.163d.2; Qt.98d.1;

praveśa **absorption, entry,** *śl.*114c; *śl.*237d; Jr.46b.1, Jr.89d.1; Qt.236d.2; see **āveśa, samāveśa;**

praśama **quietening,** *śl.*118c, *śl.*283d; Jr.119b.1;

praśiṣya **disciple of a disciple,** *śl.*35d; see **śiṣya;**

prasāda **favour,** *śl.*166c, *śl.*180c; Jr.46b.1, Jr.168d.1;

prasara **pouring out,** *śl.*42b, *śl.*42c, *śl.*49a; Jr.42d.1, Jr.50d.1, Jr.153b.5, Jr.281d.1; Qt.100b.3;

prāg-udak etc. **north-east,** *śl.*18b; **north-east and other directions**

prāṇa **subtle-breath,** ***prāṇa*****,** *śl.*7b, *śl.*46c, *śl.*91d, *śl.*108c, *śl.*178a, *śl.*179a, *śl.*180a, *śl.*253a, *śl.*278c; Jr.7d.1, Jr.48d.1, Jr.63d.1, Jr.70b.1, Jr.88d.1 - four times, Jr.89d.1, Jr.89d.3, Jr.90b.3, Jr.109b.3, Jr.146b.2, Jr.147b.1, Jr.158b.1, Jr.177d.3, Jr.208d.1, Jr.213d.1 *bis*, Jr.236d.2, Jr.247d.3, Jr.273b.1 *bis*, Jr.275d.1, Jr.278b.1, Jr.281d.1, Jr.281d.2 *bis*; Qt.70b.2 *bis*, Qt.89d.1, Qt.213d.1;

  prāṇana **subtle-breath,** *śl.*207d; Jr.70b.1;

prāyaścitta **rite of reparation,** Qt.13d.11, Qt.13d.12;

  prāyaścittī **penitent,** Qt.13d.13;

preraka **impelling,** *śl.*192b; Jr.192b.1;

  prerya **that which should be impelled,** *śl.*192b; Jr.192b.1;

prokṣa **sprinkling,** *śl.*176;

  prokṣana **sprinkling,** Jr.20d.1;

  prokṣita **sprinkled,** *śl.*202c;

  prokṣya **having sprinkled,** *śl.*187c;

procchalad **surging,** *śl.*24b; see **ucchalati;**

  procchalet **he surges,** *śl.*139d; Jr.139d.2;

bindu	**the phoneme *Ṃ*,** Jr.195d.1, Jr.213d.1; **bindu,** *śl*.239c, *śl*.244c, *śl*.245b, *śl*.245d; Jr.39d.1, Jr.247d.2 *ter*, Jr.252d.1; Qt.240b.1, Qt.247d.2 *bis*; see **baindava, *Ṃ*;**
bimba	**original, that which is reflected,** Jr.24d.2; **dot,** Qt.27b.1;
bīja	**seed,** *śl*.68a; Jr.70b.1 *bis*; Qt.46b.1, Qt.70b.1. Qt.110b.2, Qt.153b.6; **sound-seed,** Jr.216d.1, Jr.247d.1, Jr.271d.1; see **sa-bīja-dīkṣā;**
bubhukṣita	**a hungry person,** Jr.98d.3;
bubhukṣu	**a person who desires enjoyments,** *śl*.225a; Jr.127b.4, Jr.229d.1;
buddha	**aroused, enlightened,** *śl*.174a; Qt.100b.4, Qt.252d.1;
buddhi	**intellect, mind, attitude,** *śl*.263b; Jr.7d.1, Jr.48d.1, Jr.158b.1, Jr.208d.1, Jr.252d.1, Jr.271d.1, Jr.281d.2; Qt.102d.5, Qt.166b.1;
baindava	**pertaining to the *bindu*,** *śl*.37c, *śl*.261a; Jr.39d.1; see **bindu;**
bodha	**consciousness, knowledge,** *śl*.129c, *śl*.269c; Jr.95d.1, Jr.130b.1; Qt.4d.3, Qt.240b.2; see **udbodha, prabodhayet, saṃbodhayet;** see **cit, citi, citta, caitanya, saṃvit** etc.;
bodhana	**awakening,** *śl*.142d; Jr.146b.1;
bodhayet	**should light,** *śl*.226b;
brahman	***brahman*,** *śl*.97c, *śl*.286c; Jr.97b.1, Jr.98b.2; Qt.50d.1, Qt.98b.1 = Qt.128b.1, Qt.100b.4; see ***S*** 'the third Brahmā', **parabrahman;**
brahma-carya	***brahmacarya*,** *śl*.97b; Qt.100b.4;
brahma-cārī	***brahmacārī*, celibate,** *śl*.98d; Jr.98b.2; Qt.96d.4;
brahmaṇya	**pertaining to *brahman*,** Qt.100b.3;
brahma-bila	**'pit-of-Brahmā',** *śl*.88b; Jr.88d.1;
brahma-randhra,	**aperture of Brahmā,** *śl*.179b, Jr.179d.1; see **ka-randhra, ka-randhraka, randhra;**
brahma-sthāna,	**place of Brahmā,** *śl*.250b, *śl*.250c; Jr.252d.1 *bis*;

brāhman	**a brahman,** Qt.13d.11, Qt.13d.17, Qt.96d.3;
bhaga-aṅkura	**clitoris,** Qt.110b.2; see **aṅkura;**
bhāva	**Being,** *śl.*146c;
	being, mood, circumstance, becoming, object, *śl.*5b, *śl.*118d, *śl.*123c, *śl.*254a, *śl.*137d, *śl.*146d; Jr.119b.1, Jr.124b.1, Jr.135b.1, Jr.138b.1, Jr.147b.1 *bis*, Jr.182d.1; Qt.100b.6, Qt.119b.1 *ter*;
	mood, attitude, *śl.*176; Qt.22d.2 = Qt.185d.1, Qt.175d.2;
bhāvanā	**creative imagination, visualisation, contemplation, attitude, focus,** Jr.22d.2, Jr.102d.4, Jr.149b.2, Jr.156b.2, Jr.161b.2; Qt.57d.2, Qt.100b.4 *bis*, Qt.102d.5, Qt.119b.1;
bhāvayitavya	**to be contemplated,** Jr.22b.3;
bhāvayate	**one should contemplate,** *śl.*252a;
bhāvayitvā	**after contemplating,** Jr.247d.2;
bhāvayet	**should contemplate, should do,** Qt.57d.2, Qt.64d.1, Qt.102d.5, Qt.166b.1;
bhāvita	**contemplated,** *śl.*123d; Jr.124b.1; Qt.100b.6;
bhujaṅga	**cobra,** *śl.*51c; Jr.247d.4; Qt.240b.1, Qt.252d.1 *bis*;
bhujaṅgama	**cobra,** *śl.*239d;
bhūtam	**a spirit,** *śl.*287a;
bhukti	**enjoyment,** *śl.*11c, *śl.*103d; Jr.13d.2; Qt.166b.1; see **bhoga;**
bhuvana	**world,** *śl.*254c, *śl.*260d; Jr.20d.1, Jr.220d.1; Qt.24d.2;
bheda etc.	**distinction, division, multiplicity, etc.,** *passim*,
bhairava	**Bhairava, a bhairava, as a deity, as wine, as sound,** *śl.*12d, *śl.*22d, *śl.*49b, *śl.*145b, *śl.*157a, *śl.*159d; Jr.13d.3, Jr.23d.1, Jr.46b.2, Jr.50d.1 *bis*, Jr.158b.2, Jr.160b.2, Jr.160b.3, Jr.223d.1; Qt.13d.1 *bis*, Qt.13d.2, Qt.13d.5, Qt.13d.8, Qt.13d.9, Qt.13d.10, Qt.22b.1, Qt.100b.5, Qt.100b.6, Qt.110b.2;
bhairavī	**the person who is Bhairava,** *śl.*162b; Jr.22b.3, Jr.161b.2;
bhoga	**enjoyment, pleasure,** *śl.*12b, *śl.*57d, *śl.*111c = Qt.138b.1, *śl.*209c, *śl.*236a, *śl.*276d; Jr.13d.3,

	Jr.57d.1, Jr.112b.1, Jr.218d.2, Jr.277b.1 *bis*; Qt.13d.3, Qt.13d.4, Qt.102d.7; see **bhukti, ābhoga;**
upabhoga	**pleasure,** *śl.*155a,; Jr.156b.1; Qt.153b.6;
bhogyatva	**enjoyment,** Jr.13d.3;
sambhoga	**carnal pleasure,** Jr.46b.1;
bhrama	**circle, circulation,** Jr.247d.3; Qt.54d.3; see **paribhramya;**
bhramara	**circulating,** *śl.*247c;
	black bee, Qt.100b.5;
bhramaṇa	**circulating,** Jr.70b.1, Jr.281d.2;
bhramati	**circulates,** Jr.70b.1 *ter*;
bhramate	**he tours,** *śl.*40a;
bhramantam	**circulating,** *śl.*279b; Jr.281d.2;
bhramantī	**circulating,** Qt.70b.1;
bhramayet	**causes to circulate,** *śl.*279d; Jr.281d.2;
bhramet	**should circulate,** Jr.88d.1;
bhrū	**eye-brows,** *śl.*60a, *śl.*71c; Qt.100b.5 *bis*;
bhrū-madhya	**eye-brow centre, between the eye-brows,** *śl.*244d, *śl.*261a; Jr.39d.1, Jr.247d.2; Qt.39d.4, Qt.72b.2, Qt.247d.2;
maṇḍala	***maṇḍala*, circle, cycle,** *śl.*8a, *śl.*9a, *śl.*26d, *śl.*75d, *śl.*151b, *śl.*172a, *śl.*184a, *śl.*255d, *śl.*260c; Jr.9d.1, Jr.27b.2 *bis*, Jr.29b.1, Jr.54d.3, Jr.77d.3, Jr.153b.2, Jr.166b.2 *bis*, Jr.169d.1, Jr.185d.1, Jr.271d.1 *bis*; Qt.8d.1, Qt.54d.3, Qt.77d.1, Qt.166b.1, Qt.248d.1, Qt.248d.2;
mati	**mind,** *śl.*7b; Jr.7d.1;
madya	**liquor, wine,** *śl.*26b, *śl.*76a; Jr.10d.2, Jr.13d.8, Jr.13d.12 *bis*, Jr.13d.13, Jr.98b.1 *bis*, Jr.98d.1; Qt.13d.1, Qt.13d.7, Qt.13d.8, Qt.13d.11, Qt.13d.12, Qt.13d.18 *bis*, Qt.13d.19, Qt.13d.22, Qt.13d.23, Qt.13d.25, Qt.77d.1, Qt.96d.4, Qt.98d.1, Qt.100b.2, Qt.100b.4, Qt.100b.6;
madhya	**middle, centre,** *passim*;
madhya-dhāman	**central sacred place,** *śl.*280d; Jr.89d.1, Jr.89d.3, Jr.121d.2, Jr.124b.1, Jr.146b.1, Jr.147b.1, Jr.206d.1, Jr.281d.2; see **ūrdhva-dhāman, dhāman;**

madhya-nāḍī	**central channel,** Jr.7d.1, Jr.42d.1, Jr.153b.3; see **nāḍī;**
madhya-padā	**central path,** *śl.*122a, Jr.123b.1;
madhya-śakti	**central śkti,** Jr.247d.3, Jr.273b.1, Jr.274b.2 *bis*, Jr.275d.1;
manas	**mind,** *śl.*6b, *śl.*89d, *śl.*253c; Jr.89d.1, Jr.277b.1; Qt.100b.4, Qt.102d.7, Qt.175d.1;
mantra	**mantra,** *passim*;
mantra-udaya	**the arising of the mantra,** *śl.*149b; Jr.149b.1; see **udaya;**
mantra-vīrya	**the potency of the mantra,** *śl.*148b, *śl.*156b; Jr.147b.2, Jr.154b.2 *bis*; see **vīrya;**
	mantra-sādhana, mantra practice, *śl.*227d;
mantrin	**practitioner of the mantra, wise man,** Qt.55d.1, Qt.91d.1, Qt.197b.1;
manda	**weak,** *śl.*197a; Jr.197b.1 *bis*, Jr.208d.1 *bis*, Jr.209d.2; Qt.197b.1 *bis*;
	the phoneme *Ḍ*, *śl.*212c; Jr.213d.1;
mala	**impurity,** *śl.*74d; Jr.206d.1;
amala	**unsullied,** Qt.4d.3;
vimala	**unsullied** *śl.*110d; Jr.111b.1;
nairmalya	**unsullied nature,** Jr.271d.1;
nirmala	**unsullied,** Qt.110b.6;
marīci	**spark of light,** *śl.*113c = Qt.139d.1; Jr.114b.1;
marman	**vital part,** *śl.*143d; Jr.146b.1;
mahā-paśu	**human being,** Jr.54d.5; see **paśu;**
māṃsa	**meat,** Jr.98b.1 *bis*, Jr.98d.1, Jr.98d.3, Jr.100b.4; Qt.13d.12, Qt.96d.4, Qt.98d.1, Qt.100b.2;
māyā	***māyā*** *śl.*199b, *śl.*290b; Jr.70b.1, Jr.200d.2, Jr.208d.1;
	the phoneme *Ṃ*, Jr.216d.1;
	the 'seed' *HRĪṂ*, *śl.*255c; Jr.271d.1;
	see **bindu, baindava;**
mārga	**path, side,** *śl.*147b, *śl.*206a; Jr.42d.1, Jr.100b.3, Jr.130b.1, Jr.147b.1, Jr.206d.1; Qt.100b.4, Qt.114b.1, Qt.166b.1 *bis*; see **apamārga;**
mithaḥ	**reciprocal, mutual,** *śl.*104c, *śl.*128c; Jr.129b.3; see **paraspara;**
muktī	**liberation,** *śl.*11c, *śl.*91b, *śl.*103d, *śl.*276b; Jr.13d.2, Jr.21d.1; Qt.166b.1;

mukta	**free,** Jr.277b.1; Qt.127b.1; see **jīvan-mukta, mokṣa;**
mukhya-cakra	**principal circle,** *śl.*103b, *śl.*110b, *śl.*124c; Jr.107b.3, Jr.109b.4, Jr.110b.3, Jr.111b.1, Jr.112b.2, Jr.113b.2, Jr.115b.1, Jr.120b.1, Jr.125b.1, Jr.132d.1, Jr.136b.1, Jr.150b.1, Jr.160b.2, Jr.166b.1, Jr.173d.2;
mudrā	**gesture,** ***mudrā*****, sexual partner, sexual union,** *śl.*36c, *śl.*150c, *śl.*153d; Jr.39d.1, Jr.40d.1 *bis*, Jr.42d.1, Jr.150b.3, Jr.153b.6, Jr.154b.1, Jr.154b.2, Jr.156b.1, Jr.166b.2 *bis*, Jr.168d.1; Qt.39d.1, Qt.39d.3, Qt.40d.1, Qt.100b.5, Qt.198b.1; see **khecara-mudrā;**
mumukṣu	**the person who seeks liberation,** *śl.*220b; Jr.127b.4, Jr.224d.1, Jr.232d.1;
mūrti	**physical form, image,** *śl.*78a, Jr.78d.1; Qt.166b.1;
mūrta	**having physical form,** Qt.22d.2; see **amūrta;**
mūla	**root, source, total, base, perineum,** *śl.*81a, *śl.*151d, *śl.*204a, *śl.*222c, *śl.*259c; Jr.55d.2, Jr.70b.1, Jr.153b.3, Jr.206d.1 *bis*, Jr.271d.1 *bis*; Qt.91d.1, Qt.195d.1;
mūla-vidyā	**root** ***vidyā*****,** Jr.55d.2; see **unmūlana;**
melaka	**meeting, blending, mating, company,** *śl.*104b, *śl.*141d, *śl.*162c; Jr.46b.1, Jr.104b.1, Jr.142b.1, Jr.162b.1; Qt.22b.2; see **saṃmelana, sammelanā;**
melana	**meeting, blending, mating, company,** Jr.146b.2; Qt.64d.1;
melayet	**should mate,** *śl.*168d;
mithuna	**intercourse,** Jr.7d.1; see **maithuna;**
mokṣa	**liberation,** *śl.*57d, *śl.*230d, *śl.*231d, *śl.*276b, *śl.*276d, *śl.*277c; Jr.57d.1, Jr.200d.2, Jr.232d.1, Jr.277b.1; Qt.13d.2, Qt.13d.3, Qt.239b.1; see **mukti, jīvan-mukta;**
maithuna	**intercourse,** Jr.98b.1, Jr.98d.1; Qt.98d.1; see **mithuna;**
yajana	**sacrifice,** Jr.66d.2; Qt.55d.2, Qt.166b.1;
yajante	**they make sacrifice,** Jr.100b.2;

yāga	**sacrifice,** *śl.*5d, *śl.*6d, *śl.*10a, *śl.*14c, *śl.*15a, *śl.*18a, *śl.*27a, *śl.*66d, *śl.*76c, *śl.*77d, *śl.*107c, *śl.*129d, *śl.*164c, *śl.*170d, *śl.*177c, *śl.*186c, *śl.*221c, *śl.*284b, *śl.*291a *bis*, *śl.*291b; Jr.1b.1, Jr.2b.1, Jr.4d.2, Jr.5d.2, Jr.6d.1, Jr.7d.1, Jr.13d.8, Jr.13d.9, Jr.13d.12, Jr.17d.3, Jr.20d.1 *bis*, Jr.22b.3, Jr.23d.3, Jr.29b.3, Jr.46b.2, Jr.66d.2, Jr.79d.3, Jr.100b.1, Jr.100b.8, Jr.107d.1, Jr.166b.1 *bis*, Jr.285b.1; Qt.13d.21, Qt.66d.2, Qt.100b.8, Qt.166b.1 *ter*; see **anuyāga, ādi-yāga;**
yājaka	**partaking in ... sacrifice,** *śl.*99d;
yāmala	**pair, pairing,** *śl.*7a, *śl.*70b, *śl.*79c, *śl.*115c, *śl.*120d, *śl.*158b; Jr.7d.1, Jr.48d.2, Jr.50d.2, Jr.51d.2, Jr.54d.4, Jr.70b.6 *ter*, Jr.79d.1, Jr.158b.1;
yāmalī	**pair,** *śl.*53d;
yugma	**couple, group,** *śl.*32d, *śl.*49d, *śl.*63a, *śl.*78a, *śl.*131d = Qt.46b.2, *śl.*166c; Jr.33d.1 *bis*, Jr.50d.1, Jr.63d.2, Jr.168d.1, Jr.281d.2;
yugmaka	**couple,** *śl.*83d, *śl.*86a; Jr.88d.1;
yoga	***yoga*,** *śl.*166d, *śl.*225c, *śl.*236b; Jr.168d.1, Jr.229d.1 *bis*, Jr.236d.1 *bis*, Jr.273b.1; Qt.166b.1, Qt.192b.1;
yogana	**joining,** *śl.*242d;
yoginī	***yoginī*,** *śl.*28b, *śl.*72b, *śl.*150d, *śl.*183b; Jr.29b.1 - four times, Jr.40d.1, Jr.46b.1, Jr.185d.1; Qt.13d.24, Qt.22b.2, Qt.64d.1, Qt.72b.2 *bis*, Qt.129b.2;
yoginī-bhū	***yoginī*-born,** *śl.*163a;
yoginī-mukha	**'the mouth of the *yoginī*',** *śl.*221d; see **śakti-cakra;**
yoginī-vaktra	**'the mouth of the *yoginī*',** *śl.*124d; Jr.88d.1, Jr.115b.1, Jr.125b.1, Jr.129b.3 *bis*, Jr.132d.1, Jr.160b.2; Qt.126b.1;
yoginī-vadana	**'the mouth of the *yoginī*',** *śl.*40d;
yogī	***yogī*,** *śl.*206a, *śl.*219d, *śl.*230b, *śl.*270d; Jr.89.1 *bis*, Jr.89d.2, Jr.224d.1, Jr.271d.2, Jr.273b.1; Qt.100b.3, Qt.114b.1, Qt.166b.1;
yogyatā	**suitability,** Jr.20d.1, Jr.201b.2;

yogyatva	**suitability,** *śl.*219b; Jr.220d.1;
yoni	**source, womb,** Qt.166b.1;
rakta	**red, menstrual blood,** *śl.*25d, *śl.*73a, *śl.*226a; Jr.27b.2 *bis*; Qt.16d.2, Qt.54d.5, Qt.73b.1, Qt.153b.3, Qt.200d.1;
rajas	**female semen,** Jr.153b.4, Jr.153b.5; Qt.153b.6;
raṇaraṇaka	**longing,** *śl.*137c;
randhra	**aperture,** *śl.*59d, *śl.*179c; Jr.88d.1 *bis*, Jr.179d.1, Jr.247d.1; see **Ka, ka-randhra, ka-randhraka, brahma-bila;**
rabhasāt	**vigorously,** *śl.*139d, *śl.*259b, *śl.*266a; Jr.139d.2;
raśmi	**rays [of light]** *śl.*51d; Jr.51d.2;
raśmy-ogha	**stream of rays,** *śl.*24a, *śl.*50c;
raśmi-cakra	**circle of rays,** *śl.*132b, *śl.*276c; Jr.277b.1;
raśmi-gaṇa	**group of rays,** *śl.*136d; Jr.137b.2, Jr.138b.1;
raśmi-maṇḍala	**circle of rays,** *śl.*184a; Jr.185d.1;
rasa	**essence, taste,** *śl.*11b, *śl.*13a, *śl.*68a, *śl.*130d, *śl.*137c, *śl.*173c, *śl.*176, *śl.*137c; Jr.13d.1, Jr.13d.4, Jr.70b.1 - four times, Jr.104b.1, Jr.138b.1; Qt.13d.8 *bis*, Qt.13d.24, Qt.70b.1, Qt.110b.2, Qt.129b.4, Qt.153b.5, Qt.175d.2;
rasā	**essence, taste,** Jr.235d.1;
rasāyana	**revitalising fluid,** Qt.77d.1, Qt.129b.1;
rahasya	**secret,** *śl.*1b, *śl.*15a, *śl.*96d, *śl.*255b, *śl.*292a; Jr.0.2, Jr.1b.1, Jr.46b.1, Jr.117b.1, Jr.186b.2, Jr.292b.3; Qt.166b.1;
rahasyatva	**secrecy,** *śl.*169a; Jr.22b.2, Jr.168d.2, Jr.186b.1;
rātra	**night,** *śl.*76c; Jr.77d.1; Qt.77d.2 *bis*;
rāva	**roaring,** *śl.*155c;
rūddha	**restrained,** Jr.89d.1; see **nirodha, nirudhya;**
retas	**male semen,** Jr.153b.4, Jr.153b.5; Qt.17d.1, Qt.153b.2, Qt.200d.1; see **ūrdhva-retasaḥ;**
lakṣa	**one hundred thousand,** *śl.*82b, *śl.*91c, *śl.*150a, *śl.*187a; Jr.82d.1, Jr.150a.2, Jr.187b.1; Qt.100b.4;
laya	**dissolution,** *śl.*94d, *śl.*147b, *śl.*182a; Jr.4d.1, Qt.4d.2; see **vilaya;**
liṅga	***liṅga*, gender, sexual organ,** *śl.*141c, *śl.*157d, *śl.*171a; Jr.158b.1, Jr.161b.1; Qt.110b.2, Qt.153b.5;

līna	**merging,** *śl.*205c, *śl.*250d, *śl.*259d; Qt.153b.6;
līnatva	**merging,** Jr.271d.1;
līlā	**play, game,** *śl.*155a; Jr.46b.1; Qt.100b.5, Qt.166b.1;
lolī-bhāva	**interplay,** Jr.154b.2;
laukika	**worldly,** *śl.*101c; Jr.100b.3, Jr.102d.1, Jr.102d.4; see **alaukika;**
laukikavat	**worldly,** Jr.102d.4;
vaktra	**mouth,** *śl.*60a, *śl.*84c, *śl.*85d, *śl.*125d *bis*, *śl.*126a, *śl.*128c, *śl.*128d, *śl.*273d *bis*; Jr.63d.1, Jr.89d.1, Jr.126b.2 *ter*, Jr.129b.3 - five times, Qt.126b.1 *bis*, Qt.129b.3 *bis*, Qt.129b.4 *bis*; see **yoginī-vaktra, etc;**
vapuḥ	**body, substance,** *śl.*128b; Jr.22b.3, Jr.128b.3; Qt.100b.4; see **tanuḥ, deha, piṇḍa, śarīra;**
varṇa	**phoneme, caste, complexion, composure,** *śl.*55b, *śl.*55c, *śl.*101b, *śl.*255c; Jr.55d.2, Jr.101b.2, Jr.271d.1; Qt.13d.17, Qt.55d.1, Qt.70b.2 *bis*, Qt.100b.5 *bis*, Qt.195d.1, Qt.247d.1;
vastra	**cloth,** *śl.*15c, *śl.*190b; Jr.7d.1, Jr.16d.2, Jr.27b.2 *ter*;
vāma	**left,** *śl.*37b, *śl.*193a; Jr.29b.3 *ter*, Jr.46b.2, Jr.63d.2 - five times, Jr.146b.1, Jr.147b.1, Jr.195d.1 *bis*; Qt.39d.3, Qt.70b.2 *bis*, Qt.63d.2 - four times, Qt.100b.4, Qt.153b.3, Qt.195d.1 *bis*;
vāma-amṛta	**nectar-of-the-left,** *śl.*10d, *śl.*198d; Jr.13d.12; Qt.13d.21; see **amṛta;**
vāsanā	**attitude of mind, impression,** *śl.*64c; Qt.22d.1;
vikalpa	**differentiated thought,** *śl.*90d, *śl.*92a, *śl.*184c; Jr.91d.3, Jr.185d.1, Jr.200d.2, Jr.252d.2;
vikalpaka	**differentiated thought,** Jr.252d.2;
vikalpayate	**to entertain a differentiated thought,** *śl.*91a;
vikalpayitum	**to express by differentiated thought,** Jr.126b.1;
vikāsa	**expansion, opening out,** *śl.*89d, *śl.*106c, *śl.*107d; Jr.89d.1, Jr.107d.1, Jr.107d.2, Jr.109b.3, Jr.168d.1; Qt.24d.1; see **pravikāsa;**
vikāsitva	**expansion, opening out,** Qt.175d.1;

vikṣobha	**agitation,** *śl.*139b; Jr.139d.1; see **kṣobha saṅkṣobha, saṃkṣobha, kṣobhayitvā;**
vicintayet	**should reflect,** *śl.*189b, *śl.*280d; Jr.281d.5;
vijñāna	**discriminating knowledge,** *śl.*130b, *śl.*263a, *śl.*264b; Jr.133b.1; Qt.13d.17, Qt.22b.2; see **jñāna, jñānī, jñānīya;**
vidyā	***vidyā,*** *śl.*55d, *śl.*167d, *śl.*168c; Jr.55d.2, Jr.70b.3, Jr.166b.2 *bis*, Jr.168d.1 *bis*; Qt.70b.2, Qt.129b.6;
vidhi	**ritual, injunction,** *passim*;
viparyaya	**contrary direction,** Qt.27b.1;
vimarśa	**awareness,** *śl.*147c, *śl.*155b; Jr.156b.1; see **āmarśa, parāmarśa, parimarśa;**
vilaya	**dissolution,** *śl.*118d; Jr.119b.1; see **laya;**
viśeṣa	**particular,** *passim*, **esoteric**;
vīra	**hero,** *śl.*6c, *śl.*78b, *śl.*286b, *śl.*288c, *śl.*290a; Jr.78d.1, Jr.287b.1, Jr.289b.1; Qt.13d.10, Qt.13d.22, Qt.54d.2, Qt.70b.3, Qt.100b.4, Qt.101b.1, Qt.129b.4, Qt.166b.1 *bis*; see **ekavīra;**
vīra-bhojya	**the hero's meal,** *śl.*77a; Qt.77d.2;
vīrya	**potency, seed, semen,** *śl.*113d, *śl.*139b, *śl.*153a; Jr.42d.1, Jr.139d.1, Jr.150b.3, Jr.156b.1; Qt.3d.1, Qt.4d.6, Qt.129b.6, Qt.139d.1; see **mantra-vīrya;**
viloma	**upwards,** *śl.*18d; Jr.19d.1;
viśrānta	**reposing, resting place,** Jr.24d.1, Jr.127b.3, Jr.136b.2, Jr.160b.2, Jr.185d.2;
viśrānti	**repose,** *śl.*49, *śl.*138a; Jr.42d.1, Jr.48d.1, Jr.50d.1, Jr.63d.1, Jr.70b.5, Jr.79d.1, Jr.95d.1, Jr.111b.1, Jr.112b.1 *bis*, Jr.113b.2, Jr.117b.1, Jr.120b.1, Jr.135b.2, Jr.137b.1, Jr.138b.1, Jr.138b.2, Jr.138b.3, Jr.139d.1, Jr.146b.1, Jr.150b.1, Jr.278b.1, Jr.281d.1;
viśrāma	**quietening, repose,** *śl.*143a; Jr.120d.1, Jr.146b.1; Qt.64d.1;
viśva	**world, all,** *passim*;
visarga	**emission,** *śl.*116b, *śl.*127a, *śl.*140a, *śl.*142b; Jr.117b.1 *bis*, Jr.127b.3, Jr.133b.1 *bis*, Jr.140b.1, Jr.142b.1, Jr.147b.2, Jr.149b.1; Qt.141b.1; see ***Ḥ*, vaisargika, sarga;**

vedha — **penetration,** *śl.*236d, *śl.*237a, *śl.*240b, *śl.*244b, *śl.*247c, *śl.*247d, *śl.*251b, *śl.*254b, *śl.*258b, *śl.*260d, *śl.*262a, *śl.*264b, *śl.*266d, *śl.*267d, *śl.*268d, *śl.*269d, *śl.*271a; Jr.235d.2, Jr.236d.2, Jr.247d.3, Jr.247d.4, Jr.252d.1, Jr.281d.3; Qt.236d.3, Qt.240b.1 *ter*, Qt.240b.2, Qt.241b.1, Qt.247d.1, Qt.252d.1;

  vedhana — **penetration,** *śl.*241b *bis*;

  vedhanīya — **to be penetrated,** Qt.241b.1;

  vedhayet — **should penetrate,** *śl.*244a, *śl.*247b, *śl.*251a, *śl.*273d, *śl.*280b; Jr.247d.3, Jr.274b.2, Jr.281d.2; Qt.247d.1, Qt.247d.2;

vaisargika — **source of the emission,** *śl.*119b; Jr.119b.2; see ***Ḥ*****, visaga, sarga;**

vyāpta — **pervaded,** Jr.160b.2;

  vyāpti — **pervasion, succession,** *śl.*160b, *śl.*161b, *śl.*161d; Jr.54d.3, Jr.54d.5, Jr.160b.2, Jr.160b.3, Jr.161b.2;

  vyāpinī — **pervasion,** Jr.271d.1;

vyoman — **circle, space,** *śl.*25c, *śl.*207c, *śl.*249b, *śl.*259d, *śl.*264c, *śl.*281a; Jr.27b.1, Jr.46b.2, Jr.208d.1, Jr.252d.1, Jr.271d.1, Jr.281d.2; Qt.27b.1 *bis*, Qt.173d.1;

  vyoma-bimba — **dot,** Qt.27b.1;

vrata — **vow,** *śl.*166d; Jr.64d.2, Jr.168d.1; Qt.100b.6, Qt.122b.1, Qt.166b.1;

  vratin — **the person who has taken a vow,** Qt.100b.4;

śakti — **śakti, female partner, power, energy,** *passim*; **śakti, viz. one of the stages of sound,** *śl.*258a; Jr.160b.2;

  śakti-cakra — **the circle of the śakti,** *śl.*130c; Jr.132d.1, Jr.132d.2; see **yoginī-mukha** etc.;

  śakti-pāta — **descent of energy,** *śl.*197b, *śl.*207c; Jr.197b.1, Jr.200d.2, Jr.208d.1 *bis*, Jr.209d.2; Qt.197b.1;

  śakti-pātatva — **descent of energy,** Jr.211b.1;

  śakti-mān — **the one who possesses śakti,** *śl.*108b, *śl.*114a = Qt.139d.1, *śl.*119d, *śl.*154d, *śl.*246a; Jr.104b.1, Jr.105b.1, Jr.109b.1, Jr.114b.2, Jr.115b.1, Jr.119b.3, Jr.120b.1, Jr.120b.2, Jr.120d.1,

Jr.121d.1 *bis*, Jr.156b.1, Jr.161b.1, Jr.247d.3, Jr.248d.1;

śaṅkā — **doubt, question fear,** *śl.*5c; Jr.16d.5, Jr.96d.4, Jr.110b.3, Jr.229d.2, Jr.283d.2;

śaṅkha — **conch shell,** *śl.*226d; Jr.229d.1 - four times;

śarīra — **body,** *śl.*123c; Jr.48d.1, Jr.98.1, Jr.124b.1, Jr.185d.1, Jr.195d.3, Jr.271d.1 *bis*; Qt.4d.9, Qt.22d.3, Qt.213d.1;
see **tanuḥ, deha, piṇḍa, vapuḥ;**

  śarīraka — **body,** *śl.*4d;

śānta — **'rested', tranquil,** *śl.*117a *bis* = Qt.127b.2, *śl.*119c, *śl.*120b, *śl.*120d, *śl.*121c, *śl.*126c, *śl.*134a, *śl.*140b; Jr.117b.1 *ter*, Jr.119b.1, Jr.119b.3, Jr.120b.1, Jr.120d.1, Jr.121d.1, Jr.127b.1, Jr.133b.1, Jr.133d.1, Jr.142b.1, Jr.146b.2 *bis*, Jr.147b.1, Jr.173d.2; Qt.100b.4;

  śāntatā — **the 'rested' state,** Jr.120d.1;

  śāntatva — **the 'rested' state,** Jr.133d.1, Jr.142b.1;

  śānti — **resting, tranquillity,** *śl.*83a = Qt.150b.2; Jr.88d.1; Qt.13d.7;

  śānty-atīta — ***śāntyatīta***, Jr.206d.1, Jr.252d.1;

śāsana — **teaching, text,** *śl.*102b, *śl.*212b; Jr.102d.1, Jr.212b.1;

śāstra — **scripture, religious treatise,** *śl.*10b, *śl.*122b, *śl.*165a, *śl.*169c, *śl.*177b, *śl.*218c, *śl.*240c; Jr.10d.2, Jr.13d.12, Jr.13d.14, Jr.46b.1, Jr.51d.2 *bis*, Jr.54d.3, Jr.91d.1, Jr.98d.3 *bis*, Jr.102d.5, Jr.121d.2, Jr.129b.3, Jr.166b.2, Jr.192b.2, Jr.200d.2, Jr.201b.3, Jr.211b.2, Jr.218d.1; Qt.10d.1, Qt.54d.4, Qt.241b.1;

  śāstrīya — **pertaining to the scripture,** Jr.46b.1;

śikhā — **tuft of hair, flame,** *śl.*59a, *śl.*257d, *śl.*259a; Jr.63d.1, Jr.271d.1; Qt.100b.5;

  śikhi — **flame,** Qt.213d.1 *bis*;

śiras — **head,** Jr.16d.1, Jr.19d.1 *bis*; Qt.70b.2, Qt.16d.1;
see **kādya, kāya-pīṭha;**

śivatā — **the state of Śiva,** *śl.*271d, *śl.*281d; Jr.271d.2, Jr.281d.2;

  śiva-hasta — **'hand of Śiva',** *śl.*194c, *śl.*227b, *śl.*229c; Jr.192b.2, Jr.195d.1, Jr.229d.1; Qt.192b.1,

	Qt.195d.2;
śiṣya	**disciple,** *śl*.2b, *śl*.35d, *śl*.187a, *śl*.193c, *śl*.195c, *śl*.216c, *śl*.238a = Qt.236d.2, *śl*.242a, *śl*.259d, *śl*.262c, *śl*.291d; Jr.187b.1, Jr.195d.3, Jr.201b.2, Jr.208d.1, Jr.211b.2, Jr.247d.2, Jr.271d.1 *bis*, Jr.274b.1, Jr.275d.1; Qt.247d.2, Qt.202b.1; see **praśiṣya;**
śuddha	**pure, single,** *śl*.13a, *śl*.92a; Jr.13d.4, Jr.218b.1; see **śodhya;**
śuddhatama	**most pure,** *śl*.128b; Jr.128b.3;
śuddhi	**purity, cleansing,** *śl*.19a; Jr.9d.3, Jr.20d.1, Jr.240b.2;
saṃśuddha	**altogether pure,** *śl*.209d;
saṃśuddhī	**complete cleansing,** *śl*.200a; Jr.200d.2;
śūnya	**void, womb, without,** *śl*.135b, *śl*.183a; Jr.135b.1, Jr.185d.1, Jr.208d.1, Jr.281d.2; Qt.13d.12, Qt.109b.2;
śūnyatā	**void, without,** Jr.113b.1;
śūnyatva	**void, without,** Jr.146b.2;
śodhya	**to be cleansed, to be purfied,** *śl*.20c, *śl*.202d, *śl*.204b, *śl*.204c, *śl*.205a; Jr.20d.1 *bis*, Jr.206d.1 - five times; see **śuddha;**
śodhyamāna	**being purified, being cleansed** *śl*.207a;
śmaśāna	**cremation ground, sexual union, heart,** *śl*.57c, *śl*.72a, *śl*.183a, *śl*.185b; Jr.185d.1, Jr.185d.2; Qt.13d.17, Qt.72b.2;
śraddhā	**the posthumous rite, devotion,** Jr.13d.11; Qt.54d.5;
ṣaṭ	**six,** Qt.39d.3; see ṣoḍhā;
	the six [who are qualified], *śl*.41c;
	the six [fold classification of the ***dūtī*****],** *śl*.103c; Jr.102d.1,Jr.102d.4;
	six [hundrend thousand repetitions], *śl*.85b;
ṣaṭka	**set of six [senses[,** *śl*.111a;
	set of six [causal deities], *śl*.233a; Jr.235d.1;
	set of six [gestures], *śl*.36d;
	set of six [gestures, hermitages, begging places etc.], *śl*.39c;
	set of six [princes], Jr.40d.2;
ṣaḍ ... adhvan	**the six pathways,** Jr.200d.2;

ṣaḍamī **set of six who are qualified,** *śl.*33d;
ṣaḍ-ara **six beams of light,** Jr.154b.1, Jr.156b.1;
ṣaḍimāḥ **the six [śaktis],** *śl.*34d;
ṣaḍ-cakra **the six circles,** Qt.9d.1;
ṣaḍ-yugmaṃ **group of six [who are qualified],** *śl.*32d; Jr.33d.1;
ṣaṇṇāṃ **of the six [sons who are qualified],** Jr.33d.1; Qt.39d.5;
ṣaṇ-maṇḍala **the six *maṇḍalas*,** *śl.*9a; Jr.9d.1;
ṣaṣṭha **sixth,** Qt.39d.3, Qt.240b.1
the sixth [vowel, viz. *Ū*], Qt.213d.1; see ***Ū*;**
ṣaṣṭhaka **sixth,** Qt.39d.4;
the sixth [vowel, viz. *Ū*], *śl.*213b; Jr.213d.1;
ṣoḍaśa **sixteen,** *śl.*91c, *śl.*151c; Jr.88d.1, Jr.89d.2, Jr.153b.3; Qt.13d.21;
ṣoḍhā **of six kinds,** *śl.*7c, *śl.*8b, *śl.*23, *śl.*240a; Qt.240b.2; see **ṣaṭ;**
ṣoḍhātva **being of six kinds,** Jr.240b.2;
saṅketa **signal, agreement,** *śl.*40a; Jr.66d.3, Jr.185d.2;
saṃkṣobha Jr.111b.1; see **kṣobha, vikṣobha, kṣobhayitvā;**
saṅkṣobha **agitation,** *śl.*114d;
saṅga **association, attachment,** *śl.*101d, *śl.*153b; Jr.102d.1, Jr.102d.4, Jr.153b.5; Qt.100b.6; see **āsaṅga;**
saṃgama **association,** *śl.*15b;
saṅgama **joining,** *śl.*83a = Qt.150b.2; Jr.16d.1, Jr.88d.1;
saṃghaṭṭa **union,** *śl.*153d, *śl.*280a; Jr.115b.1, Jr.117b.1, Jr.126b.3, Jr.127b.3, Jr.146.1, Jr.160b.2, Jr.281d.2; see **ghaṭṭana;**
saṅghaṭṭa **union, mingling,** *śl.*49c, *śl.*53c, *śl.*116b, *śl.*136c, *śl.*140a, *śl.*145b, *śl.*152d; Jr.50d.1, Jr.79d.1, Jr.104b.1, Jr.114b.2, Jr.117b.1, Jr.133b.1, Jr.142b.1, Jr.146b.2, Jr.149b.1, Jr.153b.4, Jr.154b.1, Jr.158b.1; Qt.39d.4, Qt.100b.4, Qt.153b.4, Qt.153b.5;
saṅghaṭṭayati **he unites,** *śl.*144d; Jr.146b.2;
saṅghāta **hammering, assembly, combination,** *śl.*278b, *śl.*288c; Qt.13d.21, Qt.100b.5; see **āghāta;**
saṃcāra **transmission,** *śl.*285d;
saṃcārayet **should transmit,** *śl.*112d, *śl.*263d;

saṃcārayeta	**should transmit,** *śl.*123b;
saṃnidhāpaka	**causing [the deities] to draw near,** *śl.*170d; see **sannidhāna, sānnidhya;**
saṃpuṭa	**enclosure,** *śl.*192d; Jr.195d.1;
saṃpuṭitā	**enclosed,** Jr.191d.1;
sampuṭa	**enclosure,** *śl.*21a, *śl.*21b; Qt.21d.1;
sampuṭita	**enclosed,** Jr.21d.1;
saṃpradāya	**sacred oral tradition,** *śl.*157d; Jr.166b.2 *bis*;
sampradāya	**sacred oral tradition,** *śl.*125a; Jr.22b.2, Jr.56d.1, Jr.125b.1; Qt.22b.2;
saṃparka	**contact,** *śl.*157d; Jr.158b.1; Qt.75b.3;
saṃbodhayet	**should fully awaken,** *śl.*245c; see **udbodha, prabodhayet, bodha;**
saṃmelana	**meeting, blending, mating, company,** *śl.*158a; Jr.158b.1 *bis*; see **melaka, melana, melayet;**
sammelanā	**bringing togther,** Jr.56d.1;
saṃvit	**consciousness,** *śl.*4d, *śl.*46c, *śl.*50b, *śl.*80b, *śl.*94c, *śl.*105d, *śl.*112b = Qt.138b.1 = Qt.150b.1, *śl.*116b, *śl.*117d, *śl.*126b, *śl.*128a, *śl.*138d, *śl.*148a, *śl.*149d, *śl.*174b, *śl.*181a, *śl.*181b; Jr.4d.1, Jr.9d.3, Jr.24d.2, Jr.70b.1, Jr.80d.2, Jr.89d.3, Jr.95d.1, Jr.102d.4, Jr.102d.6, Jr.112b.1 *bis*, Jr.115b.3, Jr.117b.1, Jr.119b.2 *bis*, Jr.125b.1, Jr.126b.3, Jr.128b.2, Jr.137b.1, Jr.138b.1, Jr.138b.2, Jr.139d.1, Jr.146b.2, Jr.149b.1, Jr.150b.1 *bis*, Jr.166b.1, Jr.180d.1, Jr.181d.1, Jr.181d.2, Jr.186b.1, Jr.200d.2, Jr.235d.1, Jr.271d.2; Qt.100b.4 *bis*, Qt.128b.2; see **cit, citi, citta, caitanya, bodha,** etc.;
saṃviditatva	**recognition,** Jr.46b.1;
saṃvitti	**perception, attention, consciousness,** *śl.*133d, *śl.*146c, *śl.*221a; Jr.147b.1;
saṃsāra	**transient existence,** Jr.185d.1, Jr.211b.2;
saṃskāra	**purifying ritual,** Jr.209d.2;
saṃskṛta	**purified [for ritual],** Jr.124b.1;
saṃsthita	**permanence,** *śl.*57a;
saṃhāra	**reabsorption,** *śl.*57a, *śl.*69d, *śl.*104a, *śl.*173d; Jr.19d.1, Jr.104b.1, Jr.142b.1, Jr.173d.2, Jr.182d.1, Jr.185d.2, Jr.271d.2; Qt.57d.1;

	see **upasaṃhāra;**
saṃhṛti	**reabsorption,** *śl.*142a;
saṅkramaṇa	**transference,** Jr.42b.1, Jr.122b.3;
saṅkramanti	**they transfer,** Qt.239b.1;
sañjalpa	**murmuring,** *śl.*93a;
sakala	**composite,** *śl.*205d; Jr.146b.2, Jr.182d.1, Jr.185d.1, Jr.206d.1; see **kalā, niṣkala;**
sattā	**reality,** *śl.*127a; Jr.127b.3; Qt.166b.1;
sadya	**immediately,** *śl.*194d, *śl.*236a, *śl.*236c, *śl.*258d, *śl.*264c; Jr.195d.3; Qt.3d.1, Qt.166b.1, Qt.192b.1;
sandhā	**intentional language,** Qt.166b.1;
sannidhāna	**presence,** Qt.75b.3; **saṃnidhāpaka, sānnidhya;**
sa-bīja-dīkṣā	***sa-bīja* initiation,** Jr.232d.1; see **dīkṣā, bīja;**
samanā	***samanā*,** Jr.271d.1;
samaya	**rule, agreed teaching, time,** *śl.*159b, *śl.*200b; Jr.22b.2, Jr.46b.1, Jr.160b.2, Jr.200d.2; Qt.100b.4 *bis*;
samayi-dīkṣā	**ordinary initiation,** Jr.197b.2, Jr.200d.3;
samayī	**ordinary initiate,** *śl.*197c, *śl.*199d, *śl.*198a; Jr.200d.2; Qt.198b.1; see **sāmayika;**
samarasī	**perfectly fused,** *śl.*274b, *śl.*274c; Jr.274b.2, Jr.281d.2; see **sāmarasya;**
samādhi	**rapture,** Qt.110b.1, Qt.110b.2;
samāviśet	**becomes fully absorbed,** *śl.*110b; Jr.111b.1;
samāveśa	**entire absorption,** *śl.*143a; Jr.115b.1, Jr.125b.1, Jr.146b.1, Jr.147b.2, Jr.201b.3; see **āveśa, praveśa;**
samira	**air,** *śl.*160a;
samīra	**air,** Jr.160b.2; Qt.213d.1;
sarga	**emission,** *śl.*140c, *śl.*140d; Qt.100b.4; see ***Ḥ*, visarga, vaisargika;**
sarva	**whole,** *passim*;
sahaja	**natural,** *śl.*156c; Jr.13d.3 *bis*; Qt.13d.5, Qt.64d.1, Qt.160b.1;
sahasrāra	**thousand,** *śl.*144b; Jr.100b.3, Jr.146b.1; Qt.146b.1;
sādhaka	**Adept,** *śl.*225a, *śl.*231c, *śl.*282b; Jr.22b.3, Jr.24d.1, Jr.29b.3, Jr.40d.1, Jr.206d.1, Jr.224d.2, Jr.229d.1, Jr.232d.1; Qt.13d.4, Qt.101b.1,

	Qt.102d.5, Qt.122b.1, Qt.283d.1;
sānnidhya	**presence,** Qt.13d.23; see **saṃnidhāpaka, sannidhāna;**
sāmayika	**ordinary initiate,** Jr.289b.2; see **samayī;**
sāmarasya	**perfect fusion,** Jr.4d.1, Jr.9d.1, Jr.79d.1, Jr.117b.1, Jr.161b.1, Jr.247d.3, Jr.275d.1; see **samarasī;**
sāmarthya	**capacity, power,** *śl.*4b; Jr.4d.1, Jr.192b.1, Jr.247d.1;
sāra	**essence, outflow,** *śl.*164a; Jr.9d.2, Jr.127b.3, Jr.166b.1; see **āsāra**
sāratā	**essence, outflow,** Jr.5d.1;
sāratva	**essence, outflow,** Jr.9d.3;
siddha	**Perfected Being, perfect, complete, effective, accomplished,** *śl.*3a, *śl.*28a, *śl.*29a, *śl.*46c, *śl.*183b, *śl.*219d, *śl.*270c, *śl.*273a; Jr.3d.1 *bis*, Jr.29b.1 - five times, Jr.29b.4, Jr.33d.1, Jr.48d.1, Jr.55d.3, Jr.185d.1, Jr.211b.2; Qt.29b.2, Qt.42d.1, Qt.57d.3, Qt.123b.2, Qt.166b.1;
siddhatama	**most accomplished,** *śl.*236b; Jr.236d.1;
siddhi	**supernatural power,** *śl.*40b, *śl.*76a, *śl.*91b, *śl.*127c, *śl.*180d, *śl.*200c, *śl.*231b, *śl.*238c; *śl.*40b.1 *bis*, Jr.63d.5, Jr.64d.2, Jr.75b.4, Jr.89d.1, Jr.101b.1, Jr.128b.1, Jr.200d.2, Jr.232d.1 *bis*; Qt.13d.2, Qt.39d.6, Qt.77d.1, Qt.89d.1, Qt.96d.2, Qt.100b.1, Qt.122b.1, Qt.123b.2, Qt.129b.3, Qt.166b.1;
siddhyati	**is successful,** *śl.*185d; Jr.185d.1; Qt.24d.2, Qt.91d.1 *bis*, Qt.166b.1 *bis*;
siddhyate	**succeeds,** Jr.192b.2;
siddhyanti	**are successful,** *śl.*77b; Qt.13d.25;
siddhyet	**is successful, ascertains,** *śl.*65c; Jr.118b.1, Jr.119b.2, Jr.149b.2, Jr.191d.1;
sīt	**cry of pleasure,** Qt.100b.5;
supta	**deep sleep,** *śl.*222c; see **suṣupta;**
surā	**alcohol,** *śl.*11b; Jr.22b.1; Qt.13d.1, Qt.13d.4;
suṣi	**vein,** *śl.*143b; Jr.146b.1;
suṣupta	**deep sleep,** Jr.223d.1; see **supta;**
suṣumṇa	***suṣumṇa*,** Jr.271d.1;
sūkṣma	**subtle,** *śl.*265a; Jr.271d.1; Qt.4d.4;

Sacrifice 1 external

śl. 25-27ab	**1. The external setting**
	2. The ritual:
	A. Reabsorption into the centre:
śl. 27cd-29ab	**1. The personages on the squares of the *maṇḍala***
	Insertion of the Kula Hierarchy
śl. 29cd-32ab	**a. The 4 Perfected Beings and their wives**
śl. 32cd-33	**b. The 6 qualified gurus**
śl. 34	**i. Their śaktis**
	ii. The identifying marks of their lineages
śl. 35	**a. Definition**
śl. 36-39	**b. Examination**
śl. 40	**iii. The advantage of these marks**
śl. 41	**c. The 6 non-qualified gurus;**
śl. 42	**Difference between qualified and non-qualified**
śl. 43-45ab	**d. The bodiless gurus**
	End of the Kula Hierarchy
	Reabsorption cont.
śl. 45cd-46ab	**2. The mantras in the circle of the *maṇḍala*: Mālinī and Mātṛkā**
	3. The goddesses within the triangle of the *maṇḍala*: Parā, Parāparā and Aparā
śl. 46cd-48	**4. Kuleśvarī in the centre of the *maṇḍala***
	B. Emanation from the centre:
śl. 49-50	**1. Śakti and Bhairava at the centre**
śl. 51	**2. The deities within the triangle: 12, 64, 4, etc.**
śl. 52-54c	**3. The 8 goddesses and their consorts on the lotus outside the triangle**
śl. 54d-55	**4. The 'lamps':**
	a. According to the 64 Masters
	b. According to one's *vidyā*

SUB-TOPIC 3 — **The Ritual of Adoration**
Sacrifice 2 — **Based on the Śakti**

śl. 56	**Enunciation of the Sub-topic**	
śl. 57	**Definition: The four Stages of the Krama Cycle**	
	Examination:	
	A. Cycle I Object of knowledge	
śl. 58	**Definition of the ritual**	
śl. 59-63	**1. Emanation:**	**a. The 24 sites on one's own body**
śl. 64		**note i. 'I' am not**
śl. 65		**ii. All by recollection**
śl. 66		**b. The śakti-circle of the 9 wives**
śl. 67		**their 9 sacred sites**
śl. 68-69a	**2. Maintenance:**	**Cakriṇī / Kuṇḍalinī**
śl. 69b	**3. Reabsorption:**	**Kuleśvarī**
śl. 69cd	**4. 'Nameless':**	**Saṅkarṣiṇī**
śl. 70ab		**alone or paired**
	Cycle II Means of knowledge	
śl. 70cd-71ab	**1. Emanation:**	**24 sacred sites in 8 directions**
śl. 71cd-72ab		**the triads - their code**
śl. 72cd-73ab	**2. Maintenance:**	**'lamps' are placed there**
śl. 73cd-75ab	**- Insertion of one's private ritual -**	
śl. 75cd-76ab	**3. Reabsorption:**	**setting aside the instruments**
	4. 'Nameless':	**the goddess Kṛśā**
śl. 76cd-77	**- aside:**	**the Hymn of the Sacred Site**
	Cycle III Subject of knowledge	
śl. 78	**1. Emanation:**	**the śaktis by themselves**
śl. 79	**2. Maintenance:**	**pairing with the śaktis**
śl. 80	**3. Reabsorption:**	**a. no time**
śl. 81ab		**b. no throne**
śl. 81cd	**4. The 'nameless':**	**his śakti (*sva-śakti*)**
	B. Recitation	
śl. 82	**Enunciation and Definition**	
śl. 83-88	**1. The objects of focus**	
	2. The *haṃsa*	
śl. 89	**a. Enunciation of *haṃsa***	
śl. 90ab	**b. Definition of *haṃsa***	
śl. 90cd-91	**- note: no distinctions**	
śl. 92-95ab	**3. Oblation into the fire of consciousness**	
śl. 95cd	**Bridge: in praise of Śambhunātha**	

SUB-TOPIC 4	**The Ritual with the Sexual Partner**
Sacrifice 3	**Based on the Pair**
śl. 96	**Enunciation of the Sub-topic**
	Introduction
	1. The Participants:
śl. 97ab	**a. Enunciation of *brahmacarya***
śl. 97cd-98ab	**i. Definition of *brahman***
śl. 98cd	**ii. Definition of *brahmacarya***
śl. 99-100ab	**iii. Definition of 'bonded animal'**
śl. 100cd-101ab	**b. Definition of the term śakti**
śl. 101cd-102	**Examination of the term śakti**
śl. 103	**Concluding bibliography and effect**
	2. The Ritual
śl. 104ab	**a. i. Definition of the ritual as**
	1. Emanation,
	2. Reabsorption and
	3. Blending
śl. 104cd-105ab	**ii. Brief examination of the ritual**
śl. 105cd-106ab	**b. i. Definition of 'principal circle' and 'sub-circle'**
śl. 106cd-107ab	**ii. Etymology of *cakra* (circle)**
	Examination of the Ritual
The First Emission:	**Emanation (*sṛṣṭi*); the 'arisen' (*udita*);**
	Trajectory 1. Emphasis on action
śl. 107cd	**Definition: Satiation (*tarpaṇa*) and Expansion (*vikāsa*)**
	Examination:
	Level of bliss 3: *Parānanda*
śl. 108-109ab	**i. Satiating sub-circle with 3 M's etc.**
śl. 109cd-110ab	**ii. Satiating sub-circle with Other Means**
śl. 110cd-111ab	**Summary Quotation for levels 4-7**
śl. 111cd-112ab	**Level of Bliss 4: *Brahmānanda***
śl. 112cd-113ab	**Contrast: The egoist**
śl. 113cd-114ab	**Level of Bliss 5: *Mahānanda***
	i. Sub-circles lead to the principal circle

śl. 114cd-115ab	**ii. Principal circle impacts on sub-circle**
śl. 115cd-117ab	**Levels of bliss 6: *Cidānanda* and 7: *Jagadānanda***
	Trajectory 2. Emphasis on knowledge,
śl. 117cd-118ab	**Enunciation: Self and goddess 'consciousness'**
śl. 118cd-119ab	**Summary examination of the procedure**
	Examination in detail
śl. 119cd	**i. The differentiation**
śl. 120ab	**ii. The merging**
śl. 120cd	**iii. The identity**
śl. 121	**iv. The emission**
	Trajectory 3. Emphasis on the śakti
	1. Descriptions of the śakti :
śl. 122ab	**i. Her nature**
śl. 122cd-123ab	**ii. Her ritual preparation**
śl. 123cd-124ab	**Quote: The śakti as *bhāvā* and *bhāvitā***
	2. Summary description of the ritual
śl. 124cd-125ab	**i. At the mouth of the *yoginī***
śl. 125cd-126ab	**ii. The result : consciousness etc.**
	Examination of the ritual:
	1. For one who seeks liberation
śl. 126cd-127ab	**- focus on the ejaculating**
	2. For those who seek enjoyment
śl. 127cd-128ab	**- focus on the ejaculate**
śl. 128cd-129ab	**i. For a knowledgeable person - consuming the ejaculate**
	ii. For an officiant - anointing the organ
śl. 129cd-130ab	**Definition of the ritual**
śl. 130cd-132	**Examination**
	a. Her sex organ
śl. 133ab	**b. His own body**
The Second Emission:	**Reabsorption (*saṃhāra*) the 'rested' (*śānta*)**
śl. 133cd-134ab	**Level 1 : The 'rested' state**

śl. 134cd-135ab	**Level 2 : Non-bliss (*nirānanda*)**
	a. The principal circle stops,
śl. 135cd-136ab	**b. The sub-circles stop,**
śl. 136cd-137ab	**c. The desire for bliss.**
śl. 137cd-138ab	**levels 3, 4, 5, 6 or the Krama**
śl. 138cd-139	**level 7 : The surging**

<u>The Third Emission</u>: Union (*saṅghaṭṭa*), Blending (*melaka*)

Transition and Introduction

śl. 140	**1. Enunciation**
	a. Three forms of emission (*visarga*)
	b. Etymology of *visarga*
śl. 141-142ab	**2. Definition of the three emissions**

The Ritual

	1. The 'mantra', i.e. the practitioner alone:
śl. 142cd-146ab	**a. i. The coupling of all diversity**
śl. 146cd-147ab	**ii. Constant perception**
śl. 147cd-149ab	**iii. Creative awareness (*parāmarśa*)**
śl. 149cd-150ab	**b. Recitation**
	2. The six rayed *mudrā*, i.e. intercourse:
śl. 150cd-153ab	**a. i. Intercourse**
śl. 153cd-154ab	**ii. Stability at the Fourth**
śl. 154cd-156ab	**iii. Awareness comes (*vimarśa*)**
śl. 156cd-157ab	**b. The natural recitation: Enunciation**
śl. 157cd-158ab	**Examination: i. 8 circles (*cakra*)**
śl. 158cd-160ab	**ii. 8 phases (*uccāra*)**
śl. 160cd-161ab	**iii. 8 bhairavas (*unmanā*)**
	Results:
śl. 161cd-162ab	**1. Liberated-while-living, Bhairavī**
śl. 162cd-163	**2. The *yoginī*-child**

Conclusion:

śl. 164-166ab	**1. Etymology of *ādi-yāga* (Primordial Sacrifice)**
	2. Concluding bibliography

SUB-TOPIC 5:	**The ritual of the secret teaching**
Sacrifice 4	**Based on the body**
śl. 166cd-168	**1. Installation of the *vidyā* and the mantra**
śl. 169	**Note: There is secrecy on this matter**
śl. 170-173	**2. The *maṇḍala***
śl. 174-175	**3. The satiation of the self and the deities**
śl. 176	**- aside: a hymn**
śl. 177	**Concluding bibliography**
Sacrifice 5	**Based on the subtle-breath**
śl. 178	**1. Definition**
śl. 179	**2. Examination**
śl. 180	**3. Effect: powers of knowledge**
Sacrifice 6	**Based on the mind**
śl. 181	**1. Definition**
śl. 182	**2. Examination: i. In brief**
śl. 183-185c	**ii. In detail**
śl. 185d	**3. Effect: Perfection**
śl. 186ab	**Concluding bibliography**

PART II: THE RITUALS OF INITIATION

SUB-TOPIC 6	**Initiation**
śl. 186cd-187ab	**Enunciation of the sub-topic**
	I Ordinary initiation
śl. 187cd-192ab	**1. According to the *Mālinīvijayottaratantra* By means of mantra and flower**
śl. 192cd-195	**2. According to the *Ratnamālā* by means of mantra and 'oblation' etc.**
	Transition
śl. 196-197ab	**a. Assessing the absorption**
śl. 197cd-198ab	**b. The ordinary initiate and the Son**
śl. 198cd-199ab	**3. According to the *Ānandeśvara* by means of the 'oblation' alone**
śl. 199cd-200	**Result : The way of life for an ordinary initiate**
	II Initiation as a Son
śl. 201ab	**Enunciation**
	1. According to the *Ratnamālā*
śl. 201cd-202ab	**a. Definition of the ritual**
śl. 202cd-206	**b. Examination of the ritual**
śl. 207-208	**c. Result: i. 5 Possible effects**
śl. 209	**ii. Enjoyment**
śl. 210-211ab	**2. Another method: the surrounding fire**
śl. 211cd-212ab	**3. According to the *Sadbhāva***
śl. 212cd-213	**a. Enunciation: 3 masses of phonemes**
śl. 214-216	**b. Examination of the ritual**
śl. 217-218ab	**Results: a. He is Bhairava**
śl. 218cd	**b. He is a guru**
	III Regarding the Son who desires enjoyments
śl. 219-220	**1. a. Enjoyment within a category**
	b. Enjoyment within all categories
	c. Enunciation of the Kula sacrifice
	2. Definition of the Kula sacrifice
	3. Examination of the sacrifice
	4. Further instruction on the five states

	III Supreme penetration in the *Vīrāvalibhairava*		
śl. 272ab	**Enunciation**		
	Examination		
śl. 272cd-273ab		**i. The guru**	
śl. 273cd-274ab		**ii. Manner of penetrating the disciple**	
śl. 274cd-275		**iii. The result: disciple is one with centre**	
	IV The initiation to Śivahood of all living beings		
śl. 276ab	**Enunciation**		
śl. 276cd-277ab	**Definition**		
śl. 277cd-278ab	**Examination**	**i. In brief**	
śl. 278cd-281		**ii. In detail**	
		iii. Result: All acquire Śivahood	

RITES TO CONCLUDE THE INITIATION

śl. 282-283	**First Ritual : With the Masters and Adepts - oblation**	
	Second Ritual : With all the heroes - wine	
śl. 284-285ab	**Enunciation**	
	Examination	
śl. 285cd-287ab	**1. The ritual**	**a. Guru and initiate partake**
śl. 287cd-289ab		**b. All the heroes partake**
śl. 289cd-290	**2. Notes**	**a. Exclusion text**
śl. 291		**b. Timing the Second Ritual**
śl. 292ab	**Summation of the whole chapter.**	

BIBLIOGRAPHY

WORKS CITED IN THE THESIS AND APPENDICES

PRIMARY SOURCES

1a. Texts and Translations of Works by Abhinavagupta

Anuttarāṣṭikā: In Silburn, L. *Hymnes de Abhinavagupta.* Paris: Editions E. de Boccard, 1970. (Publications de l'Institutde Civilisation Indienne, Fasc.31) p.56.

Anubhavanivedana: In Silburn, L. *Hymnes de Abhinavagupta.* Paris: Editions E. de Boccard, 1970; (Publications del'Institut de Civilisation Indienne, Fasc.31) p.37.

Īśvarapratyabhijñāvimarśinī: Vols.1 and 2, Ed. K.A. Subramania Iyer and K.C. Pandey. Vol.3, English translation by K.C. Pandey. Delhi: Motilal Banarsidass,1986. (First published as The Princess of Wales Saraswati Bhavana Texts, nos.70, 83 and 84 in the years 1938, 1950 and 1954 respectively.)

Kramastotra: In Silburn, L. *Hymnes aux Kālī, La Roue des Energies Divines.* Paris, E. de Boccard, 1975. (Publications de Institut de Civilisation Indienne, Fasc.40) pp.125-148, 191-194.

Ghaṭakarparavivṛti: Trans. Parlier, B. *Le Ghaṭakarparavivṛti d'Abhinavagupta.* Paris, E. de Boccard, 1975: (Publications de l'Institut de Civilisation Indienne, Fasc.39) 99 pp.

Tantravaṭadhānikā: In Mukunda Ram Shastri, Ed. Kashmir Series of Texts and Studies, no.24. Nirnaya-Sagar Press, 1918. pp.111.

Tantrasāra: Delhi, Bani Prakashan, 1982. viii+9+208 p. [First edited with notes by Mukund Rām Shāstrī. Srinagar, 1918. Kashmir Series of Texts and Studies, no.17]

— Trans. Gnoli, R. *L'essenza dei Tantra (Tantrasāra).* Torino, Boringhieri, 1960. 343 p.

Tantrāloka: With the Commentary of Jayaratha. Re-edited by R.C. Dwivedi and Navjivan Rastogi, enlarged with an introduction by Navjivan Rastogi and reprinted in 8 volumes. Delhi, Motilal Banarsidass, 1987. [First edited by Mukund Ram Shastri and published in 12 volumes. Srinagar, the Publications of the Research Department of the Jammu and Kashmir State, 1918-1938. Kashmir Series of Texts and Studies, nos. 23, 28, 30, 36, 35, 29, 41, 47, 59, 52, 57 and 58]

— Trans. Gnoli, R. *Luce delle sacre scritture, (Tantrāloka).* Torino, Unione Tipografico-Editrice Torinense, 1972. 944 p.

— Trans. Silburn, L. and Padoux, A. *La Lumiere sur les tantras, chapitres 1 - 5 du Tantrāloka.* (Publications de l'Institut de Civilisation Indienne, Fasc.66) Paris, E. de Boccard, 1998. 316 p.

Tantroccaya: R. Gnoli and R. Torella, eds. 'The Tantroccaya of Abhinavagupta'. In *Indo-Sino-Tibetica.* Roma, Bardi, 1990. pp.153-189.

Dehasthadevatācakrastotra: In Silburn, L. *Hymnes de Abhinavagupta.* Paris, E. de Boccard, 1970. (Publications de l'Institut de Civilisation Indienne, Fasc.31) pp.85-86.

Paramārthasāra: Trans. Silburn, L. *Le Paramārthasāra.* 2nd revised edn. Paris, E. de Boccard, 1979. (Publications de l'Institut de Civilisation Indienne, Fasc.5) 105 p. [First edition: Srinagar, the Publications of the Research Department of the Jammu and Kashmir State. Kashmir Series of Texts and Studies, no.7]

Parātriṃśikāvivaraṇa: Mukunda Rāma Shāstrī, ed. New Delhi, Aroma Publishing House, 1991. 287 p. [First edition: Srinagar, the Publications of the Research Department of the Jammu and Kashmir State, 1918. Kashmir Series of Texts and Studies, no.18]

— Trans. R. Gnoli. *Il commento di Abhinavagupta alla Parātriṃśikā.* Roma, Instituto Italiano per il Medio ed Estremo Oriente, 1985. (Serie Orientale Roma, vol. 58) xxxiv+313 p.

— Trans. Singh, J. *Parātriṃśikāvivaraṇa.* B. Bäumer ed. Delhi, Motilal Banarsidass, 1988. xx+285 p., Sanskrit text 106 p.

Parātrīśikālaghuvṛtti: In Padoux, A. *La Parātrīśikālaghuvṛtti de Abhinavagupta.* Paris, E. de Boccard, 1975, pp.49-63. [First edition, Srinagar, the Publications of the Research Department of the Jammu and Kashmir State, 1947. Kashmir Series of Texts and Studies, no.68.]

— Trans. Padoux, A. *La Parātrīśikālaghuvṛtti de Abhinavagupta.* Paris, E. de Boccard, 1975. (Publications de l'Institut de Civilisation Indienne, Fasc.38) 138 p.

Mahopadeśaviṃśatikā: In Silburn, L. *Hymnes de Abhinavagupta.* Paris, E. de Boccard, 1970. (Publications de l'Institut de Civilisation Indienne, Fasc.31) pp.76-77.

untitled: Ed. R. Gnoli, 'Five unpublished stanzas by Abhinavagupta'. In *East and West* New Series 9: 222-223, 1958.

1b. Other primary sources

Kulacūḍāmaṇi Nigama: Ed. A. Avalon. Reprint. Madras, Ganesh and Co. 1956. 31+58 p.

Kaulāvalī: Ed. A. Avalon, Delhi, Bharatiya Vidya Prakashan, 1985. 23+4+142 p.

Manusmṛti, with the Sanskrit Commentary Manvarthamuktāvali of Kullūka Bhaṭṭa: Ed. J.L. Shastri Delhi, Motilal Banarsidass, 1983. xi+495+24+25 p.

Mālinīvijayottara Tantram: Ed. M.S. Kaul, Delhi, Butala & Co. 1984, (Kashmir Series of Texts and Studies, no.37) xxxvi+3+157 p. [First published, Bombay, 1922]

Svacchandatantram, with commentary 'Uddyota', by Kṣemarājācārya: Ed. V.V. Dwivedi, Delhi, Parimal Publications, 1985. 2 vols. (Kashmir Series of Texts and Studies, nos. 31, 37, 44, 48, 51, 56) [First edition: 1921-1935]

2. Studies and Translations

Aalto, P., 'Madyam apeyam'. In *Jñānamuktāvali* (Commemoration volume in honour of Johannes Nobel). New Delhi,

Bagchi, P. C., *Studies in the tantras,* Part I. Calcutta, Calcutta University Press, 1939. vii+114 p.

— Ed. *Kaulajñānanirṇaya.* Trans. Michael Magee. Prachya Prakashan, Varanasi, 1986. xi+94+135 p.

Banerji, S.C., *Tantra in Bengal.* 2nd edn. New Delhi, Manohar Publications, 1992. xi+352 p

Bäumer, B., *Wege ins Licht.* Zü rich, Benziger, 1992. 237 p.

— 'Vāc as saṃvāda. Dialogue in the context of advaita śaivāgamas'. In F.X. D'Sa, and R. Mesquita, eds. *Hermeneutics of encounter.* Vienna, 1994. (Publications of the De Nobili Research Library, vol.XX) pp.11-19.

Behera, K.S., 'Evolution of śakti cult at Jajpur, Bhuvaneswar and Puri.' In D.C. Sircar, ed. *The śākti cult and Tārā.* Calcutta, Calcutta University Press, 1967. pp.74-86.

Bharati, A., *The tantric tradition*. London, Rider &Co. 1965. 350 p.

Bhat, M.S., Trans. *Vedic tantrism, a study of Ṛgvidhāna of Śaunaka with text and translation*. Delhi, Motilal Banarsidass, 1987. viii+437 p.

Bhattacharya, A.K., 'A nonaryan aspect of the devī'.In D.C. Sircar, ed. *The śākti cult and Tārā*. Calcutta, Calcutta University Press, 1967.pp.56-60.

Brunner-Lachaux, H., 'Analyse du *suprabhedāgama*'. In *Journal Asiatique* 155: 31-60, 1967.

Brunner, H., 'Un tantra du nord: le Netra Tantra'. In *Bulletin de l'Ecole Française d'Extreme-Orient* 61: 125-197, 1974.

— 'Le *sādhaka*, personnage oublié du Śivaïsme du sud'. In *Journal Asiatique* 263: 411-443, 1975.

— 'Le Śaiva-Siddhānta, "essence" du Veda (Etude d'un fragment du *Kāmikāgama*)'. In *Indologica Taurinensia* 8: 51-66, 1980.

— 'The four pada of Saivagama'. In *Journal of Oriental Research (Madras)* 56-62: 260-278, 1986-1992.

Bühler, G. , Trans. *The Laws of Manu*. Delhi, Motilal Banarsidass, 1964. cxxxviii+620 p. [First published London, Oxford University Press, 1886]

Bühneman,G., 'Tantric worship of Gaṇeśa according to the Prapañcasāra'. In *Zeitschrift der Deutschen Morgenländischen Gesellschaft* 137: 357-382, 1987.

Daniélou, A. *Hindu polytheism*. London, Routledge and K. Paul, 1964. 491 p.

Das, H.C., *Tāntricism, a study of the yoginī cult*. New Delhi, Sterling Publishers, 1981. 86 p. [Includes many plates and 2 site plans]

Doniger O'Flaherty, W., *Hindu myths*. Harmondsworth, England, Penguin Books, 1975. 358 p.

Dyczkowski, M. S.G., *The canon of Saivagama and the Kubjika Tantra of the western kaula tradition*. Delhi, Motilal Banarsidass, 1989. 233 p.

— *The doctrine of vibration - an analysis of the doctrines and practices of Kashmir Shaivism*. Delhi, Motilal Banarsidass, 1989. 297 p.

— Trans. *The stanzas on vibration. The Spandakārika with four commentaries*. Varanasi, Dilip Kumar Publishers, 1994. xix+427 p.

Eliade, M., *Rites and symbols of initiation: the mysteries of birth and rebirth*. Translated by Willard R. Trask. New York, Harper and Row, 1965. 175 p. [First published in English by Harper and Row, New York, 1958. First published in France, 1959.]

Eschmann, A., 'Hinduization of tribal deities in Orissa: the śākta and śaiva typology'. In A. Eschmann, H. Kulke and G. C. Tripathi, eds. *The cult of Jagannath and the regional tradition of Orissa.* New Delhi, Manohar Publications, 1978. pp.79-98.

Esnoul, A.-M., 'Les songes et leur interprétation dans l'Inde'. In A.M. Esnoul, P. Garelli, Y. Hervouet, M. Leibovici, S. Sauneron and J. Yoyotte, Eds. *Les songes et leur interprétation, Sources orientales.* Paris, Editions du Seuil, 1959. Vol.2, pp.208-247.

Farrow, G.W. and Menon, I., Trans. *The Concealed Essence of the Hevajra Tantra, with the commentary Yogaratnamālā.* Delhi, Motilal Banarsidass, 1992. lvi+308 p.

Filliozat, J., 'Les agamas sivaites'. In N.R. Bhatt, ed. *Rauravāgama.* Pondichéry, Institut Français d'Indologie, 1961. (Publications de l'Institut Français d'Indologie, no.18) Vol.1, pp. v-xv.

Gnoli, R., 'Alcune tecniche yoga nelle scuole Śaiva'. In *Rivista degli Studi Orientali* 29: 279-290, 1956.

Gonda, J., *Change and continuity in Indian religion.* The Hague, Mouton and Co., 1965.

— *Meaning of the Sanskrit term dhāman.* Amsterdam, Maatschappij, 1967. 100 p.

Goudriaan, T. and Gupta, S., *Hindu tantric and śakta literature.* Otto Harrassowitz, Wiesbaden, 1981. (A History of Indian Literature, Vol.II - Fasc.2) ix+245 p.

Goudriaan, T., Trans. *The Viṇāśikhatantra.* Delhi, Motilal Banarsidass, 1985.

— 'Vāc. The concept of word in selected Hindu tantras, by A. Padoux' [review] *Wiener Zeitschrift für die Künde Süd und Ostasiens* 37:238-240, 1993.

Hara, M., 'La bhakti et le Stavacintāmaṇi de Bhaṭṭanārāyaṇa: texte traduit et commenté, by L. Silburn' [review] *Indo-Iranian Journal* 9: 211-218, 1966.

— 'A note on the Sanskrit phrase devānāṃ priya'. In *Indian Linguistics* 30: 13-26, 1969.

Ingalls, D.H.H., Ed. *The Dhvanyāloka of Ānandavardhana with the Locana of Abhinavagupta.* Translated by Daniel H.H. Ingalls, J. M.

Masson and M.V. Patwardhan. Cambridge, Massachusetts, Harvard University Press, 1990. vii+837 p.

Kane, P.V., *The history of Sanskrit poetics*. 4th edn. Delhi, Motilal Banarsidass, 1971. viii+446 p.

Kinsey, D., *Hindu goddesses*. Delhi, Motilal Banarsidass, 1987. viii+281p.

Kahn Ladas A., Whipple, B. and Perry, J.D., *The G Spot and other recent discoveries about human sexuality*. New York, Holt, Rinehart and Winston, 1982. xvii+236 p.

Kotru, N.K., Trans. *Śivastotrāvalī of Utpaladeva*. Delhi, Motilal Banarsidass,1985. x+172 p.

Lorenzen, D. N., *The Kāpālikas and Kālāmukhas. Two lost saivite sects*. New Delhi, Thomson Press (India) Ltd.,1972. xiv+214p.

Majumdar, P.K., 'Śakti worship in Rajasthan'. In D.C. Sircar, ed. *The śākti cult and Tārā*. Calcutta, Calcutta University Press, 1967. pp.92-100.

de Mallmann, M.-T., *Les enseignements iconographiques de l'Agni-Purāna*. Paris, Presses Universitaires de France, 1963.xii+371p.

Marglin, F. A., *Wives of the god-king: the rituals of the devadasis of Puri*. Delhi, Oxford University Press, 1985. xv+388 p.

Masson, J.L. and Patwardhan, M.V., *Śāntarasa and Abhinavagupta's philosophy of aesthetics*. Poona, Bhandarkar Oriental Research Institute, 1969.(Bhandarkar Oriental Series, no.9)xvii+206 p.

Monier-Williams, M. A., *Sanskrit English dictionary*. Delhi, Motilal Banasidass, 1993. [First edn.: London, Oxford University Press, 1899] xxxvi+1333 p.

Morinis, E. A., *Pilgrimage in the Hindu tradition*. Delhi, Oxford University Press, 1984. viii+346 p.

Muller-Ortega, P. E., *The Triadic Heart of Śiva*. Albany, State Univeristy of New York Press, 1989. xii+330 p.

Padoux, A., 'Le *Yoginīhṛdaya* et la *Dīpikā* d'Amṛtānanda: quelques problèmes'. In *Bulletin d'Etudes Indiennes* 1: 89-95, 1983.

— 'Le monde hindou et le sexe - symbolisme, attitudes, pratiques'. In *Cahiers Internationaux de Sociologie* 76: 29-49, 1984.

— 'The Ṣaṭsāhasrasaṃhitā: Chapters 1-5 edited, translated and annotated, by J.A. Schoterman' [review] *Indo-Iranian Journal* 28:140-145, 1985.

— *Vāc. The concept of word in selected Hindu tantras*. Translated by Jacques Gontier. Albany, State University of New York Press, 1990. xvi+460 p.

— 'Mantras - what are they?' In Harvey P. Alper, ed. *Understanding mantras*. Delhi, Motilal Banarsidass, 1991. pp.295-318.

— *Le coeur de la yoginī*. Paris, E. de Boccard, 1994. (Publications de l'Institut de Civilisation Indienne, Fasc.66) 427p.

Pal, P., *Hindu religion and iconology. According to the Tantrasāra*. Los Angeles, Vichitra Press, 1981. x+157 p.

Pandey, K.C., *Abhinavagupta: an historical and philosophical study*. 2nd edn. Varanasi, Chowkhamba Sanskrit Series Office, 1963. lii+1014p.

Prakash, O., *Food and drinks in ancient India*. Delhi, Munshi Ram Manohar Lal, 1961. xxiii+341 p.

Raghavan, V., *Abhinavagupta and his works*. Varanasi, Chaukhambha Orientalia, 1981. (Chaukhambha Oriental Research Studies, no.20) 201p.

Rastogi, N., *Introduction to the Tantraloka*. Delhi, Motilal Banarsidass, 1987. xxx+589 p.

Renou, L. and Silburn, L., 'Nirukta and anirukta in Vedic'. In *Sarupa Bharati. The Lakshman Sarup Memorial Volume*. Hoshiarpur (India), Vishveshvaranand Institute, 1954. pp.68-79

Rosu, A., '*Mantra* et *yantra* dans la médecine et l'alchimie indiennes'. In *Journal Asiatique* 274: 206-268, 1986.

Sanderson, A., 'Śivasūtra et Vimarśinī de Kṣemarāja: traduction et introduction, by L. Silburn' [review] *Bulletin of the School of Oriental and African Studies* 46: 160-161, 1983.

— 'The category of purity and power among the Brahmins of Kashmir'. In M. Carrithers, S. Collins and S. Lukes, eds. *The category of the person; anthropology, philosophy, history*. Cambridge, Cambridge University Press, 1985. pp.190-216.

— 'Maṇḍala and āgamic identity in the Trika of Kashmir'. In A. Padoux, ed. *Mantras et diagrammes rituels dans l'Hindouisme*. Paris, Editions du Centre National de la Recherche Scientifique, 1986. pp.169-214.

— 'Saivism and the tantric traditions'. In S. Sutherland, L. Houlden, P. Clarke and F. Hardy, eds. *The world's religions*. London, Routledge, 1988. pp.660-704.

— 'The visualisation of the deities of the Trika'. In *L'image divine*. Paris, Editions du Centre National de la Recherche Scientifique, 1990. pp.31-88.

— 'The triadic heart of Śiva: kaula tantricism of Abhinavagupta in the non-dual shaivism of Kashmir, by Paul Eduardo Muller-Ortega' [review] *Bulletin of the School of Oriental and African Studies* 53: 354-357,1990.

— 'Conférence de M. Alexis Sanderson, Directeur d'études associé'. In *Annuaire. Résumé des conférences et travaux. Ecole pratique des Hautes Etudes, Section des sciences religieuses* 100: 141-144, 1990-1991.

— 'The doctrine of the Mālinīvijayottara-tantra.' In T. Goudriaan, ed. *Ritual and speculation in early tantrism. Studies in honour of André Padoux.* Albany, State University of New York Press, 1992. pp.281-312.

— 'Vajrayāna: Origin and Function'. In *Buddhism into the year 2000. International conference proceedings.* Bangkok, Dhammakaya Foundation, 1994. pp.89-102.

— 'Meaning in tantric ritual'. In A.-M. Blondeau and K. Schipper, eds. *Essais sur le rituel III: Colloque du centenaire de la section des sciences religieuses de l'Ecole Pratique des Hautes Etudes.* Louvain-Paris, Peeters, 1995. Vol.3, pp.15-95.

Schoterman, J.A., Trans. *Yonitantra.* New Delhi, Manohar, 1980. viii+89p.

— Trans. *The Ṣaṭsāhasra Saṃhitā, chapters 1-5.* Leiden, E.J.Brill, 1982. x+232 p.

Silburn, L., Trans. *Hymnes aux Kālī, La Roue des Energies Divines.* Paris, E. de Boccard, 1975. (Publications de Institut de Civilisation Indienne, Fasc.40) 214 p.

— Trans. *Hymnes de Abhinavagupta.* Paris, Editions E. de Boccard, 1970. (Publications de l'Institut de Civilisation Indienne, Fasc.31) 103 p.

— Trans. *Le Vijñāna Bhairava.* Paris, E. de Boccard, 1983. (Publications de l'Institut de Civilisation Indienne, Fasc.15) 222 p.

— Trans. *Śivasūtra et Vimarśinī de Kṣemarāja.* Paris, E. de Boccard, 1980. (Publications de l'Institut de Civilisation Indienne, Fasc.47) vii+189 p.

-- *La kuṇḍalinī, l'énergie des profondeurs.* Paris, Les Deux Océans, 1983. 266 p.

Singh, J., Trans. *Śiva Sūtras, the Yoga of Supreme Identity.* Delhi, Motilal Banarsidass, 1979. lxvi+278 p.

— Trans. *Pratyabhijñāhṛdayam.*4th edn. Delhi, Motilal Banarsidass, 1982. x+187 p.

Sircar, D.C., *The śākta pīṭhas.* 2nd edn. Delhi, Motilal Banarsidass, 1973. vii+132 p.

Slaje, W., *Indische Schriften, Band 1, Śāradā.* Reinbek, Dr. Inge Wezler Verlag für Orientalische Fachpublikationen, 1993. 118 p.

Snellgrove, D.L., Trans. *The Hevajra Tantra.* 2 vols. London, Oxford University Press, 1959.

von Stietencron, H., 'Bhairava'. In *Vorträge / Deutscher Orientalistentag, Supplementa I,* vol.3, 1968. pp.863-71.

Varenne, J., *L'enseignement de la divine shakti.* Paris, Grasset & Fasquelle, 1995. 254 p.

Wheelock, W. T., 'The mantra in vedic and tantric ritual'. In Harvey P. Alper, ed. *Understanding mantras.* Delhi, Motilal Banarsidass, 1991. pp.96-122.

White, D. G., *The alchemical body, Siddha traditions in medieval India.* Chicago, University of Chicago Press,1996.xiii+596p.

Wojtilla, G., 'Notes on popular Śaivism and tantra in eleventh century Kashmir, (A study of Kṣemendra's *Samayamātṛkā*)'. In L. Ligati, ed. *Tibetan and Buddhist studies, commemorating the 200th anniversary of the birth of Alexander Çsoma de Körös.* Budapest, Akadémia Kiadó, 1984. (Bibliotheca Orientalis Hungarica, Vol.XXIX/2) Vol.2, pp.381-389.